A COURSE IN
MODERN LINGUISTICS

A COURSE IN
MODERN
LINGUISTICS

CHARLES F. HOCKETT

PROFESSOR OF LINGUISTICS AND ANTHROPOLOGY
CORNELL UNIVERSITY

THE MACMILLAN COMPANY

NEW YORK

THIRTEENTH PRINTING 1968

LIBRARY OF CONGRESS CATALOG CARD NUMBER: 58–5007

THE MACMILLAN COMPANY, NEW YORK
COLLIER-MACMILLAN CANADA, LTD., TORONTO, ONTARIO

PRINTED IN THE UNITED STATES OF AMERICA

To S.O.H.

To S.O.H.

PREFACE

This book is intended for those college students who take an introductory course in linguistics. If others find interest or entertainment in the work, the author will be delighted; but it is not a "popularization," and the general reader must in all fairness be warned of this. Simplicity of presentation has been sought, but not a false simplification of subject matter.

The duty of the writer of a textbook is not to explore frontiers or indulge in flights of fancy, but to present, in as orderly a way as he can, the generally accepted facts and principles of the field. This has been my aim; the tenor of the book is conservative. Nonetheless—and for this I must apologize—on some topics my enthusiasm and involvement have certainly led me to speak more emphatically than our current knowledge warrants.

Terminological innovations have been avoided as much as possible. Complete avoidance has been unattainable, because it is essential to discuss all aspects of the field in a consistent terminology, and no complete and consistent terminology has existed.

Although I have intended no adherence to any single "school" of linguistics, the influence of American linguistics, and especially that of Leonard Bloomfield, will be apparent on every page.

Linguistics is too rich a field for adequate coverage of all topics in an elementary course. The decision concerning what to include and what to omit, however, rests properly with the instructor. I have, therefore, tried to include adequate elementary treatment of all topics but two: the history of linguistics, and the detailed survey of the languages of the world. The omission reflects my own opinion that neither is a desirable topic in an elementary course; the colleague who disagrees has access elsewhere to several first-class discussions of each.

I owe a great debt to a number of my colleagues who offered me advice on one or another portion of the book, or who read an earlier version in its entirety. This earlier version was used for two successive years in our introductory course at Cornell University, and the reactions of the students have been invaluable to me. Of my colleagues, I must especially mention Frederick B. Agard, Harold B. Allen, J Milton Cowan (who taught the Cornell course during the trial runs), Gordon H. Fairbanks, Murray Fowler, Robert A. Hall, Jr., Eric P. Hamp, Sumner Ives, Norman A. McQuown, William G. Moulton, W. Freeman Twaddell. Oscar Cargill and Norman E. Eliason were especially helpful during later stages of the work. Any deficiencies remaining in the book are due to my own obstinacy, not to any inadequacy in the scholars just named. I wish also to offer my sincere thanks to the Rockefeller Foundation, for grants with which the writing was begun; to the Center for Advanced Study in the Behavioral Sciences, where the writing was completed; and, above all, to Cornell University, which, with a magic seemingly unique, makes itself a congenial home for the scholar in linguistics.

CHARLES F. HOCKETT

Ithaca, New York

CONTENTS

LINGUISTIC PREHISTORY

WRITING

LITERATURE

MAN'S PLACE IN NATURE

A COURSE IN
MODERN LINGUISTICS

1.

INTRODUCTION

1.1. This book is about *language*, the most valuable single possession of the human race.

Everyone, in every walk of life, is concerned with language in a practical way, for we make use of it in virtually everything we do. For the most part our use of language is so automatic and natural that we pay no more attention to it than we do to our breathing or to the beating of our hearts. But sometimes our attention is drawn: we are struck by the fact that others do not speak quite as we do, or we observe a child learning to talk, or we wonder whether one or another way of saying or writing something is correct.

Beyond this, many people have professional need to know something *about* language—as opposed to simply being able to use it. Here are some examples:

(1) The speech correctionist, since his job is to help people overcome difficulties or impediments in their use of language.

(2) The teacher of English composition, for a somewhat similar reason.

(3) The foreign language teacher.

(4) The literary artist, who must know his medium and its capacities just as a painter must know pigments, brushes, and colors; the literary critic for a similar reason.

(5) The psychologist, who knows that language is one of the vital factors differentiating human behavior from that of rats or apes.

(6) The anthropologist, both because language is part of what he calls "culture," and because in his anthropological field work he is often confronted by practical problems of a linguistic sort.

(7) The missionary, who may have to learn some exceedingly alien language, for which there are no ready-made primers or dictionaries—learning it not just for the management of everyday affairs, but well enough to deliver sermons and make Bible translations.

(8) The historian, because his sources of information are documents; that is, written records of past speech.

(9) The philosopher, particularly in dealing with such topics as logic, semantics, and so-called "logical syntax."

(10) The communications engineer, part of whose business is to transmit messages in spoken form (telephone, radio) or in written form (telegraph, teletype) from one place to another.

For all these people, and for others who could be added to the list, knowledge of the workings of language is a means to some end. For a small group of specialists, knowing about language is an end in itself. These specialists call themselves *linguists*, and the organized body of information about language which their investigations produce is called *linguistics*.

The relationship between linguistics and the various other fields in which some knowledge of language is useful is much like that between, say, pure chemistry and chemical engineering. Suppose that an industrial plant has been using a natural dye to color certain products. Something happens to threaten the source of the dye or to increase its cost prohibitively. It then becomes the task of the chemical engineer to find an effective substitute which requires only easily available and relatively inexpensive raw materials. In his efforts to solve this problem, he calls on all sorts of known facts of pure chemistry, many of which were discovered with no such application in view.

Similarly, suppose that an American oil company wishes to develop an oil-field in a region where the prevalent language is one not ordinarily taught in American schools. At least some of the company's personnel must learn the language. There will be no ready-made stock of experienced teachers for the purpose, as there are for such languages as French and German. Nor can one simply hire an inhabitant of the region to serve as a teacher, since native control of a language does not in itself imply conscious understanding of how the language works, or ability to teach it—any more than having cancer automatically makes one a specialist in cancer diagnosis and therapy. But there are linguists who are skilled at finding out how a language works, at preparing teaching-materials in it, and at supervising the tutorial work of native speakers. In all of this, such linguists draw on the results of pure linguistic research.

Of course, this proper relationship between "pure" and "applied" does not always work out smoothly. Sometimes those faced with a practical language problem do not bother to consult the "pure" linguists. Sometimes they ask for help, but get none. This is occasionally because the particular linguist is not interested, but more often because the organized body of information which linguists have so far gathered has nothing to contribute to the problem at hand. When this happens, the "applied" people sometimes forge ahead on their own and find a workable solution. Many a key contribution to linguistics has come about in just this way, from fields as diverse as classical philology and electrical engineering. Anything which anyone discovers about language is grist for the linguist's mill. It is his job to work every new discovery into his systematic account of language, so that those who come later will not waste their time exploring territory that has already been clearly mapped.

The above considerations reveal one reason why, in this book, we shall deal with language in the frame of reference and the terminology of linguistics, rather than in those of anthropology, philosophy, psychology, foreign language teaching, or the like. Only in this way can we be sure of serving the interests of all those readers who are, or may later become, specialists in one or another of these fields. If we were to present, say, a "psychologized" linguistics, we might serve the psychologically trained reader somewhat better (though this is not certain), but we would be doing a comparable disservice to the anthropologist, the communications engineer, the foreign language teacher, and so on.

Another and more fundamental reason is that language *deserves* autonomous treatment. The objective study of human language does not achieve its validity merely through actual or potential "practical" applications. Anything which plays as omnipresent and essential a role in human life as does language merits as careful study as possible. The more we can understand its workings, the better we shall understand ourselves and our place in the universe.

1.2. Sources of Difficulty. Linguistics is not an inherently difficult subject, but there are several points which often make trouble for the beginner. In part, these are merely matters of terminology; in part, however, they have to do with the difference between the lay attitude towards language and the orientation of the specialist.

(1) The linguist distinguishes between *language* and *writing*, whereas the layman tends to confuse the two. The layman's terms "spoken language" and "written language" suggest that speech and writing are merely two different manifestations of something fundamentally the same. Often enough, the layman thinks that writing is somehow more basic than speech. Almost the reverse is true.

Human beings have been speaking for a very long time, perhaps millions of years. Compared to this, writing is a recent invention. As late as a century or so ago, millions of people in civilized countries could not read or write—literacy was a prerogative of the privileged classes. Even today, there are large numbers of illiterates in some parts of the world. Yet there is no human community anywhere which does not have a fully developed language. Stories of peasants whose vocabulary is limited to a few hundred words, or of savages who speak only in grunts, are pure myth.

Similarly, the child learns to speak his language at an earlier age than he learns to read and write, and acquires the latter skills in the framework supplied by the former. This in itself is one of the reasons why we tend to misunderstand the relationship between language and writing. When we begin to learn to speak, the problems involved can hardly be discussed with us, since the discussion would require the very skill we have set out to achieve. But when we begin to learn to read and write, our teachers can talk with us about the task. Thus we grow up with a vocabulary for saying things about reading and writing, but with none for dealing with language itself. Of course the relationship between writing and language is close; it is only natural that we should transfer the vocabulary fitted to the discussion of writing to our remarks about language. For example, we constantly talk about spoken words (which can be heard but not seen) as though they were composed of letters (marks on paper which can be seen but not heard).

The change of orientation which is required in this connection is not an easy one to make. Old habits die hard. Long after one has learned the suitable technical vocabulary for discussing language directly, rather than via writing, one is still apt to slip. It should afford some consolation to know that it took linguistic scholarship a good many hundreds of years to make just this same transition.

(2) Much of the time devoted by the layman to language is taken up by the problem of "correctness." Is it more "correct" to say *it is I* than *it's me*? *To whom* than *who to*? What renders *ain't* incorrect? Are "incorrect" forms to be avoided under all circumstances?

It may come as a shock to learn that the linguist is not particularly interested in such questions. This statement must not be misunderstood. It does not mean that the linguist is an advocate of incorrect forms, or that he denies the reality of the distinction between correct and incorrect. As a *user* of language, the linguist is bound by the conventions of his society just as everyone else is—and is allowed the same degrees and kinds of freedoms within those conventions. In using language, he may be a purist or not. But this has little if any relationship to his special concern, which is *analyzing* language.

As an analyst of language, the linguist is bound to observe and record "incorrect" forms as well as "correct" ones—if the language with which he is working makes such a distinction. A particular linguist may become interested in the whole phenomenon of correctness, and may study this in the same objective way in which he might examine Greek verbs, or French phonetics, or the child's acquisition of speech. If he does, he may soon discover that he needs help. The sociologist or anthropologist, for example, is better prepared than he to explain the special secondary values attached to certain patterns of behavior, be they ways of speaking or points of table etiquette.

(3) The organization of affairs in our schools is such as to suggest a very close tie between language and literature. A high school English course is apt to devote some time to grammar and some time to Tennyson. The typical college French department offers instruction in that language, and in French literature, as well as—more rarely—a few courses in phonetics, philology, or the like.

The tie between language and literature is naturally close—the literary artist works in the medium of language just as the painter works in the medium of colors and the composer in that of sounds. Nevertheless, the study of the two must not be confused. A painter and a chemist are both interested in pigments. The painter's interest focusses on effective selection and placement of different colors and textures on his canvas. The chemist's interest is in the chemical composition of the pigments, whether used in one way or another by the painter. Some physicists are specialists in sound; even when they deal

with the kinds of sounds produced by musical instruments, their interest
is very different from that of the composer, the performer, or the musical audience. Similarly, the raw-materials of the literary artist are of
concern to the linguist, but he is concerned with them whether they
are used for literary purposes or otherwise.

Unlike the phenomenon of correctness, literature is apparently universal. Some sort of literature is found in almost every known human
society, and its study is proportionately important for an improved
understanding of human nature.

(4) A number of factors conspire to give us a false notion of the relationship between language, or grammar, and logic. If we carry this
notion with us into our study of linguistics, we are apt to expect some
results which are not attainable, and to miss the point of some of the
results actually attained.

One of these factors is the common assumption that any usage which
is not "logical" is therefore wrong. To say *he don't* is "illogical," for
example, since *don't* is a contraction of *do not*, and we do not say *he do*.

Such a comment reflects the fact that, in historical origin, the disciplines of grammar and of logic were close. More sophisticated reflec-
tions of this are sometimes to be found in the opinions of contemporary
philosophers. One of these recently criticized linguists for their in-
sistence that, in a sentence like *John saw Bill*, only *John* is the subject.
The critic wanted to assert that both *John* and *Bill* are subjects, since
the sentence says something about both.

Again, we often feel, as we study some language other than our own,
that its ways are most peculiar. What sense is there in the French habit
of saying *Je veux de l'eau* 'I want some water' with the definite article
before *eau* 'water,' but *Je ne veux pas d'eau* 'I don't want any water' without the article?

There are really two different points at issue here. One is the extent
to which we can expect a language to be "logical" in the sense of "consistent and sensible," and the extent to which languages differ in this
regard. The other is whether the linguist, in analyzing and describing
some particular language, should work in terms of some preconceived
notion of abstract logic or should accept what he finds.

The answer to the first point is that *every* known language shows
certain consistencies and many arbitrary inconsistencies. We do not
see the arbitrary features of our native language, because we are used

to them. Those of some other language, studied when we are adults, stand out like sore thumbs. We are quite right in doubting the sense of the French habit mentioned above: though regular, it is entirely arbitrary. But we should not be right were we to conclude that French is "less logical" than English. Is it not, in the last analysis, perfectly arbitrary that we should say *I want some water* with *some*, but should switch to *any* in making the statement negative, *I don't want any water?*

The answer to the second point is that linguistic research can accomplish nothing unless it is strictly inductive. Philosophical speculation about what language *ought* to be is sterile. In describing a language we must report actual usage, as determined by observation. In describing speech behavior in general, we must be most concerned with those features which have been empirically discovered in all the languages on which we have any information.

Thus if we observe that certain speakers of English say *I do, I don't, he does,* and *he don't,* we can only conclude that in their particular variety of English *don't* functions as the contraction of *does not* as well as of *do not.* (This does not render *he don't* "correct": its standing as "correct" or "incorrect" is here beside the point.) When we assert that *John*, and only that, is the subject of the sentence *John saw Bill*, we are not contradicting (nor confirming) what a logician may want to say about this sentence. The linguistic use of the term "subject" has relatively little to do with the logician's use of the same term; the linguist uses this term, and others, to describe how sentences are put together, rather than to describe what sentences are about and whether or not they are true.

From the linguist's point of view, the "logical" approach to language is too narrow. Language is not used just to make assertions of fact. It is used for lies as well as truth, for nonsense as well as for sense, for persuasion as well as for instruction, for entertainment as well as for business, for making war as well as for making love. Language is as broad and deep as the whole fabric of human existence; our approach to it must be comparably catholic.

1.3. Languages and Speech Communities. The linguist's range of study is not just English or just the politically important languages of the world, but every language about which we have, or can obtain, information.

The number of languages spoken in the world today is some three or four thousand. Precisely how many we cannot say. One reason is lack of accurate information on the languages of certain regions, particularly South America and parts of the Western Pacific. Another more fundamental reason is that, even when our information is adequate, we cannot always judge whether the speech of two groups should be counted as separate languages or only as divergent dialects of a single language.

Each language defines a *speech community:* the whole set of people who communicate with each other, directly and indirectly, via the common language. The boundaries between speech communities are not sharp. There are people, *bilinguals* or *polyglots*, who have a practical command of two or more languages and through whom members of different speech communities can establish contact. Most polyglots belong primarily to one speech community, and have only partial control of any other language, but there are occasional exceptions.

In many cases the boundaries of a speech community coincide with political boundaries. Thus in aboriginal times the Menomini language was spoken by all the members of the Menomini tribe, in what is now northern Wisconsin and Michigan, and by no other community. This state of affairs held for many an American Indian tribe in earlier days, and is still to be encountered in many parts of the world. But to this generalization, also, there are exceptions. Switzerland, a single political unit, includes speakers of four different languages: French, German, Italian, and Ladin or Rhaeto-Romance. Contrariwise, English, a single language, is spoken not only in Britain and in many parts of the British Commonwealth, but also in the United States.

Some speech communities of today are extremely large. English has several hundred million native speakers, and millions with some other native language have learned English for business, professional, or political purposes. Russian, French, Spanish, German, Chinese, and a few others also have vast numbers of speakers. Some specialists say that "Chinese" is a group of related languages rather than a single language, but if we break these up then at least one of them, Mandarin Chinese, still belongs in the above list. In general, speech communities of such large proportions have come into existence only recently, as a result of historical developments in the past five hundred years or so.

At the opposite extreme stands a language like Chitimacha, an American Indian language which in the late 1930's had only two speakers left. When a language reaches such straits as this, it is doomed

—no new generation will learn it, and when the old people die the language is dead too. But no such prediction can be ventured if a language has as many as even a few hundred speakers. New Guinea is packed with villages of a few hundred inhabitants each, each village or small group of villages with its own language, and all seemingly quite viable. The same is true of vast regions of South America and Africa. Most languages of today have from a few hundred to a few tens of thousands of speakers, and probably something of this sort has been the rule throughout human history.

For a very small proportion of the languages of today, there are written records which tell us something of what they were like in earlier times. Thus we have documents in English from as early as the end of the 7th century A.D. They do not look like English to us, but they are: the language in which they were written has gradually changed, in the intervening twelve hundred years, to become just the language we now speak.

We also have written records attesting to the former existence of languages which have now completely died out. From ancient Italy we have numerous inscriptions, and a few documents, in several languages besides Latin. Some of these, such as Oscan and Umbrian, were akin to Latin, while others, like Etruscan, were not. All of them were swamped by Latin as Rome rose to political supremacy—just as Chitimacha has more recently been swamped by English—and today only Latin survives, in the form of the so-called *Romance* languages: French, Portuguese, Spanish, Catalan, Italian, Rumanian, and a few others. Some of these later forms have also become extinct. We know that the last speaker of Dalmatian, a Romance language formerly spoken in what is now Yugoslavia, was killed in a mine explosion in 1898.

1.4. Language Families. All languages are constantly undergoing slight changes—in pronunciation, in grammar, in vocabulary—which, in the course of a thousand years or so, have a tremendous cumulative effect. This is why the earliest written records of English are quite unintelligible to us, as our speech would be to our linguistic ancestors of a millenium ago if in some miraculous manner they could be exposed to it. So long as the members of a speech community form a fairly tight-knit group, any change tends to spread to all the speakers of the language. But if the community is broken up, as by migration or by invasion from outside, then changes which begin in one subcommunity usually spread only within that subcommunity, and, as a result, the speech habits of the different subcommunities *diverge*. If the divergence becomes great enough, members of the different subcommunities no longer understand each other, and we must then say that each sub-community has become an independent speech community with its own language. Whenever two or more languages have developed in this way from a single earlier language, we say that they are *related*. Like-wise, we say that any group of clearly related languages constitutes a *family* of languages.

In the case of the Romance family, we are fortunate in having not only direct documentary evidence for much of the history of each sepa-rate language, but also ample written records of their common ancestor, Latin. This is a most unusual state of affairs, recurring only for the Indo-Aryan languages of India (Bengali, Hindi, Bihari, Marathi, and others): Sanskrit, known to us through a vast body of literature, was a standardized literary form of one dialect of the common ancestor. For most other families of languages the earliest written records are much more recent than the presumed common ancestor. Sometimes, by methods which we shall describe later, positive proof of relationship can be worked out even without the help of the direct evidence of written records, but in many other cases we are forced to suspend judgment. Thus some languages, so far as we know, constitute families all by themselves: for example, Basque. Similarly, it is clear that the hundred-and-fifty-odd aboriginal languages of America north of Mexico can be grouped into about fifty families, within each of which the rela-tionship is incontestable, but proposals for the further grouping of these fifty sets into a smaller number of larger families rest on more tenuous evidence and have not yet met with general agreement.

NOTES

At the end of most sections in this book will be found a paragraph or so entitled "Notes." These notes always include a check-list of the new terms which have been introduced; in some cases they contain, or refer to, problems for the reader to work on; when relevant, they include bibliographical references. The latter are given in the form of author and year of publication of the work referred to; fuller bibliographical information is presented alphabetically at the end of the book.

Insofar as possible, throughout the book, our examples will be drawn from English. Where this is not possible, we draw most heavily on German, French, Spanish, Latin, Chinese, and Menomini. These, and all other languages mentioned anywhere in the discussion, are listed alphabetically in the Appendix of Language-Names, together with information as to where, when, and by whom each language is or was spoken and the known or strongly suspected family affiliation of each.

The following terms receive somewhat sharpened meanings in §1: *language* (excludes writing), *writing, linguist, linguistics*. The following are introduced as technical terms: *speech community, bilingual* or *polyglot, divergence, related* languages, *family* of languages.

A brief but penetrating survey of the history of linguistics will be found in Bloomfield 1933, chapter 1; also, his treatment of many topics in chapters 18–27 incorporates historical discussion. More extensive is Pedersen 1931. Hall 1951b surveys developments in the United States from 1925 to 1950. Carroll 1953 describes the present state of development of linguistics in the United States, in its interrelationships with other disciplines.

The best book-length worldwide survey of languages and language families is Meillet and Cohen 1952. This treats a few areas lightly; for Latin America, one can compare McQuown 1955. Other surveys of value are Gray 1939 (especially for bibliography), Matthews 1951, Hoijer 1946.

SIGNALLING
VIA SOUND:
PHONOLOGY

2.

PHONEMES

2.1. Suppose you ask a grocer the price of eggs, and he says *sixty cents a dozen*. How do you know that he has said this, rather than *eighty cents a dozen*, or *we have no eggs today*, or something else?

The answer is obvious. The various things that someone might say in a given situation (and a given language) *sound different*. You tell one utterance from another by ear, just as you recognize the faces of your friends by sight. Of course, we are not infallible in either sort of identification. You may mistake one friend for another if the light is bad, and you may misunderstand what someone says if the surroundings are too noisy or if he mumbles his words. And just as you would have particular trouble with a pair of identical twins, so it is with a pair of English utterances like *The sons raise meat* and *The sun's rays meet*. In cases like these, context helps. You see Jean-or-Joan playing tennis, and conclude that it is Jean because Joan doesn't like tennis. You hear *The sun's rays meet* in the course of a lecture on optics, and know perfectly well that this (rather than *The sons raise meat*) is what was said. Difficulties and exceptions of this sort are marginal; they do not affect the general validity of our answer.

It follows that one subject which we must study if we wish to know how language works is *sound*—the sorts of sound used in speech, and how they are produced and detected. This part of linguistics is called *phonology* or *phonemics*.

Throughout the study of phonology, it must be remembered that sounds and differences between them have one and only one function in language: *to keep utterances apart*. This means that there is little to be learned by examining the utterances of a language one by one, trying

15

somehow to describe the sound of each. It is much more to the point to examine *pairs* of utterances to see how they *differ* in sound.

Now if we consider a pair such as *sixty cents a dozen* and *we have no eggs today*, we find the difference so extensive that it is hard to pin anything down. At the other extreme, a pair like *The sons raise meat* and *The sun's rays meet* is of no help, since, by exception, this pair cannot be kept apart by ear but only by context. Between these two extremes, however, one can find pairs which might be called "almost-identical twins." Here are some "almost-identical twins" that can be heard around the Cornell University campus:

> *She's gone to Willard Straight.*
> *She's gone to Willard State.*

Willard Straight is the student union building on the Cornell campus; *Willard State* (*Hospital*) is a mental institution not many miles away. The difference in meaning is thus very great. But the difference in sound is minimal: the first of the two has an *r*-sound in the last word which is lacking in the other. (This is the *only* difference in sound between the two. There are other differences in *spelling*, but they do not parallel anything in our pronunciation, and must not mislead us.)

Or one of a pair of almost-identical utterances may have one characteristic feature where the other has a different one:

> *That's a nice pin.*
> *That's a nice bin.*

Pairs like these yield important information about the way a language makes use of differences of sound; that is, about its *phonological system*. The second pair tells us, for example, that in English we sometimes keep utterances apart solely by having a *p*-sound at a certain point in one of them, a *b*-sound at the same point in the other. This is not very exciting information, but it is significant just the same. There are many languages in which the difference between a *p*-sound and a *b*-sound is *not* used in this same functional way. The functional use of the difference in English is therefore a characteristic feature of the language—a feature in which English differs from certain other languages.

We want to see in more detail just how the phonological systems of various languages differ from each other, but we obviously cannot explore this topic merely on the basis of the isolated information that, in English, *p*-sounds and *b*-sounds stand in contrast. We must explore the whole of the phonologic system of English.

In the two sets of almost-identical utterances so far considered, the differences in sound are located in specific words: *straight* versus *state* and *pin* versus *bin*. Now almost any word in English (or in any other language) is capable, at least on rare occasions, of occurring as a whole utterance. For example, to the question *Do you want it with soda or straight?* one might merely answer *Straight*. This suggests that a convenient way to begin our exploration of the phonologic system of English is to limit ourselves, temporarily, to one-word utterances. For the present we shall impose an even stricter limitation, considering only utterances of one syllable.

2.2. English Initial Contrasts. The pair of words *pin* and *bin* demonstrate as well as the longer utterances *That's a nice pin* and *That's a nice bin* that the contrast between a *p*-sound and a *b*-sound is functional in English. But there are various other words which are identical with *pin* except at the outset: *in, tin, din, chin, gin, kin, fin, thin, sin, shin, Min* (the nickname), *Lynn, win, spin, skin, grin*. Any pair of words drawn from this list bears testimony to the relevance in English of some difference of sound. Thus the pair *pin* and *in* shows that there is a functionally relevant difference between having a *p*-sound at a certain place and having no sound at all there. The pair *din* and *shin* demonstrates the relevance of the difference between a *d*-sound and an *sh*-sound. The pair *pin* and *spin* attests the distinctiveness of the difference between starting with a *p*-sound and starting with an *s*-sound followed immediately by a *p*-sound. And so on.

Four of the words in the list are special: *in*, since it begins with no consonant sound at all; and *spin, skin, grin*, each of which begins with a combination of two consonant sounds. Setting these four aside, we are left with a set of fourteen: *pin, bin, tin, din, chin, gin, kin, fin, thin, sin, shin, Min, Lynn, win.*

Each of these fourteen words begins with a single consonant sound, and each of the consonant sounds is different from each of the others. Thus, in place of a single two-way difference of sound (as in *pin* and *bin*) what we have is a *network of interlocking differences of sound*. Since each of the words contrasts directly with each of the others, there are ninety-one contrasts in all. Thirteen of these contrasts involve the *p*-sound: *p* is different from *b*; *p* is different from *t*; *p* is different from *d*; and so on. We shall later (§11) see that these differences are not all of the same order (*p* is *more different* in sound from *d* than it is from *b*), but at the moment this consideration is unimportant: the ninety-one contrasts are functionally all on a par.

Now does this list of fourteen words cover all the contrasts which are relevant for the fourteen consonant sounds involved? We can find out by considering some other family of partially similar words. Let us examine the family which includes *pie*, a word which obviously begins with the same *p*-sound found at the beginning of *pin*. Setting aside *eye*, which has no initial consonant-sound, and words like *pry*, *sly*, *fry*, which have two each, we find the following: *pie, buy, tie, die, guy, fie, vie, thigh, thy, sigh, shy, my, nigh, lie, rye, Wye, high*. Here we have seventeen differing initial consonant sounds, or 136 two-way contrasts, sixteen of them involving the *p*-sound. Some of these are duplications of sounds or contrasts revealed by the first list, but some of them are new: *pie* versus *guy*, for example. And a few of the sounds and contrasts represented in the first list do not recur here. What the two lists taken together show can be determined by consolidating them in the following fashion:

| *pin* | *bin* | *tin* | *din* | *chin* | *gin* | *kin* | — | *fin* | — | *thin* |
| *pie* | *buy* | *tie* | *die* | — | — | — | *guy* | *fie* | *vie* | *thigh* |

| — | *sin* | *shin* | *Min* | — | *Lynn* | — | *win* | — |
| *thy* | *sigh* | *shy* | *my* | *nigh* | *lie* | *rye* | *Wye* | *high.* |

The coupled lists show twenty different consonants, provided our pairing-off is correct, but they do not show every imaginable two-way contrast: the total number of two-way contrasts directly attested by the forms in the consolidated list is 169.

This procedure can be continued, by adding another family of partially similar words, and then another, and so on. Eventually, the addition of another new family fails to show anything not attested by those already considered. One must naturally be careful not to stop too soon, or something may be missed. Table 2.1 presents nine families, which among them both illustrate every different single consonant-sound with which English words begin and afford an example of every possible two-way contrast between those consonants. Each column is a family;

TABLE 2.1

column: 1	2	3	4	5	6	7	8	9
row:								
1 pain	pie	pooh[4]	paw	pine	pet	pat	pen	
2 bane	buy	boo[4]	baw[4]	bine	bet	bat	Ben[2]	Bess[2]
3 Taine[1]	tie	too		tine		tat	ten	Tess[2]
4 Dane	die	do	daw	dine	debt		den	
5 chain		chew	chaw	chine	Chet[2]	chat		chess
6 Jane[2]		Jew	jaw		jet		Jen[2]	Jess[2]
7 cane		coo	caw	kine		cat	ken	
8 gain	guy	goo			get	gat		guess
9 fain	fie	foo[4]		fine		fat	fen	Fess[1]
10 vain	vie			vine	vet	vat		
11 thane	thigh		thaw					
12	thy			thine		that	then	
13 sane	sigh		saw	sign	set	sat		cess
14 Zane[2]		zoo		Syne[3]			Zen[5]	
15 Shane[1]	shy	shoe	Shaw[1]	shine				
16 main	my	moo	maw	mine	met	mat	men	mess
17 nane[2]	nigh		gnaw	nine	net	gnat		ness
18 lane	lie	loo	law	line	let		Len[2]	less
19 rain	rye	Roo[2]	raw		ret	rat	wren	
20 wain	Wye	woo		wine	wet		wen	Wes[2]
21		you	yaw		yet		yen	yes
22 Haine[1]	high	who	haw			hat	hen	Hess[1]

[1] Surnames. [2] Given names or nicknames. [3] Scottish, but familiar through poetry or stories. [4] Interjections. [5] A variety of Buddhism. Other unfamiliar words in the Table can be found in any college dictionary.

each row includes only words which begin with the same consonant sound. As can be seen, there are twenty-two different consonant sounds, and a total of 231 two-way contrasts. One could add other families endlessly, but nothing new would turn up.

2.3. English Final Contrasts. So far we have sorted out only the distinctively different consonant sounds with which one-syllable English words *begin*. The pair *pin* and *bin* differ only at the beginning; but the pair *pin* and *pan* differ in the middle, and *pin* and *pip* contrast only at the end. As our next step, let us sort out the different single consonant sounds with which one-syllable English words end.

This we can do by the same procedure used for the word-initial position, except that our word families will be differently chosen: e.g., *pip, pit, pitch, pick, pig, pith, pish, pin, ping, peer, pill.* It requires a larger

TABLE 2.2

row \ column	1	2	3	4	5	6	7	8	9	10	11	12	13	14	15	16	17
1	pip		lope	rip	cope	pap	sip	cop	babe	cap	reap	leap		bub		fib	Rube[2]
2			lobe	rib			sib	cob	bait	cab							root
3	pit	late		rid	coat	pat	sit	cot		cat			mitt	but	wit	fit	
4		laid	load	rich	code	pad	Sid[2]	cod	bayed	cad	read	lead		bud			rood
5	pitch			ridge	coach	patch				catch	reach	leech			witch	Fitch[1]	
6								codge		cadge			midge	budge			
7	pick	lake		Rick[2]	coke		sick	cock	bake		reek	leak	Mick[2]	buck	wick		
8	pig			rig				cog				league	Mig[5]	bug	wig	fig	
9		Lafe[2]	loaf	Riff								leaf					roof
10		lave			cove		sieve			calf		leave					roove
11	pith		loath			path	sith			calve	wreath		myth		with[6]		ruth
12			loathe						bathe		wreathe				with[6]		
13		lace			coze	pass	Sis[2]		base	Cass[2]	Reece[1]	lease	miss	bus		fizz	ruse
14		lays	lows									leas		buzz			ruche
15	pish[3]							cosh		cash		leash			wish	fish	
16			loge						beige			liege					rouge
17		lame	loam	rim	comb	Pam[2]				cam	ream			bum			room
18	pin	lane	lone		cone	pan	sin	con	bane	can		lean	Min[2]	bun	win	fin	rune
19	ping			ring			sing						Ming	bung	wing		
20	peer			rear			cere	car					mere		weir	fear	
21	pill			rill	coal	pal	sill		bale	Cal[4]	reel		mill		will	fill	rule

[1] Surnames. [2] Given names or nicknames. [3] Interjection. [4] As in *Cal Tech* (= "California Institute of Technology"). [5] Name of a kind of airplane. [6] The word *with* has both pronunciations.

number of word families to illustrate all the possibilities here than we needed for word-initial position: Table 2.2 includes seventeen. And we encounter certain difficulties which did not turn up in initial position.

Mainly, these difficulties are due to the fact that not all of us speak English in quite the same way. Table 2.2 includes a row *peer, rear, sere, car, mere, weir, fear*. For the writer, and in general for speakers of Middle Western American English, the vowel of *peer* is quite like that of *pip, ping, pill*, and so on, so that the word is properly included in the first column. But there are some Middle Westerners, and a great many people elsewhere in the English-speaking world, for whom this does not hold—indeed, in much of New England, parts of New York City, parts of the South, and in British English, there is no terminal *r*-sound at all in such words. It is unfortunate that we should have to encounter difficulties of this sort so early in our discussion, but there is nothing which can be done about it. We are forced to choose some one variety of English, and since the writer is most familiar with the Middle Western variety he has chosen it.

The words of columns 6, 8, 10, and 17 are likewise chosen in terms of this one type of English, and require resorting for other types.

Some Middle Westerners (and some others) pronounce the four words *loge, beige, liege*, and *rouge* (row 16) with exactly the same final consonant sound that they use in *ridge, codge, cadge, midge, budge* (row 6). Others, from all areas, use two different sounds. Row 16 must be deleted for those who do not make this distinction.

Table 2.2 shows twenty-one different final single consonant sounds, and affords examples of 206 minimal two-way contrasts. One further two-way contrast is attested by the pair *seethe* and *siege*, not on the table. No minimal contrasts can be found for the final consonant sounds of the pairs

> *rouge* versus *ridge*
> *rouge* versus *ring*
> *rouge* versus *rear*.

Therefore the final consonants are defined in terms of a network of only 207 two-way contrasts.

Before passing on to an examination of the vowel sounds of mono-syllables, let us first note that to a large extent the different possible single initial consonants and the different possible single final consonants can be paired off. Thus:

> *pain* begins as *pip* ends; and likewise
>
> | | |
> |---|---|
> | *bane* and *lobe* | *Taine* and *pit* |
> | *Dane* and *laid* | *chain* and *pitch* |
> | *Jane* and *ridge* | *cane* and *pick* |
> | *gain* and *pig* | *fain* and *Lafe* |
> | *vain* and *lave* | *thane* and *pith* |
> | *thy* and *lathe* | *sane* and *lace* |
> | *Zane* and *lays* | *Shane* and *pish* |
> | *main* and *lame* | *nane* and *pin* |
> | *lane* and *pill* | *rain* and *peer.* |

These leave three initial consonant sounds (those in *wain, you, Haine*) apparently unmatched by anything final, and two final ones (those in *loge, ping*) apparently unmatched by anything initial. Occasionally one hears someone pronounce the French name *Jeanne* somewhat in the French way (though in an English context), with an initial consonant sound like the final one of *rouge*. This is so infrequent that we might almost leave it out of account altogether. Even rarer is the pronunciation of the authoress's name *Ngaio Marsh* with an initial consonant sound like the final consonant sound of *sing*.

2.4. English Medial Vowel Contrasts. The procedure which we have now used for the initial and for the final consonant sounds of monosyllables can also be used for the medial vowel sounds (demonstrated by the difference between *pin* and *pan*). On this score, dialect variation becomes really great. Table 2.3 shows, with ten families of words, those contrasts which are made regularly by most speakers of Middle Western English. Any such speaker, chosen at random, may show a few additional distinctions, but there is little agreement as to these additional ones from one speaker to another, and we omit them for the sake of greater simplicity at this stage of our discussion. The Table shows fourteen contrasting vowel sounds, and minimal two-way contrasts for every pair of the fourteen, giving an interlocking network of 91 differences of sound.

Many varieties of English show a much larger number of contrasting vowel sounds. A speaker of any of these other varieties will inevitably be disturbed by Table 2.3, and particularly by the way in which the

TABLE 2.3

column: 1	2	3	4	5	6	7	8	9	10
row:									
1 bee	ye	thee	beat	keen	beak	heel	keyed	Beal[7]	
2 bay	yea[4]	they	bait	cane	bake	hail		bail	
3 by		thy	bite	kine	bike	Hile[7]		bile	
4 boy				coin		Hoyle[7]		boil	
5 boo	you		boot	coon			cooed	Boole[7]	
6 bow[1]		though	boat	cone		whole	code	bowl	
7 bow[2]	yow	thou	bout			howl	cowed		
8 baw	yaw		bought			hall	cawed	ball	bore
9 bah			bot	con	bock		cod		bar
10 baa[3]			bat	can	back	Hal[8]	cad		
11	yeah[5]		bet	ken	beck	hell	Ked[9]	bell	bear
12		the[6]	but		buck	hull	cud		burr
13			bit	kin		hill	kid	bill	beer
14					book		could	bull	boor

[1] As for shooting an arrow.   [2] As from the waist.   [3] The bleat of a sheep; some people pronounce this the same as *bah.*   [4] As in *yea, team!*   [5] As in *Oh yeah!* Some people pronounce this so as to put it in the preceding row.   [6] One way of pronouncing the word in isolation; the other way makes it identical with *thee.*   [7] Surnames.   [8] Nickname.   [9] A trade name.

words in column 10 are aligned horizontally with those in the other columns. In the case of *bore, bar, bear, beer,* and *boor,* the reader will simply have to accept, on faith, the writer's assertion that in his speech the vowel sounds are as indicated—*bar* has the vowel sound of *bah, bot, con, bock, cod; bear* that of *bet, ken;* and so on. In the case of *burr,* the writer cannot insist that the vowel is exactly the same as that of *but, buck, hull, cud,* for, to a trained ear, it is not. But it is nearer to that of *but, buck,* and so on, than it is to any of the other vowel sounds represented in the table, and the writer is unable to find any direct contrast, in any environment, between the vowel sound of *burr* and that of *but* or *buck.* Since contrast is much more important than exact identity, the alignment is made as shown on the Table. There are certain problems connected with this that we shall not be able to deal with until much later (§40).

2.5. Summary; Phonemes and Speech Sounds. From §§2.2–4 we see that a monosyllabic utterance of Middle Western English may begin with any of the single consonant sounds sorted out in Table 2.1, or with certain combinations of two or three of them (*spin, string*), or with no consonant sound at all (*in, and*). It then continues with one or another of the vowel sounds sorted out in Table 2.3. It then ends with one or another of the single consonant sounds sorted out in Table 2.2, or with certain combinations of two, three, or four of them (*stand, text, glimpsed*), or with no final consonant at all. Of course, not all the theoretically possible combinations actually occur—if they did, then there would be no holes in our tables, and one family of words would suffice for each table. But any monosyllable which *does* occur accords with the description just given. We have sorted out all the differences of consonant and vowel sound which function to keep monosyllabic utterances apart.

Our utterances, of course, are rarely monosyllabic. Therefore we cannot be sure that we have covered every functionally relevant difference of sound in English. Before we continue our analysis of English phonology, however, let us for a moment assume that the description given above is complete, so that we can pose some crucial questions.

Just what *is* the *p*-sound (as we have been calling it) at the beginning of the word *pin*? There are two different senses in which this question can be understood, leading to two different answers.

The first (and less important) answer is to describe the *p* of *pin* in terms of what it sounds like, or in terms of how it is produced by a speaker. As we shall see in §§7–9, the *p* of *pin* can be approximately described as a "voiceless bilabial stop." This description is cast in the terminology of what is called *articulatory phonetics*. When we say that *pin* begins as *tip* ends, we are identifying the first consonant of the former and the last consonant of the latter on the basis of such description. Any two sounds, in the same language or in different languages, which fit the same description in terms of articulatory phonetics, are said to be instances or recurrences of "the same" *speech sound*. This renders the term "speech sound" relative, since our articulatory description may be either loose or precise.

The second (and more important) answer turns on the consideration mentioned in §2.1: that the sole function of sound in language is to keep utterances apart. The phonological system of a language is therefore not so much a "set of sounds" as it is a *network of differences between sounds*. In this frame of reference, the elements of a phonological system cannot be defined positively in terms of what they "are," but only negatively in terms of what they are *not*, what they *contrast* with. While it is true, and not irrelevant, that English *p* is a "voiceless bilabial stop," it is much more important that *p* is *different* from certain other elements —namely, those sorted out in Tables 2.1, 2.2, and 2.3.

Since the element *p* in English is something different from the various other elements, we are trained to pronounce it, by and large, in such a way that it cannot easily be mistaken for any of the other elements; and, as hearers, we are trained to catch even the subtlest clue of pronunciation which identifies what we hear as a *p* rather than as any of the others. But this does not mean that we must necessarily pronounce *p* in exactly the same way every time, and we do not. So long as what we say sounds sufficiently unlike any of the other elements which might occur in the same context, yielding a different utterance, our hearers will interpret what they hear as a *p*.

This affords us more leeway than we realize. It is only natural that we should be unaware of our actual variation in the pronunciation of an element like *p*, since throughout our experience with English, from earliest childhood, we have been trained to ignore certain variations in pronunciation, and to pay attention only to key differences. Accordingly, it is difficult to demonstrate to a speaker of English that his pronunciation of an element like *p* does vary quite widely. But it is easy enough to demonstrate comparable irrelevant ranges of variation in other languages. For example, if we listen to a Menomini Indian saying several times his word with the meaning 'he looks at him,' we hear in the middle of the word now a sound something like our *p* and now a sound more like our *b*. We hear the difference because English trains us to hear it. But the Menomini does not hear it, because in his language this particular difference of sound never functions to keep utterances apart—and therefore he has no reason to *need* to hear it. Conversely, a speaker of Hindi, hearing us say *pin* a number of times, will report that we fluctuate between two initial consonants, the difference between which is functional in his language, but not in English.

In this functional frame of reference, when we are dealing with the phonological system of a single language we do not ordinarily use the term "speech sound." For example, we do not call English *p* a "speech sound" in this context, because whether all occurrences of English *p* are "the same" speech sound, or some are one speech sound and some are another, depends on who is listening and on how we describe what is heard. Instead, we say that English *p* is a *phoneme*.

The phonemes of a language, then, are the elements which stand in contrast with each other in the phonological system of the language. English *p* is a phoneme, and so are the various other elements sorted out in Tables 2.1, 2.2, and 2.3. Throughout all our subsequent discussion, it must constantly be remembered that a phoneme in a given language is defined *only in terms of its differences from the other phonemes of the same language.*

NOTES

New terms: *phonology* or *phonemics*, *phonological system* of a language, *phoneme*, *speech sound*. *Articulatory phonetics* is mentioned in passing, but will not come up for detailed discussion until §7.

Hockett 1955 is a detailed treatment of the substance of §§2–13; further bibliography can be found therein.

3.

PHONEMIC NOTATION

3.1. Linguistics is one of many fields in which it is necessary to devise certain sorts of special notation.

A football coach charts plays on a blackboard with O's, X's, and arrows. Radio circuits are represented on paper by diagrams which are half pictorial and half arbitrary. Chemists have a special notation for representing elements, compounds, and reactions.

Let us for a moment consider the special notation of chemistry. At the basis of this symbolism is the assignment of a capital letter, or in some cases a capital letter followed by a lower case letter, to each element. Thus "H" represents hydrogen, "C" carbon, and "Cl" chlorine. In structural formulas, each of these symbols represents not just the element, but a single atom thereof; a dash represents a valence bond. With these conventions, the structural formula for methane or marsh gas,

$$\begin{array}{c} \text{H} \\ | \\ \text{H—C—H,} \\ | \\ \text{H} \end{array}$$

actually forms a sort of picture of a molecule of that compound. Of course, the individual symbols "H" and "C" don't "look like" atoms of hydrogen and carbon—nothing "looks like" atoms, since atoms are too small to reflect light, and thus too small to see with any physically possible microscope. But at the size-level of the whole structural formula, the geometrical arrangement of the constituent symbols is presumed to be roughly parallel to the geometrical arrangement of the constituent atoms in a molecule of marsh gas. It is to this geometrical parallelism that we refer when we call the formula a sort of "picture" of what it represents.

Now in discussing the phonologic system of any one language—and, indeed, often in discussing other aspects of the language—it is necessary to use a system of notation which will reflect the phonemic system of the language and show the phonemic composition of any utterance or part of an utterance. The way in which a *phonemic notation* for a language is developed is very much like the way in which chemists have developed their notation for structural formulas.

To start with, it is necessary to assign a different visible mark to each phoneme of the language. We could use any symbols whatsoever for this purpose; logically, all that would matter would be that we had exactly enough of them, all different in appearance. But it is helpful if, insofar as possible, we choose marks which already have some sort of association with the phonemes to be represented. The chemist's symbols have been chosen with an eye to such mnemonic help: "H" is the first letter of the written word "hydrogen," "Na" for sodium is the first two letters of Latin "natrium," and so on. In English writing, the letter "p" is often associated with the English *p*-phoneme (*pin, pull, nap, apple, bump*) and rarely with anything else. Thus the sensible choice for this phoneme in our phonemic notation for English is the letter "p."

Next, it is necessary to decide upon some proper geometrical arrangement for the symbols which represent the constituent phonemes of any utterance we want to depict. In speech, the phonemes of an utterance occur largely one after another in time. The surface of a sheet of paper or a blackboard has no time on it, but we can follow the habit of ordinary Western writing, placing the symbol for a phoneme which occurs *earlier* to the left of that for a phoneme which occurs *later*, and going on to another line when we reach the edge of the writing surface.

When these two steps have been taken, our phonemic notation for the particular language is established. We have the necessary apparatus for a graphic representation of *anything the speakers of the language ever say*.

Furthermore, our phonemic notation for the particular language is pictorial to about the same degree as are the chemist's structural formulas. There is nothing similar between the visual shape of the mark "p" and the auditory shape of the English phoneme which we choose to represent by that mark in our notation. But there is a resemblance between the geometrical arrangement of the constituent symbols in the phonemic formula displayed here:

pin

and the geometrical arrangement of the three phonemes we produce when we say the English word *pin*. In one case, the arrangement is in a single spatial dimension, and in the other it is in the single dimension of time; but, given our arbitrary equating of "earlier than" with "to the left of," the linear ordering is the same.

3.2. Special Problems in Phonemic Notations. The linguist faces one problem of notation which does not disturb the chemist. The latter needs only one notation for all possible structural formulas, for there is only one set of elements in the universe. The linguist needs as many *different* phonemic notations as there are languages to be dealt with.

It would be wasteful to make up a whole new set of visible marks for each new language. But if some of the same marks are to be used from one language to another, their assignment should not be random. What we do is to pay some attention to the similarities between phonemes of different languages *as speech sounds:* "p" in English for a certain phoneme, and "p" in our notation for French, Menomini, or Chinese for phonemes in those languages which are at least something like English *p* to the ear. Complete consistency cannot be achieved, since the phonemes of different languages are defined by different interlocking sets of contrast. But the most extremely misleading assignments of marks to phonemes can be avoided.

Formulas in phonemic notation often have to be displayed directly in the middle of a passage of written English. To set the notation off clearly from context, we shall henceforth enclose every phonemic formula between slant lines:

the English phoneme /p/
the English word /pin/ is a monosyllable
Menomini /wa·pamɛw/

and so forth. The context will always indicate what language is being discussed. But it must be remembered that "English /p/" and, say, "Menomini /p/" refer to entirely different phonemes, despite the use of the mark "p" for both.

3.3. English Phonemic Notation. We shall now assign marks to all the English phonemes uncovered by our investigation in §2. The re-

maining symbols which are needed will be added as we unravel the rest
of the English phonological system.

First the symbols for the initial consonant phonemes illustrated by
Table 2.1:

/p/	*pain, pie*	/ð/	*thy, thine*
/b/	*bane, buy*	/s/	*sane, sigh*
/t/	*Taine, tie*	/z/	*Zane, zoo*
/d/	*Dane, die*	/š/	*Shane, shy*
/č/	*chain, chew*	/m/	*main, my*
/ǰ/	*Jane, Jew*	/n/	*nane, nigh*
/k/	*cane, coo*	/l/	*lane, lie*
/g/	*gain, guy*	/r/	*rain, rye*
/f/	*fain, fie*	/w/	*wain, Wye*
/v/	*vain, vie*	/j/	*you, yaw*
/θ/	*thane, thigh*	/h/	*Haine, high.*

Nineteen of these will be used also, of course, for nineteen of the final
consonant phonemes illustrated by Table 2.2: /p/ *pip*, /b/ *lobe*, /t/ *pit*,
/d/ *laid*, /č/ *pitch*, /ǰ/ *ridge*, /k/ *pick*, /g/ *pig*, /f/ *Lafe*, /v/ *lave*, /θ/ *pith*,
/ð/ *lathe*, /s/ *lace*, /z/ *lays*, /š/ *pish*, /m/ *lame*, /n/ *pin*, /l/ *pill*, /r/ *peer*.
In addition, we need for final-position consonants the following two:

/ž/ *loge, rouge*
/ŋ/ *ping, ring.*

This totals twenty-four marks for consonant phonemes, and this is
all that is needed even for utterances longer than a single syllable.
So far as the graphic shapes of the marks are concerned, sixteen are
identical with English letters often used, in ordinary English spelling,
with the values assigned them; one, /j/, is a familiar letter used
in an unfamiliar way (though this usage is familiar in the spelling-
systems of German and some other languages); the remaining seven,
/č ǰ š ž θ ð ŋ/, are strange, but will variously recur in our phonemic
notations for certain other languages.

For the vowels sorted out in Table 2.3 we shall use the following
symbols:

/ij/	bee, ye, beat	/bij, jij, bijt/
/ej/	bay, bait	/bej, bejt/
/aj/	by, bite	/baj, bajt/
/oj/	boy, coin	/boj, kojn/
/uw/	boo, boot	/buw, buwt/
/ow/	though, boat	/ðow, bowt/
/aw/	thou, howl	/ðaw, hawl/
/ɔ/	baw, hall, bore	/bɔ, hɔl, bɔr/
/a/	bah, bot, bar	/ba, bat, bar/
/æ/	baa, bat, cad	/bæ, bæt, kæd/
/e/	yeah, bet, bear	/ye, bet, ber/
/ə/	the, but, burr	/ðə, bət, bər/
/i/	bit, beer	/bit, bir/
/u/	book, boor	/buk, bur/.

To the right we have placed the complete phonemic formula for each of the sample words.

Here even some of the symbols which are quite like English letters in shape have been assigned values for which English writing affords little mnemonic help. Our reason for this is the other mnemonic principle explained in §3.2: some of the same marks are to be used in our phonemic notations for other languages, and it is easier to maintain some degree of consistency in this, from one language to another, if the marks listed above are assigned the indicated English values.

In seven cases, we have used a combination of two marks instead of a single mark: /ij ej aj oj uw ow aw/. Linguists who have worked with English phonology are in disagreement as to the status of these seven vowel-like elements. Some believe that a word like *bay* contains a vowel which can be identified with that in *bet* (our /e/), followed by something which can be identified with the initial phoneme of *you, yes* (our /j/). For them, once the symbols "e" and "j" have been assigned the values just indicated, then the notation /bej/ for the word *bay*, or /bejt/ for the word *bait*, is a necessary consequence. A similar line of reasoning justifies the other compound notations with "w" and "j" as the second mark.

Other specialists in English phonology disagree, feeling that everything after the /b/ in *bay* is just a single phoneme, entirely on a par with everything between the initial and the final consonant of *beat*, *bit*, *bet*, *bat*, and so on.

We do not have to take sides in this argument for our present purposes. Fortunately, we can use one and the same notation whichever opinion eventually proves correct. For those who prefer to interpret the vowel of *bay* as a sequence of two phonemes, the notation /ej/ can be interpreted in that way. For those who prefer to interpret the vowel of *bay* as a single phoneme, the notation /ej/ can be interpreted as a compound mark for a unitary element, like the chemist's "He" for helium (in contrast to "H" for hydrogen). Table 2.2 shows that the initial consonants /j/ and /w/ are not matched by any final consonants; therefore we run no danger of ambiguity in monosyllables in using the marks "j" and "w" also as constituents of our compound symbols; and it will turn out that the notation remains unambiguous for utterances longer than a single syllable.

NOTES

Problems. Gleason, *Workbook* (see bibliography, Gleason 1955b), on pages 15–18, gives a list of English monosyllables for practice in transcription.

4.

ENGLISH INTONATION

4.1. In our analysis of English one-syllable utterances in §2, we pretended that two such utterances are either kept apart by some difference in constituent vowels or consonants, or else are not kept apart at all. This was an oversimplification. Consider the following dialog:

> JACK: Where're you going?
> BILL: Home.
> JACK: Home?
> BILL: Yes.

The second and third lines of this dialog are not identical to the ear, and certainly not the same in meaning. Yet the constituent vowels and consonants of the two are the same: /howm/. The difference in sound which keeps them apart lies in the changing pitch of the voice. Distinctively different features of English speech melody constitute *intonation*.

Although our conventional punctuation marks permit us to note some intonational contrasts in writing (*Home.* versus *Home?*), they do not provide for this either consistently or fully. The same mark may be used in spite of intonational differences, and, conversely, different marks may have to be used even though the intonation is the same, as it commonly would be in each of the following two utterances:

> JACK: Where're you going?
> BILL: I'm going home.

A better way of marking intonation is therefore necessary. Ideally, the marks should provide for all significant intonational contrasts, but,

33

since the precise analysis of English intonation is still a matter of some doubt, in some instances they may not.

Until recently, intonation was more or less tacitly ignored by most linguistic scholars on the assumption that it did not vary significantly from language to language, or that anything so "natural" hardly warranted serious consideration. It is perhaps true that certain features of speech melody are to be found in all languages (e.g., rise of pitch and volume under the stimulus of pain or anger), but such universal features, if they exist, are not part of intonation as we now use that term. Recent research suggests that every language has a system of basic speech melodies which is as unique to the language as is its set of vowel and consonant phonemes. It may be that the normal effect of an intonation is sometimes concealed, or overridden, by the superposition of nonlinguistic features of speech melody under the stimulus of strong emotion, but this is on a par with the fact that normal articulation of vowels and consonants is sometimes distorted by excitement, depression, or drugs.

4.2. PLs and TCs. Let us begin by examining in more detail the ways in which Bill might have said *home* in answer to Jack's question, and the ways in which Jack might have intoned his rejoinder. If Bill is offering a perfectly matter-of-fact reply, without any implication that Jack really ought to know the answer without asking, he will usually start with a relatively high pitch, and let it fall rapidly to a very low pitch at the end of the word. The relatively high initial pitch will be represented by a /^{3}/ before the word *home*, and the relatively low level reached at the end by a /^{1}/ written after the word, thus:

(1) $^3home^1\downarrow$

(The arrow at the end will be discussed later.) Instead of this, Bill may start at about the same pitch but let it fall only slightly: in this case we write /^{2}/ instead of /^{1}/:

(2) $^3home^2\downarrow$

This carries a different meaning in the present context: 'I don't particularly *want* to go home, but there's nothing else left to do.'

If Bill wants to imply 'Of course I'm going home; what else would you expect at this hour?'—then he may do one of three things. One is to start at an especially high pitch, higher than that symbolized by

/^{3}/—we shall use the mark /^{4}/—but to glide down just as far by the end of the word as in way (1):

(3) $^4home^1{\downarrow}$

Or else he may start at a very low pitch (/^{1}/), and let the pitch rise, either slightly—

(4) $^1home^1{\uparrow}$

—or more sharply—

(5) $^1home^2{\uparrow}$

The symbol /^{2}/ at the end of (5) obviously represents a level of pitch higher than /^{1}/ but lower than /^{3}/. In (4), the terminal upwards-pointing arrow means that the rise in pitch is to a level higher than /^{1}/ but lower than /^{2}/; in (5), the same terminal mark means that the rise in pitch is to a level higher than /^{2}/ but lower than /^{3}/. Thus the extent to which the pitch rises in these two is indicated jointly by the last superscript numeral and the arrow after it: the arrow means 'rise to a point higher than such-and-such,' and the last superscript numeral defines the 'such-and-such.' That these two rises are potentially different in function can be shown in another context. Suppose that Bill's answer is delivered in way (4). Jack's comment might then be delivered in way (5), with the meaning 'You don't mean *that*, do you? I hadn't expected it!' But Jack cannot achieve this meaning by using way (4), which seems never to imply any feeling of interrogation.

The intonational phonemes /^{1}/, /^{2}/, /^{3}/, and /^{4}/ are called *pitch levels* (PLs); /${\downarrow}$/ and /${\uparrow}$/ are *terminal contours* (TCs). Our examples so far do not illustrate PL /^{2}/ very well. The contrasts among /^{1}/, /^{2}/, and /^{3}/ can be more clearly shown as follows. If Jack asks *Are you going home now?* Bill may answer

(6) $^1Yes^1{\uparrow}$

which either carries the same overtones described for (4) above, or else implies that Bill is about to continue with some comment on his answer. If Jack quietly calls *Bill!* in order to get Bill's attention, Bill may indicate that he is listening by saying

(7) $^2Yes^2{\uparrow}$

Some people answer the telephone this way, or say *yes* with this intonation to a stranger who comes to the door; in these contexts it strikes many of us as brusque and a bit impatient. Lastly, suppose that Bill has asked Jack to do something, hoping for an affirmative answer, but that he does not quite hear Jack's response. He may ask 'Did you say yes?' by saying

(8) $^3Yes^3\uparrow$

In all three of these ways of saying *yes* (6, 7, and 8), there is slight rise in pitch as the word is spoken, but the pitch starts lowest in (6), somewhat higher in (7), and still higher in (8).

So far we have illustrated two TCs. There are three in all, but before introducing the third let us clarify the distinction between the two already introduced. There are two common ways for Jack to call quietly to Bill to attract his attention—assuming that both are in the same room, but that Bill is occupied with his own work or thoughts. One is like the second way (2) of saying *home:*

(9) $^3Bill^2\downarrow$

and the other is

(10) $^3Bill^2\uparrow$

The notation in (10) indicates that the pitch of the voice starts at level /³/, falls all the way to /²/, and then rises somewhat, though not far enough to reach /³/ again. Notice, thus, that the TC /↑/ *always* involves a terminal rise in pitch, even if the voice has first dipped down from a higher level.

An exaggerated variety of (9) is our usual way of calling someone from a distance; the overall increase in volume, pitch, and duration is probably part of the "natural" framework common to all languages.

Either of the following is a sort of concessive assent, implying 'that may be true, but I have doubts as to its relevance':

(11) $^3Yes^2\uparrow$
(12) $^3Yes^1\uparrow$

To the writer, the second of these tends to imply more serious reservations than the first.

Thus the key characteristic of /↑/, distinguishing it from /↓/ and from the third TC (to be discussed in a moment), is a terminal *rise* in pitch, which ends at a level somewhat higher than the PL written directly before the mark /↑/, but usually not so high as the next higher PL.

The TC /↓/ is distinguished from /↑/ basically by the absence of this terminal rise. Its positive characteristics are a fading-away of the force of articulation, often with a drawling of the last few vowels and consonants. When the immediately preceding PL is /¹/, the fade is usually accompanied by a fall of the pitch to a point somewhat *below* PL /¹/.

The third TC, /|/, is marked by the absence of the positive features for either /↑/ or /↓/. This TC most often occurs where the speaker goes right on talking, so that isolated examples, directly comparable to those that have been given for the other TCs, are harder to find and to illustrate. However, consider someone who is about to answer a complicated question, and who must think through what he is going to say before saying it. He may begin in either of the following ways:

(13)   ³*Well*³|
(14)   ³*Well*³↓

(13) is cut off suddenly without forewarning; (14) fades away from the outset. Different impressions are conveyed to the audience. Hearing (13), we sense that the speaker has realized only after beginning to speak that he must take time to think his answer out. Hearing (14), we sense that the speaker realized this necessity from the outset, and that his *well* is uttered, in part, to let us know that the necessary cogitation is under way.

4.3. Macrosegments. Utterances longer than a single syllable differ, as to intonation, in one or more of three ways from those of a single syllable.

First: a longer utterance may contain two successive intonations:

(15)   ³*No*¹| ¹*Bill*¹↑

Second: a single intonation may be stretched through two or more successive syllables, a PL at the beginning, a PL at the end, and a TC at the end; compare the following:

(16)	$^3No^1\downarrow$
(17)	$^3Never^1\downarrow$
(18)	$^3Terrible^1\downarrow$
(19)	$^3Dictionary^1\downarrow$
(20)	^3I *want to go*$^1\downarrow$
(21)	^3I *want to go there*$^1\downarrow$
(22)	^3I *want to go along with you*$^1\downarrow$
(23)	$^3Elevator$ *operator*$^1\downarrow$

Note that in all of these (16–23), the *most prominent* syllable is the very first one. (21), thus, answers the question *WHO wants to go there?*—not the question *Where do you want to go?* The most prominent syllable of an intonation, be it the first or not, and the PL which accompanies it, are said to be at the *center* of the intonation.

Third: a single intonation may include one or more syllables before its center. The PL at the center of an intonation is always the next to the last PL in the intonation, the last one being that which occurs at the end along with the TC. If there are syllables before the center, then the pitch on which they are spoken is also distinctive, and we place a mark for a PL at the beginning:

(24)	^2I *want to go* $^3there^1\downarrow$
(25)	^2I *want to* ^3go *there*$^1\downarrow$
(26)	^2I ^3want *to go there*$^1\downarrow$
(27)	^2An $^3elevator$ *operator*$^1\downarrow$
(28)	$^2He's$ *an* $^3elevator$ *operator*$^1\downarrow$

In all of these (24–28), the PL at the center is $/^3/$ (and the center is the syllable on which $/^3/$ is written).

The stretch of material spoken with a single intonation is called a *macrosegment*. We may freely speak either of the center of an intonation or of the center of a macrosegment. Everything from the center to the end, including the center, is the *head;* anything which precedes the center is a *pendant*. By definition, then, every macrosegment includes a center and a head (though the two may be coterminous, as 1–14, 16, 24), but only some include a pendant (24–28). Every macrosegment ends with a TC, which therefore automatically marks the boundary between successive macrosegments in a single utterance (as in 15, the only example so far of more than one macrosegment). Every macrosegment includes at least two PLs, one at the end and one at the center; if there is a pendant, there is an additional PL at the beginning, and there may be a fourth somewhere between the beginning and the center. Examples of the latter possibility will come later.

The commonest and most colorless intonation for short statements is /² ³¹↓/. By this abstracted notation, we mean that the pendant, if any, is spoken on PL /²/, that the head has PL /³/, and that the last PL is /¹/ and the TC /↓/. To the examples already given (1, 16–23, 24–28) we may add one here:

(29) ²*My name is* ³*Bill*¹↓

This is also the most colorless intonation for short questions built around a "question word" such as *who, where, what:*

(30) ²*What's your* ³*name*¹↓

On the other hand, questions of the sort that allow a yes-or-no answer have a different most-neutral intonation, /² ³³↑/:

(31) ²*Is your name* ³*Bill*³↑

A series of words in the proper order for a statement can be made into a question merely by using the indicated intonation:

(32) ²*His name is* ³*Bill*³↑

The following is a perfectly normal question:

(33) ³*What do you* ²*do*²| ²*with a stiff* ³*neck*¹↓

Notice what happens if we change the intonations as follows:

(34) ²*What do you do with a* ³*stiff*¹↓ ³*neck*³↑

The discovery of questions which could be distorted in this manner used to be a sort of parlor-game.

Again, notice the following two normal questions:

(35) ²*What are we having for* ³*dinner*¹| ¹*Mother*¹↑
(36) ²*What are we having for* ³*dinner*¹↓ ²*beef*²↑

Placing the intonations of (36) on the words of (35) gives a gruesomely cannibalistic effect:

(37) ^{2}*What are we having for* ^{3}*dinner*^{1}↓ ^{2}*Mother*^{2}↑

Another illustration of this difference appears in the following pair:

(38) ^{2}*What are you* ^{3}*reading*^{1}| ^{1}*Ma*^{1}*cauley*^{1}↑
(39) ^{2}*What are you* ^{3}*reading*^{1}↓ ^{1}*Ma*^{2}*cauley*^{2}↑

(38) is addressed to someone named Macauley; (39) asks about an author of that name. In (36), (37), and (39), the second intonation, given as /(^{1}) ^{22}↑/, can be replaced by /(^{1}) ^{33}↑/ without altering the effects.

To the following distorted utterance—

(40) ^{2}*He has a* ^{3}*feebly*^{1}| ^{1}*growing down on his* ^{1}*throat*^{1}↓

—the most natural response seems to be "What's a feebly?" That is, the intonational pattern seems to mark *feebly* as a noun. Replace *feebly* by *wart* or *mole* and the sentence makes sense. Or keep the words, but change the intonation as follows:

(41) ^{2}*He has a* ^{3}*feebly growing* ^{3}*down*^{1}| ^{1}*on his* ^{1}*throat*^{1}↓

The last example includes a macrosegment (the first) in which there are four PLs instead of just three or two—two before the center, instead of one. Another example of this is the second one below. One can say, quite colorlessly,

(42) ^{2}*I've been here five* ^{3}*minutes*^{1}↓

but one can also emphasize the length of time slightly by rising to PL /^{3}/ on the word *five:*

(43) ^{2}*I've been here* ^{3}*five* ^{3}*minutes*^{1}↓

This last is distinct not only from (42) but also from two others. If someone asks "Did you say *six* minutes?", you may reply

(44) ^{2}*No*^{2}↑ ^{2}*I've been here* ^{3}*five minutes*^{1}↓

And instead of (43) one can put even more emphasis on the length of time, perhaps in protest or complaint, by saying

(45) ^{2}*I've been here* ^{3}*five*^{3}| ^{3}*minutes*^{1}↓

In (44), the word *five* not only carries PL /³/, but it is also more prominent than anything before or after it; the downwards glide of pitch
begins with *five*. In (43), on the other hand, the center is the *min-* of
minutes, which is more prominent than anything around it, even though
it is spoken at the same pitch as the word *five* immediately before it.

Though the center of an intonation is by definition the most prominent syllable in the macrosegment, it need not carry the highest pitch.
Here is an example in which the center is lower in pitch than most of
the rest. Suppose a child starts to eat something that is intended for
some other use. You may admonish him by saying

(46)   ³*You* ¹*don't* ¹*eat that*²↑

This should be distinguished sharply from the following two, which are
also admonitions, but with a different force: the child is supposed to eat
something, but preferably not "that":

(47)   ³*You* ¹*don't eat* ¹*that*²↑
(48)   ³*You* ¹*don't eat* ²*that*²↑

4.4. PL /⁴/. The highest of the four PLs occurs somewhat less frequently than the other three, in a smaller variety of intonations. The
following statements subsume most occurrences of /⁴/ and will be
made as though there were no exceptions, though in fact there may be a
few. Any intonation which involves /⁴/ anywhere has /⁴/ at the center.
Furthermore, no intonation with /⁴/ at the center occurs unless it
parallels an intonation identical throughout save for the presence of
/³/ wherever the first has /⁴/. All intonations with /³/ at the center
seem to be thus paralleled. Thus one can say (24), and this is matched
by an utterance which adds some sort of special or contrastive emphasis
to *there:*

(49)   ²*I want to go* ⁴*there*¹↓

Similarly, question (31) is matched by a somewhat more surprised
query:

(50)   ²*Is your name* ⁴*Bill*⁴↑

Compare also the following two—one straightforward, the other
surprised:

(51)   ²*Is* ³*your name Bill*³↑
(52)   ²*Is* ⁴*your name Bill*⁴↑

4.5. Additional Examples. The four PLs and three TCs which have been described constitute the stock of intonational phonemes of English. The examples which follow illustrate further combinations of these elements into whole intonations.

Note the following four ways of intoning the word-sequence *it's ten o'clock I want to go home:*

(53) ^{2}*It's* ^{3}*ten o'* ^{3}*clock*^{2}| ^{2}*I want to go* ^{3}*home*^{1}↓

(54) ^{2}*It's* ^{3}*ten o'* ^{3}*clock*^{2}↑ ^{2}*I want to go* ^{3}*home*^{1}↓

(55) ^{2}*It's* ^{3}*ten o'* ^{2}*clock*^{2}↑ ^{2}*I want to go* ^{3}*home*^{1}↓

(56) ^{2}*It's* ^{3}*ten o'* ^{3}*clock*^{1}↓ ^{2}*I want to go* ^{3}*home*^{1}↓

The last of these sounds most like "two sentences": this effect is indicative of the kind of meaning the intonations /$^{2\ 31}$↓/ and /$^{2\ 3\ 31}$↓/ carry for us. The other three give the impression of a closer linkage between the two parts.

There are many strings of words which are delivered now as a single macrosegment, now as two or more. In part, this depends on the tempo of speech. For example, in normal rapid speech most of us could say either of the following two, though in slightly more careful speech we would much more often say the second:

(57) ^{2}*He has an* ^{3}*office in that building*^{1}↓

(58) ^{2}*He has an* ^{3}*office*^{1}| ^{1}*in that* ^{1}*building*^{1}↓

A more extensive breakdown would not be natural save under special conditions. If we were dictating to someone who did not know shorthand very well, we might say

(59) ^{2}*He has*^{2}| ^{2}*an*^{2}| ^{3}*office*^{1}| ^{1}*in*^{1}| ^{1}*that*^{1}| ^{1}*building*^{1}↓

And in real exasperation we might even say

(60) ^{2}*He*^{2}↑ ^{2}*has*^{2}↑ ^{2}*an*^{2}↑ ^{3}*office*^{2}↑ ^{2}*in*^{2}↑ ^{2}*that*^{2}↑ ^{3}*building*^{1}↓

An interesting intonational habit is observable in the reading of dialog, where a sentence like *"Are you going?" said Jane* is often rendered as

(61) ^{2}*Are you* ^{3}*going*^{3}↑ ^{3}*said* ^{3}*Jane*^{3}↑

Here the use of PL /^{3}/ throughout the *speaker-indication* is really not in itself meaningful, for if the direct quotation had ended with a different

PL, it would be this that would be carried through the speaker-indication. Compare the following four:

(62) ^{2}*I'm* ^{3}*going*^{1}↓ ^{1}*said* ^{1}*Bill*^{1}↑
(63) ^{2}*I* ^{3}*guess so*^{2}↓ ^{2}*replied* ^{2}*Bill*^{2}↑
(64) ^{1}*Fire*^{3}↑ ^{3}*said* ^{3}*Bill*^{3}↑
(65) ^{2}*Do you* ^{4}*mean it*^{4}↑ ^{4}*cried* ^{4}*Bertha*^{4}↑

A bit out of patience:

(66) ^{2}*I* ^{3}*told you so*^{2}↑
(67) ^{2}*I* ^{3}*told you so*^{1}↑

The first of the following is perhaps commoner than the second:

(68) ^{3}*So* ^{2}*long*^{2}↓
(69) ^{3}*So* ^{2}*long*^{2}↑

Very businesslike:

(70) ^{3}*Tell me about your* ^{2}*friend*^{1}↓

You're bound to anyway, so let's get it over with:

(71) ^{3}*Tell me about your* ^{2}*friend*^{2}↓

Choose between the alternatives:

(72) ^{2}*Do you want* ^{3}*coffee*^{3}↑ ^{2}*or* ^{3}*milk*^{1}↓

Answer yes or no:

(73) ^{2}*Do you want* ^{3}*coffee*^{3}↑ ^{2}*or* ^{3}*milk*^{3}↑

Philosophical assertion versus biological report:

(74) ^{2}*The* ^{3}*man in the* ^{3}*street*^{3}| ^{2}*is* ^{3}*my* ^{3}*brother*^{1}↓
(75) ^{2}*The man in the* ^{3}*street*^{2}| ^{2}*is my* ^{3}*brother*^{1}↓

A threat, versus mere advice:

(76) ^{2}*You'd* ^{3}*better do it*^{1}↑
(77) ^{2}*You'd better* ^{3}*do it*^{2}↓

Prediction verified, versus prediction wrong but relinquished reluctantly:

(78) $^2See^2\uparrow$ ^2I $^3thought$ $so^1\downarrow$
(79) $^3Well^2\downarrow$ ^2I $^3thought$ $so^1\uparrow$

Regretful or doubtful:

(80) $^2He's$ $^3gone^2\downarrow$
(81) $^2We'll$ $^3try^2\downarrow$
(82) $^2I'm$ $^3going^2\downarrow$
(83) ^2Nobody $^3came^2\downarrow$

Exasperated:

(84) ^2I $^3don't$ $^1know^2\uparrow$

Tired, possibly disgusted:

(85) ^2I want to go $^2home^1\downarrow$
(86) ^2I want to go $^1home^1\downarrow$

Naturally, what did you expect! (cf. example 4):

(87) ^2He ^1bought $it^1\uparrow$
(88) ^3He ^1bought $it^1\uparrow$

The first of these is more peremptory and tired than the second:

(89) $^3She'll$ ex^2plain it to $you^2\downarrow$
(90) $^3She'll$ ex^2plain it to $you^2\uparrow$

Of the following three, the first is neutral, the second emphatic, and the third helpless:

(91) ^3What a $^3man^1\downarrow$
(92) ^3What a $^1man^1\downarrow$
(93) ^3What a $^3man^2\downarrow$

Of the following two, the first signals aloofness on the part of the speaker, while the second is friendly:

(94) ^2Good $^3morning^1\downarrow$ $^1class^1\downarrow$
(95) ^2Good $^3morning^1\downarrow$ $^1class^1\uparrow$

The contrast in the next pair is somewhat similar:

(96) ^{2}*You better not* ^{3}*do that*^{2}↓ ^{2}*Mac*^{2}↓
(97) ^{2}*You better not* ^{3}*do that*^{2}↓ ^{2}*Mac*^{2}↑

Just before being interrupted, or with what follows conveyed by gestures rather than speech:

(98) ^{2}*In* ^{3}*fact*^{3}| ^{3}*my* ^{3}*friend*^{3}|

Miscellany:

(99) ^{2}*I* ^{3}*never* ^{2}*heard it before*^{1}↓
(100) ^{3}*One*^{3}| ^{3}*two*^{3}| ^{3}*three*^{3}| ^{3}*four*^{1}↓
(101) ^{3}*One*^{3}| ^{3}*two*^{3}↓ ^{3}*three*^{3}↓ ^{3}*four*^{1}↓
(102) ^{2}*One*^{2}↑ ^{2}*two*^{2}↑ ^{2}*three*^{2}↑ ^{3}*four*^{1}↓
(103) ^{1}*That's* ^{3}*all*^{2}↓
(104) ^{2}*Well*^{2}↑ ^{2}*boys will be* ^{3}*boys*^{2}↓
(105) ^{1}*I'm* ^{2}*gonna* ^{3}*tell*^{2}↓
(106) ^{1}*I* ^{3}*won't* ^{2}*tell*^{2}↓
(107) ^{3}*Right behind the* ^{1}*eight ball*^{1}↓
(108) ^{2}*The* ^{3}*man's here*^{2}↑
(109) ^{2}*I* ^{4}*hunted*^{1}↓ ^{1}*I didn't* ^{3}*fish*^{1}↑
(110) ^{2}*Miss* ^{2}*Jones*^{2}↑ ^{2}*this is Mister* ^{2}*Smith*^{1}↓
(111) ^{1}*The* ^{2}*rat*^{2}↓
(112) ^{2}*Time to get* ^{3}*up*^{3}| ^{2}*son*^{2}↓
(113) ^{2}*Well* ^{4}*look who's* ^{4}*here*^{2}↓
(114) ^{2}*That's* ^{3}*o*^{2}*kay*^{2}↓
(115) ^{2}*The* ^{2}*word*^{2}| ^{3}*pig*^{3}↓ ^{2}*is a* ^{2}*noun*^{1}↓

4.6. Intonationless Speech. Before our discussion of English intonation closes, it must be added that there are certain types of speech which show either a sharp reduction or a total loss of intonational contrasts.

Speech in an especially high and narrow register, as under certain types of emotional pressure, may compress the ordinary distances between the four PLs so as to render them difficult, perhaps impossible, to keep apart. Very low-voiced conspiratorial speech in a low narrow register can do the same. At the same time, the distinctions among the three TCs may become blurred, but it is usually still possible to tell where the TCs occur.

"Monotone" speech is prescribed for certain technical uses: a lie-detector operator is supposed to address all his questions to the subject in a uniform way, so that the crucial questions will not stand out in contrast to the trivial ones in which they are embedded. Such speech is not free from intonation. All PLs become /²/, and /↑/ is replaced by /|/ or /↓/, but other distinctions remain.

In whispering, where the vocal cords do not vibrate so as to produce a tone of precise pitch, one might expect intonationless speech. Yet in some whispering some intonational contrasts are observable. How they are produced is not understood.

Apparently the only genuinely intonationless speech occurs in singing, where the voice must follow the musical melody and cannot at the same time move according to speech melody.

NOTES

New terms: *intonation; an intonation.* Specifically for English: *pitch level* = *PL; terminal contour* = *TC; macrosegment; center, head,* and *pendant* of an intonation or a macrosegment. Of these, "macrosegment" probably applies in other languages.

In §§4–6 we follow, in the main, Trager and Smith 1951; many examples are drawn from that source and from Pike 1945. Sledd 1956 presents examples suggesting that the Trager-Smith codification of English intonation may fail to provide for certain contrasts. Our TC symbols "↑" and "↓" correspond, respectively, to Trager and Smith's "||" and "#."

5.

ENGLISH ACCENT

5.1. We are generally more aware of "accent" (or "stress") in English than we are of intonation, perhaps because we notice that it helps to distinguish some pairs of words that are alike in spelling (*ínvalid* versus *inválid*), or because it is a point on which both children and foreign learners make amusing mistakes.

As technical terms, "accent" and "stress" are not synonyms. The former term is more general. Many languages have accentual systems, whereby syllables that are identical in vowels and consonants are nevertheless kept apart. How this is done varies a good deal. The differences are sometimes in pitch level or tonal contour, sometimes in duration, and sometimes in relative loudness or prominence (§11.8). An accentual system in which the differences are largely in relative loudness or prominence is called a stress system, and the contrasting degrees of prominence are called stresses or stress-levels. The English accentual system is of this type.

From §4 we already know that the most prominent syllable of a macrosegment is, by definition, that at the center of the intonation—the syllable before which, in our notation, we write the next to the last PL numeral. The difference in prominence between this syllable and others in a macrosegment is therefore part of our intonational system. We have no right to speak of an accentual system as well as an intonational system in English, unless we can find functional differences of prominence which are not an integral part of the intonational system.

Thus the following pair of sentences bears no testimony for any separate accentual system:

(1) ^{2}*Her name is Re^{3}becca^1*↓
(2) ^{2}*Her name is ^{3}Eleanor^1*↓

47

True enough, the center of the /² ³¹↓/ intonation is differently located: on the next to the last syllable in (1), and on the third from the last in (2). Furthermore, given the two words *Rebecca* and *Eleanor*, and the specification that the center of the intonation is to fall on some syllable of each of those words, then there is no choice as to which syllable it will be. These are facts about the two *words*, but the facts can be described purely in terms of intonation: they do not show any separate accentual system.

5.2. English Stress Contrasts. However, suppose we use the same two sequences of words, but put the center of the intonation on the first word:

(3)   ³*Her name is Rebecca*¹↓
(4)   ³*Her name is Eleanor*¹↓

Or suppose we ask questions about the two girls:

(5)   ²*Isn't Rebecca* ³*going*³↑
(6)   ²*Isn't Eleanor* ³*going*³↑

In (3) and (4), the two words are in the head of the macrosegment, but not at the center; in (5) and (6) the two are in the pendant. Still, however, the second syllable of *Rebecca* is more prominent than the first or third, while the first syllable of *Eleanor* is more prominent than the second or third. And in these environments intonation cannot be responsible.

These examples show, then, that there is *at least* a two-way contrast of stress in English, apart from intonation.

Since the vowels and consonants of the words *Rebecca* and *Eleanor* are so different, one might suspect that the differences in relative prominence of the syllables of each are due to the vowels and consonants. To show that this also is not the case, let us consider some examples using the pair of words, respectively noun and verb, which are both spelled *permit*:

(7)   ²*Give me a* ³*permit*¹↓
(8)   ²*They won't per*³*mit it*¹↓
(9)   ²*The permit is no longer* ³*valid*¹↓
(10)   ²*They won't permit you to* ³*go*¹↓

Some speakers, true enough, accent the noun and the verb in the same way, thus saying

(11) $^2Give\ me\ a\ per^3mit^1\downarrow$

instead of (7). But for most of us the examples show the difference in question, and prove that it is not due to constituent vowels and consonants.

To indicate the contrast of prominence so far demonstrated, we shall put the mark // over the vowel of each more prominent syllable—including that at the center of the intonation. Thus we shall write:

(3') $^3Hér\ náme\ is\ Rebécca^1\downarrow$
(4') $^3Hér\ náme\ is\ Éleanor^1\downarrow$
(7') $^2Gíve\ me\ a\ ^3pérmit^1\downarrow$
(8') $^2They\ wón't\ per^3mít\ it^1\downarrow$
(9') $^2The\ pérmit\ is\ nó\ lónger\ ^3válid^1\downarrow$

The syllables marked // in these examples are not all equally prominent, but the remaining differences are due to intonation, in the manner already described. Thus, in the last example, per-, no, and long- are somewhat less prominent than val- because val- is at the center of the intonation.

We may still suspect that the syllables which have not been marked with // also vary in prominence, and if we hear any further variations we must check to see whether they are pertinent. When the writer says *The pérmit is nó lónger válid*, the second syllable of *permit* is regularly somewhat more prominent than any of the other unmarked syllables of the utterance. Let us test some other material. If you pronounce the words *operator* and *operation* in isolation, you will probably supply the intonation $/(^2)\ ^{31}\downarrow/$, thus saying

(12) $^3óperator^1\downarrow$
(13) $^2oper^3átion^1\downarrow$

But in (12) the third syllable, though not so loud as the first, is clearly louder than the second or fourth; and in (13) the first syllable, though not so loud as the third, is similarly louder than the second or fourth. Now let us put these two words into the pendants of longer macrosegments, with the centers of intonation after them:

(14)   *The óperator is ³síck¹↓*

(15)   *The operátion is ³símple¹↓*

Each word still retains three degrees of prominence among its syllables, as described just above. Hence an additional symbol is required. We snall use /˅/ on syllables less prominent than those marked /˝/ but more prominent than those with no mark at all:

(14′)   *The óperàtor is ³síck¹↓*

(15′)   *The òperátion is ³símple¹↓*

For some speakers of English, it is possible that the difference between the level of prominence marked /˅/ and the level left unmarked correlates with differences of consonants and vowels, particularly the latter. For example, a relatively small number of Americans say /réfjuwǰìj/ *refugee* and /éfiǰi/ *effigy*, the terminal /ij/ of the first automatically being pronounced more prominently than the terminal /-i/ of the second. In most North American English, however, both words end with /ij/. *Refugee* is then sometimes /rèfjuwǰíj/ and sometimes /réfjuwǰìj/; the end of the latter differs from the end of /éfiǰij/ only as to stress, not also as to vowel.

One might suspect the existence of even further contrasts of the stress sort in English. Theoretically, we can never prove that there are no more; but an extensive examination fails to reveal more than the three so far discussed, so that we can be reasonably confident that we have got them all.

5.3. Summary; Arrangements. Let us summarize our findings. There are *four* different *levels of prominence* for syllables in sequence in English. The difference between the most and next most prominent forms part of the intonational system. The remaining contrasts require that we recognize two *accentual* or *stress* phonemes: /˝/ *primary* and /˅/ *secondary*. Then, tabularly:

most prominent:	/˝/ *at center of intonation*
next:	/˝/ *elsewhere*
next:	/˅/
least prominent:	*no stress phoneme.*

In single-syllable macrosegments, there are no contrasts; /'/ is necessarily present:

(16)   ³Yés¹↓
(17)   ³Jóhn²↑
(18)   ⁴Héy¹↓

In two-syllable macrosegments, /'/ is necessarily present on one of the syllables; the remaining syllable may bear /'/, /`/, or no stress:

(19)   ³Jóhn stópped¹↓
(20)   ²Jóhn ³stópped¹↓
(21)   ³Bláckbìrds¹↓
(22)   ²Sàint ³Jámes¹↓
(23)   ³Jóhnny¹↓
(24)   ²a³lóne¹↓

The rhythmic differences between two-syllable sequences of the following three stress and intonation patterns,

(a) /²'³'¹↓/,
(b) /²`³'¹↓/,
(c) /² ³'¹↓/,

are most easily recognized if one says aloud a number of successive examples of each. The three columns of the following table present several illustrations of each pattern. For some speakers, a few of the items may belong in a different column, but for most people most of the expressions in each column will ordinarily have the indicated stress and intonation pattern. Read down the three columns in turn; then read across in rows:

(a)	(b)	(c)
High time.	My pen.	The rest.
Buy now.	By now.	An eye.
Sign here.	Lie down.	The eggs.
Two years.	Go home.	Some pie.
Four days.	Go in.	Some ink.
Call home.	New York.	In fact.
Les Kent.	Miss Kent.	It is.
New books.	Your books.	Goodbye.

In macrosegments longer than two syllables, an increasing number of arrangements of the stresses becomes possible; exhaustive illustrations are hardly necessary.

Any one-syllable word cited in isolation naturally carries primary stress, since it cannot be spoken at all without an intonation, and an intonation implies a center with primary stress. However, there are some one-syllable words in English which, when used with other words in longer macrosegments, customarily appear unstressed (that is, with no stress phoneme): for example, *the, a, an, is, are.* Others seem to vary freely between no stress and secondary stress: one hears either of the following:

(25)   ²*The* ³*ówl in the* ³*áttic*¹↓
(26)   ²*The* ³*ówl ïn the* ³*áttic*¹↓

If this sequence is spoken as two macrosegments, however, with /||/ after *owl,* then *in* usually or always carries /ˆ/:

(27)   ²*The* ³*ówl*³| ³*ïn the* ⁵*áttic*¹↓

Some one-syllable words rarely if ever appear unstressed, but vary freely between primary and secondary, sometimes with a contrast of meaning:

(28)   ²*Jóhnny rán* ³*óut*¹↓ (e.g., of the room)
(29)   ²*Jóhnny ràn* ³*óut*¹↓ (e.g., of money)

One normally says

(30)   ²*The wínd bléw ùp the* ³*stréet*¹↓

and

(31)   ²*The dýnamìter blèw úp the* ³*fáctory*¹↓

If one confuses these and says

(32)   ²*The wínd blèw úp the* ³*stréet*¹↓

it sounds as though the wind caused an explosion.

5.4. English Rhythm. In contrast to some other languages, English is characterized by what has been called *stress-timed rhythm.* This means that it takes about the same length of time to get from one primary-stressed syllable to the next, in speaking at a given overall tempo, whether there are no syllables between them or many. If there are none, we slow down our rate of speech slightly; if there are many we squeeze them in fast. To diagram this, we shall use long vertical lines like the bar-lines of music before each successive primary stress; these must not be confused with our intonational symbol $/|/$. The typical timing of examples (30) and (32) can then be shown as follows:

(30′) ^2The |$w\acute{i}nd$ |$bl\acute{e}w$ $\grave{u}p$ the |$^3str\acute{e}et^1\downarrow$
(32′) ^2The |$w\acute{i}nd$ $bl\grave{e}w$ |$\acute{u}p$ the |$^3str\acute{e}et^1\downarrow$

This type of timing is the rhythmic basis of English verse. The versifier makes full use of the availability in English of the stock of small words which, in some positions, can carry either secondary stress or none at all; in addition, we are accustomed in verse to having some of these carry primary stress. If the versifier requires us to put a primary stress on, say, the first or third syllable of *Rebecca*, we rebel and say his sense of rhythm is poor. But he can quite freely require a primary stress on *in* or *of* or the like. We should normally say (still using musical bar lines)

(33) ^2and| $th\acute{i}ngs$ are| $n\acute{o}t$ $wh\grave{a}t$ $they$| $^3s\acute{e}em^1\downarrow$

When Longfellow requires us to say, instead,

(33′) $^2\acute{a}nd$ $th\grave{i}ngs$| $\acute{a}re$ $n\grave{o}t$| $wh\acute{a}t$ $th\grave{e}y$| $^3s\acute{e}em^1\downarrow$

the only uncomfortable distortion is the secondary stress on *things*.

NOTES

The only new technical term is *accent*. *Stress* is one variety of accent. Accentual systems of other varieties will be mentioned briefly in §11.8.

6

ENGLISH JUNCTURE

6.1. Transition Contrasts. We have almost finished our enumeration of the phonemes of English. Only one type of contrast remains to be described. The italicized words at the ends of the following three sentences supply an example:

(1) Wait till evening and make your call at the *night rate.*

(2) It contains a lot of sodium *nitrate.*

(3) That type of pottery-decoration is called, after its discoverer, the *Nye trait.*

Assuming that we so intone these sentences as to place the center of the last intonation on the next to the last syllable, and that we use the most colorless statement intonation, then our phonemic notation, as so far developed, comes out the same way for all three: /. . . ³nájtrèjt¹↓/. It is obvious that something has been missed. We can *hear* the differences among *night rate, nitrate,* and *Nye trait.* That is, these three are kept apart by differences of sound. Any difference of sound which functions to keep utterances apart is by definition part of the phonological system of the language—and every such difference must be provided for by our analysis and our notation.

What has been overlooked is a contrast between two different ways in which a speaker of English can get from one vowel or consonant to the next—two different kinds of *transition* between successive vowel and consonant phonemes.

Suppose a speaker finishes one macrosegment with the word *night,* and then begins the next with *rates:*

(4) ²*At* ³*níght*²| ²*rátes are* ³*lówer*¹↓

The /t/ of *night* is cleanly finished, and then the speaker starts afresh with the /r/ of *rates*. This way of getting from one vowel or consonant to the next may be described as "sharp transition." Sharp transition is the only kind found across a boundary between macrosegments, so that in this circumstance there is no additional contrast: the kind of transition is simply part of the macrosegment boundary.

Within a single macrosegment, however, one finds both sharp transition and another type, which we may call "muddy." If one says

(5) ^{2}*The* ^{3}*níght ràtes*^{2}| ^{2}*are* ^{3}*lówer*^{2}↑

one almost always has sharp transition between the /t/ of *night* and the /r/ of *rate*. But in

(6) ^{2}*The* ^{3}*nítràtes*^{2}| ^{2}*are* ^{3}*bétter*^{2}↑

the transition between the /t/ and the /r/ of *nitrates* is muddy.

Our way of providing for this is to recognize *sharp transition within a macrosegment* as a phoneme. This phoneme will henceforth be represented by the mark /+/, and will be called *juncture*. Muddy transition within a macrosegment is much more common than sharp transition; we do not call it still another phoneme, but simply say that it is the way a speaker gets from one vowel or consonant of a macrosegment to the next when no /+/ is present.

The terminal portions of examples (1) through (3) can now be unambiguously represented:

(1′) /. . . ^{3}nájt+rèjt^1↓/
(2′) /. . . ^{3}nájtrèjt^1↓/
(3′) /. . . ^{3}náj+trèjt^1↓/

6.2. Distribution of English Juncture. When two successive (not necessarily adjacent) vowels within a macrosegment both bear /′/, there is always a /+/ somewhere between them, and its location is always easy to hear. Here are some examples:

(7) *frée+Dánny*   *fréed+Ánnie*
(8) *sée+Máble*   *séem+áble*
(9) *sée+zóos*   *séize+óoze*

(10)	(*Mr.*+)*Á.*+*Bénson*		(*Mr.*+)*Ábe*+*Émpson*
(11)	*sée*+*stákes*	*céase*+*táking*	*céased*+*áching*
(12)	*trý*+*spínning*	*bráss*+*pín*	*rásp*+*ín*
(13)	*trý*+*skínning*	*áce*+*kíng*	*ásk*+*ín*
(14)	*Béa*+*strúck*	*céase*+*trúcking*	*céased*+*rúnning*
(15)	*fúll*+*stóp*	*fálse*+*tóp*	*repúlsed*+*Árthur*
(16)	*Míck*+*stáys*	*míx*+*tíes*	*míxed*+*éggs*
(17)	(*óne*+) *twélfth*+*sóda*		(*thrée*+) *twélfths*+*ódor*
(18)	*síx*+*thánks*		*síxth*+*ánkle*

A librarian named *Beekman Wyatt* was known familiarly as *Beek*, giving the contrast

(19)   *Béek*+*Wýatt*   *bé*+*quíet*

If the two stressed vowels are adjacent (no intervening consonant), then no contrast is possible, and /+/ is always present: *sée*+*éight*, *trý*+*óurs*.

When a stressed vowel is preceded by one or more consonants, it is always clear whether the last consonant or so in the sequence goes with the stressed vowel or is separated from it by a /+/. All the foregoing examples illustrate this point also, but for this point it is not necessary that the next preceding vowel also bear /'/. So we have cases like the following:

(20)	*it*+*spráys*	*it's*+*práise*
(21)	*it*+*swíngs*	*its*+*wíngs*
(22)	*a pówer* (+*pláy*)	*up*+*óur* (+*wáy*)
(23)	*Sárah Báll*	(*a*) *chérub*+*álways* . . .
(24)	*a táll* (+*mán*)	*at*+*áll* (+*cósts*)
(25)	*Sárah fálls*	(*a*) *séraph*+*álways* . . .
(26)	*a vánguàrd*	*of*+*ánger*
(27)	(*a*) *máma thínks*	(*a*) *mámmoth*+*ínk* (+*wèll*)
(28)	(*a*) *púma séizes*	*púmice*+*éases*
(29)	*he zónes* . . .	*he's*+*óxly* . . .
(30)	*I máuled* . . .	*I'm*+*álways* . . .
(31)	*a níce* (+*mán*)	*an*+*íce* (+*màn*)
(32)	*it*+*síngs*	*it's*+*Énglish*

The form *it is* is often contracted to *it's*, and sometimes even further, to /s/. This supplies contrasts such as the following:

(33)	school /skúwl/	It's cool	/s+kúwl/
(34)	scold /skówld/	It's cold	/s+kówld/
(35)	stuff /stə́f/	It's tough	/s+tə́f/
(36)	spring /sprín/	It's pretty	/s+prítij/
(37)	salt /sólt/	It's always . . .	/s+ólwijz/

Similar is the following:

(38)   yacht /ját/   Ya oughta /j+ótə/

Between an unstressed vowel and a following consonant there seems to be no contrast in type of transition: the type which occurs is best classed as muddy, so that no /+/ occurs in these circumstances. *Get aboard* and *Get a board* sound the same: both are

(39)   /²gètə³bórd¹↓/

with no /+/'s.

After a stressed vowel, it is always clear whether the following consonant, if any, goes with the vowel or is separated from it by /+/. Examples (7) through (18) in part illustrate this; but it is not necessary that the next vowel also be stressed. Here are cases in which it is not:

(40)	(a) tróop aróse	(a) trúe+paráde	
(41)	(a) túbe erúpted	(a) tóo+belóved (+fríend)	
(42)	(a) dáte a wéek	(a) dáy+to wéaken	
(43)	mínus	slý+ness	
(44)	Shé's (+góing)	Béa+'s (+góing)	

Between a consonant and a following unstressed vowel there are few clear contrasts in type of transition. Normally the transition in this environment is muddy. Example (39) shows this between *get* and *a* in *get aboard* (or *get a board*); quite similarly, *Loretta* is /lɔrétə/, with no /+/ between /t/ and /ə/. However, there are some cases of contrast:

(45)   Rósa+la+Plátte   pérsonal+appéal

(that is: /ə+lə/ in the first, /əl+ə/ in the second).

From what has been said above about transitions in the vicinity of an unstressed vowel, it follows that there are few transition contrasts between successive unstressed vowels, no matter how many intervening

consonants there may be. If there are no intervening consonants at all,
the one occurrent type of transition is sharp: *the idea alarms me* thus has
/+/ between the /ə/ at the end of *idea* and the /ə/ at the beginning of
alarm. But if there is at least one consonant, the type of transition is usually muddy. In *a cherub is always* . . . one has the sequence /əbi/ (or
/əbə/); in *Sarah belongs* . . . one has the same sequence.

Secondary stress (/ˋ/) seems to work like primary stress as a conditioning factor for the occurrence of transition contrasts except in one
regard. If two successive vowels bear /ˊ/, then there is an intervening
/+/; if one of the two vowels bears /ˋ/ and the other /ˊ/, then it is
possible to have no intervening /+/, and there are clear cases of
contrast:

> (46)   (*the*) *tin tax* /tín+tǽks/   *syntax* /síntǽks/.

6.3. Juncture and Words. It is easy to fall into the error of assuming
that our mark "+" is just like the space between words that we use in
English traditional orthography. The situation is more complicated.
The factors which control where we leave spaces in writing are manifold: pronunciation is one, but grammatical and semantic considerations play a part, as does arbitrary tradition. Our phoneme /+/, on the
other hand, is defined purely in terms of pronunciation. If it turns out
that many occurrences of /+/ fall where in writing we would leave a
space, and that relatively few fall where traditional orthography does
not prescribe a space, then this is a matter of interest—mainly in the
light it sheds on our orthographic habits, since it tells us nothing new
about /+/.

To underscore this, we give some examples in which the correlation
is lacking.

If one word ends with an unstressed syllable and the next word
begins with one, there is no /+/ unless the first word ends with a
vowel and the second begins with one. Orthographically, of course, one
always leaves a space:

> (47)   *Juneau Alaska*   /ǰúwnowəlǽskə/
> (48)   *pirate savannah*   /pájrətsəvǽnə/
> (49)   *pirates of Anna*   /pájrətsəv+ǽnə/

In contractions with *is* or *has*, such as *John's* and *he's*, no space is left
in orthography. The form *he's* is usually spoken with no /+/, but

John's often has one:

(50)   *John's going.*   /²ján+z+³gówiŋ¹↓/

The /+/ in *John's* sometimes drops; in the possessive form *John's* (as *John's hat*) muddy transition is customary.

It is impossible to hear the difference between single words like *finder* and *loser* and the ordinary fast pronunciation of phrases like *find her, lose her:* the /h/ of *her* drops, and there is no /+/:

(51)   *finder, find her*   /fájndər/

Aboard and *a board* are identical in pronunciation (example 39); similarly *aloft* and *a loft, afraid* and *a frayed* (*edge*), and the like. The word *of* is often pronounced /ə/, with no following /+/: *the nine of spades* /ðənájnəspéjdz/.

The form *N.A.T.O.* is usually pronounced /néj+tòw/; it would be hard to say whether, orthographically, it is to be counted as one, two, or four words. Many people pronounce the single words *Plato* and *Cato* to rhyme with *N.A.T.O.*: /pléj+tòw/, /kéj+tòw/, as though they were two-word phrases *play toe, Kay toe.* Compare the muddy transition in *tomato* /təméjtow/, *potato* /pətéjtow/. In the Middle West everyone says /wíntər/ *winter*, /šéltər/ *shelter*. Some people in parts of New York City vary between those pronunciations and /wín+tə/, /šél+tə/.

6.4. Summary of English Phonemes. Every normal utterance in the variety of English with which we have dealt consists of one or more *macrosegments*. Each macrosegment ends with one of three *terminal contours* /|/, /↑/, or /↓/, preceded by one of four *pitch levels* /¹/, /²/, /³/, /⁴/; there is another occurrence of one of the four pitch levels at the beginning of the most prominent syllable in the macrosegment; and if this (the *center* of the macrosegment) is not at the beginning of the macrosegment, there are one or two additional pitch-level occurrences before the center.

The syllable at the center bears *primary stress:* /'/. Other syllables bear primary stress, *secondary stress* /ˋ/, or no stress at all.

A macrosegment may be broken into two or more successive smaller portions by occurrences of the *juncture* phoneme /+/. Each such smaller portion we shall for convenience call a *microsegment*. If a macrosegment includes no occurrence of /+/, then it consists of a single microsegment.

Apart from stresses, a microsegment consists of *segmental phonemes*—
that is, vowels and consonants. The vowel phonemes are:

/i/   /u/
/e/   /ə/
/æ/   /a/   /ɔ/
/ij, ej, aj, oj, uw, ow, aw/;

and the consonant phonemes are:

/p/	/t/	/č/	/k/
/b/	/d/	/ǰ/	/g/
/f/	/θ/ /s/	/š/	
/v/	/ð/ /z/	/ž/	
/m/	/n/		/ŋ/
	/l/		
	/r/		

/w, j, h/.

6.5. The Auditory Aura. Our phonemic analysis of English, and the
notation we have devised, now provide for the transcription of *everything phonemically relevant* in any utterance produced by a speaker of the
variety of English with which we have dealt. Presumably nothing else
that is detectable in the sounds produced by a speaker, even if it carries
information, is to be regarded as part of his *linguistically* organized communicative activity.

It is obvious that there are other information-carrying features in the
sounds of speech. We can often tell who is speaking even if we cannot
make out the exact words. Speakers achieve some sort of effect through
modulation of the quality of their voices, independently of their words
and intonations: we speak loudly or softly, slowly or rapidly, in a high
register or a low one, raspingly or hollowly, and so on. Without seeking
exact precision, we can perhaps class all this as *voice-quality modulation*
constituting a sort of aura around the linguistically relevant core, and
serving to identify speaker and, in some vague sense, the speaker's
mood.

Although the relevance of speaker-identifying and mood-identifying
features has long been recognized, recent intensive work suggests that
earlier formulations had missed a great deal of what may be important
in it. The main result so far of the recent work is that the functioning of

voice-quality modulation varies from community to community just as do language habits in the ordinary sense. Further research may show that we are wrong to exclude voice-quality modulation from language. Pending this, as a matter of convenience we must exclude it from further discussion in this book.

NOTES

New terms: *transition, juncture, segmental phoneme;* at least for English, *microsegment.*

Smith and Trager 1951 report more occurrences of English /+/ than are described in the foregoing. By their treatment, there is always at least one occurrence of /+/ between any two successive primary stresses in a single macrosegment. For voice-quality modulation see Smith 1955.

Problems. Gleason, *Workbook* (1955b), pp. 19–22, gives polysyllabic words and some sentences for transcription.

7.

PHONETICS

7.1. In the last five sections (§§2–6) we have described the phonemic system of one variety of English. But we have not attempted to describe what the various phonemes sound like, nor have we said anything of their mechanisms of production.

On the first score, we have to give up. What would you say to someone who asked what an orange tastes like? The best answer is to give him an orange. Similarly, if a foreigner wants to know what English /p/ sounds like, we can serve him better with an example than with a description. There is no way to print audible examples of speech sounds, any more than one can print a tastable orange.

On the second score we can do much better. Speech sounds can be described in terms of the bodily motions, called *articulation*, that produce them. We shall first delineate roughly the structure of the portion of the body that is involved in articulation. Then we shall discuss the articulation of the speech sounds of English, familiar to all of us because we speak the language. Within this framework of familiarity, we shall also describe various types of speech sound which are common in other languages but not in English.

This study is called *articulatory phonetics*. In it, we are not particularly concerned with the phonemic status of the sounds which occur in this or that language, but rather with the sounds themselves—as articulatory and acoustic events which can be directly compared from one language to another. Accordingly, it is customary to use a logically different type of notation, involving many of the symbols which appear in our phonemic notation for this or that language, but with values defined in terms of articulation, regardless of what language they have

62

been observed in, rather than in terms of networks of functional contrasts within a single language (§§2, 3). This special symbolism is called *phonetic notation*, and is marked off from context by square brackets "[," "]," instead of slant lines.

A preliminary example will help. Consider the English words *pin* and *spin*. Each contains an instance of the English phoneme /p/. But for most speakers the two instances of this phoneme do not sound alike: the /p/ in *pin* is closely followed by a puff of breath (an "aspiration"), while the /p/ in *spin* is not. This difference is not phonemically relevant in English, which is why in our phonemic notation we simply write /p/ for both. But, phonemically relevant or not, it is a clear difference in speech sound, and in phonetic notation we would often want to take note of it, by writing [pʻ] for the sound in *pin*, versus [p] (or something fancier, like [pˀ]) for the sound in *spin*. In this case, and in others where the phonetically trained investigator can hear two or three clearly distinct types of sound all representing one and the same phoneme in a given language, the different types are often called *allophones*. Thus we say that English /p/ is represented by at least two distinct allophones, an unaspirated [p] under certain environing conditions, an aspirated [pʻ] under others.

7.2. The Speech Tract. Only a restricted region of the body is involved in articulation. Some of the motions of speech are visible from outside—those of the jaw and lips, sometimes of the tongue. Other important motions occur inside, where they cannot be visually observed save with special apparatus (X-ray movies, laryngoscopes). However, to some extent, with proper training, we can detect these inner motions as we speak, sensing the position of tongue and throat just as we sense the location and posture of our hands without seeing them.

The so-called *organs of speech* consist of all the movable parts in the oral cavity (mouth), the nasal cavity, the pharynx (throat), and the lungs, together with the muscles that move these parts. Collectively, this region is the *speech tract*. All the organs of speech have other primary biological functions, such as respiration and mastication; the human habit of using them also for communication is a secondary graft on their primary functions.

Fig. 7.1 is a conventionalized sagittal section through the median plane of the speech tract, with labels as customarily used in articulatory description. Individual differences, such as in the size and precise shape of the organs, are ignored, since we know that they are irrelevant unless—as is true of a cleft palate or hare-lip—they are genuinely pathological. Barring pathology, any human has the requisite muscular and bony equipment with which to learn to pronounce any language.

In speaking, the motions of the organs must necessarily produce sounds the differences between which can be heard by others. The speech tract is roughly bilaterally symmetrical: the left-hand and right-hand halves are mirror images of each other. A pair of articulatory motions which were likewise mirror images could hardly be distinguished by ear. This explains why we can rely largely on a sagittal section for articulatory description: if we describe the motions in the median plane and to one side, we can rest assured that this subsumes also what is occurring on the other side.

We shall now survey the articulatory functions of the various portions of the speech tract, beginning with the lungs and working outwards.

7.3. The Lungs. In most speech, the lungs are neither quiescent nor loosely exhaling, but are actively pushing air outwards. The force of the pushing varies rhythmically, in a way which correlates with the successive units we call *syllables* in English and certain other languages. Rarely, a bit of speech is produced during the intake of air. Some speakers of English do this commonly

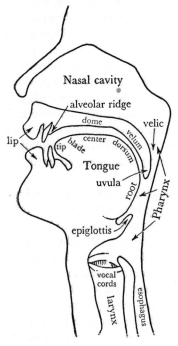

FIGURE 7.1. SCHEMATIC SAGITTAL SECTION OF SPEECH TRACT

with an assenting "grunt," something like *yeah*. In at least one reliably reported instance (Maidu), syllables pronounced with inflowing air occur in ordinary speech, interspersed among those produced during exhalation.

7.4. The Larynx. In the larynx are the *vocal cords*. In their quiescent state, these are relaxed and relatively far apart, leaving a passage so wide that air can pass through almost noiselessly. Speech sounds produced with the cords in this position are *voiceless*. English /h/ at the beginning of a word like *heap, hand, hose*, is usually pronounced simply as a brief moment of voicelessness, with the lips and tongue in approximately the position for the following vowel. The customary phonetic symbol for this is [h]. The relaxed position of the vocal cords is shown on the left in Fig. 7.2; the remaining parts of the Figure show some of the other phonetically relevant positions.

At the opposite extreme, the cords can be drawn tightly together so that no air can pass. This produces *glottal catch*, symbolized as [?]. In English, we often begin an emphatic exclamation such as *ouch!* with a glottal catch, though phonemically the utterance begins with a vowel (/áwč/). In many languages glottal catches occur frequently and in phonemic contrast to other types of articulation.

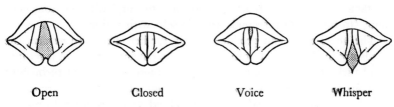

| Open | Closed | Voice | Whisper |

FIGURE 7.2.   FOUR POSITIONS OF THE VOCAL CORDS
Seen from above through the mouth of the larynx.

The vocal cords can be stretched taut, with little space between them, but so held that the passing air stream forces itself through and sets the cords into vibration, like a reed. This vibration is *voice* or *voicing*, and speech sounds which involve voicing are *voiced*. In English, the vowel phonemes are all regularly voiced, as are the consonant phonemes /b d ǰ g v ð z ž m n ŋ l r w j/; the remaining consonant phonemes, /p t č k f θ s š h/, are usually *voiceless*, though /t/ is sometimes voiced in some occurrences (*matter, batter, battle, little* as pronounced in the Middle West). An easy way to train oneself to recognize the difference between voicelessness and voicing is to cover the ears tightly with the hands and say, aloud, a pair of words like *pack : bag : pack : bag*. A strong buzz is audible throughout the word *bag*, but only for the vowel of *pack*. Or the vibration can be felt with the fingers by pressing them gently against the "Adam's apple." Like English, most of the familiar languages of Europe have both voiceless and voiced consonants but only voiced vowels. In various other languages voiceless vowels occur, though they are not widespread.

By varying the tension on the vocal cords during voicing, and the force of the passing stream of air, one can vary the *pitch* and the *volume*. Different individuals have pitch ranges of from one to three octaves. English makes phonemic use of both pitch and volume, the former in its intonational system (§4), the latter principally in its accentual system (§5). Most languages use these phenomena in one way or another, but not often just as English does. In French, for example, both pitch and volume are involved in an intonational system, and there is no separate accentual system like that of English. In Chinese, and a great many other non-European languages, on the other hand, pitch is used as a part of an accentual system: each syllable has a fixed pitch contour. Thus, in Mandarin, a syllable the vowels and consonants of which may be sketched phonetically as [mai̯] means 'to bury' with one tone contour, 'to buy' with a second, and 'to sell' with a third.

The vocal cords can produce certain further effects. In *murmur*, the cords are in vibration, but in addition the passing air stream is set into local turbulence. In one kind of *whisper*, there is this local turbulence without the voicing. In another kind of whisper, the cords are closed tightly, but the arytenoid cartilages behind them are moved apart so that the air can pass through.

7.5. The Pharynx. As in the larynx, a complete closure can be made in the lower pharyngeal region, by drawing the root of the tongue back against the back wall of the passage. This produces a *pharyngeal catch*, which occurs as a speech sound in some dialects of Arabic. Instead of complete closure, a small passageway can be left, so that the passing air stream is set into local turbulence producing a *pharyngeal spirant*, which can be either voiceless or voiced. In some dialects of Arabic both voiceless and voiced pharyngeal spirants occur, in phonemic contrast with each other and with other consonants.

A narrowing of the pharyngeal passage, instead of producing local turbulence, may simply modify the coloring of a sound produced with some motion of tongue and lips: sounds produced with this modification are called *pharyngealized*, and occur, in phonemic contrast with non-pharyngealized sounds, in Arabic.

7.6. The Velic and Nasal Chamber. The velic is the entrance from the upper part of the pharynx into the nasal cavity. This is the only structure in the nasal cavity which functions in speech, and its motions are strictly limited: it is either closed, so that air cannot pass between pharynx and nasal cavity, or open. Sounds produced with the velic open are called *nasal* or *nasalized;* those produced with the velic closed are called *nonnasal* or *oral.* In English, the consonant phonemes /m n ŋ/ are always nasal, and differ only in this way from /b d g/ which are always oral. This is why a cold in the nose, which obstructs the passage of air through the nasal cavity and alters the special coloring that is added by an open velic, tends to make /m n ŋ/ sound like /b d g/— *I'b dot bibickig you.* English /m n ŋ/, like /b d g/, are voiced; some languages have voiceless nasals contrasting with voiced ones. English vowels are often nasalized, but we do not usually notice this because it is not distinctive. In French, Portuguese, and many other languages, oral and nasal vowels stand in contrast. A convenient notation for a nasal vowel is the symbol for the corresponding oral vowel followed by a superscript "ⁿ": French *bas* /ba/, *banc* /ba^n/.

For some articulations the position of the velic is necessarily irrelevant. A glottal or pharyngeal catch, for example, cannot be nasalized, since while the passage of air is cut off completely at the glottis or lower pharynx the open or closed position of the velic produces no audible effect.

7.7. The Oral Cavity. It is within the oral cavity that the greatest variety of articulatory motion occurs. It is convenient to divide the whole range of articulatory motions in the mouth very roughly into two classes: those which have vowel-like or *vocoid* effects, and those which have consonant-like or *contoid* effects. This distinction cannot be made to rest purely on what goes on in the mouth; the two terms are acoustic or impressionistic rather than strictly articulatory. A vocoid is a sound in which resonances or colorings of one sort or another seem to be of primary importance. (Some people prefer to speak of *resonants* instead of vocoids, perhaps using the latter term in a narrower sense.) A contoid, on the other hand, is a sound involving clearly audible turbulence of the airstream at one point or another in the vocal tract, or else a complete interruption of the air stream. Use of the terms "vocoid" and "contoid" enables us to reserve the terms "vowel" and "consonant" as labels for structurally defined classes of phonemes in specific languages (§11).

In the next section we shall discuss contoid articulations, and many of those which might be classed as on the borderline between contoid and vocoid. In the section after that, we shall take up vocoid articulations, and relevant additional matters such as timing and coordination.

NOTES

New terms: *articulation, articulatory phonetics, speech tract, organs of speech.* Names of parts or regions of the speech tract: *lungs, larynx, pharynx, velic, nasal chamber* (or *cavity*), *oral chamber* (or *cavity*). Terms for articulatory properties of speech sounds: *voiceless, voiced, pitch, volume, murmur, whisper, pharyngealization, nasal = nasalized, nonnasal = oral.* Terms for certain types of speech sounds: *glottal catch, pharyngeal catch, pharyngeal spirant.* More generic terms: *allophone; vocoid* (= *resonant*), *contoid.* Terms appearing on Fig. 7.1 but not yet discussed in detail are omitted from the above lists.

8.

CONTOID ARTICULATIONS

8.1. Positions of Articulation. For the articulatory description of contoids we distinguish various *articulators*, along the lower margin of the oral cavity, and various *points of articulation*, along the upper margin. Likewise, we distinguish between *closure*, in which some articulator is pressed so tightly against some point of articulation that no air can get by, and *spirantization*, in which there is a constriction which sets the passing air stream into local turbulence.

The articulators which it is convenient to differentiate are: the dorsum, the center, and the blade of the tongue; the tip of the tongue; and the lower lip. These regions are roughly marked in Fig. 7.1. The blade of the tongue consists of the frontmost upper surface; it is sometimes necessary to specify whether the blade includes or excludes the tip.

The points of articulation are: the velum (sometimes requiring subdivision into front and back), the dome, the alveolar ridge, the backs of the upper teeth approximately at the edge of the gum, the cutting edges of the upper teeth, and the upper lip. Occasionally the last two function together.

A combination of articulator and point of articulation constitutes a *position of articulation*. Positions of articulation are labeled by a compound term, the first part designating the articulator, the second part the point of articulation. Thus we have *dorso-velar, front* and *back dorso-velar, centro-domal, lamino-domal, lamino-alveolar, apico-domal, apico-alveolar, apico-dental, apico-interdental, apico-labial, labio-dental,* and *labio-labial;* for the last of these the term *bilabial* is usually substituted. Checking in Fig. 7.1, the reader can easily test all the positions just mentioned by

69

placing his own jaw, tongue, lips, and teeth in the specified positions. Other combinations of articulator and point of articulation are either impossible (apico-velar), improbable (labio-alveolar), or simply not so far known to occur in any language (e.g., lower teeth and upper lip).

Of course there is no guarantee that every language will have only contoid articulations involving positions we have listed. The listed positions are merely a convenient frame of reference, which experience has shown usually suffices.

8.2. Stops. A *stop* is a speech sound produced by (1) a complete oral closure, and (2) velic closure. English has eight consonant phonemes which are normally stops: /p t č k/ and /b d ǰ g/. Of these, /p b/ are bilabial, /t d/ usually apico-alveolar (sometimes apico-dental), /č ǰ/ lamino-alveolar, and /k g/ dorso-velar. /č ǰ/ are also different from the other six in a way which we will describe later. One stop of each pair is voiceless, the other voiced. Phonetically, some of these phonemes differ a good deal in exact position of articulation from one environment to another. This is especially true of /k g/, which are front dorso-velar [ḵ ḡ] before /i ij/, as in *key, geese,* but back dorso-velar [q g̠] before /u uw/, as in *cool, goose.* (For the phonetic symbols see Table 8.1.) We do not hear this difference without special training, because it is not independently distinctive in our phonemic system; but a speaker of Nootka, Kwakiutl, Bella Coola, or Eskimo would hear it, since in those languages a comparable difference is phonemic.

Other languages have more or fewer positions for stops than English, or the same number of positions with differences of detail. Apico-domal or *retroflex* stops occur in many of the languages of India. Hungarian has a pair of centro-domal stops, in contrast to dorso-velar ones. Umotina has four stop positions: bilabial, apico-labial (the only reliably attested case), apico-alveolar, and dorso-velar.

The contrast between voiced and voiceless which we have for stops in English is called a contrast of *manner:* English /p/ and /b/ differ only as to manner, not as to position. There are also some other manners. *Glottalized stops* are stops made with simultaneous closure of the glottis: the muscles of throat and mouth then squeeze the air contained in the closed chamber between glottis, velic, and the oral closure; the latter is released with a sort of popping sound; then the glottal closure is released. Such sounds occur in many American Indian languages of the Northwest Coastal region and elsewhere, and in the Caucasus. *Injectives*

TABLE 8.1

PHONETIC SYMBOLS FOR STOPS, VOICED NASALS, AND SPIRANTS

	bilabial	labio-dental	apico-labial	apico-inter-dental	apico-dental, apico-alveolar	apico-domal	lamino-alveolar	lamino-domal	centro-domal, fronted dorso-velar	dorso-velar	back dorso-velar
STOPS vls	p	p̣		t̮	t	ṭ	tʲ	ṭʲ	ḵ	k	q ḳ
vd	b	ḅ		ḓ	d	ḍ	dʲ	ḍʲ	ǵ	g	g̣
NASALS vd	m	m ɱ		n̮	n	ṇ	nʲ ɲ ñ	ṇʲ	ŋ̂	ŋ	ŋ̣
SPIRANTS vls	φ	f		s̮	s	ṣ	š	ṣ̌	x ç	x	x̣ x
vd	β	v	} RILL: {	z̮	z	ẓ	ž	ẓ̌	γ̂	γ	γ̣

SLIT: {	θ̮	θ	θ̣	}			
	ð̮	ð	ð̣	}			

LATERAL: {	ɬ̮	ɬ	ɬ̣	}		
	l̮	l	ḷ	} ʎ ʎʲ	ʎ̣ ʎ̣ʲ	

Some of the sound-types for which symbols are provided in this table are discussed in later subsections and sections. The following diacritics, some of which are illustrated in the table itself, should be noted:

subposed dot: position of articulation further back than that indicated by the unmodified symbol: [ṭ] in contrast to [t].

subposed or superposed curve, concave downwards: position of articulation further front than that indicated by the unmodified symbol: [t̮] in contrast to [t].

apostrophe after voiceless symbol: glottalized: [k']. After voiced stop symbol: injective [b'].

following superscript [ʷ] and [ʲ]: labialized and palatalized, respectively: [kʷ], [tʲ].

postposed raised dot: comparatively great length: [t·] versus [t].

postposed inverted comma: aspiration: [tʻ] versus [t]. Sometimes absence of aspirate release is marked positively as follows: [t˥].

are voiced stops, during the production of which the whole glottis is moved downwards to produce a rarefaction, so that the release of the oral closure is accompanied by a sudden influx of air from outside; these are found in a number of languages of West Africa. *Clicks* are made by closing the dorsum against the velum and then making also a closure further forward in the mouth: the air in the small chamber thus established is either compressed or rarefied (usually the latter), and the frontmost closure is released first. We use clicks in one or two interjections (*tsk-tsk!*) and in signals to horses, but not in ordinary speech. A number of South African languages, and two or three in East Africa, have clicks in ordinary speech. Since the mechanism of production of a click involves only the oral cavity, a click may be voiced or voiceless, and oral or nasal.

For a *coarticulated* stop the speaker makes two oral closures simultaneously, one of them apparently always dorso-velar, and releases both at once, but without any compression or rarefaction of the air between the closures. These are most widespread in West Africa, but occur also in New Guinea.

Any part of the oral cavity not actively involved in a position of articulation is free to do something which may modify the coloring of the resulting sound. Some languages have a contrast between dorso-velars pronounced with lips spread and with lips rounded; the acoustic result is much like our contrast between /k/ and the cluster /kw/, as in *kick* versus *quick*. Many more languages, including Russian, contrast stops pronounced with the middle or rear portion of the tongue lowered and stops pronounced with that portion of the tongue raised towards the roof of the mouth: the latter are called *palatalized*.

Phonetic symbols for stops are displayed in Table 8.1. Note that we do not try to supply a completely distinct symbol for everything; instead, we use a nuclear stock of letter-like symbols, to which various *diacritics* (listed and commented on at the bottom of the table) can be added.

8.3. Spirants. Spirants are contoids produced by spirantization, as described in §8.1. In English we have eight phonemes which are normally (or always) spirants: voiceless /f θ s š/ and voiced /v ð z ž/. Some people pronounce English /h/ as a glottal spirant, but more typically it is the sort of sound described in §7.4. Of the spirants, /f v/ are labio-dental, /š ž/ lamino-alveolar; the other four all apico-alveolar, though with an additional difference about to be described.

For the front part of the tongue, certain distinctions have to be made for spirants which are not relevant in discussing stops. Both English /s z/ and English /θ ð/ are normally apico-alveolar, but the former are *rill* spirants, the latter *slit* spirants. In a rill spirant, the front edge of the tongue closes against the upper teeth or the gum on both sides, leaving only a tiny median opening through which the air stream can pass. In the second type, instead of this tiny opening there is a transverse slit.

Some speakers of English produce /s z/ as rill spirants with a laminoalveolar position instead of apico-alveolar: the tip of the tongue hangs down behind the lower teeth and does not participate. In some languages this difference in position of articulation is distinctive.

A third variety of tongue-front spirant is the *surface* spirant: English /š ž/ are neither slit nor rill, but involve close approximation of a whole area, from side to side and from front to back, of the blade of the tongue to a comparable area behind the upper teeth, perhaps including the backs of the teeth. British English /š ž/ are also surface spirants, but are lamino-domal rather than lamino-alveolar.

A fourth variety is the *lateral* spirant: a complete closure (apicoalveolar or other), is made medially, but the air is allowed to pass at one or both sides, between the edge of the tongue and the upper teeth. Such sounds are common in American Indian languages, especially of the Northwest Coast (Nootka, Kwakiutl, Salishan), and in some of the languages of the Caucasus; there is a voiceless lateral spirant in Welsh. Not all laterals are spirants, and it is only nonspirantal laterals that occur in English and other generally familiar languages (§8.5).

Spirants are subject to some of the same classification as to *manner* as are stops: voicing contrasts, pharyngealization (§7.5), labialization (rounding of lips), palatalization. Glottalized spirants are rare, if they occur at all, and there are no known instances of nasalized spirants. Table 8.1 also shows phonetic symbols for spirants.

8.4. Nasals. *Nasals* or *nasal continuants* are not clear-cut contoids, but belong rather on the boundary between contoid and vocoid. They are produced exactly like stops, except that the velic is open. English has three such phonemes: /m n ŋ/. The first is bilabial, the second apicoalveolar, and the third dorso-velar.

As just illustrated, nasals can be classified by position of articulation just as are stops. Contrasts of manner are rare, but not unknown: some languages have both voiced and voiceless nasals; and even glottalized nasals are possible, though the mechanism of production is different from that for glottalized stops. In the glottalized nasals of Nootka and Kwakiutl, one begins with a glottal closure, and releases it into the nasal continuant. Some languages have more consonant phonemes of the nasal continuant type than does English, and some have fewer— Quileute, and a very few other languages, have none at all.

Phonetic symbols for nasals are included in Table 8.1.

8.5. Lateral Vocoids. Our English /l/ is produced with the position of articulation described earlier for lateral spirants, but with a key difference: there is no local turbulence as the air passes the sides of the tongue, so that the sound is marked primarily by a certain coloring. Such lateral vocoids, usually voiced, are quite common. Various positions of articulation are found—one can even produce a bilabial lateral, by opening both sides of the lips and keeping the center closed. Many languages, including Castilian Spanish and Italian, contrast two lateral vocoids, one apico-alveolar (or apico-dental) and one lamino-alveolar. Some of the languages of India contrast an apico-dental lateral and an apico-domal (retroflex). Some speakers of English use a dorso-velar pronunciation for English /l/, instead of the more ordinary apical variety.

Apical lateral vocoids can be made to differ quite widely in color by the position in which the rest of the tongue is held: with the middle and back of the tongue held down, the result is usually called *dark*, while with the middle and back of the tongue held up, the result is *clear*. British English has a relatively clear lateral before vowels, and a relatively dark one finally, so that the two /l/'s of *little* sound quite different. In most American English the difference is far less striking. In some languages such a difference is distinctive.

8.6. Retroflex Vocoids and Trills. American English /r/ is produced in one of two ways: by curling the tip of the tongue back and up towards the dome of the mouth, or by placing it behind the lower teeth and bunching the central part up against the dome. In either case the sound is usually voiced. The first produces a *retroflex vocoid*. The second, while not retroflex in the strict sense, produces the same acoustic effect, so that the difference is usually ignored except in the closest articulatory description. Retroflex vocoids are not common, but Mandarin Chinese has one, differing from that in American English in two ways: the lips are not rounded as they are for the English sound; often the airstream is forced through fast enough to produce a buzz in addition to the retroflex coloring.

Trilling is achieved by holding some flexible bit of flesh in the passing air stream with just the right tension to allow the air to set it into rapid vibration. One can do this with the lips, but a bilabial trill is very rare as a speech sound, attested for just one word in one language (Isthmus Zapotec). An apical trill is much commoner (many varieties of French and German, and most Spanish, Portuguese, and Italian). A uvular trill is common in Europe: this is the variety of trill used by many prestige speakers of German and French for their respective /r/ phonemes.

A trill can be as short as a single *tap*, or quite long. Our American /t/ in a word like *bottle* or *automobile* often comes out as a single voiced apico-alveolar tap. In some languages a shorter trill, or tap, and a longer trill at the same position of articulation, stand in phonemic contrast: so in Spanish *pero* 'but' versus *perro* 'dog.'

Phonetic symbols for lateral vocoids, retroflex vocoids, and trills consist of the letters "r" and "l" and of any convenient typographical modifications—inverted "r" or small caps "ʀ" and "ʟ" or the Greek letters rho and lambda. For all our purposes the two most customary letters will suffice.

These sounds are often grouped together under the term *liquids;* or, together with nasals, they are sometimes called *sonorants*, in contrast with which stops and spirants are called *obstruents*.

NOTES

New terms: (1) *articulators: dorsum, center, blade,* and *tip* of *tongue; lower lip;* (2) *points of articulation: velum, front* and *back* velum, *dome, alveolar ridge, upper teeth, upper lip;* (2) *positions of articulation: dorso-velar, centro-domal, lamino-domal, lamino-alveolar, apico-domal (retroflex), apico-alveolar, apico-dental, apico-interdental, apico-labial, labio-dental = bilabial;* (4) *manner, (stop) closure, spirantization, stop, spirant; glottalized* (stops), *injective* (stops), *clicks, coarticulated* (stops), *palatalization; rill* versus *slit* versus *surface* versus *lateral(ized) spirants; labialization; dark* and *clear* (*laterals*); *retroflex* and *lateral vocoids; trills, trilling, tap; nasals = nasal continuants; liquids, sonorants, obstruents; uvula.*

The anatomist would not be dismayed by the linguist's use of any of the above terms except *dorsum;* the anatomist uses this term to refer to the entire upper surface of the tongue which touches the roof of the mouth when maximum closure is made. Our usage follows that of some contemporary linguists.

Problems. (1) Describe each of the English phonemes listed below in articulatory terms, following the model given for the first one:

/p/	voiceless bilabial stop	/v/
/t/		/ð/
/k/		/z/
/b/		/ž/
/d/		/m/
/g/		/n/
/f/		/ŋ/
/θ/		/r/
/s/		/l/
/š/		/h/

(2) Each of the following purports to be an articulatory description of a possible speech sound, but some of them are in fact impossible. Answer two questions for each: Is such a speech sound possible? Does it occur as a reasonably common representation of some English phoneme?

> voiced dorso-velar stop
> voiced dorso-velar spirant
> voiceless dorso-velar spirant
> voiceless retroflex apical rill spirant
> voiced retroflex apical rill spirant
> voiced bilabial lateral sonorant
> voiced apico-velar stop
> voiced labio-dental spirant
> voiced labio-dental nasal spirant
> voiceless bilabial glottalized stop
> voiceless bilabial nasal
> voiceless lamino-alveolar nasal
> voiceless apico-labial stop
> voiced labio-alveolar spirant.

9·

VOCOID ARTICULATIONS;
TIMING and COORDINATION

9.1. Oral Factors in Vocoids. Most pure vocoid articulations in
most languages can be described in terms of three factors: *lip position,
tongue-height,* and *tongue-advancement.*

Lip position is described along the scale *rounded-unrounded* or *rounded-
spread.* In English, the lips are spread—or, at least, not actively rounded
—in the production of the vowels /i e æ ə a ij ej aj/, but more or less
rounded in the production of /u ɔ uw ow/. In the last two, most of us
increase the amount of rounding during the production of the vowel,
and this is one factor which leads some to prefer the analysis under
which /uw/ and /ow/ are clusters of a vowel plus /w/ (§3.3). As for
/w/ itself, we shall have more to say later. In /oj/, the lips are rounded
at the beginning but not at the end; in /aw/, just the reverse.

If we compare our articulation of the vowels /i e æ/, as in *bit, bet,*
and *bat,* we find that the lower jaw is held progressively farther away
from the upper jaw, and that at least the front part of the tongue is
progressively farther away from the region of the upper teeth and the
alveolar ridge. What counts in the production of vocoid sounds is the
shape of the oral cavity; thus the position of the tongue is of primary
importance, and the position of the jaw is only a matter of convenience
in getting the tongue into proper placement. A similar difference
appears when we compare /uw ow ɔ/, as in *sue, sew, saw,* except that in
this case it is the back part of the tongue, rather than the front part,
which assumes progressively lower positions. In both cases, the scale of
contrasts involved is that of tongue-height, from *high,* through various
possible intermediate heights, *mid,* to *low.*

The third scale of contrasts is harder to describe accurately. If we compare *he* and *who*, setting aside the difference of lip-position which we have already noted, we find that in *he* the whole upper surface of the tongue, from dorsum to blade, is held high, whereas in *who* only the dorsum is high, the remainder of the tongue curving downwards and away from the roof of the mouth. Both vocoids are called "high"; when the front of the tongue, as well as the back, is high, we speak of a *front* vocoid, but where the back is high and the front is not we speak of a *back* vocoid. Intermediate between front and back are (varying degrees of) *central*. It should be noticed that the term "mid" is arbitrarily assigned to positions intermediate between high and low, while "central" is, equally arbitrarily, assigned to the intermediate range on the front-back scale. Many speakers of American English use a fairly high central unrounded vocoid in their pronunciation of the word *just* as in *I just got here* (not as in *a just man);* this pronunciation was not provided for in our phonemic analysis of Middle Western

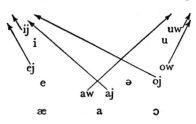

FIGURE 9.1. CHARTING OF ENGLISH VOWELS IN TERMS OF TONGUE HEIGHT AND TONGUE ADVANCEMENT
Lip-position is ignored. The arrows indicate the *direction* of tongue-motion during the pronunciation of /ij ej aj oj uw ow aw/; the *extent* of the motion varies and is *not* indicated by the length of the arrow.

English in §§2–6, since the pronunciation /jə́st/ is also common and probably always possible.

Figure 9.1 roughly displays the vowels of English in terms of the two dimensions of tongue-position, ignoring lip-position—to include the latter, we would need a three-dimensional model instead of the surface of a sheet of paper. The reader can easily verify the approximate correctness of the chart by saying appropriate English words to himself and "feeling" the position of his tongue.

In addition to the three scales of contrast which have been described so far, one often hears of a distinction between *tense* and *lax*. It is easy to demonstrate this difference in English. Hold the fingers on the bundle of muscles above and in front of the glottis within the frame of the lower jaw, and say *bit, beat, bit, beat.* For *beat,* one can feel a bunching and tension in the muscles which is either lacking or at least much

TABLE 9.2

UNROUNDED VOCOIDS

		front	central	back
high:	higher	i	ɨ ə	ɪ ɯ
	lower	i ɪ ɩ	ɨ ɨ ə	ɪ ɯ ï ɤ
mid:	higher	e	ė ə ʌ	ë ʌ ɤ
	lower	e ɛ	ė ɛ̇ ə ʌ	ë ë ʌ
low:	higher	æ ɛ	ʌ	ʌ
	lower	æ a	a ɑ	a ɑ

TABLE 9.3

ROUNDED VOCOIDS

		front	central	back
high:	higher	ü y	u̇ ʉ	u
	lower	ü ü̈ y ʏ	u̇ ʉ u̇	u ʊ ʋ
mid:	higher	ö ø	ȯ	o
	lower	ö ø ȫ œ	ȯ ɔ	o ɔ
low:		ȫ œ	ɔ̇ ɑ	ɔ ɑ ɒ

A number of the symbols appear more than once in the above tables: this is in order to indicate the most customary range of phonetic values for each symbol. Thus "i" is often used for a higher high front unrounded vowel, in contrast to "ɪ" or "ɩ" for a lower one; but if there is no relevant contrast in the high front unrounded range then "i" may itself be used for a lower high front unrounded vocoid.

less prominent for *bit*. Sometimes the same difference can be detected with *could* and *cooed;* it is harder to feel for *bet* and *bate*. Just what this bunching of the muscles accomplishes is not clear; presumably it has some effect on the precise positioning of the upper surface of the tongue, and thus bears on the shape of the oral cavity.

Basic phonetic symbols for vocoids are displayed in Tables 9.2 and 9.3, the former for unrounded vowels, the latter for rounded ones.

9.2. Modifications. For purposes of phonetic description, the specification of a vocoid in terms of the three factors mentioned first in §9.1 (excluding tenseness and laxness) is arbitrarily regarded as *basic*, and anything further that may have to be mentioned in dealing with one or another language is regarded as a *modification*. (This rough phonetic classification has nothing to do with the relative importance of different factors in specific phonemic systems, but is for convenience only.) A number of modifications are to be found. Some of them were covered in §7: a vocoid, like a contoid, can be either voiced or voiceless, or, indeed, whispered; it can be pharyngealized or nasalized. Also, vocoids can be modified within the oral chamber itself by *retroflexion* (curling back of the tip of the tongue; §8). The usual Middle Western pronunciation of the /ə́r/ of *shirt, third, furze* is a mid central unrounded retroflexed vocoid: the retroflexion represents the /r/, and the rest represents the /ə/. In Badaga, all vocoid phonemes come in sets of three, otherwise identical, differing in the presence of no, slight, or strong retroflexion.

9.3. Timing and Coordination. So far in our discussion of articulatory phonetics we have dealt almost exclusively with static positions of the various parts of the speech tract. But in actual speech all parts of the tract are constantly moving, no single position, as described ideally in the foregoing, lasting more than a brief fraction of a second. Some significant contrasts cannot be described in a purely static survey, since they turn on features of timing and coordination of motions from one articulatory position to another.

9.4. Length. The simplest timing contrast is *length*. In many languages, two utterances may be composed of exactly the same key articulatory motions, yet be distinctively different because some articulatory position is held longer in one of the utterances than in the other. Such a timing distinction may be found for a contoid or for a vocoid. In Italian, *fato* /fáto/ has a relatively long [a] and a short [t], while *fatto* /fátto/ has a shorter [a] and a longer [t]. The phonetic symbol for length is [·] after the symbol for the sound which is prolonged: thus [fá·to] and [fát·o].

9.5. Transition and Release. Somewhat different is the relative timing of two articulations or changes of articulatory function in two different parts of the speech tract. In English, utterances like *big, dig, get* begin with stops which are only weakly voiced at the outset (or even not voiced at all), but for which the voicing increases during the holding of the stop closure. In French, words like *belle*, *digne*, *gare* begin with stops that are strongly voiced from the outset. This is a subtle difference, but French spoken with the English variety of [b d g] sounds wrong to the native French ear, and this is one of the difficulties which we encounter when we are trying to learn to pronounce French well.

Again, French *pas*, *tasse*, *cas* begin with voiceless stops, and voicing begins almost exactly as the stop closure is released. English *pass*, *touch*, *catch* also begin with voiceless stops, but the onset of voicing for the vowels which follow is delayed for a perceptible length of time after the release of the stop closure, and one can clearly hear a brief phase of voicelessness, sometimes involving some local turbulence of the air at the point of articulation of the stop. Such voiceless stops are called *aspirated*, for which the phonetic symbol is [ʻ]: thus [pʻ]. The English aspirated voiceless stops sound very bad in French, and the French style of unaspirated voiceless stops sounds peculiar in English.

9.6. Timing of Chest Pulses. In many languages, if not in all, the pressure of air from the lungs occurs in a series of pulses. The timing of these pulses relative to other articulatory motions can be important. Speakers of English who pronounce *an aim* and *a name* differently probably make the difference in just this way, beginning a chest pulse after the /n/ in the first, but with it in the second.

9.7. Affricates. A special way of passing from a stop closure to a following sound or silence involves a single motion of the articulator, which leaves the position of complete closure slowly enough that a considerable amount of spirantal friction or turbulence is audible. We do not often pronounce English /p t k b g d/ in this way, but /č ǰ/ are regularly so produced; this is the other special feature of /č ǰ/ mentioned, but not described, in §8.2. Such sounds are called *affricates*. They differ from simple sequences of a stop and a spirant, in which the articulator goes through two successive motions. Thus, one may often hear the sequence [tš] between the words *hit* and *you* in a rapidly spoken *I'm gonna hit ya*, and this is quite different from the [č] of, say, *pitcher*.

Many languages have affricates at several positions of articulation instead of just a single pair as in English. Affricates are delivered in the same variety of manners as are stops (§8.2). A general way of producing a phonetic symbol for an affricate is to use a "cap" ("˄") as a diacritic over the symbol for the corresponding spirant. However, a few special

symbols are available: [c] and [ɟ] for apical affricates; [č] and [ǰ] (or
[ɟ]) for laminal ones; [ƛ] and [λ] for affricates with lateral release. To all
of these, diacritics used for stops or for consonants in general (see the
caption on Table 8.1) can be added.

9.8. Glide and Peak Vocoids. Differences of timing are important
in the distinction between *glide* and *peak vocoids*. In *bird*, as pronounced
in the Middle West, the retroflex vocoid is of the peak type; it is preceded and followed by articulations which last less long and produce
less clearly audible acoustic effects. But in *red* the same retroflex vocoid
is pronounced quickly, and with the chest-pulse only half strong,
followed by a non-retroflex vocoid which lasts longer and for which the
chest-pulse has gained full strength. The initial vocoid, in this case, is a
glide vocoid.

The same difference applies to the lateral vocoid in the second syllable of *battle* (phonemically /əl/: /bǽtəl/) and the initial one in *let*, or
to the high front vocoid /i/ in *bit* and the /j/ of *yet*. The entire difference
between the English phonemes /w j/ and /u i/ is definable only in
these terms: where vocoids of the high back rounded or high front unrounded types are the most prominent elements in syllables, they are
instances of the phonemes /u i/, but where they occur as marginal elements in a syllable with something else as the most prominent part,
they are instances of the phonemes /w j/.

A convenient way of producing as many symbols for glide vocoids as
necessary is to place a small curve under the symbol for the corresponding peak vocoid: thus [i̯ a̯ u̯]. But there are also three special symbols:
[w] pairing off with [u], [j] pairing off with [i], and [ɥ] going with [y].

9.9. Timing in Longer Stretches. In longer utterances, further
types of timing contrasts make their appearance. We saw in §4.3 (Examples 31–33) that the same sequence of words can be matched to one
and the same intonation in more than one way, depending on where the
center of the intonation is placed; phonetically speaking, this is a
matter of different timing for sequences of motions in different parts of
the speech tract.

Languages differ greatly in their characteristic rhythms, and this,
also, points to differing types of timing and coordination in longer
stretches. One example will suffice. English has *stress-timed rhythm*
(§5.4): the length of time it takes to produce an utterance depends
roughly on the number of stresses in it, so that unstressed syllables are

sometimes squeezed together and produced very rapidly, if there are a number of them between two successive stressed syllables. Spanish, on the other hand, has *syllable-timed rhythm:* regardless of the number and location of stresses, a Spanish utterance of twenty syllables takes approximately twice as long to utter as one of ten syllables.

NOTES

New technical terms: *lip position* (*rounded, spread* or *unrounded*), *tongue-height* (*high, mid, low*), *tongue-advancement* (*front, central, back*); *tense* and *lax; retroflexion* for vowels; *length, timing, coordination, transition, release, aspiration, chest pulse; affricates; peak* and *glide* vocoids; *stress-timed* and *syllable-timed rhythm.*

10·

PHONEMIC ARRANGEMENTS; REDUNDANCY

10.1. If one undertakes to learn a foreign language, a sound in the new language which is unlike anything in one's own language constitutes a difficulty. For example, English has no voiceless dorso-velar spirant [x] as a separate phoneme, but German does: *ach* /áx/ 'Oh!' *Buch* /bú·x/ 'book,' *lachen* /láxən/ 'to laugh.' Most speakers of English are inclined at first to substitute their stop /k/ for this spirant, but this will not do, since in German the voiceless spirant and stop at this position of articulation are in contrast: *Buch* as above, versus *buk* /bú·k/ '(he) baked.'

This source of difficulty in learning to pronounce a foreign language is familiar to most of us. But there is another, often overlooked. German /k/ and /n/ are individually much like English /k/ and /n/, so that one would anticipate no trouble with them. Yet a German word like *Knabe* /kná·be/ 'boy' is troublesome. The difficulty in this case is not due to anything about the individual sounds, but to the particular arrangement in which they must be pronounced. In English, unlike German, we never begin an utterance, nor a word, with /k/ followed immediately by /n/.

We see, thus, that the phonological systems of various languages may differ from each other in two ways. They usually differ as to the number of phonemes and the phonetic characteristics of each, but they also often differ as to the *arrangements* in which the phonemes occur relative to each other.

In §11 we shall deal more thoroughly with the ways in which phonemic systems differ. In the present section we shall confine our-

84

selves largely to English, in order to illustrate arrangements and limitations on arrangements and to show the communicative importance of the latter.

10.2. Phonemic Arrangements in English. The arrangements in which intonational phonemes occur relative to each other were covered in §4, and the accentual phonemes and the junctural phoneme /+/ were treated in §§5 and 6. Here, therefore, we can confine ourselves to the arrangements of segmental (vowel and consonant) phonemes within the bounds of single microsegments (§6.4).

The importance of the microsegment in this context is that there seem to be few effective limitations, on the distribution of vowel and consonant phonemes, that operate across the boundaries between successive microsegments. That is, the vowels and consonants which can occur at the beginning of a microsegment are not in any significant way limited by the vowel or consonant at the end of the preceding microsegment, or vice versa. But within the bounds of a single microsegment there are many limitations.

A few microsegments are of a special type, occurring only in macrosegments that include also one or more microsegments of what we shall call the "normal" type. These special microsegments consist of a single isolated consonant. Examples are the isolated /s/ of /s+kúwl/ *It's cool* (§6.2, example 33), the isolated /j/ of /j+ɔ́tə/ *Ya oughta* (§6.2, example 38), and the isolated /z/ of /bíj+z+gówiŋ/ *Bea's going* (§6.2, example 44).

A microsegment of the "normal" type consists of one or more *syllables: boy* (said in isolation) is one syllable; *butter* is two; *operate* three; *operator* four; *perambulator* five; *elephantiasis* six; *honorificabilitudinity* eleven. Such long ones are very rare; even six or seven syllables is unusual. The number of syllables in an English microsegment correlates exactly with the number of vowel phonemes: /bój/, /bɔ́tər/, /ápərèjt/, /ápərèjtər/, /pərǽmbjəlèjtər/, /èləfəntájəsəs/, /anərìfəkəbìlətuwdínətij/. Contrariwise, every vowel /i e æ ə u ɔ a ij ej aj oj uw ow aw/ in every occurrence, constitutes the *peak* of a syllable.

Any consonant or sequence of consonants at the beginning of a microsegment constitutes the *onset* of the first syllable. Any consonant or sequence of consonants at the end of a microsegment constitutes the *coda* of the last syllable. But the consonants and sequences of consonants which occur between successive vowels in a single microsegment are neither onsets nor codas, and cannot be assigned exclusively either to the syllable that includes also the preceding vowel or to the one which includes also the following vowel. Instead, these *interludes*, as we shall call them, belong structurally with *both* the preceding and the following vowels. Thus, syllables in English are determined by the number and location of peaks (phonetically the most prominent elements of syllables), and the exact location of the boundaries between successive syllables—except across an intervening $/+/$, where the syllables are in successive microsegments—is phonemically irrelevant. In other languages syllables have various other types of structure.

Onsets, codas, and interludes vary a great deal in complexity. "Zero" onsets occur, as in *out, in, end, awful, ooze;* likewise zero codas (*filly, window, soda, bah*), and, more rarely, zero interludes (*idea* /ajdíjə/, *reality, naive*). Non-zero onsets include from one to three successive consonants (*ray, tray, stray*); non-zero codas and interludes from one to four (*rim, ramp, ramps, glimpsed; hammer, damsel, entrance, minstrel*). However, the limitations on these longer consonant-sequences, in any of the three positions of occurrence, are stringent. If all possible sequences of one, two, or three consonants occurred as onsets, there would be a total of 14,425 different onsets (one zero onset, 24 of a single consonant, $24^2 = 576$ of two consonants and $24^3 = 13,824$ of three consonants). Actually, the total number of onsets of any frequency at all is well under one hundred. We shall list and illustrate these here, but we shall not take the space to do the same for codas and interludes, since our aim is an example rather than an exhaustive coverage of English.

All the individual consonant phonemes of the language except /ž ŋ/ occur as onsets; *pick, take, choose, kick, build, dig, jig, get, find, think, sink, shall, vat, these, zone, man, nut, ride, let, wet, yet, high.* A few speakers pronounce a French name like *Jeanne* or *Giselle* with initial /ž/, and an extremely small number pronounce the name *Ngaio* with initial /ŋ/.

Sequences, or *clusters*, of two consonants occurring as onsets often have /r l w j/ as the second. The five consonants /ž ŋ ð č j/ do not participate in onset clusters. Clusters with /r/ as second member include /pr tr kr br dr gr fr θr šr/: *pride, try, crack, bread, draw, grow, fry, thread, shrew.* Sequences with /l/ include /pl kl bl gl fl sl/: *play, clay, black, glad, flow, slow.* Clusters with /w/ are /tw kw dw gw θw sw hw/: *twenty, quick, dwell, Gwen, thwack, swell, when.* Many speakers have no /hw/, pronouncing *when* and similar words with initial /w/.

Some speakers add /pw/ in *pueblo*, or /bw/ in *bwana*, or /šw/ in *shwa*. Clusters with /j/ as second element include /pj kj bj gj fj θj vj mj hj/: *pure, cure, beauty, gules, few, thews, view, music, hew*. Many speakers have also /tj dj sj nj rj lj/, in *tune* or *Teuton, due* or *Deuteronomy, sue, new* or *neuron*, very rarely *rule, lunatic*. Many other speakers pronounce such words simply with /t d s n r l/. Those who pronounce *when* with /w/ instead of /hw/ usually pronounce *hew* and the like simply with /j/ instead of /hj/.

The clusters with /j/ show an interesting limitation between onset and peak: they occur before a stressed peak only if it is /ú/ or /úw/. A very few people break this generalization for *piano, fjord, Hjalmar*, but /pijǽnow, fijórd, jálmàr/ are more common.

A different sort of onset cluster of two consonants has /s/ as first member: /sp st sk sf sθ sm sn/ and rarely /sv/: *spill, state, skill, sphere, sthenic, smile, snare, svelte*. Recently some parallel clusters with /š/ instead of /s/ have been coming into use, especially /šm/ in *shmoo*, but also, for some speakers, /šn šl/ *Schneider, Schlitz*.

Onset clusters of three consonants all begin with /s/ and end in /r l w j/: /spr, str, skr, spl, skl, skw, spj, skj/, as in *spread, stretch, scratch, splash, sclerosis, squelch, spume, skew*.

Individual speakers are often able to add a few clusters which they use in one or two relatively uncommon words, but no onset other than those already mentioned has wide currency. As a small sample of these additional onsets, we may mention /tm/ (*tmesis*), /ts/ (*tsar, tsetse fly, Tsimshian*), /tl/ (*Tlingit*), which the writer uses. The reader may be able to discover comparably rare onsets in his own speech.

10.3. Redundancy. The full import of the stringent limitations on the arrangements in which phonemes occur can only be understood in terms of *redundancy*. In everyday parlance, this word means saying more than is strictly necessary. Teachers of English composition often criticize a student for an expression like *consensus of opinion* when merely *consensus* would do. In modern information theory, the term has much the same meaning, but freed from the connotation of undesirability, and theoretically capable of precise quantification.

We shall first illustrate information-theoretical redundancy, and its communicative function, in terms of a restricted kind of English writing, in which only the twenty-six capital letters and space are used. Suppose that someone writes the following:

(1) GO AWAY I DONT WANT TO TALK WITH YOU ANY MORE TODAY

This is easily read, given the rules of English spelling with which we are all familiar. Now suppose that we receive a message in this system which looks like this:

(2) GO AWAX I DONX WANX TO TAIK WICH YOV ANT MORE TODAX

—or like this:

(3) HTS BROYHER HAS LIUEB IN YOVNGSTOWH SINDE IANUABY

Neither of these means a thing. Yet we almost instantly understand them: we automatically assume that the sender has intended to transmit a normal "possible" message, and that there have been errors of transmission.

How is it possible for us to understand received messages which, strictly speaking, are not allowed by the conventions of the communicative system? The answer lies in the fact that not all possible sequences of letters constitute messages according to those conventions. If *every* possible sequence of letters constituted a different message, then any slightest error in transmission would change the intended message into a completely different one. We would always think that we had received a message free from errors of transmission, but would sometimes not receive and understand the message that the sender intended. Since, in actual fact, only a small portion of the mathematically possible sequences of letters is allowed, minor errors of transmission usually result, not in a completely different possible message, but rather in a sequence of letters which we know *cannot* be an undistorted message; consequently, we are able to figure out what the sender's intention was.

In a system where all possible sequences of letters constituted messages, one would have *zero redundancy*—every single letter would count. Redundancy enters actual systems in two ways: (1) absolute limitations on sequence, such as the fact that in written English Q is invariably followed by U; (2) variations in relative frequency of different sequences, such as the relatively common occurrence of ST as over against the rather rare occurrence of SCH. The communicative importance of redundancy is that errors of transmission—collectively called *noise* in information theory—are inevitable; a certain amount of redundancy prevents this inevitable measure of noise from destroying communication altogether.

What has been said above in terms of capitalized written English applies in just the same way to spoken English, or to any other language. An utterance consists of an arrangement of phonemes. If all mathematically possible arrangements of the phonemes of a language actually occurred, then the degree of clarity of articulation which would be required to prevent misunderstanding would be humanly impossible. Actually, there are always stringent limitations on the arrangements in which phonemes occur in utterances, so that there is always a measurable amount of redundancy; rough computation shows that the measure of redundancy in English is approximately 50%, and there is some reason to believe that this figure holds for languages in general.

Consequently, we are able to speak in a fairly careless natural fashion without continually being misunderstood. Speaking goes fast. In normal English one produces from twelve to fifteen successive segmental phonemes per second. We communicate via speech under all sorts of external conditions: in quiet rooms and in boiler factories. A language with relatively low redundancy would work in quiet surroundings if its speakers enunciated clearly, but would break down time and again in noisy circumstances or when people were in a hurry and had to speak faster and less carefully than usual. Redundancy in this technical sense is thus nothing to be bemoaned, but an essential ingredient of any communicative system as flexible and broad in its coverage as language.

In the discussion of redundancy and noise, it is always necessary to specify *relative to what* the determinations are being made. From one point of view, the difference between the "tone of voice" of Joe and of Bill represents noise, since this difference is superimposed on the common features which constitute the *linguistic* part of what either of them says. But from another point of view the difference is communicative, and thus not noise, for it reveals whether Joe or Bill is speaking. In a room full of people, where several conversations are going on, so long as one is trying to listen to one speaker, the sound of other speakers is noise; if one shifts attention to a different speaker, the first speaker's voice becomes noise. We thus see that, at least sometimes, no distinction can be made between "noise" and "*unwanted* message."

Another kind of overlap is illustrated by the communicative habits of the Fox Indians. Like other North American Indians, the Fox often point by protruding their lips rather than by extending a finger. Pointing is a communicative system of a minimal kind. The Fox word for 'over there' is /yo·hi/, the /o·/ produced with slight rounding of the lips but without protrusion. Now it often happens that a Fox will simultaneously point at an object and say /yo·hi/. The protrusion of the lips changes the acoustic quality of the /o·/, and thus constitutes noise relative to the language, even while it constitutes the essence of a communicative symbol in another system.

Redundancy is also relevant in the context of conscious distortion of speech. We often understand what someone is saying even if he is trying to imitate some other dialectal variety of his language, or is mocking a foreign accent. Here, as in the cases just considered, the distortion is noise in one sense, though at the same time it conveys to us the information that the speaker is imitating or mocking. A *pun* is an utterance susceptible of two (or more) different interpretations. A poor pun may be susceptible to one of the interpretations only if we allow for gross articulatory distortion:

> A: *Knock knock!*
> B: *Who's there?*
> A: *Eskimos Christians and Italians.*
> B: *Eskimos Christians and Italians who?*
> A: *Eskimos Christians and Italians no lies.*

Akin to this is *double-talk*, which sounds as if it ought to be understandable but—if heard accurately—is not. The original of the following verse parody will be obvious to anyone who is familiar with it:

> Eight of the note that kippers may,
> > Bleak as the pate from pool to pool,
> I shrink whatever goads may bay
> > For my untinkerable stool.

> It meddles naught how strut the gut,
> > How charred with blandishments the scrawl;
> I am the mister of my pfft,
> > I am the capon of my stall.

Some readers may also remember, in this context, an acoustic parody popular in the early nineteen-fifties, called *Ladle Rat Rotten Hut.* As inane as these particular examples may be, they do illustrate a functioning of redundancy which in some contexts becomes quite important (§35).

NOTES

New terms: for elements of syllables, *peak, onset, coda,* and *interlude* (developed in the above for English, but applicable in one way or another to many languages); *cluster; redundancy, noise.*

The theory of redundancy and noise, and methods for the quantification of both, are developed by Shannon and Weaver 1949. *Ladle Rat Rotten Hut:* Chace 1956.

Problem. Below is a list of clusters of two consonants. Some of those listed occur after a stressed vowel before juncture in one or another dialect of English; others do not. Find an example from your own speech of each one for which you can do so. Then make a *table* of those that occur, listing the first consonants of the clusters down a column at the left, the second consonants across in a row at the top, and marking the intersections of row and column for each cluster which occurs in your speech.

/pt pk pf pθ ps pš/
/tp tk tθ ts/
/čp čt čθ/
/kp kt kθ ks/
/bd bg bv bz/
/dθ dð dz ds/
/ǰd ǰz/
/gd gz/
/ft fθ fs/
/θt θs θm/
/sp st sč sk sθ sf/

/šp št šs/
/vd vz/
/ðd ðz ðm/
/zd zs/
/žd/
/mp mt mb md mf mθ mz/
/nt nč nd nǰ nθ ns nz/
/ŋk ŋd ŋg ŋθ ŋz/
/rp rt rč rk rb rd rǰ rg rf rθ rs
 rš rv rð rz rm rn rl/
/lp lt lč lk lb ld lǰ lg lf lθ ls lš
 lv lz lm ln/

11.

TYPES of PHONEMIC SYSTEMS

11.1. The Problem of Typology. Every language has a phonemic system. Certain features seem to be common to all phonemic systems— for example, the exclusive use of a certain tract of the human body for sound production, and the tendency towards a redundancy of about 50%. But phonemic systems also differ in various ways, and it is as important to know what sorts of differences exist, and the limits within which variation is possible, as it is to know what all languages have in common.

No report of this sort can yet be definitive. We have reasonably reliable information only on a few hundred languages, out of the three or four thousand currently spoken (§1.3). The number for which our knowledge approaches completeness, at least as to phonemics, is a mere handful. The very next language examined by trained investigators may show some phenomenon never encountered before. On the other hand, the sample for which we do have information is fairly random, so that some of the generalizations we are about to make may not be too radically modified by further research.

Another source of indeterminacy is that our reports on different systems are not always worked out in terms of the same methodology. We have seen one instance of the results of methodological disagreement: the English syllable peaks /ij ej aj oj uw ow aw/ are taken as unit phonemes by some, but as clusters by others. For the former specialists, there are 38 segmental phonemes in the Middle-Western variety of English to which our phonemic notation was adapted (§§2–6); for the latter, there are only 31. A still different approach yields a count of 33, for reasons to be discussed in §§39–40, and we shall adopt this figure for our purpose here. Problems of this sort seem to loom larger for English than for most languages—perhaps because more people have been working on English for a longer time. In any case, though this source of indeterminacy cannot be completely eliminated, most of the generalizations given below are not seriously affected by it.

11.2. Number of Segmental Phonemes. The smallest number of segmental phonemes reliably reported for any language is 13, in Hawaiian. The largest reported figure, reliable or not, is about 75, for one of the languages of the northern Caucasus. If we limit ourselves to absolutely dependable reports, the upper limit is about 45, in Chipewyan. Sixty-nine languages, selected at random, including Hawaiian and Chipewyan, show an average of slightly over 27 segmental phonemes. Of these, twenty-two have 23 or fewer; twenty-five have more than 23 but fewer than 31; and twenty-two have 31 or more.

We might naturally expect that, other things being equal, it would in general require longer strings of segmental phonemes to express given meanings in a language like Hawaiian than in one like Chipewyan. The test of this is the average length of *morphemes*—minimum meaningful elements in utterances (§14). In Hawaiian and the other Polynesian languages, only a handful of morphemes consist of a single syllable, most consist of two, and a fair number of more than two. At the opposite extreme, in some of the languages of the Caucasus practically every successive phoneme in a word is a separate morpheme.

11.3. Kinds of Segmental Phonemes. We are accustomed to thinking that every segmental phoneme must be either a vowel or a consonant, but this is not always the case—not, for example, in English, if /ij uw/ and the like are taken as clusters.

Hawaiian segmental phonemes, indeed, fall into just two classes: there are five vowels /i e a o u/ and eight consonants /p k m n w j h ?/. A syllable in Hawaiian consists of a single vowel or of a single consonant followed by a single vowel, and any Hawaiian utterance consists of a series of one or more such syllables.

In other languages, it is sometimes necessary to recognize more than two classes of segmental phonemes. The simplest sort of example is Spanish. Here every syllable includes one or another of the phonemes /i e a o u/ as its peak, but some occurrences of /i/ and /u/ do not constitute peaks of syllables: the word *buey* /buéi/ 'ox' is only one syllable, with the stressed /é/ at its peak, and the preceding /u/ and following /i/ are phonetically consonantal, like the English /w/ and /j/ of *sway* /swéj/. Here we must recognize three kinds of segmental phonemes: *full vowels* /e a o/, which are always the peaks of syllables; *consonants* (/p t č k/ and others), which are never at the peaks of syllables; and *semivowels* /i u/, which are syllable peaks in some occurrences but not in others, depending on the nature and arrangement of the surrounding segmental phonemes and the location of the accent /'/.

One language of the Spanish type, Wishram, is reported to have only one full vowel, /a/; the other vowel-like phonemes are structurally semivowels. In various other languages, nasals and liquids (phonetically like English /m n ŋ r l/) turn out to be semivowels rather than consonants.

More complicated situations also appear in those languages where one must distinguish between *simple* and *complex* peaks. Accepting the cluster interpretation of English /ij ej aj oj uw ow aw/, English is one example. These clusters are complex peaks; the unit phonemes /i e æ a u ɔ ə/ occur also as simple peaks (*sit, set, sat,* etc.). The first constituents of the complex peaks are *peak nuclei*, and the second constituents are *peak satellites*. If we group onsets, codas, and interludes together as syllable *margins*, we find that in a language with both simple and complex peaks there are the following logically possible types of segmental phonemes:

| | occurs as: | | |
	peak nucleus	peak satellite	margin
full vowel	yes	no	no
covowel	no	yes	no
consonant	no	no	yes
semivowel	yes	yes	no
demivowel	yes	no	yes
semiconsonant	no	yes	yes
omnipotent	yes	yes	yes.

Described in these terms, English has semiconsonants /w j/, full vowels, and consonants. German is similar, but German /w/ is a covowel: it occurs in complex peaks (/aw/, as in *Haus* /háws/ 'house'), but not in any marginal position. Mandarin Chinese has two full vowels, a set of consonants, three semiconsonants /m n ŋ/, one demivowel /y/, and three omnipotents /i u r/. Mandarin /i/, thus, is peak in /bǐ/ 'pen,' satellite in a complex peak in /bái/ 'white,' and marginal in /iàu/ 'want to' or /biǎu/ 'watch.' It must be remembered that its value as peak, satellite, or margin is in all cases predictable in terms of the accompanying phonemes and their arrangement.

11.4. Vowel-Consonant Ratio. For our next purpose we shall redefine the term "vowel" to include all segmental phonemes that ever occur as simple peaks or as nuclei in complex peaks, except semivowels of the nasal and liquid type. We can then ask what proportion of the whole stock of segmental phonemes of a language are likely to be vowels.

The range is wide: the highest known ratio is just under 40% (Finnish: 8 vowels out of 21 segmental phonemes); the lowest about 8% (Bella Coola: 3 vowels, 36 segmental phonemes). More significantly, there is some correlation between this ratio and the total number of segmental phonemes. Languages with the fewest segmental phonemes tend to have a middling to high percentage of vowels. Those with intermediate numbers of segmental phonemes show greater variation in the vowel percentage, but average a rather higher ratio than the first group. Languages with very large numbers of segmental phonemes have the lowest vowel ratios.

11.5. Kinds of Vowel Systems. The vowels of a language (by the definition of §11.4) usually reveal a reasonably neat system of articulatory contrasts. (Fig. 11.1).

All known vowel systems involve contrasts of tongue height. In Adyge, this is the only functioning contrast: there are three vowels, one high, one mid, and one low. Whether one of these vowels is front or back, and rounded or unrounded, depends entirely on the surrounding phonemes. This rare type of vowel system may be called *one-dimensional*.

Much commoner are *two-dimensional* systems, where some second type of contrast intersects, wholly or partly, the differentiation by tongue height. The simplest system of this sort has three vowels: two high and one low, the former pair contrasting as front unrounded and back rounded (Cree, Ojibwa, some Arabic dialects). The next-to-simplest has four vowels: two high and two low, two front and two back (Fox, Shawnee, Apachean). Latin, Spanish, Russian, and many other languages have two-dimensional systems involving three heights, in which, except at the lowest height, there is the added contrast of front-back or of unrounded-rounded: thus, in Spanish or Latin, high /i u/, mid /e o/, low /a/; front unrounded /i e/, back rounded /u o/.

The greatest number of contrasting heights reported for a two-dimensional system (or any other) is five (certain Swiss-German dialects). The greatest number of contrasts in the second dimension is three: front unrounded, front rounded, and back rounded (German,

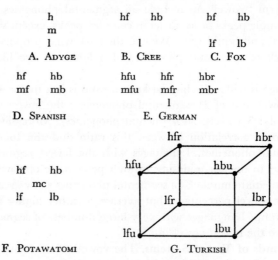

FIGURE 11.1.　SOME VOWEL SYSTEMS

The vowels are here described in terms of the relevant phonetic facts: "h" = *high*, "m" = *mid*, "l" = *low*; "f" = *front*, "c" = *central*, "b" = *back*; "r" = *rounded*, "u" = *unrounded*. System A is one-dimensional, systems B through F are two-dimensional, and system G is three-dimensional. Systems B, D, and E are triangular, C is rectangular, and F cannot be classified as either.

French, Dutch), or else front unrounded, back unrounded, and back rounded (Bulgarian, Mixteco, Rumanian). The most complex two-dimensional system has both four heights and three contrasts of the second sort, completely intersecting to yield twelve vowels. This is not attested with absolute certainty, but may occur in some dialects of Danish.

In some two-dimensional systems the second dimension of contrast is operative at all heights, so as to produce a *rectangular* system: the two-by-two system described above for Fox, Shawnee, Apachean, or the four-by-three system which may occur in Danish dialects. In others, the second dimension is operative only at some of the heights. In this case, it most often happens that there are fewer contrasts at the lowest tongue-height than at higher ones (Latin or Spanish), and the system is *triangular*. But there are exceptions: Potawatomi has two low and two high vowels, but only one mid vowel.

In one variety of *three-dimensional* system, lip position and tongue frontness or backness work independently: of the eight vowels of Turkish, four are high and four low, four front and four back, four unrounded and four rounded. In another variety, the third dimension is retroflexion: Badaga has fifteen vowels, in three sets of five, each set being like the whole system of Latin or Spanish. But the vowels of one set are unretroflexed, those of a second partly retroflexed, and those of the third strongly retroflexed.

The above survey touches only on representative examples. In addition to further varieties which are as neat and symmetrical as those described, a few languages are reported to have *skew* systems—systems in which there is no simple differentiation in terms of tongue height and the like. The reliability of these reports is not certain. It is quite common, however, for a major portion of the vowels of a language to fit a neat scheme, but with a few left over. The majority of French oral vowels fit a two-dimensional pattern (the size depending on the dialect), but there is a left-over /ə/ with some peculiarities of distribution. The French nasal vowels (four in some dialects, three in others) constitute a separate subsystem, within which only contrasts of tongue advancement and lip position are distinctive, tongue height being irrelevant.

11.6. Consonant Systems. In most languages, the consonant phonemes fall largely into two basic classes: *obstruents*, including stops, affricates, and spirants, and *sonorants*, including nasals, liquids, and glide vocoids like English /w/ and /j/. If a language has consonants produced entirely in pharynx or glottis, these stand outside this two-way classification. Obstruents often constitute a neatly patterned system, involving contrasts of position and manner of articulation. Sonorants sometimes appear to be random left-overs.

The smallest known number of contrasting positions of articulation for obstruents is two: Hawaiian has bilabial /p/ and lingual /k/, the latter freely apical or dorsal. The largest known number is nine: Nootka, Duwamish, and Snoqualmie have bilabial /p/, apico-dental /t/, front and back dorso-velar /k q/, affricates /c č ƛ/, and rounded front and back dorso-velar /kʷ qʷ/. Some of these, it will be noted, are not distinct positions in the primary articulatory sense, but constitute a proliferation of the position system via affrication and rounding. That they are functionally the equivalent of further "positions" is shown by the fact that the nine-way contrast is intersected by the manner-contrasts of each of the three languages.

<table>
<tr><td></td><td></td><td></td><td></td><td>b</td><td>d</td><td>ð̂</td><td>ǯ</td><td>ʒ</td><td>λ</td><td>g</td><td>gʷ</td></tr>
<tr><td></td><td></td><td></td><td></td><td>t</td><td>θ̂</td><td>c</td><td>č</td><td>ƛ</td><td>k</td><td>kʷ</td></tr>
<tr><td>p</td><td>k</td><td></td><td></td><td>t'</td><td>θ̂'</td><td>c'</td><td>č'</td><td>ƛ'</td><td>k'</td><td>kʷ'</td></tr>
<tr><td></td><td></td><td></td><td></td><td>θ</td><td>s</td><td>š</td><td>ł</td><td>x</td><td>xʷ</td></tr>
<tr><td></td><td></td><td></td><td></td><td>ð</td><td>z</td><td>j</td><td>l</td><td>γ</td><td>γʷ</td></tr>
<tr><td colspan="2">HAWAIIAN</td><td></td><td></td><td></td><td colspan="6">CHIPEWYAN</td></tr>
</table>

FIGURE 11.2. THE SIMPLEST AND MOST COMPLEX KNOWN OBSTRUENT SYSTEMS
Hawaiian has only a two-way contrast of position (bilabial and non-bilabial), and no contrasts of manner. Chipewyan has obstruents at eight positions of articulation (bilabial, apico-alveolar, apico-alveolar slit affricate, apico-alveolar rill affricate, lamino-alveolar affricate, apical lateral affricate, dorso-velar, and dorso-velar with rounding), and contrasts five manners of delivery (unaspirated stop, sometimes voiced; aspirated stop; glottalized stop; voiceless spirant; voiced spirant). The relatively frictionless consonants /j/ and /l/ count in Chipewyan as obstruents of this last manner of delivery.

The smallest known number of manners for obstruents is one—that is, no manner contrasts. Hawaiian has no spirants, and only the two stops /p k/. A very few other languages also lack spirants. The largest known number of contrasting manners is five: Georgian has voiceless unaspirated stops (sometimes glottalized), voiceless aspirated stops, voiced stops, voiceless spirants, and voiced spirants. Four-way and three-way manner contrasts are much commoner, and there are many varieties of each.

In Figure 11.2 we chart the simplest and the most complex reliably attested obstruent systems.

Languages which have unusually large numbers of segmental phonemes, and hence of consonants, generally achieve the higher number of consonants by a proliferation of the obstruent system: Chipewyan has 34 obstruents. Yet no one language has both the largest known number of contrasting positions and also the largest known number of contrasting manners.

A few languages (Duwamish, Snoqualmie, Quileute) have no nasal continuants. Some (Tillamook, Iroquoian, Arapaho) have just one, and all languages which have at least one have an apical nasal of the type of [n]. The largest number of nasals differentiated only by position of articulation is four; for example, in Kota. The positions of articulation for nasals are always also positions of articulation for stops, and rarely, if ever, are there more nasals than there are stops of some one manner of delivery.

Generalizations about non-nasal sonorants, and about pharyngeal and glottal consonants, are at present too limited to be worth while.

In a few languages, the consonants must in the first instance be classed differently. In Russian the basic classification should perhaps be that into *plain* and *palatal*, since most, though not all, consonants are paired off thus. Then, within each of these two subsystems, the grouping into obstruent and sonorant applies.

11.7. Syllable Types. The syllable system of English is of the *peak* type: that is (as pointed out in §10), there are as many syllables as there are syllable-peaks. This type of syllable system is quite common, though the phonemic determination of what constitutes a peak is not always, as it is in English, merely the occurrence of a phoneme of a certain class (vowel).

The *onset-peak* type differs from the peak type in that every syllable includes both an onset and a peak; it may or may not include also a coda. Yawelmani illustrates this: a syllable consists of single consonant plus single vowel, or of this followed by a single coda consonant; a single consonant between vowels goes with the following vowel as onset, while two consonants between vowels are divided, the former being a coda for the preceding vowel, the latter an onset for the following vowel. Thus there are no interludes—or, at least, no contrast (as in English) between an interlude and a sequence of coda plus onset.

The *onset* type is rare, but clearly attested for Bella Coola, where every syllable has an onset, but some syllables have no peaks. Thus the word /ɬkʼʷtx̣ʷ/ 'make it big!' consists of four syllables, each consisting of an onset consonant. There is loose transition from each consonant to the next. Phonetically this phase of transition gives the impression of a peak, but phonemically it is merely a part of the consonant.

The *duration* type has syllables defined in terms neither of peaks nor of onsets nor of some combination of these, but purely in terms of relative duration. The Japanese word /nippoñ/ 'Japan' takes about the same length of time to utter as the word /sayonara/ 'goodbye'; the syllables in the latter are /sa/, /yo/, /na/, and /ra/, while those in the former are /ni/, /p/, /po/, and /ñ/. The two special syllables /p/ and /ñ/ cannot be broken down into onset and peak, but count as syllables because they take about as long to produce as do the /yo/ and the /ra/ of the other cited word. Only a few syllables in Japanese are of this special kind, and they are highly limited in their distribution, but they define the nature of the syllable system.

Finally, there is the *syllable-juncture* type, which is, in a sense, the diametric opposite of the English system. In Cantonese, the number of syllables in an utterance is equal to the number of segments bounded by successive occurrences of a juncture phoneme /+/. Each syllable contains a single peak, though it is not always easy to locate this peak in a precise way phonetically. Contrasts of the following sort are possible: /pan+ap/ : /pa+nap/ : /pa+n+ap/, where in the first the /n/ ends one syllable, in the next it begins the following syllable, and in the third it constitutes a syllable all by itself.

11.8. Accentual Systems. Briefly, the variety of accentual systems which occur in different languages is as follows.

French, and some others, have no accentual system at all.

English, Spanish, German, Russian, and many other languages have an accentual system of the *stress* type: some syllables in context are louder than others (English /pə́rmìt/ : /pərmít/), and a monosyllabic(utterance always carries the highest degree of stress. In Spanish there are only two degress of stress in contrast; in English and German there are three; some languages may have four.

Cantonese, Vietnamese, and many other languages have an accentual system of the *tone* type: most syllables in context carry one or another of a small set of contrasting tonal contours, and even monosyllabic utterances show some of the contrasts. Some such systems involve only two tones (high and low, or rising versus falling); others show three, four, five, six, or even (in some varieties of Cantonese) nine.

Some languages show what appears to be a partial intersection of two accentual systems, involving both stresslike and tonelike features. Norwegian and Swedish belong here: Norwegian /bøn·ər/, with loud stress and one tonal contour on the first syllable, means 'peasants,' while the same segmental sequence with loud stress but a different tonal contour on the first syllable means 'beans.' But the tonal contrast is operative only on syllables with loud stress, and not in monosyllabic utterances.

Some languages show both a full-fledged accentual system of the tonal type and also one of the stress type, with few if any limitations on combinations. Mandarin /iǎn+ʒiŋ/, with stress on the first syllable, means 'eye,' while /iǎn+ʒìŋ/, with stress (and falling tone) on the second syllable, means 'glasses.'

NOTES

New terms: *simple* versus *complex* peaks; *nucleus* versus *satellite* of a complex peak; syllable *margin;* terms for classes of segmental phonemes established by their occurrent arrangements in a single language: (*full*) *vowel, consonant, semivowel, demivowel, semiconsonant, omnipotent, covowel;* types of vowel systems: *one-dimensional, two-dimensional, three-dimensional, rectangular* versus *triangular, skew;* terms for types of syllable-systems: *peak type, onset-peak type, onset type, duration type, syllable-juncture type;* types of accentual systems: *stress type* and *tone type.* The term *morpheme* enters the discussion briefly, but will not be introduced in a systematic way until §§14ff.

The typological survey in this section is condensed from §2 of Hockett 1955; bibliographical references are given in full in the latter. Work done more recently, particularly by W. S. Allen and Aert Kuipers, shows that some of the languages of the northern Caucasus indeed do have very large numbers of segmental phonemes. This modifies the assertions in §11.2, and changes the relative status of the Chipewyan obstruent system presented in Figure 11.2.

12.

PHONEMIC ANALYSIS

12.1. In the preceding sections we have been presenting certain kinds of facts—facts about the phonological system of English, about articulatory phonetics, about the known range and variety of phonemic systems in the languages of the world. It is part of the linguist's business to assemble such information. But if he is to do this, he is also forced to develop certain techniques or skills—those involved in *finding out* what the phonemic system of a particular language is. The speaker of a language "knows" the phonology of his language, in the sense that he behaves, as speaker and hearer, in conformity with it. But he cannot, without special training, describe his phonemic system to anyone else. Therefore the linguist cannot find out about the phonology of, say, Choctaw or Vietnamese merely by asking a native speaker of the language to tell him about it. Instead, he is forced to apply certain procedures of observation and experimentation. These procedures are called *phonemic analysis*.

Phonemic analysis is carried on under varying conditions. The most favorable ones are when the analyst can work through direct face-to-face contact with a speaker of the language, or *informant*—especially if the analyst and the informant both control some common language, in addition to the informant's native language that the analyst wants to study. This set-up we call *field conditions*, and we shall assume field conditions in our discussion in this section. If a language is known only through documentary records, like Latin or Old English, the basic assumptions of analysis remain the same, but the step-by-step procedures are radically different, and the degree of certainty that can be ascribed to one's results is in general lower. The special problems that are encountered under these *philological* conditions lie beyond the scope of this book. Finally, it sometimes happens that one attempts to determine the phonological system of a language that is neither currently spoken nor attested through written records, but is known only indirectly via later descendant forms of speech—for example, the language of certain Germanic tribes of some time in the first millenium B.C. (we have no way of determining either date or location precisely) which has survived, in greatly altered forms, as English, German, Norwegian, and the other so-called Germanic languages of today. The techniques used under these conditions form part of the comparative method, and will be dealt with in §§57–58.

In the field situation, it is useful to distinguish between two operations or sets of operations, which we can call *gathering* and *collation*. Gathering has to do with the process of transforming observed utterances of the informant into notations on paper, in fit form for comparison and shuffling. Collation is the kind of comparison and shuffling which then has to be done before the phonological system is revealed. In practice, one never does all the gathering first and all the collation afterwards. Early tentative efforts at collation, based on partial gathering, suggest things to be looked for in further gathering. The logical distinction between the two is essential, however, in that collation must remain tentative until gathering has been completed.

12.2. Gathering. When the analyst confronts an informant in the field, he makes certain initial assumptions: that the informant indeed speaks a language; that, therefore, the informant's utterances are largely kept apart by differences of sound (the "largely" allows for marginal exceptions like English *The sun's rays meet* and *The sons raise meat*); that only a small number of discrete differences of sound have this utterance-differentiating role. So much the analyst *must* assume. More than this, as to details, he *cannot* assume, but must determine empirically.

The analyst begins by asking the informant how to say different things: "How do you say 'man'?" "What's your word for 'dog'?" "How do you say 'two men'?" and so on. At the outset, the analyst tries to elicit only rather short utterances, for a practical reason: he must attune his own ear to the new language before he can hope to hear, with any accuracy, longer stretches of speech. Eventually, of course, he must deal with longer utterances too. The analyst transcribes each response

from the informant as best he can, in a rough phonetic form. Before
or after doing so, he may also try to imitate the informant's utterance, asking the informant to be ruthlessly critical of any errors of
pronunciation.

Even if the analyst's imitations are seemingly acceptable to the informant, the written notations which he puts down may be full of
errors. The first word-list which one assembles in this way would be
quite valueless as a permanent record of the language. But this is not
its purpose. It is merely a temporary aid to the analyst in his trial-and-
error determination of the phonological system of the language. The
process by which the analyst gradually reaches firm conclusions can
best be shown through examples.

Suppose that the first two utterances elicited from the informant lead
the analyst to put the following entries in his notebook:

(1) 'man'   [t'áli]
(2) 'woman'   [múga]

These first two items do not tell the analyst much. True enough, the
two utterances sound different, but the differences are so extensive that
they are not of much help to the analyst in his task of tabulating the
minimal functioning differences of articulation and sound. Even the
occurrence of a voiceless aspirated stop [t'] in the first item, versus a
voiced stop [g] in the second, guarantees nothing about the types of
contrast of manner for stops in the language, for it may turn out that
all medial stops are voiced, all initial stops voiceless and aspirated, or
that there are two-way or three-way contrasts in both environments.

Suppose, though, that somewhat later the following item is elicited:

(3) 'sand dune'   [dálo]

A comparison of items (1) and (3) is immediately crucial. Unless the
analyst has heard or recorded wrong, the two items begin in similar,
but not identical, ways: both with apical stops, but (1) with a voiceless
aspirated [t'], (3) with a voiced [d]. It is true that there are also other
differences in sound between the two utterances: (1) ends with [i],
(3) with [o]. But this difference is not of the sort that might reasonably
be expected to have any connection with the first. Thus the pair can
probably be interpreted as attesting to some sort of distinctive contrast
of manner between initial stops of the same position of articulation.

Tentatively, the analyst can describe this contrast as "voiceless aspirated" versus "voiced"; but this description may have to be revised as further forms are recorded and as the analyst's ears become more sharply attuned to the new language.

Next, suppose that the following turns up:

(4) 'minnow'   [tóna]

The problem presented by this item is whether there are three distinctively different manners of articulation for initial stops (voiceless aspirated in 'man,' voiceless unaspirated in 'minnow,' and voiced in 'sand dune'), or only two. If the hearing and recording are both accurate, then presumably there are three—except that an accurate phonetic record might reflect a random variation of pronunciation by the informant as he said the forms on the specific occasions when they were observed and recorded. The analyst must elicit *repetitions* of all three forms. He re-elicits (1) and (4), and (we shall say) the initial stops continue to sound quite distinct. He re-elicits (1) and (3), with the same result. But then he re-elicits (3) and (4), and it turns out that his first hearings (or the informant's first dictations) were imprecise: the stop at the beginning of (3), when the form is repeated several times, strikes the analyst's ears now as voiced, now as voiceless, though always as unaspirated; and the stop at the beginning of (4) seems to vary in the same way. He must thus revise his notation for both (3) and (4), by lining out the earlier transcriptions and replacing them, with an accompanying note:

(3') 'sand dune'   [dálo]
(4') 'minnow'   [dóna]
([d] for a stop which is always unaspirated, but which varies as to voicing: differences of voicing apparently phonemically irrelevant for utterance-initial stops)

Next, suppose that the following appears:

(5) 'envelope'   [múga]

This seems to be identical with (2). But the analyst must listen to both (2) and (5) some more, since there might be a regular difference of sound to which his ears are not yet attuned. There is a practical advantage, for ear-training, in listening to similar forms (which may or may not be identical) in immediate succession, since the acoustic impression of the first is fresh when one hears the second. In this instance the analyst discovers that they are really different, and revises his notations to:

(2) 'woman'   [múɣaˈ]
(5) 'envelope'   [múga]
(Contrast between [g] and [ɣ] distinctive.)

Finally, suppose that the analyst asks for the word meaning 'man (in contrast to woman),' and elicits

(6) 'man' (not woman)   [tʻári]

This is not quite the same phonetically as (1), but it is sufficiently similar, both in sound and in meaning, to raise some suspicions. Has the informant simply given the same word, interpreted acoustically in two different ways by the analyst (once with a lateral [l], once with a tap [r])? Or has the informant given two different words which have virtually the same meaning despite slight difference in phonemic shape? Simple rehearing may not solve this problem. If, in due course, a pair of forms like the following turns up—

(7) 'but'   [pʻélo]
(8) 'dog'   [pʻéro]

—where the only acoustic difference is just the difference between [r] and [l], then he can safely conclude that (1) and (6) are genuinely distinct forms, which simply happen to have similar or identical meanings.

The work of analysis proceeds in this trial-and-error fashion, with pairwise comparisons in instances that seem crucial, retraining of the analyst's ears, corrections and revisions of notation, and conscious omission of indication of details that prove to be phonemically irrelevant in the language. The precise style of work varies from one analyst to another. Some attempt to make the initial phonetic record as detailed and precise as possible, so that most of the process of phonemicizing will consist of deleting features that prove to be irrelevant. Others satisfy themselves with rather rough phonetics, knowing that they may well miss some distinctive contrasts to start with and have to add them later, when they have been discovered in other forms. The outcome is the same in either case. Eventually, one attains a record of a large number of forms (long as well as short) in which *all the contrasts which are relevant in each environment* are provided for, and no others. When such a record has been achieved, the first part of the analysis (gathering) has been completed, and the analyst's attention can turn fully to the second part.

12.3. Collation. The record achieved by complete and accurate gathering is, by definition, *allophonically* correct and complete. In the case of English, for example, we would know after complete gathering that initially before a stressed vowel there are contrasts between six and only six non-affricated stops: aspirated [p' t' k'] and unaspirated crescendo-voiced [ᵖb ᵗd ᵏg]. We would also know that finally after a stressed vowel there is also a six-way contrast, involving slightly aspirated to unaspirated voiceless [p t k] and diminuendo-voiced [bᵖ dᵗ gᵏ].

But there are two important and interrelated questions that gathering, unaccompanied by collation, does not answer.

(1) What allophones in *different* environments represent the same phoneme? For example, should we say that English initial [p'] and final [p] are both representations of the same phoneme /p/? Or should we associate initial [p'] and final [t]? Or initial [p'] and final [bᵖ]?

(2) How large a segment of articulation and sound should we segregate as a single allophone of a single (even if not yet recognized) phoneme? For example, should we regard English initial [t'] as a single allophone, or should we cut it into an unaspirated [t] and an aspirate release ['] or [h]?

In answering such questions, it is essential for an analyst to base his decisions on overtly stated criteria. To discuss all the criteria that have been proposed would be too complicated, but there are four fundamental principles on which almost all specialists are in agreement:

(I) *The Principle of Contrast and Complementation.* Two allophones cannot represent the same phoneme if they stand in contrast. For example, English (initial) [t'] and [ᵗd] cannot be phonemically the same, because of pairs like *ten* and *den*, or *time* and *dime*. This follows, of course, immediately from the definition of phonology.

If two allophones are not in contrast, they are said to be in *complementation* or *complementary distribution:* that is, neither occurs in any environment in which the other is found. Mere complementation is not in itself enough to assign two allophones to a single phoneme: English initial [p'] is in complementation with all six final stops [p t k bᵖ dᵗ gᵏ], as well as with various other sound-types. In order to decide which of the six possible identifications to make—if any—we have to bring in the next principle.

(II) *The Principle of Phonetic Similarity.* This principle involves the assumption that if a phoneme is represented in two or more environments, there will be a high degree of phonetic similarity among the allophones involved. We are not able to define "degree of phonetic similarity" in a really precise way, and consequently the proper application of this principle is not always clear. Yet in many cases it is. Thus English initial [pʻ] is obviously more similar to final [p] than to any other occurrent final sound-type. This similarity, accompanied by the complementation, leads almost all analysts to conclude that the two allophones represent the same phoneme, /p/.

The following analogy is often helpful to beginners. In surveying the distribution of sound-types in an alien language, the analyst is in much the same position as the detective in an old-fashioned murder mystery. He notices that the butler and the murderer are of about the same build ("phonetic similarity"), and that the former is never in evidence when the latter puts in appearance, nor vice versa ("complementary distribution"). He concludes that the butler and the murderer are one and the same.

The detective tests this hypothesis by unmasking the murderer and revealing the butler. The analyst can apply a somewhat similar test. He assumes, for example, that the strong aspiration of English initial [pʻ] is a "mask" worn by voiceless stops in initial position before stressed vowels, and that relatively weak aspiration, as in final [p], is a "mask" worn in final position. If these masks are stripped off, then what is left is identical: voiceless bilabial stop. In other words, lurking behind the similarity is an absolute identity. The points of difference are due to the difference of environment.

But this procedure does not always work. Sometimes two phonetically similar allophones stand in contrast in one environment, and do not occur at all in some second environment, where only a third allophone, also phonetically similar, is to be observed. This constitutes *multiple complementation.* Thus English aspirated voiceless [tʻ] and unaspirated voiced [ᵗd] both occur initially before a stressed vowel (*tale, dale*), but only voiceless unaspirated [t] occurs after initial /s/ before a stressed vowel (*stale*). Shall we make a phonemic identification of [tʻ] and [t], or of [ᵗd] and [t]? It depends on how we choose to differentiate between "mask" and that which is masked; the analogy with the murder mystery breaks down. In our discussion of English phonology we chose the former alternative—as, indeed, does traditional English spelling. The other alternative can also be defended, as can a third position, which holds that under the circumstances it is not proper to make *either* identification.

(III) *The Principle of Neatness of Pattern.* If we are confronted with two or more ways of identifying allophones as phonemes, both or all of which equally well meet other criteria, we should choose that alternative which yields the most symmetrical portrayal of the system. There is always the danger that in following this principle an analyst will follow a "drive towards symmetry" which resides within himself rather than within his data, but even this outcome is not necessarily undesirable, provided that others are supplied with the data on which he has based his decision.

As a first example, consider once again the English initial and final stops. With only principle I to guide us, any of the initial stops could be identified with any of the final ones, so that there would be a total of 720 different ways of "phonemicizing" the data (initial [pʻ] with any of the six final stops; then initial [tʻ] with any of the five still unassigned final stops; and so on). The principle of phonetic similarity puts an end to this range of choice, and the principle of neatness of pattern offers firm support in the same direction. By identifying initial and final [pʻ] and [p], initial and final [tʻ] and [t], and so on, we obtain a set of six phonemes /p t k b d g/ which contrast with each other on just the same phonetic basis in both environments. Furthermore, their allophones differ from each other, from one environment to the other, in parallel ways. That is, initial /p-/ differs from initial /t-/ in that one is bilabial and one apico-alveolar, and this same difference distinguishes final /-p/ and final /-t/; similarly for all other pairs. Likewise, initial /p-/ differs phonetically from final /-p/ just as initial /t-/ and /k-/ differ from final /-t/ and /-k/; and the phonetic difference between initial /b-/ and final /-b/ recurs for initial /d- g-/ versus final /-d -g/. It is this sort of parallelism or recurrence to which the term "symmetry" or "neatness of pattern" refers.

As a second example, consider the English affricates [č] and [ǰ], as in *choose, pitcher* and *juice, ledger.* One might consider interpreting these

either as single phonemes /č/ and /ǰ/, or as clusters /tš/ and /dž/. Of
course, for those speakers who have obvious medial clusters [tš] and
[dž] in forms like *hit ya*, *would ya*, in contrast with the medial sounds in
pitcher, *ledger*, the second interpretation is precluded; but there are many
who have no such contrasts. Phonetic similarity offers no decisive support for either interpretation. However, the principle of neatness of
pattern leads most contemporary analysts to prefer the first of the two.
If we interpret [č] and [ǰ] as clusters /tš/ and /dž/, then these two
two-consonant clusters are the only ones which consist of stop plus
spirant and occur initially: there is no *pattern* for initial clusters of this
type save, circularly, that established just by the two elements which
do not necessarily have to be so interpreted. By way of contrast, German
initial [č] is best interpreted as a cluster /tš/, because this is then only
one of a whole set of initial stop-plus-spirant clusters, including also
/pf ps ts ks/.

(IV) *The Principle of Economy*. The least useful and most vague of the
four principles under discussion is this last one. In one over-precise
form, it holds that one should never solve the phonemic system of a
language with 30 phonemes if an alternative solution, equally well
meeting all other criteria, requires some smaller number, say 28 or
25. Against this, it can be argued that the first phonemicization might
permit us to write a smaller average number of successive phonemic
symbols per utterance. For example, if English [č] and [ǰ] are analyzed
as clusters /tš/ and /dž/ (in a dialect where this is possible), the inventory of phonemes is smaller by two than if they are taken as units.
But in the former case we have five successive segmental phonemes in
choose /tšuwz/, whereas in the latter case we have only four (/čuwz/).
It is doubtful that one can really argue that reduction of inventory is a
greater economy than reduction in average number of phonemes per
utterance.

Instances where the principle of economy unambiguously points to
one interpretation rather than another usually turn out to be cases in
which the other three principles would eventually lead to the same
choice, without the addition of the fourth. Even if this were always
true, rendering the fourth principle logically otiose, its retention as a
practical guide in collation would be worth while. The habit of checking alternative tentative analyses for relative efficiency is a good one,

since it can reveal points which need to receive more careful consideration in the framework of the first three principles.

Using the above four principles, in ways conditioned partly by personal taste, an investigator eventually "finishes" the process of collation, in the sense that he is prepared to present his portrayal of the language's phonological system as a contribution to our knowledge of the world's languages. "Finish" is a doubtful term: residual problems often remain, sometimes for a long time. Yet a not-quite-complete description is better than none, and the public presentation of results makes it possible for others to check on the accuracy of the original investigator's work. It is not at all surprising that different analysts, working on the same language, are often in partial disagreement; the surprising—and encouraging—thing is the extent to which these disagreements concern minor details.

NOTES

New terms: *informant; field* versus *philological* conditions for analysis; *gathering* and *collation; contrast* and *complementation* (or *complementary distribution*), *phonetic similarity, multiple complementation, neatness of pattern* (often called *pattern congruity* in the literature), *economy.*

Gleason *Workbook* (1955b), pages 56–59, presents a series of problems in collation which can profitably be used at this point. Most of his phonetic and phonemic symbols are like those used in this book, or else are especially explained where they occur; but note that Gleason uses "y" for our "j."

13.

PHONEMES and SOUND

13.1. In dealing with the phonemic system of a single language, we focus our attention on *contrast*. A phoneme is defined, not as a sound produced in such-and-such a manner, but as a point of reference in an interlocking network of contrasts (§2).

In articulatory phonetics, we set aside this concern with contrast in order to describe speech sounds in terms of their mechanisms of production (§§7–9).

Using the articulatory frame of reference, we can return to the analysis of any specific phonemic system, and tell *how* the phonemes differ from each other—e.g., English /p/ and /b/ contrast along the scale voiceless-voiced, and the same contrast recurs in certain other pairs of English phonemes. We can also show how certain pairs of contrasting phonemes differ from each other more than do other pairs: English /p/ and /d/ differ distinctively not only as to manner of articulation (voiceless versus voiced) but also as to position (bilabial versus apico-alveolar). Finally, we can compare whole phonemic systems in terms of the kinds of contrasts which function in them (§11); this is a meaningful kind of comparison, whereas merely to see whether a certain type of speech sound, say [k] or [a], occurs or not in this or that language is of no particular importance.

There is another kind of phonetic study, *acoustic phonetics*. The act of speaking gives rise to a continuous train of sound waves, the *speech signal;* it is, of course, the impingement of this on the ears of a hearer that effects communication via speech. In acoustic phonetics, one studies the characteristics of speech signals by direct observation, rather than—as in articulatory phonetics—indirectly through the motions

112

that produce them. This study is conducted for various purposes, some of which are of little importance for linguistics. In what follows we confine our remarks to acoustic research of linguistic relevance.

13.2. Acoustics. The branch of physics which deals with sound is *acoustics*. Acousticians tell us that sound consists of vibrations of the air or of some other material medium; air is the medium that concerns us. Whenever air is set into vibration at a certain point, by some physical agent called the *source*, the sound travels in all directions at approximately 1100 feet per second, diminishing in energy until, in effect, it disappears.

When the vibrations are regularly spaced in time, we hear a musical tone of a definite pitch: the more rapid the vibrations (the higher the *frequency*), the higher the pitch. The range of frequencies on a piano tuned to concert pitch is from 27.5 to 4184 vibrations or *cycles* per second. This is just over seven octaves, since if one doubles a frequency, one obtains a tone one octave higher. The human ear can detect somewhat lower sounds (15 to 20 cycles per second) and somewhat higher sounds (15 to 20 thousand cycles per second) provided they are loud enough.

When the vibrations are irregularly spaced in time, we hear not a musical tone but a "noise." Noises, also, can often be classed roughly as higher or lower in pitch, as when we assert that the sound of a hammer hitting a nail is higher in pitch than the sound of surf booming along a beach.

More technically, in a pure musical tone all the energy is concentrated at a single frequency, whereas in a non-musical noise the energy is spread more irregularly through a band of frequencies.

In a pure musical tone, the amount of energy present at the frequency correlates with the *intensity* of the sound, and also, more roughly, with its "loudness" or "volume." If a bow is pulled lightly across a violin string of fixed length, the string moves back and forth through a relatively small arc, and transmits a relatively slight amount of energy per unit of time to the surrounding air: we hear a relatively soft tone. If the bow is pulled more rapidly or is pressed more heavily, the string moves through a larger arc, transmitting more energy per unit of time to the air, and we hear a louder tone of the same pitch.

The only properties of sound which can be detected by the human ear can be described physically in terms of just three factors: frequency and intensity, as mentioned above, and *duration*. The description is not always easy, for in a complex sound there may be varying amounts of energy at different frequencies, and this distribution may change

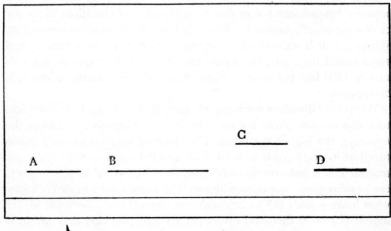

FIGURE 13.1.   IDEALIZED SPECTROGRAM

The spectrogram above shows exactly what the musical notation below does. The spectrogram shows difference of frequency by the height of the line; C is higher than A, B, or D. It shows difference of duration by length of the line: B is twice as long as A, C, or D. It shows difference of amplitude by heaviness of the line: D is more intense than A, B, or C. This last dimension is the hardest to read off accurately, just as in musical notation the marking of "p" and "f" is least precise.

rapidly. However, there are no further "ingredients": any other terms used by the acoustic phonetician can be defined with just these three.

Sound is a transient phenomenon. Unless caught and examined at just the right moment, it is gone forever. What the acoustician wants to know about sound is not anything he can determine merely by listening;

he must make accurate measurements. Consequently he uses various electronic devices, of which the most important is the *spectrograph*. When sound from any source is fed into a spectrograph, the device produces a kind of picture called a *spectrogram*, in which frequency, intensity, and duration are all represented. This picture is a permanent record, and the acoustician can measure it at his leisure. Figure 13.1 shows, in highly idealized fashion, four segments of spectrograms; the caption explains how the visual shapes correlate with features of sound.

13.3. The Speech Signal. One point should be underscored before we go on. The sound produced by a speaking human is just sound in the physicist's sense of the word. There is no special added ingredient in the sound of human speech which renders it by nature impervious to the analysis of the acoustician. The speech signal, like any other sound, can be completely specified in terms of frequency, intensity, and duration. The special features of speech do not reside in the sound of speech but in the very special equipment in the brains of human beings in their roles as speaker and hearer.

Speech occurs always in some context—the context of who is present, where they are, what they are doing, and what has already been said. The context tells the hearer to some extent what the speaker is likely to say, so that he does not have to be equally on the alert for every theoretically possible message, and often does not have to catch all of what is said in order to understand. In this defining context, the speech signal does two things, not just one: it tells the hearer what utterance has been used by the speaker, but it is also shaped in part by the speaker's voice-quality modulation (§6.5).

In examining the speech signal for linguistic purposes, we are interested only in its utterance-identifying function, and so want somehow to strain out those characteristics which are solely matters of voice-quality modulation. Only thus can we see how the remaining physical properties of the speech signal serve to tell the hearer what has been said. No machine can do this for us; the experimenter has to do it. To achieve this aim, acoustic phoneticians record utterances under conditions which tend to limit the range of voice-quality modulation, and consider multiple records from single speakers before comparing records made by different speakers. This does not eliminate voice-quality modulation, but restricts its variability of influence.

The basic procedure is approximately as follows. We make a number of spectrograms of different utterings of what is phonemically a single utterance. Then we compare the recordings, trying to discern the acoustic features common to all. Since the different utterings are phonemically identical, the acoustic features common to all must correlate with the identical phonemic structure.

Suppose, for example, that we make records of a number of utterings of *Pie is bad for me.* The spectrograms will differ to the eye, but we expect *some* measurable constant configuration to recur in all, and the initial part of this constant configuration ought to correlate with the initial /p/ of the utterance. If we then make records of *Buy a pad for me,* and compare them with each other and with the first set, we ought to be able to describe how the distinction between initial English /p/ and /b/ is represented in the speech signal.

13.4. Complexity. The most startling result is the complexity encountered. We should naturally expect that, while each segmental phoneme represented on the spectrogram would vary somewhat from one occurrence to another, it would have a recognizable and distinctive pattern. In a way, this expectation is confirmed, for it is possible, at least much of the time, to detect each successive phoneme as represented on the spectrogram. Let us call each such representation an *acoustic allophone.* The unexpected complexity lies in the fact that acoustic allophones are *numerous, diverse, intersecting,* and *overlapping.*

By "numerous" we mean that a single phoneme, instead of being represented by at most a few allophones (as, in articulatory terms, English /p/ is sometimes aspirated and sometimes not), is represented by dozens of clearly different ones.

By "diverse," we mean that the allophones which represent a single phoneme do not necessarily appear as minor variations around some single measurable constant core, but instead may seem to have virtually nothing in common.

By "intersecting" we mean that a given acoustic allophone of phoneme A may resemble some allophone of phoneme B much more closely than it does some of the other allophones of phoneme A. In an extreme instance, we find that what we know must in a certain environment be English /š/ may be absolutely identical, so far as we can measure, with what we know in another environment is English /s/.

By "overlapping" we mean that the representation of one phoneme does not necessarily end before the representation of the next begins.

Indeed, the total representation of a given phoneme in a given environment may be spread or scattered through the portion of the spectrogram which also represents several preceding and several following phonemes.

We shall not take the space to illustrate the first two points. The last two can be illustrated with a peculiarly convincing example, which will also suffice for the conclusions we shall draw.

Figure 13.2 shows four spectrographic patterns, prepared by hand and fed into a special apparatus called a *pattern playback*. Just as a spectrograph responds to sound by drawing a spectrogram, so a pattern playback responds to a spectrogram by emitting the appropriate sound. When the four patterns were played to a test audience, who were instructed to state what English syllables they thought they heard, there was a high degree of agreement on the interpretation as /píj/, /kíj/, /pá/, and /ká/. In each pattern, the lozenge-shaped dot was heard as a stop consonant, and the two parallel horizontal lines as a vowel.

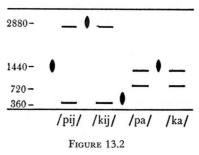

/pij/ /kij/ /pa/ /ka/

FIGURE 13.2

The crux of the demonstration is this. The acoustic representation of the /p/ of /píj/ is *identical* with the acoustic representation of the /k/ of /ká/. This does not mean that *all* occurrences of /p/ before /íj/ are identical acoustically with *all* those of /k/ before /á/, for there is wide variation in each. But the ranges of variation intersect: *some* occurrences of /p/ in /píj/ are identical with *some* occurrences of /k/ in /ká/.

Only the objective testimony of the spectrograph could demonstrate this physical fact. Our everyday experience controverts it: the /p/ of /píj/ sounds like other /p/'s to us, not like the /k/ of /ká/. And in some sense our everyday experience is right. There is something about human reception and interpretation of the speech signal which cancels out the physical fact and makes different identifications of bits of sound as "sounding the same."

Although we do not know just how this effect is brought about, the following two points are worthy of notice.

One essential difference between a spectrograph and a human hearer is that the former is, so to speak, literal-minded. If at a given moment there is a certain intensity of energy at a certain frequency, the spectrograph takes note of the fact and reports it. Earlier and later input are for the moment ignored. The human hearer pays attention to each bit of sound in terms of wider contexts: a given noise burst (represented by the black lozenges) is classed as /p/ if followed by one sort of vowel, but as /k/ if followed by another. The spectrogram ignores nothing of the signal it is built to detect. The human hearer ignores a great deal, and what is ignored and what is noted are not invariant, but depend on preceding and ensuing portions of the signal.

This tells us something, but not enough. The other clue goes deeper. A human has articulatory organs which he is skilled in using. A spectrograph has none. Any speaker hears his own speech, and feels the positions and motions of his own articulatory organs. The sound and feel of one's own speech constitute *feedback*, the former *auditory*, the latter *kinesthetic*. A speaker monitors his speech by means of feedback, just as the monitor in a radio station listens to the signal and makes predictive adjustments in it as it goes on the air. Auditory feedback can be impaired by deafness, and kinesthetic feedback can be distorted by certain drugs, such as alcohol. With any such interference, articulation deteriorates. Under normal conditions, the two sorts of feedback supplement each other, and long experience builds a very precise correlation between them.

When one is listening to someone else, the incoming speech signal consists of features more or less similar to features of speech signals which one has oneself produced in the past. Given the intimate association of articulating, feeling articulation, and hearing its results, it seems reasonable to assume that the hearer interprets an incoming speech signal, at least in part, by comparing elements of it with acoustic effects which he would achieve in certain ways with his own articulatory organs. This need not be done consciously, and need involve no subliminal motions of tongue and lips; it may take place entirely within the central nervous system. Nor do we have any reason to assume that such comparing *always* goes on. Perhaps it does, but perhaps it is a means of interpretation resorted to only under special conditions.

Let us illustrate with the /píj/-/ká/ instance. When the English-speaking experimental subject hears the first of these, he finds that the noise-burst at the beginning is one which, *in this environment*, he would match with a bilabial motion. He identifies the noise-burst, in this setting, in terms of that articulatory motion. The analyst follows his lead, and classes the noise-burst as a representation of English /p/. When the experimental subject hears identically the same noise-burst in the other setting, he finds that in *that* environment he would match it with a dorso-velar motion. Thus he identifies the same noise-burst in a different setting in terms of a different articulatory motion. The analyst accordingly classes the noise-burst in the second environment as a representation of English /k/.

The foregoing line of reasoning is in part speculative. However, perhaps our discussion is sufficiently convincing to explain why many linguists, including the writer, take the following tentative attitudes: (1) Acoustic phonetics faces a special task, for which the frame of reference of conventional phonemics is essential: the task of determining and describing the acoustic correlates of phonemes and phonemic structures. (2) This task is marginal, in the sense that progress in the rest of linguistics need not be delayed by slow development of our knowledge here. (3) The continued use of articulatory rather than acoustic description for most linguistic purposes has a justification which may be more than merely practical, in that it may reflect a certain use of the same frame of reference by the speakers of a language.

NOTES

New terms, largely those of acoustic phonetics or of general acoustics, rather than of linguistics: *speech signal; source* of a sound; (*musical*) *tone* versus *noise* (the latter here in a sense sharply different from its sense in information theory, as in §10); measurable physical properties of sound: *frequency* (in *cycles* per second), correlating with *pitch, intensity* (roughly correlating with loudness and volume), *duration; spectrograph, spectrogram; acoustic allophone; auditory* and *kinesthetic feedback*.

Acoustic phonetics is entertainingly described by Gleason 1955a, chapter 15. Results through 1954 are surveyed in Hockett 1955 §5; the standard work is Joos 1948.

PHONOLOGY AND GRAMMAR: LEVELS OF PATTERNING

14.

MORPHEMES

14.1. Definition. If the utterances of a language consisted merely of arrangements of phonemes, there would be no point in speaking or in listening. But people do speak and listen, and their oral communication transmits information and instructions and serves to coordinate their activities. That utterances can serve in this way is because they have another kind of structure in addition to the phonemic one, a structure in terms of *morphemes*.

Morphemes are the smallest individually meaningful elements in the utterances of a language.

To illustrate, we shall examine the following English sentence:

/³ján+²tríjtsiz+ówldər+sístərz+vérij+·²nájslij²↑/
(*John treats his older sisters very nicely.*)

In order to determine the morphemes of which this sentence is composed, we pull out any portion and ask the following questions about it:

(I) Does the portion recur in various utterances, with approximately the same meaning? If the answer is no, then the portion we have chosen to examine is of no use to us, and we try another. If the answer is yes, then the portion is tentatively a *grammatical form* (or, for short, simply a *form*), but not necessarily a single morpheme. (It is unfortunate that we must include "tentatively" in the preceding statement, especially since the reasons for the reservation cannot be explained until §19. In the meantime we shall proceed as though no reservation had been expressed.)

(II) Can the form be broken into smaller pieces, each of which recurs with approximately the same meaning, in such a way that the meaning

123

of the whole form is related to the meanings of the smaller pieces? If the answer is yes, then the form is larger than a single morpheme (is a *composite form*), and we must subject each of the pieces, in turn, to the same two-step examination. But if the answer is no, then the form is itself a single morpheme.

Thus each portion we choose is shown, by Test I, to be either a bad choice or a grammatical form, and each grammatical form is shown, by Test II, to be either a composite form or a morpheme. By a series of such operations, we can discover all the morphemes of an utterance.

Let us apply the tests to the following extracts from our sample sentence: /ǰá/, /ǰán+tr/, /ówldər/, and /sístər/.

The first portion, /ǰá/, fails Test I. It recurs, true enough—for example, in *Jobs are scarce here, He's a jolly old man, Two jars of shaving cream.* But we detect no common feature of meaning in these utterances which could reasonably be assigned to the recurrent portion /ǰá/.

The second portion also fails Test I. The portion recurs: *John traded his watch for a pencil, If John tries that he'll fail, From the broken demijohn trickled a stream of wine.* But the requirement of similarity of meaning is not satisfied.

Test I is quickly passed by /ówldər/. Its meaning in the original sentence is certainly much the same as in such sentences as *He is older than I; The older of the two is a girl; I do declare, I'm getting older every day!* In order to apply Test II, we must decide how to break /ówldər/ up into smaller pieces. If we were working with an alien language we might have to test many alternatives—say /ów/ and /ldər/, /ówl/ and /dər/, and so on. Since we control English natively we can avoid this complication and proceed immediately to the cut which we feel will yield positive results: /ówld/ and /ər/. The former recurs, with reasonably constant meaning, in such sentences as *He's an old man, He's the oldest of their three children, Jack is quite an active oldster.* And the latter recurs in such sentences as *When I was younger I enjoyed such things more, You should learn to enjoy the finer things of life.* The evidence seems quite clear: *older* is more than one morpheme. Similar testing of /ówld/ and /ər/ shows that each is only a single morpheme; *older*, then, is exactly two morphemes.

Finally /sístər/. This quickly passes Test I: *My sister Eileen; OK, sister, get moving!; Sister Angela will be here in a moment.* Turning to Test II, once again we have to decide what break-up to try. Let us first try *sist-* and *-er*, if only because this is much like the cut of *older* which proved fruitful.

Now there can be no doubt but that the string of phonemes /síst/ occurs in environments other than those in which it is immediately followed by /ər/, and it is equally obvious that the latter occurs where it is not preceded by /síst/. Thus, for /síst/, we have *He has a cyst which must be removed; I have a system, I can't lose; Whipped cream consists largely of air; I don't mean to insist.* And for /ər/, in addition to the examples given earlier, we could find sentences involving *brother, father, mother, daughter; hammer, butter, fetter, wither; singer, writer, actor, bettor.*

But this is not enough. We get into trouble on the score of meaning, just as we did with the portions /ǰá/ and /ǰán+tr/ which we tested first. There seems to be no reasonable similarity of meaning between the *sist-* of *sister* and any of the other /síst/'s illustrated. The words *sister, brother, father, mother, daughter* are all kinship terms, which means that they share some feature of meaning; on this basis one might want to extract the element *-er* as a morpheme carrying this shared feature of meaning. However, to do so leaves us not only with a /síst/ which—in this meaning—seems not to recur, but also with similarly forlorn elements /brə́ð/, /fáð/, /mə́ð/, and /dót/. Thus it seems reasonable to conclude that *sister* should not be regarded as a combination of smaller forms *sist-* and *-er*.

No other way of cutting *sister* into smaller pieces seems to have even the partial justification which we have found above for the cut into *sist-* and *-er*. We therefore decide to accept *sister* as a single morpheme.

Proceeding in this same way with all the different parts of our original sentence, we arrive finally at the following list of the constituent morphemes:

(1) *John* /ǰán/   (2) *treat* /tríjt/
(3) *-s* /s/   (4) *hi-* /i/
(5) *-s* /z/   (6) *old* /ówld/
(7) *-er* /ər/   (8) *sister* /sístər/
(9) *-s* /z/   (10) *very* /vérij/
(11) *nice* /nájs/   (12) *-ly* /lij/
(13) /³ ² ²²↑/.

Note the following points:

First, the intonation must not be overlooked; we have taken it as a single separate morpheme.

Second, (5) and (9) are phonemically the same, but certainly not the same morpheme, because of the difference in meaning.

Third, the breakdown of *his* /iz/ into *hi-* /i/ and *-s* /z/ may seem unconvincing. The /z/ recurs, with exactly the same meaning, in *John's book*, *the men's room*, and the like. But the /i/ recurs only in *him* (as in *hit 'im*).

If this evidence is enough to persuade us to break up *(h)is*, then maybe we want to break up *very* too, into a *ver-* which recurs in *verity*, *veritable*, perhaps *veracious*, and an element *-y* which recurs in *pretty* (*pretty well*) and perhaps elsewhere.

Marginal uncertainties of this sort are to be expected—in any language, not just in English. They must not be allowed to disturb us too much. Most problems of whether to cut or not are answered easily and quickly. Where there is conflict of evidence, it is often not very important which alternative we choose. The uncertainties lie in the nature of language, rather than in our method of attack.

14.2. Remnants. Occasionally, after we have extracted all the morphemes from some utterance by successive applications of Tests I and II, we seem to have something left over. Consider, for example,

$$^2Pléase \ páss \ the \ ^3cránbèrries^1 \!\downarrow$$

The last word of this sentence can obviously be broken into *cranberry* and a morpheme /z/ meaning "plural." *Cranberry*, in turn, seems clearly to contain an element /bèrij/ which recurs in *strawberry*, *raspberry*, *gooseberry*, *blackberry*, *blueberry*, and so on. But how about *cran-*? We look in vain for any recurrence of *cran-* with anything like the meaning it has in *cranberry*.

A strict adherence to Tests I and II would therefore force us to take *cranberry* as a single morpheme. Yet this is obviously undesirable. In the first place, the identity of the second part of *cranberry* is hardly subject to doubt. In the second place, *cran-* clearly carries a meaning, even if the element occurs nowhere save in this one combination. Cranberries are different from strawberries, raspberries, gooseberries, and so on; the meaning of *cran-* is therefore whatever it is which differentiates cranberries from these other kinds of berries. It might be hard to describe this meaning, but it is easily demonstrated in a fruit market.

What we do under such circumstances is to recognize the element in question as a morpheme of a rather special kind—a *unique* morpheme. The recognition of such special morphemes does not require any modification of our definition, but only calls for a slight change in the way we apply Tests I and II.

Other unique morphemes in English are *fro*, *kith*, *main* (as in *might and main*), *fangle* (in *new-fangled*). The line of demarcation between unique morphemes and ordinary ones is actually not so sharp as might be expected. Some morphemes which are not unique nevertheless occur in only a very limited number of combinations; e.g., *sake*, which is always accompanied by *for* (*for his sake*, *for the sake of all of us*, *Whose sake did you do that for?*). If we were to class the morphemes of a language according to the degree of freedom with which they enter into combinations, we would find a virtually continuous scale of degrees of freedom, and unique morphemes would simply be those at one end of the scale.

14.3. Recognizing Morphemes in an Alien Language. The procedures just discussed and illustrated apply to the analysis of Menomini or Burmese or French just as well as to that of English. However, some of the steps which must be taken require more conscious care when one is working with a language one does not know so thoroughly. When we work with English it is all too easy for us to jump to conclusions—and even if the conclusions are correct, the jumping obscures the logic.

If we are confronted with a single utterance in a foreign language, we can draw no morphemic conclusions at all. For example, suppose we are informed that in Potawatomi the following utterance occurs:

(1) /nkəšatəs/ 'I'm happy.'

If we learn how to say this, we are equipped to say 'I'm happy' in Potawatomi. But we have absolutely no evidence for the morphemic structure of the utterance we have learned. The whole utterance may be a single morpheme with a somewhat complicated meaning; or it may be two or three morphemes, each carrying part of the meaning of the whole.

For morphemic identification, we must have access to at least a pair of utterances—and not every pair will do. Suppose we add the following:

(2) /kčiman/ 'thy canoe.'

We are no better off than before. (1) and (2) share no obvious stretch of phonemic material, and there is no obvious common feature of meaning. On the other hand, let us add

(3) /kkəšatəs/ 'Thou art happy.'

Since (3) is partly like (1) in phonemic shape and in meaning, we can draw some conclusions: the shared portion /-kəšatəs/ must mean something like 'be happy,' and the unshared portions /n-/ and /k-/ must mean, respectively, 'I' and 'thou.'

Note that we cannot yet assert that any of these three portions is a single morpheme. In order for any of them to be a morpheme, it must be subject to no further cutting into smaller meaningful parts. Further cutting is unlikely in the case of /n-/ and /k-/, since each is only a single phoneme, but there is no such external evidence in the case of /-kəšatəs/. All that we can say for sure, at this stage, is that each of the three is a *form;* the status of each as a morpheme or as a group of morphemes remains to be determined on the basis of the comparison of many other utterances in the language.

This example underscores, in a way in which English examples cannot, the fact that the recognition of forms (and ultimately of morphemes) necessarily involves *comparison of utterances*, not just the close scrutiny of any single utterance. In English we may run through this process of comparison so easily and automatically that we are unaware of having done so.

14.4. Arrangements; Grammar. From our earlier discussion of English (in §14.1, 2) it is clear that the morphemes of a language do not occur freely in all conceivable arrangements, but only in some.

Take the short English sentence *Jim loves Jane.* Apart from the intonation, which we shall set aside here, the sentence contains four morphemes: *Jim*, *love*, *-s*, and *Jane*. Since two such morphemes cannot be pronounced at the same time, the only physically possible arrangements of these four morphemes is in a linear sequence. This yields a total of twenty-four theoretically possible arrangements. Of these, two are fully current as ordinary English sentences (*Jim loves Jane; Jane loves Jim*); two are understandable as questions, though archaic in style (*Loves Jim Jane? Loves Jane Jim?*); two are possible as emphatic statements (*Jim, Jane loves; Jane, Jim loves*—as in a longer context *Jim, Jane loves, but not Bill*). The other eighteen would not occur. (*Janes love Jim* superficially resembles a rearrangement of the four morphemes in question, but the /z/ in *Janes* is not the same morpheme as that in *loves*.)

It may seem fruitless to examine all twenty-four of the theoretically possible arrangements of the four morphemes in question in order to see which ones make sense and which do not. Why could one not simply say that any arrangement of morphemes which makes sense may occur, while an arrangement that does not make sense is not apt to occur? The objection to this inviting shortcut is that we cannot be sure which is cause and which is effect. Does an arrangement occur because it makes sense, or does it make sense because it occurs? Furthermore, the occurrent—and sense-making—arrangements of morphemes in different languages are not necessarily parallel. More than once, in learning even a reasonably close foreign language like Spanish, French, or German, we find ourselves trying to put words together in arrangements that, it seems to us, ought to make sense, but which in fact are not used by the people who speak the language. In every language there are stringent limitations on the possible arrangements of morphemes, and the limitations in one language are not to any useful degree predictable from those in another.

We summarize this by asserting that every language has its own *grammar*. The grammar, or grammatical system, of a language is (1) *the morphemes used in the language,* and (2) *the arrangements in which these morphemes occur relative to each other in utterances.*

NOTES

New technical terms: *morpheme, (grammatical) form, composite form, unique morpheme; grammar.*

Gleason, *Workbook* (1955b), pages 23–27, provides a series of problems which can profitably be undertaken at this point.

15.

MORPHEMES and PHONEMES

15.1. Shapes. In the preceding section it was tacitly implied that a morpheme not only carries essentially the same meaning wherever it occurs, but also appears everywhere in exactly the same phonemic shape. All our examples of morphemes so far have conformed to both parts of this implication. Yet the specification of identical phonemic shape was not included in our definition (§14.1).

We have encountered several instances of morphemes which are identical in phonemic shape, yet distinct because of difference in meaning. For example, /z/ marking plurality in *boys*, /z/ marking possession in *men's room*, and /z/ indicating third person singular subject in *He runs fast* are phonemically the same, but are three different morphemes. Further examples are easy to find: *bear* (animal), *bear* (give birth to), and *bare; meet* and *meat; beet* and *beat*.

This leads to a consideration of the converse: morphemes which (according to our practice so far) are distinct because of differing phonemic shapes, but which have identical meaning.

In looking for instances of this we should probably turn first to what are ordinarily called *synonyms:* words of different phonemic shape but of identical or closely similar meaning, like *big* and *large*, or *find* and *discover*. The first pair, *big* and *large*, are words of a single morpheme each, so that we could properly call them synonymous morphemes. But just how synonymous are they?

The way to find out is to put them into context. In particular, we search for contexts which can be filled in with either morpheme, yielding pairs of utterances which differ from each other only in that one contains *big* where the other contains *large*. If we can find such a *minimal pair* for *big* and *large* in which the total meanings of the utter-

130

ances are different, then we shall be forced to conclude that the two morphemes are not, after all, completely synonymous.

One test pair is *How large is it?* and *How big is it?* The reader may feel that these sentences differ in meaning, or he may feel that they are for all intents and purposes equivalent. Another pair is *He's a big man* and *He's a large man.* Here the difference in meaning is obvious: the latter would almost always refer to physical size, whereas the former could refer to social, intellectual, or political stature. In the case of *by and large* versus *by and big* we have a different situation: the first expression is common, the second hardly possible.

The test shows, then, that *big* and *large* are not entirely synonymous. This is what we find, in general, when we examine the sets of words classed as "synonyms" in a dictionary. In fact, a dictionary lists "synonyms" not because they are identical in meaning, but because of their subtle shades of difference.

Consider, however, another pair of synonymous morphemes: the /z/ meaning 'plural' in *dogs, boys, girls, tables, chairs, ideas,* and the /s/ meaning 'plural' in *cats, desks, cliffs, tops, pots.* Here, as before, it is best to assume at the start that there is some subtle difference in meaning, which could be revealed by finding an appropriate minimal pair. But in this case we search in vain. Try to replace the /z/ of *dogs, boys,* and so on, by /s/. On paper we can get the following results:

/dɔ́gs/, /bójs/, /gɔ́rls/, /téjbəls/, /čɛ́rs/, /ajdíjəs/.

The second of these is an actual English word (*Boyce*), but this has nothing to do morphemically with *boy,* and does not contain the morpheme /s/ in which we are interested. The third, fourth, fifth, and sixth are not English words at all, though they are pronounceable in English as "nonsense words." The first is not even pronounceable in English, because it ends with the cluster of consonants /gs/, alien to our phonemic habits.

Try, next, the replacement the other way round, using /z/ instead of /s/ in *cats, desks,* and so on, ostensibly producing

/kǽtz/, /déskz/, /klífz/, /tápz/, /pátz/.

These are all like the first form in the previous set—unpronounceable. The phonemic notations are fakes—the forms apparently represented do not and cannot exist.

The replacement can be tried, either way, in any other appropriate context, and the same sort of result is obtained. We can summarize by saying that /s/ 'plural' and /z/ 'plural' *do not contrast.*

The synonymity of /s/ and /z/ is thus clearly different from that of *big* and *large.* /s/ and /z/ may differ somehow in meaning, but we could not hope to discover the difference without the help of a minimal contrast; since no minimal contrast exists, any difference in meaning remains undiscoverable.

Or, to put it from the speaker's point of view: the difference between *big* and *large* affords the speaker a choice. In most environments where one of these two morphemes might be used, the speaker is free to choose the other one instead. In some environments the effective difference in meaning may be slight, or even non-existent; yet the choice is there. But the speaker has no comparable choice between /s/ and /z/ 'plural'; here the choice is made *for* the speaker, not *by* him. If he has just uttered a morpheme ending in, say, /t/, then if he chooses to add a morpheme meaning 'plural' it must necessarily be /s/. On the other hand, if he has just uttered a morpheme ending in /d/, then if he chooses to add a morpheme meaning 'plural' it must necessarily be /z/.

In any such situation, where a choice between synonymous morphemes is made *for* the speaker rather than *by* him, we prefer to describe the matter in different terms. Instead of saying that /s/ 'plural' and /z/ 'plural' are two different morphemes, we shall say that /s/ and /z/ are two different *shapes* of a single morpheme.

The difference between /s/ and /z/ is of course still *phonemically* relevant. But by this new way of speaking we eliminate the difference between shapes /s/ and /z/, specifically in the meaning 'plural,' from the *grammatical* pattern. The advantage of taking this step is that now, in describing grammar, we need deal only with differences which represent choices open to the speaker.

15.2. Examples. Here is another example of a morpheme represented now by one phonemic shape and now by another. The following three utterances consist of the same morphemes in three different arrangements:

[2]Whére are you [3]góing[1]↓
[2]Whére are [3]yóu góing[1]↓
[3]Whére are you góing[1]↓

The segmental morphemes are identical, and in identical sequence. The intonational morpheme is the same in all three, but differs in where its center is placed: on *go-* in the first, on *you* in the second, and at the beginning in the third. When the center is not at the beginning of the macrosegment, then the pendant is pronounced on PL /²/, so that the shape representing the morpheme is /² ³¹↓/. But when there is no pendant, there is no room for the /²/; this mechanical factor accounts for the representation of the intonational morpheme by /³¹↓/ instead of by /² ³¹↓/. What the speaker chooses, in this instance, is the intonational morpheme and the placement of its center; once these matters have been settled, the system decides for the speaker whether the shape will be /² ³¹↓/ or /³¹↓/.

Again, our revised orientation helps in handling the word *his* (as in the original sample sentence of §14.1). The terminal /z/ of *his* resembles the /z/ of *John's* or *men's*. If we break the /z/ off and identify it as this morpheme, we have the fragment *hi-* to deal with. The word *him* contains an element *hi-* which can be called the same morpheme; the /m/ of *him* is then another morpheme, recurring in *whom, them*. But how about the word *he*, which has such obvious affiliations with both *him* and *his*? We can break *he* /hij/ up into /hi-/ and /-j/ only if we accept the phonemic notion by which English /ij/ is a cluster of two phonemes rather than a single vowel phoneme. But even if we accept this proposal, the step leaves us with an isolated /-j/ which is hard to account for. There seems to be no reason for breaking *he* into two morphemes. It would be better if we could call *he* just one morpheme, but say that this same morpheme occurs also, in the shape /hi-/ instead of /hij/, in the words *his* and *him*. Since the shape /hij/ never occurs before the possessive morpheme /z/ nor before the /m/ of *them, whom*, and since the shape /hi-/ never occurs except with either /z/ or /m/, under our new orientation we are free to accept the proposed interpretation.

Let us consider next three tentatively distinct morphemes: the *-y* /-ij/ of *watery, milky, creamy*, the *-ly* /-lij/ of *manly, womanly, friendly*, and the *-ish* /-iš/ of *boyish, girlish, childish*. *Water, milk, man, boy* and so on are all names of things; *watery, manly, boyish* and so on are all descriptive (= 'like water' and so on). Furthermore, there is usually no choice among the three: after *water* one may use *-y* but hardly *-ly* or *-ish*.

Although a long search might fail to reveal any minimal pairs proving the three distinct, such pairs do exist, showing that caution about morphemic identifications is important. Thus *manly* and *mannish* contrast sharply in meaning: *manly* is a compliment, whereas *mannish* is sometimes rather derogatory. Similarly, there is a considerable difference between calling a woman *homely* and calling her *homey*. There is perhaps less difference between *spookish* and *spooky*, but at least to the writer *spookish* is not as spooky as *spooky*. Consequently, we must recognize *-ly*, *-y*, and *-ish* as distinct morphemes.

15.3. Morphophonemics. The preceding discussion does not require us to modify the definition of morpheme given in §14.1, but it necessitates a more careful examination of the relation between morphemes and phonemes—between grammar and phonology. If English /z/ 'plural' and /s/ 'plural' are not two different morphemes, but merely two different shapes of a single morpheme, then just what *is* the morpheme itself? And what is the relationship between a morpheme and its phonemic shape or shapes?

The answer to the first question is partly analogous to the answer to the question "what is a phoneme?" It will be remembered (§2.5) that a phoneme is defined not as a speech sound or allophone, but as a *range* of speech sound which functions as a point of contrast in an interlocking network of contrasts. A phoneme is defined not so much in terms of what it "is" or what it "sounds like," as in terms of what it is *not*—what, within the same language, it differs from. Similarly, a morpheme in a given language is defined only relative to the whole morpheme stock of the language: a morpheme is something *different* from all the other morphemes of the language. In neither case is the answer in terms of substance. One cannot point and say "there is a phoneme" or "there goes a morpheme," but can only define what either type of unit is, and what a specific phoneme or morpheme of a specific language is, in terms of the operations and criteria used in discovering them. The operations and criteria, of course, are different for phonemes and for morphemes. For the former, the criterion is identity or difference in sound of whole utterances to native speakers, without regard to meaning, while for the latter, the criteria are both meaning and (previously determined) phonemic shape.

The answer to the second question is not to be found through empirical study, but is to be supplied by definition. For the relationship of a morpheme to any of its phonemic shapes, we use the phrase *is represented by:* the English noun plural morpheme *is represented by* phonemic shape /z/ after a form ending in /d/, and *is represented by* /s/ after a form ending in /t/; the English morpheme *boy* is represented by the phonemic shape /bój/ in all environments. We have used the same phrase for the relationship between a phoneme and any of its allophones: the English phoneme /p/ is represented by a voiceless unaspirated bilabial stop after /s/, before a vowel, but by a voiceless aspirated bilabial stop initially before a stressed vowel.

The ways in which the morphemes of a given language are variously represented by phonemic shapes can be regarded as a kind of code. This code is the *morphophonemic system* of the language. When people consciously invent codes and ciphers, unless their aim is concealment of messages from those other than the intended recipients, they most often construct systems of the so-called simple substitution type. This means that each element of the message to be encoded is replaced by a fixed element in the coded form, and that the latter element always represents one and the same element in the original. The Morse code used in telegraphy is of this type: two dots represent always and only the letter "I," and so on. The morphophonemics of a language is never so simple. There are always many instances of two or more morphemes represented by the same phonemic shape (*meet* and *meat*), and always cases in which a single morpheme is represented now by one phonemic shape, now by another (/s/ and /z/ 'plural'). Therefore the morphophonemics of a language is never trivial; any systematic description of any language must cover it.

NOTES

New terms: (*phonemic*) *shape, morphophonemics, minimal pair.*

Problems. Gleason, *Workbook* (1955b), pages 28–32, gives a series of problems which can be undertaken here or can be postponed until the completion of §33. The following problem can be done now:

The English "noun plural" morpheme appears in three different phonemic shapes: /z/ in *dogs*, /s/ in *cats*, /əz/ in *faces*. The choice among these three shapes depends on the phonemic shape of the preceding (singular-form) noun. On the basis of the following list of English plural nouns, describe the conditions which require each of the three shapes:

ideas, boys, cows, sisters, rims, bags, pots, myths, messes, rouges, girls, things, ribs, sieves, tacks, patches, wishes, caps, spas, pans, fads, lathes, cliffs, judges, buzzes.

16·

THE DESIGN of a LANGUAGE

16.1. We have now established the necessary basis for describing the fundamental design features found in any and every human language.
A language is a complex system of *habits*. The system as a whole can be broken down into five principal subsystems, of which three are *central* and two are *peripheral*.
The three central subsystems are:

(1) The *grammatical* system: a stock of morphemes, and the arrangements in which they occur;
(2) The *phonological* system: a stock of phonemes, and the arrangements in which they occur;
(3) The *morphophonemic* system: the code which ties together the grammatical and the phonological systems.

These three are called "central" because they have nothing to do, directly, with the nonspeech world in which speaking takes place. It is true that an analyst—or, for that matter, a child learning a language— can deduce or learn the details of the central subsystems only by observing both speech itself and the contexts in which it takes place; but what he does deduce or learn from these observations is abstracted from the speech and the situations, and established as a set of patterns, in the brain of the child, in the brain and the notebooks of the analyst. We have already discussed phonological systems in detail (§§2–13); we have dealt very briefly with grammatical and morphophonemic systems, but shall shortly turn to each (§§17–31 for grammatical systems, §§32–35 for morphophonemic systems) for more detailed study.

The two peripheral subsystems are:

(4) The *semantic* system, which associates various morphemes, combinations of morphemes, and arrangements in which morphemes can be put, with things and situations, or kinds of things and situations;

(5) The *phonetic* system: the ways in which sequences of phonemes are converted into sound waves by the articulation of a speaker, and are decoded from the speech signal by a hearer.

The peripheral subsystems differ from the central ones in that they impinge both on the nonspeech world and on the central subsystems. The semantic system impinges, in one direction, on the directly observable physical and social world in which people live; and, in the other direction, on the grammatical system of the language. The phonetic system touches, in one direction, on the physically analyzable sound waves of the speech signal, but it also touches, in the other direction, on the phonemic system of the language. We have dealt with phonetic systems (§§7–9, 13); what few orienting remarks must be made about semantic systems will be given shortly (§16.2).

Linguistics has always concentrated on the three central subsystems, without much concern with the peripheral systems. Some scholars, indeed, prefer to define "language" so as to include only the central subsystems, regarding problems of meaning and of articulatory and acoustic phonetics as belonging to sister sciences rather than to linguistics. The choice of broader or narrower definition of the term is a matter of personal taste, and not important. Likewise, anyone is free to focus on the central subsystems or to invade the peripheral ones as he pleases. The peripheral systems are just as important as the central ones; the fact is, however, that they are much harder to study and that, so far, less has been learned about them.

This may be surprising, in the face of the obvious additional fact, already asserted, that an analyst can get at the central subsystems only by working through sound and meaning. But we must distinguish between the heuristic use of phonetics and of semantics involved in getting at the central subsystems, on the one hand, and, on the other, a detailed examination of the peripheral subsystems for their own sake. We are forced to use phonetic criteria in trying to analyze a phonemic system, for we have to discover, somehow, whether two utterances or parts of utterances "sound the same" or "sound different" to a speaker of the language. Likewise, we are forced to use semantic criteria in trying to get at the grammatical system, for we have to discover, somehow, whether two utterances or parts of utterances, differing in specified ways as to phonemic shapes, "mean the same thing" or "have different meanings" for the native speaker. It is just in the application of these criteria that we can most easily go astray, vitiating our would-be description of the central subsystems. No description of a language is free of errors stemming from this source. No description can claim more than a kind of by-and-large accuracy.

If, however, we wish to analyze in a systematic way the phonetic or semantic subsystem of a language, it is necessary first to have a careful description of the most closely related central subsystem. It is quite futile to try to analyze a phonetic system, either in terms of articulation or acoustically, without knowing about the phonemic system to which it relates. It is equally futile to try to analyze a semantic system without understanding the grammatical system to which it relates. Acousticians have sometimes attempted the former, and have ended up by making use of an inaccurate, unsystematized conception of the related phonemic system, in place of an accurate and detailed one. Anthropologists and philosophers have often attempted the latter, and have found themselves forced to invent pseudo-linguistic "mental" entities such as "ideas" or "concepts," in place of the obvious and empirically discoverable morphemes and larger grammatical forms of a language. Accurate work on phonetic and semantic subsystems is currently in its infancy, because only very recently have we recognized, even in a general way, the necessary prerequisites and appropriate angles of attack. When more has been achieved, there will be more results to report in a survey volume of the present kind.

16.2. Meaning, Antecedents, and Consequences. It is essential to distinguish between the *meanings* of morphemes and utterances, on the one hand, and, on the other, the *antecedents and consequences* of specific acts of speech. The meanings of morphemes and of combinations of morphemes are, as has been said, associative ties between those morphemes and morpheme-combinations and things and situations, or types of things and situations, in the world around us. These semantic ties are more or less the same for all the speakers of a language. The antecedents and consequences of a specific act of speech can be quite different for a speaker and for his hearers.

The same is true for some systems of communication simpler than language. The Morse Code, for example, is a convention shared by all telegraph operators, by virtue of which certain arrangements of shorter and longer voltage pulses (dots and dashes) are assigned to represent different letters and punctuation marks of written English. The meaning of a single dot is the letter "E"; this meaning is the same for all telegraph operators, whether at a given moment one of them is functioning as sender or as receiver. If on a particular occasion one operator is transmitting and another is receiving, then the antecedents and consequences of the actual transmission are different for the two: one of them is handed a slip of paper and goes through the motions which convert what is written on it into voltage pulses, while the other receives the voltage pulses via a buzzer or clicker and goes through the motions which reconvert them into a series of letters on a slip of paper. The antecedents and consequences, though different for the two operators, are tied together in a certain way, in that the series of letters written down by the receiving operator is a match of that handed to the transmitting operator. This correlation is rendered possible because of the shared *semantic* conventions of the system.

Now suppose two men are seated side by side at a lunch counter. *A* has a cup of coffee for which he wants some sugar, and the sugar bowl is out of his reach. *A* says *Please pass the sugar*. *B* passes it. This reveals, in bare outline form at least, the behavioral antecedents and consequences in which the act of speech is embedded. The antecedents and consequences are different for *A* and for *B: A* wants the sugar and gets it; *B* merely passes it. The same utterance could occur under other conditions: for example, *B* might have the coffee and ask *A* for the sugar. In the original situation, some of the behavioral consequences are not due to the linguistic structure of the utterance, but to concomitant circumstances. *B* passes the sugar to *A* rather than to *C* because it is *A*, not *C*, who has asked for it. But the semantic conventions of the language play a part, for, if *A* and *B* did not share them, *A* would have to resort to other means of getting the sugar, or go without. Thus, there is a conventional tie between the morpheme *sugar* and a certain substance: *B* does not pass the salt. There is a tie between *pass* and a familiar action: *B* does not throw the sugar bowl to the floor. And there is a shared understanding that *please,* with certain word order and intonation, is a polite request: *B* is not insulted or annoyed. Thus the *meaning* of the whole utterance *Please pass the sugar* is fundamentally the same for *A* and for *B*, despite the differences in their activities in the episode we have described.

For the child who is learning a language, or the linguist who is analyzing one, there are two and only two methods by which the semantic subsystem can be observed and utilized or described. For the child, at first, there is actually only one: the meanings which utterances and morphemes come to have for him are the result of recurrent regularities of correspondence between acts of speech of various grammatical structures and the behavioral antecedents and consequences in which the child himself participates. Later, and for the analyst, there is another method: he can be *told*—in a language or part of a language he already knows—what a newly observed form means. This second way is often very unsatisfactory. One can ask a Russian who knows some English what the Russian word /drúk/ means, and the answer will be 'friend.' This is roughly true, but the precise social circumstances under which a Russian calls another person /drúk/ are by no means the same as those under which we call someone a friend. The meaning of /drúk/, or of *friend*, for a speaker of the language involved, is the result of all his past experiences with that word. Within a single speech community, the differences between the accidents of personal history of different individuals tend to cancel out, so that if the meanings of morphemes never become absolutely identical for different speakers, they are at least sufficiently similar that communication via speech is possible. From one community to another, however, this levelling-out does not occur. Bilingual dictionaries and easy word-by-word translations are inevitably misleading; the shortcut of asking what a form means must ultimately be supplemented by active participation in the life of the community that speaks the language. This, of course, is one of the major reasons why semantic analysis is so difficult.

16.3. Language and Speaking. The summary of language design in §16.1 states that a language is a set of *habits*. An act of speech, or utterance, is not a habit, but a *historical event*, though it partly conforms to, reflects, and is controlled by the habits. Acts of speech, like other historical events, are directly observable. Habits are not directly observable; they must be inferred from observed events, whether the inferring agent is a child learning a language or an analyst seeking to describe one.

An utterance has a phonemic *structure* and a grammatical *structure*. Its phonemic structure reflects some of the phonemic *pattern* or *system* of the language. Its grammatical structure reflects some of the grammatical pattern or system of the language. The relationship of its phonemic structure to its grammatical structure reflects some of the morphophonemic patterns of the language, but note that an act of speech does not have a "morphophonemic structure." Morphophonemics resides entirely in habits, and is manifested not by another variety of structure in historical events, but by interrelationships of the two varieties of structure already itemized. Likewise, an utterance has neither a "semantic structure" nor a "phonetic structure." Semantics and phonetics reside in habits: they are made manifest not by two further varieties of structure in historical events, but, in the one case, by the relationship of the grammatical structure of an utterance to the context in which the utterance occurs; in the other case, by the relationship of the phonemic structure of an utterance to the articulatory motions and sound waves involved in the speaking.

The physiological process of speaking requires the expenditure of energy: it constitutes work in the physicist's sense. The succession of units produced by a speaker is governed constantly by the changing context, by the units already produced, and by his habits. These factors often supply conflicting directives, not only as to what unit to produce next, but also as to whether to keep on speaking or to stop. Consequently, speech is broken up by pauses, by hesitations, by interruptions, by repetitions, by sudden changes of direction. As hearers, we unconsciously edit out many of these overt manifestations of the hard work of utterance-production. In a literate community, the speaker who intends to write down what he has to say edits out the signs of hard work himself, putting into the last draft only the clean result. Our experience as hearers, writers, and readers all serves to render us unaware of the extent to which we ourselves, as speakers, hem and haw. The first exposure of anyone to a recording of his own conversational voice is usually a great shock.

Here is an example of hemming and hawing, transcribed from a tape recording of a real conversation. "*Uh*" means a hesitation with the silence filled by voicing; ". ." means a hesitation with silence:

It's uh . . it's uh not . . I mean he . . (throat cleared) *actually
well he he we we had just sort of . . in many ways sort of given up . . trying
to do very much . . until . . bedtime. Unless it's something that he can be included in . . whereupon he will . . usually isn't interested for long enough to
really . . carry through with it.*

Apart from the general impression that the speaker has a good deal of
trouble in speaking, the hearer would get much the same meaning from
this passage as he would from its edited version:

*We had (in many ways) just sort of given up trying to do much until
bedtime. Unless it's something that he can be included in, whereupon he usually
isn't interested for long enough to really carry through with it.*

This edited version is implicit within the original. It was not worked out
impressionistically, but through a careful inspection of the speaker's
habits of hemming and hawing, of inserted catch-phrases, of variations
in tempo, and the like. We indicate the end of a sentence after *bedtime*,
thus, because the speaker indicates one by using the intonation /$^{31}\downarrow$/.
The chief uncertainty is whether the phrase *in many ways* belongs in the
edited version. The speaker commonly uses this phrase to "fill silence"
while trying to think of what to say next, but it is not certain that she is
so using it on this particular occasion.

It is a matter of common knowledge that speakers in any speech community vary in fluency of control, and that the same speaker varies in
fluency from one occasion to another. Sometimes this scale of variation
is mistaken for the difference between "correct" and "incorrect"
speech, but this confusion should be avoided. Thus a speaker of "very
bad" English is sometimes a moving orator in his own brand of the
language, while many privileged speakers of "excellent" English hem
and haw a great deal. Differences in fluency thus seem not to be differences of language habits in the proper sense, but rather of habits of
some other order which are manifested, along with language habits, in
speech. *Stuttering* is a manifestation of this other order. Whatever its
causes, which are not well understood, it appears as a repetition of the
initial consonants of semantically important stressed syllables (*Please
pass the p-p-p-pepper*, in which the stutterer produces two /p/'s with no
trouble, then stumbles on that at the beginning of the key word).

Recent research suggests that much can be learned about a person
through a close examination of his unedited speech. The particular

ways in which he hems and haws, varies the register of his voice, changes his tone quality, and so on, are revealing both of his basic personality and of his momentary emotional orientation. But since (if our assumption is correct) phenomena of these sorts are not manifestations of the speaker's *linguistic* habits, it is proper to ignore them in the study of language, basing that study exclusively on edited speech.

NOTES

New terms: none, except that a number of terms already introduced are put into carefully specified relationship to each other—the *central* subsystems of a language (*grammatical, phonological, morphophonemic*), and the *peripheral* subsystems (*semantic, phonetic*).

Problems. The following are essentially problems in *point of view*, rather than of fact or of analytical procedure. Consequently they have no single "correct" answer.

(1) Distinguish, in terms of the design of languages, between the following two situations:

(a) An American singer does not want to learn French, but wishes to sing French songs. She does this in a way which satisfies speakers of French who hear her sing, without being able to speak or understand French at all.

(b) A graduate student has to learn to read French, but is not concerned with conversational ability. He accomplishes his purpose.

(2) What is the source of the misunderstanding of the nature of language when

(a) An Englishman says, "The French are such funny people. They call 'bread' *pan*." When asked why this is funny, he replies, "Oh, but it *is bread*, you know!"

(b) A small boy says, "*Pigs* are called that because they are such dirty animals."

GRAMMATICAL
SYSTEMS

17·

IMMEDIATE CONSTITUENTS

17.1. In §§14–16 we outlined the essential nature of grammar and its relationship to other aspects of language. In this and the following fourteen sections we shall investigate grammatical systems in greater detail.

Specialists have been working for a long time on the problem of analyzing, describing, and comparing grammatical systems, and the degree of accuracy achieved is much greater than the layman would suspect. At the same time, there remain many points on which precision is still impossible. Some linguists like to believe that grammatical analysis has become a completely objective operation, but this is not true. Phonemic analysis has been brought much nearer such a state: complete precision is not always possible, but we can at least pinpoint the areas of indeterminacy and usually see why they remain indeterminate. But grammatical analysis is still, to a surprising extent, an art: the best and clearest descriptions of languages are achieved not by investigators who follow some rigid set of rules, but by those who through some accident of life-history have developed a flair for it.

Consequently, the reader will find in these sections many an example which the writer has handled in one way, but which might also be handled in some other way. The writer has not sought to be ambiguous or arbitrary, but he refuses to speak definitely in cases where he cannot. Indeed, the reader should be alert for possible instances where conciseness of statement has unintentionally concealed uncertainty.

In grammatical study we are concerned with morphemes and their arrangements, but not, save in an ancillary way, with the phonemic shapes which represent morphemes. Consequently, in the present sections we shall usually cite examples in their traditional orthography, provided the language in question has one and that it involves only the

Latin alphabet. Classical Greek and Chinese examples are given in well-established *transliterations* or *Romanizations*. Genuine phonemic notation will be used only when advisable for some special reason, or for languages like Menomini which have no traditional orthography.

17.2. Hierarchical Structure. The man on the street is inclined to identify language with words, and to think that to study words is to study language. This view incorporates two errors. We obviate one when we realize that morphemes, rather than words, are the elementary building-blocks of language in its grammatical aspect, though this shift of emphasis in no sense implies that words are unimportant. The other error is more subtle: the notion, often unstated, that we need only examine words (or morphemes) as isolated units, longer utterances being simply mechanical combinations of the smaller units.

If this were the case, then all we would have to learn in studying a foreign language would be the individual morphemes and their meanings. The meaning of any whole utterance would be immediately obvious on the basis of the meanings of the ultimate constituents. Anyone who has actually studied a foreign language knows that this is not true. For a striking example of the falsity of the assumption, we turn to Chinese, which is better than French or German or Spanish for this purpose because it differs more drastically from English. Here is a commonplace Chinese sentence: *jèige yóutŭng dàgài dzài wŭfēn jūng yĭnèi néng lyóujìngle.* Apart from intonation, this sentence includes seventeen successive segmental morphemes, as follows:

(1) *j-* 'this, proximal, near the speaker';
(2) *-èi* 'thing or state';
(3) *-ge* 'discrete concrete object, animate or inanimate';
(4) *yóu* 'oil, grease';
(5) *tŭng* 'cylindrical container';
(6) *dà* 'large, great, greatly';
(7) *gài* 'generality, majority';
(8) *dzài* '(be) at, in, on';
(9) *wŭ* 'five';
(10) *fēn* 'division, section';
(11) *jūng* 'clock, hour';
(12) *yĭ* marker of modification: indicates that something which precedes modifies something that follows;

(13) *nèi* 'interior, inside';

(14) *néng* 'can, physical ability';

(15) *lyóu* 'flow';

(16) *jìng* 'clean (not necessarily dry), empty';

(17) *le* marker of completed action or completed change of state.

As is evident, some of these Chinese morphemes have meanings which are not easy to describe precisely in English. One meets similar trouble in trying to describe the meanings of some English morphemes in Chinese—or, in general, the meanings of morphemes in any one language via any other language (§16.2).

A careful scrutiny of the meanings of the seventeen constituent morphemes of the sentence can at best yield some vague notion of what the

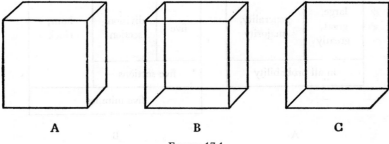

A   B   C

FIGURE 17.1

whole sentence is about. The meaning of the whole sentence happens to be 'This oil drum can be emptied in about five minutes.'

No one—not even a native speaker of Chinese—could know this merely on the basis of the meanings of the ultimate constituent morphemes. Other types of information are also required—types of information which a speaker of Chinese carries around in his head, ready to add to the information carried by what he hears. By virtue of this advance orientation, the native speaker hears the sentence not as a linear string of morphemes, but, as it were, *in depth*, automatically grouping things together in the right way.

An analogy is in order. When we look at the middle line-drawing **B** of Figure 17.1, we see it either as more like A, to the left, or C, to the right. With a bit of effort, we can make B "jell" in either way. Physically, of course, B is an assemblage of line-segments on a flat surface. The depth that we perceive lies in us, not in the figure. Yet our experience in visual perception is such that it is hard to see B as a complicated plane figure rather than in three dimensions.

The "depth" which the native speaker of Chinese "reads in" as he hears our Chinese sentence is similar, though with one important difference. All human beings, in all societies, have much the same experiences in visual perception and so would tend to react in the same way to B in Figure 17.1, but the experiences by virtue of which we read "depth" into utterances are specific to the particular language.

Thus the Chinese hearer automatically groups morphemes (6) and (7) together, as depicted in Figure 17.2A. He knows that this particular

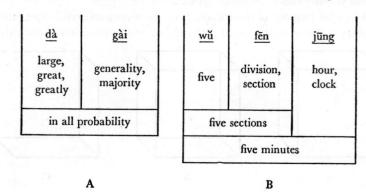

A   B

FIGURE 17.2

combination is common, and that it carries the rather special, partly unpredictable, meaning 'probably.' Likewise, he automatically groups (9), (10), and (11) together, as in Figure 17.2B, but in a more complicated way. If we were to ask him what *dàgài* (morphemes 6 and 7) means, he could tell us, and if we were to ask what *wǔfēn jūng* (9, 10, 11) means, he could tell us. But if we were to ask what *tǔng dà* (5, 6) means, he would be puzzled, for *tǔng dà* does not mean anything. He would probably be unaware that he had heard this particular morpheme sequence in the sentence, and the speaker of the sentence would scarcely realize that he had said it.

In Figure 17.3 we portray the organization of the whole Chinese sentence as the native speaker perceives it.

Diagrams of the sort shown in Figures 17.2 and 17.3 are designed to show the *hierarchical structure* or *immediate constituent structure* of composite

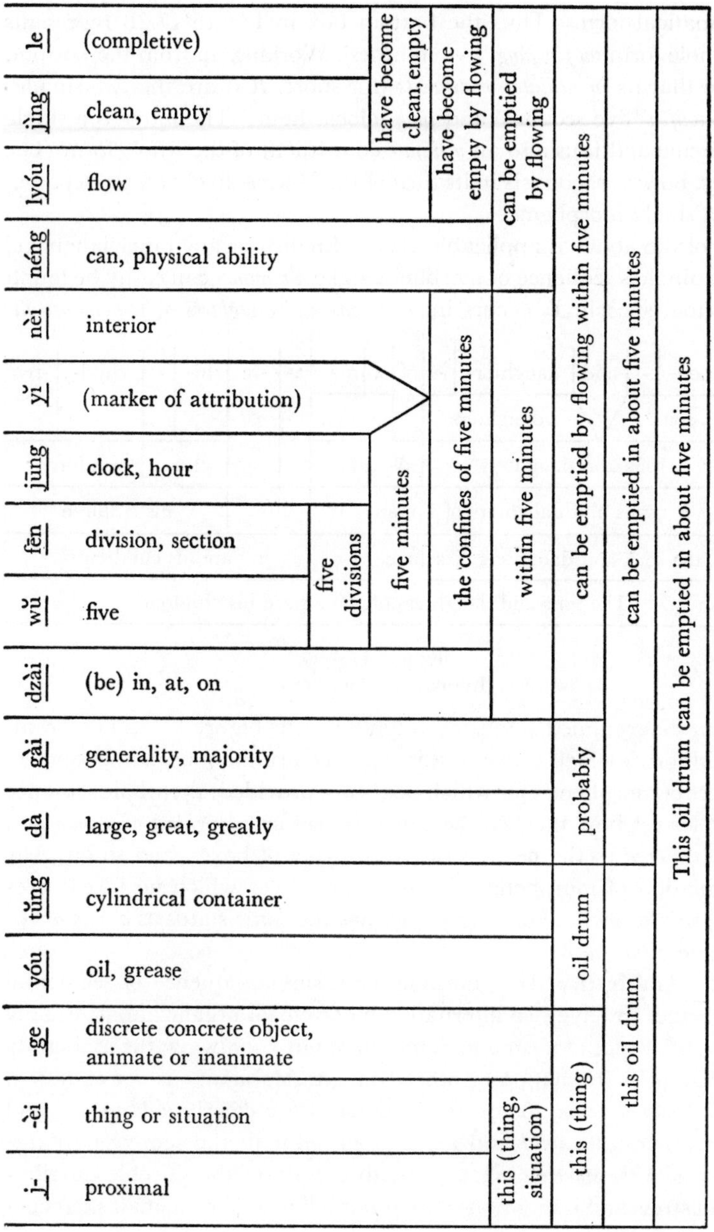

le	(completive)
jìng	clean, empty
lyóu	flow
néng	can, physical ability
nèi	interior
yǐ	(marker of attribution)
jūng	clock, hour
fēn	division, section
wǔ	five
dzài	(be) in, at, on
gài	generality, majority
dà	large, great, greatly
tǔng	cylindrical container
yóu	oil, grease
-ge	discrete concrete object, animate or inanimate
-èi	thing or situation
jì-	proximal

Bracketing structure (from inner to outer):

- wǔ, fēn → **five divisions**
- (five divisions) + jūng → **five minutes**
- (five minutes) + yǐ, nèi → **the confines of five minutes**
- dzài + (the confines of five minutes) → **within five minutes**
- lyóu, jìng, le → **have become clean, empty** / **have become empty by flowing**
- néng + (have become empty by flowing) → **can be emptied by flowing**
- (within five minutes) + (can be emptied by flowing) → **can be emptied by flowing within five minutes**
- dà, gài → **probably**
- yóu, tǔng → **oil drum**
- jì-, -èi → **this (thing, situation)**
- (this (thing, situation)) + -ge → **this (thing)**
- (this (thing)) + (oil drum) → **this oil drum**
- (probably) + (can be emptied by flowing within five minutes) → **can be emptied in about five minutes**
- (this oil drum) + (can be emptied in about five minutes) → **This oil drum can be emptied in about five minutes**

FIGURE 17.3

151

grammatical forms. Thus the bottom box in Figure 17.2B represents the whole form *wйfēn jūng* 'five minutes'. Working up from the bottom, we see that its *immediate constituents* (for short, *ICs*) are the two smaller forms *wйfēn* 'five sections' and *jūng* 'clock, hour.' The latter is a single morpheme and thus also an *ultimate* constituent of the whole form. The former, however, consists in its turn of the ICs *wŭ* 'five' and *fēn* 'section,' each a single morpheme.

All of the above is applicable also to English or any other language. A meaningless sequence of morphemes like *a man are* can easily be found in normal speech. It occurs in *The sons and daughters of a man are his*

the	son-	-s	and	daughter-	-s	of	a	man	a-	-re	hi-	-s	child-	-ren
	sons			daughters			a man				his		children	
	sons and daughters					of a man					his		children	
	sons and daughters of a man								are		his children			
	the sons and daughters of a man								are his children					
	The sons and daughters of a man are his children													

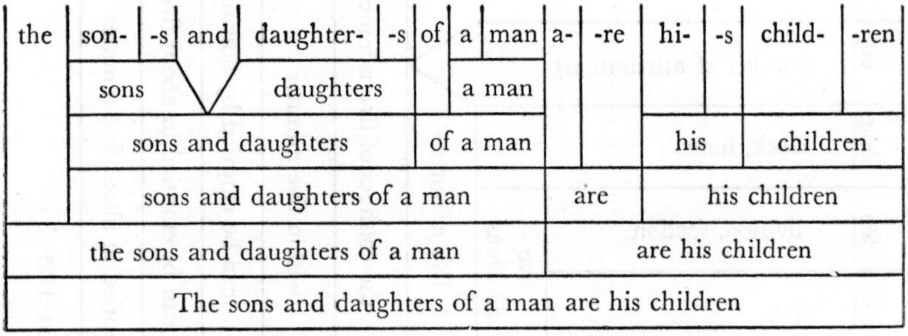

FIGURE 17.4
(Intonation is omitted)

children, diagrammed (omitting intonation) in Figure 17.4. The grammatical forms which occur in this sentence are the morphemes and sequences of morphemes for which boxes are provided: the whole sentence in the lowest box, the two segments *the sons and daughters of a man* and *are his children* in the next to the lowest row of boxes, and so on. Any combination of morphemes, in the sentence for which no box is provided, say *the sons and* or *daughters of*, has the same status as *a man are* or as Chinese *tŭng dà*.

17.3. Ambiguity. It is possible for a single sequence of segmental morphemes to have two alternative hierarchical organizations, usually with a difference of meaning. Sometimes, but not always, the ambiguity is removed by intonation or other context. Ambiguity is not common. In *wild animal house*, for example, the ICs are clearly *wild animal* and *house*, rather than *wild* and *animal house*. But in the sentence *He was dancing with the stout major's wife* (with certain of the possible distributions of stress and intonation) we cannot tell whether the man's dancing partner is stout or not. The ambiguity of its IC-structure is shown in Figure 17.5, A and B. Likewise, the expression *old men and women* can have either of two meanings, and either of two corresponding IC structures, as shown by Figure 17.6, A and B.

Ambiguity is often eliminated by context: *The stout major's wife is very thin, The stout major's wife has a very thin husband, The old men and women stayed at home while the young men went to war, The old men and women stayed at home while the young folks went dancing.*

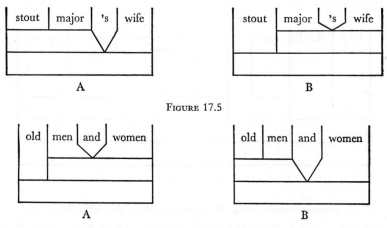

FIGURE 17.5

FIGURE 17.6

Such ambiguities remind us again of the analogy with visual perception: Figure 17.1B is ambiguous in that it looks now more like A and now more like C.

17.4. Markers. We must account for the slanting lines appearing in some of the diagrams. In Figure 17.4, for example, the diagram indicates that the ICs of *sons and daughters* are the two words *sons* and *daughters*. How about the *and*? How can a form participate in a larger form without being a constituent of it?

Of course, a different interpretation would be possible, but the one we have chosen indicates that *and*, rather than being one of the ICs of *sons and daughters*, is what we may call a *structural marker* or *signal*. Some morphemes, that is, serve not directly as carriers of meaning, but only as markers of the structural relationships between other forms. *And* marks the fact that something before it (here *sons*) and something after it (here *daughters*) are the ICs of a larger grammatical form, and *and* also marks that larger form as being of a certain type. We would choose a similar interpretation for the *or* of *sons or daughters*.

17.5. Multiple ICs. In all our diagrams so far, composite forms have been shown as consisting of just two ICs. Bipartite composite forms are extremely common, but there is no universal restriction to two ICs. English has a few cases of composite forms with three ICs; for example, *foot-pound-second* or *centimeter-gram-second*. Figure 17.7 shows the way of diagramming them.

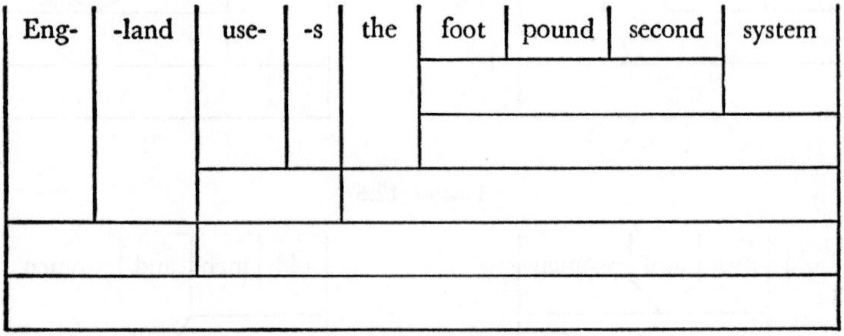

FIGURE 17.7

17.6. Discontinuous ICs. Our examples so far have had another property which is common but not universal: forms which belong together as ICs of a larger form have been next to each other in linear sequence. But *discontinuous* constituents are not at all uncommon. For example, in the English sentence *Is John going with you?*, setting intonation aside, one IC is *John* and the other is the discontinuous sequence *Is . . . going with you.*

Figures 17.8A and B show two graphic devices for handling this. In Figure 17.8A, the form *John* is entered at the beginning to render diagramming easy, but is parenthesized to indicate that it is not actually spoken there; the empty parentheses after *is* indicate the position it actually occupies in the sequence. In Figure 17.8B we avoid the duplication, but place a heavy line below the entry *John*, and mark with a dotted arrow the connection between *John* and the larger form of which it is one IC.

17.7. Simultaneous ICs. An intonation morpheme is probably always to be interpreted as one IC of the macrosegment which includes

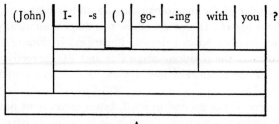

A

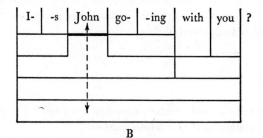

B

FIGURE 17.8

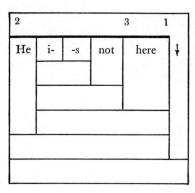

FIGURE 17.9

it, the remainder of the macrosegment, no matter how complex, constituting the other IC. In order to show this diagrammatically we have to introduce another special device, illustrated in Figure 17.9. It is necessary to mark the positions of the PLs and TC correctly, since any alternation in their position might yield a different sentence (e.g., [2]*He is* [3]*not here*[1]↓).

Diagramming is not an end in itself, but a convenient means of revealing hierarchical structure. For this, it is useful to have diagrammatic conventions. But where the structure is unusual, diagramming may become excessively complex. In such instances, we shall avoid diagrams and resort to verbal description.

NOTES

New terms: *hierarchical structure, immediate constituents* (= *ICs*), *discontinuous ICs, simultaneous ICs, structural markers*.

For ICs we follow Bloomfield 1933, p. 161, as elaborated by Wells 1947, and with modifications partly expounded in Hockett 1954.

18·

FORM CLASSES and
CONSTRUCTIONS

18.1. Recurrent Patterns. The property of language which renders it such a powerful means of communication is that one can say something that has never been said before, and yet be perfectly understood, often without either speaker or audience being aware of the novelty. A novel utterance is built from familiar raw-materials, by familiar patterns of putting raw-materials together. Neither the raw-materials nor the patterns need be new in order for the utterance to be different from any that has occurred previously.

We know from earlier discussion that the raw-materials are morphemes, and that the patterns are hierarchical rather than mere linear juxtaposition. Here we shall pursue the matter of patterns further.

Consider the two English sentences ^{2}*She bought a new* ^{3}*hat*^{1}↓ and ^{3}*He* ^{2}*likes the old* ^{2}*man*^{2}↑ diagrammed in Figure 18.1. The two are completely distinct in their constituent grammatical forms: no morpheme and no composite form of either occurs in the other. Yet they consist of the same number of constituents, in exactly the same hierarchical arrangement. Furthermore, there is a similarity in meaning beyond that of two sentences selected at random: each sentence asserts something about someone, and each assertion involves some second entity.

We summarize the similarities by saying that the two sentences are of the same pattern, and that the common pattern is responsible for the similarity of meaning. We can portray the common pattern in part without citing any forms, as shown in Figure 18.2. This "empty box" diagram is obtained from either diagram in Figure 18.1 simply by deleting all the entries.

157

On the other hand, two sentences may involve exactly the same constituents at all hierarchical levels, and yet differ in meaning because of different patterns. Figure 18.3 gives one example. The difference lies not in constituents, but in their arrangement: *John* respectively before

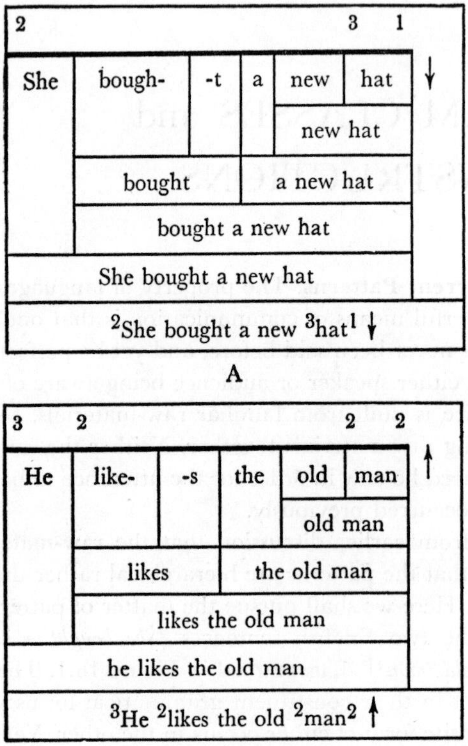

FIGURE 18.1

or within *is here.* For another example, compare the diagram of ²*She bought a new* ³*hat*¹↓ in Figure 18.1 with that of ²*She bought a* ³*new hat*¹↓ in Figure 18.4. The center of the intonation is differently placed, though the intonation, and all other constituents, are identical. (These examples are not like *old men and women,* discussed in §17.3, for in that example only the ultimate constituents were the same, the hierarchical structure being ambiguous.)

Our technique of diagramming cannot always be counted on to reveal the difference between obviously distinct patterns. Thus compare *She likes fresh milk* and *She likes milk fresh*, partially diagrammed in Figure 18.5. Insofar as the diagrams reveal the pattern, it can be shown as in Figure 18.6, but the two composite forms *fresh milk* and *milk fresh* are

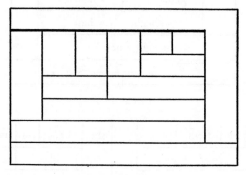

FIGURE 18.2

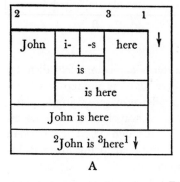

A

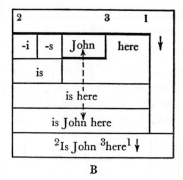

B

FIGURE 18.3

actually quite different. The former can occur in many contexts (*Fresh milk is good for you, Make it with fresh milk*); the latter is quite limited.

Suppose, however, that we had some way to distinguish between patterns that yielded the same empty-box diagram, and that we were to diagram hundreds of English sentences, delete the entries, and list all the different resulting empty-box diagrams. This would obviously give us a very large number of different whole-sentence patterns. But we

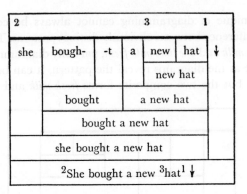

FIGURE 18.4

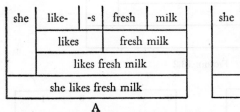

FIGURE 18.5

cannot simply assume that all these patterns are completely distinct. We must investigate a simpler possibility: that the numerous whole-sentence patterns are built up out of a smaller number of simpler ones.

In Figure 18.7 are diagrams of four progressively larger sentences,

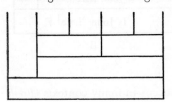

FIGURE 18.6

labelled A through D. The boxes in each are numbered in the lower right-hand corner.

Sentence A consists of only two ultimate constituents (morphemes), which are therefore also the ICs of the whole sentence: 3 and 2 are the ICs of 1.

Sentence B consists of more than two *ultimate* constituents, but, once again, of only two *immediate* constituents: 3 and 2 as in A, are the ICs of 1.

Similar remarks apply to sentences C and D.

Furthermore, the relationship between the two ICs of each whole sentence is the same. Thus, if we make just one IC-cut in each sentence, ignoring any smaller constituents for the moment, then all four sentences conform to pattern X of Figure 18.8. Box 3 in pattern X can be

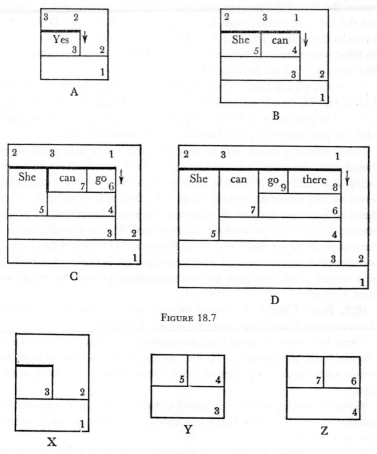

FIGURE 18.7

FIGURE 18.8

filled with any of the four intonationless morpheme-sequences *yes*, *she can*, *she can go*, or *she can go there*; Box 2 can be filled with the intonation morpheme /$(^2)$ $^{31}\downarrow$/.

Setting sentence A aside, let us examine boxes 3, 4, and 5 in sentences B, C, and D. In B, the form of box 3 has two ultimate constituents, which are therefore also its ICs: those in boxes 5 and 4. Now if, in sentences C and D, we cut the form of box 3 only into its *immediate* constituents, ignoring any finer-grained structure, we find the same thing again: the ICs of the form in box 3 of any of the sentences B, C, and D are the forms in boxes 5 and 4. This portion of B, C, and D thus conforms to the pattern labelled Y in Figure 18.8. Box 5 of pattern Y can be filled with the morpheme *she*, and box 4 with any of the morpheme-sequences *can, can go,* or *can go there.*

Similarly, setting both A and B aside, we see that the boxes labelled 4 in C and D, providing we make only one IC-cut, are identical and conform to pattern Z in Figure 18.8. Box 7 of pattern Z can be filled with the morpheme *can*, and box 6 with either *go* or *go there.*

Our treatment shows that some composite forms and some single morphemes are alike in that they can participate similarly in larger forms. For example, the single morpheme *yes* and the three composite forms *she can, she can go,* and *she can go there,* despite internal differences, share at least one *privilege of occurrence:* each can be conjoined to the intonation $/(^2)\ ^{31}\downarrow/$ to produce an utterance. The morpheme *can* and the composite forms *can go* and *can go there* share at least one privilege of occurrence: each can be used with preceding *she* to build a larger form of a certain kind. Similarly for the morpheme *go* and the composite form *go there.*

18.2. Form-Classes. A class of forms which have similar privileges of occurrence in building larger forms is a *form-class.*

Thus, by virtue of their interchangeability in box 3 of pattern X (Figure 18.8), the forms *yes, she can, she can go,* and *she can go there,* together with untold thousands of other forms, belong to a single form-class.

Similarly, ability to occur in box 2 of pattern X puts the intonation morpheme $/(^2)\ ^{31}\downarrow/$ in a form-class together with many other intonation morphemes.

Box 5 of pattern Y defines a form-class which includes *she, he, it, John, Mary, the man on the corner, my friend Bill,* and so on endlessly, but which by no means includes all forms, since we can name many which are excluded: *her, him, them, me, yes, no, ripe, find her, go with us tomorrow.*

Box 4 of pattern Y defines a form-class which includes *can, will, can go, can go there, should like potatoes, must run faster than that,* but which excludes *quickly, yes, her, him, ripe, she, he, John, Mary,* and so on.

Every other box in our diagrams similarly defines a form-class. There are not as many form-classes in a language as there are boxes in all the IC-diagrams one could draw, since different boxes often define the same form-class.

One point should be noted about the way we have chosen examples for the classes defined by boxes 4 and 5 of pattern Y. To the first (*she, he, it,* etc.) one might want to add *I, we, they, the men across the street,* all of which can occur before *can, can go, can go there.* To the second (*can, will, can go,* etc.) one might want to add *likes potatoes, finds it dull there, is trying too hard,* and others which can occur after *she.* The exclusion of these forms was intentional. Form-classes are so constituted that, if *some* member of a given class can occur with *some* member of a second class, then *any* member of the first might occur with *any* member of the second. Had we extended the lists of examples as suggested above, then this would not hold, for no one, speaking standard English, says *I likes potatoes, we finds it dull there, they is trying too hard.*

18.3. Constructions. If we were to delete the box-numbers from diagrams Y and Z (Figure 18.8), the two empty-box diagrams would be identical. This would conceal an important difference. As defined, Y subsumes composite forms like *she | can,*[1] *she | can go, the man on the corner | should like potatoes,* while Z subsumes composite forms like *can | go, can | go there, should | like potatoes.*

The difference can be underscored by regarding the numbers in the boxes in diagrams X, Y, and Z as names for form-classes. Thus, in Y, "5" means "any member of the form-class which includes *she, he, it, John, Mary,* etc." But numbers are mnemonically poor labels, and descriptive terms of some sort would be better. Let us replace "5" by *third person singular subjects,* "4" by *modal predicates,* and "3" by *predications.* Diagram

third person singular subject	modal predicate
predication	

FIGURE 18.9

Y then takes the form shown in Figure 18.9, and can be read off as follows: "any third person singular subject, followed by any modal predicate, builds a predication."

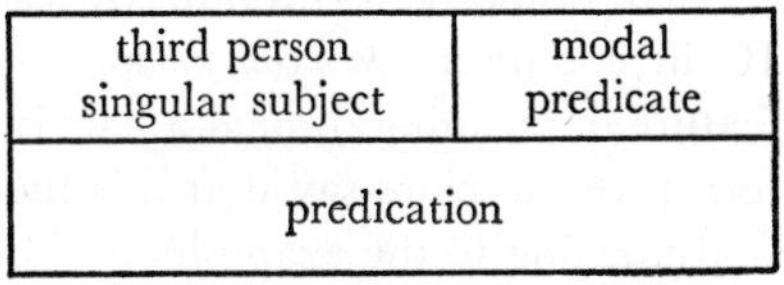

Either a statement of this sort, or a diagram of just two hierarchical

---

[1] Here and in the following sections, the vertical slash "|" is not a phonemic symbol, but an indication of the placement of the cut of the form into ICs.

levels in which the boxes contain labels for form-classes instead of for specific forms, describes a *construction*.

A construction is thus a pattern for building composite forms of a specific form-class out of ICs of specific form-classes. The description of a specific construction asserts that "any member of such-and-such a form-class, conjoined to any member of a certain other form-class, produces a form which belongs to a certain third form-class." We see immediately why care must be exercised in discriminating between form-classes. If we put *I* along with *she, he, it,* or *likes potatoes* along with *can, can go, should like potatoes,* our descriptions will have to be complicated by specification of exceptions.

The ICs of a composite form are commonly said to *stand in* a certain construction with each other, and the composite form built from the ICs by the construction is also called a *constitute*.

All constitutes built by a single construction are necessarily members of the same form-class. The form-class, however, may include also forms built by some other construction, and even single morphemes. For example, all predications are members of a larger form-class which we may momentarily call "sentence-skeletons": forms to which one can add an intonation to yield a sentence. But not all sentence-skeletons are predications: *yes, why, the more the merrier, milk for health* are the former but not the latter. Again: predications are built by conjoining a third person singular subject and a modal predicate (one construction), but are also built by several other constructions, as in *she | likes potatoes, I | can go, I | like potatoes.*

Two composite forms built by a single construction may have neither IC in common: *she | can go* and *he | should like potatoes.* The common feature of meaning of such a pair is not due to any shared grammatical form; we therefore say that it is the *meaning of the construction.*

Returning to the examples and problems discussed in §18.1, we now see that constructions are the sort of smaller pattern out of which the patterns of whole sentences are built. The two sentences diagrammed in Figure 18.1 resemble each other in that the same nesting of constructions is involved. Thus *new | hat* and *old | man* are built by a single construction. *A | new hat* and *the | old man* are perhaps both built by a second, though possibly we must say instead that they are built by two highly similar constructions. The features of meaning common to the two sentences are the meanings of the recurrent constructions.

Similarly, differences of meaning in pairs of sentences which contain the same ultimate constituents in the same hierarchical arrangement are due to differences in constructions. In *John is here*, the ICs *John* and *is here* stand in one construction; in *Is John here* the same ICs stand in a different construction (Figure 18.3). In *(she likes) fresh milk* the ICs *fresh* and *milk* stand in one construction (that of *new | hat, old | man);* in *(she likes) milk fresh* the same ICs stand in another construction (Figure 18.5).

NOTES

New terms: *privilege of occurrence, form-class, construction, meaning* of a construction, *constitute* (= composite form, but only when being discussed as the product of ICs joined by a specific construction); to *stand in* a construction.

The terms "third person singular subject," "modal predicate," and "predication" have technical status in the description of a particular language only when formally introduced in the treatment of that language. They are useful in English; there is no general guarantee that they are of value for any other language.

Some grammarians use "construct" in place of our "constitute." Some use "construction" ambiguously for our "constitute" and "construction."

19.

WORDS

19.1. The everyday use of the English word "word" is not very precise. In general, the layman looks to writing, and classes as a word whatever he finds written between successive spaces. So *matchbox* is one word, *match box* two, and *match-box* two or one depending on whether or not a hyphen is interpreted as a special sort of space. That these three spellings reflect a single combination of morphemes with a single pronunciation—/mǽč+bàks/—is ignored.

When we look at language directly rather than via writing, we must seek other criteria for the determination of words. There are several usable criteria, but they do not yield identical results. The criterion that is easiest to apply yields units most like the "words" of the layman, and it is for these that we shall reserve the term. The other criteria yield stocks of units which differ more radically from the layman's "words," and we shall not call them words, despite their wordlike properties. Instead, we shall introduce special terms for them.

19.2. Determining Words through Pause and Isolability. As the first step in determining the words in an utterance, we ask speakers to repeat the utterance slowly and carefully. Suppose someone has just said *John treats his older sisters very nicely* in the normal rapid way, as a single macrosegment (§4). If we ask for a slow repetition, he may break the sentence up into as many as seven successive macrosegments, each with its own intonation and with intervening pauses: *John, treats, his, older, sisters, very, nicely.* Or he may not pause quite so often: *his older,* or *very nicely,* might be kept as a single macrosegment. Thus we may have to elicit more than one slow careful delivery before we can be sure we have obtained the maximum break-up. Only under very artificial con-

166

ditions, however, would anyone pause at additional points, say between *old* and *-er*.

A word is thus any segment of a sentence bounded by successive points *at which pausing is possible*. The example contains seven words. It contains this number whether actually delivered as one macrosegment or as several, since words are defined in terms of *potential* pauses, not the actual pauses in any one delivery.

The pausing habits of a literate speaker of English are doubtless conditioned by his literacy, for he may pause more freely where writing habits leave a space than where they do not. But there are exceptions: many a speaker will break *matchbox* or *blackbird* into two macrosegments. Furthermore, our habits of leaving spaces in writing have not developed by mere chance. They reflect, with some distortion, speech habits, including habits of where one pauses in slow, careful speech. And the pause procedure for determining words also yields consistent results when applied to a language for which there is no commonly used writing system.

When we suspect that some factor is obscuring the results of the pause procedure, there is a supplementary procedure to which we can turn. We look for other contexts for a form, in which it will indeed occur as a whole macrosegment. Thus someone might consistently fail to break up the sentence *I'm going outside* into more than four macrosegments, *I, am, going, outside.* Yet we might hear the same person playing role *B* in the following conversation (a conversation the writer has actually heard):

> A: *Where're you going?*
> B: *Out.*
> A: *Out where?*
> B: *Side.*

From it we conclude that *outside* is two words, not one.

Words thus defined are not always identical with the layman's words. *Outside* and *don't* are single words for the layman because of the spelling, but two each for us. Yet our words have many of the properties of the layman's. They are, on the average, larger than a single morpheme: *boy, girl, man* one morpheme each, but *boyish, manly* two each, *muddily* three, and so on. At the same time, they are on the average smaller than utterances: one-word utterances like *Hi!* and *Yes?* are normal, but in the minority. We sometimes unthinkingly assume that a sentence is composed *solely* of words. This is false under either the lay definition of "word" or our own, since it leaves intonation out of account. Thus our initial example involves the intonation morpheme /³ ² ²²↑/ as well as its seven constituent words.

All morphemes can be classed according to their status relative to words. A morpheme which occurs only as part or all of some word is a *segmental* morpheme: *John, treat, -s.* A morpheme which is not part of a word is *suprasegmental:* all intonations, and some other morphemes, such as the secondary stress /ˋ/ on the second segmental constituent of /mǽč+bàks/, which is not part of the word *box.*

A form consisting of two or more words is a *phrase.*

19.3. Minimum Free Forms. Another lay expectation about words is that they are invariably grammatical units, or, in our terms, grammatical forms. This is not true under our definition. *Twenty* and *eighth* are words, so that *twenty-eighth* is two. But the ICs of *twenty-eighth* are not the words *twenty* and *eighth;* they are the form *twenty-eight,* itselt two words, and the form *-th,* less than a word.

There are two types of wordlike unit which fulfil lay expectations on the present count, at the expense of ease of determination and of some of the other properties one should like wordlike units to have. One of these is the *minimum free form.*

Some forms of one or more segmental morphemes, like English *act, John, hat, actor, actors, John's, John's hat, John's hat is on the table,* have the property that on occasion they may occur as whole utterances, requiring only the addition of a suitable intonation. Thus in answer to *Whose hat is that?* one might simply say /³ǰánz¹↓/. This property is *freedom;* forms that have it are *free.* Other segmental forms are not free, and are therefore called *bound:* the *-or* of *actor,* the *-dom* of *kingdom,* the *-s* of *sisters,* the *-ation* of *condemnation.*

Some free forms consist of ICs which are all also free. *John's hat* is an example, since both *John's* and *hat* are free. Many, however, do not consist wholly of free ICs; they are therefore *minimum* free forms. *Actor, John's, regain* qualify: in each, one IC (*act, John, gain*) is free, but the other (*-or, -'s, re-*) is bound. *Confer* also qualifies: if it is more than one morpheme (investigators disagree) then its ICs are *con-* and *-fer,* both bound. *Act* is a minimum free form because it has no ICs.

The wordlike properties of minimum free forms are clear. They are always grammatical forms, because we pay strict attention to IC structure in finding and defining them. They are on the average larger than morphemes and smaller than whole utterances. Their unwordlike property is that sometimes they are larger than single words. *Twenty-eighth* is two words, but only one minimum free form, since one of its ICs (*-th*) is bound. Even the four-word sequence *the Mayor of Boston's* (as in *the Mayor of Boston's hat*) is a single minimum free form, since the bound form *-'s* is one of its ICs.

19.4. Lexemes. The other variety of wordlike unit which fulfils the expectation that "words" should always be grammatical forms is the *lexeme*.

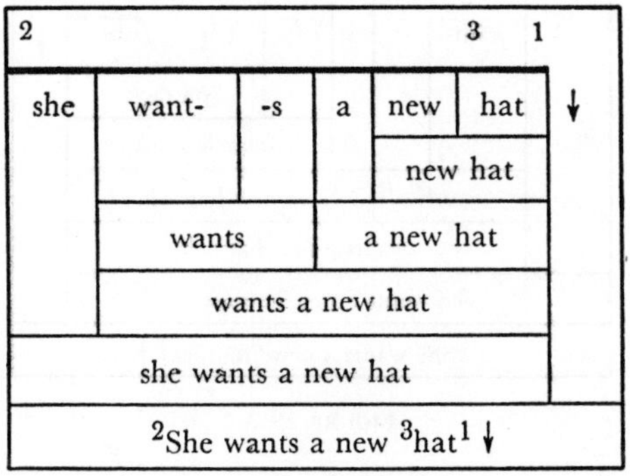

FIGURE 19.1

The sentence ²*She wants a new* ³*hat*¹↓ is diagrammed in Figure 19.1. The sentence includes only seven ultimate constituents (morphemes), but there are thirteen different grammatical forms in all, at various hierarchical levels. The diagram includes a box for each.

The morpheme-sequence *wants a new* occurs in this sentence, but only as an "accidental" concatenation (like a *man are* in *The sons and daughters of a man are his children*, §17.2). The morpheme-sequence *a new hat*, on the other hand, occurs in the sentence as a grammatical form. However, we can easily find some other sentence in which the same sequence, *a new hat*, occurs only accidentally: *She wants a new hatrack* will do (Figure 19.2).

Another morpheme-sequence in the sentence is *wants*. *Wants* is a grammatical form in this sentence just as is *a new hat*. But *wants* is different from *a new hat* in that we can find no English utterance in which *wants* occurs only as an accident. It is a grammatical form wherever it occurs. This property is manifested by every single morpheme of a language, but only by some of the occurrent sequences of morphemes.

This yields a threefold classification of all the morphemes and morpheme-combinations of a language: (1) those which occur only as accidents: *a man are, wants a new;* (2) those which occur sometimes as accidents, sometimes as grammatical forms: *a new hat;* (3) those that occur only as grammatical forms: *wants, hat.*

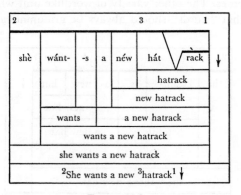

FIGURE 19.2

Let us momentarily call any morpheme or morpheme-sequence of this third variety an X. Although an X is by definition always a grammatical form, in some environments it is an IC of a larger X, whereas in other environments it is not. For example, *want* is an X; in *She wants a new hat, want* is an IC of *wants,* which is also an X; but in *I want a new hat* or *They don't want any help, want* is an IC of larger forms which are not X's.

Any X, in any context in which it is *not* an IC of a larger X, is a *lexeme. Want* is a lexeme in *I want a new hat,* but not in *She wants a new hat.* The constituent lexemes of the latter sentence are *she, wants, a, new, hat,* and the intonation morpheme $/^2\ ^{31}\downarrow/$.

Any grammatical form larger than a lexeme is a *nonce-form.* The term suggests, not inappropriately, that a speaker coins such larger grammatical forms when he needs them; if on another occasion the same larger grammatical form is again needed, he coins it afresh. The nonce-forms in our sample sentence (Figure 19.1) are *new hat, a new hat, wants a new hat,* the intonationless *she wants a new hat,* and the whole sentence. The wordlike properties of lexemes are clear. A lexeme is always a grammatical form, by definition. Lexemes are on the average larger than single morphemes but smaller than whole utterances. Many words are lexemes in many occurrences, and many lexemes are words. A minor deviation is that intonations count as lexemes: when speaking of words, or of minimum free forms, intonations have to be taken into account separately.

But lexemes are in many cases smaller than what we usually call words, even by the formal definition of §19.2. The lexemes in the two-word sequence *twenty-eighth* are *twenty, eight,* and *-th.* Those in *the Mayor of Boston's* are *the, Mayor, of, Boston,* and *-'s. Red-haired* is two words; but it is a single minimum free form, since the ICs are *red hair* (free) and *-ed* (bound); and it is three lexemes, *red, hair,* and *-ed.*

19.5. Idioms. A final lay assumption about "words," which does not actually hold either for the layman's words or for ours, is that they should always have some sort of meaning of their own, predictable in terms of their structure if they are larger than morphemes, and reasonably constant from one occurrence to another.

Minimum free forms and lexemes also do not meet this requirement. The units which do are the least wordlike of any of the types we shall discuss. The best approach to these units, which we shall call *idioms,* is via examples in some other language.

The Chinese form *yóutǔng* has as ICs the two morphemes *yóu* 'oil, grease' and *tǔng* 'large cylindrical container'; the first IC modifies the second, as *black* modifies *cat* in *black cat* or *grease* modifies *rack* in *grease rack.* Given this information, but knowing nothing else about Chinese or the culture of China, we can venture a reasonable guess as to the meaning of *yóutǔng:* 'oil container,' 'oil drum,' or the like. This guess is correct.

The ICs of Chinese *mǎshàng* are *mǎ* 'horse' and *shàng* 'space on or above, top, ascend.' As in the preceding example, the first constituent modifies the second. Reasonable guesses at the meaning of *mǎshàng* would be 'horse's back,' 'horseback,' or possibly 'on horseback.' These are wrong. The meaning is 'quickly, right away.'

This meaning is not surprising when we remember that until recently the most rapid mode of travel was by horse. But it is one thing to consider a meaning reasonable after we know it, and quite different to deduce the meaning of a form from its structure. A native speaker of Chinese is no better off than we, for he can know *mǎ* and *shàng* and still not understand *mǎshàng* unless he has learned the meaning of the latter as a separate fact about his language.

Let us momentarily use the term "Y" for any grammatical form the meaning of which is not deducible from its structure. Any Y, in any occurrence in which it is not a constituent of a larger Y, is an *idiom*. A vast number of composite forms in any language are idioms. If we are to be consistent in our use of the definition, we are forced also to grant every morpheme idiomatic status, save when it is occurring as a constituent of a larger idiom, since a morpheme has no structure from which its meaning could be deduced.

Thus *new* is an idiom in *She wants a new hat*, but not in *I'm going to New York*, because here it is part of the larger idiom *New York*. *New York*, in turn, is an idiom in the preceding sentence but not in *The New York Times* or *The New Yorker*, since in the latter expressions *New York* occurs as part of larger idioms. The advantage of this feature of our definition, and of the inclusion of morphemes as idioms when they are not parts of larger idioms, is that we can now assert that any utterance consists wholly of an integral number of idioms. Any composite form which is not itself idiomatic consists of smaller forms which are.

A composite form in another language cannot be called an idiom merely because its meaning seems queer to us. The test must be applied within the language. French *Elle est garde-malade* 'She is a nurse' may seem peculiar to us because it contains no equivalent for English *a*, but this is the regular habit in French, and the sentence is no idiom. On the other hand, though French *mariage de convenance* finds its exact counterpart in English *marriage of convenience*, both the French and the English phrases are idioms.

An idiomatic composite form may coincide in morphemic shape with a form that is not idiomatic. *White paper* is an idiom when it refers to a certain sort of governmental document, but not when it refers merely to paper that is white.

A single form can be two or more idioms. *Statue of Liberty* is one idiom as the designation of an object in New York Bay; it is another in its reference to a certain play in football. *Bear* is presumably the same morpheme in *women bear children* and in *I can't bear the pain,* but it is different idioms in these two environments.

Idioms are unwordlike especially in that they can be much larger than single words: *Now is the time for all good men to come to the aid of the party.* Yet some idioms are smaller than words. *Bought, went, paid, sold, sang, rang* consist of two morphemes each. One is, respectively, *buy, go, pay, sell, sing, ring;* the other, in all of them, is the "past tense" morpheme. In most occurrences, however, the meanings of the whole forms are predictable from the meanings of the constituents, so that the whole words are not idioms.

In theory, and largely in practice, idioms are the stuff of which dictionaries are made. The reason is obvious: a dictionary-maker need not include a non-idiomatic nonce-form, since a speaker of the language would never look up such a form. He would look up the component parts, if he needed to, and automatically know the meaning of the whole. In practice, of course, no dictionary is ever complete. There are far too many idioms in any language, and more come into existence every day.

19.6. Idioms and Morphemes. The recognition of idioms larger than single morphemes requires a modification of what has heretofore been said about morphemes as the raw-materials from which we build utterances. An idiomatic composite form, like any single morpheme, has to be learned as a whole. Thus it is equally legitimate to say that the raw-materials from which we build utterances are idioms.

Furthermore, we can often be sure that a small form is an idiom, even when it is difficult to decide whether it is one morpheme or more than one. For example, English has many words of the type *remóte, demóte, promóte, redúce, dedúce, prodúce,* each apparently built of two smaller parts, a prefix *re-, de-, pro-,* or the like, and a second part *-móte, -dúce,* or the like. But the relationships of meaning are tenuous. Grammarians are not in agreement. Some brush aside the semantic difficulties and take each word as two morphemes, following the phonemic shapes; others regard the parallelisms of phonemic shape as unconvincing and take each word as a single morpheme. Similar problems appear in the analysis of almost every language. An obvious practical step is to set the morphemic problem aside, recognizing that each form is an idiom whether it is one or more morphemes.

NOTES

New terms are the following: *word, segmental* and *suprasegmental morphemes; minimum free form, free form, bound form, phrase; lexeme, nonceform; idiom.*

The word criterion stems from current field practice. Freedom and bondage were first developed by Bloomfield (especially 1933, chapter 10). The definition of lexeme follows unpublished work of Bernard Bloch. The *term* "lexeme" has also been used in the sense of our "idiom"; e.g., by Swadesh 1946a.

Problems. The first and second series of problems below are in what may be called *pure distributional analysis.*

In the first series, each problem presents a set of "utterances," each represented by a sequence of one or more capital letters followed by a period. It is to be assumed that, within a single problem, any recurrent letter or sequence of letters has exactly the same sound *and meaning* in all occurrences. Each problem is *closed:* that is, the "language" in question included only those "utterances" which are listed. None of the "languages" involve suprasegmental morphemes. The data in each problem are to be analyzed in terms of morphemes, minimum free forms, phrases, and bound forms. The first problem is worked out to show the procedure.

(1a) A. AC. AD. ADC. B. BC. BD. BDC. C.
Solution: morphemes: A, B, C, and D (each occurs in more than one
environment; each, by definition, is insusceptible of further division).

minimum free forms: A, B, C, AD, and BD (each occurs as a whole utterance, but constituent D in the last two does not).

phrases: A|C, B|C, AD|C, BD|C (the vertical line marks the boundary between ICs; in each case, both ICs are free forms).

bound forms: D (does not occur as a whole utterance).
(1b) A. AE. AEC. AED. ACF. ADF. B. BE. BCF. BDF. BEC. BED.
C. CF. D. DF.

(1c) A. ACH. ADH. AG. AGC. AGD. B. BCH. BDH. BG. BGC.
BGD. C. CH. D. DH. EF. EFCH. EFDH. EFG. EFGC. EFGD.
(1d) A. AC. ACF. ACG. ACH. ACHFI. ACHGI. AD. ADF. ADG.
ADH. ADHFI. ADHGI. AE. AEF. AEG. AEH. AEHFI.
AEHGI. AH. AHFI. AHGI. B. BC. BCF. BCG. BCH. BCHFI.
BCHGI. BD. BDF. BDG. BDH. BDHFI. BDHGI. BE. BEF.
BEG. BEH. BEHFI. BEHGI. C. D. E. F. FI. G. GI.

In the second series, the data are the same as for the first series. In
each case, the additional analysis required is to determine the form-
classes, list the members of each, and describe all the constructions.
Form-classes can be named arbitrarily with numbers, as can constructions, and the latter can be described in terms of the labels for the
former. We illustrate with the first problem.

(2a) Data as for 1a above.
Solution: form-classes: 1 A, B. 2 C. 3 D.
constructions: 1|3→4. 1|2→5. 4|2→5.
(2b), (2c), (2d) Data as for 1b, 1c, and 1d above.

The final series of problems has to do with the recognition of idioms
in English. Remember that complete agreement between different
people can hardly be expected—idiomaticity is a matter of degree.

(3a) List all the idioms larger than single morphemes in the following
sentences:

    (a) He took off his hat.
    (b) The schoolhouse burned down last night.
    (c) I'm going to town; want to come along?
    (d) They were dancing with abandon.
    (e) He's a dirty four-flusher!
    (f) We should put a padlock on that door.
    (g) Are you afraid of ghosts?
    (h) I'll find out about that if I can.
    (i) If you can't be good, be careful.
    (j) Have you read *The Egg and I*?
    (k) Sticks and stones will break my bones but names can never
        harm me.

(l) For lunch we had our choice of toasted English muffins, Scotch broth with barley, French fried potatoes, Welsh rabbit, a Spanish omelet, Italian spaghetti, a western sandwich, or southern fried chicken, with ice cream for dessert. We went Dutch.

(m) I'm afraid your boy has two strikes against him.

(n) That new hat is extremely becoming to you.

(o) That hat becomes you.

(3b) Find ten examples of idioms larger than a single "word" (in the ordinary sense of the latter term) which involve and are used as verbs. One example: He *ran out of* money.

20·

MORPHOLOGY and SYNTAX

20.1. In many languages, words play an important grammatical role, in that they are built out of smaller elements by certain patterns, but are put together into sentences by rather different patterns. Accordingly, it is customary to regard the grammatical system of a language as composed of two subsystems. *Morphology* includes the stock of segmental morphemes, and the ways in which words are built out of them. *Syntax* includes the ways in which words, and suprasegmental morphemes, are arranged relative to each other in utterances.

To illustrate, we again use the example of §14.1:

$$^3John\ ^2treats\ his\ older\ sisters\ very\ ^2nicely^2\uparrow$$

The ultimate *syntactical* constituents of this sentence are the intonation morpheme $/^3\ ^2\ ^{22}\uparrow/$ and the seven words *John, treats, . . . , nicely.* The syntactical structure is shown in Figure 20.1; this differs from earlier diagrams only in that the breakdown stops with whole words.

Our sentence as a whole has no morphology: only the individual words in it do. *John* and *very* have the simplest possible morphological structure, since each is a single morpheme. *Treats* consists of the two morphemes *treat* and *-s; sisters* of *sister* and *-s;* and so on.

In many cases, sets of words which have similar syntactical privileges of occurrence also have parallel morphological structure, and vice versa. Consider, thus, the English verbs (I) *go, come, run, sing,* and so on, and (II) *goes, comes, runs, sings,* and so on. Verbs of type I occur freely with a subject like *I, we, you, they, the men,* but not ordinarily with *he, she, it, the man.* Verbs of type II reverse this syntactical situation: they occur with subjects of the latter variety (*he goes, the man comes*) but not with

177

those of the former. But *goes* is morphologically related to *go* as *comes* is to *come* and so on: each verb of type II consists of a verb of type I plus a suffix (in phonemic shape /-z/ in all our examples).

What this amounts to is a *morphological marking* of the syntactical privileges of some words. Some languages have little of this, and the marking is not complete in any language. In English, verbs like (III) *can, will, must, may* are single morphemes just as are those of type I. There is thus no overt morphological difference to mark the syntactical fact that verbs of type III, unlike those of type I, can occur with either variety of subject (*I can, he can*, etc.).

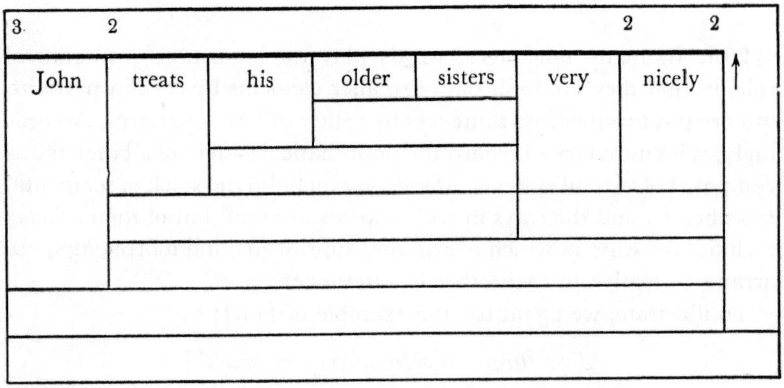

FIGURE 20.1

20.2. The Morphology-Syntax Boundary.

The line of demarcation between morphology and syntax is not always as clear-cut as our discussion so far may have suggested.

English *twenty-eighth* illustrates the difficulty. The ICs are *twenty-eight* and *-th*. The construction in which these ICs stand is not clearly morphological, because the constitute built by the construction is a phrase, not a single word. Nor is it clearly syntactical, since one of the ICs (*-th*) is less than a word. Phrases of this special structure are quite common in English, and not rare in other languages.

The best procedure seems to be to adjust the definition of "morphology" so as to include all constructions in which one IC is less than a word, even if the other IC and the constitute are sometimes phrases rather than single words or parts of words. Thus we class the English construction by which ordinalizing -*th* is added to a number as morphological, though with the special property that the number may be a phrase (*twenty-eighth, three hundred seventy-fourth*) rather than a word. We do the same with the English construction by which genitival -'*s* is added to a word or phrase (*John's, the Mayor of Boston's*). Constructions which we should hardly expect to turn up in this special use sometimes do. The formation of an adjective from a noun by adding -*ial* with a shift of stress is fairly common: *mánor* : *manórial, díctàtor* : *dìctatórial, repórter* : *rèportórial*.[1] The writer has heard (*a*) *lord-of-the-manorial* (*air*), in which -*ial* was added to the phrase *lord of the manor*, not just to *manor*.

Menomini affords a parallel:

/ahsa·ma·w/ 'he is fed'   /ke·s-ahsa·ma·w/ 'he has been fed'
/neta·hsamaw/ 'I feed him'   /neke·s-ahsa·ma·w/ 'I have fed him.'

(The alternations of vowel length are morphophonemic and here irrelevant.) The form 'he has been fed' is built by a syntactical construction from 'he is fed' with a separate word /ke·s/ 'completion.' The form 'I feed him' is built by a morphological construction from 'he is fed,' with a prefix /ne-/ 'I, me.' This same morphological construction, with the same prefix, applied to the phrase 'he has been fed,' yields the phrase 'I have fed him.'

A consequence of our adjustment in the definition of "morphology" is that we cannot always break a sentence down into successive layers of ICs, finding only syntactical constructions until we have reached the level of words, and only morphological constructions from then on. If we analyze *She arrived on the twenty-eighth day*, we find only syntactical constructions until we reach *twenty-eighth*. At this point a morphological construction appears (*twenty-eight* and -*th*). But then, at a still lower hierarchical level, we again find a syntactical construction: that of *twenty* and *eight*. In this sense, the line of demarcation between morphology and syntax remains ill-defined even though we are able to class constructions themselves unambiguously as morphological or as syntactical.

20.3. Complexity. English words rarely achieve great morphological complexity. *Ungentlemanliness* and *impressionistically* are about as far as English goes, barring a few artificial monstrosities like *honorificabili-*

[1] The colon preceded and followed by space sets off contrasting forms for comparison.

tudinity. Figure 20.2 shows the structure of *ungentlemanliness:* there are six morphemes and four layers of ICs. Fox /e·howi·kiči/, diagrammed in Figure 20.3, shows about the same complexity; but the latter word is of only average complexity for Fox.

On the other hand, English syntax can get even more complicated than the morphology of Fox or of other languages which, like Fox, tend

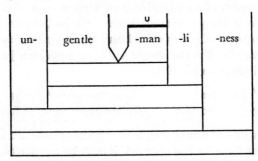

FIGURE 20.2

The absence of stress on *-man* is taken as a separate morpheme; the mark "ʊ" represents this distinctive lack of stress.

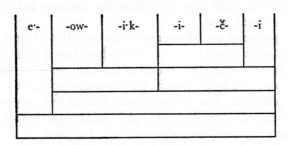

FIGURE 20.3

to put much material into individual words. The first sentence in this paragraph is average for expository English. If one diagrams it one finds about twenty IC layers.

Objective measurement is difficult, but impressionistically it would seem that the total grammatical complexity of any language, counting both morphology and syntax, is about the same as that of any other. This is not surprising, since all languages have about equally complex jobs to do, and what is not done morphologically has to be done syntactically. Fox, with a more complex morphology than English, thus ought to have a somewhat simpler syntax; and this is the case.

Thus one scale for the comparison of the grammatical systems of different languages is that of average degree of morphological complexity—carrying with it an inverse implication as to degree of syntactical complexity. The easiest rough measure of morphological complexity is the average number of morphemes per word in a representative sample. Mandarin Chinese scores very low, with barely more than one morpheme per word on the average. English shows nearer to two morphemes per word; Spanish about two and one half; Latin about three; and Fox nearly four.

Nineteenth-century scholars tried to class languages, not along a scale, but into one or another of a limited set of pigeonholes. Among their classificatory terms were *analytic*, *synthetic*, and *polysynthetic*. Thus, they thought that Chinese words were always just one morpheme, and classed the language as "analytic." Greek, Latin, and Spanish, with more morphemes per word, were "synthetic." When languages like Fox were discovered, showing an even higher count, "synthetic" seemed inadequate and the term "polysynthetic" was added. A continuous scale is better than this sort of pigeonholing. But we can conveniently use the terms "analytic" and "synthetic" in a relative way, saying, for example, that Spanish is more synthetic than Chinese but more analytic than Fox.

There is no discernible correlation between the placement of a language on the analytic-synthetic scale and anything else about either the language or other aspects of the life of its speakers. Some Nineteenth-century scholars proposed theories to the contrary, some of which have become part of the folklore about language current among educated laymen today. For that reason it is important to mention these theories and emphasize their falsity.

One false theory was that in course of time all languages tend to become increasingly analytic. There are attested instances of this direction of change: Old English to modern English, Latin to the French of the Fourteenth or Fifteenth century. But there are also instances of the opposite direction of change: French is somewhat more synthetic now than it was a few centuries ago.

A further misconception, a sort of corollary of that just mentioned, was the notion that some languages of today, especially English, are more "progressive" than others, like Spanish and German, because they have developed further in the analytic direction. For this there is no evidence at all. The Turks of today manage all the business of everyday life, and the complexities of modern technology, with a highly synthetic language; the Chinese of today do just as well with a markedly analytic language.

NOTES

New terms: *morphology* and *syntax;* (*ultimate*) *syntactical constituents* (= words and suprasegmental forms); *analytic* versus *synthetic.* "Polysynthetic" is superfluous. Some contemporary linguists use the term "morphology" to subsume all that we divide up into morphology and syntax; some logicians and semanticists use the term "syntax" or "syntactics" in this same broader way; our usage of the two terms follows that of Bloomfield 1933.

Problem. Determine and list the ultimate syntactical constituents of each of the following English sentences:

(a) The scientist walked like a man on an errand that was too important to be interrupted.

(b) His two brothers-in-law joined the Air Force.

(c) I put on my prayers.

(d) Good thirty-five to forty; utility thirty to thirty-five.

(e) I roaded the car five miles this side of Grinnell.

(f) They tape recorded the whole series of lectures.

(g) He's a swash-buckling buccaneer.

(h) These differences were noted as a fact of immediate apprehension.

(i) It looks like on this bet we're going to what they call in blackjack push.

(j) Aspirin is monoacetosalicylic acid.

21·

SYNTACTICAL CONSTRUCTION-
TYPES: ENDOCENTRIC

21.1. Construction-Types. The sentence *The old dog lay in the corner*
contains two composite forms, *old | dog* and *lay | in the corner*, built by
different constructions but nevertheless showing certain similarities. In
terms of meaning, an old dog is one kind of dog, and lying in the
corner is one kind of lying. In each case, then, one of the ICs modifies
the meaning of the other. This is not true of all composite forms. *Men
and women*, with ICs *men* and *women*, refers neither to one kind of men
nor to one kind of women; *visit Bill* refers neither to one kind of visiting
nor to one kind of Bill.

If a constitute built by one construction (say construction A) and a
constitute built by another (say B) show a certain similarity, then any
other pair of constitutes, one built by A and one by B, show the same
similarity. We can thus speak directly of similarities between constructions. A *construction-type* is a group of constructions which are similar in
some specified way. *Old | dog* and *lay | in the corner* are built by different
constructions, but the constructions are of the same type in that both
involve the modification of one IC by the other.

Construction-types are useful in comparing languages. Constructions
themselves have to be defined separately for each language: a French
composite form and an English one cannot be built by the "same" construction. But a French construction and an English one can be of the
same type.

Construction-types are also helpful in dealing with a single language,
because there are instances in which it is not easy to tell whether two

183

constitutes have been built by a single construction or only by two similar ones. English *white | house* and *little | house* illustrate this. That the constructions may not be identical is suggested by the fact that we might add *little* to the first form, giving *little white house*, but are not likely to add *white* to the second—no one says *white little house*. But the constructions are certainly of closely similar type. In some contexts this is all we need to know.

21.2. Endocentric and Exocentric. The complete specification of a construction involves (1) designation of the form-class from which each constituent is selected, and (2) designation of the form-class to which the resulting constitute belongs. Thus the construction of *old | dog* may be described (1) as involving a descriptive adjective (*new, old, young, big, friendly,* etc.) as first IC and a singular noun (*dog, cat, boy, table,* etc.) as second; and (2) as yielding a constitute which also belongs to the class of singular nouns. A form-class, in its turn, is defined in terms of a range of privileges of occurrence in larger forms.

Some constructions are such that the form-class of the constitutes is similar to the form-class of at least one of the ICs. Here "similar" means that the two ranges of privileges of occurrence largely overlap. The grammarian would prefer to speak of identity rather than similarity, but language habits are not completely tight-knit, and greater precision would be spurious.

The construction of *old | dog* is of the sort just described. *Old dog* is a singular noun just as is *dog:* the privileges of occurrence in larger forms of *old dog* are much the same as those of *dog.* Thus *The dog* (or *old dog*) *ran away; I saw the* (*old*) *dog; a big* (*old*) *dog; one* (*old*) *dog;* and so on.

The construction of *lay | in the corner* is also of this sort: *He lay there* (or *there in the corner*) *yesterday; He lay* (or *lay in the corner*) *motionless;* and so on.

Even the construction of *men and women* is of the same sort, with the difference that in this case the form class of the constitute is that of *both* of the ICs: *I saw the men* (or *women,* or *men and women*); *the men* (or *women,* or *men and women*) *have their hats; men* (or *women,* or *men and women*) *and children.*

Any construction which shows the property just described and illustrated is *endocentric.* The constituent whose privileges of occurrence are matched by those of the constitute is the *head* or *center;* the other constituent is the *attribute.* In *old dog, old* is attribute and *dog* is head. In *lay in the corner*, *lay* is head and *in the corner* is attribute. In *men and women* both ICs are heads and there is no attribute. An endocentric construction involving an attribute is *attributive* or *subordinate;* one with no attribute is *coordinate.*

A construction which is not endocentric is *exocentric.* The latter term is defined negatively, and does not imply that such a construction has a center "outside itself." An example is the construction of *visit | Bill:* the range of privileges of occurrence of *visit Bill* does not resemble that either of *visit* or of *Bill.*

Our definitions do not preclude boundary-line cases. *Blackbird* /blǽk+bə̂rd/ is clearly endocentric, with head *bird*, but *redcap* /réd+kǽp/ 'porter' is in doubt. A *redcap* is not a kind of cap, as a blackbird is a kind of bird, but a kind of person who wears a cap of the specified color. However, *redcap* is a singular noun as is *cap*, and we can find many common privileges of occurrence: *I saw the cap, I saw the redcap; The cap sat on the table, The redcap sat on the table;* and so on. On these formal grounds, it seems preferable to class the construction of *redcap* as endocentric.

All languages have both endocentric and exocentric constructions. In the remainder of this section we survey the main types of endocentric construction. In the next two sections we turn to exocentric constructions.

21.3. Coordinate Constructions. English has coordinate endocentric constructions of several subtypes. One, which might be called "additive," often but not always involves the marker *and: men and women; red and green (lights); (She walks) awkwardly and ungracefully; (He) ran up and kissed her; one hundred | twenty; twenty- | eight.* Another subtype might be called "alternative," and involves the marker *or: men or women; (Did he come) yesterday or today?; red or green (lights).* Other coordinate constructions are illustrated by *both John and Bill; neither John nor Bill; either John or Bill; (I don't know) whether he came or not; two plus two;* possibly also *two times two, two minus two.*

A very different variety of coordinate construction is the *appositive* subtype. In some instances it is clear that a construction is endocentric, and reasonable to suppose that it is attributive, but difficult to tell which IC is the head. Thus, in *Queen Mary*, one can argue that the first IC is attributive to the second, or with equal cogency that the second modifies the first. In terms of meaning, Queen Mary is a "kind" of

Queen, and also a "kind" of Mary or of person named Mary. In these circumstances we speak of apposition, not of attribution: both ICs are heads, and both are also attributes. Other examples are *Lake Michigan; Professor Jones; Mister Smith; Miss Watkins; John | the Baptist; Dick, | the boy I was telling you about; Burns | the poet; Poe, | author of "The Raven."*

Most languages seem to have much the same variety of coordinate subtypes as English, though with differences of detail. In English, alternative constructions usually involve the marker *or;* in Chinese, most alternative constructions have no marker. Thus Chinese *sān sż* 'three four' = 'about three or four' is alternative, with no marker, just as *shŕ sān* 'ten three' = 'thirteen' is additive with no marker. Some styles of colloquial English match the Chinese unmarked alternative: *He stayed three-four weeks.*

21.4. Attributive Constructions. English has a great variety of attributive constructions. We give below four sets of examples. In the first set, the attribute comes first; in the second, the head is first; in the third, the attribute is discontinuous and encloses the head; in the fourth, the head is discontinuous and encloses the attribute. In each example, the head is italicized. Parenthetical material is not part of the example, but context for clarity:

I. big *tree;* three *trees;* a *tree;* this *tree;* my *dog;* John's *dog;* stone *wall;* New York *papers;* city *street;* (the) above *remark;* no *butter;* not *bad;* very *good;* (it was) strawberry *red;* ice *cold;* fire *hot;* (the price was) mountains *high;* a great deal *better;* not *often;* quite *often;* (He decided) not *to go;* (I) seldom *go;* When you can, *come here.*

II. *number* three; *operation* Coronet; *soldiers* three; (the) *book* on the shelf; (the) *remark* above; (the) *remark* made above; (the) *man* of whom I was speaking; *much* in that book (is of interest); *afraid* of the dark; *lonesome* for you; *sick* of it all; *rare* indeed; *rarely* indeed; *is* not (here); *go* along; *walked* quickly; *found it* in the alley; *found it* last night; *lived* there; *lived there* several years; (I) *will go there* if necessary; *I will go there,* unless you object.

III. (the) latest *volume* to come out; (a) better *plan* than yours; (the) happiest *man* in the world; as *good* as that; (not) so *good* as that; so *sweet* that I can only eat a little; as *often* as you wish; too *good* to be true.

IV. *did* not *go; can* never *go.*

The attributive construction-type is apparently universal. Most of the subtypes found in English recur in the more familiar languages of Europe, though with differences of detail. Thus, often where our favored order is attribute first (*black bird, excellent dinner*), the Romance languages favor head first (French *oiseau noir, dîner excellent*).

As one example of how languages use different machinery for what is much the same relationship, we shall consider the expression of possession. English has a genitival particle which marks this relationship when the possessor is a person, animal, or period of time: *John's hat; the man's umbrella; the Mayor of Boston's wife; a day's journey*. Two pronouns, *it* and *who*, add this particle as do nouns, though our spelling conceals the fact: *its tail; whose hat*. The remaining personal pronouns have a special possessive form: *I* but *my hat*, and similarly *our, your, his, her, their*. Otherwise we reverse the order of head and attribute and use the particle *of: the top of the table, the end of the road*. But *of* is only one of a set of particles that mark various types of relationship (*the man in the street, the tree behind the house*), whereas the genitival particle is the only element of its kind in the language.

The Romance languages have special possessive forms of personal pronouns (French *je* 'I' but *mon ami* 'my friend'). Apart from this, they have only a device like English *of*, so that there is no formal peculiarity to set possession off from other types of relationship. French *la femme du boulanger* 'the baker's wife' has *de*, which is often equivalent to English *of*, but the structure is parallel to that of *boîte aux lettres* 'box for letters' = 'mailbox,' with a different particle.

Chinese resembles English in having a particle of the genitival sort (like -'s) rather than of the type of *of*. But this particle marks a much wider variety of attributive relationships than does English -'s. And in certain types of possession the particle is omitted. If the possession is *alienable*—if the relationship might be broken in the normal course of events by destroying or giving away the possessed item—then the particle is kept: *wǒ de jwōdz* 'I (particle) table' = 'my table.' If it is *inalienable*—the possessor can not rid himself of the possessed item—then the particle is optionally omitted: *wǒ de jyā* 'I (particle) family' or *wǒ jyā* 'I family' = 'my family'; *wǒ de shǒu* or *wǒ shǒu* 'my hand.' The distinction between alienable and inalienable possession is maintained, by one or another formal device, in a great many languages.

Latin had no particle of either the *of* or the -'s variety. Instead, the possessor took on a special form called the *genitive case: accūsātor* 'accuser,' but *servus accūsātōris* 'the accuser's slave'; *bellum* 'war,' but *diffi-cultātēs bellī* 'the difficulties of the war.' This device is very widespread.

Equally widespread is a device which is almost the converse: the assumption of a special form by the word denoting the possessed thing instead of the possessor. In some languages there may be a single possessed form regardless of the possessor, but more often there are a number of possessed forms, and the selection of one of them shows something about the possessor. Thus Menomini /pɛ·sekokasiw/ 'horse' has several possessed forms: /opɛ·sekokasjaman/ 'his-horse' shows that the possessor is neither speaker nor addressee, while /nepɛ·sekokasjam/ 'my-horse' shows that it is the speaker. An attributive word may then be added for specificity or emphasis: /oki·ʔsemaw opɛ·sekokasjaman/ 'the son's horse,' /nenah nepɛ·sekokasjam/ '*my* horse.'

21.5. Nesting of Attributive Constructions; Closure. Since, by definition, an attributive construction builds a constitute with privileges of occurrence much like those of one of its constituents, it is very common to find complex expressions built up by a series of attributive

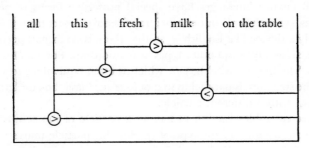

FIGURE 21.1

The marks ">" and "<" are placed at the junctions of ICs, pointing from attribute towards head.

constructions, one nesting within another. To head *milk* we can add an attribute to yield *fresh | milk*. This, in turn, can be used as head in a more inclusive form *this | fresh milk;* then we can add a postposed at-tribute, yielding *this fresh milk | on the table;* and finally, to this, we might prefix the attribute *all*, ending with *all | this fresh milk on the table.* In such a situation it is natural to extend the definition of "head" or "center" so that we call *milk* the head or center of the whole phrase. Figure 21.1 shows the phrase: the mark ">" or "<" is placed at each junction of

ICs, pointing from attribute to head. The special diagram in Figure 21.2 may be more graphic.

Languages differ as to how complex they allow such phrases to grow. Our English example could hardly be expanded further, except possibly to *all this fresh milk on the table, which you left for me this morning.* The presence of certain attributive constructions in the nesting precludes the occurrence of certain others at a more inclusive level: we can say *this fresh milk,* but not *fresh this milk; little white house* but not *white little house.* These limitations imply that eventually the process must

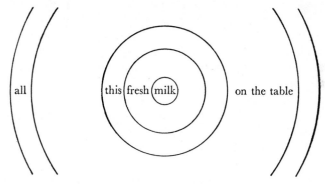

FIGURE 21.2

stop: the nesting of constructions is eventually *closed.* The whole form can then participate in still larger forms only by coordinate or exocentric constructions.

NOTES

New terms: *construction-type; endocentric* and *exocentric; head = center,* and *attribute; coordinate* versus *subordinate* or *attributive;* ("double-headed" = coordinate); *appositive* (the terms "additive" and "alternative" are usable for many languages but are less important); *alienable* versus *inalienable* possession; *closure.*

The linguistic use of the word *formal* needs to be made clear, particularly to readers who are familiar with the use of the same word among philosophers and logicians. Among the latter, a "formal" system is one developed without reference to any specific area of application, and thus contrasts with an "empirical" system. In linguistic usage, "formal" criteria contrast with "semantic" criteria: both are equally empirical. When the linguist proceeds formally, he is not ignoring empirical evidence but paying attention to one *kind* of empirical evidence rather than another.

Gleason, *Workbook* (1955b), page 47, gives a useful problem in the analysis of nesting English attributive constructions with a noun or nounlike center. Working through this problem will also help to sort out some of the attributive constructions of English.

22.

SYNTACTICAL CONSTRUCTION-TYPES: EXOCENTRIC

22.1. Major Exocentric Types. The variety of exocentric constructions in known languages is too great for any simple classification. But by setting aside constructions of marginal importance, and types found only in a few languages, the following three-way classification can be achieved. The terms used in it are largely new, since traditional grammar, based on the languages of Europe, affords few terms of sufficient generality:

> *Directive:* ICs a *director* and an *axis: in* | *the box; on* | *the table; if* | *he is going; while* | *we were there; saw* | *John; asked me* | *a question; asked* | *me.* (Discussed in detail in §§22.2–5.)
>
> *Connective:* ICs a *connector* and a *predicate attribute: is* | *a big man; is* | *tired; became* | *excited; lay in the corner* | *motionless.* (§22.6.)
>
> *Predicative:* ICs a *topic* and a *comment: He* | *is a big man; She* | *sings beautifully; I* | *saw him; That man* | *I just don't like; (She watched) us* | *cross the street.* (§23.)

All known languages have constructions of each of these types; a few languages have constructions of major importance which escape the classification.

22.2. Directive Constructions. The most widespread subtype of directive construction—found, apparently, in all languages—is the *objective* type: the director is a *verb* and the axis an *object*. English examples are *saw* | *John, asked me* | *a question, asked* | *me, wanted* | *to go.* In all other directive subtypes, one IC is a *directive particle* and the other will continue to be called an "axis." These terms lump together two

191

distinct types of directive construction in English, to be segregated shortly: *in | the box, on | the table;* and *if | he is going, while | we were there.* The number and variety of verbs used in objective constructions is usually as great as that of objects. But in other directive constructions, the number and variety of directive particles is usually small. A directive particle plays a double function. It stands in construction with its axis, but also marks the relationship of the whole constitute to the other parts of the sentence. Thus in *the pencil on the desk* and *the pencil in the desk, on* and *in* stand in construction with *the desk;* but each marks the fact that the constitute it begins is attributive to something—here to *the pencil.* We cannot call *on* and *in* markers, because a marker signals a relationship between constituents without itself being one (§17.4). But the structure-indicating role of directive particles leads us to call them *imbure markers.*

English directive particles are of two kinds, *prepositions* and *(subordinating) conjunctions;* we thus have *prepositional* and *conjunctive* varieties of the directive construction-type. *In | the box* and *on | the table* are prepositional; *if | he is going* and *while | we were there* are conjunctive.

Chinese has directive particles like English conjunctions: *yàushr* 'if,' *swéiran* 'although'; but none like English prepositions. Where English uses a preposition, Chinese uses a verb. Thus the verb *gēn,* the basic meaning of which is 'follow,' sometimes translates more naturally as 'with' or even 'from.' In *wǒ gēnje nǐ* 'I follow (continuative particle) you' = 'I'm following you,' the central verbal meaning appears. In *wǒ gēn ni chyù* 'I follow you go' = 'I'm going with you' and in *wǒ syǎng gēn yínháng jyè yidyǎr chyán* 'I plan follow bank borrow a-little money' = 'I'm planning to borrow some money from the bank,' the meanings are best expressed in English with prepositions.

Many languages differ from English in having no separate class of prepositions, but also differ from Chinese in not making special use of verbs for "prepositional" senses. Instead, they achieve equivalent meanings morphologically, within single words: Eskimo /qavuŋa/ 'to the south' and /qavani/ 'in the south.' Many languages express "conjunctive" meanings in the same way, as Hopi /níme?/ 'when he goes home' and /nímaqàjh/ 'because he went home.' But even a language which has developed this morphological device quite elaborately usually has also a few subordinating conjunctions.

On the other hand, some languages have directive particles that mark structural relationships rarely marked by either prepositions or conjunctions in English. *At night is no time to go there alone* shows the prepositional constitute *at night* functioning as a topic, but this is not a function regularly marked in English by *at* or any other directive particle. But in Japanese the directive particle /wa/, which follows its axis, marks the result as the topic in certain predicative constructions. Thus /ano hito wa/ 'that man (topic-marking particle)' is topic in /ano hito wa anata no tomodati desu/ 'That person is your friend.' Fijian has a particle /na/ which precedes common nouns (/koro/ 'village,' /sala/ 'path') whenever such a noun is the topic in a predicative construction ('The village is clean') or the specific object of a verb ('He is cleaning the village'), but not when the noun is a general object of a verb ('He cleans villages').

Even French and Spanish differ from English on this point, despite the close resemblances among the three languages. French uses constitutes built with the preposition *de* (roughly 'of') as topics: *des soldats sont arrivés* 'some soldiers have arrived' versus *les soldats sont arrivés* 'the soldiers have arrived.' Spanish marks personal objects of verbs with *a* (elsewhere 'to'): *veo a Juan* 'I see John.'

22.3. English Prepositional Constructions. The forms used as axes with English prepositions can all also occur as objects of verbs, and it is traditional to use the term "object" for both.

A few English forms function only as prepositions, for example, *against, at, from, to, with, out of.*

But the pair of sentences *He walked along* and *He walked along the road* show that some forms have other functions as well. In the former sentence, *along* is a postposed attribute to a verb; in the latter, *along* has the object *the road* and the constitute is attributive to the verb. There are more than twenty particles, sometimes called *prepositional adverbs*, which have both functions: *along, behind, below, by, across, down, off, over,* etc.

A very few particles function either as prepositions or as conjunctions: *until* is a preposition in *until tomorrow*, a conjunction in *until he comes.*

After, before, and *since* have all three functions: *Jill came tumbling after* (modifier of verb); *Jill tumbled after Jack* (preposition); *Jill tumbled after Jack did* (subordinating conjunction).

English prepositional constitutes are almost always attributive to something, and usually the head precedes: *the book | on the third shelf, the menace* | *of the dark; afraid* | *of the dark, lonesome* | *for you; (he) was sitting* | *on the desk, (she) was reading* | *in the dark.* In *At first,* | *he couldn't decide* the head follows; so also in some fixed expressions like *to the manner* | *born.*

Predicate attributes in connective constructions count as an instance of attributive use: *(He) is* | *in the corner.* In the preceding sentence, *in the corner* is a predicate attribute; in *He was working in the corner* the same prepositional phrase is attributive to the verb. In the first sentence *in the corner* could be replaced by *slow* or *dejected;* in the second, by *slowly* or *dejectedly.* The distinction between the two functions is not always clear: in *he was sitting in the corner* we could replace *in the corner* by either *dejected* or *dejectedly.*

22.4. English Conjunctive Constructions. The axis in a conjunctive construction is a *clause,* usually, though not always, a composite form built by a predicative construction.

Since clauses and objects are different kinds of forms, prepositional and conjunctive constructions can be distinguished even when the directive particle is one that can be used in either: *after, before, since, until, for,* colloquially *like, than. Until he comes* is conjunctive, *until tomorrow* prepositional, because *he comes* is a clause and *tomorrow* is not. There are also some forms which occur as conjunctions but not as prepositions: *though, although, as if, unless, whereas, if, when, whenever, while, wherever, however, lest,* and unstressed *that* (/ðət/; stressed /ðæt/ is a different word).

Some of the forms just listed also have a special use as *relatives.* In *the men that usually sit here, that* is an integral part of the clause *that usually sit here*—its topic, and subject of *usually sit here;* in *the man that I saw, that* is topic of the clause and object of the verb *saw.* Whenever a word of this sort occurs as an integral part of a clause, the clause is a relative clause and the word is a relative, not a conjunction. Conjunctions stand outside clauses, marking the relationship thereof to other material. In *the fact that she is sick* this requirement is met, and *that* is a conjunction.

Conjunctive constitutes occur as attributes, though not often as predicate attributes; as objects of verbs or prepositions; and as topics in predicative constructions. Examples of the first, with various heads: *the fact* | *that she is sick, the time* | *when John first saw her, a girl* | *like she is; bigger* | *than he is; (I) will go* | *if I want to* (or *when I want to, before she does, after she does, as if I enjoyed it, unless you tell me not to,* and so on); *after she comes* (or *when she brings the food, although I'm not hungry, whenever we like, however that may be,* etc.) | *we can eat.* As object of a verb: (*I*) *thought* | *that she was coming,* (*I*) *don't know* | *if she's coming* (or *when she's coming, where she's going, why she's coming, how she's coming*). As object of a preposition: (*I waited*) *until* | *after she got here,* (*The importance of the case lies*) *in* | *that it sets a new precedent.* Conjunctive constitutes as topics are common only with *that: That she is coming* | *is interesting;* with a special English predicative construction (§23.5), *It is interesting* | *that she plans to come.*

In *If this be true, then we must act,* each of two clauses is marked (*if . . . , then . . .*). This habit was very common in older Indo-European, for example in Greek. The paired markers are *correlatives.* One of any pair of correlatives (*if* in the example) is a subordinating conjunction. The other is not a conjunction—the traditional label is *conjunctive adverb*—: it does not stand in a directive construction with what follows, but is attributive thereto, summarizing the associated conjunctive constitute (§30.3). In current English we usually use just one of the markers: *If this is true, we must act,* or *This is true, so we must act.*

22.5. Objective Constructions. English verbs fall into various classes depending on what kind of object, if any, they can take. A list of examples best illustrates the resulting variety of objective constructions.

In the first set, the object is a single word or a phrase built by endocentric constructions: (*I*) *bought* | *roses;* (*I*) *bought* | *a razor;* (*I*) *asked* | *how to go;* (*They*) *saw* | *everything there is to see.*

In the second set, the object is a verb or a phrase built, by endocentric or exocentric constructions or both, around a verb: (*I*) *wanted* | *to go;* (*I*) *wanted* | *to go with him;* (*I*) *wanted* | *to see him during my visit;* (*She*) *stopped* | *singing;* (*She*) *stopped* | *singing the song.*

In the third set, the object is a clause, with or without a conjunction: (*I*) *can't make* | *the car go;* (*I*) *caught* | *John trying to sneak away;* (*I*) *advised* | *John to eat better meals;* (*I*) *considered* | *John to be wrong;* (*We*) *conceived* | *this plan as a way out of our difficulties;* (*I*) *put* | *the razor away;* (*I*) *got* | *it done;* (*I*) *had* | *my hair cut short;* (*We*) *elected* | *him president;* (*She*) *considers* | *him handsome;* (*We*) *call* | *him John;* (*We*) *painted* | *the barn red;* (*I*) *thought* | *that she was coming;* (*I*) *thought* | *she was coming;* (*I*) *wonder* | *whether she is coming;* (*I*) *think* | *so;* (*I*) *think* | *not.*

In the fourth set, the verb takes an object (a single vertical stroke separates the two in the examples), and then the combination in turn functions as a verb with another object (double vertical stroke): (*I*) *gave* | *him* || *five cents;* (*We*) *showed* | *her* || *how to go;* (*I*) *told* | *him* || *that she does it often.*

The role an objective constitute can play in larger forms depends not on the choice of verb or object, but on the shape of the verb. In all the examples above, the constitute is a predicate with a preceding subject (the commonest variety of topic-comment construction in English). If in the first example, we change *bought* to *buying* or *to buy*, then the constitute can perform other functions:

subject: *buying roses* | *is fun; to buy roses* | *is fun.*
object of a verb: (*I*) *enjoy* | *buying roses;* (*I*) *want* | *to buy roses.*
predicate in special kinds of predicative constructions: (*I saw*) *him* | *buying roses;* (*I want*) *you* | *to buy roses.*
object of preposition: (*I counted*) *on* | *buying roses; in* | *buying roses* (*one must be careful*).
postposed attribute: *That man* | *buying roses* (*is my father*); *His desire* | *to buy roses* (*is strange*).
preposed attribute: *Buying roses,* | *John went to his girl's house; To buy roses,* | *go to the store around the corner.*

In many languages, the shape of the verb also shows something about the object. In Menomini, for example, the sentences 'I see a bird' and 'I see a chair' require different verbs: /nenɛ·wa·w/, which specifies that the object is an animate entity other than speaker or addressee, and /nenɛ·men/, which specifies that the object is an inanimate entity. If the object is omitted ('bird,' 'chair'), the verb still contains within itself, morphologically, a construction of the objective type. This is especially clear in the forms for 'I see you' and 'you see me': the verb completely specifies the object, and a separate object word is added only for special emphasis.

22.6. Connective Constructions. In *The child grew quickly, quickly* is attributive to the verb *grew.* In *The child grew sickly, sickly* does not describe the growing, but the child: it is not a modifier of *grew,* but of *the child,* linked thereto by *grew.* So we call *grew* a "connector" and *sickly* a "predicate attribute." Most English connectors are verbs, but many verbs are never connectors. In some languages connectors are special forms, not verbs in special uses.

The commonest English connector is *be.* In sentences like *John is a man, John is tall, John is here,* this connector seems to do nothing but connect. We may therefore class it as an impure marker (like English prepositions). *As*, which is not a verb, is an equally abstract connector in (*We regarded*) *him as a friend.*

Some languages have a construction involving a predicate attribute but no connector: Russian /iván saldát/ 'John soldier' = 'John is a soldier.' In this case we cannot speak of a connective construction, since in English *John is a soldier* it is the construction of *is* and *a soldier* which is so classed. Predicate attributes without a connector appear in English in special circumstances: (*I consider*) *him one of my best friends* is parallel to (*I consider*) *him to be one of my best friends*, but with zero where the latter has *to be*. In the English situation, where connectors are usually involved, the marginal cases without them can perhaps best be described as having a *zero* connector.

Connective constitutes have the same range and variety of functions in English as do objective constitutes.

NOTES

New terms: *directive, connective,* and *predicative* exocentric constructions; *director* and *axis; connector* and *predicate attribute; topic* and *comment; verb* and *object* (*objective* construction); *directive particle* (and axis, in "directive particle construction"); *impure* markers; *preposition, subordinating conjunction; prepositional* and *conjunctive* constructions; *clause; correlatives; zero connector.* The terms "relative" and "relative clause" apply in English and some of the more familiar languages of Europe, but by no means universally.

The contrast between "pure" and "impure" markers stems from Sapir's contrast (1921) between "pure relational" and "mixed relational" elements—a contrast which has been largely neglected in grammatical theory since, though many investigators trained by Sapir have exemplified the contrast in their descriptions of specific languages.

Problem. In the following sentences, set the subject (*John, the bomb, they, it,* or *the wind*) aside, and then make a single IC cut of the remainder: e.g., cut *is a boy* into *is* and *a boy.* Then class the remainders together according to the type of construction involved: e.g., *is | a boy* goes more closely with *is | here* than either does with *found | a nickel.* Do not require any discontinuous constituents.

John is a boy.
John is friendly.
John is here.
John found a nickel.
John found a nickel in the alley.
John found a nickel yesterday morning.
John found a nickel in the alley yesterday morning.
John gave the nickel to me.
John gave me the nickel.
John goes to school.
John walked down the street.
John woke up.
John woke up his sister.
John woke his sister up.
John read a book.
John read me a book.
John read for me.
John read a book for me.
John saw me cross the street.
John saw me crossing the street.
John wants me to cross the street.
John wants to cross the street.
John likes to cross streets.
John likes crossing streets.
John painted the barn red.
It costs five dollars.
The bomb blew up the street.
The wind blew up the street.
John wants you here.
John wants you to be here.
John made a good offer.
John made me a good offer.
John made me happy.
John made me come here.
They elected John president.

23.

SENTENCES and CLAUSES

23.1. Sentences. The third major subtype of exocentric constructions (§22.1) is the predicative type. In order to deal properly with predicative constructions we must first discuss sentences.

A *sentence* is a grammatical form which is not in construction with any other grammatical form: a constitute which is not a constituent.

In English, the independence of a grammatical form from those that precede and follow, if any, is often shown by intonation. Any intonation which ends with $/^{31}\downarrow/$ signals independence. Thus if one says

$$^2It's\ ^3ten\ o'^3clock^1\downarrow\quad ^2I\ want\ to\ go\ ^3home^1\downarrow$$

one has produced two sentences in immediate succession. But if one uses some other intonation on the first half (§4.5, examples 53–56), then the parts are tied together into a single sentence, just as they would be if one inserted *and* or *but* between them. Intonation is not always an unambiguous guide. Thus $^2If\ you\ ^2like^2\uparrow$ and $^2Are\ you\ ^2going^2\uparrow$ have the same intonation, but the first would often be followed by more material in the same sentence, whereas the second would often be followed by silence. But where intonation is not decisive, segmental morphemes and their constructions help, so that one is rarely in doubt.

If we lift the intonations from sentences, the segmental remainders are highly diverse. But in any one language there are limitations. Again and again in English, the remainder consists of a predicative constitute: *John ran, I see, That's too bad, He didn't hear you, Don't you understand,* colloquially *That man I just don't like.* We class such sentences as *simple.*

In many other English sentences, the ICs, apart from the intonation, are two or more predicative constitutes standing in a coordinate con-

199

struction (§21.2): *John got here early and we left* with marker *and; John can't come but we're coming anyway* with marker *but; Either he will or he won't* with markers *either . . . or . . . ; It's ten o'clock, I want to go home*, with the intonation of the first half marking the linkage. Such sentences are *compound*.

In still others, the ICs, apart from the intonation, are a predicative constitute and a word or phrase attributive to it. Such sentences are *complex*. The attribute precedes in *So | I can't go; In that case | I can't go; If that is true | I can't go; Unless he says it's all right, | I won't*. When an attribute follows, it is often difficult to tell whether it is attributive to all that precedes or just to the second IC of the predicative construction. If our analysis is correct in the following, they are complex sentences: *He is coming | if you will let him; He is coming | if possible; He'll go | if he wants to*. But if the proper first IC cut is, say, *He | is coming if possible* (like *He | is coming tomorrow*), then the sentence is simple, and the attribute *if possible* is part of the predicate. Intonation and pausing can make the situation clear: if we say ^3He's $^3coming^2\downarrow$ (pause) ^2if $^3possible^2\uparrow$ then the attribute goes with the preceding predicative constitute. But often intonation does not help. When it does not, the ambiguity inheres in the language, and the grammarian cannot eliminate it.

More complicated sentences are possible. *John may not come and if he can't we won't come either* is a compound sentence, but its second part is in turn complex rather than simple. *If John can't and you can't, I won't* is complex with attribute first, but the attribute is in turn built (with conjunction *if*) on a form that could stand alone as a compound sentence.

All the varieties of sentences discussed above center on a predicative constitute: just one (simple sentence); two or more in coordination (compound); or just one with an attribute (complex). Most English sentences are of one or another of these varieties, or represent some combination of them. Accordingly, we class all the varieties together as the *favorite sentence-type* of the language. Any English sentence which is not of the favorite type is of some *minor* type.

One minor type consists of predicate without subject: *Come here; Go away; Please find me a larger box*. These are common as commands, but not all commands have this form (*You get out of here!*), and not all *subjectless* sentences are commands: (*What did you do?*)—*Found a nickel.*

Another minor type is the *vocative: John! Boy! Waiter! O ye faithless ones!*

Still a third minor type is the *aphoristic: The more the merrier; The bigger the better*. An example like *The bigger they come the harder they fall* is marginal between the aphoristic and favorite types.

All other minor types may be classed together as *fragments*. They occur, however, especially often in two sets of circumstances. If something other than a favorite sentence is added as an afterthought to what has already been said, either by the same speaker or by some other, or is offered by one speaker as answer to another's question, the fragment is *completive: (Where are you going?)—Home; (I'm going to do that now.)—If I can. Yes* and *No* occur as special completive fragments in answer to certain kinds of questions. Strong emotion, or its simulation, may produce *exclamatory* fragments: *Ouch! Goodness gracious! The devil you say!*

23.2. Predicative Constructions. The kernel of an English sentence of the favorite sentence-type is a predicative constitute. This is true also in most other languages, and quite possibly in all, though there are subsidiary differences to be noted shortly.

The most general characterization of predicative constructions is suggested by the terms "topic" and "comment" for their ICs: the speaker announces a topic and then says something about it. Thus *John | ran away; That new book by Thomas Guernsey | I haven't read yet.* In English and the familiar languages of Europe, topics are usually also subjects, and comments are predicates: so in *John | ran away.* But this identification fails sometimes in colloquial English, regularly in certain special situations in formal English, and more generally in some non-European languages.

In the second example given above, *That new book by Thomas Guernsey* is spoken first because it specifies what the speaker is going to talk about: it is the topic of the sentence, though not its subject. The topic is at the same time the *object* of the verb *haven't read (yet)*, and the subject of that verb is *I*, part of the comment of the whole sentence.

In formal *the man whom you visited here yesterday*, the relative clause *whom you visited here yesterday* has *whom* as topic, the remainder as comment. But *whom* is object of *visited*, and *you* is its subject.

Menomini /nɛ·wɛ·w enoh enɛ·niw anenoh metε·mohsan/ 'he-sees-the-other that man that woman' = 'the man sees the woman' begins with a verb that specifies morphologically that its subject is a more important third person singular animate entity, and that its object is some subsidiary third person entity. /enoh enɛ·niw/ 'that man' is both sub-

ject of the verb and topic of the sentence; /anenoh metɛ·mohsan/ 'that
woman' is object of the verb and part of the comment. But in /niak
enoh enɛ·niw anenoh metɛ·mohsan/ 'the-other-sees-him that man that
woman' = 'as for the man, the woman sees him,' the verb /niak/ shows
that its subject is the subsidiary entity and its object the more important
one. In this case /enoh enɛ·niw/ is still the topic (as shown both by its
morphological shape and by its position directly after the verb), though
it is object of the verb, and /anenoh metɛ·mohsan/ 'that woman' is
part of the comment, though also the subject of the verb. The two types
of sentence arrangement are equally common.

When the topic and comment of a predicative constitute are not also
the subject and predicate, then usually the comment in turn is a
predicative constitute consisting of subject and predicate. In *That new
book by Thomas Guernsey | I haven't read yet,* the comment consists of sub-
ject *I* and predicate *haven't read yet;* in *whom | you visited here yesterday,* the
comment consists of subject *you* and predicate *visited here yesterday;*
similarly in the Menomini example. Thus subject-predicate constructions are one variety of topic-comment constructions, but by no means
the only kind.

In Chinese the preceding generalization does not hold. The favorite
sentence-type of Chinese is different from that of English. If we delete
the subject from a simple English sentence, say *We | visit them often* or
I | found a nickel, the lone predicate cannot function as a sentence of the
favorite type, but only as a subjectless sentence (a command *Visit them
often!,* completive *Found a nickel*). If we delete the topic from a simple
Chinese sentence that has one, the comment still can stand, in most
cases, as a sentence of the favorite type. Thus in answer to the greeting
Nǐ hǎu ma? 'You OK eh?' = 'How are you?' the reply is usually simply
Hǎu 'Am-OK' or *Hěn hǎu* 'very am-OK.' It is not at all necessary to in-
clude *wǒ* 'I' and say *Wǒ hěn hǎu* 'I very am-OK' = 'I'm OK.' The
English short reply *OK* or *fine* is not comparable; the analog would be
Am OK or *Am fine,* which we do not say.

Furthermore, many Chinese comments consist in turn of a topic and
comment, so that one can have a sentence built up of predications
within predications, Chinese-box style. *Wǒ jīntyan chéngli yǒu shr̀,* freely 'I
have business in town today' has topic *wǒ* 'I' and the remainder as
comment. *Jīntyan chéngli yǒu shr̀* 'There is business in town today' in turn

has topic *jīntyan* 'today' and the remainder as comment. *Chéngli yǒu shr̀* 'There is business in town' consists of topic *chéngli* 'in town, town's interior' and comment *yǒu shr̀* 'there is business.' Even *yǒu shr̀*, which contains no topic, can easily stand as a whole sentence. The tie in Chinese between topic and comment is to us unusually loose, particularly if we compare it only with the usual tie between subject and predicate in English. This is shown by a sentence like *Wǒ | shr̀ sānmáu chyán*, literally 'I | am thirty cents,' freely 'As for me, my bill (or the money in my pocket, or the like) amounts to thirty cents.'

Superficially this Chinese state of affairs seems to be matched in languages like Latin, Spanish, or Menomini, where, also, the overt separate-word subject of a predicative constitute can be deleted, leaving in many cases a form that can stand as a sentence of the favorite type. In Latin one may say *Puer puellam amat* 'The boy loves the girl,' or simply *Puellam amat* 'He (or she) loves the girl.' But the structure is quite different. The verb *amat* specifies morphologically that its subject is singular and third person. The sentence *Puellam amat* still includes both subject and predicate, though the subject is represented only by morphemes within the verb. The Chinese sentence *hěn ài nèige nyǔhár* 'very-much love(s) that girl' includes no topic at all, either in separate words or within the verb; in context, the unspecified lover or lovers might be the speaker, the addressee, someone else, or any combination of these.

Since the favorite sentence-type of Latin, like that of English, turns on a predicative constitute, and since Latin verbs regularly include a subject within their own morphological structure, we call Latin verbs *sentence-words*. A sentence-word is a word which contains within itself the nuclear construction of the favorite sentence-type of its language. Menomini, Spanish, and many other languages are like Latin in having sentence-words; many others are like Chinese and English in having none.

23.3. Clauses. In the remainder of §23 we survey the range and variety of English predicative constructions. We can only hint at the total complexity of this phase of English grammar. The complexity in other languages is just as great, though exact parallelism of details is rare.

A simple English sentence (*Birds sing*) consists, apart from intonation, of a single *clause*. A compound sentence consists of two or more clauses; a complex sentence has a clause as head and often has a clause included in the attribute. English clauses are often topic-comment constitutes (those that are not, such as the *so* in *if so*, do not concern us at present), very often of the subject-predicate type.

Limiting ourselves first to clauses of the subject-predicate variety, we can outline one classification of English clauses as follows:

I. The predicate is a verb, with or without attributive elements: *John | ran away, I | sat down, She | was weeping, They | were left alone, (I asked) John | to sit down, (I saw) her | weeping loudly.* These are *intransitive* predicates, and hence intransitive clauses.

II. The predicate is an objective constitute (§22.5), with or without attributive elements: *John | saw me, He | put the box in the corner, I | asked John to run away, I | saw her weeping loudly, She | gave me a cookie last night when I called on her, (I saw) John | crossing the street.* These are *transitive* predicates, yielding transitive clauses.

III. The predicate is a connective constitute (§22.6), with or without attributive elements. The resulting clauses are *equational*. There are three subtypes:

A. The predicate attribute is a noun: *John | is a big man, The boy | became a giant, (We asked) him | to be chairman, (I consider) him | one of my best friends.*

B. The predicate attribute is an adjective: *John | is big, The boy | grew tall, (I consider) him | to be correct, (She likes) milk | fresh, (We regard) this milk | as fresh.*

C. The predicate attribute is adverbial (a form which might occur as an attribute to a verb): *John | is here, The meeting | was last night, They | were in the room, (He put) the box | on the table.*

For instances like *It costs five dollars, It weighed ten pounds, We walked three miles* some grammarians set up a fourth category: these fit easily into neither type II nor type IIIA.

Cutting across the above is a classification into *active* and *passive* clauses. A passive clause may be intransitive or transitive, but it matches another clause (usually a transitive one) in the following way:

intransitive passive	transitive active
*They	were left alone on the island.*	*Someone	left them alone on the island.*
*The job	was done by Bill.*	*Bill	did the job.*

transitive passive

transitive active

John | was given a book.

A book | was given John.

}

Someone | gave John a book.

In these cases the subject in the passive clause is equivalent to the object, or one of the objects, in a corresponding active clause. The correspondence is different in:

intransitive passive

intransitive active

The baby | was sung to by her mother.

The mother | sang to her baby.

Here the subject in the passive corresponds to the object of a preposition in the active. Equational clauses are not matched by passives. But if an equational clause is the object of a verb in a transitive clause, as in *I consider him correct* (*him | correct*, an equational clause, object of *consider*), then a corresponding intransitive passive may separate the ICs of the included equational clause: *He | is considered correct.* The result is similar to an equational clause (*He | is correct*), except that one could expand the predicate of the passive clause, yielding, say, *He | is considered correct by me*, and this is not done with an equational clause.

Different from all the foregoing are clauses in which the topic is not a subject: *John | I saw* (*but Bill I didn't see*) *James | we asked to be chairman, Him* (colloquially often *He*) *| I consider one of my best friends, This milk | we consider strictly fresh, Last night | was the meeting!?, Ten pounds | it weighed!* Just as passives correspond to actives, clauses of this variety correspond to one of the subject-predicate variety: *James | we asked to be chairman* corresponds to ordinary *We asked James to be chairman.* The topic of the special clause is some element drawn from the predicate of the ordinary clause (*James*). The comment then consists of the subject of the ordinary clause (*we*) plus what is left of the predicate (*asked to be chairman*). The comment thus consists in turn of subject and predicate; but the predicate is often a form which could not stand as the predicate of an ordinary clause—*asked to be chairman* could not.

23.4. Dependent and Independent Clauses. A further classification of English clauses, which cuts across those already set forth, is into *dependent* and *independent*. An independent clause is one in proper shape to occur as a simple sentence: *John ran.* An independent clause can be rendered dependent with a subordinating conjunction: *if John ran*, occurring as a whole sentence, is a fragment.

Otherwise, dependent clauses are shown to be so by the verb, or by the absence of any verb (or the presence of the particle *as*) instead of the verb *be*. Thus *John is there* is independent, but *John be there, John were there* (both often used in formal discourse after *if*), *John being there, John to be there, John there* are dependent. The examples given in §23.3 under I, II, and III include the following further instances: *John | to sit down, her | weeping loudly, John | crossing the street, him | one of my best friends, him | to be correct, milk | fresh, this milk | as fresh.*

Each variety of dependent clause has its own range of use. The variety in which the verb appears with suffix *-ing* is thus used: as subject (*John singing that song annoys me*); as object of certain prepositions (*Don't count on John singing that song, I thought of John singing that song*); and as object of certain verbs (*I heard John singing that song*; likewise with *see, find, enjoy, detest, hate,* and others). The variety with the bare verb is used as object with a partly different array of verbs: *I heard John sing that song; see, help,* but not *find* or others of the preceding list. *As* replaces some form of *be* largely after certain verbs or prepositions: *We regard this milk as fresh, We considered him as a friend, We thought of you as very competent, We shall take this one as an example.*

23.5. Classification by Order. A final classification of English independent clauses is by *order*.

In *direct order* clauses, the subject precedes all of the verb: *John is going, John does go, John has been going.* In *normal inverted order* clauses, the verb, or the first word of a verb longer than one word, precedes the subject: *Is John going, Does John go, Has John been going.*

If the verb is just one word, normal inverted order occurs only with *be, have, can, could, may, might,* and a few others. The normal inverted parallel to *John can go* is *can John go;* that of *John goes today,* however, is not *goes John today* but *does John go today.* The verb is expanded into a phrase with *do* (*does, did*), and this is what precedes the subject. In direct order, the expansion with *do* is used only with special stress, as *John DOES go today,* and in the negative, as *John doesn't go.*

Normal inverted order is common in questions, but many questions do not have it. Normal inversion is also regular after introductory elements *only thus, only in this way, seldom,* and a few others: *Only thus can we achieve our purpose.* In elevated style some dependent clauses have inversion instead of a conjunction: *Were we there, (we should know the answer).*

Special inverted order clauses place various verbs of motion before the subject: *Away ran John, Here comes the train, There go all my hopes.* Only a few patterns of this sort are common; an introductory word (*away, here, there*) seems always to be present.

Related to the preceding are two common types of English clauses of more complicated structure.

In one, an "empty" subject *it* occupies the subject position, but refers to an "expanded" subject placed later in the clause: *It's hard to do that* with expanded topic *to do that; Is it common for people to act that way?; It was John that I meant; It became difficult to get a ticket.* These tie in with clauses of type III (§23.3): the predicate is a connective constitute, most often with an adjective as predicate attribute, and the expanded subject follows it.

In the other, a "dummy" subject *there* (usually unstressed /ðər/) occupies the subject position, and the real subject comes later: *There's a circus in town; There're some pencils in that drawer; Is there a doctor in the audience?; Are there any restaurants in this town?; Then there arrived a long cavalcade.* The verb is usually *be*, and its form shows that the postposed subject is the real one: *is* with *a circus, are* with *some pencils.* These also relate to clauses of type III (§23.3): the predicate is usually a connective constitute, most often with an adverb as predicate attribute, but the real subject comes before the predicate attribute.

NOTES

New terms: *sentence, sentence-type; favorite sentence-type, minor sentence-type; simple, compound,* and *complex* (favorite) sentences; *vocative* and *aphoristic* minor sentences (in English); *fragments (completive* and *exclamatory); sentence-word. Subject* and *predicate* versus *topic* and *comment.* The following four terms were introduced specifically for English, but have potential applicability elsewhere: *intransitive, transitive,* and *equational; passive.* The following terms were introduced specifically for English, and may or may not be applicable in comparable ways for other languages: *dependent* and *independent* clauses; clause *orders: direct, normal inverted,* and *special inverted;* "empty" subject *it* and "dummy" subject *there;* "expanded" subject (with "empty" *it*).

The simple operational definition of "sentence" was presented by Meillet 1912, p. 339, was adopted by Bloomfield (e.g., 1933 p. 170), and is now generally accepted in practice if not always in theoretical discussion.

The relation between English active and passive clauses, discussed briefly in §23.3, is one example of what have recently been called *grammatical transformations*. The transformational approach in grammatical analysis is developed by Chomsky 1957, Harris 1957, Lees 1957, too late to be worked into our treatment.

Problem. English verb phrases involve, in addition to ordinary verbs, certain special verbs: (1) *be* (*am, are, is, was, were, been, being*); (2) *have* (*has, had, having*); (3) *do* (*does, did*); (4) *can, could, shall, should, will, would, may, might, must.* Almost all types of English verb phrase are illustrated by the italicized portions of the sentences listed below. Classify the examples and describe the patterns involved.

> He *finds* things.
> He *found* something.
> He *is finding* it now.
> He *was finding* it then.
> It *is found* all around here.
> It *was found* in the alley.
> He *has found* a new friend.
> He *had found* a new friend.
> He *does find* things (despite what you think)!
> He *did find* it (despite what you think)!
> He *can find* it for you.
> He *could find* it for you.
> He *has been finding* life rather hard.
> He *had been finding* life rather hard.
> It *has been found*.
> It *had been found*.
> It *can be found*.
> It *could be found*.
> He *can be looking* for it while you wait.
> He *could be looking* for it while you waited.
> He *may have been finding* things hard.
> He *might have been finding* things hard.
> It *may have been found* by now.
> It *might have been found* if we had hunted harder.

24.

INFLECTION

24.1. In Japanese /anata no tomodati/ 'you (particle) friend' = 'your friend,' the genitival relationship between /anata/ 'you' and /tomodati/ 'friend' is shown by a separate word /no/. In Latin *servus accūsātōris* 'slave of-accuser' = 'the accuser's slave,' the same relationship is shown not by a separate word but by the morphological shape of the possessing noun: *accūsātōris* instead of *accūsātor* 'accuser.'

Japanese /no/ is a marker (§17.4). The Latin element *-is* in *accūsātōris* is not a marker, because markers are defined as separate words. Instead, it is an *inflectional affix*. Inflectional affixes are thus much the same as markers, except that, whereas markers are separate words, inflectional affixes are bound forms.

Some elements are on the boundary between markers and inflectional affixes. English genitival *-'s* is a bound form, but it is freely joined to phrases (*the Mayor of Boston's hat*) as well as to single words (*John's hat*). In this respect it resembles Japanese /no/, which often follows a phrase, and differs from Latin *-is*, which is never so used. As we describe a language we can lean either way in handling such boundary cases—the language itself is quite indifferent to our choice. The writer's preference is to treat English *-'s* as a marker rather than an inflectional affix.

Inflection is that part of morphology which involves inflectional affixes. The remainder of morphology is *derivation* (to be taken up in §28).

When all inflectional affixes are stripped from a word, what is left is a *stem*. In some cases the stem itself occurs as a complete word, as in English *boys*, where stripping the inflectional affix *-s* 'plural' from the word leaves just the singular form *boy*. In such cases, it is convenient

209

to distinguish between mention of the stem and mention of the morphemically identical whole word by writing the former with a hyphen: *boy-* but *boy*. In other cases the stem is a bound form. This is generally so in Latin: the nominative singular *amīcus* 'friend' and the nominative plural *amīcī* 'friends' share only *amīc-*.

The whole set of words built with inflectional affixes on a stem, together with the bare stem if it occurs as a whole word, constitutes the *paradigm* of the stem. The paradigm of *boy-* thus consists of the two words *boy* and *boys*. Some languages, such as Chinese, have no inflection. For them, the distinction between stem and word, and the term "paradigm," are superfluous. But languages which have inflection always have some *uninflected* words: English *to, and, if, when*, Latin *novem* 'nine,' *sī* 'if,' *nōn* 'not' contain no inflectional affix and none can be added. Here the distinction is not superfluous. Such forms are both stems and words, and their paradigms consist each of a single word.

If a paradigm includes two or more words, and the stem without inflectional affixes belongs to the paradigm, we extend the meaning of "inflected form" to include the latter also: *boy*, as well as *boys*, is an inflected form of *boy-*.

Some cases remain uncertain under our initial definition. If the bound form in an uncertain case is used with stems in much the same way as are one or more clearly inflectional affixes, then the marginal case is counted as inflectional too. English *-ly*, as in *prettily*, is an instance. It is not unreasonable to say that in *She sang prettily* the *-ly* marks the fact that *prettily* is attributive to *sang*. Furthermore, *-ly* is mutually exclusive with *-er* and *-est* (*prettier, prettiest*), in the sense that at most one of the three occurs at a time in a word. Since *pretty : prettier : prettiest* belong to a single paradigm, we are led to add *prettily* to the paradigm, and to class *-ly* as an inflectional affix.

Another supplementary criterion is also helpful. Inflectional constructions are exocentric (§21.2) in a strong sense: the total range of privileges of occurrence of an inflected form, in further morphological constructions and in syntax, is not exactly matched by that of any morphologically simpler form. *Boys* is only two morphemes: a morphologically simpler word would have to be just one. *Boys* occurs in environments like *these* _____, *the* _____ *are*, but not in *this* _____, *the* _____ *is*. Some words of a single morpheme occur in the latter environments but not in the former: *boy, cat, child*. Some words of a single morpheme occur in both sets of environments: *sheep, fish, people.* But no single-morpheme words occur in just the first set, as *boys* does. If we did not already know that *boys* is inflectional, these facts would tell us so.

By way of contrast, this criterion quickly shows that *boyish* is not inflectional. In all such sentences as *She was wearing a boyish bob, She looks very boyish*, the word can be replaced by a morphologically simpler word such as *nice, good, pretty.* The occurrence of *boyish* in the larger word *boyishly* is matched by the occurrence of *nice* in *nicely. More boyish* and *most boyish* are matched by *more happy, most happy.* So *boyish* is derivational rather than inflectional.

Allowance has to be made for irregular formations. *Good* does not yield an adverb of shape *goodly* as *pretty* yields *prettily*—the actual word *goodly* is another adjective, formed with a different element *-ly* (as in *manly, kingly*). But *well* relates in meaning and in syntactic use to *good* as *prettily* does to *pretty.* The parallelism leads us to regard *well* as the irregularly formed adverbial inflection of *good*, just as *prettily* is the regularly formed one of *pretty.* Similarly, *fast* (in *He walked fast*) can be taken as the irregularly formed adverbial inflection of *fast* (*a fast walk*), the irregularity in this case consisting in the absence of the customary affix *-ly*. In such cases, it is the statistical prevalence of certain patterns, as well as the parallelism, which leads to the decisions.

24.2. Inflectional Categories. The forms of a paradigm often fall into two or more intersecting classes called *inflectional categories.* The paradigms of some Spanish adjectives afford a simple example. There are four words in each paradigm: e.g., *bueno, buena, buenos, buenas*, all meaning 'good.' One of the inflectional categories represented in these is *number:* the first two words are *singular*, the second two *plural.* The other inflectional category represented is *gender:* the first and third are *masculine*, the second and fourth *feminine.*

In the case of the English paradigm *pretty : prettily : prettier : prettiest*, one category is *degree:* the first two forms are *positive*, the third *comparative*, and the fourth *superlative.* The further contrast within the positive degree constitutes a second category, not operative for comparatives and superlatives. It has no traditional label, but its members can be called *adjectival (pretty)* and *adverbial (prettily)*.

In some cases a paradigm involves only one category. English and Spanish nouns show only number, as *muchacho* 'boy' versus *muchachos* 'boys.' The stem of the Spanish noun is *muchacho-; muchacha* 'girl' and *muchachas* 'girls' are the two inflected forms of a different stem *muchacha-*, though the two stems (*muchacho-* and *muchacha-*) are in turn related derivationally.

24.3. Inflectional Phrases. Two of the inflectional categories of Latin verbs are *voice* and *aspect*. There are two voices, *active* and *passive*, and two aspects, *imperfective* and *perfective*. The two voices and two aspects would be expected to intersect to yield four combinations: active imperfective, passive imperfective, and so on. In fact they do not: the passive perfective is lacking. Thus *amō* 'I love,' *amor* 'I am loved,' and *amāvī* 'I have loved,' but no inflected form of the stem *am-* for the meaning 'I have been loved.' Yet it makes sense to speak also of a Latin passive perfective. Wherever an inflected form with passive perfective meaning and syntax might be expected, what actually occurs is a two-verb phrase: *amātus sum* 'I have been loved.' These phrases are not part of the inflectional morphology of the Latin verb, because the structure of phrases is syntax, not morphology—and hence not inflection. But they fill an obvious hole in the inflectional pattern, and so may be called *inflectional phrases*. The traditional term is "periphrastic inflection," but this is misleading because it suggests, contrary to the facts, that the phrases were morphological formations.

English phrases like *more beautiful* and *most beautiful* can be taken as inflectional phrases. Short adjectives of the type *fine, pretty, small, dry, happy, thin, big, free, polite* have inflectional comparatives and superlatives made with the affixes *-er* and *-est*, sometimes with irregularities (*good : better : best*). Many longer adjectives (*beautiful, intelligent, dangerous, antediluvian*) reject *-er* and *-est*. This leads to no syntactical gap, however, because the phrases built with preceding *more* and *most* have the same range of syntactical functions. A few adjectives allow both formations (*handsome : handsomer* or *more handsome*), in which case the difference in meaning between the two is largely stylistic.

Inflectional phrases can be recognized only where there is a clear gap in the inflectional patterns, which the phrases serve to fill. English verb phrases like *am loved, have loved, have been loved* are not inflectional phrases, because English verb inflection does not define the roles which these phrases play. The fact that many such English phrases translate into single inflected verb forms in Latin is of course beside the point.

NOTES

New terms: *inflection* (vs. *derivation*), *inflectional affix, stem, paradigm, un-inflected* (stem or word), *inflectional category; inflectional phrase* ("periphrastic inflection"). Other terms are specific to one or another language, and label inflectional categories or members of them: number (singular, plural); gender (masculine and feminine in Spanish); degree (positive, comparative, superlative for English); adjectival and adverbial forms in English; voice (active and passive for Latin); aspect (imperfective and perfective for Latin).

Problems. Gleason Workbook (1955b) pages 42–46, provides three excellent problems in the analysis of inflectional sets of forms. We present one simpler problem here:

Divide each of the italicized words in the following English sentences into stem and—if any—inflectional affix. Write the stem in each case with a terminal hyphen. Where possible, write the inflectional affix in phonemic notation, with a hyphen before or after it depending on whether it follows or precedes the stem. Where this is impossible, devise some other notation, and explain what it means.

> *Judge* not that ye be not *judged.*
> *Darts* is an *interesting* game.
> *That* is the *fundamental* problem.
> *Gentlemen* prefer blondes.
> I *thought* I *saw* a pussy cat.
> The *more* the *merrier.*
> He doesn't *like us* any more.
> *Those data* concern electrical *phenomena.*

25·

KINDS of SYNTACTICAL LINKAGE

25.1. When words or phrases stand in a certain construction, the fact may be marked in any of several ways. These ways are *kinds of syntactical linkage.*

The weakest kind of linkage is that which depends only on the form-classes from which each IC is drawn. Thus *black | cat* consists of two ICs, each a single morpheme. We know that the two belong together, and that the first is attributive to the second, simply because that is the way in which forms like *black* and *cat* work. This may be called linkage by *selection.*

When the only linkage is by selection, grammatical ambiguities may appear. *Yellow | clothes* consists of the same ICs in the same order in *She likes yellow clothes* and in *Strong soap will yellow clothes.* The constructions are different: in the first, attribute plus noun head; in the second, verb plus object. But the construction is not shown within *yellow clothes* itself. When a potential ambiguity of this sort is removed by context, we can speak of linkage by *context.*

A stronger kind of linkage is by *marker: men and women* with marker *and;* Japanese /anata no tomodati/ 'your friend' with marker /no/. Earlier sections have supplied many examples of this, as also of linkage by *impure marker: on* in *the pencil on the table; if* in *I'll go with you if you like.*

All languages use linkage of the above kinds. A further kind, linkage by *inflection,* is obviously possible only in some languages. There are several varieties of this.

25.2. Concord. Concord (often called *agreement*) is found in endocentric constructions, and in a tie that cuts across hierarchical structure to link certain predicate attributes to subjects.

214

In Spanish, both nouns and adjectives are inflected for number. When an adjective is used as attribute to a noun, the noun and the adjective *agree*, or are in *concord*, as to number: *muchacho bueno* 'boy good' = 'good boy'; *muchachos buenos* 'good boys.'

In Latin, nouns and adjectives share not only the inflectional category of number but also that of *case*, and nouns and adjectives used together show agreement in this respect also: *puer bonus* 'good boy' (nominative singular); *puerī bonī* 'good boys' (nominative plural); *puerōrum bonōrum* 'of the good boys' (genitive plural).

In Spanish *Ese libro grande no es mío* 'That big book is not mine,' the subject is *ese libro grande* 'that big book,' singular, *no es* is the connector in a connective predicate, and *mío* 'mine,' singular, is the predicate attribute. The subject and the predicate attribute agree in number. In *Esas mesas grandes no son mías* 'Those big tables are not mine,' both subject and predicate attribute are plural.

25.3. Governmental Concord. This variety of linkage by inflection is often found in the company of the preceding, and is often classed merely as "concord," but there is a difference.

Some Latin and Spanish adjectives are inflected for gender, though nouns in those languages are not. However, any Latin or Spanish noun *belongs* to a gender: Spanish *muchacho* 'boy,' *rey* 'king,' *lápiz* 'pencil' are masculine, while *muchacha* 'girl,' *reina* 'queen,' *mano* 'hand' are feminine. When a Spanish adjective of the sort that is inflected for gender is used with a noun, it shows the proper gender for that noun: *lápiz bueno* 'good pencil' but *mano buena* 'good hand.' *Lápiz* 'pencil,' a noun, is not masculine because it has been inflected to be so, but because it is inherently and unavoidably so. Only for the accompanying adjective, *buen-*, is there any inflectional choice of gender, and the choice is governed by the gender of the noun. In, say, Spanish *muchachos buenos* 'good boys,' the agreement as to number is a matter of ordinary concord, while the agreement as to gender is governmental concord, the noun doing the governing.

Similarly, the gender of a subject in Spanish governs the selection of gender-inflection of an adjectival predicate attribute: in *Ese libro grande no es mío* 'That big book is not mine,' since the subject is masculine, the predicate attribute appears in its masculine inflected form *mío;* while in *Esa mesa grande no es mía* 'That big table is not mine,' where the subject is feminine, the predicate attribute appears in its feminine inflected form *mía*.

Governmental concord does not appear only in the company of ordinary concord. Menomini nouns are inflected for number, while numerals are uninflected words. It is the habit to use the singular of a noun with the word for 'one,' but the plural with the words for 'two,' 'three,' and so on. This is governmental concord: the numeral governs the number-inflection of the accompanying noun.

The inflectional categories involved in either sort of concord depend on the language, and even in one language different circumstances may involve concord for different categories. In Latin *Ad eam partem pervēnit quae nōndum flūmen trānsierat* 'To that part he-came which not-yet the-river it-had-crossed' = 'He came to that part which had not yet crossed the river,' the word *eam* 'that' agrees with *partem* 'part' in gender (governmental concord) and in number and case (ordinary concord). But *quae* 'which' agrees with *eam partem* 'that part' only in gender and number; its case is determined by its function in the clause it begins.

25.4. Government. This variety of linkage by inflection appears only in exocentric constructions of the directive subtype; otherwise it resembles governmental concord. In the Latin sentence cited above occurs the phrase *ad eam partem* 'to that part,' with ICs *ad*, a preposition, and *eam partem*. The construction is prepositional, thus exocentric. The object of *ad* regularly appears in the accusative case; we say that the preposition *governs* the accusative.

Similarly, most Latin verbs which can take an object govern the accusative case, though a few govern some other case: *oblīvīscī* 'to forget' the genitive, *ūtī* 'to use' the ablative.

When the governing word completely determines the inflected form (within a specified inflectional category) of the governed word, the inflected form in which the latter appears serves no independent function, but merely helps to mark the syntactical connection. In some instances the governing word does not completely determine the inflected form of the governed word, but only narrows down the range of choice. Thus the Latin preposition *in* governs either the accusative or the ablative: *in urbem* 'to the city,' and *in urbe* 'in the city.' We still speak of government, because there are five other Latin cases, none of which can occur after *in*. But in such instances the inflectional affix in the governed word is comparable to an impure marker (like English prepositions) rather than to a pure marker (like English *and*, *or*) since, in addition to helping mark the syntactical connection, the inflectional affix carries some meaning of its own. Thus, with the Latin preposition *in*, the ablative of the governed noun adds the meaning of location, the accusative that of end-point of motion.

25.5. Cross-Reference. This variety appears in certain endocentric constructions and in several types of exocentric construction.

In Menomini, the appearance of a noun in an inflected form which shows, not only that the noun is possessed, but also something about the possessor, leads to instances of cross-reference. Thus in /enoh enɛ·niw oti·hsɛhsan/ 'that man his-dog' = 'that man's dog,' the inflectional affix /o-/ in /oti·hsɛhsan/ 'his-dog' indicates that the possessor is a third person singular animate entity. The separate words /enoh enɛ·niw/ 'that man' designate a third person singular animate entity. The affix /o-/ stands in cross-reference with the separate words. If we replace /enoh enɛ·niw/ 'that man' by /akoh enɛ·niwak/ 'those men,' then the inflectional affix must be changed also: the appropriate form for the word 'dog' is now /oti·hsɛhsowa·wan/ 'their dog,' where the affixes /o-/ and /-owa·w/ combine to specify that the possessor is third personal plural animate. If the separate phrase designating the possessor (/enoh enɛ·niw/ 'that man,' /akoh enɛ·niwak/ 'those men') is omitted, as it often is when context obviates potential ambiguities, then there is no cross-reference.

In Latin, the use of the genitive case of one noun to indicate that it stands in a possessive relationship to some other noun can also be interpreted as giving rise to instances of cross-reference. Thus in *difficultātēs bellī* 'difficulties of-war' = 'the difficulties of the war,' the genitive ending -*ī* can be said to stand in cross-reference with *difficultātēs* 'difficulties.' There is, however, a difference between this and the situation in Menomini: in Menomini, different persons and numbers of the possessor require different inflectional affixes on the noun denoting the possessed item, while in Latin the same genitive case appears for the possessor regardless of the nature of the possessed item.

In a Latin predicative constitute such as *puer puellam amat* 'the boy loves the girl,' there is cross-reference between the subject *puer* 'boy' and the inflectional affix -*t* in the verb, which specifies that the subject is third person singular. As in the case of Menomini possession, a change in the subject may entail a change in the inflectional affix in the verb:

pueri puellam amant 'the boys love the girl,' with third person plural subject and with inflectional affix *-nt* instead of *-t*.

Cross-reference appears in some languages also in objective constructions. Menomini is again an example. /nenɛ·wa·w/ 'I see him or her' indicates inflectionally that its subject is the speaker and its object some third person singular animate entity; /neniak/ 'He or she sees me' indicates just the reverse. Thus in /nenɛ·wa·w enoh enɛ·niw/ 'I-see-him-or-her that man' = 'I see that man,' there is cross-reference between the verb and its object.

25.6. Inflectional Linkage and Constructions. Now that inflection and inflectional linkage have been discussed, we can slightly simplify the definition of "construction" given in §18.3.

According to that definition, *I | like potatoes* and *she | likes potatoes* are built by two distinct constructions, though the two constructions are of very similar type. The definition was so phrased in order to avoid the implication that combinations like *I | likes potatoes* or *she | like potatoes* might occur, since in fact they do not. Now, however, this implication can be provided for in terms of habits of inflectional linkage: in this case, of cross-reference between subject and verb.

The revised description of a construction is as follows: Any member of such-and-such a form-class, conjoined to any member of a certain other form-class, produces a form of a certain third form-class, provided that the selections from the first two form-classes are compatible with regard to concord, governmental concord, government, or cross-reference, whichever is relevant. *I* and *she* are then assigned to the same form-class, though to different subclasses thereof because of their behavior in cross-reference; *like potatoes* and *likes potatoes* are assigned to a single form-class, though likewise to different subclasses because of their different behavior in cross-reference. Thereupon we can say that *I | like potatoes* and *she | likes potatoes* are built by the same construction—one of the predicative type, with ICs a subject and a predicate—and provide for cross-reference separately.

NOTES

New terms: *syntactical linkage;* linkage by *selection,* by *context,* by *marker,* by *impure marker,* by *inflection; concord* = *agreement, governmental concord, government* (and *to govern*), *cross-reference.* Terms specific to one or another language: *case* (for Latin), including *nominative, genitive, accusative, ablative; number* and *person* (for Latin). A few of these terms have occurred earlier, but are discussed from some slightly new angle in the present section.

Problems. Gleason *Workbook* (1955b), pages 48–50, gives a Swahili syntax problem which illustrates how complex certain types of syntactical linkage can get. We give a problem of a rather different sort here:

Discuss the extent and nature of cross-reference between subject and verb in English, in the light of the following examples. A vertical line marks the end of the subject, and the verb is italicized:

I | *go* there regularly	We | *go* there regularly.
You | *go* there regularly.	They | *go* there regularly.
He | *goes* there regularly.	She | *goes* there regularly.
It | *goes* like this.	John | *goes* there regularly.
The clock | *goes* well.	The men | *go* there every day.
I | *went* there yesterday.	We | *went* there yesterday.

(etc. with subjects *you, they, he, she, it, John, the men*)

I | *can* do it.	We | *can* do it.

(etc. with subjects *you, they, he, she, it, John, the man, the men*)

I | *am* tired.	We | *are* tired.
You | *are* tired.	They | *are* tired.
The boys | *are* tired.	He | *is* tired.
She | *is* tired.	It | *is* here.
The man | *is* tired.	
I | *was* tired.	He | *was* tired.
She | *was* tired.	It | *was* here.
You | *were* tired.	They | *were* tired.
We | *were* tired.	The boys | *were* tired.

John and Mary \| *were* tired.
The sheep \| *was* crossing the road.
The sheep \| *were* crossing the road.
My family \| *is* coming to see me.
My family \| *are* coming to see me.
Darts \| *are* made with feathers.
Darts \| *is* an interesting game.

Some | *is* better than this.
Some | *are* better than this.
Who | *is* coming?
Who | *are* coming?
All | *was* quiet.
All | *were* quiet.
My goldfish | *is* dying.
My goldfish | *are* dying.
Singing and shouting | *is* a waste of time.
Singing and shouting | *are* a waste of time.
A son and heir | *was* born to him this morning.
The people of Europe | *are* interesting.
The peoples of Europe | *are* highly varied.
Six fingers per hand | *is* common in some parts of the world.

26·

PARTS of SPEECH

26.1. A *part of speech* is a form-class of stems which show similar behavior in inflection, in syntax, or both. The *part of speech system* of a language is the classification of all its stems on the basis of similarities and differences of inflectional and syntactical behavior. Since every whole word contains, by definition (§24.1), just one stem, a part-of-speech system can also be interpreted as a classification of whole words: the part of speech of a word is that of its stem.

Although it is rare to find two languages with identical part of speech systems, a great many languages show the same basic plan and differ only as to details. A few languages deviate more drastically. After describing the most common fundamental plan, we shall give two examples of wider deviations: Nootka and English.

26.2. The Tripartite Plan. The most revealing way to view a part-of-speech system is as a few large stem classes, the stems in which resemble each other in basic ways, divided into successively smaller classes on the basis of additional criteria. No matter what criteria are chosen as basic, it almost always turns out that the assignment of a few stems must be changed when further criteria are considered. If we treat Latin in this hierarchical manner, the result is as follows:

Stems inflected for case (*nouns* in a broad sense):
Stems belonging to a gender or indifferent to gender (*substantives*, or nouns in a narrower sense, and *pronouns*): *puer* 'boy' (masculine), *puella* 'girl' (feminine), *cīvis* 'citizen' (indifferently masculine or feminine), *ebur* 'ivory' (neuter). Certain stems, such as that of *ego* 'I' (indifferent to gender),

221

show special features which lead to their segregation as pronouns.

Stems inflected for gender (*adjectives*):
Stems having an adverbial form (*descriptive adjectives*):
clārus 'clear' (adverbial form *clārē* 'clearly').
Stems having no adverbial form (*pronominal adjectives*): *hic* 'this,' *tōtus* 'all.'
Stems having inflected forms which show person and number of a subject (*verbs*):
Stems inflected for voice: *amāre* 'to love' (passive voice *amārī* 'to be loved').
Stems not inflected for voice:
Always active in form: *facere* 'to make, do.'
Always passive in form: *sequī* 'to follow.'
Uninflected stems (*particles*): *in* 'in, into,' *postquam* 'after.' Syntactical criteria establish various subclasses, suggested by the traditional terms *prepositions, adverbs, conjunctions, interjections.*

All parts of the above classification could be carried further by specifying additional criteria. A few stems which show no inflection show syntactical behavior so nounlike that we class them as nouns rather than as particles: *nihil* 'nothing,' *quattuor* 'four.'

The main advantage of hierarchical presentation is that it brings out facts which tend to be concealed by a mere listing of eight or ten smaller stem-classes all on a par. Thus it is a fact that Latin substantives and adjectives resemble each other more in their behavior than either resemble verbs or particles.

A second advantage is that it usually provides for the assignment of stems with peculiarly limited paradigms or syntactical uses. We shall see a demonstration of this in §26.5 below.

A third advantage is that the hierarchical procedure renders easier the comparison of the part of speech systems of different languages. Setting all subclasses aside, the basic scheme of Latin is tripartite: nouns (in the broadest sense), verbs, and particles. This is the most widespread basic scheme in the languages of the world.

Differences within the basic scheme appear, however, with the very first subclassification. In Latin, and in many of its kindred languages in the Indo-European family, stems with "descriptive" or "adjectival"

meanings ('red,' 'big,' 'little,' and so on) belong to the same fundamental class with names of objects ('boy,' 'table,' 'sky'). In Georgian,
which is not Indo-European, and in Armenian, which is, such words do
not even form a separate subclass from other nouns: for 'red' one uses
either a noun meaning 'red thing' or, more rarely, a noun meaning
'redness.' In Japanese, some words with what to us are descriptive
meanings are nouns, while others are verbs. By far the commonest situation, however, is for all such words to be verbs. In Menomini, /mɛhko·n/
'he is red' belongs to the same subclass of verbs as /pa·pɛhcen/ 'he falls,'
while /mɛhki·w/ 'it is red,' together with /pa·pɛhnɛn/ 'it falls,' belong
to a different subclass of verbs. Chinese *húng* 'red,' *dà* 'big,' *syǎu* 'small,'
and the like form a separate subclass of verbs, but with the same
basic syntax as words like *lái* 'come,' *chr̄* 'eat,' and *yàu* 'want,
want to.'

As a further illustration of how details vary, we shall survey the subclassification of nouns in Menomini and Chinese, which differ in this
respect as much from each other as either does from Latin.

(1) Menomini nouns fall into two principal subtypes: nouns proper
and pronouns. The segregation of pronouns is much as in Latin. Nouns
proper are further classed as *independent* or *dependent*, and as *animate* or
inanimate.

Independent nouns are inflected for *possession:* /neto·s/ 'my canoe,'
/oto·s/ 'his canoe,' and so on; but also have *unpossessed* forms: /o·s/
'canoe.' Dependent nouns have only possessed forms: /ne·k/ 'my dwelling,' /ke·k/ 'thy dwelling,' /ke·kowaw/ 'your dwelling,' and so on. In
the main, dependent nouns refer to body parts, types of kin, and a few
items of intimate possession.

Animate and inanimate are gender classes, comparable in grammatical function to those of Latin. Animate nouns include all those
that refer to people, animals, and spirits; some body parts but not
others; some plants and plant products but not others; and a few objects that neither we nor the Menomini think of as alive, such as 'kettle,'
'doll,' 'high bluff along a river.' All other nouns are inanimate. Animate
nouns form the plural with one suffix (/enɛ·niw/ 'man,' /enɛ·niwak/
'men'), inanimates with another (/we·kewam/ 'house,' /we·kewaman/
'houses'). Animates have an inflected form which inanimates lack: one
which shows the subsidiary importance in the context of that named by
the noun (/enɛ·niwan/ 'the other man or men'). As objects of verbs

and as subjects of intransitive verbs, animates and inanimates require different verbs.

Little of this is reminiscent of Latin. A sharper difference is the total absence in Menomini of anything like the Latin inflectional category of case.

(2) Chinese nouns are all uninflected. They fall into five main classes: *demonstratives, numerals, measures,* nouns proper or *substantives,* and (*personal*) *pronouns*. The first four are differentiated by their relative positions in a nest of attributive constructions involving one of each: *jèi sān jāng jwōdz* 'this three flat-thing table' = 'these three tables.' The first IC cut in this four-word phrase is before the last word, *jwōdz* 'table,' a substantive. The next one breaks the first word, *jèi* 'this,' a demonstrative, from the middle two. The third one separates *sān* 'three,' a numeral, and *jāng* 'flat-thing,' a measure. In briefer forms, such as *jèi jāng jwōdz* 'this table' or *sān jāng jwōdz* 'three tables' (or even merely *jwōdz* 'table, tables'), the words of course retain the part-of-speech affiliation determined by their position in the longer phrase. The pronouns (e.g. *wǒ* 'I') do not occur in this nest of attributive constructions.

Measures and substantives cannot be distinguished in terms of meaning, but only in terms of syntax. Measures occur directly after numerals, while substantives do not. To count something named by a measure, one merely prefixes the number to it: *sān gwó* 'three countries,' *sān tyān* 'three days.' To count something named by a substantive, one must insert an appropriate measure between the numeral and the substantive: *sānge gwójyā* 'three fatherlands,' *sānge lǐbài* 'three weeks.' In both of these, the measure *ge* carries virtually no meaning, but simply fills the measure position, which is necessarily occupied by some form. In other cases the choice of measure is semantically relevant: *sān kwài chyán* 'three hunk money' = 'three dollars,' but *sān fēn chyán* 'three division money' = 'three cents'; *yíge syānsheng* 'a gentleman' but *yí wèi syānsheng* 'an honorable gentleman.'

26.3. Bipartite Systems. At least one language, Nootka, is known to have a bipartite system. One significance of this system is that it disproves any assumption that the contrast between noun and verb is universal on the level of parts of speech.

Nootka stems are either *inflected* or *uninflected:* these are the two major parts of speech. Inflected stems all have the same potential range of inflectional possibilities, whether from their meanings we should expect them to be nouns or verbs or something else. Some of the inflected forms are nounlike in their syntax, while others are verblike. Thus consider the four stems /wała·k-/ 'go,' /qo·ʔas-/ 'man, person,' /ʔi·ḥ-/ 'large,' and /ʔatḥija-/ 'at night.' With no overt inflectional affix these all have nounlike syntactical uses and can be translated 'a going, a trip,' 'a man, a person,' 'a large thing,' and 'the night time.' With inflectional affix /-ma/, all four have an implicit third person singular subject, are used syntactically in verblike ways, and can be translated 'he goes,' 'he is a man,' 'he is large,' and 'he does it at night.'

26.4. Multipartite Systems. A number of languages, including English, have more than three basic parts of speech. English is not like Latin because many English stems are used in ways that parallel two or more of the Latin parts of speech: *fancy* in *a strange fancy* (noun, like a Latin substantive), in *fancy dresses* (adjective), and in *They fancy themselves dancers* (verb). Equally, English is not like Nootka, because by no means all stems have such a wide range of use: *strength* is used only as a noun, *icy* only as an adjective, and *describe* only as a verb.

Setting aside the particles of all three languages, we can compare the remaining stocks of stems to three athletic squads, coached in different ways to play much the same game. Several skills are required for the game. The Latin coach trains specialists. The Nootka coach tries to make an all-'round player or triple-threat man of every member of the squad. The English coach combines these techniques, producing some specialists but also good numbers of double-threat and triple-threat men. In a pinch, a specialist may be thrown into a game to do something for which he is not well equipped (*son* in *That nice young man really sonned the old lady*), on the analogy of *That nice old lady really mothered the young man*), but this is very different from the genuine versatility of *fancy* or *faint*.

A player is a stem. A skill is a pattern of use in inflection or syntax or both. The set of players on a single squad who all have the same range of skills, wide or narrow, is a part of speech.

The terms "noun," "adjective," and "verb," when English is discussed, refer to skills rather than to the players that have the skills.

Thus the pattern of use indicated by the word "noun" involves most or all of the following: Inflection for plural (*boy*:*boys*), though this is not inevitable—*music* follows the rest of the pattern but is rarely pluralized. Use as head in nests of attributive constructions, often with initial *a* or *an*, *the*, *this* or *these*, *that* or *those*, or unstressed *some* (/səm/): *a boy*, *an elephant, the boy, this boy, these boys, that boy, those boys, some boys, some milk.* The resulting endocentric phrase, or sometimes the bare word, occurs typically as a subject (*The boy is here*), as an object of a verb (*We saw the boys*), as an object of a preposition (*Look at the boys*), and as a nominal predicate attribute (*My children are boys*).

English stems which follow the noun pattern of usage just described, but do not also follow the adjective pattern or the verb pattern yet to be described, belong to a part of speech we shall call *class N*. Examples are *strength, food, action, day, friend, art, danger, music, boy, elephant*.

The adjective pattern of use turns mainly on inflection for degree (*pretty : prettier : prettiest*) or on participation in equivalent inflectional phrases (*beautiful : more beautiful : most beautiful*); and on inflection with *-ly* for adverbial use (*prettily, beautifully*); without *-ly*, the whole words are used as or in adjectival predicate attributes: *She is pretty, Jane is more beautiful than Mary*. English stems which follow the adjective pattern but not also the noun or verb pattern belong to a part of speech we shall call *class A*. Examples are *long, false, likely, certain, icy, sleepy, short, soft, civil, beautiful*.

Both stems of class N and those of class A (as well as those of some of the classes yet to be described) are often used as preposed attributes to a noun head: *action program, long program; art student, sleepy student*. This usage is followed by such a wide variety of stems, differing from each other so greatly as to their other uses, that it does not help us in determining the part-of-speech affiliation of stems.

However, there are many stems which follow both the noun and the adjective patterns, though not the verb pattern described below. These stems belong to *class NA*. Examples are *American, sweet, savage, private, human, male, white, red, innocent;* thus, *a good American, He is an American, They are Americans* (all noun pattern), but *He is American, They are American, John is more American than his sister* (all adjective pattern). In *American life* we see a class NA stem functioning in a way typical also of both class N stems and class A stems. This function does not fall within either the noun pattern or the adjective pattern.

The verb pattern in general involves inflection. *Be* has eight inflected forms: *be, am, are, is, was, were, been, being*. Many have five: *sing, sings, sang, sung, singing*. Most have only four phonemically different ones: *describe, describes, described, describing*. A few have only two: *can, could*. And the syntactical use of *must, ought* classes them with verbs despite the absence of inflection. Syntactically, the typical uses are as verb in an objective construction (*saw John*), as verb in an intransitive predicate (*I see, John was singing loudly*), and as connector in a connective construction in an equational predicate (*They seem tired*). Stems which show this pattern of usage but not the noun nor adjective pattern belong to *class V: describe, admit, punish, bury, strengthen, falsify, penetrate, collaborate, denazify*. Class V stems do not often occur as preposed attributes to nouns, but in their inflected forms with *-ed* or *-ing* they do: *an admitted fault, a penetrating remark*.

Stems which show both the noun pattern and the verb pattern belong to *class NV: walk, love, cure, change, air, eye, nose, beard, elbow, finger, cut, build*.

Stems showing both adjective and verb patterns belong to *class AV: clean, dry, thin, slow, clear, busy, idle, true*.

Finally, stems showing all three patterns belong to *class NAV: fancy, faint, black, yellow, blue, brown, gray, damp*.

Use as preposed attribute to a noun is not the only function which is indecisive for part-of-speech affiliation. There is an affix *-ed*, much like the verb inflectional affix *-ed*, which occurs in expressions like *a blooded hound, a fluted column, a windowed house, a gifted student*, though it is more typically added to phrases, as in *a full-bodied flavor, a many-windowed house, a four-footed animal*. This is not the same as the verb inflectional affix, and the mere occurrence of a stem with this affix does not place the stem in class V, AV, NV, or NAV rather than in one of the other classes.

English stems which do not belong to one of the seven major classes described above (N, A, V, NA, NV, AV, and NAV) belong to an eighth class of *particles*, with many subclasses differentiated by syntax. Even a few of the particles are versatile enough to play subsidiary roles as noun, adjective, or verb: thus *up* and *down* are particles in *He went up, He walked down* (adverbs); *He went up the street, He fell down the hill* (prepositions); but verbs in *He upped the price, He downed the medicine* and nouns in *We all have our ups and downs*. The seven major classes are all quite large; the class of particles is relatively smaller and its subclasses smaller still. Words like *he, she, it, this, that, every, each* belong marginally to one or another of the major classes, but show special features of behavior (inflectional or syntactical or both) which set them off from the other major-class stems (§30.3).

26.5. Stems of Limited Occurrence. Every language has some stems which do not share the full range of inflectional or syntactical behavior of any of the major parts of speech, or even of any of the most important subclasses. The limitations put them into special smaller subclasses, but usually they can be shown to belong clearly to one or another of the ordinary major classes.

Thus English *afraid* is one of a dozen or so words used only as adjectives, and only in some of the ways typical of adjectives. We use *afraid* as an adjectival predicate attribute (*He is afraid*), and in that position it participates in inflectional phrases for comparative and superlative (*He was more afraid, most afraid*). We do not add *-ly*, and we do not use the word as preposed attribute to a noun, as we do most stems in classes A, N, NA, NV, AV, and NAV. *Afraid* and its kindred can hardly belong to any class but A, but they constitute a special small subclass of that class.

English *neo, paleo, proto, dextro, levo* are used as preposed attribute to a noun or adjective head (*neo-Platonic, paleo-Siberian, dextro-rotation*), occasionally to a verb head (*This compound dextro-rotates*), and fairly often alone as predicate attribute (*His attitude is neo, This compound is dextro*). They are never inflected for degree nor used in equivalent inflectional phrases, but sometimes they are pluralized (*The neos think thus-and-so*). We may treat them as a marginal subclass of class N stems.

Most English nouns are inflected for number. Some are not. Some are always plural: *scissors, shears, trousers, pants, clothes*. Some are almost invariably singular: *music*. Some are used syntactically as singular or plural but show no change in shape: *sheep, deer, trout, bass, carp, fish, people*. These features of behavior place the words in special subclasses of class N, NA, NV, or NAV.

English *fro, main,* and *kith* are far more restricted, occurring only in *to and fro, might and main, kith and kin*. The clue to the part of speech of the three words is *and*, which usually joins coordinate ICs into a larger form of much the same form-class as the ICs. Lacking other evidence, we may assume that *and* functions here as it usually does. Hence *fro*, like *to*, is a particle; *main* and *kith*, like *might* and *kin*, belong to class N.

NOTES

New terms: *part-of-speech system; parts of speech; tripartite, bipartite,* and *multipartite* systems. Terms like "noun," "verb," "substantive" are technical only as defined and applied in the discussion of a single language.

The standard full-length discussions of English (Jespersen 1909–49, 1933; Curme 1931, Palmer 1924, Kruisinga 1925) and most shorter recent treatments (Fries 1952, Trager and Smith 1951) do not break with the Latinizing tradition by which English has nouns, verbs, and adjectives as separate parts of speech. We follow Whorf 1945 (in Carroll 1956).

27

GRAMMATICAL CATEGORIES

27.1. We have remarked several times on the difference between nouns and adjectives in Spanish (or Latin) as to gender. Nouns *belong* to a gender; some adjectives are *inflected* for gender. For adjectives, then, gender is an inflectional category (§24.2). For nouns, the genders are rather what we shall call *selective* categories.

The membership of a word in a selective category is often not shown by the word itself, and may not be revealed in all the larger environments in which the word occurs. Thus, though many Spanish masculine nouns end in -*o* and many feminines in -*a*, this marking is not consistent: *lápiz* 'pencil' and *patriota* 'patriot' are masculine; *mano* 'hand' is feminine. And a sentence like *Dos lápices, por favor* 'two pencils, please' does not tell us the gender of *lápiz*. But gender comes into play as soon as the noun is used with an article or a gender-showing adjective: *el lápiz* 'the pencil,' *un lápiz bueno* 'a good pencil,' with *el, un,* and *bueno* rather than their feminine counterparts *la, una,* and *buena.*

In this Spanish example of a selective category, inflection plays an indirect role, since *el* and *la, un* and *una, bueno* and *buena* are different inflected forms of the same stems. But selective categories do not invariably depend on inflectional ones. A language with no inflection at all nevertheless has many selective categories. A language with some inflection has many selective categories which do not turn on inflection. In Fijian, /mata/ 'day' is preceded by /na/ when it is the subject of a clause, but /viti/ 'Fiji' is preceded instead by /ko/. /na/ and /ko/ are two distinct particles, not different inflected forms of a single stem. Yet the choice of /na/ or /ko/ establishes a twofold classification of all Fijian

230

nouns and noun phrases: names of specific people and places belong to the /ko/ class, common nouns to the /na/ class. Since a common noun or noun phrase is sometimes adopted as the name of a person or place, the classification is not quite mutually exclusive: /na vanua levu/ would mean '(a) big island,' while /ko vanua levu/ is the name of a specific large island in the Fijian archipelago.

Inflectional and selective categories are all *grammatical* categories. A *generic* category is a whole system or classification: English number, Spanish gender, Latin case. A *specific* grammatical category is an element in a system or a class in a classification: English plural, Spanish masculine, Latin accusative.

Some selective categories are very small, and come into play only in highly specific grammatical circumstances. In English, only a dozen or so stems can occur in the environment *go* ____-*ing* in the sense of 'go to a place, carry on the specified activity, and (perhaps) return.' Thus we say *Let's go swimming*, *He went fishing*, and likewise with *boat*, *hunt*, *golf*, *skate*, *row*, *canoe*, *walk*, *hike*, *dance*, *camp*, *ice-skate*, *ride*, and a few others. There seem to be two semantic requirements: an element of recreation or sport, rather than merely of physical activity, and an element of motion from one place to another rather than activity in one place. The former bars *Let's go marching;* the latter bars *Let's go eating* or *Let's go tennising*. All this seems obvious to us who speak English. But neither this nor any of the other many small selective categories of English is obvious to the speaker of some other language, nor are his peculiar small classes of forms obvious to us.

On the other hand, many generic categories are so extensive that every stem of some major part of speech belongs to one or another of the associated specific categories (if the generic category is selective), or is invariably inflected for one or another of the specific categories (if the generic one is inflectional).

27.2. Gender. Genders are classes of nouns reflected in the behavior of associated words. To qualify as a gender system, the classification must be exhaustive and must not involve extensive intersection: that is, every noun must belong to one of the classes, and very few can belong to more than one.

Under this definition, some languages have no gender at all. Chinese substantives (§26.2) fall into classes in terms of what measure is used when the substantive is counted, but there are so many measures (hundreds), and so many nouns used with two or more measures with different resulting meanings, that the classification is not usually thought of as a gender system. In languages where the gender system is obvious, the number of classes may be as few as two or as many as twenty or thirty. There is usually some element of semantic consistency in the system, turning on sex, animateness, size, shape, degree of abstraction, and the like, but almost always some of the gender affiliations are arbitrary.

Thus the masculine and feminine genders in Spanish, French, Italian, and Portuguese are semantically consistent in that nouns referring clearly to males are masculine, those referring clearly to females feminine; but the gender of other nouns is for the most part arbitrary. Other varieties of two-gender system occur in Dutch, the Scandinavian languages, and Algonquian. In the latter the categories are *animate* and *inanimate:* though here, also, some assignments are arbitrary, for the most part names of living things are animate in gender and others inanimate. Fijian and Tagalog show a different two-gender system, described briefly for Fijian in §27.1: appropriate labels would be *common* and *proper.*

German, Latin, Greek, and Sanskrit have three genders: in German, masculine (*der Mann* 'the man,' *der Tisch* 'the table'), feminine (*die Frau* 'the wife,' *die Erle* 'the alder tree'), and neuter (*das Weib* 'the woman,' *das Kind* 'the child,' *das Blut* 'the blood'). German nouns referring exclusively to human females are never masculine in gender, and those referring exclusively to human males are never feminine in gender; this is about as far as semantic consistency goes.

Russian has a similar three-gender system, but also, partly intersecting it, a two-way contrast of animate and inanimate. An animate noun, whatever its affiliation in the three-way system, is referred to by /któ/ 'who,' an inanimate noun by /štó/ 'what.' Also, masculine and neuter animate nouns show a feature of inflectional pattern for case different from masculine and neuter inanimates.

We may speak of gender in English either by relaxing the requirement of non-intersection of the gender-classes, or by recognizing seven genders instead of three. The cue is reference to that named by the noun with *he, she,* or *it,* or optionally with more than one of those pronouns:

> *he* only: *John, boy, man;*
> *she* only: *Mary, girl, woman;*
> *it* only: *road, street, paper;*
> *he* or *she: citizen, president, dean, doctor;*
> *he* or *it: billy-goat, ram, drake;*
> *she* or *it: nanny-goat, boat, car, ship;*
> *he, she,* or *it: baby, child, cat, dog, robin.*

Where there is a choice of pronoun, there are factors, subtle but theoretically describable, which determine it. *Baby* is usually referred to by
he or *she* if the sex is known or thought to be known, more often by *it*
if the sex is not known or the speaker does not care (as adults other than
the child's parents often do not). *Boat* is referred to by *she* if the particular
boat is large or has a name (and watercraft are most often given names
which belong to the *she*-class), but by *it* if it is both small and nameless.
In certain colloquial expressions, *she* is used for practically any noun,
breaking the associations listed above: of a truck trailer, *Back her in here;*
of any vehicle or activity, *Hold her a minute, Mac.*

Distinctions of number are often worked into gender systems. In
Russian, German, and English, gender classification applies only in
the singular: all plurals work alike (English reference merely by *they*).
In the Bantu languages, which have as many as twenty-five or thirty
genders, there is some tendency for the classes to pair off as corresponding singular and plural.

Korean, Japanese, and some of the languages of Southeast Asia have
selective and inflectional categories which are more similar to gender
systems than to any of the other types of category we shall describe:
differentiations reflecting the relative social status of speaker, addressee,
and subject of discourse. In Korean, six different types of social relationship between speaker and addressee are distinguished by choice of
verb inflectional patterns; intersecting this, certain other choices correlate with the relative social status of the speaker and the topic of
discourse.

27.3. Number. There is much semantic consistency in English number, but here, also, one finds arbitrary assignments: *wheat* is singular,
oats plural.

In Turkish, Hungarian, and Georgian there are two numbers only slightly different from our own. The "singular" refers to a specified number of items, and to just one unless added words indicate the contrary; the "plural" refers only to an indefinite plurality. If English worked this way we should say *three boy* rather than *three boys*, but otherwise choose between singular or plural just as we do (*a boy, the boy, one boy, some boys, the boys, boys*).

Classical Greek and Sanskrit have a singular and a plural much like ours, and also a *dual* which refers to just two as, often, in speaking of paired body-parts. Some languages have a four-way number system: the distinctions may be singular, dual, *trial* (exactly three) and plural (more than one, or more than three, depending on the language); or singular, dual, *paucal* (a few) and *multiple* (many). Fijian has the latter system, but only in its personal pronouns: nouns show no number at all.

27.4. Person. This generic category sorts out entities relative to the speaker (*first* person) and the addressee (*second* person). In the more familiar languages, anything other than speaker or addressee is simply *third* person, but in some languages there are further distinctions.

Thus Algonquian has a subsidiary distinction within the third person, for animates, between a "proximate" and an "obviative": the former is used for the third person nearer the center of attention, the latter for any subsidiary animate third person which may come into the discourse (§26.2). Eskimo and the Athapaskan languages have a similar arrangement.

Person and number are tied together in a very widespread distinction, not applicable in the singular, between first person *inclusive* (speaker, addressee, and perhaps others) and first person *exclusive* (speaker and others but not hearer). In Chinese this distinction is optional with personal pronouns. In the Algonquian languages and many others, the distinction is necessarily made whenever a speaker uses a first person non-singular form.

27.5. Case. Cases are inflected forms for nouns which fit them for participation in key constructions relative to verbs. Many case systems include also specific categories of other kinds—for example, the Latin genitive—but unless the system includes specific categories of the kind just described we do not call the generic category "case."

Thus the case system of Latin qualifies as such because, of all the specific categories, only one, the nominative, is appropriate for the subject position in ordinary independent subject-predicate constructions:

puer puellam amat 'the boy loves the girl,' with nominative *puer* 'boy.'
Another case, the accusative, is the only one to appear, with most verbs,
as the object: *puellam* 'girl' in the above example.

We class the Latin case system as of the *accusative type* because one
case is used for the subject of any sort of verb, while a second is used
for the object of a transitive verb. There are three other types of case
systems. Eskimo has the *ergative* type: a case which we shall call the
nominative appears for the subject of an intransitive verb and for the
object of a transitive verb, while a second case, the ergative, appears
for the subject of a transitive verb. The Latin and Eskimo systems can be
contrasted as follows:

> Accusative type:
> *The boy*(nom.) *is singing*(intr.).
> *The boy*(nom.) *is running*(tr.) *the car*(acc.).
> Ergative type:
> *The car*(nom.) *is running*(intr.).
> *The boy*(erg.) *is running*(tr.) *the car*(nom.).

A third type of case system, the *nominative* type, appears in Hindi:
a single case (by definition the nominative) appears both for the
subject of any verb and for the object of a transitive verb. The system is
a case system because there is also an inflected form of nouns which
cannot occur in either of these syntactical positions. If we consider
Latin neuter nouns as a class apart, rather than simply as nouns, then
we have another instance of a nominative type system: *hoc ebur bonum est*
'this ivory is good' with nominative *hoc ebur; ille ebur fert* 'he is carrying
ivory' with the same form *ebur.*

The *accusative-ergative* type is found in Georgian. Georgian has two
types of verbs which are used with two connected nouns: transitives
and "causatives." The distribution of the three key cases in Georgian
can then be shown as follows:

> *The car*(nom.) *is coming*(intr.).
> *The boy*(erg.) *is bringing*(caus.) *the car*(nom.).
> *The boy*(nom.) *is singing*(tr.) *a song*(acc.).

The number of cases in a system runs from two up to twenty or thirty.
Hindi has two, Latin seven, Finnish and Hungarian a much larger,

number. Cases which do not participate in the essential noun-verb syntax that marks an inflectional category as a case system have various other usages, with innumerable quirks specific to each language. Very often some of the additional cases are used where in English we use a preposition: Eskimo /qavuŋa/ 'to the south' and /qavani/ 'in the south.'

27.6. Allocation or Possession. We have seen examples from Menomini (§26.2) of a noun inflected to show the person and number of a possessor: this illustrates the generic category of allocation or possession.

In Armenian and Arabic this type of inflection is applied to words which are like English prepositions or adverbs rather than nouns. Thus a meaning like 'behind me' is expressed by a stem 'behind' inflected to specify first person singular allocation.

27.7. Subject and Object Reference. Latin verbs, in so-called "finite" forms (§27.10), are inflected to show the person and number of a subject. Similar inflection is very widespread, with various differences: for example, in Yuma the inflection shows only number of subject, not person. In many languages transitive verbs are also inflected to show the person and number of the object: thus Menomini (§22.5).

English has very limited inflection for subject-reference. Most verbs distinguish, in the present tense, only between third person singular subject (*goes*) and all others (*go*); past tense verbs and a few special verbs like *shall, can, must* show no differentiation at all; *be* shows a different two-way contrast in the past tense (*was, were*), and a three-way contrast in the present (*am, is, are*).

27.8. Voice. Voice-distinctions apply to verbs, and have to do with the relationship between the subject and the verb, the verb and its object, or the verb and some other noun tied to it in an intimate way. Latin verbs have two voices, active (*puer amat* 'the boy loves') and passive (*puer amātur* 'the boy is loved'). Greek and Sanskrit have three: active, passive, and *middle* or *medio-passive*, the latter with a more or less reflexive meaning: 'I see myself' or 'I see my hand' versus active 'I see (him)' and passive 'I am seen.'

Semantically similar distinctions are often made syntactically instead of inflectionally. Thus voice in English is not an inflectional category but is determined by the structure of the verb phrase (§23.3). Similarly, the distinction between transitive and intransitive, which is selective rather than inflectional in both Latin and English, is inflectional in some languages.

27.9. Tense, Mode, and Aspect. *Tenses* typically show different locations of an event in time: *I am eating lunch, I was eating lunch.* English verbs are inflected only for a two-way tense contrast, present and past; future time is expressed by other devices. This holds also in the other Germanic languages and in Slavic. A three-way contrast is common: past, present, and future. Sometimes there are further refinements, say immediate past versus remote past. Hopi has three tenses: one used in statements of general timeless truth ('Mountains are high'), a second used in reports of known or presumably known happenings ('I saw him yesterday,' 'I'm on my way there right now'), and a third used of events still in the realm of uncertainty, hence often where we would think of the event as in the speaker's future ('He's coming tomorrow').

Aspects have to do, not with the location of an event in time, but with its temporal distribution or contour. They show contrasts of meaning of the following sorts: 'He is singing,' 'He has been singing,' 'He sings habitually,' 'He sings repeatedly,' 'He is beginning to sing,' 'He is bringing his song to a close.' English has no inflectional aspects, but it shows two two-way aspectual contrasts by the structure of the verb phrase:

he sings	:	*he is singing*
. .		. .
he has sung	:	*he has been singing*

or again:

he sang	:	*he was singing*
. .		. .
he had sung	:	*he had been singing*

Modes show differing degrees or kinds of reality, desirability, or contingency of an event: *He is here* (fact), (*If*) *he were here* or *Were he here* (contrary to fact). Fox has a large number of modes: one of them means, in effect, 'God forbid that such-and-such should happen!' and another 'So what if it did happen! What do I care!?' Menomini has a five-way contrast largely of the mode type, though semantically there are traces of tense-like meaning also: /pi·w/ 'he comes, is coming, came' : /pi·wen/ 'he is said to be coming, it is said that he came' : /pi·ʔ/ 'Is he coming? Did he come?' : /piasah/ 'so he *is* coming after all (despite our expectation to the contrary)!' : /piapah/ 'but he was going to come! (and now it turns out that he is not!).'

An allocational inflection of nouns is sometimes intersected by an inflectional category reminiscent of tense or aspect: Potawatomi /nkəšatəs/ 'I am happy' (verb) and /nos·/ 'my father,' /nčiman/ 'my canoe' (nouns) versus /nkəšatsəpən/ 'I was formerly happy (but not now),' /nosp·ən/ 'my deceased father,' /nčimanpən/ 'my former canoe, now lost, destroyed, or stolen.'

27.10. Predication or Finiteness. Latin verbs are inflected for five formally parallel "tense-modes" (usually taken as three tenses in one mode and two in another), two aspects, and two voices. Within each combination of tense-mode, aspect, and voice, there are six forms differentiating person and number of subject. All of these forms are used at the center of clauses forming or participating in sentences of the favorite type: they are *finite* or *predicative* forms.

In addition, however, the paradigm of a Latin verb stem includes two smaller sets of forms:

(1) Semi-finite or semi-predicative forms, with less differentiation of person and number of subject and virtually none of tense-mode, used in commands. These are conventionally called "imperatives": *amā* 'love thou!' *amātē* 'love ye!' *amātō* 'do thou later love; let him later love!'

(2) Non-finite or non-predicative forms, with no distinctions of tense-mode and no indication of subject, used in clauses of certain dependent types and in some adjectivelike and nounlike ways. Three of these are the infinitives, which show aspect and voice: *amāre* 'to love' (imperfective active), *amārī* 'to be loved' (imperfective passive), and *amāvisse* 'to have loved' (perfective active). Other non-finite forms are the gerunds, participles, and supine.

It is quite common for the paradigms of verbs to involve some non-finite forms alongside the finite ones. The Menomini system is in part like that of Latin, in part quite different. The verb paradigm includes forms in four so-called "orders." In the "independent order," verbs are inflected for the five modes mentioned in §27.9, and to indicate person and number of subject and (if transitive) of object. All these forms are finite. The "imperative order" is quite like the semi-finite imperative system in Latin. The "negative order" forms are not finite: the verbs show subject and object reference, but no mode, and occur in construction with an inflected negative word which shows the mode and which is the predicative word: /kan opianan/ 'he is not coming' : /kawen opianan/ 'it is said that he is not coming' : kan-ε·ʔ opianan/ 'is he not coming?' : /kasaʔ opianan/ 'so he's not coming after all! (despite our expectation that he would)' : /kapaʔ opianan/ 'but he wasn't going to come! (yet here he is!).' Finally, "conjunct order" forms are used in dependent clauses of several sorts and in some nounlike ways: these forms differ from the Latin non-finite forms in that these also are inflected for subject and object reference.

Other words than verbs may show non-finite and finite forms. The Menomini negative word is not a verb, but, as illustrated in the preceding paragraph, has finite forms which show mode: it also has a non-predicative form /kat/ or /kan/ used in clauses in which the verb is in the independent or conjunct order. Most Menomini pronouns also have both non-predicative and predicative forms, the latter showing mode: /kenah/ 'thou,' but predicative /kenεʔ/ 'thou art the one : /kenεwen/ 'thou art said to be the one' : /kenεt/ 'art thou the one?' : /kenεsaʔ/ 'so *thou* art the one!' : /kenεpaʔ/ 'but *thou* wast to be the one!'

In a different way, Sierra Miwok nouns have predicative inflectional forms which specify the person and number of a subject which 'is' that named by the noun: 'thou art a man' based on the stem 'man'; even 'thou art my father,' based on a smaller inflected form 'my father' in turn based on the stem 'father.'

NOTES

New terms: *selective* vs. *inflectional categories; generic* vs. *specific* categories; *grammatical categories.* Terms used for grammatical categories in the treatment of many languages: *gender* (specific: masculine, feminine, neuter, animate, inanimate, common, proper); *number* (specific: singular, plural, dual, trial, paucal, multiple); *person* (specific: first, second, third; inclusive vs. exclusive first person non-singular); *case* (specific: nominative, accusative, ergative); *case-systems* (of nominative, accusative, ergative, and ergative-accusative types); *allocation* or *possession; subject-reference, object-reference; voice* (specific: active, passive, middle = medio-passive; transitive, intransitive); *tense; mode; aspect; predication = finiteness.*

28.

DERIVATION

28.1. When all inflectional affixes are stripped from the words of a language, what is left is a stock of stems. The stem which appears in the paradigm (*we*) *sing*, (*he*) *sings*, *sang*, *sung*, *singing*, (*a community*) *sing*, (*community*) *sings* may be represented as *sing-*. This stem is a single morpheme. The stem of the paradigm *singer*, *singers* is *singer-*. This stem is more than one morpheme: it includes the smaller stem *sing-* as one IC, and also an element *-er* 'agent.'

The construction involved in the composite stem *singer-* is morphological, since a bound form *-er* is involved; but it is not inflectional. Therefore (§24.1) it is derivational. Derivation, then, deals with the *structure of stems*.

28.2. Structural Classification of Stems. The stems of a language can always be classed as follows, it being understood that no one language necessarily has stems of every type, and that in some languages some of the distinctions are of little practical value:

I. *Simple stems:* consisting each of a single morpheme.

II. *Derived stems* or *derivatives*, consisting of more than one morpheme:

    IIA. *Secondary derived stems*, in which at least one IC is itself a stem:

        IIA1. *Secondary derivatives*, in which only one IC is itself a stem; the other IC is a *derivational affix*.

        IIA2. *Stem compounds*, in which both (or all) ICs are themselves stems.

    IIB. *Primary derived stems*, in which no IC is itself a stem:

        IIB1. *Primary derivatives*, in which one IC is a derivational affix; the other is a *root*.

        IIB2. *Root compounds*, in which neither IC is a derivational affix.

Most of the above can be illustrated from English:

Simple stems: *boy-*, *girl-*, *man-*, *sing-*, *red-*, *green-*, *like-*, *go-*, *hammer-chrysanthemum-*(?).

Secondary derivatives: *girlish-*, *boyish-*, *manly-*, *womanly-*, *singer-*, *actor-*, *actress-*, *likable-*, *performance-*, *befriend-*. The smaller stem which appears as one IC of a secondary derivative is the *underlying form:* in our examples, *girl-*, *boy-*, *man-*, *woman-*, *sing-*, *act-*, *actor-*, *like-*, *perform-*, *friend-*. The derivative is said to be *derived from* or *built on* the underlying form *with* the derivational affix. In our examples the affixes are *-ish*, *-ly*, *-er/-or*, *-ess*, *-able*, *-ance*, *be-*.

Stem compounds are better illustrated from Latin. *Agricola* 'farmer' has the stem *agricol-*, composed of the stem *agr-* of *ager* 'field' and the stem *col-* of *colere* 'to cultivate'; *gemellipara* 'twin-bearing' has stem *gemellipar-*, composed of *gemell-* (*gemellus* 'twin-born') and *par-* (*parire* 'to bring forth'). The inserted *-i-* (*agr-i-col-*) is an automatic connective element.

Primary derivatives: *detain-*, *retain-*, *defer-*, *refer-*, if we interpret them as containing more than one morpheme (§19.6), consist of derivational affixes *de-* and *re-* and underlying forms (roots) *-tain*, *-fer*. The two affixes occur also in secondary derivation: *deform*, *reform*. The roots recur only in other primary derivatives.

Root compounds: *telegraph*, *telephone*, *phonograph*, *photograph*, *gramophone*, *photostat* may belong in this category (§28.5).

28.3. Layers of Derivation. Our definitions of the various structural types of stems do not imply that the ICs are necessarily single forms: any IC may itself be composite.

If the underlying form in a secondary derivative is not a single morpheme, its structure is also covered by the classification. Thus the underlying form of *actress-* is the secondary derivative *actor-*, built in turn on the simple stem *act-; telegraphic-* is a secondary derivative from *telegraph-*, which is perhaps a root compound.

However, if a derivational affix or a root is composite, then its structure is not covered by the classification. Composite roots are rare, and where found the details are specific to the language, not warranting general discussion here. Composite derivational affixes are more common and can be illustrated from English.

Alteration- looks superficially like a parallel to *creation-*, *oration-*, *iteration-*, *fixation-*. The latter are secondary derivatives, built with the affix *-ion* on stems *create-, orate-, iterate-, fixate-*. But there is no stem *alterate-;* only the shorter stem *alter-*. Likewise, *damnation-, condemnation-, conservation-, formation-, information-* and many others are not matched by shorter stems ending in *-ate,* but only by still shorter ones (*damn-, condemn-, conserve-, form-, inform-*).[1] We recognized a *coalescent* affix *-ation* which consists, true enough, of two smaller affixes *-ate* and *-ion,* but which in many cases functions as a unit in secondary derivation. *Alteration-* is then a secondary derivative from the stem *alter-,* built with this coalescent affix.

28.4. Deficient Stems. Suppose, for a moment, that *alteration-* stood alone in English, as the only stem in *-ion* not matched by a shorter stem in *-ate.* In this hypothetical case we should handle the matter differently. We should insist that its ICs were *alterate-* and *-ion,* but we should not call *alterate-* a root, since it is too complex to fit well into the class of English roots. Instead, we should call *alterate-* a *deficient stem:* that is, an element which is stemlike in its structure and in further derivational patterns, but which does not participate directly in inflectional or syntactical constructions as normal stems do.

The English example is hypothetical; in Menomini we find genuine instances. The word /ni·swasa·ʔsow/ 'deuce-card' is in appearance a regular secondary derivative, with affix /-w/ 'agentive,' from what looks like a verb stem /ni·swasaʔsi-/. This apparent verb stem is in turn quite regularly built from smaller constituents, but does not happen to occur directly in inflected forms. Nor does the word /ni·swasa·ʔsow/ end with any string of affixes which might be regarded as forming a coalescent affix. We therefore call the underlying form /ni·swasaʔsi-/ a deficient stem. Its deficiency is more understandable when we learn that it would mean, if used directly in inflection, something like 'he writes himself as two, he is written as two'—neither our own way of life nor that of the Menomini is apt to present a speaker with circumstances in which he would need to express that meaning.

28.5. English Compounds. It is not always easy to tell whether a derived stem should be viewed as primary or as secondary. The exam-

---

[1] *Damnation-* and *condemnation-* include an /n/ (/dæmnéjšən/, /kàndemnéjšən/) which does not appear in the inflected forms of the underlying stem (*damn* /dæm/, *damning* /dæmiŋ/, etc.) This /n/ is part of the stem; its appearance or non-appearance is a matter of morphophonemics: see §33.1. Likewise, the difference in shape between *-ate* /éjt/ and *-at(ion)* /-éjš-/ is morphophonemic, and therefore not of concern to us here.

ples discussed just above bear witness to the difficulty. Another example is the status of such English stems as *telegraph-*, *telephone-*, and so on. Most such stems contain at least one constituent which is clearly not itself a stem: *tele-*, *phono-*, *gramo-*. But many contain one constituent which is either a stem or is the same in shape as, and similar in meaning to, some stem: *graph*, *phone*, *photo*, *stat*. Some of the constituents which are not stems seem to contain, in turn, a stem: *phono-* thus contains *phone*.

Yet English stems of the kind just dealt with are different from English *phrasal compounds*, like *blackbird*, *bluebird*, *blackboard*. The latter are a special sort of sequence of two words, with a lowering of stress on the second word (thus /blǽk+bə̀rd/): their structure is syntactical, not morphological. It seems best, for English, to bypass the theoretically definable difference between stem compounds and root compounds and speak simply of *close compounds* (*telegraph* and the like) in contrast to phrasal compounds. The important fact about elements like *tele-*, *phono-*, *photo-*, *graph-*, *phone-*, *gramo-*, *stat-* is that they occur quite freely in close compounds; whether each of them is or is not a stem then assumes secondary importance.

28.6. Part of Speech Affiliation. A stem, by definition, belongs to some part of speech. In the case of a simple stem, its part of speech is simply one of the facts about the morpheme. In the case of a derived stem, however, the part of speech to which it belongs can often be predicted in terms of one or another of its ICs. This is especially true in the case of forms built with derivational affixes.

In some languages derivational affixes fall into two sets, which have been called "restrictive" and "governing." A restrictive affix stands in an attributive relationship to the underlying stem to which it is added, and the derivative belongs to the same part of speech as the underlying stem. A governing affix stands in some other relationship to the underlying stem, and determines the part of speech of the derivative. We give examples from Eskimo, where this classification has been well worked out.

One type of restrictive affix is added only to noun stems. From 'stone' different affixes yield derivatives with such meanings as 'large stone,' 'small stone,' 'new stone,' 'old stone,' 'group of several stones,'; from 'blanket,' one obtains 'home-made blanket,' 'purchased or obtained blanket,' 'ruins or remnants of a blanket, blanket-remnants.'

A second type of restrictive affix is added only to verb stems: 'sing' yields 'sing a lot,' 'sing badly,' 'sing properly,' 'sing thoroughly,' 'sing uninterruptedly,' 'sing energetically,' 'sing repeatedly,' 'sing in the future,' 'sing in the past,' 'sing customarily.'

A third type, much rarer, is added to either noun stems or verb stems: from 'house' one gets 'only a house, nothing else'; from 'to talk,' with the same affix, one gets 'just talk, without doing anything else.'

Some governing affixes are added only to noun stems and yield larger noun stems: 'goods, property' yields 'someone or something having goods'; a place-name X yields 'inhabitant of X,' 'place near X.'

Other governing affixes build verb stems from noun stems: from 'father' one gets 'to be a father,' 'to have a father,' 'to supply with a father.'

Still others build noun stems from verb stems: 'to sing' yields 'one who has sung,' 'instrument for singing.'

Finally, some governing affixes build verb stems from verb stems: 'to hunt' yields 'to be engaged in hunting,' 'to begin to hunt.'

The classification of derivational affixes into restrictive and governing is not always useful. A more general classification, of the affixes of secondary derivation, turns on two considerations: (1) the part of speech of the underlying form, and (2) the part of speech of the derivative. Thus English *-ion* is added only to stems of classes V, AV, NV, or NAV, and yields stems of classes N, NA, NV, or NAV, usually the first of these (§26.4): *create-* (V) : *creation-* (N); *orate-* (V) : *oration-* (N); *fixate-* (V) : *fixation-* (N); but *vacate-* (V) : *vacation-* (NV); *correct-* (AV) : *correction-* (N).

The major part of speech affiliation of a derivative may be determined in one way, the membership of the derivative in one or another subsidiary stem-class in another. In Menomini, diminutivizing suffixes are added only to noun stems, and yield only nouns, but the gender (animate or inanimate) of the derivative is that of the underlying form: /ahkɛ·h/ 'kettle' is animate, and therefore /ahkɛ·hko·hsɛh/ 'little kettle, can' is animate too. Compare the situation in German, where a diminutive derivative of a noun is neuter regardless of the gender of the underlying form: *der Tisch* masculine 'the table' : *das Tischchen* neuter 'the little table'; *die Frau* feminine 'the married woman' : *das Fräulein* neuter 'the young lady'; *das Haus* neuter 'the house' : *das Häuschen* neuter 'the little house.'

NOTES

New terms: *simple stem, derivative, secondary derived stem, secondary derivative, stem-compound, primary derived stem, primary derivative, root-compound; derivational affix, underlying form, root; coalescent affix, deficient stem.* For English, *close* vs. *phrasal* compounds. *Restrictive* vs. *governing* affixes (may apply more widely than Eskimo).

Problem. Some of the English stems listed below are secondary or primary derivatives. Determine the ICs of each; class each as secondary or as primary and show why; give another example or so for each derivational affix.

roadster-, currency-, different-, deference-, sequential-, digital-, baggage-, braggart-, brassy-, breadth-, brazen-, lioness-, sluggard-, guardian-, guileless-, kingdom-, suffragette-, gusto-, hackney-, oxide-, bulbous-, cupric-, fungus-, monad-, Americanism-, Brazilian-, physicist-.

29.

SURFACE and DEEP GRAMMAR

29.1. In the preceding eight sections we have been discussing grammar largely in terms of constructions, working roughly from large to small (that is, first syntax, then inflection, and finally derivation). But the specification of the forms and constructions in a sentence does not always tell everything of grammatical relevance about the sentence. A pair of forms in a sentence which do not stand in construction with each other may nevertheless be tied together, in a rather different way.

For our first illustration of this it is best to draw on an unfamiliar language. The Chinese morpheme *kāi* has, to our way of thinking, a very wide range of meaning: 'to open' (a door, window, box), 'to turn on' (a light), 'to boil,' 'to open up for tilling' (land not previously used agriculturally), 'to break' (a fast or dietary pledge), 'to cut with' (a knife, in surgery), 'to start' (a meeting officially), 'to start, drive' (a vehicle). True, there is a common thread of meaning in all this wide range: some literal or metaphorical opening or coming-apart. However, which specific meaning emerges in a given context is a function not alone of *kāi*, but also of the context.

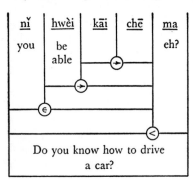

FIGURE 29.1

Thus consider the sentences diagrammed in Figures 29.1, 2, and 3. The marks at the points of junction of boxes for ICs specify the con-

246

struction-type: "ϵ" topic-comment, "$\rightarrow$" directive with director first, "$>$" attributive with attribute first, "$<$" attributive with attribute second. The first sentence means "Do you know how to drive a car?" The morphemes *kāi* and *chē* 'wheeled vehicle, car' stand in construction, the second as object of the first, and the context narrows the meaning of

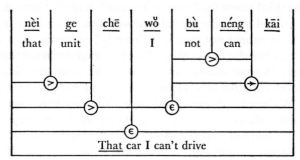

FIGURE 29.2

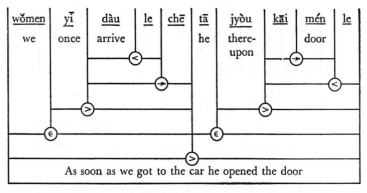

FIGURE 29.3

kāi to 'drive.' The second sentence means '*That* car I can't drive.' *Kāi* and *chē* are not here in construction with each other, but neither stands in any overriding construction with anything else, and the special meaning still emerges. The third sentence means 'As soon as we got to the car he opened the door.' *Kāi* and *chē* are still both present, though not in construction with each other; the special meaning does not emerge, however, because *kāi* is preempted by the nearby element *mén* 'door,' while *chē* is similarly preempted by *dàu* 'to arrive at.'

We see thus that the special meaning of *kāi* ('drive') does not emerge only when that morpheme stands directly in construction with *chē* 'car.' It emerges provided (1) that the two morphemes are sufficiently near to each other, and (2) that neither is in some overriding construction with some other morpheme. The first two sentences fulfil these requirements; the third meets the first requirement but not the second. The tie between *kāi* and *chē* in the second sentence is not a matter of constructions, but we cannot say that it is "merely" semantic. It is a grammatical tie: otherwise the speakers of the language could not understand each other. In some sense, though not at the most superficial grammatical level, *chē* is the *object* of *kāi* in the second sentence as in the first.

29.2. "Valence." A metaphorical terminology that suggests itself at this point is that of "valence." The morpheme *kāi*, so to speak, has a "positive" valence of a special directive kind: it seeks something in the context to seize on as its object. In the first sentence (Figure 29.1), that

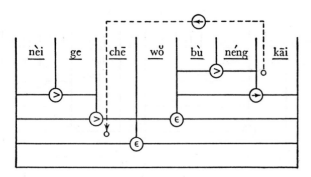

FIGURE 29.4

something is immediately at hand: the ordinary grammatical requirements of constructions and the special requirements of "valence" are fulfilled at the same time. In the second sentence (Figure 29.2) there is nothing in the immediate vicinity of *kāi* to attract its valence. The participation of *kāi* in ordinary constructions leaves it "unsaturated," and the valence has to stretch further into the context. We could diagram the result by modifying Figure 29.2 as shown in Figure 29.4. Figure 29.5 demonstrates an even more remote stretching-out for an appropriate object. Here we assume that two people have just walked up to a car and that one says the sentence: "I'll drive." The sentence contains no element anywhere fit to be the object of *kāi*, so the valence of that morpheme reaches into the non-speech environment. The figure inverts the graphic device used in comic-strips: in those, space is stolen from a picture of a situation to provide a "balloon" for what someone says; here we steal space from the portrayal of what is said to provide a "balloon" for a feature of the non-speech situation.

"Valence" is not a technical term, and the preceding discussion is also not technical: the phenomena hinted at by the discussion are not yet well enough understood for the development of a precise terminology. It is also entirely metaphorical to speak, as we have, as though

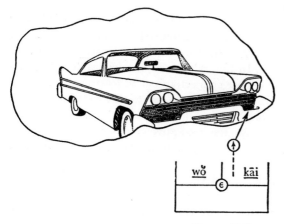

FIGURE 29.5

morphemes had "purposes": the purposes are presumably rather in the speakers and hearers. Yet the phenomena themselves, however discussed, are important. It is as though the whole network of structural relationships between forms, overlapping sometimes into the non-speech context, constituted a complex intertwining of various kinds of valences, only one layer of which is immediately apparent to the analyst. This most apparent layer constitutes, we shall say, *surface grammar*. Beneath it lie various layers of *deep grammar*, which have much to do with how we speak and understand but which are still largely unexplored, in any systematic way, by grammarians. It is the surface grammar, and it alone, which is diagrammed in Figures 29.1, 2, and 3; in Figure 29.4 the diagram shows also one item of deeper grammar.

29.3. Differences Among Languages. Languages differ as to what is on the surface and what is deep. We give three examples of such differences.

In English, as in Chinese, forms in construction with each other are usually (though not invariably) next to each other. Thus surface grammar in both languages is basically shown by linear order, while deeper connectivities between forms often cut across intervening material. But this is not true in all languages. In Latin, for example, relationships shown by linear order are largely stylistic in their semantic effects and belong in deep grammar, the surface-grammatical relationships being shown inflectionally.

Thus in English, as in Chinese, one may say either *I don't like to drive such a large car* or, in a common colloquial style, *Such a large car I don't like to drive.* The two sentences differ in surface grammar, but are much the same at deeper levels. In Latin, however, a comparable rearrangement of words modifies deeper connectivities and leaves surface grammar unaltered. The surface grammar of *puer puellam amat* and of *amat puer puellam*, both roughly 'the boy loves the girl,' is shown by the nominative case of *puer* 'boy,' the accusative case of *puellam* 'girl,' and the kind of verb *amāre* 'to love' is—a transitive verb governing an accusative object.

For the second example, consider the four English sentences (a) *She's singing*, (b) *She's running*, (c) *She's singing a hymn*, and (d) *She's running the car.* In surface grammar these go in pairs: (a) and (b) are alike (Figure 29.6), as are (c) and (d) (Figure 29.7). On deeper levels the parallelism does not hold. Thus one deeper relationship—call it *N*, for a reason which will appear in a moment—holds between *is singing* and *she* in (a) and (c), between *is running* and *she* in (b), but between *is running* and *the car* in (d). Another deeper relationship, *E*, holds between *is running* and *she* in

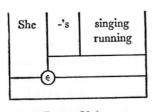

FIGURE 29.6

(d), and still a third, *A*, between *is singing* and *a hymn* in (c). The differences turn on, and reflect, a deep-level difference between *run* and *sing.* Both of these forms are freely used as verbs, and both are freely used either intransitively or transitively. But they belong to different selective categories as to types of valence. The valence tie between *sing* and its subject is the same whether the verb is followed by an object or not. The valence tie between *run* and its subject, when no object follows, is *not* the same as that between *run* and its subject when an object follows, but rather the same as that between *run* and its object when it has one.

Precisely these three types of valence, found in English only at a deep level, appear immediately on the surface in a language like Georgian. It will be more convenient to illustrate with a Georgian-like modified English, in which nouns and pronouns have three cases: nominative,

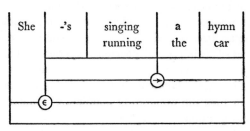

FIGURE 29.7

ending in -*N*, ergative, ending in -*E*, and accusative, ending in -*A*. In this Georgian pseudo-English, the four sentences are phrased as follows:

(a) *SheN is singing* (or *Is singing SheN*).
(b) *SheN is running* (or *Is running SheN*).
(c) *SheN is singing a hymnA* (or *Is singing SheN a hymnA* or *A hymnA is singing sheN*, etc.).
(d) *SheE is running the carN* (or *Is running sheE the carN* or *The carN is running sheE*, etc.).

The case inflection frees word-order for deep-level uses, and the alternatives given for each sentence differ only as to deep grammar.

Finally, consider English *Atoms are too small to see by any possible technique* and *They are too much in love to see clearly*. The surface grammar of the two sentences is much the same, though not identical. But cutting across the surface grammar is a difference in the deeper connections of *to see*. In the first sentence, *atoms* and *see* are related as they are in *You can't see atoms;* in the second, *they* and *see* are related as they are in *They see you*. In Latin this distinction would be shown inflectionally: *see* in the first sentence would be a passive infinitive, *vidērī* 'to be seen,' and in the second sentence an active infinitive, *vidēre* 'to see.' Certain Latinate literary styles of English maintain the distinction, or try to, by insisting on rephrasing the first sentence as *Atoms are too small to be seen by any possible technique*. This Latinizing hamstrings English, and does not tell us which form to use in a sentence like *It was too dark to see*, where the valences of *see* may well be left unsaturated or have to reach out into the non-speech context.

29.4. Differences Among Grammarians. Just as languages differ as to what is assigned to surface grammar and what is handled at deeper levels, so, not unexpectedly, equally competent grammarians often disagree in the analysis of a single language. The disagreements stem from differences of training and previous experience. They should be regarded not as conflicts demanding resolution, but as enrichments in our understanding of the language in question: both sides can be right in a dispute, in that the apparently conflicting opinions may reflect facts at different grammatical depths.

A single English example will serve. Consider the sentence *John, leaping onto the runaway horse, quickly brought it under control*. Some grammarians would assign *leaping onto the runaway horse* to the subject, as a postposed attribute to *John*. Others would take *John* alone as the subject, all the rest as predicate. There is a genuine question as to which of these ties belongs to surface grammar and which to deep; but there can be no outright acceptance of one and total rejection of the other. Both are part of the total structure of the sentence; both reflect the grammatical pattern of the language.

30.

SUBSTITUTES

30.1. In the preceding section we asserted that deeper levels of grammatical patterning are not yet well understood. To this there is one outstanding exception: the valence behavior of forms called *substitutes*.

The Chinese morpheme *kāi* 'open,' used in the examples of §29.1, has a valence of the directive type: it seeks something which can stand to *kāi* in the role of object. When substitutes have a valence (not all of

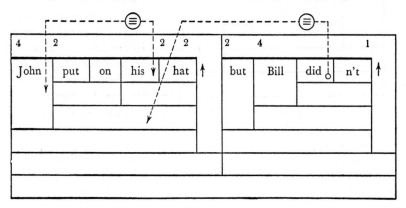

FIGURE 30.1

them do), it is invariably of the *appositive* type: we shall symbolize this as "≡". The sentence diagrammed in Figure 30.1 contains two examples. The substitutes in this sentence are the morpheme *he* (in the word *his*) and the morpheme *do* (in the word *did*). *He* refers to *John:* it is John's hat which John puts on, and it would be possible, though awkward, to paraphrase the first part of the sentence as *John put on*

253

John's hat, with no substitute. Similarly, *do* refers, as indicated in the diagram, to the whole phrase *put on his hat:* this is the action the sentence asserts Bill did not perform.

Like other valences, the appositive valence of a substitute may fail to find any appropriate form in the linguistic context, and thus be forced

into the non-speech environment. If we say *John put on her hat*, the substitute *she* (the stem of the word *her*) cannot refer to anything in the sentence, and is forced outside: see Figure 30.2. Even when we say *John put on his hat*, context may show that it is not John's own hat, but someone else's, and in this case also the valence from *his* leads into the non-speech environment.

Thus there is often some ambiguity in what is actually said, and it may or may not be eliminated by the situation in which the speaking takes place. Sometimes the ambiguities remain. The diagram in Figure 30.3 shows an instance: the valences and the listener are equally

FIGURE 30.2

unsure as to who couldn't wait for whom.

The form, if any, on which the valence of a substitute seizes is called its *antecedent*. In the first example, *John* is the antecedent of *his*, and the phrase *put on his hat* is the antecedent of *did*. In the example of Figure 30.3, the antecedent of *she* must be *Jane* or *Mary;* only the speaker knows which. The hearer knows only that, whichever it is, the other is the antecedent of *her*. The antecedent need not precede the substitute: in *Taking his hat, John strode from the room*, the antecedent *John* follows. The antecedent can be in a preceding or following sentence: *John just arrived. He brought his car.* The antecedent may occur in a sentence spoken by someone else: *Is John here yet!—No, he isn't.*

Substitutes usually used with an antecedent are called *anaphoric*.

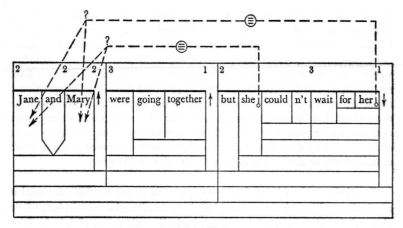

FIGURE 30.3

30.2. The Definition of Substitutes. Why is it that, as speakers of English, we can state with such confidence, when confronted with the sentence *Jane and Bill were going together but she couldn't wait for him,* that *Jane* is the antecedent of *she* and *Bill* that of *him?*

The answer lies in the inherent nature of all substitutes—the special properties by virtue of which certain grammatical forms are classed as substitutes:

A *substitute* is a form which, under certain conventional circumstances, replaces any member of a given form class.[1] Thus, in English, the substitute *I* replaces any singular noun or noun phrase, providing that this word or phrase denotes the speaker of the utterance in which the substitute is used.

(Thus if John Brown says *I'm hungry,* *I* "replaces" the singular noun phrase *John Brown;* if Mary Turner says it, *I* "replaces" *Mary Turner;* if, in a children's story, an animal, train, or toy says it, *I* "replaces" *the bear* or *the little green locomotive* or *the tin soldier.* Bloomfield's term "replace" is unfortunate: it does not imply that the "replaced" phrase might occur instead of *I,* but only that *I* in the given situation denotes exactly what the singular noun or noun phrase "replaced" would denote if it *were* used.)

The grammatical peculiarity of substitution consists in this: that the substitute replaces only forms of a certain form class, which we may call the *domain of*

[1] Paraphrased from page 247 of *Language,* by Leonard Bloomfield. By permission of Henry Holt and Company, Inc., Copyright 1933.

the substitute; thus, the domain of the substitute *I* is the English form class of singular nouns and noun phrases. The substitute differs from an ordinary linguistic form, such as *thing, person, object,* by the fact that its domain is grammatically definable, rather than requiring any sort of practical knowledge of the world in which the speakers of the language live. Whether an ordinary form, such as *thing,* can be used of this or that practical situation, is a question of meaning; the equivalence of a substitute, on the other hand, is grammatically determined. For instance, no matter whom or what we address, we may mention this real or pretended hearer in the form of a noun expression by means of the substitute *you*—and for this we need no practical knowledge of the person, animal, thing, or abstraction that we are treating as a hearer.

To reinforce the above, let us compare *thing,* not a substitute, and *it,* a substitute. There is a structural tie between *it* and a certain large form class of singular noun expressions, including *the paper, John's head, my house, bread, the sky, sex, honor, truth, a thing.* No speaker of English argues about the propriety of using *it* to refer to any of the forms listed. But one can get into all sorts of arguments as to whether that designated by a certain singular noun expression, say *sky,* or *sex,* or *honor,* or *truth,* is a "thing" or not.

In the sentence *Jane and Bill were going together, but she couldn't wait for him,* we know that *Jane* is the antecedent of *she* because the domain of *she* includes *Jane* and does not include any other form in the sentence. In the sentence *Jane and Mary were going together, but she couldn't wait for her,* there is ambiguity because both *Jane* and *Mary* belong to the domain of *she.*

In some instances we are able to determine that all the members of the domain of some substitute have a feature of meaning in common. When this is the case, then we say that the substitute has, as one feature of its own meaning, this *class-meaning* shared by all the members of its domain. More often, no such common feature can be discerned. Consider the domain of *she.* A great many members of this domain designate a single female human or obviously female animal: *Jane, Mary, my daughter, the girl on the corner, the brown-and-white cow.* If a form which does not ordinarily or exclusively have this designation occurs, in a specific context, with such meaning, then that places the word for the nonce in the domain of *she: Max,* as a nickname for a girl named *Maxine,* is referred to by *she.* But this class-meaning, 'single female human or animal,' is not an invariable part of the meaning of *she* because so many members of the domain of *she* do not share the meaning: *the old boat is on her last legs* and the like (§27.2). This situation seems to be typical: many of the members of the domain of a substitute will have some clear feature of meaning in common, but the domain will also include forms which do not share that semantic feature.

30.3. Kinds of Substitutes. There are two aspects to the behavior of any substitute: its *domain-tie*, as expounded above, and what may be called its *type*. For example, the domain-tie of *I* is its connection with the form class of singular nouns and noun phrases; its type is that it is used only when the noun expression designates the speaker of the utterance in which the substitute occurs. These two aspects generate a twofold classification for the substitutes of any language.

As to domain-ties, the most widespread variety of substitute is that which "replaces" nouns, or one or another subclass of nouns and noun phrases. When such substitutes are words or stems, rather than bound affixes, they are called *pronouns*. The chief types of pronoun in English, recurring usually with only minor modifications in other languages, are the following:

Personal: I, me, my, mine; you, your, yours; we, us, our, ours; he, him, his; she, her, hers; it, its; they, them, their, theirs. The defining characteristics of these are elementary aspects of the relation between speaker and addressee, plus certain simple features of number; in the third person singular we have also gender.

Demonstrative: this, these; that, those. The type turns on relative distance (in time or space) from the speaker and hearer, and on number.

Interrogative: who, whom, whose; what; which. The type is indicated by the label: the forms request a specification with a (non-interrogative) noun expression.

Relative: who, whom, whose; which; unstressed *that* (note the partial coincidence in form with interrogatives). The type turns on use in clauses which are attributive to the antecedent of the pronoun.

Negative: nobody, no one, nothing. These deny the validity of any member of their domain in the utterance in which they occur.

Indefinite: (1) *any, anybody, anyone, anything;* (2) *some, somebody, someone, something.* The first group imply that whatever member of the domain be chosen, the resulting utterance is intended: *Anybody knows that*—therefore John knows that, Bill knows that, you know that, and so on. The second group assert the existence of at least one member of the domain which will render the utterance valid: *Someone has been stealing my parsnips*—if not Bill, then John, or, if neither, then Dick, and so forth.

Inclusive: all, everyone, everybody, everything. In a context where John, Bill, Marie, Ronald, and Vanessa are involved, and no one else, *Everyone is here* means *John is here and Bill is here and . . . and Vanessa is here.* The inclusives differ from the first set of indefinites only in connotation.

There are also some scattered pronouns which do not come in sets: *same, other, each, one, ones.* Numbers higher than *one* have some substitute-like properties and are perhaps to be so classed.

The division into anaphoric and non-anaphoric cuts across the classification into types given above. Of the personal pronouns in English, those of the third person are anaphoric. The demonstratives are sometimes so: *Here are two eggs: this is for you, and that for me* (more often we say *this one* and *that one*). The relative pronouns are usually anaphoric: *My mother was the one who baked the cake* has relative *who* and antecedent *the one*.

Part of the classification of English pronouns into types reappears for substitutes with other sorts of domain-ties. Thus *here, now, there, then* are of the type of the demonstrative pronouns, but their domains are adverbs and adverbial expressions of time and place: *John is here : John is in the room; I did it then : I did it last night. Where, when,* and *why* are interrogatives, but not pronouns; *nowhere, never* are negative adverbial substitutes; *anywhere, somewhere,* indefinites; *everywhere, always, ever,* inclusives. *So* functions as an adverbial substitute (*He did it so : He did it poorly*), but also as a *clause substitute: If so, we must get out of here : If that is the case, we must get out of here.* The second members of pairs of correlatives (*if . . . , then . . .* ; §22.4) are clause substitutes, with the subordinate clause as antecedent: *If so, then we must leave.*

Do and its inflected forms serve as verb substitutes. *Do* is anaphoric, as shown, for example, in Figure 30.1, but is not of any of the types which have been described for pronouns. In a sentence like *He doesn't like her, but I do,* the terminal *do* has as its antecedent the phrase *does like her:* the *not* of *doesn't like her* is not part of the antecedent.

The domain of substitutive *do* excludes certain verb phrases beginning with *be, have, can, would, will,* and a few others. Thus we do not say *He is sick, but I don't,* or *He will be here at eight, and so do I.* Instead, we repeat the finite verb of the preceding part of the sentence: *He is sick, but I am not; He will be here at eight, and so will I.*

30.4. Zero Anaphora. This leads us to a phenomenon often called *zero anaphora:* the use, not of a special grammatical form, but of a special construction of ordinary grammatical forms, as an anaphoric substitute. The first part of *She couldn't have been thinking of me, could she?* contains the long verb phrase *could have been thinking.* In the second part of the sentence, the speaker does not use a special substitute form (like *do* or *did*), nor does he repeat the entire verb phrase; instead, he uses the first word of the verb phrase as a substitute for the whole. The rest of the verb phrase is "replaced by zero." Similarly, though we say *I like the big book better than the small one,* with pronoun *one* (antecedent *book*), we say *I like fresh candy better than stale,* where an adjective, *stale,* followed by no noun at all, occurs substitutively for the phrase *stale candy.*

It will be remembered that one subclass of nouns in Chinese are "measures," and that measures, unlike substantives, occur directly after numerals (§26.2). Measures are of two kinds, autonomous and auxiliary. The latter are most regularly used between a numeral and a substantive, as a grammatical aid in counting what is named by the substantive. Autonomous measures are quite regularly used without a following substantive: *jèi tyān* 'this day,' *sān shěng* 'three provinces.' When an auxiliary measure occurs without a following substantive, the construction is substitutive: *jèige rén hǎu* ('this-unit man is-good'), *kěshr nèige buhǎu* ('but that-unit is-not-good') = 'This man is good but that one is not.' Here the second occurrence of measure *ge* 'unit,' without a substantive, has the preceding substantive *rén* 'person, man' as its antecedent.

30.5. Bound Substitutes. All our examples so far have been of substitutes which are stems, whole words, or phrases. In many languages there are also bound substitutes, usually inflectional affixes. In Menomini /newiahkwan/ 'my hat' and /owiahkwan/ 'his hat,' the affixes /ne-/ and /o-/ are substitutes quite like English *my* and *his.* Menomini also has the words /nenah/ 'I' and /wenah/ 'he, she' which are personal pronouns, but not quite of the same type as those of English: /nenah/, for example, is used not merely to designate the speaker of the utterance in which it occurs (since the prefix /ne-/ is often used under these circumstances), but to *emphasize* that designation.

The variety of linkage by inflection called cross-reference (§25.5) regularly involves bound substitutes. Even the vestigial inflection of English verbs for person and number of subject—involving, usually, only the -*s* suffix for third person singular subjects in the present tense—conforms to this: the -*s* is a bound substitute.

30.6. The Surface Grammar of Substitutes. In many languages the surface grammar of substitutes which are stems or whole words is somewhat different from that of the most similar non-substitute forms. In English, for example, the contrast between *I* and *me* recurs in certain other pronouns (*he* : *him*, *she* : *her*, *we* : *us*, *they* : *them*, and, in very formal English, *who* : *whom*), but does not appear in nouns or noun phrases. The contrast between *my* and *mine* recurs only in *our* : *ours*, *your* : *yours*, *her* : *hers*, *their* : *theirs*.

In Eskimo, where ordinary nouns have a case system of the ergative type (§27.5), personal pronouns have, instead, one of the accusative type. In Georgian, where ordinary nouns have a case system of the accusative-ergative type, personal pronouns (which exist, as in Latin, only for the first and second persons) have a single undifferentiated form where a noun would appear in nominative, accusative, or ergative.

These differences in surface grammar are sometimes such that certain substitutes are properly regarded as belonging to different parts of speech from non-substitutes: thus in English, where pronouns cannot conveniently be assigned to any of the classes N, NA, NV, and so on (§26.4), and in Chinese, where demonstratives and personal pronouns constitute two of the five subclasses of the major class of nouns (§26.2). In Japanese, on the other hand, there is apparently no surface-grammar reason to set personal pronouns apart from the class of nouns. And in English, substitutive *do* is in the first instance simply a verb among other verbs.

NOTES

New terms: *substitute; antecedent, anaphoric; domain* (and *domain-tie*) and *type* of a substitute; *class-meaning* of a substitute (if any substitutes actually have one); *pronoun, clause substitute; bound* substitute; "*zero*" *anaphora*. For English, and with varying applicability to other languages: *personal, demonstrative, interrogative, relative, negative, indefinite,* and *inclusive* types.

A recent and insightful discussion of substitutes and certain related matters is Jakobson 1957.

31·

THE GRAMMATICAL CORE

31.1. Comparing Grammatical Systems. It is not too difficult to compare the phonemic systems of two languages: §11 showed in a sketchy way how this can be done. It is much harder to compare grammatical systems, because they are so complex. Yet it is clear that some differences between grammatical systems are much more important, for purposes of such comparison, than others.

Consider, for example, the words *tea* and *write*, *he* and *she*. In present-day Menomini, there are words for 'tea' and 'write'; in the Menomini of 1700 there were not. Yet Menomini is hardly closer to English in its grammatical system today than it was in 1700. And if we could delete the words *tea* and *write* from English, the system manifested by the remainder would not essentially differ from English as it actually is. On the other hand, Menomini does not now have, nor did it have in 1700, any pair of forms comparable to English *he* and *she*. This is a systematic difference of real importance. If we could delete the words *he* and *she* from English, or replace the two by a single word, the system of the modified language would be markedly changed.

Roughly, then, the total stock of elementary forms of a language can be split into two unequal portions: *tea*, *write*, and all other grammatically "unimportant" forms go into one portion (by far the larger), while *he*, *she*, and all other grammatically "important" forms go into the other. The deletion of any one or two forms from the first portion would leave the grammatical system of the language essentially unchanged; the deletion of even a single item of the second kind would have drastic consequences. Equally drastic consequences could not be

261

achieved by tinkering with the first portion unless we deleted all the members of some large form-class.

By way of illustration, here are two English sentences which have certain features in common despite their differences. The reason for the slightly poetic style will be apparent in a moment:

'Twas morning, and the merry sunbeams did glitter and dance in the snow; all tinselly were the treetops, and the happy fairies frolicked.

'Twas stormy, and the tall pines did quiver and tremble in the gale; all dark were the streets, and the weary villagers slept.

These two sentences are built by clothing one and the same grammatical "skeleton," as it were, with two different kinds of "flesh." In part, the skeleton could be indicated simply by listing, in order, the grammatically important forms which are shared by the two sentences, with blanks for the flesh-words. In part, it could be indicated via an empty-box diagram of the common IC-structure of the two sentences. In Figure 31.1 we combine these two devices, by filling in such boxes of the diagrams as contain skeletal forms, but leaving those for flesh-forms empty. Intonation is left out of account. Some of the constructions are marked as to type: "ε" stands for predicative with topic first, "϶" for the same with topic second; "+" for additive; ">" for attributive with attribute first, "<" for the same with attribute second; "→" for directive.

It was just this grammatical skeleton which Lewis Carroll clothed with flesh in the form of nonsense-syllables in the first stanza of *Jabberwocky:*

'Twas brillig, and the slithy toves
Did gyre and gimble in the wabe;
All mimsy were the borogoves,
And the mome raths outgrabe.

(Humpty Dumpty explains that *outgrabe* is the past tense of a verb *outgribe.*) When Alice heard this stanza she said:

"Somehow . . . , it seems to fill my head with ideas—only I don't know exactly what they are!"

To a large extent, Alice's unrecognizable "ideas" were just the abstract framework of relationships which is shown in Figure 31.1. The framework itself asserts nothing about anything, but it is familiar to Alice, and to us, because as we speak English we constantly use bits of it in utterances which *do* purport to deal with the world around us. We can leave to philosophers the argument whether the abstract relationships

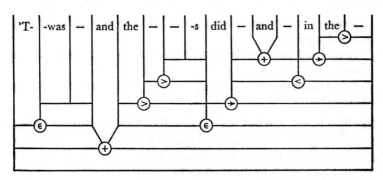

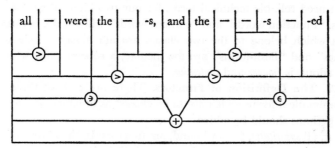

FIGURE 31.1
The syntactical connection of the two halves graphed separately above is not clear: perhaps additive, or perhaps, structurally, there are two sentences.

themselves have any sort of existence in the world outside of speech. Whatever they may decide, it is clear that the "meaning" of a word like *and* or *the*, or of a construction like that of attribution, is a very different sort of thing from the meaning of a word like *morning* or *sunbeam*. One might at first suspect that the "meaning" of *and* is no more abstract or peculiar than that of *unicorn*, but this is probably not the case. *Unicorn* designates a horselike or antelopelike mammal with a single horn in the middle of its forehead, while *and* does not designate anything. (It is linguistically quite irrelevant that no unicorns exist.)

Having pulled the flesh from the bones and examined the latter, we must also see what the flesh looks like when not draped over the skeleton. Since we have already been exposed to the flesh of the first two sentences, in the structure shown by the skeleton, we add a third set of flesh-forms which will also fit the framework:

> morning merry sunbeam glitter dance snow tinselly treetop happy fairy frolic;
> stormy tall pine quiver tremble gale dark street weary villager sleep;
> father happy child jump shout yard ready present birthday festivity begin.

The effect is easier to feel than to describe—like an extreme variety of headline English, or like certain types of Chinese poetry (particularly in word-by-word English translation), where many of the structural relationships are left to the reader's imagination.

We need reliable technical terms for our two kinds of grammatical forms. "Function words" and "content words" will not do, because the forms which belong to the two classes are not always whole words. "Bones" and "flesh-forms" are too jocular; a soberer pair, which we shall adopt, is *functor* and *contentive*.

31.2. The Definition of Functors. There are at least three types of grammatical forms which are to be classed as functors, and a fourth type perhaps should be added.

First, all *substitutes*, free or bound, are functors. In the abstract framework of Figure 31.1, the substitutes are *it* ('*t* in '*twas*) *all*, *the*, and the inflectional affixes in *was*, *were*.

Second, all *markers*, pure and impure, are functors. In the example, the markers are *was* (the stem: marker of connective construction), *and*, *do* (in *did*), *in*.

Third, all *inflectional affixes* are functors. In the example, the inflectional affixes are *-s* (plural), *-ed* (past tense), and the special person-number inflectional indications in *was* and *were*.

As we see, some morphemes are functors on more than one basis: the inflectional affixes in *was* and *were* are also bound substitutes.

Fourth, it may be that abstract governing derivational affixes should be counted as functors. It will be remembered (§28.6) that a derivational affix is governing if it determines the part of speech of the derivative built with it. Such an affix is abstract if it does little or nothing else —that is, if it adds no other discernible element of meaning to the underlying form. This can be difficult to judge. If we do not insist on unattainable precision, then we might regard the *-y* of *slithy* and *mimsy* (in the Lewis Carroll original) as a functor: this suffix makes adjectives (*creamy, milky, watery, swishy, gluey*) and seems not to add much meaning of its own.

31.3. The Grammatical Core of a Language. We can now return to the problem that was posed at the beginning of §31.1.

The essential grammatical tenor of a language, and the key differences between the grammatical systems of different languages, lie in what we shall call the *grammatical core*. By this we mean, for any language,

    (1) its part-of-speech system;
    (2) its grammatical categories;
    (3) its functors;
    (4) its construction-types and constructions.

The grammatical core of a language plays much the same role relative to the whole grammatical system that our skeleton of abstract relationships, depicted in Figure 31.1, plays relative to the various full sentences built on it. The grammatical core can be described using not more than a few hundred contentives—just enough to serve as examples of how all other contentives work too. A language can (and does) acquire new contentives, and lose old ones, without changing its essential machinery; so long as the core remains unaltered, the language continues to operate in much the same way as before. Similarly, an individual speaker of a language masters its grammatical core fairly early in life, and from that time on there is little change of pattern worth talking about, though he constantly acquires new contentive vocabulary, and sometimes ceases to use words or phrases because he outgrows them (adolescent slang) or because conditions change (automobiles replace the horse and buggy).

The grammatical core plays an important role in effective foreign-language teaching. Apart from pronunciation and morphophonemic difficulties, which vary greatly depending on the language to be learned and the native language of the learner, the chief obstacle to the mastery of a foreign language is the difference between its grammatical core and that of the learner's own language. The main reason for the customary restriction of vocabulary (that is, contentives) in elementary foreign-language-learning materials is not that vocabulary is itself hard—indeed, vocabulary is certainly the easiest phase of a foreign language to learn. The reason is rather that there is no point in learning large numbers of contentives until one knows what to do with them. After the grammatical core has been mastered, the acquisition of new vocabulary hardly requires formal instruction. It can be done by reading or speaking the language.

Those quasi-linguistic systems which we call *logic* and *mathematics* stem from the grammatical cores of languages. Just as the abstract grammatical framework diagrammed in Figure 31.1 asserts nothing about the world around us, so no purely mathematical or logical proposition says anything about anything—it is an empty vessel, into which one can place any contents that will fit. Logic and mathematics represent, in the first instance, a discarding of many of the complexities of the grammatical core of any real language, and then an ultimately vast network of additional abstract relationships built up on this base. To a considerable extent, the central features of logic and mathematics are features shared by the grammatical cores of many or most languages: the history of logic from Aristotle down to the present represents a succession of eliminations of features which proved to be too specific to a particular language. As a result, logical and mathematical works are more accurately translatable from one language to another than is any other type of discourse.

NOTES

New terms: the *grammatical core; functors, contentives*. *Abstract* governing derivational affixes.

The illustrative use of *Jabberwocky* is taken from Fries 1952, who gives credit for the device to Aileen Traver Kitchin.

Fries (1952 and earlier works) has been most insistent on the functor-contentive contrast. Something like this contrast is recognized by such modern logicians as Carnap 1937 and Quine 1951; see, especially, the first fifty-odd pages of the latter work, in which Quine derives his elementary terms for symbolic logic from an analysis of certain English functors. The logician's contrast is not directly transferable to linguistics because his procedure is not empirical, as the linguist's must be.

Problem. The reader who knows a language other than English fairly well can profit by devoting a few hours to a comparison of their grammatical cores. A full-scale comparison, of course, would require years of work.

MORPHOPHONEMIC SYSTEMS

32.

MORPHOPHONEMICS

32.1. In the past sections (§§17–31) we have surveyed the ways in which grammatical systems work. This means that the smallest units of concern to us have been morphemes. We have been concerned with the ways in which morphemes are put together into utterances; but we have had no interest in the phonemic shapes which represent the morphemes.

For example, in §19.5 we listed five English words, *bought, went, paid, sold,* and *sang,* and stated that each consists of two morphemes: one, respectively, was asserted to be the verb stem *buy, go, pay, sell,* and *sing,* while the other, common to all five, was asserted to be the past tense morpheme. We made no mention at all of the obvious differences between the phonemic shapes representing these various morphemes in the different words, because at the time it would have been beside the point to do so.

Now, however, we are ready to concentrate on the phonemic shapes which represent morphemes. There are morphemes which are represented in all occurrences by a single phonemic shape: for example, *pay,* represented by /péj/ in *pays, paid, paying, payer, payee, payment,* and so on, as well as in the whole word *pay.* If all the morphemes of a language were like this, then the morphophonemics of the language would be trivial. But there are complications in every language. Thus, in English, the past tense morpheme is represented by a suffixed /d/ in *paid,* but by a combination of infixed /ow/ and suffixed /d/ in *sold,* and in various other ways in *bought, went, sang. Sell* is represented by /sél/ in most contexts, but by /s..l-/ when accompanied by the past-tense morpheme

(/s.´.l-/ plus /...ow...-d/ yields /sówld/); *sing* is usually /síŋ/, but is also represented by /s.´..ŋ/, into which fit infixed representations of certain inflectional morphemes, to yield *sang, sung.*

The fact of multiple representation of single morphemes gives rise to one aspect of morphophonemics, which in turn has two sides: (1) the methods by which an investigator attempts to decide which shapes are to be taken as representations of which morphemes; (2) the different types of relationships between representations.

Beyond this, there are two other aspects of morphophonemics deserving discussion: (3) the typical shapes of representations (in any one language) and the economy of utilization of the available phonemic arrangements; (4) the direct semantic effects of phonemic shapes. In the present section we shall deal with (1) and with the simplest parts of (2); in the following three sections we shall take up the rest of (2), (3), and (4).

32.2. The Terminology of Morphophonemics. When a morpheme is represented sometimes by one phonemic shape and sometimes by another or others, we say that the shapes stand in *alternation* with each other, or, more briefly, that the morpheme *manifests* alternation. Each representation is a *morph;* all the morphs which represent some given morpheme are called *allomorphs* of that morpheme. Thus /sél/ and /s...l/ are both allomorphs of the morpheme {*sell*}. This statement also illustrates a graphic device by which we shall differentiate, in this and the next few sections, between mention of a morpheme and mention of a morph: in mentioning a morpheme, we shall enclose some label for it between braces.

It is in many cases useful to apply the terminology of alternation in a uniform way to all the morphemes of a language, including even those which are represented only in a single way phonemically. We manage this by a verbal trick, saying, for example, that English {*pay*} manifests *invariant alternation*—being represented, in all environments, by a single allomorph /péj/.

Two morphs are distinct if they differ in phonemic shape, as /sél/ and the /s...l/ of *sold*. They are also distinct if they are allomorphs of different morphemes, even if they are identical in shape: /sél/ representing {*sell*} and /sél/ representing {*cell*} thus count as two different morphs.

Sometimes it is necessary to deal with alternations in shape of forms larger than morphemes—for example, of words. Our examples of this, however, will not require any additional terms.

32.3. Sporadic Alternation. Certain kinds of alternation are systematic and predictable, and require to be described in any treatment of a language which shows them. There is another sort, however, which is harder to handle, and which we shall discuss first, mainly in order to get it out of the way.

The best approach to *sporadic alternation* is to point out a couple of the mechanisms by which an instance may arise. Suppose we find the speakers of a language neatly divided, by some geographical line of demarcation, into two groups: those on one side of the line pronounce a certain word in one way, while those on the other side pronounce it in another way. To be concrete, let us say that the word is English *root*, and that the two pronunciations are /rúwt/ and /rút/. Now so long as the difference is correlated with dialects, we do not speak of sporadic alternation. But situations of this kind are not stable. Some people, in due time, hear both /rúwt/ and /rút/, and sooner or later some speakers acquire both habits of pronunciation, using now the one and now the other in a quite random and unpredictable way. When this has happened, we have sporadic alternation.

The difficulty with this sort of sporadic alternation is in being certain that a pair of forms constitute a genuine example. Many speakers of English use both *hoist* and a more colloquial form *heist* (/hájst/); this pair has the same origin as that described above for /rúwt/ and /rút/. But in this case there has been a semantic differentiation: *hoist* and *heist* are not two shapes of a single morpheme, but different morphemes, with similar but distinguishable meanings. Any proffered example of sporadic alternation of this source is under suspicion, for there may be some differentiation of meaning which the investigator has missed.

Another source of sporadic alternation yields firmer examples. Suppose someone sets out to say *That clock's an hour fast*, but that, since he is speaking in our normal sloppy way, he slips and says (in objective physical terms) *That glock's an hour fast*. We will probably understand his utterance. But we may understand without even noticing the deviation from normal pronunciation, or we may understand despite the fact that we hear and note the deviation. If we do not notice it, then phonemically the speaker has said what he planned to say. But if we notice it, then the event involves an actual substitution of the phoneme

/g/ for the phoneme /k/. And in the latter case, it follows that we have an occurrence of the unusual phonemic shape /glák/ representing the morpheme {*clock*}, instead of its customary representation /klák/. Every one of the "normal" allomorphs of every morpheme in a language is thus surrounded by a vaguely defined family of phonemically similar shapes which, in a random way, sometimes occur in its stead.

The unpredictability of such sporadic alternation sets it off as very different from the kinds of alternation with which we shall deal in §33. And in our further discussion of morphophonemics we shall set this special variety of alternation aside and speak only in terms of "normal" allomorphs.

32.4. The Investigator's Problem. A neatly-packaged description of a language can set forth its phonemics, its morphophonemics, and its grammar in separate compartments. But a description can only be produced by the hard work of trained investigators, and the guise in which the language appears to them, as they set out on their analytical task, is not neatly packaged at all. They are forced to sort out bits of evidence, collating by trial and error, until the facts begin to emerge.

The investigator cannot directly observe morphemes. What he can discover in the first instance is morphs. (Cf. §16.) His problem is then that of deciding which morphs are properly to be interpreted as allomorphs of the same morpheme. The way in which he solves this problem will determine both his ultimate portrayal of the grammatical system of the language, and his eventual description of its morphophonemics. Grammar and morphophonemics are separate subsystems of a language, but grammatical and morphophonemic *analysis* necessarily proceed hand in hand.

The operating assumptions involved in this joint analysis have only in part been codified; there is as yet nothing like complete agreement among specialists. However, there are a few principles which are almost universally accepted. The three listed and discussed below can profitably be compared with the first three criteria for phonemic analysis listed in §12.3:

(I) Two morphs cannot be allomorphs of a single morpheme if they contrast. For example, *stricken* and *struck* both appear to be past participles of the verb *strike*, one formed like *ridden* from *ride*, the other like *stuck* from *stick*. But *stricken* and *struck* cannot be morphemically identical; so, if they are based on the same stem, the inflectional affixes are necessarily different morphemes.

(II) Two morphs cannot be allomorphs of a single morpheme unless they have the same meaning. Since determinations of meaning are at best rough, this criterion represents a possible source of disagreement, and yet in practice uncertainties are not numerous. The /s/ of *cats*, the /z/ of *dogs*, and the /ən/ of *oxen* are all similar enough in meaning that we do not hesitate to assign them to a single morpheme if the other criteria are satisfied. It is possible that the /ən/ of *oxen* is not, in fact, the same morpheme as the /z/ of *dogs;* but if this is true, the decisive factor is not divergence of meaning. On the other hand, the separate word /plúrəl/ also means 'more than one,' but there is obviously a difference in meaning between the affixes and the separate word, at least in that the latter has all sorts of connotations which the affixes do not carry.

(III) Even if other criteria are satisfactorily met, one does not assign two morphs to a single morpheme unless the resulting morpheme fits into the emerging grammatical picture of the language in a sensible way. One does not simply strive to see how small a stock of morphemes can be ascribed to the language by clever manipulation of one's data.

Thus one might find two ostensibly different derivational affixes, say -*dom* (as in *kingdom*) and -*y* (*duchy*), of "identical" meanings, and with such distribution that neither occurs with any stem with which the other has been found. But it would complicate our view of the language, rather than simplify it, to insist that the two affixes are only different allomorphs of a single morpheme. Many derivational affixes have a highly limited distribution at best, and are not freely used in coining new derivatives. Yet new derivatives *are* occasionally coined even with the most limited affix, and the lack of contrast between the two suffixes in question may be only apparent, or only temporary or accidental.

On the other hand, though *went* and *go* differ from each other in shape just as radically as do -*dom* and -*y*, recognizing *went* as the past tense of *go* makes good sense. There are endless numbers of verbs in English, and almost invariably they have a past tense—for the most part formed quite regularly from the stem by a suffixed morpheme. *Went* must be a past tense form, since it works syntactically like other forms which undeniably are; *go* has to be a present tense form for a similar reason. If we go in the face of this evidence and keep *go* and *went* apart, then we are left with a forlorn verb *go* which lacks a past tense, and a forlorn past tense form *went* which lacks a present tense.

The three criteria just described are not enough, for any single language, to yield determinate results. They represent a minimum frame of reference for handling data in all languages, but for any given language it is always necessary to seek further criteria of a realistic and fruitful sort. The achievement of a uniform methodology for application to all languages lies in the future.

NOTES

New terms: *morph, allomorph; alternation; invariant* and *sporadic* alternation. Note the special use of braces { }.

The simultaneous process of grammatical and morphophonemic analysis is sometimes called *morphemics*. This term thus applies to a *kind of procedure*, and does not (as do "grammar" and "morphophonemics") label a phase of language design.

33·

TYPES of ALTERNATION

33.1. Internal and External Sandhi. Morphophonemic alternations are subject to a number of different classifications, some of them partly intersecting each other. We take these classifications up one by one.

In many languages, the morphemes which enter into a single word vary in their phonemic representation depending on the other morphemes present in the same word; at the same time, the shapes of whole words vary depending on their position relative to each other and on the shapes of adjacent words. The most convenient way to describe the alternations involved is in terms of *internal* and *external sandhi;* the term *sandhi* (pronounced /sə́ndij/ in English, literally 'a placing together') was used for just these phenomena by the ancient Hindu grammarians. We give a simple illustration from Fox.

Every Fox word has, potentially, two shapes. One shape ends in a short vowel; the other shape is identical except that the terminal short vowel is missing. The fuller shape appears before pause, or before a word which begins with a consonant; the shorter shape appears before a following word beginning with a vowel. Thus 'and' is both /mi·na/ and /mi·n/: one says /ihkwe·wa mi·na šeka·kwa/ 'the woman and the skunk,' but /ihkwe·wa mi·n anemo·ha/ 'the woman and the dog.' The short form can be predicted if one knows the full form. The full form cannot be predicted from the short form, since there are four different short vowels in the language and one would not know which to add. For this reason we call the fuller form the *base form.* The habit just described is one of external sandhi only; when, within a word, vowels of successive morphemes come together, more complicated things happen.

One simple fact of internal sandhi in Fox is that every morpheme which ends in /t/ (this is a short way of saying "every morpheme represented on some occasions by an allomorph ending in /t/") has potentially a matching allomorph ending instead in /č/. The latter appears, instead of the former, whenever the next element in the word begins with /i/, /i·/, or /j/. Thus /pja·te/ 'if he comes' and /pja·či/ 'that he comes' both contain, after the stem {/pja·-/}, an inflectional morpheme {/t/}; in the first, this is followed by a further inflectional element represented by shape /e/, whereas in the latter the added element is represented by /i/, calling for the replacement of /t/ by /č/.

This habit, in its turn, is purely one of internal sandhi: the conditions for the replacement cannot even be met between successive words. One has to imagine that all the habits of internal sandhi apply "before" any of those of external sandhi: thus, if the word /pja·či/ stands in a phrase before a word beginning in, say, /a/, the /i/ drops by external sandhi, but the /č/ remains even though the /i/ which elicits it is not spoken.

A contrast similar to that between external and internal sandhi is often found within words, some successive morphemes being bound together more loosely than others. In Nootka and Eskimo, for example, inflectional suffixes elicit one sort of variation in shape of the preceding stems, while derivational suffixes elicit a different and more complex kind. Something like this holds in English. The suffixes of noun and verb inflection, the adverbializing -ly, and the derivational affix -er 'agentive' are added more loosely; the comparative and superlative -er and -est, and most derivational suffixes, are added more tightly. Thus stems like damn-, bomb-, long- 'not short' and long- 'be desirous' have full shapes /dǽmn-/, /bámb-/, /lóŋg-/, /lóŋg-/. The final consonants are dropped when nothing follows in the same word, and also when "looser" suffixes follow: damning /dǽmiŋ/, bomber /bámər/, longing /lóŋiŋ/ 'desire,' longer /lóŋər/ 'one who longs.' They are retained before "tighter" suffixes: damnable /dǽmnəbəl/, bombard /bàmbárd/, longer /lóŋgər/ 'more long.' Similarly, when the derivational prefix a- (as in acquire, attest) precedes the stem know-, a latent initial /k/ in the latter appears (acknowledge /æknáliǰ/) which is otherwise omitted (know /nów/, knowledge /náliǰ/).

33.2. Optional External Sandhi. This is a phenomenon akin to ordinary external sandhi, but radically different from the latter in that it is not morphophonemic. We can illustrate from English.

Consider the three English sentences *John's going*, *Jack's going*, and *Rose's going*. In these there occurs the *short-form* of the word *is*, although it appears in three phonemically distinct shapes: /z/, /s/, and /əz/. Once we know that the short-form of *is* is to be used, then we can predict which of these three shapes will represent it, since the selection depends entirely on the phonemic shape of the preceding word.

However, we do not always use the short-form. It is also possible to say *John is going*, *Jack is going*, *Rose is going*. As a result, the pair of utterances *John is going* and *John's going* stand in contrast with each other: there must be not a morphophonemic but a grammatical difference between them. One of them, at least, must include some morpheme not present in the other.

No one knows exactly how to interpret pairs of this sort. The bulk of the grammatical structure of *John is going* and *John's going* is the same, a fact which our treatment must not conceal. One suggestion is that the difference be ascribed to a "style morpheme" with the meaning "deliberate and careful speech." The presence of this morpheme in *John is going* is signaled not just by the /i/ of *is*, but by the appearance of the full form, phonemically with preceding juncture, instead of the short form. In the second of a pair like

> *He's gonna find 'er.*
> *He is going to find her.*

the same style morpheme occurs just once, stretched through the whole utterance (in the manner of an intonational morpheme), rather than three times. Other solutions have also been proposed, but none of them—including this one—is entirely convincing.

33.3. Automatic and Non-Automatic Alternation. It has been noticed that some alternations are such that if they did not take place, the phonemic pattern of the language would be different from what in fact it is. Our example of Fox external sandhi will serve here. Nowhere within a Fox phrase do sequences of vowels occur; this is a fact of the Fox phonemic pattern. Now if, in the expression meaning 'the woman and the dog,' one used the full form of /mi·na/ 'and,' giving /ihkwe·wa mi·na anemo·ha/, one would have two adjacent vowels within a phrase.

Alternations of this kind are called *automatic*. One of the alternate shapes is the *base form*, and the other or others are said to replace the base form under specific conditions where, otherwise, there would be an arrangement of phonemes contrary to the phonemic pattern of the language. It is to be noted that the term "automatic" refers to the fact that the base form is replaced, but not to the particular replacement which is made. Thus, in Fox, the phonemically impossible sequence of two vowels could be avoided just as well in the expected sequence of /mi·na/ and /anemo·ha/ by inserting an /h/, or indeed any other consonant, between the two /a/'s, or by dropping the initial vowel of the second word. These other devices are in fact not used, but it remains true that there is nothing about the *phonemic* system of the language which renders the actually-used device any more natural than one of these alternatives.

Non-automatic alternation is any alternation which is not automatic. The replacement of Fox /t/ by /č/ in internal sandhi, though quite regular (see below), is not automatic, because the phoneme-sequence /ti/ occurs: /nekoti/ 'one.'

33.4. Regular and Irregular Alternation. An alternation is *regular* if it is what occurs most frequently under stated conditions, any other alternation which occasionally occurs under the same conditions then being *irregular*. Most automatic alternations are regular, though exceptions are not logically impossible. But some non-automatic alternations are regular too, as witness the Fox /t/-/č/ situation just mentioned.

The English noun-plural morpheme is represented by a number of different shapes: /z/, /s/, and /əz/; /ən/ in *oxen;* infixed /e/ in *men;* a scattering of others. The regular pattern involves /z/, /s/, and /əz/; these three stand in automatic alternation with each other, the base-form being /z/. Replacement of this by any other shape is irregular: e.g., in *oxen, men, children, data, phenomena, oases, gladioli,* and so on. It would be impossible to make a complete list of the noun stems which follow the regular pattern, but it is quite possible to approach an exhaustive listing of the irregular ones.

Regularity is a matter of degree. No other verb in English works like *go* in forming the past tense (*went*); indeed, it is hard to see what one could do with a verb like *come* or *see* or *find* to make its past-tense formation parallel to that of *go*. Such an isolated pattern constitutes the high-water-mark of irregularity, called *suppletion* or *suppletive alternation*. A less irregular pattern is that of the seven common verbs which, in forming the past tense, lose everything but the initial consonant or consonant cluster of the stem, add /ɔ/, and then the past tense morpheme in the shape /t/: *brought, thought, sought, taught, bought, caught, fought.* Any pattern for which two examples can be adduced is at least slightly less irregular than one for which only an isolated instance exists.

33.5. Phonemically and Morphemically Conditioned Alternation. In English the indefinite article occurs in two different shapes, conventionally written *a* and *an.* The choice between these shapes depends in no wise on what kind of word (grammatically speaking) comes next: in *a man,* a noun follows; in *a rich man,* an adjective; in *a thinking man,* the ing-form of a verb; in *a quickly-growing movement,* an adverb; compare also *a not-to-be-forgotten experience, a rah-rah-shouting crowd, a to-the-hills movement.* The only relevant feature of what follows is the nature of the first phoneme of the next word: if it is a consonant, the article appears in shape *a*; if it is a vowel, the article appears in shape *an.* The alternation between *a* and *an* is therefore said to be *phonemically conditioned.*

On the other hand, the alternation between /wájf/ (in the singular *wife*) and /wájv/ (in *wives*) for the morpheme {*wife*} is *morphemically conditioned.* The shape /wájv/ is required when the noun-plural morpheme follows. There are other morphemes which appear in the same shapes (/s/ and /z/) as the noun-plural morpheme, but none of these requires the alternate shape /wájv/: *my wife's hat, my wife's coming with me,* and *my wife's never been there* all show /wájf/.

Morphemically conditioned alternation is always non-automatic; automatic alternation is always phonemically conditioned. There are also phonemically conditioned alternations which are not automatic. The English *a/an* alternation is of this sort. Use of *a* rather than *an* before a vowel would not yield a phonemically impossible sequence: witness (*the*) *idea isn't* (/ajdíjə+ízənt/), (*a*) *soda always* . . . (/sówdə+ólwijz/). Likewise, use of *an* rather than *a* before a consonant would not yield a prohibited phonemic arrangement: witness (*John*) *and Mary,* where the unstressed alternant of *and* is usually /ən/, identical with the usual pronunciation of *an.*

33.6. Base Forms. Several times in the preceding survey we have made mention of "base forms." The recognition of one representation of a morpheme (or of a larger form, say a word) as base form is sometimes merely a matter of descriptive convenience, but sometimes it has deeper significance.

Thus in the case of *wife : wives,* we take /wájf/ as base form. The reason is obvious. In describing the alternation we must state, somehow, the conditions which elicit each alternate shape. The conditions which call for the shape /wájv/ are easy to state: when the noun-plural morpheme follows, this shape occurs. To say that /wájf/ is the base form means nothing more than that this is the shape which appears *except* under the specific conditions which we itemize. It would be much more complicated to work in the other direction, describing the conditions which call for /wájf/ and saying that, except under these conditions, the shape /wájv/ appears.

This is a good practical working principle, but in some cases other considerations take precedence. If an alternation is automatic, we have no option. The base form in automatic alternation is the alternant which appears in those environments in which the phonemic habits of the language do not force the choice. In English, the phonemic shapes /z/, /s/, and /əz/ all occur after a vowel: *seize* /síjz/, *cease* /síjs/, and *ideas* /ajdíjəz/ show the three after the vowel /íj/. When the noun plural morpheme follows a noun stem ending in a vowel, it appears in shape /z/: *boy* : *boys* /bój/ : /bójz/; *fee* : *fees* /fíj/ : /fíjz/; and so on. So far as phonemic habits are concerned, the noun plural morpheme could be represented in this environment by /s/ or by /əz/, but it is not. /z/, then, is the base form. /z/ is replaced by /s/ after voiceless consonants after which /z/ is phonemically impossible: *cliffs, myths, cops, tots, clocks*. It is replaced by /əz/ after six consonants after which neither /z/ nor /s/ is phonemically possible: *matches, judges, passes, wishes, buzzes, rouges*. If we attempt, instead, to set up either /s/ or /əz/ as the base form, then the replacement of either of these by /z/ after a vowel-final stem turns out not to be automatic. The discovery that an alternation is automatic, and the discovery of the base form, go hand in hand, each implied by the other.

It can thus happen that the base form in some instances is considerably rarer than its replacements. Indeed, in some instances the most conveniently recognized base form never actually occurs; under these conditions we call it a *theoretical base form*. We can illustrate from Latin. Consider the nouns *rēx* /re·ks/ 'king,' genitive *rēgis, lūx* /lu·ks/ 'light,' genitive *lūcis* /lu·kis/, and *nix* /niks/ 'snow,' genitive *nīvis* /ni·wis/. The stems of these three nouns can be set up with base forms /re·g-/, /lu·k-/, and /nigw-/. The first two of these are not theoretical: /lu·k-/ occurs, for example, in both the nominative and the genitive singular, while

/re·g-/ occurs in the genitive singular (the change from /g/ to /k/ before the /s/ of the nominative is then automatic, since the word-final cluster /-gs/ is impossible). But the base form /nigw-/ does not occur anywhere in the inflection of the noun. In the nominative, where /-s/ follows, the /w/ is automatically lost between consonants, and the /g/ is replaced by /k/ just as for *rēx*. In the genitive, and before other vowel-initial endings, the theoretical sequence /gw/ between two vowels is contrary to the phonemic habits of Latin, and the /g/ is lost with "compensatory lengthening" of the preceding vowel (/i/ replaced by /i·/). Yet this actually non-occurrent shape is the most convenient one to set up as base form for the stem; the treatment is supported also by the verb *ninguit* (/ningwit/) 'it snows,' where our base form seems to occur interrupted by an infixed /n/, an element which turns up elsewhere in Latin verb morphology.

NOTES

New terms: *internal* and *external* sandhi, *automatic* and *non-automatic* alternation, *regular* and *irregular* alternation, *phonemically conditioned* and *morphemically conditioned* alternation; *base form, theoretical base form, suppletion* or *suppletive alternation; optional external sandhi.*

Morphophonemic alternation is discussed extensively by Wells 1949. We confine the term "automatic alternation" to only one of the several types of alternation Wells subsumes under this term. Our definition of "regular" and "irregular" follows Bloomfield 1933; of "phonemically conditioned" versus "morphemically conditioned," Nida 1949. Internal and external sandhi: Bloomfield 1933.

Problems. Gleason *Workbook* (1955b), pages 28–32, gives problems which can be undertaken now if they were not done at the end of §15; those on pages 33–40, and problem 8.A on page 41, can be done now. In the last problem, the three forms to be transcribed and analyzed for each of the listed English verbs are those that fill the blanks of *I want to* _____, *He* _____ *yesterday,* and *I've never* _____.

In a Latin dictionary or glossary, one finds verbs listed with four (sometimes three) *principal parts:* for example, *facio, facere, fēcī, factus.* What morphophonemic information is conveyed by this listing of principal parts? What grammatical information?

34.

CANONICAL FORMS and ECONOMY

34.1. Canonical Forms. Two morphs in a language may be identical in shape: for example, /bér/, a morph representing the morpheme {*bear*} 'to suffer, to give birth to,' and /bér/, a different morph representing the morpheme {*bear*} 'ursus.' Two morphs which are not identical in shape may nevertheless be similar in easily describable ways: /bér/ (either one) and /síŋ/ are alike in that each consists of a single syllable, whereas /bátəm/ is two syllables with stress on the first, and /kǽləndər/ is three syllables with stress on the first. We say in this case that /bér/ and /síŋ/ are of the same *canonical form*, whereas /bátəm/ and /kǽləndər/ are of two other canonical forms. A canonical form, then, is a sort of generalized phonemic shape.

If we make a list, more or less at random, of a hundred or so morphs from a single language, an interesting fact seems always to emerge: there are certain canonical forms which are *favored* considerably more than others which the phonemic system of the language would equally well allow.

Let us consider Fijian as a first example. Literally hundreds or thousands of Fijian morphs are of the canonical forms

$$C_1V_1C_2V_2$$

or

$$C_1V_1C_2V_2C_3,$$

where "C" stands for any consonant phoneme or for none at all, and "V" for any vowel phoneme, while the shapes involving C_3 occur only

284

when a vowel-initial suffix follows in the same word. Here are a few examples: /vola-/ 'to write,' /viri(k)-/ 'to throw,' /rai(ð)-/ 'to look, to see,' /muri-/ 'to follow,' /tau(r)-/ 'to take,' /taa(j)-/ 'to chop,' /loma(n)-/ 'to love,' /lutu(m)-/ 'to stumble, to fall,' /ðabe(t)-/ 'to ascend,' /kaði(v)-/ 'to call.' Contentives (§31.1) in Fijian are rarely, if ever, represented by morphs of some shorter canonical form. Shorter morphs are found among the functors: suffixes like /-a/, /-i, /-na/; particles like /na/, /e/, /ko/, /ni/. But some functors are represented by shapes of the favored canonical type: suffix /-taka/, predicative particle /saa/, /sai/. And a minority of contentives are represented by even longer shapes: /rotuma/ (name of an island), /vanua/ 'land,' /tamata/ 'people,' /taŋata/ 'man,' /jalewa/ 'woman,' all of which conform to a canonical form

$$C_1V_1C_2V_2C_3V_3(C_4).$$

In English, one favored canonical form is a single stressed syllable, normally preceded by juncture: symbolize this by Ś. Examples are *bear, sing, find, trounce, jump, judge, edge, land, take, man, girl*. Morphemes represented by shorter shapes are largely derivational or inflectional. A second favored canonical form is ŚS, in which the shape of the unstressed second syllable is very often /ər/, /əl/, /əm/, /ən/, /ij/, /ow/: *hammer, scatter, mortar, bottle, pestle, whistle, bottom, tandem, forum, button, gallon, foreign, busy, early, pillow, meadow, window, bureau*. Single morphs longer than this are relatively rare (*calendar, nasturtium, furbelow, chrysanthemum*). Words of three or more syllables in general show at least some marginal possibility of breakdown into two or more morphs.

This generally recurrent phenomenon is of great help to the investigator who works on a hitherto unanalyzed language. Usually it does not take long to catch on to the prevalent pattern, and thereafter the investigator is not completely blind in his trial-and-error analysis. Suppose, for example, that the prevalent pattern seems to be that stems are of shape CVC- and suffixes of shape -V or -VC. Suppose that the investigator records a new word, say /kanap/, the meaning of which suggests that it includes stem and suffix, though neither is one which has obviously turned up in previously recorded material. Instead of being forced to try all possible breakdowns—/k-/ plus /-anap/, /ka-/ plus /-nap/, and so on—the investigator can at least try the most likely breakdown first (that into /kan-/ and /-ap/), and turn to the alternatives only if this proves fruitless.

34.2. Positional Classes. Closely allied to the matter of canonical forms, if not, indeed, part of it, is the *positional classification* of morphs. The term "affix," which was used in §§24 and 28, is grammatical: it subsumes bound forms of certain kinds. But the apparently parallel terms "prefix," "suffix," "infix" are not grammatical; they refer, rather to positional classes of the morphs which represent bound forms. Thus in *boys*, the noun-plural affix is represented by a morph /z/ which is suffixed to the representation of the stem; in *men*, exactly the same affix is represented by a morph /e/ which is infixed within the discontinuous representation /m.'.n/ of the stem.

The positional class to which a morph belongs must be taken into consideration in recognizing canonical forms of morphs. Prefixed affixes (prefixes) and suffixed affixes (suffixes) may be of the same generalized phonemic shape, and yet they belong to different canonical forms. Thus English elements like *be-* (*befriend*), *re-* (*regenerate*), *un-* (*unmannerly*), *in-* (*ineffable*) are to be kept separate from elements like *-er* (*singer*), *-er* (*larger*), *-est* (*largest*), *-ist* (*Communist*). In quite the same way, the Fijian suffixed affixes /-a/, /-i/, /-na/ must be separated from particles like /na/, /e/, /ko/, /ni/.

The reason for this is that, generally speaking, the position occupied within the word by a constituent morpheme, just like the precise phonemic shape which represents that morpheme, is determined *by* the language *for* the speaker, not by the speaker (§15.1). We can say *boys*, with the noun-plural morpheme represented by a suffixed morph, but we cannot alternatively say /zbój/ with the noun-plural morpheme first, in order to convey some other shade of meaning. We say *befriend*, but never /fréndbij/.

In many languages with complex morphologies, the three terms "prefix," "infix," and "suffix" are not enough to provide for a complete positional classification of morphs; instead, successive prefix positions or suffix-positions have to be recognized. The inflection of Menomini verbs involves morphs (representing inflectional affixes) of ten successive suffix-positions, though all ten are never occupied in a single word. Oneida involves almost thirty positional classes; Totonac more than sixty. As a simpler example, consider Potawatomi /kčimannanən/ 'our (inclusive) canoes.' There is a prefix /k/ 'thy' in this word, and a stem /čiman/ 'canoe.' There are then two successive suffixes, the positions of which cannot possibly be reversed: /nan/ 'possessor is plural and includes speaker,' and then /ən/, which pluralizes the stem 'canoe.' If /nan/ is replaced by zero, the meaning is 'thy canoes'; if it is replaced by /wa/ 'possessor is plural and excludes speaker,' the meaning is 'your (pl.) canoes'; if /ən/ is dropped, the meaning is 'our (inclusive) canoe.'

34.3. Reshaping and Metanalysis. Canonical forms have reality for the speakers of a language, not just for the analyst. From time to time it happens that a form of an unusual shape—say an unusually long single morph, or an idiomatic combination of morphemes in which the shapes are highly irregular—will be reinterpreted as though it consisted of a sequence of more familiar morphemes represented by more familiar shapes. The general term for this is *metanalysis*. If, as sometimes happens, the reinterpretation involves an actual change of the phonemic shape, then the phenomenon is known as *reshaping*.

Some examples are intentionally humorous: *OK, if it's feasible, let's fease it*, where the primary derivative *feasible* is treated as though it were secondary (§28.2).

Sometimes reshaping takes place because the speaker is insufficiently familiar with the form he wishes to use. There is no general label for this, but if the form intended is a learnèd one, the mistake is known as a *malapropism*. The effect on others may be humorous, but the intention is not. Examples are *We would be reminisce* (for *remiss*) *in our duty if we did not investigate; I'm simply ravishing* (for *ravenous*).

Quite a number of English words and phrases are known to be the result of reshaping at some time in the past history of the language, though only rarely do we know the attendant circumstances. Were it not for reshaping, the words *crayfish* or *crawfish, female*, and *mushroom* would be, respectively, something like /krévəs/, /féməl/, and /múwsəràn/. We can guess at the circumstances in that *crayfish* or *crawfish* does name a kind of fish, and in that *female* and *male* are often paired in speech; in the third instance it is hard to see any similarity in meaning, but at least *mush* and *room* are familiar syllables. Another example, more recent, and with the older form still in use alongside the reshaped form, is *Welsh rarebit* for *Welsh rabbit:* some literal-minded soul, failing to detect any rabbit in the dish, concluded that he must not have heard its name aright.

But metanalysis need not, in the first instance, involve any reshaping. The plurals *peas* and *cherries* are older than the singulars *pea* and *cherry:* formerly the longer forms were singulars like *wheat* or *sand*. The reinterpretation of the final /z/ of the words as representing the noun-plural morpheme was metanalysis. Children can be observed to do the same thing:

> Older Sister: *He's got poise.*
> Little Brother: *What's a poy?*

Another used to be—and for many speakers doubtless still is—*an* plus *other*, irregular only in that there is usually no juncture between the *n* and the /ó/ as there is in, say, *an apple*. But because of that irregularity, one will occasionally hear something like *I could eat a whole nother apple*. By the same mechanism we have *a newt* from earlier *an ewte*, and, in the reverse direction, *a nickname* for earlier *an ekename*. The earlier morphemic structure of *execute* and *chandelier* is not too clear—the latter was probably *chandel-* plus a suffix *-ier*—but when, a few decades ago, the words *electrocute* and *electrolier* were coined, the former pair were being metanalyzed as *exe-* plus *-cute* 'put to death legally,' and *chande-* plus *-lier* 'hanging light-holder.'

Akin to metanalysis, but distinct from it, and different particularly in that there is no necessary effect on the pattern of the language, is *folk-etymology*. A folk-etymology is an invented explanation of why a certain form means what it does, and the invention, no matter how far-fetched, usually turns somehow on the same sort of vague similarity of shape which underlies metanalysis and reshaping. A student asked: "Are *affricates* called that because they are extremely common in the languages of *Africa?*" The Chinese word for 'thing' is *dūngsyi*, which is a single morpheme, though longer than the most favored canonical shape; but *dūng* is a morpheme meaning 'east' and *syī* is one meaning 'west,' and some Chinese actually believe that the word for 'thing' is a compound of these two shorter forms. (In accordance with this folk-theory, the word for 'thing' is written with two characters, the first that used also for *dūng* 'east' and the second that used also for *syī* 'west.') Folk-etymology need not be accompanied by metanalysis, but we might guess that every instance of the latter at least potentially involves the former.

34.4. Economy. It is not entirely accidental that the favored canonical form for morphs in Fijian should be at least as long as it is. The language has sixteen consonants and five vowels, and the phonemic structure is such that a syllable consists either of a lone vowel or of a vowel preceded by a single consonant; most possible combinations of consonant and vowel occur, though a few, such as /ji/ and /wu/, do not. This means that there are only eighty-odd possible syllables in the language. The number of single-syllable shapes is too small for any large number of morphemes to be represented by them. On the other hand, there are on the order of 6400 possible two-syllable sequences, which gives more "room."

Not all of these available two-syllable shapes are necessarily used. The details are not available, but we can state the matter hypothetically. If a very high percentage of the favorite shapes were used, we should say that the language manifested a fairly efficient morphophonemic *economy*. If, despite the availability of 6400 two-syllable shapes, only some relatively small percentage were used, many morphemes being represented by even longer morphs, then we should say that the morphophonemic economy showed low efficiency.

Let us consider the same problem in English. The total number of monosyllables which would be in accord with the phonemic pattern of the language is in the tens of thousands. A shape like /stíjf/ conforms just as closely to the favored canonical form in English as does /stíf/; yet the latter is, so to speak, "inhabited," while the former is not. And one can coin a seemingly endless list of other acceptable but "uninhabited" shapes: /bík, kéb, bówp, čélb, čém, kúwm, kráb, íjp, fáwz, fríŋ, frúw, gríč, hóws/, and so on. It is obvious that the morphophonemic economy is relatively inefficient.

Mandarin Chinese stands in sharp contrast. The favored shapes for morphs in Chinese, as in English, are single syllables, excluding those which end in /r/ (since in most cases this constitutes a separate morph). The total number of these is about 1600, and a very high proportion of these phonemically possible 1600 are actually "inhabited."

A more accurate estimate of morphophonemic economy would allow for two additional factors: (1) the "density of population" of various shapes—as, in English, the fact that at least three different morphemes are represented by morphs of the shape /bér/, while only one is represented by /síŋ/; and (2) the relative frequencies of the morphemes which share a given representation. With a given percentagewise utilization, we should be inclined to say that a heavy piling-up of morphs in just one portion of the used shapes was less efficient than a more even spread. Little work has been done along this line, but probably the edge of greater efficiency which Mandarin seems to show over English would be somewhat diminished if we could allow accurately for these factors.

It must be emphasized that the measurement or estimate of the morphophonemic economy of a language is not a value judgment. We cannot assert that greater economy is "better" in any logical, ethical, or esthetic sense. It is possible, indeed, that too efficient an economy, with some phonemic systems, might impair communication. Morphophonemic economy is simply one of the ways in which languages can differ.

NOTES

New terms: *canonical forms* of morphs; *positional class; reshaping, metanalysis, malapropism, folk-etymology;* morphophonemic *economy.*

Problem. The workings of complex morphological systems can often be displayed in a diagram. The three types of diagram most often used have been nicknamed the *maze,* the *freightyard,* and the *rollercoaster* (see Harris 1951, Hoenigswald 1950a). These are illustrated in Figures 34.1, 34.2, and 34.3, the pattern chosen being the inflection of Spanish gender-showing adjectives; this pattern is too simple to need diagrammatic display, and is therefore a good one with which to demonstrate the diagramming techniques.

In Figure 34.1, one is to proceed from left to right, never crossing any lines, and picking up certain elements as one passes through the chambers in which they are stored. The chamber marked "STEM" contains all the stems of Spanish gender-showing adjectives, so that in passing through this chamber one is to pick up one, and just one, of this set of forms: say *buen-* 'good.' Next one has a two-way choice, either to pass through the upper chamber and pick up *-o-* 'masculine' or to pass through the lower chamber and pick up *-a-* 'feminine.' Next one has another two-way choice, either passing through the upper chamber and picking up no more inflectional material (so that one ends up with *bueno* or with *buena*), or else passing through the lower chamber and picking up *-s* 'plural' (so that one ends up with *buenos* or with *buenas*).

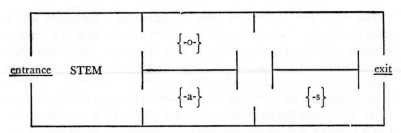

FIGURE 34.1.   THE MAZE

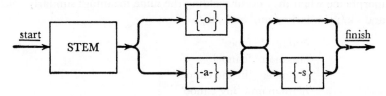

FIGURE 34.2.   THE FREIGHTYARD

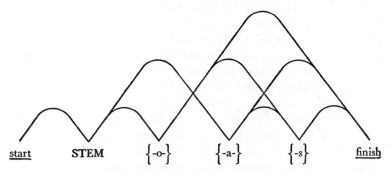

FIGURE 34.3.   THE ROLLERCOASTER

The Spanish gender-showing adjective has just these four forms: all of them are generated by the diagram, under our rules, and no others can be so generated.

The freightyard is quite like the maze, except that the possible routes are along the tracks—with no turning back—and items are stored in the sheds.

The rollercoaster is different. One starts at "start," up the first slope; one can turn down wherever there is a curved top, but not at an angle; one keeps going until one finishes with "finish."

The maze and freightyard have the advantage of showing which inflectional affixes belong in a single positional class: those in chambers or sheds aligned vertically with each other belong in a single such class. The rollercoaster has the advantage of listing all the inflectional affixes along the bottom for ease of checking against inadvertent duplications. Below we give the paradigm of a Potawatomi inanimate independent noun. Determine the constituent stem and affixes. Draw two diagrams, one a maze or freightyard, the other a rollercoaster, to display all the inflectional possibilities. Consider /ən/ and /n/ allomorphs of a single morpheme when they occur yielding the same meaning; similarly /ək/ and /k/; similarly /əm/ and /m/.

/čiman/ 'canoes'
/čimanən/ 'canoe'
/čimanək/ 'in the canoe'
/nčimanəm/ 'my canoe'
/nčimanmən/ 'my canoes'
/nčimanmək/ 'in my canoe'
/kčimanəm/ 'thy canoe'
/kčimanmən/ 'thy canoes'
/kčimanmək/ 'in thy canoe'
/wčimanəm/ 'his canoe'
/wčimanmən/ 'his canoes'
/wčimanmək/ 'in his canoe'
/kčimanmənan/ 'our (inclusive) canoe'
/kčimanmənanən/ 'our (inclusive) canoes'
/kčimanmənanək/ 'in our (inclusive) canoe'
/nčimanmənan/ 'our (exclusive) canoe'
/nčimanmənanən/ 'our (exclusive) canoes'
/nčimanmənanək/ 'in our (exclusive) canoe'
/kčimanməwa/ 'your canoe'
/kčimanməwan/ 'your canoes'
/kčimanməwak/ 'in your canoe'
/wčimanməwa/ 'their canoe'
/wčimanməwan/ 'their canoes'
/wčimanməwak/ 'in their canoe'

35.

SECONDARY EFFECTS of
PHONEMIC SHAPES

35.1. By the description of language design of §16, communicatively
the phonemic shapes which represent various morphemes ought to be
arbitrary: the only function of a morph is to represent a morpheme.
However matters are not so simple. Perhaps, in one sense, the habitual
assignments of phonemic shapes to morphemes is arbitrary, but in addition to this the phonemic shapes apparently have some communicative
side-effects.

A good way to demonstrate this is to explore a possible proposal for
increasing the morphophonemic efficiency (§34.4) of English. Suppose
that we obtain an accurate account of the relative frequency of all
English morphemes and of the most important short idiomatic groups
of morphemes. Then we reassign morphs to morphemes (and to short
idioms) in a more rational way. Assuming that there are fifteen thousand monosyllables which conform to our phonemic pattern, we arrange for these to be the representations of the fifteen thousand most frequent morphemes and short idioms. Current monosyllables which are
not among the fifteen thousand most frequent must be assigned longer
shapes. In this way, we do not change in the slightest either our grammatical or our phonological habits, but we arrange for things that are
said most often to be said most briefly.

Like most proposals for language reform, this one is utterly unrealistic
from many points of view. However, let us carry it through to see
what the purely linguistic results would be. To start with, since *English*

293

is a very common word (among the thousand most frequent), let us call the revised language *Ing*. Is it true that Ing and English differ only in trivial ways?

The answer lies in the realm of puns, plays on words, verse, slang, so-called "onomatopoeia," and the like. We must not think of such uses of language as in any way inferior to its use in writing treatises on bacteriology or delivering lectures on civil law.

Consider Longfellow's poem "The Day is Done." There are forty-eight morphemes or short idioms in this poem which, under the recommendations for Ing, are too long. For example, *feather* ranks somewhere in the second thousand most frequent words, and anything which we say that often should, according to the proposal, be said in a single syllable. On the other hand, *lay* 'song' is quite rare, and does not deserve a monosyllabic representation. Making up and assigning new shapes—in one of many possible ways—we get the following Ing version of the poem; the original is placed to the right in lieu of a lexicon of new Ing forms:

The day is done, and the darkness
 Falls from the wings of Night
As a bick is wafted downward
 From a keb in his flight.

I see the lights of the steek
 Gleam through the rain and the
 mist,
And a loog of sadness comes morve
 me
That my soul cannot fump:

A loog of sadness and taykling,
 That is not preck to pain,
And stads rooch crob
 As the mist stads the rain.

Come, read to me some froo,
 Some jup and fring rappy

The day is done, and the darkness
 Falls from the wings of Night
As a feather is wafted downward
 From an eagle in his flight.

I see the lights of the village
 Gleam through the rain and the
 mist,
And a feeling of sadness comes
 over me
That my soul cannot resist:

A feeling of sadness and longing,
 That is not akin to pain,
And resembles sorrow only
 As the mist resembles the rain.

Come, read to me some poem,
 Some simple and heartfelt lay

That shall soothe this restless loog
And skal the thoughts of day.

That shall soothe this restless feeling
And banish the thoughts of day.

. . .
      . . .

Then read from the spoited tem

The froo of thy choice,
And lend to the rhyme of the trut
The sugg of thy voice.

Then read from the treasured
volume
The poem of thy choice,
And lend to the rhyme of the poet
The beauty of thy voice.

And the night shall be filled with
bope,
And the cares, that coom the
day,
Shall fold their tents, like Roafts,
And as yibbly steal orch.

And the night shall be filled with
music,
And the cares, that infest the
day,
Shall fold their tents, like Arabs,
And as silently steal away.

The most obvious fact about the Ing version is that Longfellow's rhythm and rhyme are generally lost. This, of course, does not imply that poetry could not be composed in Ing, but it does mean that the poetry of Ing is not that of English: different phonemic shapes for morphemes imply different sets of rhyming or rhythmically comparable words.

Beyond this, most of us feel that some of the shapes newly assigned to certain grammatical forms are not fit to carry the meanings of the forms. *Sugg* strikes the writer as an absolutely impossible syllable to use in the sense of 'beauty'; *skal* seems equally inept for the meaning 'banish.' There will certainly be disagreement about details in such re-actions, but the reactions are undeniable; the puzzle is, where do they come from?

One extreme theory holds that the inappropriateness of the sound /ság/ for the sense 'beauty' is a general matter, so that any speaker of any language would agree. Similarly, proponents of this theory try to show that words meaning 'little' tend to have a high front vowel (English /i/, /ij/), while words with the opposite meaning tend to have a low vowel (English /æ/, /a/, /ɔ/). English *big* and *small* reverse this association, but one exception is not very important when the theory is proposed only as a statistical tendency. Yet it seems unlikely that the theory can be carried very far. If we list the forms meaning 'beauty' or something like it, in fifteen or twenty languages chosen more or less at random, we find that we have also a large variety of phonetic shapes. Here are some of them, each spelled out in a rough approximation to a phonemic notation for the particular language: /bote/, /bejésa/, /ermosúra/, /beléza/, /frumuséce/, /šố·n+hàjt/, /hássan/, /Jamaal/, /měi/, /féw/, /lélé/, /pagɔ/, /wə·/, /kwalci·n/.

Proponents of the same theory claim that in a line of poetry such as *the murmuring of innumerable bees*, the very sound of the words is suggestive of their meaning. One dissenter pointed out that two minor changes of the sound can result in a total change in the meaning: *the murdering of innumerable beeves*.

At the opposite extreme one finds the theory that the apparent aptness of the shapes actually used in a language for the meanings they carry is due entirely to their individual familiarity. *Sugg* sounds wrong for 'beauty' because we are not used to it: give us a while to accustom ourselves to the new shape, and *sugg* will "sound" as beautiful as *beauty* does now.

Both of these extreme theories go too far. We cannot be sure where the truth lies, except that it certainly lies somewhere between the extremes, and in the following discussion we shall search for it there.

35.2. The Theory of Secondary Associations. To begin with, recall our discussion of redundancy and intentional distortion at the end of §10.3. If we listen to the parody poem given there, beginning *Eight of the note that kippers may*, we have no difficulty in following the familiar original (*Out of the night that covers me*, . . .): few of the words are phonemically identical with their opposite numbers in the original, but they are sufficiently similar that, in the sequence in which they come, redundancy comes into play, and we quickly associate the shapes that strike our ears with the appropriate original words.

We can say that two words or phrases are *acoustically similar* if, under conditions of some extraneous noise, and lacking defining context, one might be misheard as the other. Acoustic similarity is a matter of degree, since with enough noise any word could be misheard as any other; but we are concerned only with the closer similarities. Any given *focal* word (that is, a specific word in which we are interested) is thus surrounded by a vaguely defined family of words which are more or less acoustically similar to it. The members of the family will in general have the widest variety of meanings, and yet it may often happen that some members of the family will resemble the focal word not only in acoustic shape, but also in meaning. For example, the family surrounding the focal word *vanish* includes *banish*, which is somewhat similar in meaning, as well as *vantage* and *Spanish*, which show little semantic relationship.

Some of the paralleling resemblances in both sound and meaning are accounted for by the grammatical structure of the forms. Thus *sighting* and *lighting* share the terminal shape -*ing*, as well as a feature of meaning, and we find this shape so widespread in association with this meaning that we break the -*ing* off as a separate morph, occurring in both *sighting* and *lighting* as well as in many other forms. But beyond the grammatically induced resemblances, there is a vast and complex tracery of subsidiary resemblances which we do not regard as due to the grammatical structure of the forms; they are, as it were, "accidental." Once the -*ing* is broken off from *sighting* and *lighting*, we are left with a pair *sight* and *light*, which still resemble each other partly in sound and in meaning; but we do not find it feasible to recognize morphs *s*-, *l*-, and -*ight*. And yet there is really no sharp line of demarcation between parallel resemblances which we choose to account for grammatically and those which we do not—this is borne out by the frequent disagreements, among laymen and specialists alike, as to the "proper" grammatical analysis of some forms.

Now we can suppose that when we hear a given word in a given context, there is a double effect: (1) principally, the phonemic shape of the word, plus the narrowing-down help of the context, tells us what morpheme or larger grammatical form is being said; (2) at the same time, the phonemic shape of the word sets up reverberations, by virtue of its acoustic similarity to some other words. These secondary associations will tend to be reinforced in the case of acoustically similar words which also are somewhat similar to the focal word in meaning, and will tend to be cancelled out in the case of those which are alien in meaning.

The inappropriateness of *sugg* for the meaning 'beauty' can be accounted for within this framework. It is true that, if we were accustomed to this shape, its similarity in sound to words of definitely 'unbeautiful' connotations might not worry us. But since *sugg* is just being brought into consideration, its secondary associations with words like *plug, mug, jug, ugly, tug, sag, suck* are too great: they overpower any effort we may make to accept the proper primary association with the assigned meaning.

Conversely, replacing the shape *banish* by *skal* destroys the secondary associations of the former with *vanish, Spanish, vantage,* and the like. The loss of some of these associations does not matter much, but the first tie, reinforced as it is by similarity of meaning, is such that the change of shape would represent a distinct change in the more subtle workings of the language.

35.3. Onomatopoeia and Synesthesia. In addition to the effect of secondary associations, which are mediated through other forms in the same language, we must also make at least one concession to the first of the two extreme theories discussed earlier. Some words and phrases, claims the theory, actually *sound like* that which they mean: such a form is *onomatopoetic.*

Far too many forms in different languages have been called onomatopoetic by the unwary; in many cases, the responsible factor must be the sort of secondary associations we have already discussed. Yet there can be no question but that onomatopoetic forms exist. A form with a meaning like 'sun,' 'man,' 'chair,' or 'bright light' cannot be onomatopoetic, because the only way in which the sound of a word can physically resemble its meaning is for the meaning itself to be a sound, or, at the very least, something which produces a characteristic sound. Thus a word which means 'sound of a dog barking' or 'sound made by a cat,' or 'loud noise of pieces of metal striking together,' or possibly 'cat' or 'dog,' stands some chance of being onomatopoetic. Even in these instances, there is also often a large arbitrary element in the phonemic shape of the word. In English a bell says *ding-dong;* in German it says *bim-bam.* The difference between *ding-dong* and *bim-bam* represents the arbitrary element. The fact that each form consists of two syllables, with a high front vowel in the first and a low vowel in the second, an initial voiced stop and a final nasal in each syllable, is indicative of the onomatopoeia.

If *the murmuring of innumerable bees* involves onomatopoeia, it lies in the continuous voicing of the phrase from beginning to end, which, with the minor variations of stress and pitch, causes the phrase to sound vaguely like what it describes. (At least the sound of the phrase is more similar to the sound it describes than it is to the sound of thunder, and the given phrase sounds more like the murmuring of bees than would a phrase like *pontifical pachyderms practising polkas* or *the full-throated buzzing of hundreds of stinging insects.*) The existence of the phrase *the murdering of innumerable beeves,* so similar in sound but so different in meaning, is irrelevant. The latter phrase is not onomatopoetic; the first perhaps is. A judge who knew no English obviously could not tell which was onomatopoetic and which was not, for onomatopoeia can be judged only in terms of sound *and* meaning.

Some psychologists want to push the theory of cross-language appropriateness further than our discussion of onomatopoeia would allow, on grounds called *synesthesia.* The theory of synesthesia proposes that there are certain types of resemblance from one sense modality to another: that is, that certain sounds, like certain lights, can be classed as "bright," versus other sounds and lights which are "dull." If so, then a linguistic form which means a "bright sound" and which is onomatopoetic because it *sounds* like a "bright sound" could still be onomatopoetic if it meant, instead, a "bright light." It is exceedingly difficult to gather proper evidence for the testing of this theory, and no one can say yet whether, or to what extent, it is valid. In English we use the pair of words *high* and *low* both for relative altitudes and for relative pitches. In Chinese the pair of words *gāu* and *dī* are used in just the same way; that is, *gāu* means 'high' in either altitude or pitch, and *dī* means 'low' in either connection. It would not be valid to use this as evidence for synesthesia. Even if this particular instance of synesthesia tests out with English-speaking and Chinese-speaking subjects, it is possible that the cross-sensory identification is the *result* of their linguistic habits, rather than the cause, and that the linguistic habits, in turn, are similar only by accident. We shall not know the answer to the problem of synesthesia until we have made extensive cross-language comparisons. Pending this, "explanations" in terms of synesthesia can hardly be given credence.

NOTES

Investigations and discussions of "sound symbolism," as the topic of this section is often called, include Brown 1955 and the works mentioned therein; also Bolinger 1950 and Read 1949. The writer learned the theory of secondary associations largely from Professor M. H. Abrams of Cornell University.

Problem. The English words listed below are often thought to show a particularly apposite matching of sound and meaning. Classify them into sets showing recurrent similarities of sound *and* meaning. Discuss (e.g., secondary associations, genuine onomatopoeia, or both?).

bang, bash, bat, batter, biff, blare, bounce, bump, chatter, clang, clap, clash, clatter, crack, crash, crunch, drop, flame, flare, flash, flicker, flimmer, flop, glare, gleam, glide, glimmer, gloom, glow, gnash, jounce, mash, rap, ride, shatter, shimmer, simmer, slap, slash, slide, slip, slop, slush, smash, splash, trounce.

IDIOMS

36·

IDIOM FORMATION

36.1. Synchronic and Diachronic. The study of how a language works at a given time, regardless of its past history or future destiny, is called *descriptive* or *synchronic* linguistics. The study of how speech habits change as time goes by is called *historical* or *diachronic* linguistics. Our major concern so far has been with the former, but we are now drawing our survey of it to a close and preparing to concentrate on the latter.

It is a mistake to think of descriptive and historical linguistics as two separate compartments, each bit of information belonging exclusively in the one or in the other. There are certain matters which are relevant both in understanding how a language works at a given time and also in connection with linguistic change. One clear example of this is *idiom formation.*

In every living language, new idioms are constantly being created, some destined to occur only once or twice and then to be forgotten, others due to survive for a long time. This fact sets a limit on the possible completeness of a description of a language, since one cannot list idioms which have not been observed, and cannot observe those which will not be coined until the day after one's work is completed. Nor can one, with any reliability, predict what new idioms will be coined. Observation shows, however, that each language favors certain patterns in the creation of new idioms. This favoritism is part of the design of the language at the time of observation, and is therefore properly reported in a descriptive study of the language. But any actual new coinage may constitute a change, no matter how small, in the grammatical system of the language, and in course of time the cumula-

303

tive effect of many such *small* changes can be great. Thus it is that idiom formation is also an important matter in historical linguistics.

36.2. The Birth of Idioms. The reader will recall the fundamental fact (§18.1) that a speaker may say something that he has never said, and never heard, before, to hearers to whom the utterance is equally novel, and yet be understood. Indeed, this is a daily occurrence. The way in which it comes about is basically simple: the new utterance is a nonce-form (§19.4), built from familiar material by familiar patterns. If the occasion arises and I say *That enormous old house of theirs requires one hundred and nineteen pairs of nine-foot curtains*, I am probably saying something that has never been said before in the history of the human race. But even if precisely this utterance has by some chance occurred before, the previous occurrence and the present one have nothing to do with each other: I am not remembering and quoting the utterance, but am coining it anew because the circumstances call for it.

However, the mere occurrence of a nonce-form for the first time does not in itself constitute the creation of a new idiom. An additional ingredient is required: something more or less unusual either about the structure of the newly-produced nonce-form, or about the attendant circumstances, or both, which renders the form memorable. As we go about the business of living, we constantly meet circumstances which are not *exactly* like anything in our previous experience. When we react via speech to such partially new circumstances, we may produce a phrase or an utterance which is understandable only because those who hear it are also confronted by the new circumstances. Alternatively, an individual may react to conventional circumstances with a bit of speech which is somewhat unconventional—once again being understood because of context. Given any such novelty, either of expression or of circumstances or of both, the event bestows special meaning on the linguistic form which is used, and the latter becomes idiomatic.

Here are two examples. Recall first, from §34.3, the little boy who said *What's a poy?* This utterance is unusual in its form; the members of the family who overhear him are apt to remember the event and tell the story to others. They may even use the new form *poy* in family jargon. Just what the form will mean will depend on the circumstances in which the boy used it; perhaps it will not *denote* anything but it will certainly have *connotations*. Even if the form is not destined to survive for long or to spread very widely, it is none the less a new idiom. Probably this particular coinage has occurred many times, quite independently, in different family circles in the English-speaking world. (All the other instances of metanalysis, with or without reshaping, described in §34.3, are also examples of idiom-formation.)

Next imagine a rather different set of circumstances: Mrs. X comes home with a new blouse, of one of those indeterminate blue-green shades for which women have a special fancy name, but which they class definitely as a shade of green, not of blue. Mr. X compliments her by saying *That's a nice shade of blue*. For days thereafter, Mrs. X teases her husband by pointing to any obviously green object and saying *That's a nice shade of blue, isn't it?* Here there is nothing unusual about the form of the utterance, only about the original attendant circumstances; yet the utterance has taken on, at least temporarily, idiomatic value.

The total context, linguistic and nonlinguistic, in which a nonce-form takes on the status of an idiom is thus the *defining context* of the idiom. In the two examples given above, the defining contexts are informal. But formal contexts of various sorts may equally well serve. The poet or other literary artist may quite consciously strive for the unusual; so may any of us, in our puns, clever repartee, and so on. A mathematician, having explored a new field of modern algebra, may write "A *distributive lattice* is a lattice in which each operation is distributive over the other"; those of his readers who understand the rest of the sentence now know what he will henceforth mean by the phrase *distributive lattice*, which has just been defined as a technical term—that is, as one sort of idiom. On the other hand, those of us who do not understand the rest of his sentence are not enlightened: *distributive lattice* is neither an understandable idiom for us, nor does it seem to make any sense if taken simply as a nonce-form. This is akin to another familiar experience: verbal humor which is quite funny when it first happens, at least to those who directly observe it, often falls flat when told to outsiders.

36.3. Idioms and Non-Linguistic Signalling Systems. The imparting of special new meaning to a familiar linguistic form (or a form composed of familiar parts) is but one version of a phenomenon which manifests itself throughout human behavior. The phenomenon is largely responsible for our essential humanness: it occurs slightly, if at all, among other animals; and it is made possible ultimately only through the existence and nature of language.

Paul Revere and his unnamed friend agreed that one light in the Old North Church should signify that the British were approaching by land, two lights that they were coming by sea.

You tell your friend "I'll honk twice when I come, so that you won't have to be watching for my car all the time."

The counter-intelligence agent agrees with his confederates that he will pull down the window-shade when they should enter the apartment in order to catch the enemy spy with the incriminating evidence in his possession.

A conclave of government representatives from all over Europe agree that certain marks on road-signs, throughout Europe, shall signify certain conditions and contours of the road ahead.

A brace of bridge-players agree that scratching the left ear shall mean "The bid I am making is a fake, to confuse the opposition"; this agreement is against the rules of the game and constitutes cheating. Or they agree that a jump-bid to four clubs shall mean "show me how many aces you have by your next bid"; this is not against the rules of the game, and constitutes a convention, not cheating.

The members of a tribe "agree" (though not through any formal conclave) that the first thunderstorm of spring shall be the signal for the holding of a certain ceremonial dance.

Thus, any event which is observable, and the occurrence or location of which can be controlled or, at least, predicted, can be assigned any meaning whatsoever, and hence serve, for a shorter or longer period, as an element in a signalling system. It is almost exclusively through the use of language, or of its complex derivatives such as writing, that human beings establish the conventions of such signalling systems, though this is not always overtly and obviously the case. At least, we must admit that the verbal discussion by virtue of which a thing or event takes on a given symbolic value is in many cases entirely informal. There are parts of Europe where a young woman dare not walk with the free stride customary in the United States: this gait has taken on a special value, and observers would immediately class her as a hussy, if not as a fille de joie. The agreement that this value should be assigned the particular stride was obviously not reached in a convention, and yet it took some kind of communication to bring the agreement about.

The crucial role of language is also in no way derogated by the fact that, in some cases, the communication involved in establishing new agreements is carried on via writing or via some more recent system like telegraphy: for these systems, in turn, were developed in the first place by just the same mechanism, with human language already at work to make their development possible. All of what the anthropologist calls human *culture* involves shared conventions of the sort we have illustrated. It is no accident that the only animal with more than a bare minimum of culture is also the only animal with the power of speech.

When the "thing or event" which is given special symbolic value by this mechanism is itself a speech-form, we have the phenomenon with which we are primarily concerned: the coining of an idiom. Theoretically, we must recognize this status even for forms which are habitually assigned roughly the same special value over and over again. Thus, if in pouring a drink a host says *Say when!* or if someone in charge of a group lifting a heavy load says *Lift when I say "Now!"* both *when* and *now* become momentary idioms.

Similar temporary idioms appear in parlor magic. In one stunt, the magician leaves the room, while the audience and the magician's confederate agree on the name of some city or town. When the magician returns, the confederate asks a series of questions of the shape "Is it _____?"—each time putting a place-name in the blank. The magician says "no" until the right one comes along. The clue rests in the use, by the confederate, in the question directly before the one to which the magician is to respond affirmatively, of a place-name the shape of which includes an animal-name: *Deer*field, *Mans*ville, *Elk*ton, and so on. By convention between the magician and the confederate, this special class of place-names has been assigned the special idiomatic value.

36.4. Idiom Formation and Derivation; Productivity. There has been a tendency in the technical literature of linguistics to confuse idiom formation and derivation. It is important for us to understand clearly not only the distinction between these two, but also the reason for the confusion.

To start with, we need the notion of *productivity*. The productivity of any pattern—derivational, inflectional, or syntactical—is the relative freedom with which speakers coin new grammatical forms by it. Thus the formation of English noun-plurals with /z s əz/ is highly productive.

The addition of -*ly* to produce an adverbial is fairly productive; the addition of -*dom* to form a noun from a noun is quite restricted.

The productivity of a pattern varies in time: some of our freer patterns were highly limited five hundred years ago, and conversely. There are also shorter-termed variations, of the sort we might call "fashion." For example, twenty-odd years ago, when the type of restaurant called a *cafeteria* was spreading across the country, there was a short explosion of similarly-formed names for stores in which there was an element of self-service: *groceteria*, *booteteria*, *booketeria*, and so on, to a total of well over a hundred, most of which are now completely in limbo.

Setting such brief fads aside, we find that, by and large, syntactical patterns tend to be the most productive, inflectional patterns next, and derivational patterns least.

It also appears that, the *less* productive a pattern is, the *more* likely it is that if a new form does get coined by the pattern it will have idiomatic value. We do have idioms involving highly productive patterns: e.g., *the coast is clear*. But it is relatively difficult to create a new idiom by the subject-predicate pattern, as in the instance just given. On the other hand, consider the English derivational suffix -*ward* or -*wards*. We inherit a double-handful of perfectly ordinary words containing this suffix: *northward(s)*, and so forth with names of compass-points, *inward(s)*, *backward(s)*, *sunward(s)*. We do not freely say such things as *He walked tablewards* or *on my Chicagoward journey*. Therefore, when P. G. Wodehouse wrote *Lord Emsworth ambled off pigwards*, the stretching of the pattern beyond its ordinary limits achieved some sort of special effect: *pigwards* was a new idiom.

In the above we see one reason why there has been the confusion between derivation and idiom formation: derived stems are often idioms, and newly-created derived stems tend to have idiomatic value because of the relatively unproductive nature of the majority of derivational patterns. Clearly, however, the association between idiom formation and derivation is not identity. Derived stems are not always idiomatic; idioms are not always derived stems. Currently the formation of adjectives with a suffix /-ij/ is rather productive: one hears new combinations like *Chinesey*, *pavementy*, *New Yorky*, and even phrase derivatives like *a paper-boxy sort of contraption*—the forms are highly colloquial and do not turn up in print. But they are not idioms: the special value adheres to the suffix, not individually to each new combination.

Awful is both a derivative (stem *awe-* and affix *-ful*) and an idiom. *Darts*, as the name of a game, is an idiomatic fixation of the ordinary plural of the noun *dart*, and is thus an idiom but not a derivative.

Another factor which has promoted the confusion is that interest has tended to focus on formations at smaller size-levels, largely on morphological formations. This has concealed from view the existence of vast numbers of larger idioms—short phrases like *blackboard*, whole utterances such as *Now is the time for all good men to come to the aid of the party*, or even conversations:

> Lady: *Are you copper-bottoming 'em, my man?*
> Workman: *No, I'm aluminiuming 'em, mum.*

Indeed, as one passes to larger and larger size-levels, idioms merge imperceptibly into the sorts of discourse which, as we shall see in §64, can reasonably be called *literature*.

NOTES

New terms: the pair *synchronic* and *descriptive* are for the moment synonyms; in §38.1 we shall distinguish between them. Similarly for the pair *diachronic* and *historical*, which can be taken as synonymous until §41.1. The other new terms are the *defining context* for an idiom, and *productivity* of a grammatical pattern.

Many articles in the journal *American Speech* report on changing fashions of idiom formation in American English. Fashion (largely non-linguistic) has been carefully analyzed by A. L. Kroeber; see especially Kroeber 1919, Kroeber and Richardson 1940.

37.

TYPES of IDIOMS

37.1. Substitutes. In §36.1 we asserted that in each language there are certain patterns which are most favored in the formation of new idioms. A few channels for idiom formation are either widespread or, it may be, universal; others are quite specific to one or a few languages. The information available on this subject is still too spotty for a really systematic survey, but we shall generalize our discussion as much as possible.

Anaphoric substitutes (§30.1) are almost by definition forms which turn up in each new context with a new idiomatic value. If I say, totally out of context, *He didn't get here on time,* you do not know whom I am talking about, save that he is male and probably human. In context, the preceding speech or factors of the non-speech environment establish what specific male human (or, perhaps, animal) the substitute *he* is going to designate until further notice. Of course, the convention can alter rapidly and often.

Numbers, which are probably to be classed as substitutes, show a similar variation of specific reference. The answer *three* can be given to a great variety of questions: *How many children have you? How old are you? What time is it? How many pounds does that roast weigh? What page is that on? How much are two and one?*

This sort of constant shifting qualifies as idiom formation, though not of the sort which can accumulate to change the grammatical pattern of a language. It is of the very nature of an anaphoric substitute that it should behave in this way. In order for the grammatical pattern of the language to be altered, the substitute would have to be modified as to its domain-tie or its type (§30.3), or both.

310

However, substitutes are not exempt from the more customary sort of idiomatic specialization. In English, *it* was at one time idiomatically a noun with the meaning 'sex and/or personality appeal'; it is also a noun meaning 'that one of a group who must chase the others, in tag or hide-and-seek.' *He* and *she* have idiomatic uses in *she-camel*, *he-man*, *Is your cat a he or a she?* Freud wrote a book the English title of which, *The Ego and the Id*, does not involve idiomatic uses of substitutes; but the German original bore the title *Das Ich und das Es*, with special uses of the ordinary German pronouns *ich* 'I' and *es* 'it.' When a news-announcer says *Good night and thirty*, the last word does not refer to twice fifteen.

37.2. Proper Names. In all human communities there are certain recurrent idiom-creating events called *naming*. People are named; places are named; sometimes certain individual animals, spirits, or vehicles are named. There are various formally prescribed ceremonial activities in connection with naming, the details of which are of interest to the anthropologist; but here we must concentrate on the purely linguistic aspect.

If the language has a noun-like part of speech, then names are almost invariably nouns, except that place-names sometimes appear to be loca-tive particles. However, before the actual name-giving, the linguistic form which is to be used may not have this status. We have all heard of Indians with names like *Sitting Bull* (real) or *Big Chief Rain-in-the-Face* (invented); this reflects, in English, a genuine habit in many Indian languages. Menomini has as men's names /ɛ·kosewɛ·t/, literally 'that he hangs people up,' /ana·hko·hsɛh/ 'little star,' /ana·ma·nahkwat/ 'under a cloud,' /wasɛ·ʔ ɛ·pet/ 'that he sits on the nest,' /awa·noh-ape·w/ 'he sits in fog.' These are all ordinary words and phrases, of various part-of-speech affiliation; some of them become substantival, and participate in larger constructions like nouns, only in their idio-matic function as proper names.

The grammatical properties of proper names may also deviate from those of the most similar "ordinary" words. In English, names of cities, rivers, and lakes either are never preceded by an article, as *New York*, *Lake Michigan*, or else have the article *the* permanently fixed alongside, as *The Hague*, *The Mississippi* (*River*); river names are apparently all of the latter sort. In Fijian, a word used as a proper name of person or place is marked by the preceding particle /ko/, while words used as "ordinary" names of things are marked in the same syntactical circumstances by /na/ : /na vanua levu/ 'the (or a) big land, big island' but /ko vanua levu/ 'Big Island' as the name of the largest island of the Fiji group (§27.1).

A language may also have a stock of forms which have no function save that of being used as the proper name of one or another individual: English *Mary, William, Robert, Elizabeth.* These words are not substitutes, since they do not meet the criteria which define the latter; but in their behavior they are much like anaphoric substitutes, shifting their specific denotation from context to context—though less kaleidoscopically than do substitutes. If I say, out of context, *Robert didn't get here on time,* you are hardly more informed than if I had used the substitute *he* in place of the proper name *Robert.* By way of apparent exception to the special status of these names in English, and perhaps in other languages, any of them can be "deproper-ized," as it were, to mean 'person or other entity with the proper name in question': we freely say *But there are two different Roberts in our group.*

We may say that there are as many different idioms of the shape *Robert,* in the dialect of a particular speaker of English, as there are men and boys—and perhaps goldfish—of that name in his circle of acquaintances. However great this number may be, there is still just a single *morpheme* of that shape, even as there is just one English substitute *he* despite the way in which its denotation shifts.

Peculiar and amusing habits of naming are found, in our society, for race-horses (almost any word or phrase: *Aquaduct, Came First, Never Any Better, Bootstraps,* etc.) and for books. The sentence *Have you read the egg and I?* is ridiculous unless the hearer knows that a certain book has the title *The Egg and I;* even with this knowledge, the occurrence of *I* after a verb like *read* is disturbing.

To logicians, a "proper name" or "proper noun" is a symbol which designates an entity of which there is only one. It should be clear from our discussion that in actual languages there are no forms which can be so described, save possibly through pure accident. By this exception we mean, for example, that a family might invent a completely new name for a newborn child, so that at least temporarily the word would designate that child and nothing else. In principle, however, other parents might at any time decide to use the same name, whereupon the uniqueness would vanish. There are many Mary's; there are many Jones's; there are even many Mary Jones's. There are many Al's—for nicknames, too, belong here, though with different cultural ramifications. There is a widely known Flatbush in Brooklyn, but there is another in western Canada.

Here, also, may be mentioned the "*x*" of the algebra textbook. In one problem after another, the author says "let *x* represent such-and-such," but the such-and-such varies. Thus, though /éks/ is a perfectly ordinary linguistic form, it works like a substitute or a proper name: we cannot define it once and for all, but can only describe the circumstances in which it is used, newly defined each time.

Proper names and "*x*," like substitutes in their ordinary use, do not involve idiom-forming behavior of the language-changing kind. A change in the design of the language would be, for example, if *Robert* fell into disrepute and disuse, or if the new name invented by the parents mentioned above became popular.

37.3. Abbreviation. One widespread mechanism of idiom formation is *abbreviation:* the use of a part for a whole.

Behind abbreviation lies the fact that, whenever any grammatical form is actually used by a speaker, some of its connections with the circumstances of use, and with the grammatical forms used with it, adhere to it, and turn up as more or less forceful connotations whenever the form is used again. Even when used in the discussion of interior decoration, the word *red* carries along, momentarily hidden, its connotation of political radicalism, and *blue* its connotation of unhappy mood, and these connotations may erupt from hiding into awareness if the circumstances give the slightest push in that direction. In a group thoroughly familiar with poetry, the reciting of any characteristic phrase from a poem is enough to elicit all the rest of the poem in the awareness of the hearers: *Tell me not in mournful numbers* . . .. This last is called *allusion*, and is a variety of abbreviation.

In English, whenever an endocentric phrase with a noun head is used frequently with some special sense, it may happen that the noun will be dropped, the prior part of the form thus taking on the meaning of the whole. At the least noticeable end this verges on, or becomes indistinguishable from, zero anaphora (§30.4): *You take the red cloth, and I'll take the yellow.* But we cannot evoke zero anaphora in a case like *Massachusetts General* for *Massachusetts General Hospital,* or *I'm going up to maternity* for *I'm going up to the maternity ward,* where the conditioning context is not in the immediate environment.

If the original phrase is one in which the noun may be pluralized, then the abbreviated form may likewise be: *You take the white pieces, and I'll take the reds*. The most startling instance of this which has come to the writer's attention is a use of *abridgeds* for *abridged dictionaries:* the spelling of the abbreviated form implies a terminal consonant cluster /jdz/otherwise unknown in English.

A comparable phenomenon is observable in the Romance languages and in Latin. The frequency with which former adjectives in these languages have taken on specialized idiomatic substantival functions is such as to render the distinction between substantive and adjective hard to discern. In Latin, for example, the names of the months in classical times were masculine substantives; but earlier they had been adjectives, masculine to agree with the substantive *mēnsis* 'month': *mēnsis Aprīlis* 'Aprilian month' was abbreviated to *Aprīlis* 'April.'

Something similar occurs in Chinese. We know that formerly *Jūnggwo* meant 'middle kingdom': *jūng* meant, and in some contexts still means, 'middle, center,' while *gwó* is 'country, kingdom.' This is what the Chinese call their own country, earlier thought to be at the center of the world. But by virtue of the meaning of the combination *Jūnggwo*, as the idiomatic designation of a specific country, the first participating morpheme has taken on the meaning of the whole, and is now used in other combinations with that meaning rather than merely the meaning 'middle': *Jūng-Měi* 'China and the United States,' *Jūng-syī* 'China and the West.' Likewise, a morpheme *jī*, earlier simply 'machine,' participates in the two-morpheme idiom *fēijī* 'fly-machine' = 'airplane,' and from this context it has taken on also the meaning 'airplane.' Thus *hùngjàjī* 'bomber' is not even literally to be interpreted as 'hurl bomb machine,' but rather as 'hurl bomb airplane.'

Sapir has reported a closely comparable abbreviative phenomenon from the northern Athapaskan languages.

With these widely separated and structurally dissimilar languages or groups of languages as points for triangulation, we can probably conclude that in one form or another the mechanism is universal.

In English we find also a rather different pattern of abbreviative idiom formation, not attested for many other languages: that of replacing a long word or phrasal compound by its first, or its stressed, syllable, whether or not that syllable has previously been a morpheme. Thus we have *cab* and *bus* from earlier *cabriolet* and *omnibus;* similarly *cello* from *violoncello*, *piano* from *pianoforte*, *plane* from *airplane* or *aeroplane*, and *gent*, or more often the plural *gents*, from *gentleman* or *gentlemen*. The pattern exhibits some variation: *cello* is two syllables, and *plane* is not the most loudly stressed syllable of *airplane*. Some people still write " 'plane" and " 'cello" with an apostrophe as graphic indication of the abbreviation, as though there were something slightly improper about it.

In some circles abbreviations of this sort abound and new ones are freely coined. From the college scene we have many:

/sówš/	for	*sociology*
/ǽnθ/, /ǽnθrow/		*anthropology*
/ékow/		*economics*
/hówm ék/		*home economics*
/kém làeb/		*chemistry laboratory*
/fíz éd/		*physical education.*

The results of this type of abbreviative idiom formation can sometimes not be distinguished from those of another type, found in many literate communities, in which a spoken abbreviation stems from a reading-off of a written abbreviation. The Cornell student word /rówtəsij/ must be of this sort, from the written abbreviation "R.O. T.C." = *Reserve Officers' Training Corps*, because no sort of abbreviative effort on the spoken phrase would yield the shape of the slang term. /kém làeb/ might be of either origin, since the written form "Chem. Lab." could hardly be read off otherwise. /sówš/ is certainly invented without writing, since the written abbreviation "Soc." would yield something like /sák/.

In the administration of F. D. Roosevelt and during World War II, the custom of calling governmental and military agencies and programs by abbreviative nicknames, derived (usually via writing) from their full official titles, became very popular. Two special developments should be noted. If the abbreviated written form can be read off as though it were an ordinary English word, the abbreviated nickname is often produced in this way: /ǽmgàt/ from "AMGOT" for "Allied Military Government of Occupied Territories." In a number of cases, the official long title has been worked out with a conscious view to this kind of abbreviation: thus "Women's Auxiliary Volunteer Emergency Service" was chosen because its initials, "WAVES," spell an ordinary English word of apt denotation and connotation; "United Nations Educational, Scientific, and Cultural Organization" was originally to have a designation minus the word *Scientific*, and that word was added especially to make the written abbreviation "UNESCO" yield what was thought to be an appropriate (though not theretofore meaningful) pronunciation, /juwnéskow/. The second special development is akin to the first: when circumstances lead an organization to change its official name, it may stick to one which yields the same abbreviation, so that the publicity value of the latter will not be sacrificed. "Transcontinental and Western Air" changed to "Trans-World Airlines," preserving the initials "TWA"; the "Committee on Industrial Organization" became the "Congress of Industrial Organizations," preserving the initials "CIO."

37.4. English Phrasal Compounds. An English phrase such as *hatrack, paperweight, bookcase, matchbook, book match*, has three constituents of immediate relevance: *hatrack* has ICs *hat* and *rack*, plus the feature of reduced stress on the second IC. The latter feature seems to be some sort of structural signal or marker (§17.4), but there is a problem as to what it marks. To find out, let us compare some pairs of phrases which differ only in that one of each pair is ordinary whereas the other is a phrasal compound:

a whíte hóuse	*The Whíte Hòuse*
a wóman dóctor	*a wóman dòctor*
a bláck bírd	*a bláckbìrd*
a bláck bóard	*a bláckbòard*
a fíne stóne	*Mr. Fínestòne*
a whíte cáp	*a whítecàp*
a réd cáp	*a rédcàp.*

The difference of meaning for each pair is clear. A *whíte hóuse* is any house which is white; the *Whíte Hòuse* is white, and a house, but also specifically the President's residence. Similarly, a *wóman dóctor* is any doctor who is a woman, a *wóman dòctor* (not rare as a colloquialism) is a gynecologist of either sex. But if we try to discern any parallelism between the successive differences, we fail. About all we can say is that usually a phrasal compound is idiomatic. In the particular examples above, the paired ordinary phrases are not idiomatic, but this is not necessarily the case, as witness *brówn bétty*, a kind of dessert, or *bést mán* at a wedding. In other words, the marker indicates idiomaticity, but by no means all idioms have the marker.

There is also a second type of phrasal compound in English, examples of which likewise seem usually to be idioms; in this type the reduction of stress is on the prior member:

a lóng ísland	*Lòng Ísland*
Sóuth Ohío	*Sòuth Dakóta*
a néw hát	*Nèw Yórk.*

If there were a magazine called *The Yorker*, a huckster could cry out *Get your néw Yórker here;* this is not the same cry as *Get your Nèw Yórker here*, or as *Get your néw Nèw Yórker here*.

We conclude that in each type of phrasal compound the structural signal has no particular meaning save precisely that of marking the form as idiomatic. This conclusion is strengthened when we observe that, in the ordinary course of speaking, people freely produce new phrasal compounds, particularly those of the first type, though usually when there is some special meaning to be signalled. A woman was once heard to comment on the large number of new infants in her neighborhood by saying *Why, it's a veritable báby fàrm.*

These particular channels of idiom formation are favored in English, and are specific to English and certain closely related languages. We have evidence that the first of the two has been in use for many centuries: some common modern English words, now certainly single morphemes, trace back to early idiomatic phrasal compounds. *Housewife* is a relatively recent coinage; *housewife* /hózəf/ 'sewing-kit,' now obsolescent, dates back to a Middle English coinage with elements which have come down separately as *house* and *wife; hussy* comes from an Old English compound /hú·s-wì·f/, coined from the even earlier forms of the same elements.

37.5. Figures of Speech. Students of rhetoric are dealing with idioms, and with patterns of idiom formation, when they talk of *figures of speech*. When we say *he married a lemon*, the morpheme *lemon* 'sour-dispositioned woman' is obviously a different idiom from the same morpheme meaning 'kind of fruit,' and the former usage developed from the latter by a particular figure of speech.

The traditional classification of figures of speech into "hyperbole," "litotes," "oxymoron," "irony," and the like, is based primarily on the literary usages of classical Greek and Roman authors. Some of these figures are found in the more recent literature of the West because of its classical heritage. No one yet knows how universal the valid application of the traditional terms may be. Chinese, Choctaw, colloquial

English, or Menomini may or may not have any figure usefully describable as "irony" or as "metaphor"; any of these may have figures not comfortably subsumed by the classical terms. Individual idiomatic specializations, of course, are almost always unique to a language or group of languages: to speak of the *foot* of a mountain makes no sense whatsoever to an Ojibwa.

In any case, to the classical roster ought to be added the *pun*. A perfect pun involves semantic and grammatical ambiguity in the face of absolute phonemic identity, with both interpretations sensible in the context in which it occurs. A wry lecturer on American history once said *The European missionaries moved westwards through the American wilderness, converting the Indians, mainly to dust,* . . . When the Department of Classical Languages at Cornell was housed in the topmost floor of the oldest and dustiest building on the campus, it was entirely appropriate that they taught *Attic* Greek.

37.6. Slang. It is not certain whether slang is universal or even widespread, but, wherever it is found, its idiomatic nature is clear. Slang depends for its effect on the striking and far-fetched nature of its semantic overtones and its secondary associations (§35). With constant use, the special effect of a slang expression becomes dulled. As this happens, the expression is either abandoned or retained in the "respectable" non-slang vocabulary of the language. This accounts for the short average life of most slang, and for the rapid rate of replacement. *Absquatulate* was once slang for 'go away'; it gave way to *vamoose*, the latter in turn to *scram;* in the early nineteen-fifties teen-agers were using such expressions as *Here's your horn: blow* or *Here's your drum: beat it.* By the date of publication of this book, these last will probably also be old and tired, used only by adults trying to pretend to be teen-agers.

NOTES

New terms: *proper name; abbreviation, allusion; figure of speech.*

On substitutes and proper names, see Jakobson 1957.

An excellent brief survey of Latin figures of speech is given in Hale and Buck 1903. For English one must turn to nineteenth-century discussions of rhetoric; most modern textbooks of Freshman English have little to say about the topic.

SYNCHRONIC
DIALECTOLOGY

38.

IDIOLECT, DIALECT, LANGUAGE

38.1. Descriptive and Synchronic. In §36.1 we introduced the two terms "descriptive" and "synchronic" as though they were synonyms. But there is a distinction. *Descriptive linguistics* deals with the design of the language of some community at a given time, ignoring interpersonal and inter-group differences. Such differences are always to be found in any language spoken by more than one person, since no two people have exactly the same set of speech habits. *Synchronic linguistics* includes descriptive linguistics, and also certain further types of investigation, particularly *synchronic dialectology*, which is the systematic study of inter-personal and inter-group differences of speech habit. Synchronic dialectology is the subject of this and the next two sections.

The firmest point of departure for synchronic dialectology is the *idiolect*. Generally speaking, the totality of speech habits of a single person at a given time constitutes an idiolect. There are certain exceptions. For example, someone born of English-speaking parents in Germany, who learns the one language from his family and the other from his playmates, possesses two idiolects rather than one. It is even convenient to say that an educated Swiss-German, who can converse both in his local dialect and in so-called "Standard" German, possesses two idiolects. In some cases it is impossible to decide whether a speaker has two rather similar idiolects or just one relatively flexible idiolect; fortunately, such marginal cases are not numerous enough to impair the practical utility of the approach.

There are few aims which might lead us to study a single idiolect in detail. Usually we are concerned with the by-and-large habits of some group of people. Yet the notion of idiolect is important, because in the

321

last analysis a language is observable only as a collection of idiolects. Language is the basic instrument by which human beings achieve and carry on collective behavior, but speaking itself (with a few stylized exceptions, such as choral recitation) is not collective behavior. We cannot directly observe the by-and-large speech habits of a whole community. We cannot even observe the *habits* of a single individual: all that is directly observable is the speaking *behavior* of individuals (or its physical results, such as written records); all the rest must be inferred (§16.3).

A language, as just asserted, is a collection of more or less similar idiolects. *A dialect* is just the same thing, with this difference: when both terms are used in a single discussion, the degree of similarity of the idiolects in a single dialect is presumed to be greater than that of all the idiolects in the language. This precludes certain theoretically possible uses of either term: no one would put the German idiolects of Hamburg and the English idiolects of Liverpool into one dialect or language, as over against all other German and English idiolects; nor can we allow a use of "dialect" whereby some speakers of a language speak a "dialect" (e.g., Brooklynese, Southern, rustic) while others speak the "real" language—everyone speaks one dialect or another. Yet we have considerable leeway in the application of both terms. Though usually we speak merely of the "English language," it is not wrong to distinguish, when the occasion arises, between the "British language" and the "American language." Similarly, some specialists speak of a "Central-Atlantic-Coast dialect" of American English, while others do not segregate the idiolects of that region from those further to the north— and both opinions can be defended. The relative looseness of the two terms is a merit, not a defect, for one can add as many precisely delimited technical terms as one needs, based on various criteria of similarity between idiolects.

In the present section we shall use only two criteria, both of which are, so to speak, external, not requiring that the investigator know anything of the design of the idiolects involved. Both criteria stem from an everyday assumption about language: that people who "speak the same language" can understand each other and, conversely, that people who cannot understand each other must be speaking "different languages." The facts are not so simple, yet the everyday expectation can be modified to yield more formal grounds for idiolect-grouping.

Suppose that we are confronted by two individuals, chosen at random from the present population of the world, save that each is a monolingual. By definition, then, each has just one idiolect. If the two speakers can understand each other about everyday matters with no difficulty, we say that their idiolects are *mutually intelligible*. If they cannot understand each other at all, their idiolects are mutually unintelligible. If they can understand each other part of the time, or with one or another degree of difficulty, or only after having listened to each other's speech for a while, then there are two different ways of handling the facts.

One way is to force a clearcut yes-or-no answer for every pair of idiolects. This is not so artificial as it may seem, since most pairs of idiolects, chosen at random, yield results near one end of the scale or the other. Besides, one can set up some minimum degree of ease of intercommunication which will determine an affirmative judgment.

The other way, of course, is to quantify degrees of mutual intelligibility.

38.2. All-or-None Mutual Intelligibility. If we select an initial idiolect, and put with it all the idiolects we can find which are mutually intelligible both with the first one and with each other, the resulting set of idiolects constitutes what we shall call an *L-simplex*. This is illustrated in Figure 38.1. Each dot represents an idiolect; a line connects each

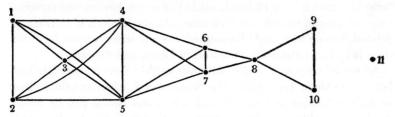

FIGURE 38.1

pair which are mutually intelligible. The set shown in the Figure includes five L-simplexes: 1-2-3-4-5 form one; 4-5-6-7 another; 6-7-8 a third; 8-9-10 a fourth; the lone 11 a fifth. 1-2-3-4-5-6 do not constitute an L-simplex, since 6 is not mutually intelligible with 1, 2, or 3. 1-2-3-4 do not constitute one, because these four are not only all mutually intelligible with each other, but also with 5.

If two idiolects are not mutually intelligible, then sometimes we can discover one or more other idiolects that, together with the first two, constitute a *chain* in which each successive pair are mutually intelligible. Normally one would find the shortest possible chain. Thus, in Figure 38.1, idiolects 1 and 10 are not mutually intelligible, but we can find a chain consisting of 1, 5, 6, 8, and 10 (or with 4 instead of 5, or 7 instead of 6): 1 and 5 are mutually intelligible; likewise 5 and 6; 6 and 8; 8 and 10. If two idiolects are either mutually intelligible or are connected by at least one such chain, they are *linked*. An *L-complex* consists of any idiolect plus all other idiolects which are linked both to the first and (consequently) to each other. In Figure 38.1, all the idiolects but 11 constitute one L-complex, the lone 11 another.

In many cases it turns out that a set of idiolects which has traditionally been called a language, with an established language name, is both an L-simplex and an L-complex. This is probably the case for Menomini, for Choctaw, and for many another language spoken in aboriginal times by some small and relatively autonomous tribe.

In other instances the correlation is not so neat. If by "German" we mean what is usually meant by the term—all the idiolects of Germany, German-speaking Austria, and German-speaking Switzerland—then this "language" is more than a single L-simplex but less than an L-complex. There are pairs of idiolects in "German" which are not mutually intelligible: a speaker from Switzerland and one from the boundary region near Holland, neither of whom has learned standard German, cannot understand each other. All the idiolects of German, as defined, belong to a single L-complex, but the latter is more inclusive, since it includes also all the idiolects of Dutch and Flemish.

All the idiolects of what are ordinarily called "French" and "Italian" belong to a single L-complex. The Norman or Parisian and the Roman or Sicilian cannot understand each other, but chains can be found, passing from village to village across the French-Italian border.

The German situation and the French-Italian situation are different. Within the L-complex that includes German, there is a large L-simplex that includes a high percentage of the idiolects; pairs of mutually unintelligible idiolects are relatively few, and are usually linked by many rather short chains. This is true also of English: the Yorkshireman and the Kentucky mountaineer would have trouble understanding each other, but the former can get along with a Londoner, a Londoner with a New Yorker, and a New Yorker with a Kentucky mountaineer. We can represent the German or English situation with a type of picture: a large circle for the vast numbers of mutually intelligible idiolects (the large included L-simplex) with a few bulges for the minority of extreme types (Figure 38.2). A similar representation of French-Italian takes the shape of a bumpy dumbbell (Figure 38.3): the two halves are for the

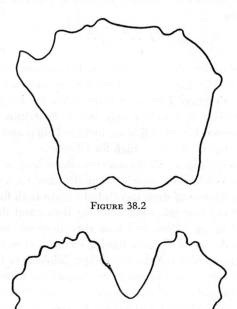

FIGURE 38.2

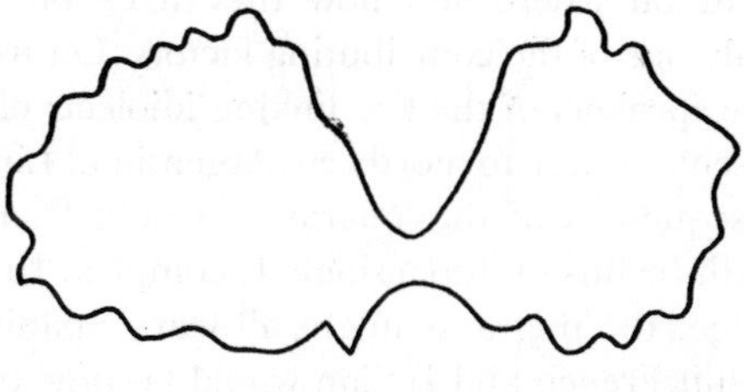

FIGURE 38.3

two large included L-simplexes, and the neck is for the small group of idiolects marginal to both and linking them together.

A representation of Chinese would be much more complicated. All Chinese idiolects form a single L-complex, but within it one can find at least five varieties so divergent from one another as to be mutually quite unintelligible. One of these, Mandarin, is relatively more uniform for some 300,000,000 speakers, though not even all these idiolects are mutually intelligible; the other four involve, all in all, only half as many individuals, and the variation is greater.

Another useful notion in this connection is that of *dialect flexion*. If there are N idiolects in a set, then the number of pairs of idiolects is

$$P = \frac{N(N-1)}{2}.$$

Let M be the number of mutually intelligible pairs of idiolects in the whole set. Then

$$F = \frac{P-M}{P}$$

is the index of dialect flexion of the set. If most pairs of idiolects are mutually intelligible, the flexion is low; if many pairs are mutually unintelligible, it is higher. The index is quite low for English, and even lower if we arbitrarily consider only North American English. It is higher for German, higher still if we include Dutch and Flemish with German; presumably it is very high for Chinese.

It is to be noted that in all the above we have largely ignored geography. The ease with which people can understand each other, and the degree of resemblance of their speech habits, are both functions of the amount of talking that takes place among them, and this, in turn, is partly dependent on where and how they live—on geography. But geography is only one of the contributing factors. Let us in imagination transport all the speakers of the key linking idiolects of French-Italian from their present homes to northern Argentina. Linguistically, the immediate consequences of this migration would be nil. French and Italian would still be linked into a single L-complex. In time, of course, this might change: the migrants might all learn Spanish, or might all die, and as a result French and Italian would become two L-complexes instead of one. But this might happen without the migration. Thus we must distinguish between the state of idiolect-differentiation in a population and its geographical distribution, if only in order to see clearly how the latter, and changes in it, function as causal factors in bringing about changes in the former.

38.3. Degree and Kind of Mutual Intelligibility. There are parts of West Africa where dialect flexion is quite high, though all the idiolects are supposed to belong to a single L-complex. It is said that in some of these regions overt recognition is given to the existence of varying degrees of mutual intelligibility. The inhabitants of village A describe the dialect of adjacent village B as a "two-day" dialect, that of the somewhat more remote village C as a "one-week" dialect, and so on.

What is meant is that in the first case two days of working towards the goal are enough to establish a basis for easy intercommunication about practical matters, whereas in the second case the adjustment requires a week.

The exact nature of the mutual adjustment is not known. It may be that each individual continues to speak in his own way, merely learning to understand the differing speech patterns of the other. Or it may be that each individual modifies his own productive habits as well.

In some other cases we know, in part, the mechanism of adjustment. A Dane who had never heard Norwegian, and a Norwegian who had never heard Danish, would be hard put to it to communicate. Among educated Danes and Norwegians, however, communication is quite unimpeded: each speaks his own personal variety of his own language, but has learned by experience to understand the speech pattern of the others. The result may be called *semi-bilingualism:* receptive bilingualism accompanying productive monolingualism. Similarly, speakers of Chinese from all over the Mandarin area understand the Mandarin of Peiping, with which they have had a great deal of experience (since Peiping is an important cultural and political center), but the man from Peiping cannot understand some of the other varieties of Mandarin without settling down in a region and working at an adjustment of his receptive habits.

In actuality, then, "mutual intelligibility" is not only a matter of degree, rather than of kind, but is not always even mutual.

Some recent studies have tried to face these facts and to quantify, at least roughly, the degree of intelligibility of one dialect or language for a speaker of another. The investigator first makes short recordings in each of the dialects or languages to be tested. A count is made of the *points of content* in each recorded text. Then speakers of each dialect or language are exposed in turn to each of the recordings, including that in their own variety of speech, and a percentagewise determination is made of the number of points of content each subject derives from each text. Since the speaker of dialect A, listening to the recorded text in dialect A, may not catch all the points, his score on his own dialect establishes a base-line for the measurement of his success with the texts in the other dialects.

One such study was made with the current dialects of four Central-Algonquian communities: Shawnee, Kickapoo, Sauk-and-Fox, and

Ojibwa. The resulting percentages of mutual intelligibility were reported as follows: Kickapoo and Sauk-and-Fox, 79%; Shawnee and Kickapoo, 6%; Shawnee and Sauk-and-Fox, 2%; all the remaining pairs, 0%. These results conform to the expectations of anyone acquainted with the four varieties of speech and with the kinds of contacts their speakers have had in the last decades. Kickapoo and Sauk-and-Fox have usually been regarded as closely similar dialects of a single language; Shawnee is regarded as a separate Central Algonquian language, but is shown by analysis to be more similar to Sauk-Fox-Kickapoo than to any other language still spoken. The Kickapoo, Sauk-and-Fox, and Shawnee live not far from each other in Central Oklahoma, but the Sauk-and-Fox have many connections with a linguistically almost identical group of Indians several hundred miles away near Tama, Iowa; the Ojibwa community used in the test is near Mt.

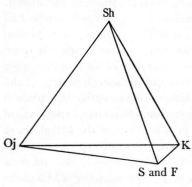

FIGURE 38.4

Pleasant, Michigan. In Figure 38.4 we represent the dialects of the four communities, separated by distances which are, insofar as possible, proportionate to the percentagewise mutual *un*intelligibility. All but Ojibwa are properly spaced to this scale, and Ojibwa is placed just far enough from the other three to be at least distant enough on the same scale: exact scaling proves impossible in a two-dimensional diagram.

The neat figures of percentage of mutual intelligibility were obtained by averaging, for example, the measure of Shawnee understanding of Kickapoo (12%) and that of Kickapoo understanding of Shawnee (0%). The separate figures are even more important. No one but the Shawnees understood more than a negligible percentage of the Shawnee text; no one but the Ojibwas understood much of the Ojibwa text; and the Ojibwas understood virtually none of any of the other texts. The Sauk-and-Fox scored 82% with the Kickapoo text, but the Kickapoos only 76% with the Sauk-and-Fox text. Obviously this reflects a measure of semibilingualism, Kickapoo being the language others learn to understand but not to speak. And the Kickapoos are the perennial wanderers among the Central Algonquians of today: their communities are scattered from northern Mexico to central Oklahoma, with outliers as far northeast as Michigan, and some of them are constantly visiting back and forth.

NOTES

New terms: *descriptive* and *synchronic* are distinguished; *synchronic dialectology; idiolect, a dialect, a language; mutual intelligibility;* "L-simplex" and "L-complex"; dialect "flexion"; *semi-bilingualism.*

Note that *language* (an "uncountable" noun with no plural, like *milk*) and *a language* (a "countable" noun with a plural, like *box*) are different technical terms. English and French are both *language* (uncountable noun), but they are different *languages* (countable noun). In this section and the next it is the meaning of the count-noun *a language* which concerns us.

Measurement of degrees of mutual intelligibility: Hickerson and others 1952; Pierce 1952; Voegelin and Harris 1951. On idiolects, dialects, languages, see Jespersen 1925.

Problem. An anthropologist comes to a mountain valley, in which there are eleven villages. He finds that in all eleven villages different languages or dialects are spoken, but that all eleven are quite obviously related, though none are closely related to any dialects spoken outside the valley. Call the villages (and their dialects) $A, B, \ldots, K$. Experimentation shows that people from different villages can sometimes understand each other and sometimes not. Specifically, the dialects of the following pairs of villages are mutually intelligible: $AB, AC, BC, BD, BE, CD, CF, DE, DF, DI, DJ, EI, EJ, FG, FI, FK, GH, GK, IJ, IK$.

Assuming that the population is all sedentary, so that adjacent villages have dialects showing greater similarity than those of villages further separated, sketch a rough map to show the most probable location of the villages relative to each other. Do not mark "north," because there is no information for this detail of "absolute" geography.

A few people in each village also speak a second language, known to the anthropologist. He wishes to do anthropological work in as many of the villages as possible. If he must use only a single interpreter, what is the best he can do, and from which village should he choose the interpreter? If he can use several interpreters, what is the minimum number which will enable him to work in all eleven villages, and from which villages should they be chosen?

Pretending that each village contains only a single speaker (or that all contain exactly the same number of speakers), compute the index of dialect flexion.

39.

COMMON CORE and
OVERALL PATTERN

39.1. Code Noise. Our discussion of idiolect differentiation in §38 turned entirely on the test of mutual intelligibility. This is an external test: in order to apply it to a pair of idiolects, we do not have to know or say anything about their design (§16.1). But we must go deeper. What correlation is there between degree of mutual intelligibility and similarity of design of the idiolects involved? As might be expected, close similarity implies mutual intelligibility; a certain amount of difference, on the other hand, need not imply mutual unintelligibility. People manage to understand each other even though they signal by divergent codes. An investigation of the reasons for this will show us certain further useful ways of classing idiolects into language-like sets.

To track down the first reason, we must bring up once again the matter of *noise* (§§10.3, 35.2). People whose idiolects are virtually identical often understand each other despite the presence of a good deal of external noise—sound of various sorts which strikes the ears of a hearer along with the speech signal. Such *channel noise* sometimes renders communication difficult or impossible, but often it does not. When it does not, it is because the speech signal, as it leaves the speaker, actually contains far more evidence as to what message the speaker is transmitting than the minimum which the hearer must receive to interpret the message accurately. Channel noise destroys some of that evidence, but does not seriously impair communication so long as a sufficient percentage remains undistorted.

Divergence between the codes of two people who communicate with each other via speech can be regarded as another sort of noise: *code noise*. The reason why people can understand each other despite code noise is exactly the same as the reason why channel noise, up to a point, does not destroy communication. The speech signal which leaves one person contains, in terms of his own total set of habits, more evidence as to what message he is transmitting than the minimum which he himself would have to receive to understand the message. Some of this evidence may be irrelevant for a particular hearer, whose speech habits deviate from those of the speaker, but if a sufficient proportion of the evidence falls within the shared portions of the two sets of habits, the hearer will still understand.

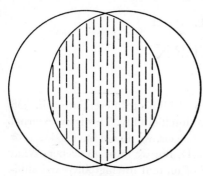

FIGURE 39.1.   TWO IDIOLECTS WITH A COMMON CORE

Each circle represents an idiolect; the hatched area represents their common core.

The effect of the two sorts of noise on communication is the same. If, for a certain pair of idiolects, there is virtually no code noise (that is, if the two sets of habits are virtually identical), then communication is possible despite a relatively great amount of channel noise. If, for another pair of idiolects, there is a larger amount of code noise, then communication is possible only if the channel noise is less. All sorts of everyday experiences bear this out: we understand native speakers of our own variety of English over poor telephone circuits, and people with thick foreign accents when we are face-to-face with them, but have trouble if people of the latter sort talk with us over the telephone.

39.2. Common Core. If any group of people regularly communicate via speech, then the first possible responsible factor is that their idiolects involve shared features; the total set of shared features we shall call the *common core* of the idiolects. Barring channel noise, speech in any of the idiolects is understandable to speakers of all the others as long as it remains within the common core, while any momentary resort to the features peculiar to the speaker's idiolect and not shared by the others constitutes code noise. For example, *A* may pronounce *can* 'container' and *can* 'be able' differently, while *B* does not distinguish them. *A* and *B* nevertheless agree in keeping both words distinct from *con* and *ken*. The agreement belongs to the common core of the two idiolects; the disagreement represents an idiosyncrasy for each.

In Figure 39.1 we show, in a very simple way, two idiolects which have a common core. Theoretically, a set of three idiolects might be mutually intelligible and yet not have, as a whole set, any common core. We show in Figure 39.2 how this is theo-
retically possible: idiolects *A* and *B* have a common core; likewise *A* and *C*; like-wise *B* and *C*; but *A*, *B*, and *C*, taken to-gether, have none. If speech is produced in idiolect *A*, the speakers of *B* and *C* may both understand, but on the basis of differ-ent portions of the whole signal. In prac-tice, however, this sort of situation does not seem to turn up. More typical is the situation in which hundreds, thousands, or even millions of different idiolects share a discernible common core, which can be observed approximately (via sta-tistical sampling) and described subject to some degree of indeterminacy. Thus our phonemic notation for English (§§2–6) comes close to being a notation for those contrasts which are shared by all speakers of North American English,

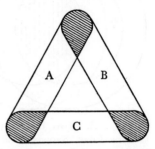

FIGURE 39.2. THREE MUTU-ALLY INTELLIGIBLE IDIOLECTS WITH NO COMMON CORE

Each of the elongated lozenges represents an idiolect. Each two share a common core, repre-sented by the hatched areas, but three taken together share nothing. (There is, of course, no "scale" to such diagrams: all that counts is regions, bounda-ries, and intersections.)

and for no other contrasts; it deviates from this mainly in that it pro-vides for the contrast between *cot* (/a/) and *caught* (/ɔ/), which a good many millions of speakers in Central and Western Canada and adja-cent portions of the United States do not have.

39.3. Semi-Bilingualism. There is, however, a second important reason for mutual intelligibility in the face of divergence of idiolect design. A given speaker may constrain his speech to the bounds of his own code, and yet be trained to understand things that he would not say. In Figure 39.3 we elaborate the representation of Figure 39.1 to allow for this. For each speaker, the inner circle marks the bounds of his *productive* idiolect, while the outer circle marks the bounds of what he is trained to understand. Speech from *A* may thus fall outside the productive idiolect of *B* without automatically constituting code noise; it is code noise only if it falls outside the larger circle for *B*. This sort of situation is immediately reminiscent of semibilingualism (§38.3).

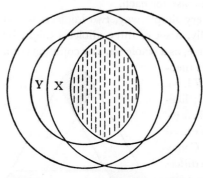

FIGURE 39.3. TWO IDIOLECTS WITH A COMMON CORE, SHOWING THE DISTINCTION BETWEEN PRODUCTIVE AND RECEPTIVE CONTROL

The left-hand circles represent A's idiolect: the smaller circle for his range of productive control, the larger for his receptive control. The right-hand circles similarly represent B's idiolect. The hatched area is their common (productive) core. If something A says falls in region X, it is still understandable to B, though B would not have said it; if it falls in region Y, it is code noise for B.

It would even be possible for two people to communicate without any common core at all between their productive idiolects. Imagine a Frenchman who understands, but cannot speak, German, and a German who likewise has receptive but not productive control of French. This is depicted in Figure 39.4: the circles representing the productive idiolects do not intersect, but the larger circles representing the boundaries of receptive control do. As might be suspected, it is considerably easier to draw an abstract picture of this situation than it is to find an actual case of it—just as for the theoretically possible case depicted in Figure 39.2. The easy intercommunication of educated Danes and Norwegians (§38.3) is not a case, for Danish and Norwegian show a sizable common core.

39.4. Overall Pattern. All our pictures must be interpreted as instantaneous snapshots: in even short periods of time, the boundaries of an individual's productive and receptive control change, for they are highly labile. A private uses the word *sir* oftener than a commissioned officer, but the latter knows the word just as well as the former: if the private is commissioned, or the officer demoted, his productive system is slightly changed. Language-learning never ceases. What stands outside an individual's sphere of receptive control today may be within it

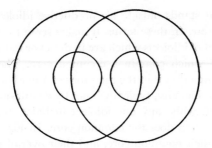

FIGURE 39.4.   MUTUAL INTELLIGIBILITY WITH NO COMMON CORE

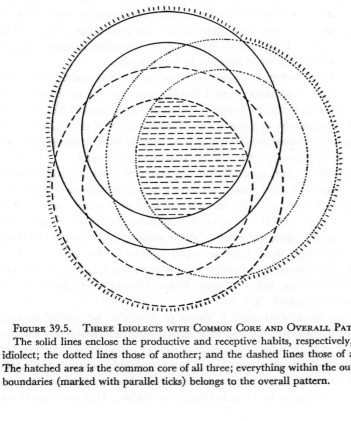

FIGURE 39.5.   THREE IDIOLECTS WITH COMMON CORE AND OVERALL PATTERN
The solid lines enclose the productive and receptive habits, respectively, of one idiolect; the dotted lines those of another; and the dashed lines those of a third. The hatched area is the common core of all three; everything within the outermost boundaries (marked with parallel ticks) belongs to the overall pattern.

tomorrow; what stands outside his productive idiolect today may be within it tomorrow. In these terms, it makes sense to speak of an *overall pattern* for any set of idiolects which are in direct or indirect contact with each other and which contain a common core. The overall pattern includes everything that is in the repertory of any idiolect, productively or receptively. It includes, typically if not by definition, more than does any one idiolect, while any one idiolect includes, typically if not by definition, more than does the common core. In Figure 39.5 we show three idiolects, their common core, and their overall pattern, to make the statements just given more graphic.

In a literate community such as our own, it is even possible in effect for the overall pattern to include features not found in any idiolect—though this is in part a matter of definition. Written materials may contain words which no one in the community actively uses, and yet someone may draw a word from such sources and start using it again, thus introducing it at least into his own idiolect. Theodore Roosevelt is said to have revived the word *strenuous* in just this way.

39.5. Application. Common core and overall pattern do not afford us, any more than does mutual intelligibility, a way of determining really sharp boundaries between different "languages." Yet they do supply another way of recognizing language-like sets of idiolects, and, perhaps more important, show that sometimes descriptive statements which are apparently contradictory can be equally valid.

On the first point, note that we can take any single idiolect as point of departure and class with it all those idiolects which share a discernible common core both with the first and with each other, excluding all those which do not. We imagine that all idiolects of what is normally called English would belong to a single such set, and that no idiolects usually excluded from English would belong to the same set. It is possible, though not certain, that by this test French and Italian would come out separate, not as a single linked idiolect-group as under the L-complex approach (§38.2).

Having established such a group of idiolects, we can then take several different approaches in studying and describing it. One approach is to study some one idiolect or dialect without reference to other idiolects. Some have asserted that this is the only possible approach, and that it thus does not make sense to talk about, say, phonemes, except with reference to a single idiolect or dialect. This assertion is not convincing, for a second alternative is to describe the whole group of idiolects in terms of their common core: so long as one remains within *this* frame of reference for North American English, it makes perfect sense to say that the vowels of *can* 'container' and *can* 'be able' are phonemically identical, despite the fact that some speakers regularly distinguish the words.

Still a third approach attempts to determine the overall pattern of the whole group of idiolects, by taking a statistical sample of idiolects (one obviously could not work with every speaker of English in North America) and operating on them together. Under this approach, the vowels of *can* 'container' and *can* 'be able' are phonemically distinct, despite the fact that many people do not distinguish them—because *some* people do. Furthermore, if a particular speaker has the first vowel in some words, the second in others, but with such distribution that within his idiolect the two are not in contrast, we still, under this third approach, regard them as phonemically distinct. The basis of functional contrast, under this approach, is not only the difference between *A*'s pronunciation of one utterance and *A*'s pronunciation of another utterance, but also the difference between *A*'s pronunciation of one utterance and *B*'s pronunciation of the same or another.

The third approach—via overall pattern—is particularly useful in that it affords us an excellent frame of reference for dealing with pattern differences between idiolects or dialects. The overall pattern of a language is a sort of arsenal; each idiolect represents a selection from it, sometimes symmetrical and sometimes skew. As an example of this we shall present, in the next section, a description of the phonological overall pattern of North American English insofar as it concerns stressed syllabics, and show how certain key regional dialects fit into it.

NOTES

New terms: *channel* and *code* noise; *common core* and *overall pattern; productive* versus *receptive* idiolect.

In the days before the phonemic principle had emerged clearly, the overall pattern approach in phonology was foreshadowed by specialists who devised sets of phonetic symbols for the handling of specific families of languages or dialects with which they had had some experience. One such system was devised by Lundell for the study of Swedish dialects (referred to by Bloomfield 1933, p. 87); another by Meinhof for the Bantu languages. These sets of phonetic symbols did not attempt to provide for all the articulatory differences which might prove distinctive in this or that language in the world, but focussed primarily on types of differences known to be "important" (that is, probably, phonemic) in one or another of the dialects in question. The fact that we now undertake a comparable task in rather more rigorous fashion does not prevent these earlier cases from being anticipations of modern methods.

40

AMERICAN ENGLISH STRESSED SYLLABICS

40.1. The Overall Pattern. The stressed syllabic nuclei (syllable peaks, §11.3) of American English are of two types, *simple* and *complex*. A simple syllabic consists of one or another of nine vowel phonemes:

	front unrounded	central to back unrounded	back rounded
high	/í/	/ɨ́/	/ú/
mid	/é/	/ə́/	/ó/
low	/ǽ/	/á/	/ɔ́/;

while a complex syllabic consists of one of these nine vowels plus one of three glides, /j w ˅/. The first of these is a glide towards high front tongue position, the second a glide towards high back tongue position with progressive rounding of the lips, and the third a glide towards mid or low central tongue position.

Some words are pronounced in identical ways by almost everyone. Using these words, we can illustrate many, but by no means all, of the syllabics of the system:

/í/: *bit, hiss, hip, kick, hitch, riff, myth.*
/é/: *kept, bet, neck, mess, Jeff.*
/ǽ/: *cap, hat, batch.*
/ú/: *book, put, look, foot, puss.*
/ə́/: *but, bud, bun, bus, buzz, cup, luck.*

339

/á/: *cot, lock, hop, botch, bosh* (except in Eastern New England,
where, as in Southern British English, these words have /ó/).
/íj/: *beet, peep, leak, reach.*
/éj/: *pate, cape, sake.*
/úw/: *boot, spook.*
/ów/: *cope, boat, roach, poke.*
/áᵛ/: *spa, hah, bah, fa, la.*

These examples illustrate only eleven of the syllabics, out of a total of
thirty-six. To illustrate the rest, we have to consider certain individual
words or families of words, which are pronounced with one or another
syllabic in various different parts of the country.

A fundamental distinction for this survey is among: (1) words in
which virtually no one has an /r/ after the syllabic (all those listed for
the examples above); (2) words which have an intervocalic /r/, as
spirit, marry; (3) words in which, in Middle Western pronunciation, the
syllabic is followed by /r/ and then by another consonant, as *spurt,
mark;* (4) words in which, in Middle Western pronunciation, the syllabic is followed by a word-final /r/, as *spur, mar.* Dialectwise, we distinguish between *rful* and *rless* varieties of English: the rless dialects are
located in Eastern and Coastal New England, New York City and
environs, along the east coast southwards, and in various parts of the
South. Rless speakers elsewhere are either recent arrivals or are acquiring (or trying to acquire) rless speech because of the prestige influence
of stage, screen, radio, television, or the like. In words of type (1), no
one has an /r/; in words of type (2), everyone does; in those of type
(3), rful speakers have an /r/ and rless speakers do not. In words of
type (4), rful speakers have an /r/, but rless speakers fall roughly into
two groups. Some have an /r/ if the next word begins with a vowel
(*spear it, the war is*) and not otherwise (*spear them, the war was*); others
often have no /r/ even when the next word begins with a vowel. In the
discussion below, "rless" will refer to the first of these groups, since the
behavior of the other group of speakers is easily deduced from wnat we
say about the first.

40.2. The High Front Region. Words like *with, his, is, if, this,* which
often occur without stress, quite commonly turn up in stressed position
with /í/ instead of /í/.

Children, silver, milk, and perhaps some other words in which the vowel is followed by /l/ plus a consonant, often have /ɨ/; *milk* is /mélk/ for some speakers.

In *pretty good,* the pronunciations /prítij/ and /pɨrtij/ are both common; in *a pretty girl* one is more apt to hear /prítij/, but for some people /ɨ/ is over-precise even for this use of the word.

In the South, *sister, dinner,* and some other two-syllable words often have /ɨ/.

In words like *crib, bid, ridge, big, rim, shin, live, is,* where the syllabic is followed by a voiced consonant, many speakers in the southern Middle West and in the north central parts of the South have /ɨˇ/ rather than /ɨ/.

In all the words so far considered, /í/ will be heard from at least some speakers—even those who in natural speech use some other syllabic may use /í/ in precise enunciation.

In many parts of the South, /í/ and /é/ do not contrast before /n/. *Bin* and *Ben* thus sound the same, as do *fin* and *fen, pin* and *pen.* Usually the syllabic used in both words of the pairs is /í/, but in some regions it may be /é/.

We next consider several sets of words where /é/ is often heard, but not always.

The same speakers who often have /íˇ/ instead of /í/ before voiced consonants also tend to have /éˇ/ instead of /é/ in the same circumstances: e.g., in *web, dead, fez, hedge, peg.*

Many Middle Westerners have /éj/ rather than /é/ in *leg, egg,* though words like *peg, beg, dregs, keg, Meg* seem to have only /é/. On the other hand, some speakers (South? Far West?) do not have /éj/ anywhere before /g/, saying not only /lég/, /ég/ but also /vég/ *vague,* /plég/ *plague.* Akin to this is /í/ instead of /íj/ in *league,* found occasionally in southern New Jersey.

Yeah is /jéˇ/ or /jæˇ/ for various speakers, perhaps more often the former. Another casual form of *yes* is /jéw/.

Most words which have /íj/ for anyone have it for almost everyone. However, in Philadelphia and some adjacent regions, down to Baltimore and perhaps up through central New Jersey, one hears /ɨj/ in *me, he, see, we,* and, for some speakers, also before a voiced consonant as in *mean, heed, seed, heave.* Some rural Rhode Island speech, and that of

Martha's Vineyard, have /ív/ in *beans, teeth.* Many speakers in many areas have /ív/ before /l/, as in *feel, real,* and some of these have a contrast between /ríjl/ *reel* and /rívl/ *real* (both different from /ríl/ *rill*). *Idea, theater, museum* are often /ajdíjə θíjətər mjuwzíjəm/, but the sequence /íjə/ is replaced by /ív/ in "higher-class" East Coast speech in *idea* and *theater;* the writer has /ív/ in *museum* /mjuwzívm/, but this is apparently idiosyncratic.

There is also widespread agreement on the use of /éj/ in many words. Certain "finishing-school" types in and near New York City have /ǽj/ in a few words, such as *gray,* where /éj/ is most usual. Charleston has /ív/ in some common words like *eight, ate,* where most speakers have /éj/. Before /l/, some speakers have /év/ instead of /éj/: /pévl/ *pale.*

Spirit, mirror generally have /í/. *Fierce, fears, feared* generally have /ívr/ in rful speech, /ív/ in rless. *Fear, dear, spear* have /ívr/ in rful speech, /ív/ in rless save when the next word begins with a vowel, when an /r/ appears. Thus *spirit* and *spear it* generally contrast, as /spírɨt/ and /spívrɨt/. However, many or most Middle Westerners have only /ír/ in all such words, with no contrast, except that occasionally a rare word or two may have /íjr/: *eerie,* perhaps, pronounced /íjrij/ in contrast to *Erie* /írij/.

40.3. The Low Front Region. *Cap, hat, batch, tack,* and other words with a stop /p t č k/ after the syllabic, have /ǽ/ almost everywhere; but in the writer's speech, and for some others from the southern Middle West, *tack* and others with following /k/ have /ǽj/.

In words where a voiced consonant follows the syllabic and another vowel follows that, and in which there is no morpheme boundary after the consonant—*cabinet, Cadillac, flagon, Savarin*—/ǽ/ is quite general. In monosyllabic words with a final voiced consonant, and in polysyllabic words where there is a morpheme boundary after the medial consonant, /ǽv/ and /év/ are very common in the Middle West and in the Central Atlantic Seaboard, and /ǽv/ in New England. In the Central Atlantic Seaboard, minimal contrasts between /ǽ/ and /ǽv/ or /év/ are quite common. *Can* 'be able' may have /ǽ/, *can* 'container' the complex nucleus. Likewise *Cab* (*Calloway*) with /ǽ/ but (*taxi*)*cab* with a complex nucleus; *hand* (verb) with /ǽ/ but *hand* (noun) with a complex nucleus; *have* versus *halve,* the name *Manning* versus *manning, hammer* (tool) versus *hammer* 'ham actor.' Sometimes the assignments of syllabics to these pairs are reversed. At least some Middle Atlantic Seaboard speakers have both diphthongs: *have* with /æ/, *salve* with /ǽᵛ/, *halve* with /éᵛ/.

All words which in the regions just mentioned have a centering glide may in the South have /ǽj/: /pǽjs/ *pass*, /hǽjnd/ *hand*. The writer has /ǽj/ in *ashes, bag, sang*, which represents a northwards upthrust of this habit into central Ohio.

Some complex nucleus, instead of the vowel /ǽ/, seems to be commonest before /f s v z/, then /b d/, then /m n/, and rarest before /ŋ l/.

British English, of course, has /áᵛ/ rather than /ǽ/ in a number of words where /f v θ s nd/ follows: *calf, calves, path, pass, command*. In Boston and northern coastal New England most of these words have a slightly fronted centering nucleus which we take to be /áᵛ/, since it contrasts with a clearly more fronted centering nucleus /ǽᵛ/ in a word like *lather*.

Catch has /é/ instead of /ǽ/ in some Southern speech and in some northern rural speech, usually alongside a more "elegant" pronunciation with /ǽ/.

Merry, ferry, Terry, herald usually have /é/. *Marry, Harry, Harold, harrow* have /ǽ/ in New England, the Middle Atlantic region, and the South Atlantic region, so that *merry* and *marry* contrast as /mérij/ and /mǽrij/. In most of the Middle West, however, all of these words have /é/. Some older-generation Middle Western speech has /éj/ in a few words: /méjrij/ *Mary*. South central Pennsylvania and western Maryland seem to have /áᵛ/ in *marry*.

In New England and the South Atlantic region, *Mary, hairy, fairy, daring* have /éᵛ/; in the Middle Atlantic region they usually have /é/, as is the rule in the Middle West. Some parts of the South show /éj/.

Scarce, scares, scared, and such imported words as *bairn, cairn, laird*, generally have /éᵛr/ in rful speech, /éᵛ/ in rless. *Scare, fair, wear* work the same way, allowing for the presence of /r/ in rless speech only before a vowel, as in *scare 'em*. Here, also, most Middle Western speech has simply /ér/.

40.4. The High Back Region. Words which are often unstressed in context, like *could, would, should*, turn up stressed with /í/ as well as with /ú/. This is true also of *good;* all four words sometimes are heard with

/ɨ̆/ instead of either /ɪ̆/ or /ŭ/. Some words often pronounced with /ŭ/ before a voiced consonant have /ŭˇ/ for those speakers who tend to have /ɪ̆ˇ/ rather than /ɪ̆/ in *did*, *bib*, and the like.

There is one set of words, *room*, *root*, *soot*, *hoop*, *food*, *bosom*, and a few others, which vary quite erratically between /ŭ/ and /úw/: two speakers from a single region may not agree as to the assignments of one or the other syllabic to the different words. In the region from Philadelphia to Baltimore the complex alternant is often, or perhaps usually, /ɨ̆w/ instead of /úw/; this may extend into New Jersey.

Push has /új/ for a good many Middle Westerners, particularly in the more southern parts (Ohio, Indiana, Illinois); elsewhere it generally has /ú/.

Do, *lose*, *loose*, *boon*, *booed*, *boot*, *spook* generally have /úw/. The Baltimore-Philadelphia region often has /ɨ̆w/ instead of /úw/ when no consonant follows (*do*, *too*), or when a voiced consonant follows (*moon*, *spoon*).

Some older-generation rural Middle Westerners have /ɨ̆w/ or /jɨ̆w/ in words like *cute*, *cube*, *abuse*, *few*, *yew*, *ewe*, instead of /júw/. For some, *yew* and *you* contrast as /jɨ̆w/ and /júw/, but for others both are /jɨ̆w/.

In the Eastern Coastal regions generally, /úw/ and /júw/ are kept distinct: /túw/ *two*, /tjúwn̥/ *tune*. The distinction is also generally maintained in Canada. In much of the Middle West, and even in western New York, the distinction is lost after apical consonants /t d s z n l/: *tune*, *dune*, *assume*, *newel*, *lucid* all have /úw/ without a preceding /j/. The loss of the /j/ is most widespread after /l/, and least after /t d n/. Some Middle Western speakers who have only /úw/ in the above words retain the /j/ in another family: *Teuton*, *Deuteronomy*, *deuteron*, *neuron*, *neurotic;* others have /úw/ in these words too.

Before /l/, some speakers have /úˇ/ instead of /úw/: /fúˇl/ *fool*.

Most words which have /ów/ in the Middle West (*coat*, *bone*, *code*, *road*, *phone*, etc.) belong to a single family, in the sense that in any one dialect region they all have the same nucleus. The nucleus is /ów/ in much of the East and South as well as in the Middle West, but /ɔ́w/ in upper-class New England and New York City speech (as in Southern British, where there are even instances of /éw/), and in upper and lower class Philadelphia speech.

However, Charleston has /úˇ/ instead of /ów/ in some homely words: *coat*, *note*. And one set of words, including *road*, *coat*, *home*, *whole*, *stone*, have /ó/ in older-generation rural New England speech. The word *whole*, particularly in some set expressions like *the whole thing*, has /ó/ instead of /ów/ quite generally over the country. *Shone* apparently has /ó/ instead of /ów/ in much of Canada.

Some speakers have / óᵛ/ instead of /ów/ before /l/, as in /kóᵛl/ *coal*.

Fury, jury generally have /ú/. *Boors, Bourse, assured* have /úr/ in the Middle West, /úᵛr/ fairly generally in Eastern rful speech, and /úᵛ/ in rless. *Booʳ, poor, sure* have the same, rless adding an /r/ before a vowel. /r/-final monosyllables tend to keep the same syllabic when a suffix is added, so that in the East *boorish* and *poorest* may contrast with *jury, jury*, the former with /úᵛr/, the latter with /úr/.

40.5. The Low Back Region. *Cot, lock, hop, botch, bosh*, and other words in which the syllabic is followed by a voiceless consonant, regularly have /á/; before a voiced consonant, as in *cod, hob, dodge, Oz*, many speakers have /áᵛ/ either regularly or else optionally instead of /ä'/. However, in eastern New England, as in Southern British, all these words have /ó/. Thus, where the Middle Westerner contrasts *cut* and *cot* as /kót/ and /kát/, the eastern New Englander says /kót/ and /kót/, and the Englishman says /kát/ and /kót/.

After /w/, or before /g/ or /ŋ/, /ó/, or in the Middle West often /óᵛ/, is usual instead of /á/: *watch, waffle, want, hog, dog, log, fog, cog, long, strong*. The writer, and sporadically a few other Middle Westerners, pronounces the *l* in the words *balm, calm, alms, psalm, palm*, and uses /ó/ rather than /á/ before it. *Wash* is highly variable: in the Middle West one will hear /wáš/, /wóš/, /wóš/, /wóᵛs/, /wórš/, or /wójš/— the latter apparently only from those who say /pújš/ for *push*.

In the east, and occasionally in the Middle West, *bomb* and *balm* contrast, with /á/ in the first, /áᵛ/ in the second.

Law, paw, laud, awning, fawn, hawk, saw, pause have /óᵛ/ generally in the Middle West and along the East Coast except in the South. In New York City, Philadelphia, and Baltimore, as well as in some British speech, the syllabic is /óᵛ/ in all these words. In many parts of the South it is /ów/.

Father usually has the same syllabic as *balm*, but in educated Baltimore speech, and perhaps in Philadelphia and some adjacent regions, *father* has /óᵛ/.

In the northernmost Middle West (northern Michigan, Wisconsin,

Minnesota), in Ontario, in Canada west of Ontario, and in an indeterminately large region of the American northwest stretching into Utah, there are no contrasts between /á/ and /ɔ́/. The possible syllabics in the words we have just discussed are /á/ and /áˇ/: the former in *cot, lock, hop, botch, cosh, watch, waffle, want, hawk;* the latter in *law, paw, saw, spa, pa, fa, la;* perhaps /áˇ/ and perhaps free variation in *cod, hob, dodge, Oz, hog, dog, log, fog, cog, long, strong.*

The words *spa, pa, fa, la, bah* seem to have /áˇ/ everywhere.

The natural-speech form *gonna* (for *going to*) varies a great deal: /ɔ́/ is common, but so also are /ɔ̌/, /ɔ̌/, and even /á/.

Part, harp, hark, larch, farce, harsh, hearth have /ár/ in rful speech, /áˇ/ in rless. *Card, large, Marg, carve, bars, harm, barn, Carl* have /áˇr/ in rful speech, but /áˇ/ in rless; in rless speech, *father* and *farther* are usually alike. In the Middle West, all the words listed usually have /ár/, rather than /áˇr/. In parts of the East one may have /ɔ́ˇ/ (rless) and /ɔ́r/ or /ɔ́ˇr/ (rful) in some of these words.

Far, par, star, car have /ár/ in the Middle West, /áˇr/ in rful speech in the East, and /áˇ/ in rless, save before a vowel.

Fort, porch, pork, north, force have Middle Western /ór/ or /ɔ́r/, Eastern rful the same, and Eastern rless /óˇ/ or /ɔ́ˇ/, generally the former. *Ford, form, horn, whorl* have Middle Western /ór/ or ɔ́r/, Eastern rful /óˇr/ or /ɔ́ˇr/, Eastern rless /óˇ/ or /ɔ́ˇ/. In New York city, *lord* = *laud* = /lóˇd/; in Eastern Coastal New England *chordata* = *caudata* = /kɔ̀ˇdátə/.

Some dialects contrast *hoarse* and *horse, mourning* and *morning,* and some other pairs, generally with /ó/ or a complex nucleus beginning with /ó/ in the first member of the pair, and /ɔ́/ or a nucleus beginning therewith in the second. This is found even in the Middle West, but there some older-generation speakers have /ówr/ in *hoarse, mourning.*

For, store, core have /ór/ in the Middle West, /óˇr/ or ɔ́r/ in Eastern rful, and /óˇ/ or /ɔ́ˇ/ in Eastern rless (save before a vowel). Thus in rless speech *lore* and *law* may contrast as /lóˇ/ and /lɔ́ˇ/, or may be identical—New York City both /lóˇ/, New England both /lɔ́ˇ/.

When a suffix beginning with a vowel is added to a monosyllabic word ending in /r/, the nucleus before the /r/ is usually kept unchanged: /stáˇr/ *star* and /stáˇrij/ *starry* in Eastern rful speech. But in words of the type of *sorry, sorrow, borrow, tomorrow,* with no active morpheme boundary after the /r/, other things happen. The four just listed almost universally have /á/ (/sárij/ and so on); the one exception is among some Northwestern speakers, who have /ó/: /sórij/ and so on. Words like *orange, porridge, forest, Morris, chorus, Lawrence* have variously /á/, /ɔ́/, or /ó/, save that in the Northwest /ɔ́/ does not occur. Even two speakers from a single region often will not agree in their assignment of syllabics in these words.

40.6. The Mid Central Region. American English is highly uniform in its use of /ə́/ in words like *but, bud, bun, bus, buzz, come, cup, luck, other, mother,* and the like; here Southern British English deviates sharply, having /á/.

Just, as in *He just got here,* has /ə́/ quite commonly in deliberate speech, but /ɨ/ is extremely common everywhere in more natural speech. The adjective *just* (*a just man*) is normally pronounced with /ə́/. This gives a four-way contrast between /í/, /é/, /ɨ/, and /ə́/: *gist, jest, just* (adv.) and *just* (adj.).

Tulsa is /tɨ́lsə/ for some speakers; likewise *come* is /kɨm/ for some— probably as a restressing of the unstressed form of the word in such expressions as *come on, come here.*

The word *the* is occasionally cited in isolation, or stressed in context; many people use the pronunciation /ðíj/ under these conditions, but one also hears /ðə́ˇ/.

Hurt, twerp, church, lurk, mirth, nurse have /ə́r/ in the Middle West and in Eastern rful speech, /ə́ˇ/ or /ɨˇ/ in Eastern rless. *Blurb, heard, urge, berg, verve, stirs, worm, fern, curl* have /ə́r/ in the Middle West, /ə́ˇr/ or /ɨˇr/ in Eastern rful, and /ə́ˇ/ or /ɨˇ/ in Eastern rless. *Fur, sir, cur* have /ə́r/ in the Middle West, /ə́ˇr/ or /ɨˇr/ in Eastern rful, and /ə́ˇ/ or /ɨˇ/ in Eastern rless, adding an /r/ before a vowel. Minimum contrasts for any one speaker are rare, but one New Jersey speaker has /pɨ́rtij/ *pretty,* /θə́rtij/ *thirty.*

Where a vowel follows the /r/ (in the same word), contrasts are found. One Rhode Island speaker contrasts *furry* and *hurry* as /fɨˇrij/ and /hə́ˇrij/; some speakers in the Middle Atlantic region contrast the same pair as /fə́rij/ and /hə́ˇrij/.

Older-generation New York City speech, and that of certain small regions in the South, including New Orleans, have /ə́j/ in *hurt, twerp, blurb, urge,* and so on. In words like *fur, sir,* /ə́j/ is very rare, but does occur. A few extreme New York City types seem to have /ój/, but the parody-Brooklynese *thoid*, *boid* is inaccurate, the actual forms having /ój/.

40.7. Syllabics with Extensive Glides. Middle Western has /áj/ in a great many forms: *mine, thine, my, lie, pipe, sight, hike, ride,* and so on. In many parts of the South, these words have /áˇ/, though some Southern speakers have a few with /áj/ as well. New York City generally has /ój/ in all these words. In the northern Middle West and Ontario (and perhaps in more of Canada), /áj/ is common finally or before a voiced consonant, but /ój/ is heard generally before a voiceless consonant: *lie, lied, line, lies* with /áj/, but *light, mice, spike* with /ój/. Some speakers in this region use /ój/ in some of the first set of words also.

Before /l/, /æˇ/ or /áˇ/ occurs for some speakers who do not have the Southern habit of using this more generally in place of /áj/: *I'll* /æˇl/ or /áˇl/, *file.*

Middle Western English also has many words with /ój/: *hoist, boil, boy, coy, coil, Coyne,* and so on. In a few rural regions all homely words of this sort have /áj/, just as in *buy, high, height,* /ój/ occurring only in recent importations—thus *hoist* 'lift' and *boil* may be /hájst/ and /bájl/, whereas *hoist* 'type of road or mining machinery' may be /hójst/. In parts of the South, one hears /óˇ/ instead of /ój/ before /l/: /óˇl/ *oil.*

Middle Western English has /áw/ in *about, loud, down, house, rouse, now;* so does New England. In parts of the South, in the southern Middle West, and in all of New Jersey and eastern Pennsylvania, these words have /æw/. In Tidewater Virginia they have /ów/, sometimes even /éw/. In the northern Middle West and in much of Canada, /ów/ is usual before a voiceless consonant, as in *about, house, out,* while /áw/ occurs before a voiced consonant and finally, as in *houses, loud, down, now.* This distribution of /ów/ and /áw/ in this region is often disturbed: thus some say /hóws/ and /háwzɨz/, others /háws/ and /háwzɨz/, still others /hóws/ and /hówzɨz/.

40.8. Alternation between Simple and Complex Nucleus. In a number of cases, we have seen words which are pronounced by certain speakers in two different ways, one of them often involving a simple syllabic, the other a complex one. For example: /á/ and /áˇ/ in Middle Western *cod, hob, bomb, balm,* or /æ/ and /æˇ/ or /éˇ/ in some other cases.

It should be noted that the speaker's choice of one or the other form is often conditioned by the location of the word relative to stress and pitch phonemes. The writer would say ²*bomb and de³stroy*¹↓ with /bám/, but ²*shell and* ³*bomb*¹↓ with /báˇm/. A colleague, originally from Illinois, speaks regularly of /²hǽfin+³hǽˇf¹↓/ *half-and-half.* /²hǽnd+in+³hǽˇnd¹↓/ *hand in hand* is quite common. One Rhode Island speaker cites the word *bother* in isolation as /³báð̇ər¹↓/ and *father* as /³fáˇð̇ər¹↓/; but in saying ²*You don't need to* ³*bother*¹↓ (or ³*You* ²*don't need to* ²*bother*²↑) he uses /áˇ/ in *bother*, and in saying ²*My father can't* ³*come*¹↓ he uses /á/ in *father*. In the southern Middle West, *Did he go?* may have /díd/, and ²*He* ⁴*did*²↑ may have /díˇd/.

The conditioning factor, as these examples show, is the intonation. In any ordinary sentence (not a special one-word sentence which is simply citation of a word), the word has the complex nucleus if it is at the center of the intonation, the simple vowel otherwise.

NOTES

The great bulk of the observations here reported were made by Trager and Smith 1951. These investigators posit that the glide /ˇ/ is phonemically the same as the prevocalic consonant /h/; the truth or falsity of this is irrelevant for our treatment. Any over-all pattern analysis is, of course, only a statistical approximation. The situation as presented in this section will more likely than not have to be modified— mainly by way of being rendered more complex—as more observations are made. Perhaps we shall be forced to recognize more vowels, perhaps more glides, and perhaps "hypercomplex" nuclei in which a vowel is followed by two successive glides. The reader whose interest is challenged should consult Sledd 1955.

Problem. The reader should analyze his own idiolect, or as much of it as he has time for. Use the words given as illustrations in this section. Examine them in context rather than in isolation; at best, work in pairs, each observing the pronunciation of the other.

As syllabics turn up, tabulate them. For this purpose, prepare a chart with at least nine rows and at least four columns; some extra rows and columns are advisable. Mark the rows, at the left, with the symbols for the nine vowel phonemes listed in §40.1. Mark the first four columns for no glide, [j], [w], and [ˇ] respectively. Mark an extra column with

[·], representing added length without perceptible glide in any direction. Leave room for columns for "hypercomplex" nuclei with two successive glides, in case any turn up. After everything is tabulated, it may turn out that the reader's distribution of [ˇ] and [·] is in complementation (§12.3), as it is for the writer, or that some other phonemic regrouping of the phonetically distinguished glides is possible.

LINGUISTIC
ONTOGENY

41·

LINGUISTIC ONTOGENY

41.1. Diachronic linguistics, defined in §38.1, has two aspects. The process of development of speech habits in a single person, from birth to death, is *linguistic ontogeny*, the study of which is one aspect of diachronic linguistics. The histories of languages as wholes through successive decades and centuries is linguistic *phylogeny*. For the study of the latter, the term *historical linguistics* is customary. Our concern for the moment is ontogeny; in §42 we shall turn to phylogeny.

One approach to linguistic ontogeny is child-centered, concerned with what the acquisition of communicative habits does to the child. Another approach is system-centered, concerned rather with the impact of the child on the communicative systems he is acquiring. These approaches are complementary, not contradictory; but we shall concentrate on the second, partly because direct attack from the first angle is extremely difficult, and partly because the second attack is more in keeping with the approach taken in the rest of this book.

41.2. Developments before Speech. The newborn infant has a specifically human stock of genetically transmitted capacities, but participates, to start with, neither in language nor in any other communicative system of his community. His congenital reactions are gross responses (crying, wriggling) to gross stimuli (hunger, pain, loud noises, falling). But the differentiation of stimuli and the refinement of responses begin immediately. As maturation completes the anatomical structure of the nervous system, the child's behavioral sequences get both more complex and also, for a time, more random. The randomness is never completely eliminated subsequently, but only canalized so as to produce a degree of statistical predictability.

The earliest communicative conventions in which the child comes to participate are not linguistic. They are established, inevitably, between the infant and the mother or mother-substitute. (Though the older person who cares for the infant is not always the biological mother—in some cultures it is regularly an older sibling—we shall hereafter use the term "mother" for simplicity's sake.) Sucking may be congenital, but seeking the nipple, and the context in which the search can be successful, are learned. The closing of the nursery door may become a signal for going to sleep, or for crying. A certain touch on the shoulder may come to stimulate turning-over motions. The completion of the bath may come to indicate the impending arrival of the doll, so that the child reaches for the doll before seeing it. Crying becomes differentiated to correlate with different factors—hunger, wet—and the mother learns to differentiate the cries.

All such understandings between infant and mother are communicative conventions. They differ from the communicative conventions involved in language in several important ways:

(1) The signals of the infant and of the mother are not *specialized:* that is, there is a "natural" biological or physical connection between the signal and its antecedents or consequences. The child's movements in searching for the nipple signal the mother that it is hungry: with or without the mother's help, the search may be successful. An older child's assertion *I'm hungry,* on the other hand, has only the arbitrary culturally-defined tie to its antecedents, its consequences, and its meaning, for the child and for those to whom the child addresses the remark.

(2) The early signals mean what they do largely because of some geometrical resemblance between signal and meaning (the semantic relation is "iconic"). The touch on the child's shoulder which triggers him into turning over is a vestige of the full-fledged manipulation by which the mother herself turns the child over. On the other hand, there is no geometrical resemblance at all between the words *Please turn over* and the act of turning over: the semantic relation here is purely arbitrary.

(3) The early signals are not transmitted when they are not meant seriously. The infant cries from hunger when it is hungry, not otherwise. An older person may say *I'm hungry* when he is not hungry at all. Linguistic signals are often *displaced:* we refer to things when they are

not around. Early communication between infant and mother is not at first displaced, though in time it can become so.

(4) The understandings between mother and infant are not based on a sharing of repertories of *transmitted* signals, but only on the mother's correct understanding of the signals from the child and the child's correct understanding of the quite different signals from the mother. The child may turn over when the mother touches his shoulder; the mother does not turn over when so touched by the child. The mother may attend to the child's toilet in response to a certain cry; the mother does not cry and is not thus administered to by the child. Logically, this is like conversation between a Frenchman and a German each of whom can understand, but not speak, the language of the other. In contrast, when two people speak the same language, then in theory either one *may* produce any utterance produced by the other.

From this base, a slow approach towards the sharing of communicative systems by child and mother, or child and other adults, is rendered possible because the child starts to *imitate*. We dare not take "imitation" as an undefined explanatory term: all we can safely mean by it is a matching of the contours of perceptible behavior of one organism to those of another. Just how the learning of imitation takes place is not known. The young of non-human hominoids (chimpanzees, gorillas, and so on) also imitate, but never so elaborately as do human children: this may point to a difference in genetically transmitted capacity. Perhaps the inception of imitation, in any infant, is accidental. Every child plays by wriggling all its muscles, soon in repetitive patterns where each cycle may be a self-imitation of the preceding. It must also be important that adults imitate children, as well as each other.

With imitation, a further factor comes to play a crucial role: *adult misinterpretation*. Every mother believes, or pretends, that she knows what the world is like to her child. But no matter how accurate a mother's understanding of her child, a signal or apparent signal from the child occupies one functional status in the communicative repertory of the child, a different and generally more complex status in the mother's repertory or in her partly inaccurate interpretation of the child's systems. In every culture, adults willy-nilly play the game of ascribing more complexity to their children's behavior than is factually *yet* there; though also, by way of contrast, adults will sometimes assume *less* complexity in their children than the latter have achieved. The first of these means that imitative or other adult reactions to a child's behavior will be more narrowly defined, in context and in physical contours, than the child's own signals. This imposes narrowing constraints on the conditions for success of the child's efforts, and presses the child towards greater precision it its own responses and towards closer matching of its responses to those of adults. This is a necessary adjustment of the child to the community, though it may involve emotional maladjustment for the child. Often enough, the first vocal sound interpreted by the child's mother as a "word" is not a linguistic signal at all for the child, but an accident. But it would be sad indeed if the mother reacted to the truth instead of to her own desires.

41.3. The Acquisition of Grammar. Reciprocal imitation eventually builds into the child a repertory of vocal signals which have the force of reports or commands or both, which superficially resemble certain short utterances of adult language (including, of course, adult "baby talk") in sound and meaning, and which the surrounding adults call "words." They are not "words" in our technical sense (§19). The most important property of true words is that, like the generally smaller elements, morphemes, they are used as constituents in building complex messages, according to grammatical conventions. In the communicative economy of the child at the earliest speech stage, his vocal signals are not words in this sense, but the indivisible and uncompoundable signals of a *closed repertory:* each utterance from the child consists wholly of one or another of these signals. Each signal has been learned as a whole, in direct or indirect imitation of some utterance of adult language. For a while the repertory is increased only by the holistic imitation of further adult utterances. This does not "open" the closed system, but merely enlarges it.

In time, the child's repertory includes some signals which are partially similar in sound and meaning. Suppose, for example, that the child already uses prelinguistic equivalents of adult /^{3}mámə^1↓/ and /^{3}mámə^2↑/, and of /^{3}dǽdij^1↓/, but not, it so happens, of /^{3}dǽdij^2↑/. The adult forms are structured: each consists of a recurrent word plus a recurrent intonation. The child's analogs, at the moment, are unitary signals. But then comes the most crucial event in the child's acquisition of language: he *analogizes*, in some appropriate situation, to produce an utterance matching adult /^{3}dǽdij^2↑/, which he has never heard nor said before. As of this first analogical coinage, both the new utterance and those on which it is based are structured: the child's system is (to some slight extent) an "open" or "productive" system rather than closed; and the child has begun to participate in genuine, if still highly idiosyncratic, language.

The first analogical coinage is exceedingly difficult to observe with certainty. Indeed, a child probably produces a number of analogical coinages which meet with no understanding because they deviate too radically from anything in adult speech, before he hits on his first communicatively successful coinage. We can know that the leap from closed system to open system is well in the past, however, when we hear a child say something that he could not have heard from others: usually a regularization of a morphophonemically irregular form of adult speech, say *mans* instead of *men* or *hided* for *hid*.

The above assumes that the child's first analogizing is in his own production; it may, however, be in his reception of what is said by others. That is, the child may react appropriately to an utterance he has never heard before, because of its partial resemblances to signals already in his receptive repertory. Receptive and productive control do not keep in step, as was pointed out in §39.4.

Once successful analogical coinage has taken place, the habit of building new utterances with raw-materials extracted from old ones is reinforced by the success. The leap is often extremely sudden and is followed by an amazingly rapid proliferation of what the child says. Coinages which deviate too radically from what is provided for by the grammatical system of the adult language do not meet with understanding: the coinages, and the specific analogies on which they are based, are abandoned for lack of reinforcement. Before long it becomes impossible, in general, to tell whether a particular utterance on a particular occasion is repetition from memory or new construction from remembered parts and patterns.

41.4. The Acquisition of Phonemic Habits. The correlation between the development of phonemic and of grammatical habits is not clear. For some children, the signals of the prelinguistic "closed" stage already have a phonemic structure; for others, it may be, the inception of phonemics trails behind the step from "closed" to "open." It is known that some children make a holistic false start on pronunciation, learning to imitate a few adult utterances with remarkable phonetic accuracy, but then losing this accuracy temporarily as true phonemic habits begin.

The mechanism by which phonemic habits begin is not known. Perhaps, as the closed repertory of vocal signals is increased by new borrowings from adult speech, it simply becomes imperative for the signals to be kept apart by attention to recurrent smaller articulatory-acoustic partials, if the system is to continue to be enlarged.

The child's earliest phonemic system involves only a few of the contrasts functional in the adult system around him. At 16 months, one child in an English-speaking environment had a closed repertory of about two dozen utterances, in which, for stops, only the contrast between labial and non-labial was functional. By 20 months, the repertory, though still closed, was larger, and the stops showed a three-way differentiation: labial, apical (/t/ : /č/ contrast still undeveloped), and dorsal. Voicing contrasts were added about a month later, giving a six-stop system as over against the eight-stop system of adult English. Only somewhat later did grammatical patterning begin.

The development of a child's phonemic system from one stage to the next thus takes the form of a splitting of some articulatory range into smaller contrasting subranges: in a range where earlier there was but one phoneme (say a voicing-irrelevant dorso-velar stop /k/) there come to be two (voiceless /k/ versus voiced /g/). Sometimes there is temporary backsliding. Often, some forms acquired during an earlier stage are not immediately reshaped when the phonemic system is restructured, so that for a while one finds multiple matching of adult phonemes by the child's phonemes. Thus one child, at one stage, had a voicing-irrelevant /p/ for some adult /b/'s, a nasal /m/ for others. The former matching was a survival from an earlier stage in which voicing-contrasts were irrelevant for the child, so that he imitated both adult /b/ and adult /p/ with his /p/, but adult /m/ with his /m/; the latter reflected the new habit, by which the child matched adult /p/ by his own /p/, but both adult /b/ and adult /m/ by his /m/. Later the forms that had been learned by imitation during the earlier stage were readjusted; and in due time, of course, the child proceeded to the three-way differentiation of /p/ : /b/ : /m/ characteristic of adult English. But the reshaping of forms learned earlier is sometimes not complete, and adult speech can show traces of its incompletion. One subject says /wúrm/ idiosyncratically for *worm*, retaining an unadjusted early childhood pronunciation. Such doublets as *Polly* and *Molly*, or *Peg* and *Meg*, may have this origin.

The child's utterances are not, in general, a routine phoneme-by-phoneme transformation of the adult form. Rather, consonant clusters may be mapped into single consonants, unstressed syllables are often omitted, and a single consonant may be repeated in successive syllables to do duty not only for the adult consonant it usually matches but also for some other. Thus one child said [kékə], in his own phonemic system of the time probably /kíka/, for adult *Rebecca:* the unstressed *Re-* is omitted, the second /k/ matches the /k/ of the adult form, and the first /k/ conforms to the habit of non-matching repetition just described.

The exact sequence of successive splits in the phonemic system of a child varies somewhat from child to child, though not drastically. The end of the process, of course, depends on the phonemic habits of the surrounding adults. The English-speaking child eventually introduces contrasts of voicing for stops; the Menomini-speaking child does not, because the surrounding adults do not have them.

As in grammar, adult misinterpretation and the distinction between productive and receptive control play crucial roles. The child understands forms kept apart phonemically by differences of speech sound which he does not yet use in his own speech. Parents understand from context rather than from performance, usually "reading in" articulatory distinctions that the child is in fact not using: the mother hears adult /p/ in the child's voicing-irrelevant /p/ if in the context it *should* be adult /p/, and adult /b/ similarly. This supplies the child both with a model and with a reward for success. In a remarkably few years the child's phonemic system is almost completely congruent with that of the adults, though it is not unusual for a few distinctions of minor importance—that is, distinctions which play relatively minor roles in keeping utterances apart—to remain unacquired until the age of ten or twelve.

41.5. Semantic Aspects. The emotional contexts of the child's earliest communicative participation—long before his earliest speech—establish a pattern of connotations that are germinal for the personality of the eventual adult. This is too important a fact to leave unmentioned; but the details of the process must be left to psychiatrists and genetic psychologists.

As true language begins, the child's first "definitions" of forms are operational, because there is nothing else for them to be. Verbal definitions elicited from older children show this: "a *newspaper* is a thing that gets thrown on the porch and Mama wraps up the garbage in it." But verbal explanations of new forms are also supplied the child very early: "See, Johnny! That's a *cow*. That's where our milk comes from"— where demonstration, directly or with a picture, is supplemented by words. Verbal explanations are unavoidable if language is to serve as a substitute for direct experience and is to coordinate collective enterprise. There is an unavoidable side-effect of verbal nonsense, which is not altogether unfortunate, since poetry and literature operate in the realm of what, from an overly mechanical operational point of view, might unthinkingly be classed as nonsense.

The child's experience with communication, especially language, tends to blur for him the distinction between what we may call *direct* and *trigger action*. Direct action is, for example, going out and killing a rabbit; trigger action is telling someone else that one is hungry so that the other person catches the rabbit. If the child is hungry, he is not forced to go hunting himself: he can make appropriate sounds, and others feed him. If this result can be achieved by triggering, can one not also obtain rain, or good crops, or the sweetheart one desires, by the right sort of triggering? The child thus slides easily into an acceptance of the magical element of his community's technology, which, in human history, has grown out of communication in just this way. The child learns to knock wood for luck, to go on a vision quest, to pray for rain, to say *Gesundheit* to someone who sneezes, or to bury a slave under the first post of a new house. These are triggering actions intended to achieve certain desired results, and often the results do follow: there is nothing more unnatural about them, to the growing child, than there is about asking for food when one is hungry. It has taken the human race untold thousands of years to learn, slowly and laboriously, the distinction between the realm in which "wishing can make it so" and the realm in which it cannot.

41.6. Later Developments. By the age of four to six, the normal child is a *linguistic adult*. He controls, with marginal exceptions if any, the phonemic system of his language; he handles effortlessly the grammatical core; he knows and uses the basic contentive vocabulary of the language. Of course there is a vast further vocabulary of contentives that he does not yet know, but this continues to some extent throughout life. He may get tangled in trying to produce longer discourses, as in describing the activities of a morning at school, but clarity in extended exposition is a point on which older people also vary greatly.

At the age of four to six, in our culture and in some others, the child has passed beyond the "cradle stage," in which his communicative habits are shaped mainly by mother or mother-substitute, and is in a period where his most crucial contacts are with *other children*. The blood-and-bone of many languages is transmitted largely through successive generations of four-to-ten-year-olds: the fires of childhood competition and the twists of childhood prestige do more to shape a given individual's speech patterns, for life, than does any contact with adults. "As the twig is bent"—and it is bent by other twigs.

Two later developments require mention. If a child has not yet reached the verge of adolescence and is transplanted to an environment in which a different language is spoken, he usually accommodates to the new language with little emotional difficulty and eventually with high accuracy. Children of immigrants to this country, whose exposure to English has been continuous since the age of four or five or so, show little or no trace, as adults, of their original training in some other language. But if the child has passed this crucial biological point, the task of learning a new language is emotionally difficult and learning is hardly ever perfect.

Ten or fifteen years later, an individual goes through a comparable narrowing-down in adaptability to new local varieties of his own language. An American woman of about nineteen, or man of about twenty-five—there are many personal differences and these figures are rough estimated averages—if taken to a new part of the United States or Canada, will adjust to the different dialect of English in a few months, and earlier habits may become completely submerged. Past those ages the adjustment is slower and usually never complete.

It is not yet known whether the last two generalizations apply significantly to cultures other than our own. Post-adolescents in our culture are supposed to undergo certain emotional crises and reorientations, in order to qualify as adults: the second transition-point in speech adaptability may be causally connected with this cultural fact.

The idiolect of any individual, even past all the transition points that have been mentioned, continues to change at least in minor ways as long as he lives. However, the mechanisms of this continued change are quite indistinguishable from those responsible for phylogenetic change, and their description is therefore left for our detailed discussion of the latter.

NOTES

New terms: *diachronic* and *historical* linguistics are now distinguished. *Ontogeny* vs. *phylogeny* (terms transferred from genetics, not carrying with them, of course, the limitation to genetically controlled development that they have for the biologist).

On displacement: Bloomfield 1933, p. 30. The statements made in §41.6 reflect research of Martin Joos and of Henry Lee Smith, Jr., not yet published; but see Hall 1951a. On child speech in general, see Jakobson 1941 and Leopold's extensive bibliography 1952.

PHYLOGENY

42·

PHYLOGENETIC CHANGE

42.1. Were it not for written records, we should probably not realize that the design of any language changes as time goes by. But with written records proof is easy. Below are given nine passages, all in English, but originally written at different times. The first is from the eighteenth century, the second from the seventeenth, and so on, so that the last dates from approximately one thousand years ago:

(1) When these thoughts had fully taken possession of Jones, they occasioned a perturbation in his mind, which, in a constitution less pure and firm than his, might have been, at such a season, attended with very dangerous consequences. (Henry Fielding, *The History of Tom Jones*, 1749.)

(2) I have now don that, which for many Causes I might have thought, could not likely have been my fortune, to be put to this under-work of scowring and unrubbishing the low and sordid ignorance of such a presumptuous Lozel. (John Milton, *Colasterion*, 1645.)

(3) Then the Spanish Friars, John and Richard, of whom mention was made before, began to exhort him, and play their parts with him afresh, but with vain and lost labour. (John Foxe, 1563.)

(4) Ryght reverent and worchepfull broder, after all dewtes of recomendacion, I recomaunde me to yow, desyryng to here of your prosperite and welfare, whych I pray God long to contynew to Hys plesore, and to your herts desyr; letyng you wete that I receyved a letter from yow, in the whyche letter was viij*d*, with the whyche I schuld bye a peyer of slyppers. (The Paston Letters, 1479.)

365

(5) As to lawe, trewe men seyn þat þei willen mekely & wilfully drede & kepe goddis lawe up here kunnynge & myȝt, & eche lawe of mannes makynge in as myche as þei witen þat it acordiþ wiþ goddis lawe & reson & good conscience & to þe riȝtful execucion þer-of; & god him self may bynde man no more to his owen lawe for his endeles riȝtwisnesse & charite þat he haþ to mannes soule. (*How Men Ought to Obey Prelates*, attributed to John Wyclif, d. 1384.)

(6) And nis ha witerliche akast, t in-to þeowdom idrahen, þat,—of se swiðe heh stal, of se muche dignete t swuch wurðschipe, as hit is to beo godes spuse, Ihesu cristes brude, þe lauerdes leofmon, þat alle kinges buheð,—(*Hali Meidenhad*, C. 1300).

(7) Wrecce men sturuen of hungær, sume ieden on ælmes þe waren sum wile ricemen. sume flugon ut of lande. Wes næure gæt mare wrecce hed on land. ne næure hethen men werse ne diden þan hi diden. For ouer sithon ne for baren hi nouther circe ne cyrce iærd. oc namen al þe god ð þar inne was. (Peterborough Chronicle, 1137.)

(8) Ða com Harold ure cyng on unwær on þa Normenn. and hytte hi begeondan Eoforwic. æt Stemford brygge. mid micclan here Englisces folces. and þær wearð on dæg swiðe stranglic gefeoht on bá halfe. Ðar wearð ofslægen Harold Harfargera and Tosti eorl. and þa Normen þe þær to lafe wæron wurdon on fleame. and þa Engliscan hi híndan hetelice slógon. oð þ hig sume to scype coman. sume adruncen. and sume eac forbærnde. (Worcester Chronicle for 1066.)

(9) Uton we nu efstan ealle mægene godra weorca, ond geornfulle beon Godes miltsa, nu we ongeotan magon þæt þis nealæcþ worlde forwyrde; for þon ic myngige ond manige manna gehwylcne þæt he his agene dæda georne smeage, þæt he her on worlde for Gode rihtlice lifge, ond on gesyhþe þæs hehstan Cyninges. (Aelfric, Blickling Homily, 971.)

The first thing we notice as we move back a few centuries is that some of the spelling is queer. Even in (2), from Milton, we find *don* where we spell *done*, and *scowr* for our *scour*. This might lead us to think that nothing else has changed—just the spelling. When we examine passage (4) this theory is weakened. Though most of the words are familiar, the spelling is so different that it could hardly represent the pronunciations we now use. And we will probably puzzle over *wete*—it meant 'know,' and has now passed out of use, though we still have a poetic or archaizing *wot* related to it. *Whych* and *whyche* are obviously both our modern *which*, but are these two spellings for a single word, or, perhaps, two inflected forms of a single stem? In (5), all these problems increase. In the spelling, we find letters no longer used. Go back the full thousand years, and the passage might as well be in Icelandic or Swedish.

We see, then, that a millenium of phylogenetic change has sufficed to alter English so radically that if a tenth-century Englishman and a twentieth-century Englishman or American could meet face to face, they would not understand each other at all.

To some extent, the degrees of difference and rates of change are concealed, rather than revealed, by the spelling in the above passages. The spread of printing and the development of general literacy in England led, after some delay, to a standardization of spelling, which not only rode rough-shod over the regional differences of the time, but also became ossified and has been very little altered since. If we can read Milton and Foxe, it is in part because we still spell words in ways more appropriate for their pronunciation than for ours. If the phonograph had been invented a few centuries earlier than it was, so that we could hear a recording made in the days of Milton or Shakespeare, we should find our ears much less attuned to their pronunciation than our eyes are to their spelling.

Because of the ossification of spelling, we may get the impression that our language had changed much more between 950 and, say, 1450 than it has since the latter date. This impression is perhaps illusory. Of course, it is dangerous to speak of the rate of phylogenetic change, since —with a tentative exception to be dealt with later (§61)—we have no reliable yardstick with which to measure it. To the extent that we can measure it at all, the rate would appear to be approximately constant, not only for English, but for every language. Only under unusual circumstances does the rate appreciably increase or decrease, and then only for brief intervals.

One point is certain: conscious efforts to impede the natural slow change of speech habits have always failed. For example, the French and Spanish Academies have succeeded, in the last few centuries, only in temporarily fixing certain minor habits of spelling and of the formal style of the language used in writing, and even in these peripheral matters writers have in time rebelled, changing their style to suit the changed language, whether or not the conservative Academies were persuaded to revise their edicts. Religious motives sometimes lead to a retention of styles of speech and writing which do not otherwise survive: this is illustrated by the continuing use in the Catholic Church of a late form of Latin, and quite similarly by the millenia-long survival of Sanskrit in India for religious and learnèd purposes. Yet the survival of Latin in this way is very different from the continuing use of a living language. The descendants of the Classical Romans went on, generation after generation, speaking what had at one time been Latin, and in two thousand years has become variously French, Spanish, Italian, and so on. Shortly after classical times, relatively unchanged Latin survived only as a special religious idiom: it was no one's native language, but was acquired by those who needed it after they had achieved linguistic adulthood in their native language. Hebrew was maintained in this special status for more than two thousand years, having otherwise died out altogether. During this time, it changed only slowly and in minor ways. Now that it has again acquired the status of a living language in Israel, we can be certain that it will undergo all the kinds of change experienced by any living language.

42.2. Divergence and Relatedness. Gradual change in the design of a living language is part of its life and is inexorable. Equally inevitable is divergence, whenever a single language comes to be spoken by groups of people out of touch with each other. A century or so of divergence produces aberrant dialects of what is still a single language. A millenium or so produces two or more languages where before there was but one; but because of their common origin the two or more are *related* (§1.4).

Strictly speaking, two successive stages of a single language, say Old English and modern English, could also be called "related." The term is rarely used in this context, not because it would be incorrect, but because it is unnecessary. However, this simplest sort of relatedness has a negative implication of importance. Modern English is a direct continuation of the Old English of a millenium ago. It also contains a vast number of words, and some other features, which came into the language from French after the Norman Conquest in 1066; but this in no sense implies that Anglo-Norman French was an "ancestor" of modern

English. Modern English does not have two "parents," but only one: Old English.

Indeed, in speaking of relatedness, we must not be confused by the sort of thing that characterizes genetic relationships of organisms. Animals show an individuation in time as well as in space, by virtue of which an individual can correctly be said to be the offspring of two other individuals (sexual reproduction) or of one other individual (asexual reproduction). Languages show no such individuation through time: languages do not "reproduce" either sexually or asexually, but simply *continue*. It is meaningless to ask when Old English ceased and the next stage began. No language known to us has had a "beginning" discoverable through the available evidence, but only earlier and earlier preceding history. The institution of human language as a whole must have had its beginnings sometime in the remote past, but this is a different matter. It is also a different matter that a language sometimes becomes *extinct:* that is, all its speakers die off or learn other languages, without transmitting the language to any succeeding generation.

Thus even the figure of speech involved in saying that Old English is a "parent" or an "ancestor" of modern English is shaky: Old English is simply what modern English was a thousand years ago, and modern English is simply what Old English has become. There seems to be no way to discuss linguistic relatedness and change save with figures of speech like "parent," "ancestor," and "descendant," but we must not read in implications which are not validly carried by such terms in this context.

At a given point in time, then, a set of related languages is merely what would be a set of dialects of a single language except that the links between the dialects have become very tenuous or have been broken. This means that if languages A and B, spoken at a given time, are related, then their later forms will always continue to be related, just as long as both continue to be spoken. The mere fact of relationship thus becomes of secondary importance. More important is the *degree* of relationship. French, Italian, and English, all spoken now, are all related. But the relationship of French and Italian is closer than that of either of those and English: the latest common ancestor of the first two was spoken only about two thousand years ago, while the latest common ancestor of all three was spoken at least twice as long ago. Latin is more closely related to current English than is French, because to get from Latin to English one first traces back a certain distance into the past and then forward to English; the comparable trip from contemporary French to contemporary English is two thousand years longer.

In a few instances where we have direct documentation of common ancestors, we might be able to say that languages X and Y are more closely related than languages Z and W, all four being contemporaries. In general this sort of judgment is difficult and uncertain. We know that Menomini and Fox are related, as are English and German, or French and Italian, but to say (as the writer would tend to) that the first pair are more closely related than either of the others is to speak impressionistically.

We can also never assert, in any absolute sense, that two languages are *not* related. The most skillful methods available do not enable us to push our horizon back more than a few thousand years earlier than the oldest documentary records. Relationships which antedate this earliest attainable horizon necessarily remain unproved—and also incapable of disproof. Nobody would suspect that Menomini and English are related; but if, in fact, the two had a common ancestor some twenty-five to fifty thousand years ago, we have no way of knowing it. This being so, the overt statement that languages A and B are "not related" takes on a modified meaning: it means that the actual relationship, if any, lies too far in the past for proof. Of course, scholars do not always agree as to whether such a judgment can be validly passed. For example, some believe that Indo-European and Semitic may be *demonstrably* related; their opponents believe, not that the two families are unrelated, but only that the relationship, if real, is too remote for clear proof.

NOTES

New term: *extinction*. A number of terms appear here for the first time since §1: divergence, related languages, closeness or degree of relationship.

Problem. Each of the assertions given below contains a germ of truth, but none is clearly expressed and all are easily misunderstood by the layman. Clarify:

(1) Chinese is one of the oldest languages in the world.

(2) French, Spanish, Portuguese, Italian, and Rumanian are just modern dialects of Latin.

(3) Latin is not a dead language because it is used in the Roman Catholic Church.

(4) German is more conservative than English.

(5) The Norman Conquest brought French scribal habits into England, resulting in the end of Old English and the beginning of Middle English.

(6) Old English is now extinct.

$43 \cdot$

OLD and MIDDLE ENGLISH

43.1. External vs. Internal History. In historical linguistics it is important to distinguish between the *external* and the *internal* history of a language.

The external history of a language concerns the location and migrations of its speakers, the episodes in which they have had various sorts of contact with speakers of other languages, the circumstances under which it has acquired new groups of speakers (other than by normal transmission to children born within the community) or lost old groups, and so on—indeed, anything about the history of the speakers of the language which has some bearing on the history of the language itself.

The internal history of a language concerns what happens to the design of the language as time passes.

In our discussion of historical linguistics we shall use examples from the history of English wherever we can, turning to other languages only when necessary. It therefore seems advisable to devote time at this point to a brief description of part of the external history of English and of the phonological systems of two earlier stages of the language.

43.2. The External History of English. The Romans, who had first come to Britain in 55 B.C., under the leadership of Julius Caesar, officially withdrew the last of their troops about 400 A.D.; the inhabitants who remained were speakers of Celtic dialects. Half a century later, the Germanic-speaking Angles, Saxons, and Jutes began to invade the island, and in the course of a hundred years or so pushed the Celts westwards into Wales and Cornwall and northwards towards Scotland. We use the term *English* for the Germanic speech of these invaders and their descendants, as of their arrival in England, though

372

there was, of course, no sharp break in their speech habits at the time of migration. When convenient, the term *pre-English* is used for their speech before the migration, as well as after it until the earliest stage for which we have documentary records.

The invaders brought with them a knowledge of *Runic writing*, and a sparse scattering of Runic inscriptions in English have survived to the present; two of these, consisting each of a single personal name, may date from the 5th century. Christianity was brought into Saxon England during the first half of the 7th century, and with it came the use of Latin, spoken and written, for religious and learnèd purposes. Before long, English came to be written with the Latin alphabet; the earliest surviving documents of this sort date from the last part of the 7th century, and from the 8th century down to the present the record is continuous and ever-increasing in volume.

Between the 8th and the 11th centuries, large numbers of Scandinavians ("Danes") came to Britain, first merely raiding, but later settling there. We have no written records of the speech of these later arrivals. It was not mutually intelligible with the English of the time, but it must have been sufficiently similar that communication was possible with some effort. Speakers of Scandinavian and of English lived intermingled, but for centuries there was no permanent fixation of one group as ascendant over the other. It was primarily due to a series of military victories over the Danes that Alfred the Great, and his native region of Wessex, achieved political supremacy towards the end of the 9th century. But the see-saw between Saxon and Dane continued, and in the early 11th century the whole country was ruled by Danish kings.

The restless Scandinavians did not confine their attentions to England; in the 9th and 10th centuries they also struck at the northeastern parts of France, and, in time, became the ruling aristocracy of Normandy. In the process, they took on many Gallic ways, including the French language, losing their own Germanic speech. Then, in 1066, the descendants of these same people, now French in language and largely in culture, invaded England under William the Conqueror, defeated Harold at the Battle of Hastings, and took over the country. For well over two hundred years, French was the language of the rulers of England, while the masses of the people continued to speak English. But eventually the language of the conquerors, that of a minority despite its greater prestige, once again disappeared. The Normans made

London, rather than Wessex, their seat of government—a fact of no little importance in the history of our language.

The English of the period from the first written records down to about 1066 A.D. is called *Old English*, abbreviated "OE." That of the ensuing period, down to about the end of the 15th century, is called *Middle English* ("ME"); from the 16th century to the present we speak of *Modern English* ("NE," with "N" for "new" because "M" is pre-empted for "middle"). So far as the language itself is concerned, these dates are purely arbitrary: there were no sudden restructurings of speech habits, and it is foolish to argue whether, say, 12th-century English is better regarded as "late OE" or as "early ME." Each of the three indicated periods is rather long, and to pin things down we shall always mean, by "OE," unless there is specific indication to the contrary, the speech of approximately King Alfred's day; similarly, "ME," unless there is an overt statement otherwise, will always mean the speech of the London and Midlands region at the time of Chaucer (late 14th century). "NE" will regularly refer to our own English of today.

Never throughout its history has English been free of dialect differences. The Angles, Saxons, and Jutes came from different parts of the Continental lowlands, bringing more or less divergent dialects with them, and they settled in different parts of England. During the hegemony of Wessex, the local dialect of that territory, called *West Saxon*, carried more prestige than that of any other part of England, and we have more documents in that dialect than in any other for the whole OE period; writers after Alfred tended to write in the West Saxon manner even if they were not natives of Wessex. Later, when French was on its way out as the language of the upper classes, London had become the political center of the country and was achieving cultural and commercial supremacy. Consequently, the dialect of the Midlands acquired prestige, becoming first a provincial standard and then a national standard. Most English of today, all over the world, save for a few local varieties largely confined to the British Isles, is more nearly the lineal descendant of the ME of London than of the ME of any other district. And London ME was in turn the descendant of the OE of the Midlands, not that of Wessex. Fortunately, we do have some documents in Midlands OE, though the OE writings of the greatest literary importance are largely West Saxon.

Our knowledge of the design of OE and ME depends on our ability to interpret the surviving documentary evidence, plus what clues we can get from an examination of NE and of documents in the older stages of the Germanic languages akin to English. There are many unsolved problems of detail, and many points on which scholars are not in agreement. The portrayals of the phonological systems of OE and ME which are given below were worked out by the writer, and differ in some ways from the traditional interpretations.

43.3. The Phonological System of OE. The vowel phonemes of OE were perhaps as follows:

/i ɨ y u
e ə ö o
æ a ɔ/.

This system involved three tongue-heights, the contrast between front (/i e æ y ö/) and back (the rest), and the contrast between unrounded (/i e æ ɨ ə a/) and rounded (the rest, except that /ɔ/ may simply have been further back than /æ/ and /a/). In the late 8th-century OE of Wessex and the Midlands, /ö/ had disappeared, words in which /ö/ would be expected showing /e/ instead, but /ö/ survived past this period in some of the other dialects. In later West Saxon there were some peculiar developments not taken into account here; they did not particularly affect the speech of the Midlands, and thus have little bearing on NE.

Examples: *hlid* /hlíd/ 'lid,' *bedd* very early /bédd/ but 8th-century /béd/ 'bed,' *baec* /bǽk/ 'back,' *liornian* /lírnian/ (later *leornian* /lórnian/) 'to learn,' *meolcan* /mólkan/ 'to milk,' *healt* /hált/ 'halt,' *cynn* /kýn/ 'kin,' early *oexen* /öksen/, later West Saxon and Midlands *exen* /éksen/ 'oxen,' *cruma* /krúma/ 'crumb,' *crop* /króp/ 'crop,' *crabba* /krɔ́bba/ 'crab.'

As in NE (§40.1), there were complex nuclei consisting of one or another of the eleven vowels plus a glide element. The details are not clear. Ten of the eleven vowels occurred with a lengthening glide which we can write as /·/; /ö/ did not, for, in all dialects, where we would expect /ö·/, we find /e·/. Examples of the others are: *bliþe* /blí·θe/ 'blithe,' *grene* /gré·ne/ 'green,' *haelan* /hǽ·lan/ 'to heal,' *lioht* /lí·xt/ (in early West Saxon; apparently /lí·xt/ in the Midlands) 'light,' *seoþan*

/só·θan/ 'to seethe,' *deaf* /dá·f/ 'deaf,' *dryge* /drý·ŷe/ 'dry,' *ful* /fú·l/ 'foul,' *scoh* /sḵó·x/ 'shoe,' *ban* /bó·n/ 'bone.' There may have been also some complex nuclei with a glide /w/: *feower* 'four' and *feawa* 'few' may have been /féwwer/ and /fáwwe/ rather than /fó·wer/ and /fá·we/. There were none with a glide like NE /j/.

By the end of the 10th century, the dialect of the Midlands seems to have lost the three vowels /i ə a/ altogether: /a/ fell together with /æ/, /ə/ for the most part with /e/, and /i/ with /i/ or /e/. Since there was no /ö/ in this region, the vowel system was reduced to /i e æ y u o ɔ/.

The consonant phonemes were

/p	t	ḵ	k	
b	d	ĝ	g	
		ŷ		h
f	θ	s	x	
m	n			
	l			
	r			
w/.				

/p t ḵ k/ were voiceless stops. /ḵ/ was a *k*-like sound produced with a more fronted position of articulation than /k/, and, in fact, at least by the eleventh century may have been quite like our /č/. Examples: *pol* /pó·l/ 'pool,' *ta* /tó·/ 'toe,' *ceosan* /ḵó·san, ḵó·san/ 'to choose,' *cunnan* /kúnnan/ 'to be able.' /b d ĝ g/ were the corresponding voiced stops: *botm* /bótm/ 'bottom,' *dumb* /dúmb/ 'mute,' *ecg* /éĝ/ 'edge,' *frogga* /frógga/ 'frog.'

/ŷ/ was a voiced spirant in the position of articulation of /ḵ ĝ/: *geong* /ŷúng/ 'young,' *dæges* /dǽŷes/ 'day's,' *byrg, byrig* /býrŷ/ 'cities.'

/h/ was like NE /h/, but occurred only initially in a stressed syllable: *helpan* /hélpan/ 'to help,' *hlid* /hlíd/ 'lid.'

/f θ s x/ were spirants, but were voiced or voiceless depending on environment: voiced (and the first three thus like NE /v ð z/) between voiced sounds medially, but voiceless at the beginning of a stressed syllable, finally in a word, next to a voiceless consonant (like /t/), or when doubled. They were thus voiced in words like *lofian* /lófian/ 'to praise,' *aþe* /ó·θe/ 'oath,' *husl* /hú·sl/ 'eucharist,' and *dagas* /dóxas/

'days'; but voiceless in words like *fugol* /fúxol/ 'bird' (the /f-/), *deaf* /dá·f/ 'deaf,' *scaeft* /sḳǽft/ 'shaft,' *þancian* /θɔ́nkian/ 'to thank,' *muþ* /mú·θ/ 'mouth,' *oþþe* /óθθe/ 'or,' *sae* /sǽ·/ 'sea,' *wordes* /wórdes/ 'word's,' *wissian* /wíssian/ 'to direct,' *cniht* /kníxt, kníxt/ 'boy,' *hlihhan* /hlíxxan, hl̥íxxan/ 'to laugh.' /x/ did not occur initially.

The other consonants need little comment. /r/ was certainly a tap or trill, not like modern American /r/. It should be noted that there was no dorso-velar nasal /ŋ/ as a separate phoneme in OE. In words like /θɔ́nkian/ 'to thank' or /síngan/ 'to sing,' where OE /n/ was followed by a dorso-velar stop, the /n/ was itself probably pronounced as [ŋ], but it was still phonemically /n/.

We know nothing of OE intonation, and little of OE stress and juncture. We are sure that there was a contrast between stress (/'/ over a vowel in our notation) and its absence; there was probably also a secondary stress in compounds like *daedbot* /dǽ·d bò·t/ 'penance,' *raedbora* /rǽ·d bòra/ 'counsellor,' and perhaps in words like *adraefan* /ɔ̀· drǽ·fan/ 'to expel.' Certainly the OE analogs of NE words like *the, that, is, at, with, I*, which are often atonic in context, showed this same characteristic.

It would take too much space to describe in detail the arrangements in which OE phonemes occurred relative to each other. But we should note that certain clusters of consonants occurred which are alien to NE: initial /hl hr hn kn gn wr wl/; medial doubled consonants /pp tt ḳ̂ḳ̂ kk bb dd ĝĝ gg ss xx θθ mm nn ll rr/; final clusters such as /mb ng sl tm/.

43.4. The Phonological System of ME. The vowel system of Chaucerian ME was in some ways much simpler than that of OE described above. There were five vowel phonemes /i e a o u/ which occurred in stressed syllables; a sixth, /ə/, occurred mainly in unstressed syllables, though possibly also with stress (there are no certain examples). In illustrating these we cite also the OE forms:

OE	ME
drincan /drínkan/	/drínkə(n)/ 'drink'
helpan /hélpan/	/hélpə(n)/ 'help'
crabba /krɔ́bba/	/krábbə/ 'crab'
oxa /óksa/	/óksə/ 'ox'
sunu /súnu/	/súnə/ 'son'.

There were four complex nuclei with glide /j/:

OE	ME
ridan /rí·dan/	/ríjdə(n)/ 'ride'
swete /swé·te/	/swéjtə/ 'sweet'
daeg /dǽɣ̂/	/dáj/ 'day'
—	/bój/ 'boy.'

There were four complex nuclei—perhaps five—with glide /w/:

OE	ME
hus /hú·s/	/húws/ 'house'
foda /fó·da/	/fówdə/ 'food'
þohte /θó·xte/	/θáwxtə/ 'thought'
—	/ríwdə/ 'rude.'

Finally, there were three diphthongs with a lengthening and centering glide /ˇ/:

OE	ME
haeþ /hǽ·θ/	/héˇθ/ 'heath'
nama /nóma/	/náˇmə/ 'name'
stan /stó·n/	/stóˇn/ 'stone.'

The consonants included /p t č k b d ǰ g/; separate sets of spirants with contrast of voicing, /f θ s š x/ versus /v ð z/; /h/ as in OE and NE; /m n l r w j/ as in NE.

NOTES

New terms: *External* vs. *internal history*. Note the abbreviations *OE*, *ME*, *NE*, and note the use of the prefix *pre-* as in *pre-English*. If a language *X* is known to us through written records or by direct observation only as of a certain date, any earlier stage of the language is referred to as *pre-X;* in general, though not always, the term *pre-X* refers to relatively recent earlier stages.

The external history of English is described in very full form in

Baugh 1935; this book does not get deeply into the internal history, save for vocabulary. The deviations in our portrayal of OE phonology from that generally accepted are based on an examination of the sources, particularly the early glossaries and the Vespasian documents, consulted via Sweet 1885. The interpretation is influenced about equally by Kuhn and Quirk 1953, 1955, and by Stockwell and Barritt 1951, 1955. The handling of ME is based only on secondary sources—the standard manuals, particularly Moore 1951.

44·

KINDS of PHYLOGENETIC
CHANGE

44.1. We saw in §16.1 that a language can be viewed as composed of several subsystems: centrally, a phonemic system, a grammatical system, and a morphophonemic system; peripherally, a semantic system and a phonetic system. Within the grammatical system it is important to distinguish between the grammatical core (§31) and the remainder. Within the morphophonemic system, it is similarly important to distinguish between alternation (§33) and canonical forms of morphs (§34).

Episodes in the internal history of a language can always be classed according to the subsystem or subsystems affected. It is this classification which yields what we mean by different *kinds* of change. Such a classification says nothing, in itself, about the *causes* or *mechanisms* involved, except that, as we shall see, a change of one kind sometimes entails a change of another kind.

We have, then, the following kinds of change:

    I. Central:
        A. *Phonemic change:* any change in the repertory of phonemes or in the arrangements in which they can occur.
        B. Change in the grammatical system:
            1. Change within the grammatical core: we shall use the term *grammatical change* exclusively for this.
            2. Change in the grammatical system outside the grammatical core: *lexical change.*

> C. Change in the morphophonemic system:
>   1. Change in the phonemic representations of morphemes or larger forms: *shape change*.
>   2. Change in habits of alternation: *alternation change*.
> II. Peripheral:
>   A. *Semantic change:* any change in the meanings of grammatical forms.
>   B. *Phonetic Change:* any change in habits of pronunciation and hearing.

We now give examples of all these kinds of change, all drawn from the history of English.

44.2. IA. Phonemic Change. OE (§43.3) had four spirants, /f θ s x/, voiced or voiceless depending on environment, and one, /ɣ̂/, always voiced. NE has lost /ɣ̂/ and /x/ altogether, and has split the other three into three pairs of spirants with voicing contrast: /f v θ ð s z/. We have also gained a fourth pair, /š ž/, the former in part from an OE consonant cluster (/sk̯/), the latter only in words from other languages. Almost any other portion of the phonemic systems of OE and NE shows comparable restructurings.

44.3. IB1. Grammatical Change. OE nouns were inflected for case. The inflection of /stɔ́·n/ 'stone' was as follows:

	singular	plural
nom. and acc.	/stɔ́·n/	/stɔ́·nas/
gen.	/stɔ́·nes/	/stɔ́·na/
dat. and instr.	/stɔ́·ne/	/stɔ́·num/.

This system of case-inflection has been lost in NE, save for traces in the pronouns. The forms of this particular OE stem have had the following history:

OE	NE	
/stɔ́·n/		(*This stone is heavy*)
/stɔ́·ne/	/stówn/ *stone*	(*He hit me with a stone*)
/stɔ́·na/		(*He weighs ten stone*)
/stɔ́·nes/	/stównz/	*stone's*
/stɔ́·nas/		*stones*
/stɔ́·num/ (lost altogether).		

If we interpret the /z/ of the NE form *stone's* not as a case-ending, but as a particle, then no case distinctions remain at all. Historically, the form *stone* after a number (*he weighs ten stone*) comes from the old genitive plural; in the functioning grammatical system of NE this is simply a special syntactical position for the singular form.

44.4. IB2. Lexical Change. OE had many words which have been completely lost; we list only a small handful: /bádu/ 'fighting, battle,' /kɔ́·f/ 'bold, brave,' /kɔ́mp/ 'battle,' /ɣífan/ 'to give.' The NE word *give* is not the continuation of the last word in this list, which would come down rather as /jív/. NE *give* is one of thousands of words which, so far as we can tell from the manuscript evidence, were not in the vocabulary of OE, but have come into the language since. Others, to mention only a few, include *skirt, they, chair, table, vest, veal, potato, tobacco, hominy, typhoon*.

The OE word /skádu/ 'shadow, darkness' survives in NE, but as two distinct words: *shade* and *shadow*. These are from different inflected forms of the single OE stem. The converse of this—distinct OE stems falling together in NE—is harder to be sure of. OE /blɔ́·wan/ 'to blow' (as of the wind) and /blɔ́·wan/ 'to bloom' have both given NE *blow*, and for some speakers *blow* 'bloom' may count as a marginal use of *blow* as of the wind, but it is also possible that the NE forms should be regarded as two homonymous morphemes. A safer case (though the forms do not trace back all the way to OE) is the *by* of *by-laws* and that of *by-path, by-pass, by-form:* all of these are just one element now, but in origin the first is quite distinct from the others.

44.5. IC1. Shape Change. We have already seen that the shape of the word meaning 'stone' changed from OE /stɔ́·n/ to NE /stówn/. Quite similarly, we have

OE	NE	OE	NE
/bɔ́·n/	bone	/bɔ́·t/	boat
/gɔ́·d/	goad	/tɔ́·ken/	token
/skɔ́·n/	shone	/pɔ́·pa/	pope
/hɔ́·liğ/	holy	/hɔ́·l/	whole
/hɔ́·m/	home	/hlɔ́·f/	loaf.

In some of these the meaning has altered too—indeed, we could hardly assert that it has remained completely invariant in any case. /hlɔ́·f/

meant not exactly what we mean by *loaf*, but rather 'loaf of bread, bread,' and, by extension, 'food.'

One notes an important regularity in the words just listed: in all of them, OE had /ɔ́·/ and NE has /ów/. This difference is so great that the change of shape is obvious. But even in cases where the word in NE has much the same shape, phonetically speaking, that it probably had in OE, we must assert that the shape has changed phonemically. Thus OE /klíf/ 'cliff' has become NE *cliff* /klíf/. The *pronunciation* has scarcely been altered. But the /i/ of OE /klíf/ was a vowel in one vocalic system, whereas the phonetically similar /i/ of NE /klíf/ is a vowel in a different vocalic system. OE /i/ contrasted, for example, with a front rounded vowel /y/; NE does not, because there is no front rounded vowel in the NE phonemic system. Thus, strictly speaking, we must recognize that any change in any part of a phonemic system implies that the phonemic shapes of *all* grammatical forms have been altered.

44.6. IC2. Alternation Change. OE /bó·k/ 'book' had the nominative-accusative plural /bé·ķ/. /bó·k/ survives as *book;* /bé·ķ/, had it survived, would now be /bíʃč/, but we do not use this form. Instead, we form the plural of *book* in the regular way: *books*. Thus some of the habits of alternation in the formation of plurals from singulars have changed. This is not in itself an instance of grammatical change, since NE has inflection for number just as did OE; but it is tied in intimately with the sweeping grammatical change which has eliminated inflection for case.

The inflection of OE /hú·s/ 'house' was such that the stem-final /s/ was sometimes word-final, and thus phonetically [s] (§43.3), and sometimes followed by an unstressed vowel, thus phonetically [z]. For example, the nominative singular /hú·s/ was [hú·s], while the dative singular /hú·se/ was [hú·ze]. At this stage, there was no morphophonemic alternation, since the *phonemic* shape of the stem was the same throughout the paradigm. Later, however, the difference between voiceless and voiced became phonemic for spirants. When this had happened, then the difference between /s/ in /hú·s/ and /z/ in /hú·zə/ constituted a morphophonemic alternation; we still retain this in NE *house* /-s/ versus *houses* /-z-/. The /f/ : /v/ alternation in *calf* : *calves*, *wife* : *wives*, *loaf* : *loaves* and the /θ/ : /ð/ alternation in *mouth* : *mouths*, have this same history. Thus NE has acquired certain habits of alternation which OE did not have.

44.7. IIA. Semantic Change. We have already seen that OE /hlɔ́·f/ did not cover the same range of meaning as its NE descendant *loaf*. OE /séllan/ meant 'to give,' with 'to sell' as a marginal sense; NE *sell* means only the latter. OE /mó·d/ meant 'mind, heart, courage, pride,' not *mood*. OE /mýrxθ/ survives as *mirth*, but the OE word meant 'pleasure' in a rather more general sense. OE /kwéllan/ meant 'to kill, murder, execute'; now we *quell* a revolt, a rebellion, an uprising, or turbulent emotions. OE /klýppan/ 'to hug, embrace, accept' is now *clip* 'to fasten together.'

44.8. IIB. Phonetic Change. There are two distinct sorts of phonetic change, and no standardized terminology with which to keep them apart. We shall here speak of *sound change* and of *sudden phonetic change*.

Sound change is a gradual change of habits of articulation and hearing, which we have good reason to believe takes place constantly in every human community. We shall describe it in more detail later. Under IC1 (shape change) above we listed some words all of which had /ɔ́·/ in OE and /ów/ in NE. These words have been in constant use from Alfred's day (and earlier) to our own. Any speaker, living at any time during that millenium, would learn the words, use them, and pass them on to the next generation, without in the slightest realizing that his pronunciation of them was undergoing any modification. Yet in a thousand years the gradual change has added up to a clear structural difference: the structural position of /ów/ in the NE phonemic system cannot in any sense be identified with that of /ɔ́·/ in the OE phonemic system.

Sudden phonetic change is a very different matter, which we shall illustrate rather than try to describe. After the Norman Conquest, speakers of English were exposed to hundreds of Norman French words, many of which contained sounds alien to the English pronunciation of the time; in due course, many of these words came to be used in English as well as in French. Norman French had, to give just one instance, a word-initial contrast between voiceless /f/ and voiced /v/, whereas the English of the time had in initial position only the voiceless spirant. We can imagine large numbers of individual Englishmen mispronouncing French words that began with /v/—probably mainly by using their initial voiceless /f/ instead of the French /v/—and some of them never managing to master the new and alien sound. Others, however, would in due time succeed, and would thenceforth use the voiced spirant initially in such words even when placing the words in an English embedding context. To begin with, such events did nothing save to render the individual Englishmen more or less bilingual. But the borrowed words were gradually working into the inherited fabric of English, carrying some of their hitherto alien features of pronunciation with them. In the end, the phonemic system of English had been modified by the events: English now had a contrast between voiced and voiceless spirants in initial position. And, of course, pronunciation and hearing habits had been rather suddenly modified. In this context the word "sudden" does not mean instantaneous—only markedly less gradual than sound change.

We can see the same sort of thing happening today. For example, some Americans learn some German, and use some German words, with more or less German-like pronunciation, in their English. A speaker of NE who says *Zeitgeist* with an initial /ts-/ has that initial cluster in his idiolect. A speaker who regularly pronounces the composer *Bach*'s name with a final /x/ has that phoneme in his idiolect. The essential difference is one of scale. If millions of Americans came to use dozens of German words with /x/, we could not for long regard it purely as an idiolectal "aberration"—we should have to recognize that NE had acquired a new phoneme by sudden phonetic change.

NOTES

New terms: labels for *kinds* of phylogenetic change: *phonemic* change, *grammatical* change, *lexical* change, *shape* change, *alternation* change, *semantic* change, *phonetic* change, the last subsuming both *sound change* and *sudden phonetic change*. Most of these terms, and a number to be introduced in subsequent sections, are used constantly in historical linguistics; but in this book we make rather more precise distinctions than has in general been customary.

Problem. Below is a list of thirty OE words which have survived into NE. Each OE word contains either /d/ or /θ/ after the stressed vowel. Each NE descendant contains either /d/ or /ð/ in the same position. Describe what has happened to OE /d/ and /θ/ in this position by NE times, in such a way that if we were presented with an OE word not on the list, we would be able to assert *definitely* what would happen to any properly-located /d/ or /θ/ in it.

/ódela/ *addle*
/ǽ·ŷθer/ *either*
/bodiŷ/ *body*
/brí·del/ *bridle*
/bró·θor/ *brother*
/fǽder/ *father*
/fǽθm/ *fathom*
/féθer/ *feather*
/fórθung/ *farthing*
/fúrθor/ *further*
/gǽderian/ *gather*
/hǽ·θen/ *heathen*
/híder/ *hither*
/hrǽθor/ *rather*
/hwéθer/ *whether*
/léθer-/ *leather*
/mǽ·dwe, -wa/ *meadow*
/mó·dor/ *mother*
/nǽ·del/ *needle*
/néθera/ *nether*
/nórθerne/ *northern*
/ó·θer/ *other*
/rǽ·diŷ/ *ready*
/rúdiŷ/ *ruddy*
/skǽdwe, -wa/ *shadow*
/sú·θerne/ *southern*
/trédel/ *treadle*
/θíder/ *thither*
/wéder/ *weather*
/wíduwe/ *widow.*

45·

MECHANISMS of
PHYLOGENETIC CHANGE

45.1. The examples of different kinds of phylogenetic change given in the preceding section show that in many instances changes in different subsystems of a language are tied together. Is this tying-together ever causal? That is, can we ever say that a change of one kind is either the sole cause, or one of several contributory causes, for a change of another kind?

We shall seek the answer to this question by looking more thoroughly into some of the examples. We shall find that there are three main *mechanisms*—that is, *types* of causes—for the various kinds of phylogenetic change, together with a number of subordinate mechanisms that are not so well understood.

45.2. Sound Change as a Mechanism. OE dative singular /stó·ne/ ('stone') and genitive plural /stó·na/ fell together in pronunciation by ME times, as /stóvnə/. By the same ME times, OE genitive singular /stó·nes/ and nominative-accusative plural /stó·nas/ had both become /stóvnəs/. Several different *kinds* of change are involved in this sequence of events. Continuous sound change had gradually lessened the acoustic difference between OE unstressed /e/ and /a/ until in late OE they had become identical. When they became identical, a restructuring of the phonemic system (a phonemic change) had occurred, since certain contrasts which earlier had been part of the system were now lost. The sound change, and the resulting phonemic change, led to a shape change in countless forms, including those cited above. In the inflection of 'stone' and of many other nouns, the genitive singular and

387

the nominative-accusative plural had now become identical (ending in /-əs/); likewise the dative singular and genitive plural (ending in /-ə/). Such a falling-together of the shapes representative of different inflectional forms, brought about by sound change, is known as *syncretism*. The specific instances of syncretism just mentioned did not in themselves constitute a grammatical change, since some nouns still maintained distinct shapes for the inflectional categories in question. However, it was one of the factors contributing to the eventual total loss of case inflection in English.

In this first example, then, we see sound change functioning as a mechanism for the production of certain other kinds of change: phonemic change, shape change, and, in part, grammatical change.

In OE the noun meaning 'back,' like a number of others, had two stem-shapes differing as to vowel: the singular had /ǽ/, as in nominative-accusative /bǽk/, while the plural had /ɔ́/, as in nominative-accusative /bɔ́ku/. Now in early ME times the two stressed short vowels /ǽ/ and /ɔ́/ had fallen together, as a single low vowel /á/, so that the two forms cited had become respectively /bák/ and /bákə/. The disappearance of the /ǽ/ : /ɔ́/ distinction was the result of sound change; but as a further result, there was an alternation change: a certain irregular alternation common in OE was lost.

Shortly after the events just described, early ME /á/ was lengthened to /áˇ/ when followed by a single consonant in turn followed by an unstressed vowel. /bák/ and /bákə/ thus became respectively /bák/ and /báˇkə/; likewise, /fádər/ 'father' (from OE /fǽder/) became /fáˇder/, but its genitive /fádrəs/ (from OE /fǽderes/) retained the short /á/. In this case sound change brought about a new set of irregular morphophonemic alternations. The immediate consequences have now been obscured by subsequent events: the vowel of our NE *back* reflects ME /á/ rather than /áˇ/; some modern British dialects have /féjðər/ 'father,' showing the ME form with lengthened /áˇ/, but standard NE *father* is from the form with ME unlengthened /á/ (with, however, a lengthening of a later date).

It is clear from these examples that sound change, in addition to being one *kind* of phylogenetic change, must also be recognized as one of the *mechanisms* involved in other kinds of phylogenetic change. The truth of this is underscored when we search in vain for any sequence of historical events in which sound change can be shown to be the *result* of some other sort of change. This does not mean, of course, that gradual modification of habits of pronunciation and hearing is "uncaused," but it does mean that the causes of sound change cannot be found *within the system of habits we call language*.

45.3. Borrowing. Under IB2 (lexical change) in §44.4, we listed some words which were not part of the vocabulary of OE but have come into the language since. These words were taken from various other languages: *skirt* and *they* from Scandinavian in early times; *chair*, *table*, and *veal* from Norman French after the Conquest; *vest* much later from Italian; *potato*, *tobacco*, and *hominy* from various American Indian languages (sometimes via another European language rather than directly) after the voyages of Columbus; *typhoon* from South Chinese in the early days of the China trade. French words coming into English after the Norman Conquest brought with them some new phonemic distinctions, such as the contrast between /f/ and /v/ which we discussed under IIB in §44.8. Here, then, is a second important mechanism of phylogenetic change: technically it is called *borrowing*.

Borrowing is not always from one language into another; sometimes it is merely between dialects. Our words *vat* and *vixen* began with /f-/ in OE (/fǽt/, /fýksen/), and if they had the same continuous history as *father*, *four*, *foot*, they would begin with /f-/ today. But there is an area in the southeast of England in which all OE initial /f-/'s were voiced to /v-/: to this day people in this area pronounce *father*, *four*, *foot*, as well as *vat*, *vixen*, with an initial /v-/. Our contemporary NE has come down largely from the London English of ME times, and documentary records show that in ME times the two words in question, having fallen into disuse in London, were reintroduced from the rustic dialects in which initial /v-/ was regular.

45.4. Analogical Creation. The OE singular /bó·k/ 'book' and irregular plural /bé·ḳ/ 'books' both survived into ME, respectively as /bówk/ and /béjč/. In ME times there were vast number of nouns in which the plural was formed from the singular by adding /-əs/. On the analogy of these, a new ME plural form /bówkəs/ was coined; for a time, both /bówkəs/ and /béjč/ were used, but eventually the latter died out, leaving *books* as the only plural one hears today.

The mechanism of analogical creation is obviously that involved in most instances of idiom-formation, which we discussed in §§36 and 37 from a synchronic point of view. It is by the same mechanism that a child, or a foreigner learning English—or, indeed, an adult native speaker of English when he is overly tired—may say *foots* instead of *feet:* we may portray the situation as follows:

boat	is to	*boats*	as
back	is to	*backs*	as
cliff	is to	*cliffs*	as
root	is to	*roots*	as

. . .

foot   is to   *X.*

The three dots stand for countless other nouns which work the same way. Solving the proportions, *X* is obviously *foots*.

45.5. Minor Mechanisms. Working individually and in various combinations, the three mechanisms itemized above can bring about every kind of phylogenetic change described in §44. However, not all known changes in the design of languages can be ascribed to just these three mechanisms. There are seemingly a number of minor mechanisms, none so well understood as the principal three, but all allied more closely to analogy than to borrowing or to sound change. Each of the three principal mechanisms will be discussed in greater detail in subsequent sections; the minor mechanisms are itemized and illustrated here but will not be dealt with further.

Contamination is the reshaping of a word on the basis of constant association with some other word. It is supposed, for example, that we say /fíjmèjl/ *female*, rather than the historically expected /fémǝl/ or /fíjmǝl/, because of the habitual pairing of this word with *male*. Efforts have been made to show how this reshaping might have come about analogically, but the arguments are not convincing.

Metanalysis is akin to contamination, except that an older form is actually replaced by one which makes "more sense" to the speakers who introduce the new shape. Examples were given in §34.3; we may cite again the replacement, by some speakers, of *Welsh rabbit* by *Welsh rarebit*. A more obscure example, which is perhaps not what is usually meant by metanalysis, is the expression *prose laureate*, used in an advertisement as an epithet for a certain New York writer. Obviously this is based somehow on *poet laureate*. Historically, in the expression *poet laureate* the first word is a noun and the second an attribute; but the coining of *prose laureate* must imply an interpretation of the older phrase as though *poet* were attribute and *laureate* head. The ordinary association of *prose* with *poetry* is involved, but the new coinage cannot be purely analogical, since the analog to *poet* is not *prose* but something like *writer of prose*.

The remaining varieties are all observable as "slips of the tongue," and it has been suggested that a more thorough study of such lapses might teach us more about them. This suggestion was made years ago, however, and so far a good deal of work has yielded very little information.

Metathesis replaces an old form by a new one which differs in that two parts have been interchanged: *disintregation* for *disintegration,* /stǽnd sòwn/ for *sandstone, whipser* for *whisper, it steams to sick* for *it seems to stick.* One would not expect such slips of the tongue to have any lasting effect on a language, but in some cases, apparently, they do. Latin *parabola* (borrowed from Greek) has come down into Spanish as *palabra* 'word,' with the position of the /r/ and the /l/ interchanged; there are other instances of *r-l* interchange in the history of the languages of Europe. OE had both /ɔ́·skian/ 'to ask' and /ɔ́·ksian/; the latter still survives in some dialects. OE also showed a frequent pairing of forms with /r/ respectively before and after a syllabic nucleus: e.g., /bǽrnan/ and /brǽnan/ 'to burn.' NE *bird* reflects a metathesized form of OE /bríd/ 'young bird'; NE *horse* has metathesis as compared with the ancestral form beginning with /hr-/.

In *haplology* one of two more or less similar sequences of phonemes is dropped. One of the writer's colleagues regularly says *morphonemics* instead of *morphophonemics;* the writer once heard a child say /helówis/ for *Hello, Lois.* Latin *nūtrīx* 'nurse' and *stīpendium* 'wage-payment,' according to the regular patterns of derivation by which they were built, ought to have been respectively *nūtrītrīx* and *stīpipendium,* but the longer forms are not attested.

Assimilation makes one part of an utterance more like some nearby part in phonemic shape. When the two parts are adjacent, this may occur gradually as a part of sound change. But in *distant assimilation* other material intervenes. In Proto-Indo-European the words for *four* and *five* began with different consonants. The distinction was maintained, for example, in Sanskrit, which had /čatur/ 'four' (from Proto-Indo-European /kʷ-/) and /pañča/ 'five' (from /p-/). But in Latin, 'five' begins with the consonant expected only for 'four': *quīnque* with the *qu-* of *quattuor*. And in Germanic, 'four' begins with the consonant expected only for 'five'—/f-/. We assume that the reshapings in Latin and Germanic were relatively sudden, and that they occurred in the context of counting, where the words are used successively. Contamination may well be a special variety of distant assimilation.

Dissimilation works in just the opposite way: where one would expect the same phoneme or sequence of phonemes twice, something else occurs in one of the positions. Latin *peregrinus* 'foreigner, stranger' thus appears in the Romance languages with /l/ instead of the first /r/: Italian *pellegrino* (English, borrowed from Romance, *pilgrim*).

NOTES

New terms: the distinction between *mechanism* and *kind* of phylogenetic change. Labels for mechanisms: *sound change* (also a kind of change), *borrowing*, and *analogical creation;* and minor mechanisms: *contamination, metanalysis, metathesis, haplology, assimilation, distant assimilation, dissimilation.* Note also *syncretism* and our use of the word "reshaping." And note the use of the prefix *Proto-:* if a group of languages, collectively called the *X* languages, is related, then the term *Proto-X* designates their latest common ancestor, the "parent" language of all of them.

Sturtevant 1947 gives probably the fullest discussion of "lapses" or "slips of the tongue," with a great many examples.

46·

INNOVATION and SURVIVAL

46.1. Whatever mechanism or combination of mechanisms may be involved in an innovation in the design of a language, it is essential to distinguish between the innovating event itself and the subsequent spread of the new feature—if it does spread—to other speakers of the language.

There must have been some single small community—perhaps a village, or a family group—in which the OE unstressed vowels /e/ and /a/ first fell together in pronunciation, rendering pairs like /stó·ne/ and /stó·na/ phonemically identical (§45.2). Only in course of time did this habit of identical pronunciation spread through the rest of the late-OE-speaking world.

There must have been one or more specific individuals who first—and independently, if there were several—uttered the analogical plural /bówkəs/ 'books' instead of using the inherited form /béjč/ (§45.4); before long, though, many people were saying /bówkəs/ through imitation of the innovators, or because they had never heard /béjč/.

There must have been some first individual to use the Norman French word *chair* in an otherwise English utterance; before long, the word was being used in the speech of many who knew no French at all.

Our records of past speech are extremely sparse, so that we cannot usually know the exact identity of the innovating individual or group. In a few recent cases we do know who started a form: *gas* was invented in the 17th century by the Dutch chemist Van Helmont; *physicist* and *scientist* were coined about 1840 by William Whewell of Cambridge,

393

England; *chortle* was one of a number of new words used by Lewis Carroll, the rest of which remain alive today mainly in the context of his own writings; *kodak* was invented by George Eastman, *blurb* by Gelett Burgess, and *Frigidaire* by some advertising copywriter working for General Motors. Furthermore, in earlier instances where we cannot pin down the precise date and place of an innovation, our records occasionally at least show that it was in use earlier in one region than in others. All this leads us to believe that the distinction between innovation and spread is in principle sound.

At the same time, it must be recognized that the mechanism by which a new usage spreads is just one of the mechanisms by which an innovation may come about to begin with: borrowing. The habit of pronouncing /stó·ne/ and /stó·na/ identically developed in some one village; it spread because people in other villages imitated the new usage. A few Englishmen borrowed *chair* from Norman French; others borrowed the word from the first few. We cannot in principle distinguish between borrowing which introduces a new form into a whole language or dialect, on the one hand, and, on the other, borrowing by which the new form spreads to other speakers of the language or dialect. However, we are free to look at any given instance of borrowing from either of two angles, depending on our interest at the moment. We may be interested in the *history of a form* (often called *etymology*): from this angle, any borrowing of the form from one language or dialect into another is an episode in its spread. We may be interested in the *history of a system* (say a language or a dialect): from this angle, the same episode is an innovation in the system. Thus, if we are dealing with the collective history of the languages of Europe, we will speak of "innovation" in connection with the first importation of the word *algebra* from Arabic, and only of "spread" thereafter, even when the word passes from one European language to another. If, on the other hand, we are dealing only with the history of English, then the arrival of the word *algebra* in England is an "innovation." If we are focussing on a specific idiolect, then the acquisition of any word from others is an "innovation," and "spread" is meaningless.

From the point of view of the dialect or language in which an innovation occurs, it is possible to class innovations roughly into two types. The analogical ME plural /bówkəs/ 'books' illustrates one, and the imported *algebra* the other. When /bówkəs/ first occurred, the language already had a perfectly serviceable plural for the noun *book:* the inherited plural /béjč/. The two forms /bówkəs/ and /béjč/ were thus immediately in *competition* with each other: it did not make much practical difference whether a speaker said the one or the other, and it would have been very risky at the time to predict which of the two competing plurals would eventually survive and which—if either— would be lost. The word *algebra*, on the other hand, was brought to England along with the branch of mathematics to which it refers; there was no older form, with roughly the same meaning, to compete with it.

It is clear that the factors which make for the survival or non-survival of an innovation are different in these two cases. Some of these factors are best discussed in the specific context of one or another mechanism of phylogenetic change; but some of them can be dealt with in more general terms.

46.2. Factors Favoring Survival. Languages differ as to the sort of welcome they offer innovations of various kinds, and within a single language this seems to change, through successive periods of history, much as do fashions of dress or etiquette.

Thus in ME times a large number of analogically formed regular plurals, like /bówkəs/, made their appearance and survived, the older irregular plurals dying out. In addition to *books* we may mention *cows* and *days;* the OE plural of the former would now be /káj/ and of the latter /dóⱽz/. Regularized plurals still are to be heard from time to time—*mans, sheeps, womans.* The analogical basis for their appearance is with us—but they meet with a cold reception, and are not imitated by others save in a purely jocular way. Here, then, is one area in which there has been a change of fashion between ME times and the present.

In another area, earlier English was unreceptive but the contemporary language is hospitable. Phrasal compounds of the type of *hóusekèeping, hóusekèeper, méat-èater, dréssmàking* have been common for centuries. No doubt the pattern of relationship between *singing* or *singer* (used as nouns) and *to sing* (verb) has from time to time led speakers to use a phrasal compound verb like *to méat-èat,* but until recently such coinages, if they indeed occurred, did not spread into general usage. Today, however, forms like *to hóusekèep, to bábysìt, to báckbìte* are on the increase, both in variety and in frequency of occurrence.

The two examples above both involve innovations by analogy, but the phenomenon of fashion is just as apparent in connection with borrowing. In the nineteenth century a fashion of strong resistance to borrowed words developed in Germany, at least in educated and official circles; the consequence, as we shall see later, was not the cessation of borrowing but an increase of borrowing of one kind rather than of others. At the opposite extreme, English and the Romance languages have long had the fashion of borrowing learnèd words from Latin and Greek; similarly, Japanese and Korean from Chinese, Persian from Arabic, and Turkish from Arabic and Persian.

But to bring fashion into the picture is not to explain the matter, because we still have to account for the changes of fashion. On this score little is known. A great many non-linguistic factors must play a part—the social standing of the innovator, the general conservatism or progressivism of the community in its attitude towards speech, and so on. Two more purely linguistic factors are suspected of having some bearing: the *frequency* of any older competing form, and the *unobtrusiveness* of the innovation.

46.3. Frequency. One common consequence of analogical creation is that a morphophonemically irregular form is replaced by a more regular one: this is called *analogical levelling*. Other things being equal, irregular forms of high frequency are less apt to be so replaced than are rarer ones. Before discussing why this should be the case, let us give some evidence.

OE had more irregular verbs than does NE. Of those which have survived at all, a good many are now quite regular. Below are two lists of NE verbs which were irregular in OE. After each appears a figure, which indicates roughly the relative frequency of the word in NE: "1" means that the word is among the thousand most frequent in the language, "2" that it is the thousand next most frequent, and so on. Those with no figure are not in the most frequent twenty thousand. Both lists were chosen at random:

I. Irregular both in OE and in NE:
bite 2, *ride* 1, *rise* 1, *write* 1, *fly* 1, *choose* 1, *freeze* 2, *bind* 2, *drink* 1, *find* 1, *grind* 2, *sing* 1, *swim* 2, *run* 1, *swell* 2, *fight* 1, *bear* 1, *steal* 2, *tear* 1, *break* 1, *come* 1, *speak* 1, *treat* 2, *eat* 1, *see* 1, *lie* 1, *sit* 1, *draw* 1, *stand* 1, *shake* 1, *slay* 4.

II. Irregular in OE, regular in NE:
glide 3, *bow* 1, *seethe* 8, *help* 1, *delve* 12, *melt* 2, *swallow* 2, *yield* 2, *yell* 2, *yelp* 8, *carve* 3, *smart* 3, *warp* 5, *thresh* 5, *mourn* 2, *spurn* 5, *quell* 6, *shear* 4, *fret* 3, *fare* 2, *bake* 2, *grave, wade* 6, *shave* 4, *wax* ('grow'), *flay* 11, *laugh* 1, *step* 1, *dread* 2, *fold* 2, *well* (*up*).

Of course there is overlap in the frequencies, but the average difference is too great to be ascribed to experimental error.

To account for the bearing of frequency on analogical levelling, let us note that if an irregular form is frequently used, a child learning his native language will hear it many times, and may never come out with any analogically produced regular alternant. Even if he does, he probably already knows the inherited irregular form and may reject his own innovation. For a rarer irregular form this argument applies in reverse. This is doubtless part of the story; the rest turns on the other factor—unobtrusiveness, which will be discussed in a moment.

Under some circumstances, extreme rarity may preserve an irregularity instead of helping to lose it. The process, however, is quite different. The words *spake* (past tense of *speak*) and *beholden* still occur from time to time; it would seem that the rarity and irregularity of the forms constitute an integral factor in their peculiar archaic flavor, and it is because of the latter that the forms are used.

46.4. Unobtrusiveness. A highly divergent innovation often achieves temporary popularity precisely because it stands out so sharply against the backdrop of ordinary speech. Often such extreme forms count as slang, and we have already seen (§37.6) that a slang form tends to die out rapidly: its punch is lost through overuse and some new innovation takes its place.

For this reason, less obtrusive innovations are more likely to survive as part of the ordinary machinery of the language. Today we fluctuate between the plurals *hoofs* and *hooves*, *roofs* and *rooves*, *laths* and *paths* with /θs/ or /ðz/. In the light of this, an innovating plural *chieves* or *handkerchieves* might escape notice.

Similarly, we must suspect that when the analogical regular plurals /bówkəs/ and /kúws/ (or /kúwz/) 'cows' were first uttered in ME times, they were inconspicuous because of the large numbers of conflicting patterns for plural-formation in ME and the large numbers of nouns for which more than one plural was in use. People were attuned to a good deal of fluctuation, and understood what they heard without paying much attention to the speaker's selection of one or another of about equally common variants.

The rarity of a form, up to a point, similarly makes for unobtrusiveness of a competing innovation: this is the rest of the story of the bearing of frequency on analogical levelling. *Two mans* is conspicuous because we hear *men* dozens of times a day. But of the pair *macrodonts* and *macrodonta*, neither stands out as noticeably queerer than the other.

A new formation may be inconspicuous because it occurs in an environment which is itself novel or otherwise striking. The past tense of *sit* is always *sat*, but the new phrasal compound *to bábysìt* yields either *bábysàt* or *bábysìtted*. In the Romance languages, a number of irregularly inflected simple verbs underlie derivations, formed with a prefix, which have been partly or wholly regularized. The imperative of Spanish *decir* 'to say, speak' is irregularly *dí*, but that of *bendecir* 'to bless' is *bendíce*, quite regular. The extreme example is Spanish *ir* 'to go', which is highly irregular; yet *subir* 'to go up, ascend' is a completely regular verb of the so-called "third conjugation."

It would seem that an innovation brought about by sound change is always completely unobtrusive, so that, if it does not survive, we cannot appeal to undue obtrusiveness as the reason. When OE unstressed /e/ and /a/ fell together, probably no one noticed the event. The "functional load" carried by this phonemic contrast had been very small: that is, hardly ever would a pair of utterances, both possible in the same practical situation, have differed only in that one had unstressed /e/ while the other had unstressed /a/. But in making this generalization about innovations through sound change, we must remember that there may have been untold hundreds of such innovations, in the last thousand years of English, of which we have no record because they were abortive—that is, they affected some small community, but did not spread, and the surviving older pattern in due time covered them up even in the village or region originally affected. In the nature of the case, we cannot know how blatantly obtrusive these abortive innovations may have been.

Occasionally, of course, an innovation survives where neither of the favoring conditions we have discussed can have been operative. This underscores the importance of non-linguistic factors which escape our observation. German *Kaiser* 'emperor' and Russian /cár₁/ with much the same meaning are ultimately loans from late Latin *caesar;* the latter was originally the name of a particular Roman, *Gaius Julius Caesar.* A change of meaning, such as that of Latin *Caesar* (man's name) to *caesar* 'ruler, emperor,' takes place by a sort of analogy; at first the new meaning must have been a striking novelty. Our word *whore* formerly meant 'dear' (compare the cognate Latin *carus* 'dear'); its first application in what is now the only meaning must have been similarly striking.

46.5. Factors Favoring Non-Survival. When two forms—say an inherited one and an innovation—are in competition, then the non-survival of one of them may simply be the negative aspect of the survival of the other. Of course, sometimes both survive indefinitely. When this happens, we usually find that some semantic distinction has arisen, so that, in effect, they have ceased to be in competition. *Wrought* and *sodden* are old past participles of the verbs *work* and *seethe;* we now use *worked* and *seethed* ordinarily, *wrought* and *sodden* only in special transferred senses or in fixed phrases (*What hath God wrought?*). *Shade* and *shadow* are from a single OE noun (§44.4); in ME some of the inflected forms developed a long stem vowel /áᵛ/ while others kept the short /á/, and then the paradigm was filled out analogically for each shape of the stem. Had there not been some semantic differentiation, probably by now we would be using only one of the words, the other being lost (like the plural /béjč/) or surviving only in special contexts (like *wrought*). In the case of *mead* and *meadow*, which have a parallel history, the former is indeed largely confined to poetic usage. The competition between the Norman French loans *beef, veal, pork, mutton* and the inherited native English words *ox, calf, swine, sheep* did not lead to the loss of either set; the semantic differentiation which helped to retain them all is discussed by Sir Walter Scott in a famous passage in *Ivanhoe.*

But a form may also be lost when there is no special competing form. The principal cause of such obsolescence is change in conditions of living, which removes the need for the word. We still have many words referring to horse-drawn vehicles and related matters, but they are used much less than formerly, and in another generation or so some of them may be dead.

Various sorts of taboo may lead to the non-use of a form. More often, the form which disappears is not the tabooed word itself (some of our "Anglo-Saxon monosyllables" are extremely hardy), but words which are similar in phonemic shape. The animal names *rooster* and *donkey* are now far commoner in American English than *cock* and *ass;* earlier English and French both had a word for 'rabbit' which has disappeared, save perhaps in local dialects, because of its similarity to a tabooed word of sexual reference.

Finally, one of two words sometimes disappears because the two have come to have the same shape (*homonyms*), despite distinct meanings, and misunderstandings and embarrassment accompany the continued use of both. OE /lǽ·tan/ 'to permit' and /léttan/ 'to prevent' both became late ME /lét/ by sound change. That one or the other should have virtually died out is understandable, but it is hard to see why it was the word meaning 'to prevent' rather than the other. The OE words for 'plow' and 'portion' both come to us as *share;* in the former sense we now use *plow* or at least the compound *plowshare,* though we do not know in just what context the homonyms would give rise to confusion. In one region of southern France the Latin words for 'rooster' and for 'cat' would both come down as /gat/, but this shape is actually in use only for 'cat'; various other forms have been adopted for the meaning 'rooster.' In this case we can see, in part, why one rather than the other should have survived: /gat/ 'rooster' would stand isolated, whereas /gat/ 'cat' is accompanied by a number of derivatives with related meanings.

46.6. The Extinction of a Language. The extinction of a language, or of its dialects in some isolated region, is quite a different matter from the obsolescence of a single word.

The Germanic conquerors of Normandy in the 9th and 10th centuries lost their Germanic speech and took on French; when some of them proceeded in the 11th century to conquer England, they ultimately lost what had become their language (French), and took on English. This is, of course, not necessarily the fate of a politically ascendant language. A number of American Indian languages have disappeared, even though their speakers were not all slaughtered. A number of others, such as Navaho, Ojibwa, and many in Mexico and further south, show no signs of losing ground; yet we can hardly expect them in the future to supplant the ascendant languages imported from Europe. The languages of European immigrants to the

United States are often quite vigorous for a generation or so, but most of them are now on the wane.

While it is thus quite impossible to state in any general terms the conditions under which one of two competing languages will survive, we do know something of what takes place when a loss is occurring. Fifty-odd years ago many Norwegians settled in the United States, particularly in Wisconsin and Iowa. At the start, most of them were monolingual in Norwegian, or, at most, could use a little English for highly practical purposes. The second generation once again included some such monolinguals, but also many who knew both Norwegian and English, using the former in the home, the latter, for example, in school. In succeeding generations the proportion of bilinguals to monolingual Norwegians increased, and also, of the bilinguals, those whose "preferred" language was English grew more numerous and those whose "preferred" language was Norwegian grew rarer. As of today, monolingual Norwegians are very rare and usually are of the oldest surviving generation; the youngest generation includes many who are virtually monolingual in English. If nothing happens to interfere with the trend, in another half-century Norwegian will have disappeared altogether in these communities.

Such a very slow community-wise shift from one language to another is obviously very fertile ground for the borrowing of forms from one language into the other, but the abandonment of the one language and the adoption of the other is *not* in itself a manifestation of borrowing.

NOTES

New terms: *innovation* versus *spread* and *survival; history of a form* (*etymology*) versus *history of a system* (language, dialect, idiolect); *competition* of forms; *frequency* and *unobtrusiveness* as factors in survival; *analogical levelling* of morphophonemic irregularities.

The frequency figures for NE verbs in §46.3 are taken from the *Thorndike Century Senior Dictionary*. On the extinction of languages, see Swadesh 1948; for Norwegian in the United States, Haugen 1953.

47·

THE CONDITIONS for BORROWING

47.1. From our discussion of §46 we see that borrowing stands somewhat apart from the other mechanisms of phylogenetic change: any of the mechanisms can bring about an innovation, but if the innovation survives and spreads to other speakers only borrowing can be responsible. It is therefore especially important for us to understand the conditions under which borrowing is likely to occur.

Whenever two idiolects come into contact, one or both may be modified. In face-to-face communication, either speaker may imitate some feature of the other's speech; when the contact is indirect, as in reading, the influence can of course pass only in one direction. The feature which is imitated is called the *model;* the idiolect (or language) in which the model occurs, or the speaker of that idiolect, is called the *donor;* the idiolect (or language) which acquires something new in the process is the *borrowing idiolect* (or language). The process itself is called "borrowing," but this term requires some caution. Thus, that which is "borrowed" does not have to be paid back; the donor makes no sacrifice and does not have to be asked for permission. Indeed, nothing changes hands: the donor goes on speaking as before, and only the borrower's speech is altered.

From our definition, we see that the conditions for borrowing are present constantly, as a natural accompaniment of every use of language except genuine soliloquy. In the contact of idiolects A and B, the chances that borrowing will actually occur depend on several factors, one of which is the degree of similarity of A and B. If the two idiolects

402

are very similar, borrowing is unlikely, since neither speaker is apt to use any form unknown to the other. If A and B are so divergent that the speakers cannot understand each other, borrowing is equally unlikely. Between the two extremes we find the situations in which borrowing is more probable. In practice, these situations can be classed roughly into two types. In one type, the two idiolects share a common core (§39); under these conditions we speak of *dialect borrowing*. In the other, there is no common core but rather some degree of bilingualism or semibilingualism (§38.3); in this case we speak of *language borrowing*.

47.2. Individual and Mass Effect. A single act of borrowing affects, in the first instance, only the borrowing idiolect. This is in itself important for linguistic ontogeny; borrowing is presumably the most important mechanism by which an idiolect continues to change during adult life. But if such a single act of borrowing were not followed or accompanied by others, it could lead to no measurable results in the later history of the language as a whole. If I take a fancy to the French word *ivrogne*, and start to use it in my English, my idiolect is modified. The future of the language is not affected unless others imitate me, so that the newly imported word passes into more or less general usage and is transmitted to subsequent generations. This would be more probable if a number of speakers of English who knew some French were, at more or less the same time, to start using the French word in their English. Such mass importation from another dialect or language is very common, and in historical linguistics is the kind of borrowing that interests us most.

Consequently, it is customary to speak loosely of a "single" borrowing even in cases where thousands of individual acts of borrowing from one idiolect to another must have been involved. Thus we say that the Latin word *vīnum* has been borrowed into English just twice (not thousands of times); once into pre-English, giving OE /wí·n/, NE *wine;* later, via Norman French, giving ME /víjnə/, NE *vine*. Even if the factor mentioned in the preceding paragraph were not operative, this sort of mass-statistical approach would be forced upon us by the limitations of our documentary evidence.

47.3. Conditions for Borrowing. The mere contact of idiolects A and B does not guarantee that one will borrow from the other. For a borrowing to occur, say from B to A, two conditions must be met·

(1) The speaker of A must understand, or think he understands, the particular utterance in idiolect B which contains the model.

(2) The speaker of A must have some motive, overt or covert, for the borrowing.

The first condition need not detain us long. Our reference must be to apparent rather than genuine understanding, because in many known instances there is really some measure of misunderstanding. An amusing example is the following. In the Philippines, the names of saints are often bestowed on infants. After World War II, one child was named *Ababís*, supposedly the name of the patron saint of the United States. The child's father had repeatedly heard American soldiers, in moments of emotional stress, call on this saint: *San Ababís*.

The second is more difficult. We cannot profit from idle speculation about the psychology of borrowers, but must confine ourselves to such overt evidence as is at hand. This may lead us to miss some motives of importance, but we can be much surer of those which we do discern. These are two in number: *prestige* and *need-filling*.

47.4. The Prestige Motive. People emulate those whom they admire, in speech-pattern as well as in other respects. European immigrants to the United States introduce many English expressions into their speech, partly for other reasons, but partly because English is the important language of the country. Upper- and middle-class Englishmen, in the days after the Norman Conquest, learned French and used French expressions in their English because French was the language of the new rulers of the country. Bobby-soxers imitate, in one way or another, the latest and most popular radio or TV singer.

Sometimes the motive is somewhat different: the imitator does not necessarily admire those whom he imitates, but wishes to be identified with them and thus be treated as they are. The results are not distinguishable, and we can leave to psychologists the sorting out of fine shades of difference.

However, there is one negative variety of prestige which must not be overlooked: that of conformity with the majority. Naturally, this is more operative under some social conditions than others. A child moved at an early school age from one part of the United States to another changes his style of English in the direction of that of his new age-mates in school and playground. This is not necessarily through direct imitation of some single outstanding playmate, but simply be-

because it is discomforting to be in the minority. Here, as often, different prestige models may disagree. The child's parents and teachers probably say *John and I are going*, while the predominant usage of the child's age-mates is *Me and John are going*. For a time, at least, the drive for conformity within the age group is apt to take precedence.

The prestige motive is constantly operative in dialect borrowing; it becomes important in language borrowing only under special conditions. When speakers of two different languages live intermingled in a single region, usually one of the languages is that spoken by those in power: this is the *upper* or *dominant* language, and the other is the *lower*. Such a state of affairs has most often been brought about by invasion and conquest, more rarely by peaceful migration. In the long run one or the other language may disappear, but the factors which determine which will survive seem to be so subtle and complex as to escape accurate observation (§46.6). In the meantime, however, the prestige factor leads to extensive borrowing *from the dominant language into the lower*. Borrowing in the other direction is much more limited and largely ascribable to the other principal motive.

47.5. The Need-Filling Motive. The most obvious other motive for borrowing is to fill a gap in the borrowing idiolect.

We can imagine a British sailing-vessel in China waters in the earliest days of the China trade, manned by a mixed crew. A Chinese crewman notices a cloud-formation on the horizon and in terror cries out his word for the kind of storm that impends. After the storm, the English-speaking members of the crew are all too willing to admit that it is unlike anything in their previous experience and needs its own name; they adopt the Chinese word *typhoon*.

Thus new experiences, new objects and practices, bring new words into a language. It does not matter whether the new objects and practices come to the community, by way of what anthropologists call *diffusion*, or the community goes to the new objects and practices, by way of migration; the result is the same. *Tea, coffee, tobacco, sugar, cocoa, chocolate, tomato* have spread all over the world in recent times, along with the objects to which the words refer. Typhoons and monsoons have not spread, but direct or indirect experience with them has.

Among the new things which migrants or conquerors encounter are natural and artificial topographical features, and place-names are often passed down from the earlier inhabitants of a region to later

arrivals. Slavic place-names in eastern Germany, such as *Berlin,*
Leipzig, Dresden, Breslau, attest the earlier presence of Slavic-speaking
peoples in that region. *Vienna, Paris,* and *London* are of Celtic origin.
Schuylkill, Catskill, Harlem, The Bowery were taken from Dutch into
English when New Amsterdam became New York. *Michigan* 'big
lake,' *Wisconsin* 'where it is cold,' *Chicago* 'skunk weed,' *Illinois* 'man,'
Oshkosh 'claw,' *Mississippi* 'big river,' and many others, are Algonquian;
these were names of lakes, rivers, and Indian settlements before they
became by transfer the names of cities and states.

Immigrants to the United States in the last seventy-five years have
drawn heavily on English for new words, partly on the prestige basis
and partly for need-filling purposes: the two motives must often be
mingled, and we cannot always say which was more important in a
given instance. In exchange, however, American English has acquired
only a sparse scattering of need-filling loans from the various languages
of the immigrants: *delicatessen, hamburger, wiener, zwieback* from immigrant German, *chile con carne, tortilla* from Mexican Spanish, *spaghetti,*
ravioli, pizza, grinder (sandwich) from Italian (the last perhaps from
grande 'big one'), *chow mein, chop suey* from Chinese—to stick to the
sphere of humble foodstuffs. More elevated loans from these languages
have usually entered English via other routes: the immigrants are not
responsible for *Zeitgeist, Weltanschauung* (German, philosophy), *allegro,*
andante, sonata, piccolo (Italian, music), *demi-plié, grand plié, barre,*
arabesque (French, ballet).

Our examples of borrowing under the need-filling motive have been
of borrowing from one language to another. But the same variety of
borrowing takes place constantly among the dialects of a single language. American baseball, or something much like it, was first played
in this country about a century ago in cities on the east coast; a similar
game is reported from earlier in England. The game spread in an
accelerating fashion through the United States, and its terminology
spread along with it, though both game and terminology underwent
modifications from time to time. (Of course both game and terminology
have now also spread to certain other speech communities, Japan and
Central America in particular.) Expressions like *corn pone, corn bread,*
spoon bread are known wherever the types of food are prepared, but
seem to have got their start in the South.

If a local dialect gains ascendancy for political and economic reasons, then one expects extensive borrowing *from* that dialect for prestige reasons, but forms borrowed *into* the ascendant dialect have to be explained—and usually, if the records are not too scanty, explanation on the need-filling basis is possible. When the ascendant ME of London imported the words *vat, vixen,* and perhaps *vane* (as in *weather vane*) from the local dialects of the south and east, it was borrowing words that occurred mainly in cultural contexts of little importance in city life. The words may have been carried to London by Kentish tradesmen who settled in the city, or, at least in the case of *vixen* and perhaps in that of *vane,* might have been picked up by London aristocrats while on hunts in the south.

NOTES

New terms: the *model,* the *donor,* and the *borrowing idiolect* (or *dialect* or *language*); *dialect borrowing* versus *language borrowing; prestige* motive and *need-filling* motive for borrowing; *upper* or *dominant* versus *lower* language; *diffusion.*

In this and the next two sections we follow Bloomfield 1933 chapters 25–27, but incorporate the newer and closer-fitting elaboration of Haugen 1950. An excellent and thorough recent study of all phases and types of borrowing is Weinreich 1953, with an exhaustive bibliography.

The persistent rumor that American baseball was invented by Abner Doubleday in Cooperstown, N. Y., is now considered false; see Menke 1953. The rumor that chop suey was invented in New Orleans, not in China, may have some truth in it—the dish in its present form may have spread through the United States from New Orleans—but the term *chop suey* is from Cantonese, in which language it designates a common type of prepared food, similar to if not identical with what we call by the term.

48·

KINDS of LOANS

48.1. The examples of borrowing given in §47 involve in most cases the development of an *idiom*—be it word or phrase—in one language or dialect on the basis of one already current in another. There are several different ways in which this can come about, and there are also known or suspected cases of borrowing of other than lexical items. In this section we shall sort these out, and also specify the kinds of phylogenetic change that can be brought about, directly or indirectly, by the different kinds of borrowing.

Whenever the need-filling motive plays a part, the borrower is being confronted with some new object or practice for which he needs words. Under these conditions it does not always happen that the borrower imports bodily the words already used by the donor; in fact, three rather distinct things may happen, giving rise respectively to *loanwords*, *loanshifts*, and *loanblends*.

48.2. Loanwords. The borrower may adopt the donor's word along with the object or practice: the new form in the borrower's speech is then a *loanword*.

The acquisition of a loanword constitutes in itself a lexical change (§44), and probably we should say that it constitutes or entails a semantic change. A shape change is sometimes involved at least in the sense that a shape theretofore "uninhabited" (§34.4) by any form may have been brought into use. English acquisition of *wiener* /wíjnər/ involved no such change, since the language already had a morpheme represented by the shape /wíjn/ and several morphemes represented by suffixed /-ər/. Our acquisition of *allegro* /əlégrow/, on the other hand, entailed a shape change of the type just described.

408

Other kinds of phylogenetic change are not directly implied by a single new importation, but they may come about as the result of a whole wave of loanwords from some single source, along the following lines:

Grammatical change. ME acquired a large number of Norman-French adjectives containing the derivational suffix which is now *-able/-ible: agreeable, excusable, variable,* and others. At first, each of these whole words must have functioned in English as a single morpheme. But English had also borrowed some of the verbs which in French underlay the adjectives, and in due time there came to be a large enough number of pairs of borrowed words for the recurrent termination to take on the function of a derivational affix in English. This is shown by the subsequent use of the suffix with native English stems: *bearable, eatable, drinkable* (the stems tracing back to OE /béran/, /étan/, /drínkan/).

At a much earlier time, before the migration of our Germanic-speaking ancestors into England from the Continent, pre-English borrowed a good many Latin words which included the suffix *-ārius* 'he who has to do with such-and-such,' together with some of the Latin words which underlay derivational formations with this suffix. From these borrowed words, a suffix paralleling the Latin *-ārius* was in due time peeled out, and used on native as well as imported stems: OE /wǽγnere/ 'wagoner.' Within OE the affix was extended to use with verb stems: /rá·fere/ 'robber,' /rǽ·dere/ 'reader,' /wrí·tere/ 'writer,' from the stems of /rá·fian/ 'to rob,' /rǽ·dan/ 'to read,' /wrí·tan/ 'to write.' This is the source of our NE agentive affix *-er.*

In both of these examples it is to be noted that the derivational affix was not borrowed as such: it occurred as an integral part of various whole words, and only the latter were actually borrowed. Apparently we can generalize on this point: *loanwords are almost always free forms* (words or phrases); *bound forms are borrowed as such only with extreme rarity.* The generalization is not perfect, though, as shown by the occasional occurrence of a form like English *cuteheit* /kjúwt+hàjt/ 'bit of cute behavior or speech,' where the German affix *-heit* has been imported bodily and added to the English word *cute.*

Alternation Change. Our learnèd vocabulary, borrowed directly or indirectly from Latin and Greek, includes a good number of words like *datum* : *data, phenomenon* : *phenomena, matrix* : *matrices.* What has happened here is that we have borrowed both the singular and the plural forms of the word, using the singular as an English singular and the plural as the matching English plural. Since English already had the inflectional category of number, these importations do not imply any grammatical change, only additional patterns of alternation. In such cases there is usually competition between the imported and native patterns. Most of us tend to use *data* as a singular "mass-noun," like *milk,* saying *this data is* . . . rather than *these data are* . . .. Doublet plurals in competition are even commoner: *matrixes* /méjtriksəz/ and *matrices* /méjtrəsìjz/, *automata* and *automatons, gladioluses* and *gladioli.* One cannot safely predict which alternative in such a case will in the end win out; currently, in English, the imported plural has a more learnèd connotation than the native one. The extension of an imported pattern of plural-formation to a native word is much rarer, but some sociologists and psychologists have been heard to say /prówsesìjz/ for *processes;* presumably this is supported by the erudite connotation of the foreign-style plural.

Phonemic and Phonetic Change. The first few members of a community to use a word from another language, or from a highly divergent dialect of their own, may imitate the pronunciation of the model accurately. Any isolated borrowing which spreads into general usage, however, is unlikely to retain its foreign pronunciation if that in any way goes against the pronunciation habits of the borrowers. Such an isolated loan in English is the Maori name *Ngaio,* which in Maori begins with a dorso-velar nasal. The English pronunciation is /nájow/ or /əŋgájow/. Some of us pronounce initial /ts/ in *tsetse fly, tsar;* most, however, begin the words with /z/. Even French words like *rouge, garage, mirage,* probably end more commonly in English with /ǰ/ than with /ž/.

However, it would seem that a great flood of loanwords from some single source, involving many bilinguals as the channel for the borrowings and with a major prestige factor, can have some striking consequences in articulatory habits. The stock example, once again, is the influence of Norman French on English: it was through this influence that English acquired initial /v z ǰ/, and, consequently, the phonemic contrast between /v/ and /f/, /z/ and /s/. Although classic, the instance is not isolated. A number of studies have shown how thoroughly the phonemic systems of several Latin American Indian languages have been transformed via Spanish loans; for example,

Quechua probably had only a three-vowel system /i a u/ before the arrival of the Spaniards, but now, by virtue of completely assimilated loans from Spanish, has a five-vowel system /i e a o u/.

48.3. Loanshifts. When confronted with a new object or practice for which words are needed, the borrower may not accept the donor's words along with the new cultural item. Instead, he may somehow adapt material already in his own language. The precise adaptation, however, may be in one way or another patterned on the donor's verbal behavior. In any case, a new idiom arises, and since it arises under the impact of another linguistic system, it is a *loanshift*.

The spread of Christianity into England in the 7th century carried many Latin words into OE as cultural loanwords: *abbot, altar, canon, cowl, noon, pope, cap, sock, cook*, to cite but a few. A few earlier loans were brought into more active use: *church, bishop*. But for some of the fundamental notions of the new religion, old Germanic words were used: *God, heaven, hell* were merely stripped of their heathen connotations and invested with the meanings described by the missionaries. The influence on the borrowing language is minimal in cases of this kind: the only change directly entailed is semantic.

Portuguese *grosseria* means 'a rude remark.' But Portuguese immigrants in the United States now use the word in the sense 'grocery (store)'; obviously the similarity in shape of the English word has played a part, but the result, once again, is a semantic change. Portuguese *livraria* 'bookstore, library in a home' has similarly come to be used among the immigrants in the sense 'public library,' replacing the usual Portuguese word *biblioteca;* the responsible model is the English word *library*.

If the model is a form with two different ranges of usage, only one of which is matched by a form in the borrowing language, the borrower may extend his native form to the other range of usage of the model. Yiddish has a form *ver* 'who?' (interrogative) and another form *vos* 'who' (relative). On the basis of the range of usage of English *who*, some Yiddish speakers in this country will say *der ments ver iz do* instead of *der ments vos iz do* for 'the man who is here.' The complementary extension of *vos* into *ver* territory might be expected, but is not on record. Immigrant German has a new verb *gleichen* 'to be fond of,' formed from *gleich* 'like' on the basis of the verbal use of English *like*. The Greek word *aitía* had two ranges of meaning, 'cause' and 'fault, blame'; a verb derived from it, *aitiáomai*, came to mean 'I charge, accuse.' The Greek term for the case of a noun used as object of a verb was *aitiātikḗ ptôsis* 'the case pertaining to what is caused or affected'; the Roman grammarians made a loanshift extension of the stem of the Latin verb *accūsō* 'I accuse,' and coined *accūsātīvus* as the Latin equivalent of the Greek grammatical term.

If the model in the donor language is a composite form, then the borrower may build a parallel composite form out of native raw material: the result is a *loan-translation*. English *marriage of convenience* and *that goes without saying* are loan-translations from French; *long time no see* and *can do* (as affirmative response to a request) are loan-translations, with some distortion, from Chinese; *loanword* is a loan-translation from German *Lehnwort*. American immigrant Portuguese *responder para tras* is a loan-translation of English *to talk back;* immigrant Norwegian *leggja av* 'to discharge' is based on English *lay off*. French *presqu'île* and German *Halbinsel* are modeled on Latin *paenīnsula* ('almost-island' = 'peninsula'); French *gratte-ciel* and Spanish *rascacielos* are both modeled on English *skyscraper*.

If all borrowing is a phase of what anthropologists call *diffusion*, then the acquisition of loanshifts is an instance of the particular kind called *stimulus-diffusion:* a member of a borrowing community gets the general notion for something from some donor community, but works out the details himself. Good nonlinguistic examples are to be found in the history of writing. The Latin alphabet spread into England and was adapted for the writing of English in the 7th century; this was ordinary diffusion. Much later, the Cherokee Indian Sequoia got the general notion of a writing-system from Europeans, but worked out the details of his system for Cherokee, including many of the shapes of the individual graphic symbols, on his own.

Loanshifts involve lexical and semantic change, and in some cases may lead to minor grammatical change. The latter is effected if the literal following of a foreign model in the creation of a new idiom gives rise to some type of construction previously alien to the borrowing language. The English pattern of two nouns in succession, the second attributive to the first, as in *operation Coronet*, seems to have come in from French in this way. Other kinds of phylogenetic change are probably not brought about by this particular type of borrowing.

48.4. Loanblends. A loanblend is a new idiom developed in the borrowing situation, in which both the loanword and the loanshift mechanisms are involved: the borrower imports part of the model and replaces part of it by something already in his own language.

American immigrant Portuguese borrows English *boarder* as *bordo:* the stem, *bord-*, is imported from English, but the agentive suffix *-er* is replaced by the structurally and semantically comparable Portuguese element *-o*. The same immigrants use *alvachus* 'overshoes' and *alvarozes* 'overalls'; the initial *al-* is recurrent in Portuguese. Pennsylvania German changes *bossy* to *bassig*, *funny* to *fonnig*, *tricky* to *tricksig*, replacing the English adjective-forming *-y* by the similar German *-ig*. Similarly, Pennsylvania German *bockabuch* 'pocketbook' borrows the first word of the phrasal compound but replaces the second part.

An interesting case is the common substandard English *chaise lounge*, where the first word of the French model *chaise longue* 'long upholstered chair of a certain kind' is imported, but the second part is mistranslated so as to seem to make sense.

Records of earlier borrowings often do not permit us to determine whether a hybrid word is the result of loanblending at the time of borrowing or a later coinage of native and well-assimilated foreign elements. In most of the above examples we have reason to believe that loanblending was involved. In the case of English *talkative* and *bearable* (§48.2) we have documentary evidence to show that they were later hybrid formations. But in many other instances we cannot be sure.

48.5. Pronunciation Borrowing. If a speaker imitates someone else's pronunciation of a word which is already familiar to the borrower, we may speak of *pronunciation borrowing*. Usually the donor and borrowing idiolects are mutually intelligible, and the motive is prestige. A Southerner who comes to the North and begins to say /gríjsij/ instead of /gríjzij/ is borrowing a pronunciation. A Middle-Westerner who goes East and begins to say /mǽrij/, /hǽrij/, /kǽrij/ instead of /mérij/, /hérij/, /kérij/ (*marry, Harry, carry*) is doing the same thing.

Something like this may have been involved in some of the instances in which earlier Latin loans in OE, surviving in ME times, were replaced by later loans via Norman French. OE had /férs/ 'verse,' and /kré·kas/ 'Greeks,' which doubtless survived into the ME period. The later borrowings, via Norman French, had initial /v-/ and /gr-/, but were otherwise quite similar in sound to the other forms. A speaker who abandoned the /f-/ and /kr-/ forms in favor of the /v-/ and /gr-/ forms may simply have been changing his pronunciation of what was in effect a single word in each case. The same may have been true as ME /gív/ 'give,' from Scandinavian, supplanted the inherited form /jív/.

A style of pronunciation can also be imitated, usually for prestige reasons, without specific reference to a particular word. Modern Castilian Spanish /θ/ was formerly a spirant of the general type of [s]; the change to [θ] is said to have arisen because the king had a lisp, which others found it advisable to imitate.

Pronunciation borrowing of this sort can operate across language boundaries. A few centuries ago the languages of Western Europe all had a phoneme of the /r/ type, pronounced as a tongue-tip tap or trill. Today, upper-class French and German both generally use a uvular trill, or, in certain environments in German, a centering glide; British English uses the latter or has lost the /r/ altogether in non-prevocalic position; the Russian military caste in training during the first decade or so of the 20th century likewise use the uvular trill. In current French and German the tongue-tip trill is rustic; in English any pronunciation of non-prevocalic /r/ is substandard or American. The story behind this is apparently that of the spread of a fashion of pronunciation among the more educated and privileged classes in the various countries, which of course had a good deal of contact with each other and included many individuals who spoke more than one of the languages.

There are other geographical areas in which certain features of pronunciation recur in unrelated or only distantly related languages, and though we lack historical records we can suspect a similar cause. For example, glottalized stops and affricates are found in languages of the most varied affiliations in a large region of aboriginal North America, centering on the Northwest Coast; many of the languages of southern Mexico have tones; both Indo-European and Dravidian languages in India have retroflex consonants.

48.6. Grammatical Borrowing. We have seen that grammatical change can be brought about indirectly by borrowing—via sets of related loanwords. There is some doubt that grammatical change can result from borrowing *from another language* in any other way, but the issue is not settled. We shall consider two cases.

Our definition of "grammatical change" is "change in the grammatical core" (§44.1). The grammatical core includes, among other things, forms which we collectively call "functors" (§31.2), and some functors are separate words. If a functor in one language should be borrowed into another as a loanword, retaining its functorial status, then we might naturally expect the immediate consequence to be a grammatical change in the borrowing language—albeit a minor one.

This has happened in the history of English. Scandinavian loans into OE include many of the most everyday sort: *sky, skin, skill, scrape, scrub, bask, whisk, skirt, kid, get, give, gild, egg, gift, hale, reindeer, swain, plow, bloom* ('flower') are merely representative. Among these Scandinavian words are the following functors: *they, their, them, both, same, till, fro, though.* The modern third person singular ending of verbs (/z s əz/) may also be of Scandinavian origin: OE had endings involving /θ/, which still survive in archaizing English (*goeth, singeth, doeth, doth*).

However, we cannot be certain that the importation of these words entailed essential grammatical change. OE had its own functors with just the functions of those listed above: for example, /hi·/ 'they,' /híra/ 'their,' /hím/ 'them.' In ME the descendants of these OE forms were in competition with the Scandinavian borrowings. Chaucer used *they* as the subject form, but *hir* (*her, hire, here*) and *hem* otherwise. Our current unstressed form /əm/, as in *hit 'em*, belongs descriptively with the full form *them*, but historically is a survival of OE /hím/. It would seem that, rather than involving any grammatical change, the borrowing of the Scandinavian functors merely presented speakers with alternative shapes for certain morphemes. In *shape*, modern *they* stems from Scandinavian; but in *grammatical function* it is just as much a continuation of OE /hí·/ as NE *he* is of OE /hé·/.

This argument about English does not settle the issue, because at other times and places more direct grammatical borrowing may have occurred, even if the phenomenon is rare. In certain areas, unrelated or only distantly related languages seem to share key grammatical features which can hardly have developed in complete independence. Turkish, Armenian, Georgian, Ossetic, and several other languages of the Caucasus and vicinity all show the following phenomenon in their noun inflection: a plural base is formed from the singular stem by the addition of a suffix; the cases of the plural are then produced by adding, to the plural base, just the same suffixes used in the singular. At least for Georgian and Ossetic we have historical evidence showing that some centuries ago the number and case situation was otherwise. The actual endings do not point to borrowing, but the *system* seems to have spread from one language to another.

NOTES

New terms: *loanword, loanshift* (including the special case *loan-transla-tion*), *loanblend; pronunciation borrowing;* and, if such occurs, *grammatical borrowing.*

An excellent report of the impact of one language (Spanish) on phonetic and phonemic habits in another (Zoque) is given in Wonderly 1946.

Problem. Look up each of the following words in the *New English Dictionary* (also called the *Oxford*), and determine the origin of each and the date of its first attested appearance in English. Other dictionaries will often give the former item of information but not the latter:

algebra, bungalow, burnoose, caboose, calaboose, chair, Eskimo, ginseng, jungle, kaolin, kayak, moose, monsoon, mongoose, piccolo, scrape, skirt, scandal, scan, scarp, skunk, sandhi, safari, snoop, stoop (in front of a house), table, trombone, totem, taboo, vest, cheese, wine, cap, sock, noon, pope, red.

49.

ADAPTATION and IMPACT

49.1. Adaptation. Once a borrowed word has been thoroughly "naturalized," its subsequent history is like that of any form already in the language. OE /pó·pa/ 'pope' was a Latin loan, while /stó·n/ was inherited; but the sound change that has led from the shape /stó·n/ to modern /stówn/ has changed OE /pó·pa/ in the same way to /pówp/. French *state, navy, danger* came into ME with stressed /á·/, also found at the time in such inherited words as /ná·mə/ 'name,' /šá·kə/ 'shake,' /bá·ðə/ 'bathe'; we now have /éj/ in all these words.

The fact just illustrated is sometimes obscured by *reborrowing:* the example of OE /férs/ 'verse,' replaced by the later loan from Norman French, is a case in point (§48.5). In this instance the documentary evidence clearly shows the reborrowing and the replacement; this supports us in believing that the same sort of thing must have happened in many other instances, where direct evidence is lacking.

However, during the period of importation, the shape of an incoming word is subject to more haphazard variation. Different borrowers will imitate a foreign word in slightly different ways. Monolinguals to whom the word is passed on will alter its shape even more, though not always in the same direction. This modification of the shape of the incoming word is called *adaptation:* usually it leads to a shape more in keeping with the inherited pronunciation habits of the borrowers, though, as we have seen, the latter may also be altered.

The buffeting-about of the incoming word often results, in the end, in a single surviving and fixed shape, but sometimes two or more shapes become more or less equally naturalized and survive, side by side, in competition. Thus *garage* has three current pronunciations: /gərá·ž/,

417

/gərá·ĭ/, and /gǽriĭ/, the last primarily British. In the future, one of these may spread at the expense of the other two until finally only one survives.

If a language or dialect takes only scattered loans from a single donor, one is not apt to find any great consistency in the adaptation. The few English words from Chinese, such as *chop suey, chow mein, typhoon, amah, kow tow,* entered English at various periods and from different Chinese dialects, and show no regularity of correspondence with the shapes of the Chinese models.

On the other hand, if many loanwords come from a single source over a relatively short period, there may develop a *fashion* of adaptation. which then makes for greater consistency in the treatment of further loans from the same source. The Normans, later the North French, had such a fashion for the importation of learnèd loans from book or clerical Latin. English borrowed many of the words which had come into French from Latin in this way, and in time developed its own fashion of adaptation for words taken directly from Latin: this fashion stemmed from the earlier French habit plus what happened to French words when they were imported into English. *Procrastination* came into English directly from Latin; it does not occur in older French, yet has just the shape it would have had if it had been borrowed via French. Indeed, we are now able to make up new English words from Latin (or Latinized Greek) raw materials, even where Latin or Greek did not have the word, and the shapes taken by the coinages depend ultimately on the fashions of adaptation just mentioned: *eventual, immoral, fragmentary, telegraph, telephone, siderodromophobia* 'fear of railroads.'

Japanese and Korean went through periods of very easy and regular borrowing from Chinese. Chinese nouns were borrowed as nouns, with predictable modifications of shape. Chinese verbs were also borrowed, but were made into Japanese or Korean verbs only by virtue of an established fashion of loanblending: the borrowed verb was used as the first element of a compound, the second element being the stem of a native verb of very general meaning (Japanese *suru* 'to do,' Korean *ha-* 'to do, make, say'). Thus Chinese *sànsàn bù* 'to take a stroll' is actually reduplicated verb plus object; Japanese has the loanblend *sañsañ-busuru* for the same meaning. The use of the native verb stem renders easy the addition of the inflectional apparatus of Japanese and Korean —something lacking in the Chinese prototypes.

A comparable fashion of loanblending has developed in Persian for the accommodation of verbs borrowed from Arabic. Arabic, on the other hand, though currently it accepts western scientific and technological nouns with ease, has developed no simple pattern for the introduction of the necessary verbs (*titrate*, *anastomose*); some specialists seem to feel that this has slowed down the technological development of the Arabic-speaking countries.

Detailed knowledge of a language which is a constant source of learnèd and technical loans, combined with a kind of veneration of the culture of its speakers, can produce a type of "bilingual purism." When classical erudition was at its height in England, a word like *sociology*, the first half from Latin and the second half from Greek, would have been eyed askance. The technical terms *morpheme*, *phonemics*, *morphemics*, *allophone*, *allomorph* are all English, and none the less so because the stems and affixes which participate in them were once carried into English from Greek. The bilingual purist, of which there are still a few, frowns on these words: the proper "Greek" forms would be *morphome*, *phonematics*, *morphomatics*, *allelophone*, *allelomorph*. As in other matters of correctness (§1.2), we are free to agree or dissent; but it should be recognized that the bilingual purist pursues an unattainable ideal. His knowledge of the languages from which English has borrowed is inevitably limited. He objects to *morpheme* because he knows Greek; he passes in silence over the equally "objectionable" expression *The Mississippi River* because he does not know that, when literally translated from Fox, this expression becomes *The Big River River*.

49.2. The Impact of Borrowing on a Language. In theory, one language might influence another so drastically that subsequent scholarship would be unable to determine which of the two had played the role of borrower and which that of source. English, despite its tremendously heavy load of French loans, is really a very poor candidate for this theoretical possibility: the grammatical cores of ME and NE trace back uninterruptedly to that of OE. A more serious contender is modern Albanian, in which there are so many loans from Latin, Romance, Greek, Slavic, and Turkish that only a few hundred "original" Albanian stems are still in use. This delayed scholarly recognition of the historical status of the language, but it was at last demonstrated that Albanian constitutes an independent branch of the Indo-European family. The best current example is Vietnamese: some scholars believe that it is basically Khmer, with a heavy overlay of loans from Thai, while other specialists believe just the reverse.

As was pointed out in §46.2, the *receptivity* of a language to loanwords changes, fashionwise, with the passage of time. In the nineteenth century, a fashion of strong resistance to loanwords developed in educated and official circles in Germany; the consequence, however, was largely an increase in the number of loanshifts and loanblends.

To the historian, the English words *chair* and *table* are loanwords *as of a certain date*, while, *as of that date, stone, bench*, and *pope* are not. Viewed descriptively, of course, all five of these words are today simply ordinary English. In some instances, however, the vocabulary of a language can be divided, even on a purely descriptive basis, roughly into two portions, the elements in one portion showing certain features of morphophonemic or grammatical behavior not shown by those in the other; and one of the portions may in fact be comprised largely of relatively recent loanwords. Sometimes it does not even require the critical eye of the specialist to make this analysis. Despite the fashion of rejection, German contains a good many loanwords; but even the educated German layman seems to be aware of their status. They follow divergent patterns of stress and, to some extent, of consonantism and vocalism, which mark them off from the ordinary vocabulary. Whenever some portion of the vocabulary has such clear marking, then even in synchronic discussion, it can properly be called the *foreign vocabulary* of the language.

Foreign vocabularies are not found exclusively in the "major" languages of civilization. A certain number of Menomini words differ from the bulk of the vocabulary in their morphophonemic behavior and, in part, in phonemic shape. Many of these are loans from Ojibwa, and others were coined within Menomini to resemble the actual loans. The set includes one verb, /anohki·w/ 'to work,' a number of ordinary nouns like /ko·hko·h/ 'pig' (ultimately from French, but directly from Ojibwa), and, interestingly, many personal names. In the absence of documentary records, we do not know the circumstances attending the borrowing of these words.

49.3. Pidgins, Artificial Languages, and Creoles. So-called *pidgins* represent the most extreme results of borrowing known to us.

During the expansion of Europe and the development of worldwide trade by European merchants, circumstances often arose in which it was essential for Europeans and others to communicate, neither knowing anything of the language of the other. This happened, for example, in the China trade. In a desperate attempt to be understood the British or Yankee merchant would often speak artificial "broken English" or "baby talk," on the mistaken assumption that it was easier for the Chinese to understand. The Chinese would make an equally desperate effort, imitating the already badly distorted English. After enough of such give-and-take, conventions became established, and there had evolved what in this case is known as *Chinese Pidgin English*. The English word *pidgin*, used in the designation of Chinese Pidgin English and of other languages which have arisen in the same way, is a borrowing into English from Chinese Pidgin English; the latter, in turn, got the word from English *business*. A number of other pidgins are known, many but not all based on English.

The most important thing descriptively about a pidgin is that it is a language. Despite the circumstances of its origin, once it is well established a pidgin has a life of its own. The native speaker of English cannot today make himself understood in an English-based pidgin merely by mixing up his grammar and pronouncing his words in some personally invented "simplified" way. The task of mastering a pidgin must be approached with the same degree of seriousness involved in the successful learning of any other language.

And yet any pidgin, as long as it continues to be that, has certain peculiarities not to be found in other languages. The chief of these is extremely high redundancy. The phonemic system is loose, so that great variation in actual pronunciation—even to the point of several phonemically distinct shapes for many morphemes—can occur without necessarily impairing understanding. The grammar is as regular as is that of any language, and not necessarily simple. The vocabulary is normally small, designed primarily for the handling of trade negotiations and for the conveying of practical commands from master to servant or of reports in the opposite direction. Yet, by sufficient paraphrase, almost any meaning can be expressed. Furthermore, a pidgin can increase its vocabulary by the same means available to "normal" languages—particularly, of course, by continued borrowing. In many parts of Melanesia, where there are literally hundreds of distinct native languages, the widest imaginable variety of activities in the realm of politics, sport, literature, religion, and education are conducted in Melanesian Pidgin English.

It was at one time thought that, for example, Chinese Pidgin English was simply "English vocabulary with simplified pronunciation and Chinese grammar." This is not the case. Its vocabulary, true enough, is largely English, but a few Chinese words are to be found, and a scattering of words from other sources (e.g., Spanish and Portuguese). We have already commented on the pronunciation. The grammar, however, is in actuality no more Chinese than English. A point-by-point comparison of the grammatical patterns of Chinese Pidgin English with those of English and of Chinese shows that in most cases the Pidgin has followed a pattern which is roughly comparable in English and in Chinese—for example, the habit of using a sequence of two nouns, the first attributive to the second, which is a common habit in English and even commoner in Chinese. In a few cases a Chinese pattern not paralleled by anything of importance in English is included, but in a few cases the reverse holds. Finally, in a few instances the pidgin has struck out on its own and developed patterns not closely matched in either Chinese or English.

It may at first seem strange to turn from pidgins to artificial or "invented" languages, but shortly we shall see that the discussion of the latter belongs here. In origin, to be sure, an artificial language is seemingly different from a pidgin: a pidgin arises under the pressure of practical circumstances in a bilingual situation, while an artificial language is invented by a scholar sitting quietly in his study. A good many such artificial languages have been devised, largely in Europe, in the past hundred years. Most of them have had no real life outside the brains of their inventors and a few devotees; but one, Esperanto, has gone further. To the inventor of an artificial language, the process of invention may seem like a manifestation of his own free will; looked at from outside, however, we see that the inventor's decisions are based on his own habits of speech, his knowledge, accurate or inaccurate, of various other languages, and his general understanding or misunderstanding of how language works. It is no accident that most of the last hundred years' crop of artificial languages, including Esperanto, are clearly classifiable as *European* languages in their semantics, their grammar, and their phonology. If an investigation of Esperanto were carried on by specialists who were ignorant of its origin, they would class it as an aberrant form of Romance. They might even venture the guess that the features which render it aberrant were due to pidginization. This guess would not be far wrong, for the process of inventing actually involves a continual borrowing of forms and features from this, that, or the other natural language, with irregular and unpredictable distortions of shape.

The resemblance goes even further. A pidgin, by definition, is nobody's native language: it is learned by linguistic adults as a second language. The same is true of an artificial language. Thus both lack the layer of childish forms and usages found in every natural language and passed down from one generation of children to the next, and also the special nursery forms used between adults and children as the latter are learning to speak. However, in some cases communities composed of individuals of divers first languages have taken a pidgin as their common language, and have raised children for whom it is native. When this happens, we cease to call the language a pidgin, and say that it is *creolized*. Creolization quickly fills out a pidgin with childish and nursery forms: the difference should not be underestimated. There are several examples of creoles in the Caribbean area, spoken largely by the descendants of escaped Negro slaves. As of 1955, Melanesian Pidgin English shows clear signs of incipient creolization, though no one can know how far the process will carry. An artificial language which has really been learned by adults of differing first languages can be creolized in just the same way, and with comparable results. This has happened, to some extent, to Esperanto.

In this context, if anywhere, one might expect mention of a genuine "mixed language." Yet the most recent studies suggest that no such language exists. Haitian Creole French is highly aberrant, and yet is properly classifiable as a variety of North French. Chinese Pidgin English is an extreme type of English, not of Chinese. Melanesian Pidgin English is likewise a variety of English, not of any of the many languages of Melanesia. One simple test of this is the relative ease with which different people can learn a given pidgin or creole. Any native speaker of English can learn to understand and read Chinese Pidgin English in a relatively short time, provided that he takes the matter seriously. The task is much harder for the Chinese.

NOTES

New terms: *adaptation; reborrowing; fashion* of adaptation; *impact* of borrowing; *foreign vocabulary* as a synchronically observable phenomenon. *Pidgin, artificial language,* and *creole;* creolization. Note the pattern by which "pidgin" and "creole" are used in the designations of specific languages of the sort: *X-Pidgin-Y* or *X-Creole-Y* means a pidgin or creole based on Y as the dominant language which has supplied at least the bulk of the vocabulary, with X, or the languages of the X region, as the most important second contributing factor. The most extensive and useful recent studies of pidgins and creoles have been made by Hall (1943, 1944, 1953). The comparison of the grammatical pattern of Chinese Pidgin English with those of Chinese and of English was made by Hall and the present writer, and has not been published in full. On artificial languages, Guérard 1922.

Problem. Each of the following is a specimen of a pidgin; the specimens are given in only a quasi-phonemic notation, since the precise details are not known. In both, English is involved as one of the contributing languages, but one is English Pidgin X and the other is X Pidgin English. Which is which?

(1) kóm na ínij-sej. míj sæ gíj juw wan sánij fow júw de njám.
    'Come inside. I'll give you something to eat.'
(2) héjlow nájk kómtəks. 'I don't understand.'
    ká májkə mítlajt? 'Where do you live?'
    jǽkə klǽtəwə kówpə lǽpij kówpə čók kówpə bówt. 'He wades to the boat.'

50·

ANALOGICAL CREATION

50.1. It has been said that whenever a person speaks, he is either mimicking or analogizing. Often we cannot know which is the case. A few years ago we might have heard someone say *shmoos*, under circumstances which led us to believe that he had never said it before. We would still not know, however, whether he had previously heard the plural form *shmoos*, or had heard only the singular *shmoo* and was coining the plural on his own.

When we hear a fairly long and involved utterance which is evidently not a direct quotation, we can be reasonably certain that analogy is at work (§36.2). There is even more certainty when a speaker produces some form which deviates from what he could have heard from others. Examples are especially common in the speech of children. Regularized plurals, like *mans* and *sheeps*, probably are produced by every English-speaking child. *Clothes* (usually pronounced /klówz/) is today an isolated plural; one child supplied the singular /klów/. Interpretation of singulars ending in /z/ or /s/ as though they were plurals is likewise common. *What's a poy?* (§34.3) is one instance. Another is the following. At breakfast, a woman said *Daddy, please pass the cheese.* Her small daughter then said *Mummy, I want a chee too.*

Having frequently heard his father say *Don't interrup(t)*, one boy returned the admonition in the form *Daddy! You're interring úp!* On the basis of *look at* /lúkət/ *this*, some children have said *I'm looketing.* As a five-year-old girl was improperly sliding from her chair to go under the lunch table, her parents said *Don't disappear;* she continued the motion, saying *I'm dissing a peer.* When told *You must behave*, a child may reply *I'm being haive.* One child used *bate* as the past tense of *beat* (= 'finish first'); compare our approved *eat : ate*. Four planes overhead are in a *formation;* two planes are therefore in a *twomation.* When it was more excessively hot than would warrant the comment *It's too hot,* one child said *It's three hot.* (All of these instances are attested.)

Adults produce forms like these too, but they are more apt to be received either as slips of the tongue, perhaps through weariness, or as feeble attempts at humor. Examples of the former are the writer's *I could eat a whole nother apple,* or what he has twice caught himself saying after answering the phone: *It's for she.* An example of the latter is *You're looking very couth and kempt today.*

In all the cases so far cited, a clear analogical basis for the coinage can be discerned. *A whole nother apple,* thus, solves a phonemic proportion like

a big apple	:	*a whole big apple*	: :
a second apple	:	*a whole second apple*	: :
another apple	:	*X.*	

It's for she is based on sets like

John is wanted on the phone	:	*It's for John*	: :
You are wanted on the phone	:	*It's for you*	: :
She is wanted on the phone	:	*X.*	

For some novel forms, however, we cannot find any such basis. No doubt this is often due to our lack of detailed information about the workings of the language, but when due allowance is made for this an unexplained residue still remains. It is because of this that the various minor mechanisms of change, named and illustrated in §45.5, must be recognized. For the same reason, the aphorism with which we began this section cannot be wholly accepted: speaking turns largely on mimicking and analogizing, but not completely.

The ordinary kind of analogical innovation, which is illustrated by most of our examples so far, can bring about most, but not all, of the kinds of phylogenetic change. The two kinds which do not seem to result are phonemic and phonetic change, but these are effected by a somewhat divergent variety of analogy to which we shall turn in the next section.

50.2. Grammatical and Shape Change through Analogy. In OE vast numbers of nouns were identical in shape in the nominative and accusative: always in the plural, always for singular neuter nouns, and quite often for singular masculines and feminines. By early ME times, the two cases had fallen together save in pronouns. In part, this was due to sound change, which had led to homonymy of some paired nominatives and accusatives which were distinct in OE. But in part we must ascribe the loss to analogical levelling (§46.3). We see the beginning of the loss already in OE, where some nouns fluctuated between two shapes for the accusative: /kwé·n/ 'queen' appeared in the accusative singular sometimes as /kwé·ne/ but sometimes as /kwé·n/, the latter form identical with the nominative.

In this example, analogy leads to shape changes, and ultimately to a grammatical change, since an inflectional distinction is lost.

The ME coining of regular plurals like *cows*, *books*, *days* implies shape change and alternation change, the latter mainly by way of loss of some earlier patterns of irregular alternation, but not any grammatical change, since the inflectional category of number remained.

The predecessors of many current American dialects of the South lost word-final (that is, strictly speaking, prejunctural) /d/ after /n/ and /l/, by sound change, so that *find* became /fá·n/, *found* became /fǽwn/, *old* yielded /ówl/, and *told* yielded /tówl/. The /d/ has in part been restored by borrowing from dialects which did not experience the loss, and in words of a certain type it has generally been restored by analogy: namely, words in which the final /d/ is the only mark of the difference between past tense (or participle) and present tense of a verb. Thus many Southerners currently say /fá·n/*find*, /ówl/ *old*, /fǽwn/ *found*, and /tówl/ *told*, where, in the latter two, the difference from the present tense is shown by a different vowel, but pronounce the /d/ in /sínd/ *sinned*, /bó·ld/ *boiled*. Here analogy has brought about shape change and alternation change; also, in a small way, phonemic change, in that certain *arrangements* of phonemes (the final clusters /nd/, /ld/) are restored to the system.

The OE suffix /-ere/, ultimately a borrowing from Latin *-ārius* (§48.2), was for a long time added only to noun stems. But in OE there were a number of instances where a noun that underlay a formation in /-ere/ was paralleled by a verb: for example, /rá·f/ 'spoils, booty,' with the derivative /rá·fere/ 'robber,' stood beside a verb /rá·fian/ 'to despoil, rob.' On this basis, /-ere/ came to be added to verb stems where no parallel noun existed: /rǽ·dan/ 'to read' : /rǽ·dere/ 'reader.' It is

primarily in this latter function that the derivational affix has survived
into NE. The change effected is grammatical.

Examples of analogical innovations in syntax are harder to find,
though the mechanism surely works here as in morphology. The recent
colloquial pattern *I'm going home and eat* presumably stems from such
proportions as the following:

> *I'm going to go home* : *I'm going to go home and eat* ::
> *I'm going home* : *X.*

The complexity of the part-of-speech system of NE (§26.4) stems
largely from the fact that in each of the basic paradigms (nominal,
verbal, and adjectival) the bare stem is itself a free form. In OE the
inflectional patterns were more elaborate: with little trouble, OE inflected stems can simply be classed as nouns, verbs, or adjectives. The
more complicated inflectional apparatus of OE was stripped away, bit
by bit, partly by sound change and partly by analogy, until even in
ME there were only vestiges. This process left some homonymous nouns
and verbs, related in meaning in one way or another. On the basis of
those, many words which in OE had been only noun, or only verb, were
analogically extended to the other range of use; quite similarly for
nouns and adjectives, verbs and adjectives, and any of these and some
types of particles. The ultimate outcome was a grammatical restructuring of the first order. Literary Tudor English, as in the works ot Shakespeare, incorporated freer and more extensive interchange than is customary now: one could *happy* a friend, *malice* or *foot* an enemy, *fall* an ax
on someone's neck, speak or act *easy*, *free*, *excellent;* speak of *fair* instead
of beauty, of a *pale* instead of pallor; a *he* was freely a man, and a *she* a
woman (*the fairest she he has yet beheld*)*;* one could *askance* one's eyes, and
speak of the *backward* (*the backward and abyss of time*), or of a *seldom*
pleasure. Much of this was poetic play with the potentialities of the
grammar of the time, but it goes beyond what is now usual. In the
intervening centuries the newer and more elaborate part-of-speech system of the language has become stabilized.

50.3. Back-Formation and Recutting. We saw in our original set
of examples from children that analogy sometimes leads to the peeling-
out of a form shorter than that which previously was current: *boys* is to
boy as *cheese* is to *chee*. This particular version of analogy is called *back-
formation*.

Back-formation leads to a new construction in the case of *keeper* : *keep* :: *singer* : *sing* :: *hóusekèeper* : *X;* or *a recording of that song* : *let's record that song* :: *a tape-recording of that song* : *X.* Given enough composite verbs consisting of noun (or the like) plus simpler verb, like *to housekeep, to tape-record, to cross-refer*, new instances may arise other than through the back-formation which at first is their sole source. Again, we have a scattering of forms in which a noun precedes and modifies an adjective: *fire-hot, ice-cold, stone dead*, and occasionally a new one is heard; some sort of back-formation may play a part here, though the details are not clear.

Back-formation can also lead to lexical change, in the form of new morphemes. If *chee* were to come into currency in the meaning 'piece of cheese,' or if *clo* 'individual garment' were established as the singular of *clothes*, we would have lexical change, though admittedly of a minor sort. Back-formation gave us our present singular nouns *pea* and *cherry* (§34.3), and substandard *a Chinee, a Portugee*.

Akin to back-formation is *recutting*, where a form which historically has a morpheme boundary in one place is treated as though the boundary were elsewhere. *Lozenges* is the plural of *lozenge* /lázinǰ/; but some people, having heard the plural oftener than the singular, consistently form a singular /lázinǰə/, on the analogy of *ideas* : *idea*, *sodas* : *soda*, and the like. Mainly this seems to reshape morphemes rather than to bring new ones into existence. French *argent* /aržaⁿ/ 'silver' does not now end in /t/, but it used to, and the /t/ which appears today in the derivative *argentier* /aržaⁿtje/ 'silversmith' belongs historically to the stem, not to the derivational affix (Latin *argentum* : *argentārius* with suffix *-ārius*). Since the loss, by sound change, of the /t/ of the underlying noun, the point of morpheme division in *argentier* has been shifted, and the reshaped suffix *-tier* appears with stems that never had a final /t/: *bijoutier* 'jeweler,' where *bijou* 'jewel' is an old loan from Breton *bizun*. The common German abstract suffix *-keit* is the result of the recutting of forms where the older suffix *-heit* was preceded by a stem ending in a dorsal stop; *-heit* also survives, so that in this case, at least, lexical or grammatical change has been brought about, in that we have two suffixes where before there was but one.

50.4. Rhythmically Conditioned Analogical Change. Because our records of earlier speech seldom indicate such matters as stress, juncture, and intonation, we may forget that suprasegmental morphemes of various sorts may play a part in analogical change.

In §40.8 we mentioned the Rhode Island speaker who cites *bother* as /báðər/, *father* as /fá·ðər/, but who has /á·/ in both words ordinarily when they occur at the center of the intonation, and /á/ in both ordinarily when they occur elsewhere. We may probably assume that at an earlier stage this dialect had the variation for *father* but not for *bother*. If so, then the development of intonation-center /bá·ðər/ could have come about in the following way:

not at center of intonation		at center of intonation	
/fáðər/	:	/fá·ðər/	::
/báðər/	:	*X.*	

We can suspect that this type of conditioning played a part in many earlier developments in English; but the suspicion has to remain just that because of the inadequacy of our records.

On the other hand, we do have some information about the stress-patterns of earlier English, and know that variations in the level of stress of certain words have given rise to analogical new forms. Between OE and ME, unstressed /-ik̯/ lost the /k̯/ and became /-ij/. This is shown by such words as OE /ɔ́·nlik̯/ 'only,' ME /ó·nlij/. The OE first person singular pronoun, in the nominative, was /ík̯/, but this word, like our present personal pronouns, was in context sometimes stressed and sometimes unstressed. The unstressed form, by the sound change already described, gave ME /ij/. Then, on the analogy of words which consisted of the same vowels and consonants whether stressed or unstressed, the shape /ij/ was extended to stressed positions in the phrase, so that ME had two stressed forms, /íč/ and íj/. In the ensuing competition the former finally disappeared in Standard English; the latter has become our NE /áj/, which has in the meantime developed its own unstressed byforms.

The same sort of restressing of unstressed alternates accounts for our initial /ð/ in words like *the, they, them, thou, thee, thy, that, those, this, these, then, than, there*. In fact, extension to stressed position of the pronunciation with an initial voiced spirant may have been the first appearance in English of a contrast between voiced and voiceless apical slit spirants, which in OE had been subphonemic variants of a single phoneme /θ/. We cannot be sure of this, since it is also possible that the shortening of the medial doubled cluster /θθ/ of OE (voiceless) first yielded a medial contrast between short voiceless /θ/ and short voiced /ð/. The facts are obscured by orthographic habits: never in the history of the language has there been any orthographic indication of the difference. In OE times two symbols were available, þ and ð, but since there was only one phoneme they were used interchangeably in all positions. After the Norman Conquest the digraph *th* came into use, and to this day we write both /θ/ and /ð/ with *th*—though now we would have good use for a pair of distinct letters.

NOTES

New terms: *back-formation* and *recutting*.
Tudor English: Abbott 1872.

51·

FURTHER VARIETIES of ANALOGY

51.1. Semantic Change through Analogy. The type of analogy which brings about semantic change is sometimes a bit different from those dealt with in the preceding section: in our proportional equations, we have to take into consideration the practical situation or the emotional connotations as well as the speech forms themselves.

Until a few decades ago, *house* meant a structure with rooms and doors and windows, in which one could live and keep one's belongings; *home* meant one's place of residence and the kinfolk with whom one lived, together with the whole pattern of interpersonal relationships among the members of the family. Thus, to say *Smith has a lovely house* meant one thing, and was relatively colorless; to say *Smith has a lovely home* had far warmer connotations. Yet in some practical situations one might equally well make either remark. On this model, a real-estate salesman would replace *a lovely new eight-room house* by *a lovely new eight-room home*, though referring in fact to a bare uninhabited structure. Events of this kind have led to a clear shift in the meaning of the word *home*.

We can imagine similar circumstances in other cases. OE /méte/ meant 'food'; its lineal descendant *meat* now refers only to flesh food except in a few idioms like *sweetmeats* and *meat and drink*. ME *bede* /béˑdə/ meant 'prayer,' whereas its NE descendant *bead* means a pellet on a string. The German word *Kopf* 'head' formerly meant 'cup, bowl.' We know the general circumstances in which the meaning of *Kopf* began to shift: texts from the end of the Middle Ages refer to warriors smashing the *Kopf* of an opponent. Likewise, the extension

432

of *bede* from 'prayer' to 'pellet on a string' seems to have occurred in the context of using a rosary as a mnemonic aid in praying: one *counted one's bedes*.

51.2. Conflict of Analogies. In many a situation in which a person speaks, there are several models which might be followed, leading to different results. If a child knows *sing : sang* and *swing : swung*, as well as the regular pattern (*sigh : sighed*), he may, on first learning the word *swim*, coin as past-tense form either *swam* or *swum* or *swimmed*. Occasionally it happens that a speaker follows two models at once. Having hesitated between *Don't shout so loud* and *Don't yell so loud*, one may actually come out with *Don't shell so loud* or *Don't yout so loud*. (The first of these was actually observed by the writer.) If the result survives, it is called a *blend*. Blending has traditionally been regarded as a mechanism of change allied to, but not identical with, analogy—and has thus usually been classed with contamination, metanalysis, and other minor mechanisms (§45.5). But its kinship to ordinary analogy is perfectly clear.

A number of NE words which appear in documents only in relatively recent centuries are believed to have originated as blends. *Bash* is first attested in 1641; it is perhaps a blend of *bat* and *mash*, both of which are earlier. *Clash* (1500) may be from *clap* and *crash* or *dash*. *Flare* (1632) may be a blend of *flame* or *fly* and *glare* or *bare*, though there is also a possible Scandinavian source. *Glimmer* (1440) may be from *gleam* and *shimmer*. *Smash* (1778) may be from *smack* and *mash*. *Crunkle*, which the writer has seen only in the works of L. Frank Baum (published in the first quarter of the present century) is perhaps a blend of *crinkle* and *crunch*. Contemporary /skwúš/ is perhaps *squash* and *push*.

Phrasal blends are sometimes to be observed. One child, for a period of months, said *do it like this way*, presumably blending *like this* and *this way* (similarly with *that*). Some syntactical constructions may have this origin, but there seem to be no sure examples.

51.3. Allophonic Analogy. In certain varieties of Caribbean Spanish, the consonant /s/ when not followed by a vowel has been weakened by sound change to [h]—about like the English /h/ of *he, hate*. In some dialects this [h] is still a member of the /s/ phoneme, since there is no contrast: the [s]-like variety of the /s/ phoneme occurs initially in the phrase and medially before a vowel, while the [h] occurs medially before a consonant and at the end of a phrase. Thus what sounds like

[lasánimah] 'the souls' still ends phonemically in /s/ : /lasánimas/,
and what sounds like [lahmučáčah] 'the girls' is still phonemically
/lasmučáčas/.

Note, however, that in these two phrases the article *las* appears in two
allophonically different shapes, even if phonemically they are the same:
[lah] before a word beginning with a consonant, and [las] before a word
beginning with a vowel.

Since many words in Caribbean Spanish are quite the same, allophonically as well as phonemically, regardless of the shape of neighboring words, some dialects of this type have developed a contrast between
the [s]-like and the [h]-like sounds, giving rise to separate phonemes /s/
and /h/. What happens is that the allophonic shape of a word fit for
occurrence finally in a phrase, or before a consonant, is analogically
extended to use before a word beginning with a vowel: the shape [lah]
comes to occur before words beginning with a vowel. Once this happens, the two phrases given earlier have a new phonemic structure:
/lahánimah/ and /lahmučáčah/. The intervocalic /h/ of the former
contrasts with an intervocalic /s/ in such a phrase as *hacer* /asér/ 'to do'
or *la ciudad* /lasiudád/ 'the city.'

This type of analogical innovation is *allophonic analogy*. It differs
essentially from the types which we have considered up to now, for, in
all of those, the smallest units with which we were concerned were
phonemes. Extension of the regular English plural suffix to occurrence
after *man* yields nothing new phonemically: not only is the cluster /nz/
not new, but even the whole shape of the regularized plural *mans* occurs
in the language already (*if he mans the boat, . . .*). But in allophonic
analogy one allophone of a phoneme comes to occur in positions previously open only to some other allophone of the same phoneme, and a
new phonemic contrast is thus created.

Except for cases like the analogical restoration of final /ld/ and /nd/
in the English of the South (§50.2), which at least introduces a new
(or older but lost) *arrangement* of phonemes, allophonic analogy seems to
be the only kind that can bring about a phonemic change. If the contrast between voiceless /θ/ and voiced /ð/ did come into English first
through the restressing of atonic words like *this, that, the*, then that event
also constituted an instance of allophonic analogy, and the example
belongs here rather than in §50.4.

51.4. Analogy and Borrowing. Now that we have discussed analogy in some detail, it will be worthwhile to mention briefly certain ways in which analogy operates in conjunction with borrowing. The most obvious instance is in loan-translations (§48.3). The operation of analogy in this case cuts across from one language (or dialect) to another, about as follows:

French		English	
mariage	:	*marriage*	::
de	:	*of*	::
convenance	:	*convenience*	::
mariage de convenance	:	*X.*	

The bilingual, solving the proportion, finds that *X* is *marriage of convenience*.

Analogy comes into play, secondly, when a regular fashion for the reshaping of words borrowed from some single donor has become established (§49.1):

Latin		English	
actiōnem	:	*action* /ǽkšən/	::
afflictiōnem	:	*affliction* /əflíkšən/	::
sepārātiōnem	:	*separation* /sèpəréjšən/	::
procrastinātiōnem	:	*X.*	

The first three forms are the accusatives of Latin nouns, known to the borrower, which obviously parallel the already existent English words on the right. The -*tion*- part of the first three Latin forms is matched by /-šən/ in English: this will then likewise be so in the new borrowing. The final -*em* of the Latin forms is missing in the English: so will it be for the new borrowing. The Latin forms are accusatives, rather than the nominatives *actiō, afflictiō, sepārātiō;* the new borrowing similarly turns on the accusative, which shows the terminal *n* of the stem, rather than on the nominative. The stress is regularly on the next to the last syllable in the Latin forms, and with equal regularity on the syllable before the /-šən/ in the English. All of these cross-language patterns participate in determining what *X* shall be: *procrastination* /prowkrǽstənéjšən/.

When a suffix or other bound form common to a number of borrowings from a single source is cut off and becomes productive (§48.2), we again have the operation of analogy, but in this case the words have already been assimilated, and the analogy involved does not cut across from one language to another.

In dialect borrowing, an individual who is attempting to improve the outward symbols of his social status often develops regular habits—that is, analogies—for modifying his earlier pronunciations of words. Let us suppose that his natural speech involves the pronunciations /túwn dúwn núw túwzdij/ for *tune, dune, new, Tuesday,* and that he comes to the conclusion that /tjúwn djúwn njúw tjúwzdij/ are "better." He will make a conscious effort to use the initial clusters /tj- dj- nj-/, instead of his earlier simple consonants /t- d- n-/, and it often happens that the analogy will be carried too far. Thus one radio announcer regularly introduced a 12:00 news program as /ðə wɔ́rld ǽt njúwn/, using /nj-/ in the word *noon* where no native speaker of a /tjúwn djúwn njúw/-dialect would. Such forms as /njúwn/ are called *overcorrections* or *hyperurbanisms.*

We can also class under this rubric certain forms in which language borrowing rather than dialect borrowing is involved. Speakers of English who know no French get some vague notion of the differences between French and English pronunciation, and may overcorrect the usual English /téjtətèjt/ *tête-a-tête* to /téjtətèj/, on the mistaken assumption that "in French you leave the final consonant off." Nor are foreign languages necessarily kept properly apart: the German actress's name *Rainer* has sometimes been pseudo-Frenchified in English as /ràjnijéj/.

NOTES

New terms: *blend; allophonic analogy; overcorrection* or *hyperurbanism.*
The examples of blends are taken largely from Sturtevant 1947. Sturtevant has more examples and some interesting discussion.
Problems. (1) Describe how it comes about that a college freshman will write (or even speak, under some circumstances) the following:

  (a) Between you and I.
  (b) Everyone should get a square deal, no matter whom they are.

(2) Can you find or invent an example of what might reasonably be called a *hyberruralism?* How about *hyper-Brooklynese?*
(3) The following two problems have to do with change of meaning

through analogy. In each case we describe a sequence of events; the reader is to formulate in precise fashion the mechanism by which the events come about:

(a) In the year 2019, the first Earth settlers on the edge of a vast plain on Venus find in the fields a small rodent-like creature, about four

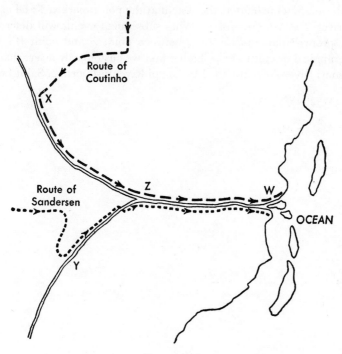

FIGURE 51.1

inches long, with large ears, which they call a *flapple*. Between 2019 and 2069, the settlers drift westwards, reaching the mountains at the far edge of the plain by the latter date. As they move west, the rodents they encounter are gradually different, their ears growing progressively shorter and their bodies longer, so that in 2069 the people living by the mountains are accustomed to using the word *flapple* for a creature about ten inches long with very small ears. A man goes on a trip from the mountains to the east coast in 2069, and is much surprised to hear those who stayed behind use the word *flapple* for the small long-eared animal.

(b) Figure 51.1 shows an outline map of a river-system discovered by the early explorers of the largest continent on Venus. Coutinho, with his party, first comes to the system at the point marked X on the map: he names the river he has discovered *The New Amazon*. Sanderson first encounters the system at the point marked Y: he names the river *The New Mississippi*. What subsequent events will determine the "proper" name of the river between point Z and point W? Is it geographical or cultural—or both—that we customarily assert that the Missouri River flows into the Mississippi River just north of Saint Louis?

52.

THE NATURE of
SOUND CHANGE

52.1. We have now discussed all the known mechanisms of phylo-genetic change save one: sound change.

In §44.8 we described sound change as a gradual change in habits of articulation and hearing, taking place constantly, but so slowly that no single individual would ever be aware that he might be passing on a manner of pronunciation different from that which he acquired as a child. This gradualness is extremely important. No one has yet observed sound change: we have only been able to detect it via its consequences. We shall see later that a more nearly direct observation would be theoretically possible, if impractical, but any ostensible report of such an observation so far must be discredited.

For example, observers have reported that in France today the difference between two nasal vowels, that of *fin, demain, craindre* (/e^n/, unrounded) and that of *un, chacun, humble* (/ö^n/, rounded, but otherwise much like the first), is disappearing. Older-generation speakers keep the difference, but younger people are more and more using the former in words which used to have only the second; in time, it is supposed, the difference may disappear altogether. Now this is not sound change. The mechanism is borrowing, largely of the type which in §48.1 we called "pronunciation borrowing." Some words have two alternative phonemic shapes, one with /e^n/, the other with /ö^n/, and the shapes with /e^n/ are gaining ground, via borrowing, at the expense of those with /ö^n/. It is probable that sound change played a part in

439

getting the competition between these alternative forms started, but it is a serious mistake to confuse the two matters.

52.2. How Sound Change Comes About. When a person speaks, he aims his articulatory motions more or less accurately at one after another of a set of bull's-eyes, the *allophones* of the language. For example, if he says *time to go*, the first bull's-eye at which he aims can be described, in articulatory terms, as a relatively strong voiceless apico-alveolar stop with a considerable amount of aspiration. This allophone is a member of the English /t/ phoneme. If he says *I forgot*, the last bull's-eye aimed at is another member of the /t/ phoneme, but not the same one: in this case it is again a relatively strong voiceless apico-alveolar stop, but with less prominent aspiration. If he says *doughnuts are good*, the first bull's-eye is a relatively weak apico-alveolar stop, voiceless at its inception but with increasing vibration of the vocal cords until, as the stop closure is released, the voicing is strong. This bull's-eye, of course, belongs to the English /d/ phoneme.

When another speaker of the language listens to what is being said, he listens for the successive allophones, but he does not have to hear them all, under most conditions, in order to understand. The reason for this is one which we have discussed before: redundancy—allophones occur only in certain arrangements relative to each other, so that a correct identification of any fair percentage of them leads, first, to a correct identification of the whole utterance and, subsequently, to the illusion that *all* of the allophones in the utterance have been heard quite clearly and distinctly. The hearer is charitable. If the speaker says *time to go*, but misses aim badly on the initial /t/, so that physically (as could be determined on a spectrogram) it is more like a /d/, the hearer will very often not even notice the discrepancy.

This charity on the part of hearers leads the speaker to be quite sloppy in his aim most of the time. The shots intended for the initial-/t/ allophone will be aimed in the general direction of that bull's-eye, but will fall all about it—many quite close, some in the immediate vicinity, a few quite far away. If we were to collect and accurately measure a large sample of shots fired at the initial-/t/ bull's-eye, we should expect their distribution about the bull's-eye to be more or less as shown in Figure 52.1. Here, for simplicity, we pretend that a "miss" can be separated from the bull's-eye only by falling to the "left" of it or to the "right" of it; in actuality the matter is more complicated.

The dispersion of shots aimed at the initial-/d/ allophone, or at any other, would give a similar graph. Now, since the initial-/t/ and initial-/d/ allophones have something in common, let us graph together the dispersion of shots aimed at these two bull's-eyes—Figure 52.2. The composite graph shows two *maxima*, indicating that more

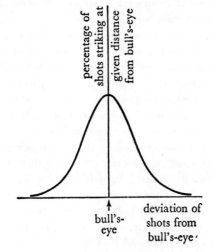

FIGURE 52.1

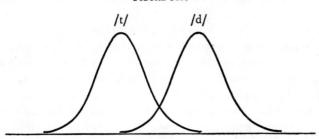

FIGURE 52.2

shots aimed at /d/ come close to that bull's-eye than at any given distance from it, and similarly for /t/. It also shows that some shots intended as /t/'s, and correctly so interpreted by the hearer, are physically closer to the /d/ bull's-eye than some intended /d/'s, and vice versa. This does not mean that some intended and correctly understood /t/'s are "really" /d/'s. We have two matters to compare: the *physical properties* of a given shot, as measurable by a spectrogram; and the phonemic classification of a given shot. The latter depends not on what the physical measurements show, but on *what the hearer makes of it.*

Let us imagine a much larger and more complicated graph, which will provide for all the allophones of the language at once. Since bits of speech sound can differ from each other in a number of different ways, our large graph must have a good number of dimensions—not just the single horizontal dimension of the two simplified partial graphs in Figures 52.1 and 52.2. But it will show the dispersion of all shots aimed at all bull's-eyes, and in each case the actual shots will cluster around a single point, at which there will be a *frequency maximum.*

We must now ask why it is proper to assume that of the shots aimed, for example, at the initial-/t/ allophone, more will strike very close to the bull's-eye than at any distance from it. Why do we assume that the center of dispersion of actual shots is at the bull's-eye? In gunnery this is by no means the case. A gun crew can fire a succession of shells at a fixed target, aiming and correcting with great diligence, and yet find that the shellbursts have centered around a point at some distance from the intended target. Why should it be otherwise in the present context?

The reason is simple to state, but will then require some supporting discussion. The center of dispersion of shots aimed at a given allophone is squarely at the bull's-eye *because the location of the former determines the location of the latter.*

To see how this is so, we must return to a consideration of the hearer, and then remember that any hearer is also, at times, a speaker, and that he hears his own speech. As a child learns a language, he learns to react differentially to utterances which are phonemically, and therefore allophonically, distinct. He acquires a set of acoustic and articulatory points of reference in terms of which he categorizes the incoming speech-signal when he is functioning as a hearer, and at which he aims his own articulation when he is functioning as a speaker—monitoring the result because he hears what he says. The points of reference are the allophones of his idiolect. They can be determined for him *only* by the physical nature of the speech which he actually hears, first from others, later also from himself. If the speech of those about him has a frequency maximum at a certain position in the range of all possible speech sound, then he will develop a point of reference at precisely that position. The frequency-distribution of the physical characteristics of heard speech becomes for him an *expectation distribution:* he expects shots to come close to the center of dispersion of preceding shots, and comes to interpret them as though they had even when they do not. In other words, the frequency maxima *are* the points of reference; both of these *are* the bull's-eyes towards which articulation aims; all three of these *are* the allophones of the language.

One more factor must be considered before we show how all this is related to sound change. We must assume that the instances of the initial-/t/ allophone (for example) that an individual heard ten years ago carry less weight in determining the precise momentary state of his expectation distribution for this allophone than the instances which he heard yesterday. There is a sort of decay effect. As time passes, any given bit of heard speech makes a smaller and smaller contribution to the picture. On the other hand, new speech is constantly being heard, and is adding its relatively greater weight to the expectation distribution.

Thus, if some speaker of English, over a period of years, were to hear a relatively large number of initial /t/'s with unusually inconspicuous aspiration, his expectation distribution would be altered: the location of the frequency maximum would drift, and his own speech would undergo the same modification. We would not, of course, expect any *single* speaker of English to have such an experience. In general, individuals who are in constant communication with each other will experience essentially parallel changes in their expectation distributions, and, thus, also in their articulatory habits.

It is just this sort of slow drifting about of expectation distributions, shared by people who are in constant communication, that we mean to subsume under the term "sound change."

In order to see why we should believe that sound change, so defined, is constantly going on, we need only consider the vast multitude of factors which can contribute to the determination of the physical properties of any bit of heard speech. These physical properties depend only in part on the "speaker's intention." Before the sound reaches the inner ear of the hearer, other variables come into play. A list would have to include the following: the amount of moisture in the throat, nose, and mouth of the speaker, random currents in his central nervous system, muscular tics, muscle tonus, emotional state, possible presence of alcohol or drugs, the care with which the speaker is enunciating; the amount and nature of the extraneous noise which reaches the hearer along with the speech signal; the condition of the hearer's outer ear (presence of wax or dirt), the amount of attention the hearer is giving to the speaker. The list could be extended. Since the physical properties of each actually heard bit of speech in turn condition the expectation distribution of the hearer—and thus his articulation and, ultimately, the expectation distribution of the whole community—every one of the factors we have named bears indirectly on sound change. The situation is so complex that it is hard to imagine how sound change could *not* go on all the time.

52.3. Sound Change and Other Mechanisms. In either borrowing or analogy (or in any of the minor mechanisms of change, §45.5), what happens in the first instance is a *sudden event:* a single speaker borrows a form from some other community, or creates a new form analogically; if it survives, it is because others do the same, or because others in turn borrow it from him. Sound change is not sudden, but very gradual and continuous; only certain of its consequences can, in a sense, be sudden.

Borrowing and analogy can bring about marked reshaping of a single idiolect. Sound change, so far as we know, does not *noticeably* do this, though in theory we must assume it does.

We may properly speak of *a* borrowing or of *an* analogical innovation. The phrase "sound change," on the other hand, is like the word "milk": we do not ordinarily speak of *a* milk, because the noun refers to a continuous mass, not (as do *book* and *chair*) to something which comes naturally in individuated hunks; and we cannot properly speak of *a* sound change for a similar reason. It is true that the expression "*a* sound change" occurs in the manuals of historical linguistics, but this is because the term is being used in senses for which we have reserved other terms: "*a* shape change," "*a* phonemic change."

If we are lucky, we can observe an act of borrowing or an analogical innovation as it happens. Only indirect methods could show us sound change in progress. Suppose that over a period of fifty years we made, each month, a thousand accurate acoustic records of clearly identifiable initial /t/'s and /d/'s, all from the members of a tight-knit community. At the end of the first five years we could compute and draw the curve representing the sixty thousand observations made up to that time: the resulting graph would be a reasonably accurate portrayal of this portion of the community's expectation distribution. After another year, the first year's observations would be dropped, the sixth year's added, and a new curve drawn. Each subsequent year the same operation would be performed. The resulting series of forty-six curves would show whatever drift had taken place. The drift might well not be in any determinate direction: the maxima might wander a bit further apart, then come closer again, and so on. Nevertheless, the drift thus shown would constitute sound change.

At this point, before we proceed to describe how sound change can lead to modifications in the design of a language, it must be admitted that many scholars do not believe that it has any effect on language-design at all. These scholars use the term "sound change," but they use it for other matters, not as we have defined and described it. They do not deny that sound change in our sense may go on, but they deny its relevance—particularly since, as asserted above, the direct observation of sound change is impossible. They believe that it is futile to posit a process insusceptible to direct observation, and make that process explanatory for directly observed events, at least if directly observable mechanisms can be made to explain the events. Instead of our sound change, they base their explanations largely on an especially intimate sort of borrowing between only slightly different dialects.

On this subject there are not just two opposed opinions, but a whole spectrum of slightly differing points of view, merging imperceptibly into each other. The scholars involved use some of the same terms in minimally differing senses, so that the literature on the subject over the last eighty years is exceedingly difficult to follow.

Although it would be improper to pass over these disagreements in silence, it would serve no purpose to complicate the present survey by trying to spell out all the different opinions in detail. The writer has tried to formulate a description of sound change and of its consequences which is consistent both within itself and also with the rest of the portrayal of language given in the book.

53.

COALESCENCE and SPLIT

53.1. From the description of sound change given in the preceding section, it should be clear that gradual random drift in pronunciation and hearing habits could go on indefinitely without leading to any notable consequences—in particular, without bringing about any re-structuring of the central subsystems of the language. So long as the frequency maxima of a community's expectation distribution merely wander about, there can be no results of any interest to us. But there are two things that sometimes occur, in the course of this meandering, which may have either immediate or delayed consequences. One of these is: *two maxima drift closer together and finally coalesce.* The other is: *a single maximum splits into two, which then drift apart.*

53.2. Two Maxima Coalesce. The consequences of coalescence depend on the status, relative to each other, of the two allophones. If the allophones are members of a single phoneme, and thus never in contrast, their coalescence does nothing to the language. Careful phonetic examination reveals that the kind of initial /t/ which most of us use before a stressed vowel and the kind of final /t/ which we use after a stressed vowel are slightly different. If these minor differences were to disappear, the phonemic system of the language would not be affected. There are, indeed, some speakers for whom the two seem to be quite indistinguishable, at least by ordinary techniques of observation.

But if the allophones are members of two different phonemes, their coalescence implies a phonemic change. This is clearest in the case where, before the coalescence, the two allophones stand in direct contrast.

One example is the loss, in the English of the South, of the terminal

446

/d/ in the clusters /ld/ and /nd/. What happened here, in phonetic terms, was a coalescence of the features typical of terminal /ld/ and /l/, and of those typical of terminal /nd/ and /n/: the resulting merged pronunciations clearly belong respectively to /l/ and /n/. The phonemic change was that certain arrangements of phonemic units disappeared—the number of phonemes in the repertory was not reduced. Overt shape changes were brought about in that such pairs of words as *field* and *feel*, *find* and *fine*, *hold* and *hole*, came to be homonymous. Even now, when analogy has restored the /d/ which marks past tense and participle (*sinned*, *killed*), and thus also restored the phonemic system to its earlier state, such pairs of words as *field* and *feel* remain homonyms.

In other instances, the number of phonemic units in the stock is reduced. For some group of French speakers, at some time in the past, somewhere in France (probably in the south), sound change led to the merger of *all* allophones of /e^n/ and *all* allophones of /ö^n/: the system then included one fewer phoneme than before. The change of pronunciation apparently affected /ö^n/ more than /e^n/, presumably by way of progressive loss of rounding, for the single resulting unit seems to have been more similar to the /e^n/ than to the /ö^n/ of those dialects which still retained the distinction. Speakers of the latter sort, whose phonemic patterns still maintained the distinction, would learn some words from speakers of the former, and thus pronounce some words with /e^n/ which, were it not for the interdialectal borrowing, ought to have /ö^n/. For that matter, some speakers whose dialect had been directly affected by the change would restore the /e^n/ : /ö^n/ contrast through pronunciation-borrowing from those who had not lost it. In this way, many words acquired competing pronunciations. It is only the last stage of this—the competition between alternative pronunciations—which has been directly observed. But it is only the first stage which illustrates coalescence via sound change.

A coalescence can bring about an immediate and drastic restructuring of a phonemic system, even though no other major change in pronunciation is involved. A striking example is a restructuring which was brought about in this way in late OE or early ME—perhaps, in the London area, as late as the 13th century. Prior to the change, the stressed nuclei of the dialect seem to have been twelve in number:

$$/i/ \quad /u/ \qquad /i\cdot/ \quad /u\cdot/$$
$$/e/ \quad /o/ \qquad /e\cdot/ \quad /o\cdot/$$
$$/æ/ \quad /ɔ/ \qquad /æ\cdot/ \quad /ɔ\cdot/.$$

Possibly there were still stressed nuclei /y/ and /y·/, but this does not materially change the picture. Sound change led to a complete merger of the short nuclei /ǽ/ and /ɔ́/. The long nuclei, and the four other short vowels, probably did not undergo striking change of pronunciation, but their structural positions were altered; the new system was:

$$/i/ \quad /u/ \qquad /ij/ \quad /uw/$$
$$/e/ \quad /o/ \qquad /ej/ \quad /ow/$$
$$\quad /a/ \qquad /eᵛ/ \quad /oᵛ/.$$

(The /aᵛ/ listed in §43.3 was a later addition, as described in §45.2.) Thus earlier /θǽt/ 'that' and /krɔ́bbə/ 'crab' became /θát/ and /krábbə/, both pronunciation and phonemic shape being altered; but the change of earlier /klǽ·nə/ 'clean' to /kléᵛnə/ and of earlier /stó·n/ 'stone' to /stóᵛn/ was a phonemic restructuring which involved no change of pronunciation *of those words*. Their shapes were restructured because a change *in any part* of a phonemic system alters the structural position of *every* form in the language. (For this same reason, the validity of the example is not dependent on our particular way of phonemicizing the two stages of English—a way with which some scholars would disagree.)

53.3. One Maximum Splits. A single allophone may split, and the resulting pair drift apart, *only if the different directions of drift involve distinct phonetic environments.*

Consider, for example, an English dialect (imaginary if not real) in which initial /t/ before a stressed vowel and final /t/ after a stressed vowel are quite indistinguishable. This means that the same allophone is being used in *tin, two, tap* and in *pat, sit, hot*. The initial-position occurrences and the final-position occurrences might become different, through sound change, so that there would be two allophones instead of one.

On the other hand, let us consider occurrences of initial /t/ before a stressed vowel in, say, words used as verbs (*take, turn, tackle*) versus the same phoneme in the same position in words which are never verbs (*two, task, torpid*). It would be quite impossible for the /t/'s of the first sort to drift off one way, those of the second sort in another direction:

the difference between occurrence in a verb and occurrence in some other kind of word is *not* a difference in phonemic and phonetic environment.

Whenever we find what at first looks like a violation of this principle, we can confidently search for some other factor. Thus OE initial/θ/ gives NE /θ/ in most words, like *thank, thatch, thane, think, thief, thing, thorn, thousand, thirst,* but /ð/ in some: *the, this, that, there, though, thou, thee, thy, thine,* and a few others. The /θ/-words are contentives (§31); the /ð/-words are functors. But we soon realize that all the functors in which /θ/ has become /ð/ are words which often occur, in context, without stress, whereas contentives rarely so occur. But this implies that there *was* a difference of phonetic environment involved in the two directions of drift: initial OE /θ/ in a stressed syllable remained voiceless, while initial OE /θ/ in an unstressed syllable became voiced. The spread of /ð/ to the stressed forms of the words was a matter of analogy (§50.4).

An allophonic split cannot unaided bring about a phonemic restructuring. The single allophone before the split belongs to a single phoneme, and the allophones after the split still belong to a single phoneme. However, splitting can *set the stage* for a phonemic change, which then comes about—if at all—in one of three ways: (1) a coalescence, via sound change, of sounds in the environment of the two allophones; (2) analogy; (3) borrowing. The example discussed immediately above illustrates the second of these; we shall give one example of each of the other two.

In pre-English, and possibly in the earliest stage of recorded OE, there was a phoneme /ĝ/ with two allophones: one allophone was a stop [ĝ], and one was a spirant [ɣ́]. The former occurred after /n/, as in /sénĝan/ 'to singe,' and when doubled, as in /éĝĝ/ 'edge.' Otherwise the latter occurred: for example, in /dǽĝ/ 'day,' phonetically [dǽɣ́]. This state of affairs had been brought about by a number of earlier developments, including, in all probability, the split of a single earlier allophone (we are not sure whether it was a stop or a spirant before the split). Of course the two allophones did not contrast at this stage— there was no environment in which some words had one, other words the other.

Now between very early OE (or very late pre-English) and the stage of OE which we described in §43.2, a phonemic restructuring took place which at first would not seem to have anything to do with the two allophones of /ĝ/. Sound change led to a shorter and shorter pronunciation of word-final double consonants after a stressed vowel, until finally the contrast between a single and a double consonant in that position was lost: earlier /mónn/ 'man' became /món/, ending quite like /wí·n/ 'wine,' which had never ended with /nn/; earlier /bédd/ 'bed' became /béd/; and so on. This change affected final /ĝĝ/ just as it affected other final double consonants, but as [ĝĝ] was shortened, it was not also spirantized. Therefore, after the change, short [ĝ] and short [ŷ] contrasted with each other in one position: finally after a stressed vowel. For earlier /ĝ/ we must at this later stage write sometimes /ĝ/ and sometimes /ŷ/. Earlier /dǽĝ/, though its pronunciation had not altered, was now phonemically /dǽŷ/; earlier /éĝĝ/, changed in pronunciation, was now phonemically /éĝ/. The new phonemic contrast has stayed in the language ever since: we still end *edge* with a stop, but not *day*.

A good example of restructuring through borrowing, more or less closely on the heels of splitting, is the change of the English spirantal system brought about by loans from Norman French. Splits of a considerably earlier date had led to a situation in which /f/ and /s/ had both voiced and voiceless allophones, in distributions which we can indicate roughly as follows:

| /f/: | [f-][1] | [-v-][2] | [-ft-][3] | | [-f][4] |
| /s/: | [s-][5] | [-z-][6] | [-st-][7] | [-ss-][8] | [-s][9]. |

Here "[-ft-]" means "/f/ was voiceless before a voiceless consonant," "[f-]" means "initial /f/ was voiceless," and so on; the superscript numbers are for cross-reference to the next table. Many incoming Norman French words kept their own type of spirant, voiced or voiceless, even when the distribution went counter to the traditional English habits. The loans gave rise to two new phonemes, /v/ and /z/, and in so doing brought about a reassignment of some of the allophones of the earlier /f/ and /s/. In the following table, an asterisk means "in French loans"; the reassignment of older allophones is indicated by the superscript numbers:

/f/:	[f-][1]*	[-f-]*	[-ft-][3]		
/v/:	[v-]*	[-v-][2]*			
/s/:	[s-][5]*	[-s-]*	[-st-][7]	[-ss-][8]	[-s][9]
/z/:	[z-]*	[-z-][6]*.			

NOTES

New terms: *coalescence* (of two allophones); *split* (of one allophone). The statement at the beginning of §53.3, of the conditions under which splitting may occur, contains, in the light of our definitions, the essence of the so-called neogrammarian assumption of the "regularity of sound change."

The effect of sound change on a phonemic system is sometimes to render the system less symmetrical than it was. Some scholars believe that there is a sort of *drive towards symmetry* in phonemic habits, whereby whenever skewness develops, there is a tendency to restore symmetry via analogy (probably allophonic, §51.3), borrowing, or further sound change. See especially Martinet 1955.

54.

THE CONSEQUENCES of
SOUND CHANGE

54.1. We have now seen how sound change, working alone (coalescence, or splitting followed by environmental coalescence) or in conjunction with other mechanisms (splitting followed by borrowing or analogy), can lead to the restructuring of a phonemic system and concurrently to shape change. These are the only *immediate* consequences which sound change can have. Any other kind of phylogenetic change is an indirect consequence of the reshaping and the phonemic restructuring. We shall consider one example each of alternation change, of grammatical change, and of lexical and semantic change, in which sound change is known to have been among the ultimately responsible factors. Some of the cases we are about to examine have been mentioned before, but we now approach them from a different angle.

54.2. Alternation Change. The simplification of early OE final double consonants after stressed vowel (§53.3) brought it about that some nouns which had earlier had only a single stem shape now had two. 'Man,' for example, had been /mónn/ in the nominative-accusative singular, and /mónnes/ in the genitive singular; in the OE of Alfred's time the former had become /món/, but the latter retained the double consonant and was thus still /mónnes/. Therefore the stem at this period had both the shape /món-/ and the shape /mónn-/, depending on what followed. The same thing happened to 'bed': earlier /bédd/ : /béddes/, but later /béd/ : /béddes/. And the same happened to a great many other nouns.

452

Phonemic restructuring seems very often to produce morphophonemic irregularities of this kind: indeed, probably most of the inflectional irregularities found at any stage in the history of any language can be traced to this ultimate source. However, we know (§46.3) that as soon as an irregularity has developed, it may then at any subsequent time be leveled out analogically. Sometimes this happens very quickly. Later OE shows the spelling *mann* for the nominative singular, as well as the spelling *man;* this may have been a purely graphic restoration of the double-*n* spelling on the basis of the continued pronunciation of a double /n/ in the other case-forms, or it may indicate an actual analogical restoration of the final double consonant on the basis of the pre-suffixal alternant of the stem. By ME, however, we find only single final consonants—indicating another simplifying restructuring of any analogically restored final doubles. The irregular alternation of /béd/ : /béddəs/, /mán/ : /mánnəs/ remained throughout ME, and was only finally wiped out more recently, when double medial consonants were shortened—yielding, in the end, the current regular *bed* : *bed's, man* : *man's.*

The interplay of sound change and analogy in matters of this kind can be summed up aphoristically: sound change tends to irregularize, while analogy tends to regularize.

54.3. Grammatical Change. The very extensive grammatical changes which have occurred in English in the last thousand-odd years are not the result solely of phonemic restructurings, but the latter have played an important role. This is probably normal; we should not expect phonemic restructuring to produce such results unaided.

Between OE and early ME a series of phonemic restructurings took place, largely by way of coalescence, which did much to abolish the distinctiveness of the different inflectional forms of OE nouns. The phonemic changes were as follows:

(1) Unstressed /a e o u/ coalesced into /ə/;
(2) Then final /m/ after an unstressed vowel coalesced with /n/, the result belonging phonemically to the /n/ that occurred in other positions;
(3) Then final /n/ after an unstressed vowel was lost except when immediately followed (in the next word with no intervening pause) by a vowel;

(4) Then final /ə/, in three-syllable words with stress on the first syllable, was lost.

As a result of these changes, the various inflected forms of OE /óksa/ 'ox' were reshaped as shown by the following chart:

		OE	early ME
Sg. Nom.		/óksa/	/óksə/
	Gen. Dat. Acc.	/óksan/ ⎫	
Pl. Nom. Acc.		/óksan/ ⎬	/óksə(n)/
	Dat.	/óksum/ ⎭	
	Gen.	/óksena/	/óksən/.

Here the /n/ of /óksə(n)/ was present if a vowel followed, lacking before a consonant or a pause; but the /n/ of the plural genitive was always present. However, pairs of forms with and without final /n/ were soon analogically freed from the specific conditioning by what followed, so that both occurred in any surroundings. Our present *ox* is of course from the earlier singular nominative; *ox's* and *oxen's* are analogical new formations; *oxen* is from the ME genitive plural and from the form with terminal /n/ of the nominative-accusative-dative plural. The ME form /óksə/ has died out altogether in its competition with /óksən/.

Here, again, we see a sort of interplay between sound change and analogy. As sound change ate away at the distinctiveness of the OE inflected forms of nouns, syntactical relationships and shades of meaning which had been shown in OE, at least in part, by the case of the noun, came to be expressed in other ways instead. We cannot suppose that the loss of some bit of inflectional machinery was ever the source of any conscious embarrassment.

54.4. Lexical and Semantic Change. Changes of the lexical and semantic sort caused ultimately by sound change are of very minor importance. Phonemic restructuring can lead formerly related forms to be so different in shape that the relationship between them ceases to pertain. We thus have, as mentioned in §44.4, both *shade* and *shadow* from different inflected forms of one OE noun; similarly, both *mead* and *meadow* from those of another. The separation of the two in each case occurred during ME times when case-relationships, as we have seen, were rapidly becoming less important: /šáˇdə/, from the OE nominative /skǽdu/, served as the base for new analogical case forms and plural, while /šádwə/, from the old oblique forms, served as the base for an analogical new nominative singular. This produced two separate stems, each inflected just as much as most ME nouns were, and the vicissitudes of usage have developed distinct meanings for them. The *-lorn* of *forlorn* and *love-lorn* is all that is left of what was once the past participle of the verb *to lose; lost*, though irregular today, was an analogically created regular past participle when it first entered the language. Descriptively, NE *-lorn* is hardly to be related to *lose*. In quite the same way, *worked* is an analogically regularized past participle of *to work;* the older irregular past participle *wrought* still survives, but is not by most speakers of today taken as related to *work*.

Contrariwise, phonemic restructuring can operate on forms that are phonemically distinct at one stage to render them homonymous at a later stage. This may or may not result in lexical and semantic change: we still have plenty of homonymous pairs and triads of words, like *bear, bear, bare*, and this is equally true of most languages at most known stages of their histories. We have already seen, in §46.5, the factors which may lead to the loss of one of a set of homonymous words, or to its replacement by some longer alternative form. If neither, or none, of such a set is lost, then descriptively at the later stage one of the historically distinct words may be felt to be a peculiar marginal use of the other. To some speakers of NE, the poetic *blow* 'bloom' is probably a marginal meaning of *blow* 'move air,' and *ear* (of corn) may be taken as the same word as *ear* (on head), though both pairs were quite distinct in OE.

54.5. Direction of Sound Change. We have now discussed both the nature of sound change and the various ways in which it can bring about immediate or ultimate consequences. There remain several questions to which we should like to know the answers, if the answers are available.

The first of these is: is there any general *direction* in sound change? We have seen how manifold are the factors that can contribute to sound change, and it is not surprising that, with our present techniques of observation, any prediction, either of a specific trend in sound change or of a specific resulting structural change, should be quite out of the question. However, by gathering many examples of phonemic restructurings which have come about as the result of sound change, we can at least discover that certain outcomes are more frequent, and hence more probable, than others.

For example, the gradual fronting of the position of articulation of a dorso-velar stop or spirant ([k g x γ]), particularly in the vicinity of front vowels like [i e], is extremely common. The gradual retraction of a relatively front [k g], or of a [č] or [ĵ], is much rarer indeed, even in the vicinity of back vowels like [u o]. In general, when sound change leads to a phonemic restructuring, the key phoneme in the new scheme is fairly similar, in articulation or acoustically or both, to its immediate predecessor in the old scheme. We should not expect sound change to lead *directly* to a change from, say, earlier [p] to later [g]. Given time enough, and a long enough sequence of intervening changes, anything *can* become anything else; but the changes of any great frequency show less erratic variety than such a statement would imply.

These facts perhaps imply that despite the large number of factors which play an indirect contributing role in sound change, there is a single factor of greatest importance: the tendency to speak sloppily, doing no more work than is necessary to make oneself understood. Under these conditions, the pronunciation of any given phoneme in a given environment tends to carry over articulatory motions involved in the immediately preceding and following phonemes. A [k] becomes more and more fronted before front vowels because the tongue is put into something approaching the position for the front vowel while the [k] is being made; and so on.

The tendency towards sloppiness of articulation does not, of course, lead to a complete loss of all phonemic contrasts so that speech is reduced to a continuous undifferentiated *uh-h-h-h*. A contrast is lost hither or yon in the system, but there is always some sort of compensation, so that the communicative business of speech can still be carried on. It is probably legitimate in this connection to speak in teleological terms, and to say that it is because the communicative business of speech *must* be carried on that the complete degeneration of articulation never comes about. This is simply the historical analog of the matter of redundancy and noise, which we discussed synchronically in §10.3.

54.6. Suddenness and Obtrusiveness. Secondly, how sudden and how obtrusive is the actual phonemic restructuring to which a trend in sound change may lead?

Sound change itself is constant and slow. A phonemic restructuring, on the other hand, must in a sense be absolutely sudden. No matter how gradual was the approach of early ME /ǽ/ and /ɔ́/ towards each other, we cannot imagine the actual coalescence of the two other than as a sudden event: on such-and-such a day, for such-and-such a speaker or tiny group of speakers, the two fell together as /á/ and the whole system of stressed nuclei, *for the particular idiolect or idiolects*, was restructured.

Yet there is no reason to believe that we would ever be able to detect this kind of sudden event by direct observation. In the first place, the actual moment of coalescence might be today for one speaker in a community (say in a certain village), tomorrow for another, a month from now for a third, so that even in a small village the *collective* pattern would be changed more slowly, perhaps requiring a period of years. In this sense there is no suddenness. In the second place, the event is certainly very unobtrusive. People do not listen to pronunciation; they listen to meanings. Those in whose speech the restructuring has not yet quite occurred will not notice it. They will interpret the speech-sound that they do not, usually, hear clearly anyway, in terms of what it *ought* to be according to their own habits.

54.7. Frequency. Thirdly, how frequent are the phonemic restructurings brought about by sound change? We can begin to find an answer by counting the attested restructurings between the OE of Alfredian times and modern "standard" American English, neglecting all sorts of attested developments which show up today only in local dialects, if at all. The number is apparently on the order of one hundred, which means, on the average, one every ten or fifteen years. When we remember that this figure also represents the speech of a large and steadily increasing number of people, we conclude that such events are quite rare. At least, they are rare as compared with successful analogical innovations, or with borrowings from other languages or widely divergent dialects: in the three centuries which immediately followed the Norman Conquest, some *twelve thousand* French words found their way into English.

Of course, the figure for phonemic restructurings given above cannot, in the nature of things, include those which, so to speak, "died a-borning": a small group of people undergo the change, but borrowing from the unchanged pattern of other communities completely submerges the results.

54.8. Importance. Finally, how important is sound change as a mechanism of phylogenetic change?

Here we find an interesting contradiction, depending on relative to whom we are judging importance. For the speakers of a language, sound change is certainly the least noticeable and important of all the mechanisms. Borrowings and analogical creations are sometimes noticed and commented on, or even undertaken consciously, but sound change never is.

But for the linguistic historian, who wishes to investigate the history of a language or a family of languages, sound change is of supreme importance. It achieves this importance for the following reason: if a coalescence does not "die a-borning," but gets a good start in the speech pattern of a considerable community of people, then *its effect is irreversible.* The restructuring which has come about *cannot be undone by sound change,* and is highly unlikely to be completely undone by any other mechanism. This stems logically from the conditions, stated in §53.3, under which an allophone can split. The irreversibility of successful coalescences constitutes the most powerful single tool of the historian of language; in the following sections we shall see why.

LINGUISTIC
PREHISTORY

55.

INTERNAL RECONSTRUCTION

55.1. History without Written Records. Our earliest surviving documents in English date from the end of the seventh century A.D. (§43.1). The history of English from that time to the present can be based on the interpretation of written records. But if we wish to push our perspective further into the past, we are forced to turn to other methods. These other methods have to be brought into play more quickly when we seek to determine something of the history of, say, the Bantu languages of Africa, or the Algonquian languages of North America: the speakers of these languages (and of hundreds of others) knew nothing of writing until the coming of Europeans in recent times, so that the oldest written records, if any, are for all practical purposes contemporary.

In seeking a deeper time-perspective than direct documentation affords, we make use of several interrelated techniques: *internal reconstruction; dialect geography; external reconstruction* or the *comparative method;* and *glottochronology.* Collectively, these can be thought of as the methods of *linguistic prehistory*—using the word "prehistory" in its familiar sense of that part of the past for which written records are lacking, in contrast, therefore, with what is best called *recorded history.* The first and third of the techniques are time-honored, though the first has only recently been carefully codified. The second technique is by no means always applicable, and serves more as a corrective for results achieved from the first and third than as an independent approach. Glottochronology is quite new, and not yet fully reliable, but it holds great promise. It does not in any sense duplicate what is accomplished with the other

461

techniques, but builds thereon to yield a more precise dating than the others can supply.

In the absence of written records, these indirect techniques are our only way to obtain historical information. But there is nothing to prevent us from using them in cases where written records do exist, and there are two reasons why the duplication is worth while. One reason is that the validity of the indirect methods can thus be checked. For example, we examine the modern Romance languages, apply the comparative method, and reconstruct a picture of their common ancestor; then we compare this indirectly achieved picture with our direct documentation of Latin. The agreement is so good that we gain confidence in the results of the comparative method where no such direct check is possible. The other reason is that even when written records are available, they do not tell everything: a sparse portrayal achieved purely through documentary evidence can often be rendered sharper by adding the results of indirect methods. The Romans did not write down—in documents that have managed to survive two thousand years of copying—all the words they knew and used in their speech; the evidence of the Romance languages attests to a fair number of Latin words that are not found in the available direct documentation, and we are quite confident that the Romans did know and use these additional words.

In this and the following sections we shall discuss the methods of linguistic prehistory one by one, in the order in which they are listed above. In general, none of these techniques is used to the exclusion of the others; we separate them only for clarity of exposition. For the reasons given in the preceding paragraph, we shall not confine our examples to cases where documentary evidence is lacking.

One warning must be given at the outset. Many of the early nineteenth-century investigators who first developed the comparative method—and, to some extent, the method of internal reconstruction—hoped that a systematic application of such methods might carry our perspective of human language appreciably nearer the actual beginnings of the institution. This hope was vain and must be abandoned. Our earliest written records, in any part of the world, date back only a few millenia; the best that linguistic prehistory can do in any detail is to extend this horizon back a few millenia further. But there are good reasons for the belief that our ancestors have possessed language for much longer, perhaps millions of years. The deepest attainable detailed temporal horizon thus represents a mere scratch on the surface. Any deductions that can currently be made about the *evolution* of language, in contrast with the history of specific languages or language families, require very different techniques, involving the study of the communicative behavior of our non-human ancestors and cousins.

55.2. Internal Reconstruction. The technique of internal reconstruction is applied to descriptive (§38.1) information about a single language at a single stage of its development: say modern English, or classical Latin, or contemporary Choctaw. The fundamental assumption is that some events in the history of a language leave discernible traces in its design, so that by finding these traces one can draw inferences as to the earlier incidents which are responsible for them.

One fact of phylogenetic change is of key importance in this connection. As we saw in §54.2, phonemic restructurings brought about by sound change tend to make for irregularities of morphophonemic alternation; and, conversely, many morphophonemic irregularities found in a language at a given stage reflect an earlier regularity disrupted by phonemic restructuring. Therefore, a careful examination of morphophonemic irregularities in a language, and of the distributional aspect of its phonological system, should yield reasonable deductions about its earlier history.

Potawatomi affords a striking example. Many Potawatomi stems show a variation in the location of vowels depending on the inflectional prefixes and suffixes which are present. Thus the word for 'paper' is /msən?əkən/; but the word for 'my paper,' which has a prefix meaning 'I' or 'my' before the same stem, appears as /nməsnə?kən/. The contrast in shape is revealed more clearly if we present the two words spread out as follows, with the identical portions of the two vertically aligned:

/m sən ?əkən/
/n məs nə? kən/.

An endless number of Potawatomi stems show a comparable variation in shape, but we can discuss the matter with just the one example. In describing how Potawatomi now works, without any regard to its past history, it is convenient to set up theoretical *base forms* (§33.6) for stems and inflectional affixes, in which we indicate more "potential" vowels than are actually heard. Thus we set up the base form of 'paper' as /məsənəʔəkən-/, where the terminal hyphen tells us that this is not intended to be the transcription of a form as spoken, but rather something abstracted from the actually spoken forms; the prefix for 'my' we similarly set up as /nə-/. We can then state rather simply which of the "potential" vowels will be heard in actual speech: the controlling principle is a rhythmic one, by which the "potential" vowels of alternate syllables are omitted. Thus if a whole word includes just the stem /məsənəʔəkən-/, the second, fourth, and last "potential" vowels are actually spoken, yielding the phonemic shape /msənʔəkən/; but if the whole word includes /nə-/ followed by /məsənəʔəkən-/, then exactly the same rhythmic principle leads to the loss of a different set of the "potential" vowels, yielding the phonemic shape /nməsnəʔkən/.

So far we have said nothing of the history of the language. But the sort of situation we have just described immediately suggests the following historical interpretation: At some earlier time—in what we shall call "pre-Potawatomi"—the phonemic shapes of words included all the vowels which we now set up as "potential" vowels in our theoretical base forms. The word for 'paper' in pre-Potawatomi was thus something like /məsənəʔəkən/, and the word for 'my paper' something like /nəməsənəʔəkən/. Between pre-Potawatomi and contemporary Potawatomi, sound change led to the gradual weakening of certain vowels, in positions within words specified by a certain rhythmic principle, until finally they were lost altogether—yielding the current phonemic shapes.

In other words, internal reconstruction proposes that what poses, in a purely synchronic view, as a statement of morphophonemic alternation, may in a historical view be a description of a chronological sequence of events.

We have no written records of earlier Potawatomi (at least, none early enough for our purposes), so that we cannot test our hypothesis directly. But there are a number of languages still spoken which are obviously related to Potawatomi, and by applying the comparative method to these we can achieve just as good an independent check as documents would supply. Indeed, all we need do is to examine the relevant Fox forms: /mesenahikani/ 'paper,' and /nemesenahikani/ 'my paper.' Compare, further, the following:

	Fox	Potawatomì
'I am happy'	/nekeša·tesi/	/nkəšatəs/
'he is happy'	/keša·tesiwa/	/kšatsə/
'skunk'	/šeka·kwa/	/škak/
'woman'	/ihkwe·wa/	/k·we/
'man'	/ineniwa/	/nənə/
'stone'	/aseni/	/s·ən/.

The Fox forms of today seem to retain various short vowels, from the common ancestor of the two languages, which have been lost in Potawatomi. Of course there is a converse hypothesis: that the common ancestor was more like contemporary Potawatomi, and that Fox has "grown" new vowels. Languages do indeed "grow" new vowels, but detailed investigation in the present instance shows that this alternative is impossible. If a language "grows" a new vowel, then what precise vowel is developed is predictable from the surrounding consonantism or other phonemic environmental factors. In the Fox forms cited above we find three different short vowels, /i/, /e/, and /a/, where Potawatomi has no vowel at all; the development of the Potawatomi forms can be explained on the basis of our original assumption about the common ancestor, but the development of the Fox forms cannot be explained on the converse assumption. Finally, most of the other contemporary Central Algonquian languages agree with Fox, not with Potawatomi, as to location and variety of vowels.

A second example can be drawn from modern German. German has six stop consonants, /p t k b d g/; these all occur initially and medially, but in prejunctural position one hears only /p t k/. Noun and adjective stems which end in a stop show two different patterns of behavior when inflectional endings are added:

first pattern:	/tý·p/ 'type'	:	/tý·pen/,
	/tó·t/ 'dead'	:	/tó·te/,
	/dék/ 'deck'	:	/déke/;

second pattern:	/táwp/ 'deaf'	:	/táwben/,
	/tó·t/ 'death'	:	/tó·de/,
	/tá·k/ 'day'	:	/tá·ges/.

Descriptively, we account for this in a very simple way. We set up base forms for the stems with the final stop that they show before a vowel ending, thus /tý·p-/, /tó·t-/, /dɛ́k-/, /táwb-/, /tó·d-/, tá·g-/. We then account for the replacement of stem-final /b d g/ by /p t k/, when no ending follows, on the basis of the phonemic limitation on the voiced stops which precludes their occurrence in word-final position.

This situation, once again, immediately suggests a historical interpretation: that in earlier German, the stops /b d g/ did occur in word-final position; and that sound change has led to a falling-together of the final voiced stops with the corresponding voiceless ones.

We have copious written materials from earlier stages of German, so that the hypothesis can be checked, and once again our internal reconstruction is shown to be correct *in general*—not, indeed, in all particulars. The current noun /bánt/ 'band, ribbon,' with longer inflected forms like /bánde/, /bándes/, would be set up as basic /bánd-/; and we would infer, by our hypothesis, that the earlier form with no ending was /bánd-/; but Old High German documents attest clearly to /bánt/, /bánte/, /bántes/, and the current alternation in this particular instance is due to a subsequent change of medial /-nt-/ to /-nd-/, rather than to the change of final /-nd/ to /-nt/.

In this example, again, it should be noted that no other historical inference is realistically possible on the basis of the observed current situation. One could not conceivably propose, for example, that at an earlier stage all such stems ended in voiceless stops /p t k/ whether final or followed by an inflectional ending, and that between the earlier time and now some of these stops have become voiced in word-medial position. This alternative is impossible because we cannot find any phonemic conditioning factor which would govern the splitting of the postulated earlier single allophones /-p- -t- -k-/ into two, the two subsequently becoming phonemically distinct (§53.3). Our knowledge of what is probable and of what is possible in sound change guides us inevitably to the correct inference.

55.3. Internal Reconstruction on Old English. Preparatory to our discussion of the comparative method, it will be convenient to describe here a few inferences about the probable prehistory of English which can be made from the state of affairs known for OE.

We start with the inferred earlier history of Alfredian OE /ǧ/ and /ᵹ̌/. In the OE of Alfred's time, these two were in what is called *partial complementation:* they contrasted in one environment—at the ends of words, as in /éĝ/ 'edge' versus /dǽɣ̂/ 'day'—but in all other environments at most one of the two occurred, to the exclusion of the other. Such a distribution, plus the close phonetic similarity of the two phonemes (one a stop, the other a spirant, but both voiced and both pronounced with the same position of articulation), immediately suggests that the contrast was recent. Now we also find some stems in Alfredian OE alternating between a single and a double final consonant: single when nothing follows in the same word, as /mɔ́n/ 'man,' /béd/ 'bed,' but double when more material follows in the same word, as the genitives /mɔ́nnes/, /béddes/. This suggests that at an earlier stage such stems had ended in the double consonants even when nothing followed in the same word: /mɔ́nn/, /bédd/, and likewise /éĝĝ/ for Alfredian /éĝ/; and that in the intervening period the final double consonants had been shortened by sound change. In the earliest OE texts there is a sufficient sprinkling of spellings like *mann*, *bedd*, to support the theory, and comparison with the other old Germanic languages supports it even more strongly.

But if all Alfredian OE final /ĝ/'s trace back to a somewhat earlier doubled [ĝ̂ĝ̂], then at the earlier time [ĝ̂] and [ɣ̂] were in complete complementary distribution, and thus certainly members of a single phoneme, which was always voiced and always fronted dorso-velar, but was stop or spirant depending on environment. Either symbol would do to represent this single earlier phoneme; arbitrarily, we have chosen /ĝ/.

The reader will recognize this example: it was used in a different connection—though presented in the opposite order—in §53.3. The line of reasoning described directly above is what supplies us with this particular illustration of what was being discussed in §53.3.

In our further applications of internal reconstruction (and of the comparative method, in §§57–60) to OE, we can assume the results of this particular inference, writing only /ĝ/, but also indicating final double consonants where appropriate. This means that we will be citing relatively early OE forms, either as attested in the early documents or as achieved through internal reconstruction applied to the language of Alfred's time.

A second suspicious looking thing in OE is the distribution of the stressed vowels /ǽ/ and /ɔ́/ (stressed /á/ also comes into the picture, but is more complicated, and we shall leave it aside). Stressed /ǽ/ and

/ɔ́/ are in partial complementation; furthermore, many stems appear now with one, now with the other, depending largely on the endings. Thus we find /dǽ͜g/ 'day,' retaining /ǽ/ throughout the singular (/dǽ͜ges/, /dǽ͜ge/), but showing /ɔ́/ in the plural (/dɔ́xas/, /dɔ́xa/, /dɔ́xum/). The same happens in the inflection of /pǽθ/ 'path,' /stǽf/ 'staff,' /hwǽl/ 'whale,' /fǽt/ 'vessel,' /bǽk/ 'back,' /bǽθ/ 'bath,' /blǽk/ 'ink,' and a number of other nouns and adjectives; a similar phenomenon appears in some verbs, as /hɔ́bban/' to have': /hǽbbe/ '(I) have' : /hɔ́faθ/ or /hǽfθ/ '(he) has.' However, a few stems appear in both shapes regardless of what follows: /ɔ́sk̲e/ or /ǽsk̲e/ 'ashes,' /hnɔ́ppian/ or /hnǽppian/ 'to doze,' /lɔ́ppa/ or /lǽppa/ 'lappet.'

The basis for the partial complementation is not entirely clear, but certainly consists in part of what vowel (if any) follows in the next syllable: before /e/ in the next syllable, and in monosyllables, /ǽ/ is commoner; before /a/ and /u/ in the next syllable, /ɔ́/ is commoner. The historical inference is clear, and more detailed investigation supports it: OE /ǽ/ and /ɔ́/ were at some earlier time allophones [ǽ] and [ɔ́] of a single phoneme (we might symbolize it as /á/), which had developed these relatively disparate allophones in two different sets of environments; then other changes led to the loss of the conditioning factors in some of the environments, setting the two allophones into contrast as separate phonemes.

Finally, we shall consider the distribution of OE /k/ and /k̲/. Again we find partial complementation: flanked by a front vowel, and after /s/, /k̲/ is commoner, while, not so flanked, /k/ prevails. Thus the singular /bó·k/ 'book' changes not only its stem vowel but also the following consonant in the plural /bé·k̲/ 'books.' There are exceptions: /k/ occurs before the front vowels /y/, /y·/, /ö/, /e/, and /e·/, and at least in late OE /k̲/ appears before the back vowel /ó·/ in /k̲ó·san/ 'to choose.' But the last-cited word has an earlier attested shape /k̲ɔ́·san/, pointing to an even earlier /k̲éwsan/ with a front vowel. And there is some evidence that the vowels /y/, /y·/, /ö/, and some occurrences of the front vowels /e/ and /e·/, came from earlier back vowels. This latter evidence is limited within OE; only when we apply the comparative method to OE and its sister Germanic languages does the argument become decisive. Nevertheless, the situation in OE at least *suggests* that /k/ and /k̲/ may at an earlier time have been allophones [k] and [k̲] of a single phoneme (say /k/), which had split into these allophones in clearly distinct environments, and that subsequent environmental changes had thrown the two allophones into contrast.

We might expect that a similar examination of OE /g/ and /ğ/ would reveal a parallel situation, suggesting a comparable historical interpretation; but it does not. All that we discover in this case is that the earlier history of /g/ and /ğ/ must have been more complicated; only the comparative method shows what that history was.

55.4. Summary. We see that the method of internal reconstruction yields results of varying value. In the Potawatomi case, and in the case of Alfredian OE /ğ/ and /γ̂/, the conclusions we reach appear incontrovertible. In the German case, they seem equally sure, and yet the documentary evidence shows us that they are only in general correct, some of the details actually having been different. The instance of OE /ǽ/ and /ɔ́/ is somewhat more convincing than our brief discussion of it above implies; the instance of OE /k/ and /ḵ/ is weakest of all. It is thus obvious why the linguistic historian does not, through choice, work exclusively with internal reconstruction, but rather conjoins this technique to any and every other which circumstances allow.

NOTES

New terms: *linguistic prehistory* (vs. *recorded history*); methods, including *dialect geography, internal reconstruction, external reconstruction* or the *comparative method,* and *glottochronology; partial complementation.* Note that the term "comparative method" does not mean simply comparison of any sort, for any purpose, but specifically a kind of comparison of *related* languages for the purpose of determining as much as possible about their common ancestor. For "comparison" in the sense of typological study and classification (§§11, 31), some other term has to be used, even though outside linguistics the word "comparison" often means this.

Earlier discussion of internal reconstruction (not by that name) led to Bloomfield's examples of so-called *reminiscent sandhi* (see in the index in Bloomfield 1933). More recent codification of the method is supplied by Hoenigswald 1943 and 1946.

Problem. Below are listed a set of pairs of words in Fijian. Note that in Fijian every word ends in a vowel and that every consonant is immediately followed by a vowel. The forms on the left are used of general action, while those on the right are used when there is a specified definite object: e.g., /ðabe/ is used meaning 'go upwards, ascend,' while /ðabeta/ is used meaning 'ascend (something, e.g., a hill)' when the word for 'hill' is actually included in the sentence. Do two things with the data. (1) Synchronically, extract base forms for the stems, and describe the morphophonemics involved in the forms that actually appear in speech. (2) Diachronically, make an inference by the technique of internal reconstruction about the state of affairs in "Pre-Fijian."

/ðabe/	'to go upwards'	/ðabeta/
/kaði/	'to call, call out'	/kaðiva/
/vola/	'to be writing'	/volaa/
/viri/	'to throw'	/virika/
/rai/	'to look (for)'	/raiða/
/muri/	'to follow'	/muria/
/tau/	'to take'	/taura/
/taa/	'to chop'	/taaja/
/loma/	'to love'	/lomana/
/lutu/	'to fall down'	/lutuma/

56·

DIALECT GEOGRAPHY

56.1. Gathering Dialect Information. If a language is spoken by at least two people, then there are always some differences of usage which an observer can detect if he looks closely enough. If a language is spoken, as many are, by thousands or millions of people, then variations of usage show some degree of correlation. with the social and geographical structure of the society to which the speakers belong. People who are daily in contact with each other, either because they live in a single village or because they belong to the same social or economic class, tend to share usages, while those who rarely or never have occasion to speak directly with each other show greater divergences of speech pattern.

The amount and nature of social stratification varies greatly from one society to another, so that this factor in dialect differentiation is not always operative. Where it is operative, we often find that the speech of the privileged classes is more uniform from one locality to another than is that of the less fortunate: educated British English is much the same in London, in Manchester, and in Southampton, but the local dialects in and near those three cities show great divergence. This, also, is a function of how much people intercommunicate: the privileged classes travel about more, and in their travels come into contact largely with other members of the same class, while the less fortunate stay closer to home. The matter of "correctness" in speech is closely tied in here, for standards of correctness derive largely from the natural habits of speech of the privileged classes and are promulgated mainly for the guidance thereof. Adherence to the rules becomes one symbol of class membership. In a stratified society with little vertical motility—that is,

471

one in which the son of a farmer is predestined to become a farmer himself, and knows it—the special connotation of correctness does not arise: the privileged class has its usages, and the lower classes have theirs, and that is that. But when there is the belief that humble origin is no necessary barrier to social advancement, the doctrine of correctness comes into the picture, with its whole panoply of rationalizations and justifications. The acquisition of "correct" habits of speech and writing becomes one of the rungs in the ladder of social success. The doctrine may then survive long after the social structure which gave rise to it has been altered. This seems to be largely what has happened in the United States.

Whether a society of thousands or millions of people shows social stratification or not, the factor of geographical proximity and separation is always operative in contributing to the dialect picture. In an unstratified society it affects everyone, and in a stratified society it operates at least on the lower strata. Consequently, the student of dialect variation can always make some determinations of the sort that can be displayed on maps.

In dialect geography, one attempts to draw historical inferences from the geographical distribution of linguistic forms and usages, either as the only sort of evidence or in conjunction with evidence of other kinds. Before any deductions can be attempted, it is necessary to collect and organize the geographical information. The customary procedure for the preparation of a *dialect atlas* is as follows:

(1) A preliminary survey of a region is made, to get some notion of the ways in which usage varies from subregion to subregion, and some impression of the way in which the region is broken up by variations of usage.

(2) Two basic frames of reference are then prepared. One is a list of the geographical *points* at which usage will be checked in more detail. The other is a list of *items* of usage to be checked at each point; this latter takes, in due time, the form of a questionnaire. (The two words "point" and "item" will be used in the following in the special senses just indicated: the first for a geographical location, the second for an observable unit of usage.)

(3) Field workers travel through the region, stopping at each preselected point, finding suitable informants, and filling out a copy of the questionnaire for each informant. Only one or two informants can

usually be used at each point, and they are generally chosen from the oldest living generation of people who have resided at or near the point since early childhood. The collected material thus represents only a tiny sampling of the total population of the region.

(4) When all information is in, maps are drawn, showing the distribution of each alternative usage for the items in the questionnaire.

The items which are selected for survey can be of various sorts. Here are some representative examples:

(1) The word or phrase customarily used for a certain meaning: *bucket*, *pail*, or something else as the common name for the metal container for carrying water; the word or phrase for cottage cheese; the word for the see-saw.

(2) The meanings for a certain word, provided that the word is known: the type of object referred to by *doughnut*, or by *milkshake*, or by *pail*. Thus in parts of the South, where *bucket* is the word for the metal water container, *pail* is used for a similar utensil made of wood.

(3) The pronunciation (in terms of factors known to be generally of phonemic relevance in the language) of a given word: *orange* with a rounded or with an unrounded first vowel; *greasy* with /s/ or with /z/.

(4) The phonemic identity or difference of two forms: (*I*) *can* and (*a tin*) *can* same or different; *cot* and *caught* same or different.

Dialect atlas work done so far shows some minor variations within, or slight deviations from, the schema outlined above. One sharply deviant survey, which has proved invaluable in the study of English, was based not on direct observation of informants but on an examination of a body of documents of known provenience dating from Middle English times. Another useful study, the results of which have appeared only piecemeal in articles, is a survey of the United States by counties, using as many informants as possible but only a small number of items. The main advantage is that a different sort of map can be drawn from those to be discussed below, a map showing how the prevalence of one usage over another gradually increases or decreases along any route.

The more customary types of maps are as follows. One type (Figure 56.1) has differently shaped symbols each representing a specific usage. Another type (Figure 56.2) has lines representing *isoglosses:* the geographical boundaries of usages.

When isogloss-maps are superposed, the lines representing the different isoglosses sometimes appear to criss-cross in the wildest manner; yet

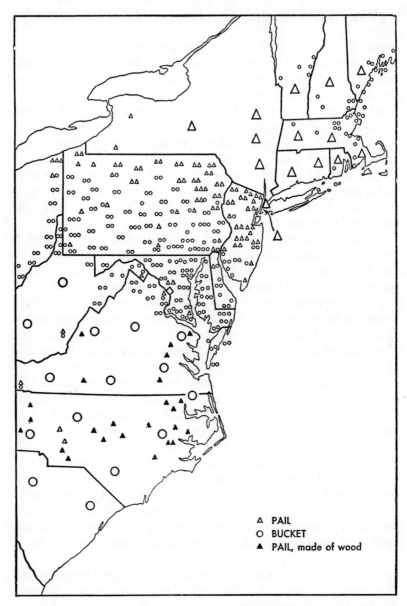

FIGURE 56.1.   ONE KIND OF DIALECT MAP

(Adapted from Map 66 of Hans Kurath, *A Word Geography of the Eastern United States*, University of Michigan Press, by permission. Copyright 1949 by The University of Michigan.)

474

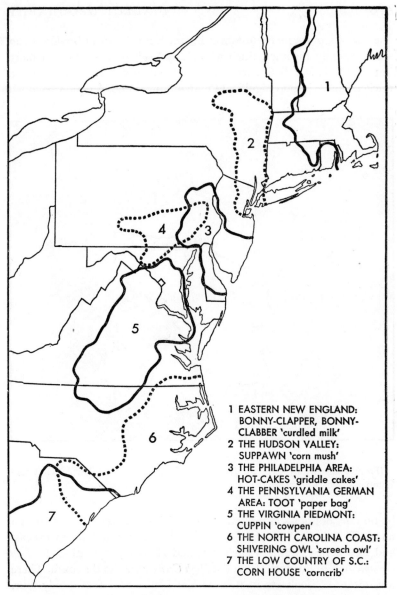

1 EASTERN NEW ENGLAND:
BONNY-CLAPPER, BONNY-
CLABBER 'curdled milk'
2 THE HUDSON VALLEY:
SUPPAWN 'corn mush'
3 THE PHILADELPHIA AREA:
HOT-CAKES 'griddle cakes'
4 THE PENNSYLVANIA GERMAN
AREA: TOOT 'paper bag'
5 THE VIRGINIA PIEDMONT:
CUPPIN 'cowpen'
6 THE NORTH CAROLINA COAST:
SHIVERING OWL 'screech owl'
7 THE LOW COUNTRY OF S.C.:
CORN HOUSE 'corncrib'

FIGURE 56.2.   ANOTHER KIND OF DIALECT MAP, SHOWING ISOGLOSSES
(Adapted from Map 2 of Hans Kurath, *A Word Geography of the Eastern United States*, University of Michigan Press, by permission. Copyright 1949 by The University of Michigan.)

475

one also discovers many instances in which a number of isoglosses run along roughly together. Such a *bundle of isoglosses* constitutes a more important dialect boundary than does any isolated isogloss, and a thicker bundle is more significant than a thinner one. A region bounded

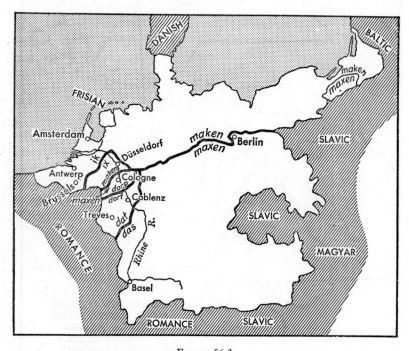

FIGURE 56.3

(From *Language*, by Leonard Bloomfield. By permission of Henry Holt and Company, Inc., Copyright 1933.)

by bundles of isoglosses is often called a *dialect area*, and may be given a name. The classic example of an isogloss bundle is that which runs east and west across Germany, Belgium, and Holland, separating the *Low German* area to the north from the *High German* area to the south. There are dozens of isoglosses in this bundle; Figure 56.3 shows only four, which run along very close together except in the west, where they fray out. Figure 56.4 shows a convenient segregation of dialect areas and subareas in the Eastern United States, based on the locations of thicker and thinner isogloss bundles.

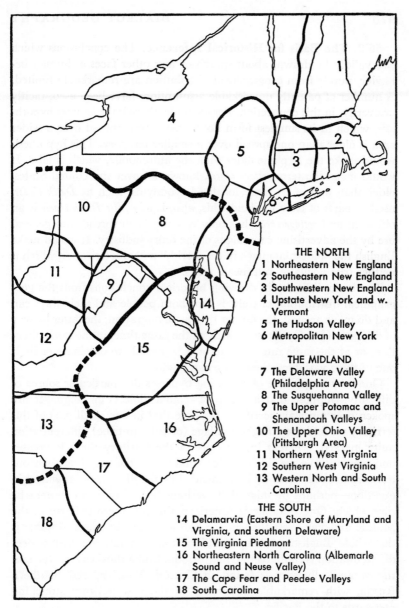

THE NORTH
1 Northeastern New England
2 Southeastern New England
3 Southwestern New England
4 Upstate New York and w.
  Vermont
5 The Hudson Valley
6 Metropolitan New York

THE MIDLAND
7 The Delaware Valley
  (Philadelphia Area)
8 The Susquehanna Valley
9 The Upper Potomac and
  Shenandoah Valleys
10 The Upper Ohio Valley
   (Pittsburgh Area)
11 Northern West Virginia
12 Southern West Virginia
13 Western North and South
   Carolina

THE SOUTH
14 Delamarvia (Eastern Shore of Maryland and
   Virginia, and southern Delaware)
15 The Virginia Piedmont
16 Northeastern North Carolina (Albemarle
   Sound and Neuse Valley)
17 The Cape Fear and Peedee Valleys
18 South Carolina

FIGURE 56.4. DIALECT AREAS IN THE EASTERN UNITED STATES

(Adapted from Map 3 of Hans Kurath, *A Word Geography of the Eastern United States*, University of Michigan Press, by permission. Copyright 1949 by The University of Michigan.)

56.2. The Basis for Historical Inference. The conclusions which can validly be drawn, about speech or any other facet of human behavior, purely from geographical distribution are remarkably limited. A number of patently unworkable assumptions have been used, tacitly or overtly, in this connection. For example, there is the *age-area* hypothesis, which in its simplest form holds that a trait spread over a wider area is older than one spread over a smaller territory. This hypothesis would make the airplane older than the automobile, which is false. It would make the term *cottage cheese*, known all over the United States, older than any of its more localized synonyms, such as *Dutch cheese*, used in parts of New England: this, also, is false, for *Dutch cheese* is an old term and *cottage cheese* has only recently been spread into general use by the advertising campaigns of the dairy industry. It would make English the "oldest language in the world," a characterization which is neither true nor false, but meaningless.

The basic difficulty in drawing historical conclusions from the geographical distribution of traits is that both people and their ways can and do move around, the former by way of migration, the latter by way of diffusion (§47.5), not necessarily at the same time, in the same direction, or at the same rate. Whenever it is possible to eliminate or limit one of these variables, then more can be done.

One very simple line of reasoning bypasses this particular source of difficulty. Suppose that a group of related dialects or languages are spoken over a certain territory. Suppose that in one small part of this territory we find the village-to-village (or tribe-to-tribe) differentiation quite marked, whereas in the bulk of the territory there is greater homogeneity. We are able to deduce that *most* of the large homogeneous territory has only recently been invaded by the dialects or languages in question—perhaps by migration, perhaps by diffusion, we cannot be sure which. One example is American English, more uniform in the Middle and Far West than in the East and the Old South. Another is the whole English-speaking world of today: really marked dialect differentiation is confined to Great Britain. Still a third case is Russian: the greatest diversity is found in Central, Western, and Southern Russia, with remarkable uniformity in the vast territory stretching eastwards to the Pacific.

It should be noted that we can draw no deduction at all about the subregion of greater diversity. This may have been the center from which the dialects or languages have spread, but it also may represent recent migrations of many different groups from elsewhere, settling next to each other. One can often tell which is the case by a more detailed comparison of the dialects or languages involved, but this means that one is using information beyond the purely distributional.

A second valid basis for historical deduction requires only one sort of information in addition to the geographical. The Athapaskan languages were spoken, in recent aboriginal America, in a discontinuous region: a vast stretch in the interior of Alaska and western Canada, several isolated spots in Oregon and California, and a fair-sized area in the Southwest. Since the languages are all related, the antecedents of the present speakers must at some time have been distributed over a single continuous region. We can go no further purely on the geographical evidence. We cannot know, for example, whether the "proto-territory" of the Athapaskans was in the North, or the Southwest, or on the Pacific coast, or, indeed, elsewhere.

The inference of earlier continuous distribution, in the example just given, is rendered valid by the fact that the "trait" in question is not one which could possibly come about by *parallelism:* that is, by two or more groups of people, out of touch with each other, making the same discovery or invention. The same judgment can often be made of items of usage in a single language. As Figure 56.1 shows, the word *bucket*, for a metal container used to carry water, is known in eastern and northern New England, throughout the Old South, and in parts of Pennsylvania, but not in the Hudson valley and upstate New York, where *pail* is the prevalent term. Since the use of *bucket* for this specific article could hardly develop independently in two or more places, we can infer that at some earlier time its geographical distribution must have been continuous. Naturally, we cannot say how long ago that time was, nor can we deduce the location of the proto-territory.

Few problems in dialect geography, unfortunately, are amenable to solution on the basis of the two valid lines of deduction just described. Yet such problems are often solved. The reason is that in the parts of the world where the methods of dialect geography have mostly been applied, it is possible almost to eliminate one of the variables mentioned earlier: migration. The lower social strata in the population of western Europe—the "folk"—are largely sedentary, and have been for a number of centuries. Thus if we find a certain usage in the folk speech of a continuous region within, say, the Dutch-German area, we can with reasonable certainty assume that the usage originated at some specific point, and that it has reached its observed distribution via diffusion rather than migration. The methodological observations that follow are all based on work done with sedentary populations. There is no guarantee that the same methods would be feasible in an essentially migratory region, such as the aboriginal Plains of North America, or pre-European Polynesia; they perhaps require modification even for English-speaking North America, because of the relative recency of occupation of much of the continent.

56.3. Inferences in Sedentary Areas. The first question that the dialect geographer must ask about any isogloss is the following: Is this isogloss currently migrating, or is it temporarily fixed? If it is migrating, in which direction?

An isogloss, or a bundle of isoglosses, which runs along some obvious barrier to intercommunication can normally be assumed to be temporarily fixed. The usage or usages involved have spread from centers somewhere, passing from speaker to speaker and from village to village until they encountered the barrier, where they stopped. The barrier may be a natural one, like a mountain range or a broad river, or—apparently more important—it may be political.

Conversely, if an isogloss does not coincide at least roughly with some communicative barrier, then one can surmise that diffusion is currently going on. But this conclusion is not nearly so sure as the first, and supplementary evidence is needed. One obvious way of finding out is to make a resurvey of the usages involved after some interval, say a decade. A comparison of the earlier and later distributions at least shows any migration of the isogloss that has occurred in the intervening years, and this is sometimes enough to extrapolate the most probable direction of earlier diffusion and the most likely direction for the future. The original German atlas was based on data gathered in the 1870's and 1880's: Figure 56.3 shows a few of the results. A resurvey of a few crucial items in the 1930's showed that some of the isoglosses of the great east-to-west bundle have moved further north in certain localities, whereas virtually none have moved southwards. This confirms what most specialists in German have believed for a long time: that High German usages have been spreading northwards for many centuries.

Apart from resurveying, deductions as to direction of motion can sometimes be based on the relative location of isoglosses and of likely centers of prestige, such as politically or culturally important cities. Let us suppose that we find, on one side of an isogloss, a probable center of prestige influence, and that on closer examination we find that the first isogloss is but one of a number which run more or less concentrically about the same center. The dialect atlas of New England shows a number focussing on Boston in just this way. One of them marks the

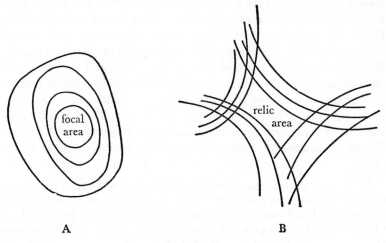

A   B

FIGURE 56.5

limits of the region in which *tonic* is the usual term for fruit-flavored carbonated soft-drinks, and historical research has revealed that a Boston soft-drink company used this term, for many years, in the trade name of its products. A region bounded by such a group of concentric isoglosses, and enclosing a center of probable prestige, is called a *focal area*. We cannot be sure that the isoglosses around a focal area are continuing their spread outwards, but we can be reasonably sure that the earlier motion was from the focus.

Sometimes we find, in a sense, the converse of a focal area: a region containing no obvious center like Boston, and surrounded, not by more or less concentric isoglosses, but by segments of various isoglosses that point to diverse centers elsewhere. The difference is shown in a highly idealized way in Figure 56.5, which greatly exaggerates the ease with which one can distinguish between a focal area and a so-called *relic area.* In the relic area situation, we surmise that usages outside the area are crowding in on it, and that, barring political or cultural upsets, they will continue their encroachment.

Thus isoglosses make immediate sense if they run along some clear barrier to intercommunication, or if they point to a focal center, or both. There remain many isoglosses which do not make sense in either of these obvious ways and which require more searching study. The most fruitful direction for deeper exploration of these has proved to be the earlier political and cultural state of affairs in the region involved. Cities and towns rise and fall as centers of prestige, and political boundaries, if not natural ones, are moved about by wars and treaties. All these changes are reflected in dialect distribution, but usually with some delay. An isogloss that cannot be understood in terms of the current political scene may therefore mirror an earlier one. There are many examples of this in the German-Dutch area. The following presentation is rephrased from Bloomfield; the map referred to is our Figure 56.3, showing isoglosses, it will be remembered, as of the 1880's:

Some forty kilometers east of the Rhine the isoglosses of the great bundle that separates Low German and High German begin to separate and spread out northwestward and southwestward, so as to form what has been called the "Rhenish fan."[1] The isogloss of northern [k] versus southern [x] in the word 'make' crosses the Rhine just north of the town of Benrath . . .. It is found, now, that this line corresponds roughly to an ancient northern boundary of the territorial domains of Berg (east of the Rhine) and Jülich (west of the Rhine). The isogloss of northern [k] versus southern [x] in the word 'I' swerves off north-westward, crossing the Rhine just north of the village of Ürdingen. The Ürdingen line corresponds closely to the northern boundaries of the pre-Napoleonic Duchies, abolished in 1789, of Jülich and Berg—the states whose earlier limit is reflected in the Benrath line—and of the Electorate of Cologne. Just north of Ürdingen, the town of Kaldenhausen is split by the Ürdingen line into a western section which uses [x] and an eastern which uses [k] in 'I': we learn that up to 1789 the western part of the town belonged to the (Catholic) Electorate of Cologne, and the east part to the (Protestant) County of Mörs. Our map shows also two isoglosses branching southwestward. One is the line between northern [p] and southern [f] in the word 'village'; this line agrees roughly with the southern boundaries in 1789 of Jülich, Cologne, and Berg, as against the Elec-

---

[1] From pages 343f of *Language*, by Leonard Bloomfield. By permission of Henry Holt and Company, Inc., Copyright 1933.

torate of Treves. In a still more southerly direction there branches off the iso-gloss between northern [t] and southern [s] in the word 'that,' and this line, again, corresponds with the old southern boundary of the Electorate and Archbishopric of Treves.

It is clear that in areas for which we have no documentary information about the location of earlier political boundaries, at least some tentative inferences about them can be drawn from the materials of dialect geography. But we must also be careful not to read too much into the word "political" in this context: the cultural, as against the natural, factors which establish barriers to communication, in parts of the world other than Western Europe, may not be of the sort to which the common-vocabulary term "political" would readily apply.

56.4. Conclusion. Dialect geography, as a technique for recon-structing past history, is obviously limited. It is at its best only under special conditions (long-settled sedentary population) and when used in conjunction with documentary evidence. Even then it can operate only on a relatively small scale of time and space.

It would be very wrong, because of these limitations, to scorn or dis-card dialect geography or to underestimate its value. Apart from the fact that more powerful techniques may be developed within this field at any time, the following points should be made.

In the first place, dialect geography leads to certain useful results that do not fall into what we would usually call history or prehistory. Since our discussion has been oriented in that direction, we have not had occasion to discuss these results. About a decade ago a searching study was made of the correlation between social structure and habits of pronunciation in South Carolina. This study revealed that so simple a matter as the use or non-use of retroflexion after vowels before con-sonants (e.g., *part* pronounced as /párt/ or as /pá˅t/) is a good index of certain social attitudes deriving from differences of class background.

In the second place, certain varieties of geographical survey— whether they would count, in traditional terms, as "dialect geography" is here irrelevant—can be of great value in revealing just what his-torical problems there are in a region, even if other methods then have to be brought to bear in seeking the solutions. There are regions of Mexico and Central America where we have only spotty information about the aboriginal languages. We know, let us say, that all the local dialects of a given region are ultimately related, but do not know which of them belong to one language and which to another—if, indeed, there are any major lines of cleavage. A fairly simple survey would give us part of the answer to this. We could then make an intelligent selection of key villages for more intensive gathering of materials, looking towards an application of the comparative method.

In the third place, a problem is not necessarily trivial simply because it is limited in time and space. Many scholars are intensely interested in the details of recent history in this or that locality, and to this dialect geography can often make a contribution. Furthermore, detailed recent local history helps us to understand the *kinds* of things that occur on such a small scale elsewhere, and at earlier times. Dialect geography has the virtues of concreteness and specificity; sweeping generalizations not based on concrete small-scale facts are bootless. It is along this last line that dialect geography has, so far, made its greatest contribution.

NOTES

New terms: *dialect atlas; isogloss, bundle of isoglosses; dialect area;* "proto-territory"—that is, the geographical region inhabited by the speakers of the parent language of some group of related languages; *focal area* and *relic area; parallelism* in cultural or linguistic developments.

Bloomfield's discussion (1933, chapters 18, 19) highlights the history of dialect-geographical and comparative methods. Pop 1950 is a very full survey, with bibliography, of dialect geography throughout the world. Wallace 1945 completely demolishes the simple form of the age-area hypothesis. The first valid inference from geographical distribution described in §56.2 has been formulated (not in print) by Isidore Dyen. Our examples of American dialect distributions are taken largely from Kurath 1949. The cultural significance of postvocalic /r/ in South Carolina: McDavid 1948. The Middle English study via documents of known provenience: Meech and Whitehall 1935. The U. S. survey by counties: unpublished materials of C. K. Thomas.

Problem: Gleason, *Workbook* (1955b), pp. 77–79.

57.

THE COMPARATIVE METHOD

57.1. The comparative method is by far the most powerful of our techniques in linguistic prehistory. It is applicable when we are faced with two or more clearly distinct languages which are nevertheless related, or look as though they might be. If the relationship is not certain, application of the method can sometimes render it so. If we are comparing more than two languages, then the method is sometimes able to show us not only what their common ancestor was like (and, thus, something of the separate prehistory of each of the languages, back as far as the time of the common ancestor), but also in what ways their degrees of relationship differ—say, that languages A and B are closer to each other than either is to language C.

Distinct but related languages are, as we have emphasized, merely the later continuations of what were at some earlier time dialects of a single language. On the other hand, the fact that a language at a given stage in its history has a good deal of dialect variation in no way guarantees that the different dialects are destined to diverge until eventually they are separate languages; nor does diversity of *dialects* at a given stage necessarily imply that at some earlier time the language was more uniform. English has dialects now; it has had dialects as far back as we can trace things—certainly since before the migration of the Angles, Saxons, and Jutes from the continent. While it is true that a uniform dialect may become differentiated, as when some of its speakers migrate and others stay at home, it is not by any means true that this is the only way in which dialect differentiation can have come about— it may not have "come about" at all, but simply have *been*, for an indefinitely long period in the past history of the language. And while

485

divergent dialects can grow into distinct languages, given enough separation and enough time, they do not have to: if their speakers maintain just the right amount of direct and indirect contact, the degree of differentiation may become neither greater nor less for an indefinitely long time.

In the face of these facts, when we wish to employ the comparative method we are forced to make a potentially false working assumption: that the distinct languages which we are comparing trace back not merely to a single parent language, but to a single language *free from dialect variation*. We shall see shortly why this assumption has to be made. It is not exactly a contrary-to-fact assumption, because in some instances it may actually be true. But we can hardly ever know whether it is true or not, so that it is a source of unavoidable uncertainty. The comparatist does not stop work because of this, but he has to remember at all times the potentially misleading nature of his working assumption.

Whenever we compare two forms of speech—two dialects of a single language, two related languages, or even any two languages chosen at random—we encounter some words which are similar in sound and in meaning. This double similarity may be due to (a) accident (German *nass* 'wet' : Zuni *nas* 'wet'), (b) borrowing, from one form of speech into the other or into both from some third (German and English *rouge*, both from French), or (c) direct inheritance in both forms of speech from an earlier form of speech which was the common ancestor of the two. In the third case, we call the words *cognates*.

In the comparative method, we work first and foremost with cognates. Often, at the outset, we cannot be sure whether certain sets of words are cognates or not; the procedures of the comparative method help us to decide. But if we try to apply the method not to distinct languages but merely to dialects of a single language, we find ourselves in trouble. In the case of distinct languages, at least some similarities due to borrowing are easily eliminated: English *Weltanschauung* is obviously a loan from German, and German *Motorpool* equally obviously a loan from English. In the case of dialects of a single language, the sorting out of cognates from loans or accidental resemblances is exceedingly difficult: should we compare New England /kóʳs/ with Middle Western /kórs/ or /kós/? When the answers to such questions are obtainable, they are obtained through the methods of dialect geography, not through the comparative method. And when we remember that a

EXAMPLE   487

group of related dialects need by no means be descendants of an earlier more homogeneous form of speech, we see that the logical basis for the contrast between cognates and loans is lacking—the distinction simply cannot be made. This is why the comparative method is applicable only to distinct languages.

57.2. Example. For our example of the comparative method we shall turn to the oldest attested stages of the Germanic languages: OE, *Old Icelandic* = OI, *Old Saxon* = OS, *Old High German* = OHG, and *Gothic* = G.[1]

The relationship of these languages is obvious on casual inspection: they have closely similar grammatical cores, somewhat similar phonemic systems, and—most important—hundreds of shared items of vocabulary. The only possible conclusion is that they are divergent forms of an earlier single language: this parent language we call *Proto-Germanic*. The comparative method cannot tell us where, when, or by whom this language was spoken, but it can tell us many structural facts about the language, and we can rest assured that it was indeed spoken somewhere, at some time, by someone.

Let us begin with a single shared item of vocabulary:

	G	OI	OE	OS	OHG
(1)	/físks/	/fískr/	/físk/	/físk/	/físk/
	'fish'				

Each of these is in the nominative singular, an inflectional category shared by all the languages. Their resemblance in sound and meaning is obvious, but does not in isolation prove anything. Perhaps it would be too much of a coincidence for the resemblances to be accidental, but they could easily be due to borrowing.

To test this, we look for *recurring correspondences*. Thus, each of the five words for 'fish' begins with /f/, so that the correspondence can be represented in phonemic terms as /f- f- f- f- f-/: here, and later, we put the symbols down in the same order in which the forms from the five different languages were cited in (1) above—that is, first G, then OI, then OE, then OS, and finally OHG. Since in each of the languages the respective /f/ phonemes, initially before a stressed vowel, were pho-

[1] The provenience and dates for all of these are given in the *Appendix of Language Names*, under INDO-HITTITE.

netically voiceless labial spirants, we can represent the correspondence phonetically as [f- f- f- f- f-].

Now this correspondence recurs in a good many other instances:

	G	OI	OE	OS	OHG
(2)	/fádar/	/fáθir/	/fǽder/	/fáder/	/fáter/
	[fáðar]	[fáðir]			
	'father'				
(3)	/fáran/	/fára/	/fóran/	/fáran/	/fáran/
	'to go'				
(4)	/fó·tus/	/fó·tr/	/fó·t/	/fó·t/	/fú·ş/
	'foot'				
(5)	/féhu/	/fé·/	/fóx/	/féhu/	/féhu/
	'cattle'				
(6)	/fló·dus/	/fló·θ/	/fló·d/	/fló·d/	/flú·t/
	[flo·ðus]	[flo·ð]			
	'flood, stream'				

In the above, and in all further examples, we transcribe phonetically as well as phonemically whenever there are allophonic facts of special relevance—as, for example, in the above, the fact that G /d/ between vowels, and OI /θ/ between vowels, were phonetically voiced spirants. The OHG /ş/ was some sort of spirant distinct from /s/, but no one knows just what it was phonetically.

In the original set, (1), the second correspondence can be symbolized phonemically as /í í í í í/, and phonetically as [í í í í í]. This correspondence, again, recurs in many other sets:

(7)	/bídjan/	/bíθja/	/bíddan/	/bíddian/	/bítten/
	[bíðjan]	[biðja]			
	'to pray, beg, entrust'				
(8)	/wítan/	/víta/	/wítan/	/wítan/	/wíşşan/
	'to know'				

Also, in (1), we have the correspondence /s s s s s/, phonetically [s s s s s]; in this phonetic shape it recurs in, for example:

(9)	/sé·tun/	/sá·to/	/sǽ·ton/	/sá·tun/	/sá·şşun/
	'they sat'				

EXAMPLE 489

	G	OI	OE	OS	OHG
(10)	/séˇan/	/sá·/	/sɔ́·wan/	/sá·ian/	/sá·en/
	'to sow'				
(11)	/stílan/	/stéla/	/stélan/	/stélan/	/stélan/
	'to steal'				
(12)	/skí·nan/	/skí·na/	/sk̲í·nan/	/ski·nan/	/skɪ·nan/
	'to shine'				

In some of this last group, the [s s s s s] correspondence turns up in a distinctly different environment (e.g., initially before a stressed vowel), but in (12), as in (1), it is followed by the next correspondence that concerns us: /k k k̬ k k/, phonetically [k k k̬ k k]:

	G	OI	OE	OS	OHG
(13)	/kóˇs/	/káws/	/k̬á·s/	/kóˇs/	/kó·s/
	'I, he chose'				
(14)	/kíwsan/	/kjó·sa/	/k̬ó·san/	/kíwsan/	/kíwsan/
	'to choose'				

For OE, OS, and OHG, this is as far as we can go, since in those languages the words involved in (1) consist of just four successive segmental phonemes. The G and OI forms are longer, and we can find other sets in which the correspondence /-s -r — — —/ (phonetically [-s -r — — —]) turns up—the dashes meaning "zero." One example is (4), and note the following:

	G	OI	OE	OS	OHG
(15)	/hárdus/	/hárθr/ [harðr]	/hárd/	/hárd/	/hárt/
	'hard'				
(16)	/húnds/	/húndr/	/húnd/	/húnd/	/húnt/
	'dog'				
(17)	/líwfs/	/ljú·fr/ [ljú·vr]	/lɔ́·f/	/líwf/	/líwb/
	'dear'				
(18)	/lángs/	/lángr/	/lóng/	/láng/	/láng/
	'long'				
(19)	/róˇθs/	/ráwθr/ [rawðr]	/rá·d/	/ró·d/	/ró·t̥/
	'red'				

These examples are either masculine nouns, or the masculine forms of adjectives, in the nominative singular: G had an ending /-s/ for this inflection; OI an ending /-r/; the other three languages, usually no ending at all.

We see, thus, that the successive correspondences in the words of set (1) all recur in many other sets of words. The great regularity with which the correspondences recur renders it very unlikely that the resemblances—in set (1) or in any of the other sets—are due to borrowing. When we find a family of words that have spread, via borrowing, through several languages, we usually find that the differences of phonetic shape are relatively haphazard; but in the words we have examined they are not haphazard at all. The conclusion is that the five words of set (1) are indeed cognates: that is, that there was a single word in Proto-Germanic, which by direct tradition in the five separate languages has come down in just the shapes listed in (1). Not only do we reach this conclusion; we also venture to reconstruct first the allophonic shape, and eventually the phonemic shape, which the word had in the parent language, as follows:

The parental word began with a consonant sound which has been inherited in each of the daughter languages as [f-]. The phonetic testimony of the five languages is in agreement. It is customary to assume that if all of a set of related languages share a feature, that feature was present in the parent language. Consequently, we assume that the Proto-Germanic word for 'fish' began with [f-].

The parental word continued with a stressed vowel which has been inherited in the daughter languages as [í í í í í]. By the principle asserted just above, we assume that the second sound in the parental word was something like [í].

In the same way, we posit parental [s] on the basis of the correspondence [s s s s s].

The fourth correspondence in the word makes more trouble, since the languages do not agree. Four of them have a voiceless dorsal stop. But OE has a fronted dorso-velar stop, which, as we know from §44.2, contrasted in OE with a similar stop pronounced at a more retracted position of articulation (OE /k/). Now we also find instances of a recurring correspondence /k k k k k/, phonetically [k k k k k], as in,

	G	OI	OE	OS	OHG
(20)	/kníw/	/kné·/	/knɔ́·/	/kníw/	/kníw/
	'knee'				

—and it is obviously for this correspondence that we should reserve a posited parental [k]. So, tentatively, we assume a separate parental [ḳ] for the fourth correspondence in 'fish.'

The problems at the ends of the G and the OI words are too intricate for us to discuss. So far we have justified a reconstructed phonetic shape beginning with *[físḳ-] for the parental word for 'fish'; the reasoning about the end of the word, which we omit, finishes this as *[físḳaz] or *[físḳoz]. The asterisk at the beginning of these transcriptions has nothing to do with the phonetic notation, but is simply a warning: it tells us that the form being transcribed has not been directly observed nor found in some document, but only inferred indirectly. It is the custom in historical linguistics to mark any indirectly inferred form in this way.

57.3. Phonetic Similarity versus Regularity of Correspondence.
The five daughter words for 'fish' which we examined above are very similar phonetically, and this may tend to conceal one essential point of the comparative method. In searching for genuine cognates, it is *not* close phonetic similarity that counts, but rather *regularity of correspondence*. To underscore this, consider the stressed syllable nuclei in the following set:

G	OI	OE	OS	OHG
(21) /hévtan/	/héjta/	/hó·tan/	/hévtan/	/héjşşan/
'to name, call'				

We see, in the correspondence /év éj ó· év éj/, a great deal of diversity from one language to another—in particular, the OE /ó·/ seems quite divergent. But for this correspondence, also, one can find many examples:

(22) /hévls/	/héjll/	/hó·l/	/hévl/	/héjl/
'whole, sound'				
(23) /évns/	/éjnn/	/ó·n/	/évn/	/éjn/
'one'				
(24) /stévg/	/stéjg/	/stó·x/	/stévx/	/stéjg/
[stévx]				
'he ascended'				
(25) /stévns/	/stéjnn/	/stó·n/	/stévn/	/stéjn/
'stone'				

The regularity of recurrence assures us in this case, just as much as in a case where there is less phonetic variety, that the words are cognates:

that the prototype word in the parent language had some sort of stressed syllabic which has been inherited in the various daughter languages in just the shapes we find. True enough, it is much harder to decide in this instance just what the parental sound may have been. Early in our work, we would probably settle for some arbitrary symbol, which would not be assigned any phonetic value but would merely represent the correspondence. Thus one might represent the prototype word for (21) as *[hÁtana], where "Á" is not a phonetic symbol but shorthand for the correspondence /éᵛ éj ó· éᵛ éj/. But arbitrary symbols of this sort are temporary props, to be eliminated as soon as evidence is accumulated pointing to the actual phonetic shape in the parent language. In the present instance, after a great deal of work, Germanicists have come to the conclusion that our "Á" was something like [áj] or [ój]. Consequently, we reconstruct the word 'to name, call' as *[hájtana] or *[hójtɔnɔ].

NOTES

New terms: *cognates; correspondence, recurring* correspondences, *regularity* of correspondence. Note also the use of the asterisk, described at the end of §57.2. In this book we restrict the asterisk to forms reconstructed for a proto- or pre-language; in some circles it is customary to mark even a non-occurrent form of an attested stage of a language (say, English *She like potatoes*) in this way.

Our interpretations of the old Germanic languages are based largely on the standard manuals; Moulton 1954 lists most of them. The reanalysis of Moulton 1954 has been largely worked into our approach in this and the next section.

Problem. The actual historical relationship of two languages is not always apparent from casual inspection, but sometimes it is. Gleason, *Workbook* (1955b), page 86, lists the words with twenty-five different meanings from each of six unidentified languages. It is good experience to examine these and venture guesses as to which of the six languages are most probably related, which less probably.

58·

RECONSTRUCTING PHONEMICS

58.1. Our notation *[fiskɔz] for Proto-Germanic 'fish' is at the moment only in rough phonetic or allophonic form. We are sure that the parental word began with something like [f], but we do not know what Proto-Germanic phoneme that [f] represented, nor what other allophones the same phoneme may have had, nor where else, besides initially before a stressed vowel, the same phoneme may have occurred. The OE /f/, as in /fisk/, had also a voiced variant between vowels, as in /néfa/ [néva] 'nephew'; the G /f/, on the other hand, seems to have been voiceless in all positions—e.g., medially in /háfjan/ 'to raise.' Was Proto-Germanic like OE, or like G, or perhaps different from both?

In other words, our task of reconstructing the *phonemic* system of the parent language has only begun. To complete it, there are two other sorts of operations which must be performed, comparable in general to the operations we perform in determining the phonemic system of a language observed by direct contact (§12), but necessarily differing in details:

(1) We must tabulate all the sounds which stood in contrast with each other in any given position: e.g., all the single consonants which occurred in the parent language initially before a stressed vowel. When we remember that the elements of a phonemic system can ultimately be defined *only* in terms of contrast (§2.5), it is easy to see why this step is necessary.

(2) We must compare the elements which stood in contrast in any

493

one position with those which contrasted in each other position, in order to decide which element in each position belonged to the same phoneme as which element in other positions.

58.2. Pretonic Consonants in Proto-Germanic. To illustrate the first of the steps described above, we shall concentrate on the position directly before a stressed vowel ("pretonic" position).

To tabulate the sounds which contrasted in this position in the parent language, we first list all the correspondences in that position, and then check to see whether some sets of two or more of these correspondences might not reflect one and the same parental sound, the multiplicity of correspondence being due to special changes in one or another of the daughter languages.

The Germanic correspondences which we find in pretonic position are listed below. Each is supplied with a number preceded by "C"; to the right, we refer to word-sets, in the preceding section and this, which illustrate the correspondence in question. Each correspondence is given phonemically, and then also phonetically if the phonetics are not obvious:

(C1)	/p- p- p- p- pf-/	(26, 27)
(C2)	/t- t- t- t- tš-/	(28)
(C3)	/k- k- ḳ- k- k-/	(13, 14)
(C4)	/k- k- k̂- k- k-/	(29)
(C5)	/b- b- b- b- b-/	(7)
	(OHG /b-/ may have been voiceless unaspirated rather than voiced)	
(C6)	/d- d- d- d- t-/	(30)
(C7)	/g- g- ĝ- x- g-/ [g- g- γ̂- γ- g-]	(31, 32)
(C8)	/g- g- g- x- g-/ [g- g- g- γ- g-]	(33)
	(OE initial /g-/ may possibly have been spirantal, or have varied freely between voiced spirant and voiced stop)	
(C9)	/f- f- f- f- f-/	(1, 2, 3, 4, 5)
(C10)	/θ- θ- θ- θ- d-/	(34)
(C11)	/s- s- s- s- s-/	(9, 10)
(C12)	/h- h- h- h- h-/	(15, 16, 21, 22)
(C13)	/m- m- m- m- m-/	(35, 36)
(C14)	/n- n- n- n- n-/	(37, 38)
(C15)	/l- l- l- l- l-/	(17, 18)

(C16) /r- r- r- r- r-/   (19)
(C17) /w- v- w- w- w-/   (8, 39)
(C18) /w- — w- w- w-/   (40, 41)
(C19) /j- — ĝ- j- j-/ [j- — ĵ- j- j-]   (42)
    (OE /ĝ-/ may have been phonetically quite like G, OS, and
    OHG /j-/. The dash represents "no consonant at all.")
(C20) /— — — — —/   (23, 43).

The additional examples we need are:

	G	OI	OE	OS	OHG
(26)	/pévda/ [pévða] 'cloak'	—	/pó·d/	/pévda/	/pféjt/
(27)	'penny'	/pénningr/	/péning/	—	/pfénning/
(28)	/túngo·/ 'tongue'	/túnga/	/túnge/	/túnga/	/tʂúnga/
(29)	/kórn/ 'grain'	/kórn/	/kórn/	/kórn/	/kórn/
(30)	/dóhtar/ 'daughter'	/dó·ttar/	/dóxtor/	/dóxtor/	/tóxter/
(31)	/gíban/ [gívan] 'to give'	/géfa/ [géva]	/ĝifan/ [ĵívan]	/xéfan/ [ɣévan]	/géban/
(32)	/gáf/ [gáv] 'I, he gave'	/gáf/	/ĝáf/ [ĵáf]	/xáf/ [ɣáf]	/gáb/
(33)	/gó·θs/ 'good'	/gó·θr/ [gó·ðr]	/gó·d/	/xó·d/ [ɣo·d]	/gúvt/
(34)	/θáta/ 'that, the'	/θát/	/θǽt/	/θát/	/dáʂ/
(35)	— 'mouse'	/mú·s/	/mú·s/	/mú·s/	/mú·s/
(36)	/múnθs/ 'mouth'	—	/mú·θ/	—	/múnd/
(37)	/nímiθ/ 'he takes'	—	/nímeθ/	/nímid/	/nímit/

	G	OI	OE	OS	OHG
(38)	/nám/	/nám/	/nóm/	/nám/	/nám/
	'I, he took'				
(39)	/wérθan/	/vérθa/	/wórθan/	/werθan/	/wérdan/
		[verða]	[wórðan]	[wérðan]	
	'to become'				
(40)	/wórθun/	/úrθo/	/wúrdon/	/wúrdun/	/wúrtun/
		[úrðo]			
	'they became'				
(41)	/wúlfs/	/úlfr/	/wúlf/	/wúlf/	/wólf/
		[úlvr]			
	'wolf'				
(42)	/júngs/	/úngr/	/ǧúng/	/júng/	/júng/
	'young'		[ɣ́úŋg]		
(43)	/óˇgoˇ/	/áwga/	/áˑge/	/óˇxa/	/ówga/
	[óˇɣoˑ]	[áwɣa]	[áˑɣ́e]	[óˇɣa]	
	'eye'				

Of the twenty correspondences listed and illustrated, ten are of the simple sort for which all the languages are phonetically in agreement or nearly so. Accordingly, we reconstruct as follows:

for	Proto-Gmc.	for	Proto-Gmc.
C4	[k]	C13	[m]
C5	[b]	C14	[n]
C9	[f]	C15	[l]
C11	[s]	C16	[r]
C12	[h]	C20	(zero).

In C1, C2, C6, and C10, all the languages agree except OHG. The policy in such a case is to try to follow the majority rule. This policy, like that of assuming that the parent language had any feature which is common to all the daughter languages, is only a working principle: in some instances other evidence eventually shows that a conclusion based on the simple working principle is wrong. In the present cases, however, no such conflicting evidence turns up, and we accordingly reconstruct as follows:

for	Proto-Gmc.	for	Proto-Gmc.
C1	[p]	C6	[d]
C2	[t]	C10	[θ].

Correspondences C17 and C18 are identical save in OI, which shows /v/ in C17 but zero in C18. For both, all the other languages agree in having /w/. As a first step, we could arbitrarily reconstruct with [w₁] for C17 and [w₂] for C18: our notation means that both correspondences point to some sort of [w]-like sound, but that the twofold reflex in OI has to be accounted for: whatever the phonetic difference between Proto-Gmc [w₁] and [w₂] may have been, it is possible that the two were in contrast, and that in all the languages save OI the contrast has been lost.

The next step is to examine the distribution of [w₁] and [w₂], both in Proto-Germanic (when we have reconstructed enough different proto-type words to make this possible) and in the OI reflexes. We soon discover that [w₁], kept in OI as /v-/, appears only before unrounded vowels in OI, which presumably trace back to unrounded vowels in the parent language, while [w₂], lost in OI, appears only in words where OI has a rounded vowel, presumably tracing back to a rounded vowel in the parent language. That is, the distinction between [w₁] and [w₂] need not be ascribed to the parent language: it can be accounted for realistically within the separate history of OI. Consequently, we put the two correspondences together, and reconstruct both with a parental [w]:

for   Proto-Gmc.
C17, C18   [w].

We have already examined correspondence C4, but let us now take it up again, in connection with C3. These two correspondences, once again, differ only in one language—OE, which has /ḵ/ for C3 but /k/ for C4. As in the case just discussed, we would at first posit two different parental sounds, in contrast initially: say [k₁] and [k₂], or, since the OE situation affords a clue, [ḵ] for C3 and [k] for C4. The details of the argument about these two are much more intricate than those for correspondences C17 and C18, but in due time a comparable conclusion is reached. That is, we need not posit more than one parental allophone, [k], explaining the split of this into OE /ḵ/ and /k/ within the separate history of English. Roughly speaking, the parental [k] was fronted to [ḵ] at some time between Proto-Germanic and historic OE, before vowels which were, at the time, front; but was kept as a back dorso-velar [k] in other environments. (It was fronted always after [s], regardless of what vowel followed, but this position is not the one here under consideration.) The vowels which brought about the fronting of parental [k] had not all been front vowels in Proto-Germanic, and by historic OE times some of them were once again not front vowels; but the history of the OE vowel system is such as to render realistic the assumed intervening stage when the distribution was as we have stated above. It will be remembered that in §55.3 we showed, in part, how internal reconstruction applied to OE suggests that /k/ and /$\underset{\wedge}{k}$/ had earlier been only allophones of a single phoneme; the evidence we get from the comparative method supports that deduction.

Consequently, we put C3 and C4 together:

> for   Proto-Gmc.
> C3, C4   [k].

This also revises our prototype for 'fish' from *[fískɔz] to *[fískɔz].

We are now left with correspondences C7, C8, and C19. All the languages except OE show the same initial consonant for C7 and C8, though OS has a spirant where the other three show a stop. C7 and C19 are the same in OE, but are distinguished in the other four languages. It turns out that we can safely posit just two parental consonants, [g] for C7 and C8, and [j] for C19. The split of parental [g] in OE into /g/ and /$\hat{g}$/ is parallel to the pre-OE split of parental [k] into /k/ and /$\underset{\wedge}{k}$/, with one difference: the more fronted allophone of parental [g] in time fell together with the pre-OE reflex of parental [j]. Consequently, we assert:

> for   Proto-Gmc.
> C7, C8   [g]
> C19   [j].

It should be added that we cannot be entirely sure about the phonetic nature of the parental [g]. We have used a stop symbol, but the OS evidence, and what happened to the more fronted allophone in OE, suggest that it may instead have been a voiced spirant.

Tabulating the results, we find the following single consonants in contrast in Proto-Germanic in the position directly before a stressed vowel. In the table, we enclose the symbols in slant lines, since all the sounds were phonemically distinct in that they contrasted in this particular position. The phonetic descriptions, however, specify only what the consonant phonemes were like in this position; we do not yet know where else any of them occurred, nor what allophones they had in other positions:

voiceless stops: /p/ /t/ /k/
voiced stops: /b/ /d/
voiced stop or spirant? /g/
voiceless spirants: /f/ /θ/ /s/
aspiration: /h/
liquids: /l/, /r/
nasals: /m/ /n/
semivowels: /w/ /j/.

In addition to this sixteen-way contrast among single consonants, the pretonic position also allowed the occurrence of no consonant at all (correspondence C20), and of any of a number of consonant clusters. The sets of cognates we have cited do not suffice for reconstructing all the clusters, but (11), (24), and (25) certainly point to a parental /st-/, (12) to /sk-/, and (20) to /kn-/.

58.3. Intervocalic Consonants in Proto-Germanic. In order to illustrate the second of the two operations described in §58.1, we must tabulate the contrasts in some second position in the parent language. We choose for this second position that after a stressed vowel (or with an intervening /r/ or /l/) and before an unstressed vowel. We shall not repeat in detail the lines of reasoning by which the contrasts in this position in the parent language are determined, since the methods involved are exactly the same as those presented in §58.2. Instead, we shall merely list the results, confining ourselves, furthermore, to stops and spirants.

Eleven correspondences suffice for the present discussion (omitting some complications, particularly in OE, that can be explained within the separate histories of the daughter languages):

(C21) /-p- -p- -p- -p- -ff-/ (44)
(C22) /-t- -t- -t- -t- -ss-/ (8, 9, 21)
(C23) /-k- -k- -k- -k- -xx-/ (45)
(C24) /-f- -f- -f- -f- -f-/ [f v v v f] (46)
(C25) /-θ- -θ- -θ- -θ- -d-/ [θ ð ð ð d] (39)
(C26) /-h- —— — -h- -h-/ (5)

(In OE and OI the intervocalic [h] drops, its effects usually showing in some modification of the preceding vowel.)

(C27)	/-b- -f- -f- -f- -b-/	[v v v v b]		(31)
(C28)	/-d- -θ- -d- -d- -t-	[ð ð d d t]		(2, 15, 26)
(C29)	/-g- -g- -x- -x- -g-/	[γ γ γ γ g]		(43)
(C30)	/-s- -s- -s- -s- -s-/			(14)
(C31)	/-z- -r- -r- -r- -r-/			(47)

Additional examples:

	G	OI	OE	OS	OHG
(44)	/sle·pan/	—	/slǽ·pan/	/slá·pan/	/slá·ffan/
	'to sleep'				
(45)	/ga-lú·kan/	/lú·ka/	/lú·kan/	—	/lú·xxan/
	'to lock'				
(46)	—	/ņéfe/	/néfa/	/néfo/	/néfo/
		[néve]	[néva]	/névo/	
	'nephew'				
(47)	/méˇza/	/méjre/	/mǒ·ra/	/méˇro/	/mé·ro/
	'more'				

The medial stops and spirants which we reconstruct for Proto-Germanic on the basis of these correspondences are as follows:

for	Proto-Gmc.	for	Proto-Gmc.
C21	[p]	C27	[v]
C22	[t]	C28	[ð]
C23	[k]	C29	[γ]
C24	[f]	C30	[s]
C25	[θ]	C31	[z].
C26	[h] or [x]		

58.4. The Proto-Germanic Consonant Phonemes. There were, of course, more different phonetic environments for consonants in Proto-Germanic than the two we have discussed above; but it appears that no position other than the two dealt with allowed a greater number of contrasts than did these two. We can therefore proceed to set up the consonant phonemes of the parent language on the basis of the contrasts in just these two positions.

First we can set aside reconstructed /m n l r w j/: these occurred in various positions, but present no particular problems.

Pretonic [p- t- k-] and intervocalic [-p- -t- -k-] are obviously to be paired off as members of the same phonemes: /p t k/, always voiceless and always stops.

Pretonic [f- θ- s-] and intervocalic [-f- -θ- -s-] are likewise to be paired off: /f θ s/, always voiceless and always spirants.

There are no medial voiced stops to match the initial voiced stops [b- d-]; and there are no initial voiced spirants to match intervocalic [-v- -ð-]. The initial [g-] may have been a spirant rather than a stop, as indicated towards the end of §58.2; the medial [-γ-] was not matched by any initial voiced spirant unless [g-] was indeed also a spirant. In any case, it seems clear that we should assign pretonic [b- d- g-] and inter-vocalic [-v- -ð- -γ-] to a single set of three phonemes /b d g/, which were always voiced but were stops or spirants depending on environment. This is a realistic conclusion to reach: many languages which can be directly observed show the same sort of alternation—for example, modern Spanish.

The initial [h-] and the medial [-h-] or [-x-] can be assigned to a single phoneme if the medial sound was [-h-], but if it was [-x-] (and there is some evidence to suggest this), then one might hesitate to do so. We have to leave this matter unsettled. We shall use initial /h-/ and medial /-x-/ (the latter also in some other positions, such as final) in any further phonemic transcriptions of Proto-Germanic forms, but this choice of symbols is no guarantee that the conclusion it implies is correct.

The medial [-z-] is not matched by anything in initial position with which it can be grouped into a single phoneme. We have no recourse but to recognize /z/ as a separate phoneme, which never occurred directly before a stressed vowel.

Summarizing tabularly, we have, as the consonant phonemes of Proto-Germanic:

Voiceless stops:	/p/	/t/	/k/	
Voiceless spirants:	/f/	/θ/ /s/	/x/	(/h/)
Voiced stops/spirants:	/b/	/d/	/g/	
Voiced spirant:		/z/		
Nasals:	/m/	/n/		
Liquids:		/l/ /r/		
Semivowels:	/w/	/j/.		

To this we add, without discussion or proof, the reconstructed vowel system:

Vowel phonemes:

$$/i/ \qquad /u/$$
$$/e/ \qquad /ɔ/.$$

Complex nuclei:

/ij/	/iw/	
/ej/	/ew/	/eˠ/
/ɔj/	/ɔw/	/ɔˠ/
	/uw/,	

all of which occurred stressed, and many of which occurred also without stress.

NOTES

The step from allophonic to phonemic reconstruction is systematized by Hoenigswald 1950b. We write "ɔ" for the proto-Germanic vowel usually represented as "a," for the sake of symmetry; the phonetic implication (a more retracted and possibly rounded low vowel) may not be defensible.

Problems. Gleason, *Workbook* (1955b), p. 85.

Using Germanic cognate sets (1) through (48), in the preceding section and this, plus sets (49) through (80) below, reconstruct the initial consonant clusters before a stressed vowel of proto-Germanic.

	G	OI	OE	OS	OHG
(49)	—	/kvíkr/	/kwíku/	/kwík/	/kwék/
	'alive'				
(50)	—	—	/hní·xan/	/hní·xan/	/hní·gan/
	'to bend down'				
(51)	/bró·θar/	/bró·θer/	/bró·θor/	/bró·θar/	/brú·der/
	'brother'				
(52)	/brá·xta/	—	/bró·xte/	/brá·xta/	/brá·xta/
	'I brought'				
(53)	/blínds/	/blíndr/	/blínd/	/blínd/	/blínt/
	'blind'				
(54)	/kwíman/	—	—	—	/kwéman/
	'to come'				

	G	OI	OE	OS	OHG
(55)	/frákunθs/	—	/frókuθ/	—	—
	'despised'				
(56)	/drínkan/	—	/drínkan/	/drínkan/	/trínkan/
	'to drink'				
(57)	/skájdan/	—	/sḱá·dan/	/ské·dan/	/skéjdan/
	'to divide'				
(58)	—	/fróskr/	—	—	/frósk/
	'frog'				
(59)	—	/fróst/	—	/fróst/	/fróst/
	'frost'				
(60)	/fló·dus/	/fló·θ/	/fló·d/	—	/ˈflúᵛt/
	'flood, tide'				
(61)	/grás/	—	/grǽs/	/xrás/	/grás/
	'grass'				
(62)	/hlájfs/	—	/hló·f/	—	/hléjb/
	'bread, loaf'				
(63)	—	—	/sḱélx/	—	/skélx/
	'oblique'				
(64)	/stáθs/	/stáθr/	/stéde/	/stád/	/stát/
	'place'				
(65)	/swí·n/	/sví·n/	/swí·n/	/swí·n/	/swí·n/
	'pig'				
(66)	/θwérhs/	—	/θwɔ́rx/	—	—
	'perverse'				
(67)	/kwé·ns/	—	/kwé·n/	—	—
	'queen, wife'				
(68)	—	/hríngr/	/hríng/	/hríng/	/hríng/
	'ring'				
(69)	/wráka/	—	/wrɔ́ku/	—	—
	'revenge'				
(70)	—	/spínna/	/spínnan/	—	—
	'to spin'				
(71)	—	/smókkr/	/smókk/	—	—
	'smock'				
(72)	—	/stráwmr/	/strá·m/	/stró·m/	/stró·m/
	'stream'				

	G	OI	OE	OS	OHG
(73)	/tríggws/	/trýggr/	/(ĝe)trówe/	/tríwwi/	/(gi)tríwwi/
	'true'				
(74)	/twálif/	—	/twélf/	—	—
	'twelve'				
(75)	—	/θrí·r/	/θrí·/	/θrív/	/θrí·/
	'three'				
(76)	—	—	/dwéllan/	—	/twéllan/
	'to tarry'				
(77)	/snútrs/	/snótr/	/snóttor/	/snóttar/	/snóttar/
	'wise'				
(78)	/hwás/	—	/hwó·/	/hwé·/	/hwér/
	'who?'				
(79)	/kwíno/	—	/kwéne/	/kwéna/	—
	'woman, wife'				
(80)	/wlíts/	—	/wlíte/	/wlíti/	—
	'face'		'form, beauty'		

59.

RECONSTRUCTING
MORPHOPHONEMICS
and GRAMMAR

59.1. As we saw in the preceding two sections, the comparative method proceeds by finding sets of possible cognates, attempting the reconstruction of parental prototypes, and eventually achieving a portrayal—often with some holes—of the phonemic system of the parent language, of the phonemic shapes of the prototypes of the sets of cognates, and of the changes which have led from the forms of the parent speech to the forms in each of the daughter languages. The discovery of recurrent correspondences lends support to the hypothesis that the possible cognates are really such, and with sufficient regularity of recurrence we abandon all doubt. In the process, some of the sets with which we began usually fall by the wayside as spurious—that is, as accidental resemblances, as the result of borrowing, or as forms that would be exact cognates save for some analogical reshaping. One instance of the last appears in set 40 (§61.2): G /wórθun/ 'they became' is not the unaltered cognate of the forms in the other four languages, because the G form (if it had not somehow been reshaped) would have been /wórdun/. This deviation does not impair the value of the form for the purpose we were seeking when it was listed, but it must nevertheless be accounted for. A more striking example is the resemblance between the Germanic word which appears in English as *have* and in German as *haben*, and the Latin word *habēre* 'to have.' The Germanic and the Latin words are not cognates.

505

A general requirement of the comparative method is *realism*. This requirement applies in two ways. In the first place, the portrayal of the parent language which we achieve must make it look like a real language, of the sort with which we are familiar by direct contact or through documentary evidence. The phonemic system of Proto-Germanic, as we reconstructed it in §58.4, meets this requirement quite satisfactorily: the number of phonemes is reasonable, and the allophonic variation between stop and spirant postulated for /b d g/ is familiar from various directly known languages.

A more stringent form of this part of the requirement of realism is that the parent language should be reasonably similar to each of the daughter languages. If anything—measuring in a rough impressionistic way—the parent language should be expected to be somewhat more like each of its descendants than they are like each other. It is easy to see why: if the parent language is separated in time by n years from each of the descendants, then the descendants are, in effect, separated by $2n$ years from each other—since to get from one to another we must first go back to the common parent and then down to the other.

The other aspect of the requirement of realism is that the postulated prehistory of each of the separate languages, from the parental form down to the time of our observations or our documentary records, must involve only the kinds and mechanisms of phylogenetic change which we know to be operative in languages in general. We are not allowed to assume, let us say, that between Proto-Germanic and OE the phonemic system changed whimsically and at random, when between OE and NE—as in every other case known through written records—we know that phonemic systems have changed only as the result of certain specifiable mechanisms. *To forget this requirement is not just a minor error; it is to abandon the comparative method altogether.*

Although our knowledge of how phonemic systems change, and particularly of the nature of sound change, constitutes the mainstay of the comparative method, it is not necessary for us to stop with a reconstruction of the phonemic system of the parent language and of the phonological shapes of the prototype vocabulary. Under favorable conditions—that is, if the daughter languages are not too distantly related—we can go far beyond this. We can determine some of the details of morphophonemic alternation in the parent language; we can discern the major outlines of its grammatical system; we can even make some tentative inferences about the nonlinguistic habits of the speakers of the parent language. In the present section we shall illustrate the first two of these points; in the next, the third, together with some related matters.

59.2. Reconstructing Morphophonemic Alternations. Certain OE verbs showed a variation in the final stem consonant. Thus /sní·θan/ 'to cut' kept the stem-final /θ/ in most inflected forms, but had /d/ instead in the preterit plural /snídon/ 'we (ye, they) cut' and in the past participle /sníden/. Again, /ḳǿ·san/ 'to choose' had preterit plural and past participle /kúron/, /kóren/, with /r/ instead of /s/. A number of verbs shared each of these alternations, though the vast majority— including some with stem-final /θ/ and /s/—kept the same consonant in all inflected forms.

This is the sort of situation which tempts the historian to apply internal reconstruction if he can (§55). We want at least to guess that at some pre-English stage these alternating stems showed the same final consonant in all inflected forms, and that some sequence of sound change and resulting rephonemicizations had given rise to the OE irregularity. But this vague guess is about as far as the OE evidence can carry us.

And when we turn to the other Germanic languages, we soon discover that the postulated pre-English stage of regularity for these verb stems must have been also pre-Proto-Germanic, rather than some stage between Proto-Germanic and OE. For some of the same alternations appear in some of the other attested languages. The OHG equivalents of the OE verb forms cited above are, respectively, /sní·dan/ : /snítum/, /gisnítan/ and /kíwsan/ : /kúrum/, /gikóran/. In OHG we also find the second alternation in the verb /rí·san/ 'to rise,' with /rírum/ and /giríran/, though in OE this verb keeps the stem-final /s/ in all forms. OHG also attests to a third alternation of the same general sort: /tṣí·han/ 'to draw, accuse' : /tṣígum/, /gitṣígan/, showing /h/ in alternation with /g/. This has been obscured in OE by specifically pre-English changes: the corresponding forms are /tǿ·n/, /tíxon/, and /tíǧen/. These are exact cognates of the OHG forms: in pre-OE, intervocalic /x/ was lost after influencing the quality and quantity of the preceding stressed vowel, and the intervocalic /x/ and /ǧ/ of OE, like the intervocalic /g/ of OHG, are the regular reflexes of Proto-Germanic intervocalic /g/.

We must conclude that in Proto-Germanic all four of the verbs we
have illustrated, as well as some others for which there is comparable
evidence, showed an alternation:

*/tíjx-/	:	*/tíg-/ 'to drag, accuse'
*/ríjs-/	;	*/ríz-/ 'to rise'
*/kíws-/	:	*/kúz-/ 'to choose, test'
*/sníjθ-/	:	*/sníd-/ 'to cut.'

In each of the daughter languages, some of the verbs of this set have
been analogically regularized. This accounts for OE 'to rise,' where the
/s/ of most of the inflected forms has been analogically extended to the
preterit plural and the past participle, where /r/ would be expected.
The regularization went furthest in G, where seemingly no verbs show
the alternations: for the four we have used as examples, G shows
/gatí·han/ : /gatéhum/, /gatéhans/; /urrí·san/ : /urrísum/, /urrísans/;
/kíwsan/ : /kúsum/, /kúsans/; and /sni·θan/ : /sníθum/, /sníθans/—
with the commoner stem-final consonant in all cases replacing the
rarer one. Despite this constant tendency towards analogical regularization, a few traces of the Proto-Germanic alternation survive to this
day in English: *lose* but *for-lorn; seethe* but *sodden.*

We have thus reconstructed one pattern of irregular morphophonemic alternation for Proto-Germanic. Many other examples could
be added, but we do not need them for our purpose, which is simply to
show how the comparative method can achieve such results.

59.3. The Reconstruction of Grammatical Patterns. As an illustration of how grammatical features can be reconstructed, we shall
consider the distinctions of case in singular nouns in Germanic.

In OE, all nouns showed a nominative case, used when the noun was
the subject in a predication: /wúlf/ 'wolf,' /dǽĝ/ 'day,' /túnge/
'tongue.' This case was also the one used in direct address ("vocative"),
a point worth mentioning only because the situation was different in
some of the sister languages. For the vast majority of nouns, identically
the same form was used when the noun occurred as the object of a
verb, but to this there were a few exceptions: /túngan/ 'tongue' (as
object). Therefore it is necessary to speak of a separate accusative case.
Another form, usually distinct, was used when the noun was object of
certain prepositions, or occurred as the indirect object of a verb, or
expressed the instrument or agent of an action: this is traditionally

called the dative case (/wúlfe/, /dǽǧe/, /túngan/, in the third word identical with the accusative but in all instances distinct from the nominative). And there was a clearly distinct genitive case: /wúlfes/, /dǽǧes/, /túngan/. In personal pronouns the dative case of nouns was split two ways, into a so-called dative (/θǽ·m/ or /θɔ́·m/ 'that' neuter) and a so-called instrumental (/θý·/ or /θón/). But this greater differentiation in pronouns does not require us to speak of more than four cases for nouns (§30.6).

Between the earliest OE documents and those of several centuries later one can discern an increasing tendency to use the dative instead of the accusative for the object of a verb. One might want to extrapolate on the basis of this trend, and to guess that in pre-OE the accusative had perhaps more often had a form distinct from the nominative, and that the loss of distinctiveness was one of the factors leading to the use of the dative in its stead. This would be a highly tentative guess if based on OE alone; it is worthy of consideration only if we find support outside of OE.

Such support is forthcoming. In both G and OI the accusative is much more commonly distinct from the nominative: G /wúlfs/ 'wolf' nominative but /wúlf/ accusative, OI /hírθer/ 'shepherd' nominative but /hírθe/ accusative. With the traces of the distinction found in OE, OS, and OHG, it is clear that we must look for a full-fledged contrast in Proto-Germanic.

In G, the form of a noun used in direct address was often like the nominative, but in a few instances it was instead like the accusative: /wúlf/ 'Oh wolf!' like accusative /wúlf/, not like nominative /wúlfs/. We may therefore suspect that a separate vocative case may have to be recognized for Proto-Germanic.

In the earliest OHG documents we find for nouns a situation like that retained in some pronouns in OE: a form distinct from the ordinary dative case, for use to express agent or instrument. An example is dative /táge/, later /tága/ 'day,' versus instrumental /tágu/, later /tágo/. After the earliest period, one can observe in OHG an increasing disuse of the separate instrumental, the dative replacing it. Once again, one may be tempted to extrapolate, assuming both dative and instrumental for Proto-Germanic, with a trend, beginning perhaps even in Proto-Germanic times, to use the dative instead of the instrumental (or at least to destroy the formal differentiation). This trend would then have worked itself out to completion before the earliest records in most of the languages, but not quite completely in the case of OHG nouns, or in the case of pronouns in several of the languages.

We see, thus, evidence pointing towards a six-case system for singular nouns in Proto-Germanic: nominative, vocative, accusative, genitive, dative, and instrumental. But we also have to look at the actual shapes in the daughter languages, in order to see which of the inflectional endings representing these cases in the daughter languages may be cognates. Here is a table, showing typical masculine singular nouns in four of the daughter languages, but not always the same noun; the inflectional ending, when overt, is separated by a hyphen:

	G	OI	OE	OHG
Nom.	/wúlf-s/	/árm-r/	/wúlf/	/tag/
	'wolf'	'arm'	'wolf'	'day'
Voc.	/wúlf/	(= Nom.)	(= Nom.)	(= Nom.)
Acc.	/wúlf/	/árm/	/wúlf/	/tág/
Gen.	/wúlf-is/	/árm-s/	/wúlf-es/	/tág-es/
Dat.	/wúlf-a/	/árm-e/	/wúlf-e/	/tág-e/
Inst.	(= Dat.)	(= Dat.)	(= Dat.)	/tág-u/.

The working-out of correspondences in unstressed syllables is quite difficult in Germanic and the answers so far available are not certain. However, for the singular inflection of the largest class of masculine nouns, the Proto-Germanic endings seem to be reconstructable as follows:

Nom.	*/-ɔz/
Voc.	*/-e/ (or */-i/ or zero?)
Acc.	*/-ɔ/
Gen.	*/-esɔ/, */-ɔsɔ/
Dat.	*/-ɔj/
Inst.	*/-ɔᵛ/, /-ej/.

In the typical G pattern, all the endings listed above have been inherited with only regular sound change, except that the instrumental form has for the most part fallen into disuse. In the other languages, some forms which descriptively must be called datives are actually from the Proto-Germanic instrumental: the two cases have fallen together grammatically, but the form that represents the single coalesced case is sometimes the earlier instrumental instead of the earlier dative. The loss of the separate vocative, other than in G, is in part due to sound change (syncretism, §45.2), and probably in part due to the analogy of nouns where the vocative and nominative were already identical in shape.

The above is only a small sample of grammatical reconstruction. Specifically for Germanic, the data are such that we can achieve almost as thorough an understanding of the *morphological* system of Proto-Germanic as we have for any of its daughter languages. Syntax, in Germanic and elsewhere, is another matter. It is probably possible to achieve more syntactical reconstruction than anyone yet has, but the amount of labor involved is necessarily enormous, and even under the best possible conditions large gaps and uncertainties would remain.

60·

FURTHER RESULTS of the COMPARATIVE METHOD

60.1. Inverted Reconstruction. The discussion of §59.2 was intended to demonstrate how some patterns of morphophonemic alternation of a parent language can be reconstructed by the comparative method. In the course of the demonstration, a question was asked which has not yet been answered: whether the consonant-alternating verbs of OE might not reflect an earlier state of affairs in which the verbs in question did not show the alternation. All that we were able to discover on this point, via both the comparative method and internal reconstruction, was that the earlier state of regularity for these verbs must have antedated even Proto-Germanic.

The pattern of alternation in Proto-Germanic may now be described more fully. Not only in verbs, but in some other instances, there were morphemes which ended now in one consonant, now in another; the full set of alternations was as follows:

$$
\begin{array}{ccc}
/f/ & : & /b/ \quad [v] \\
/\theta/ & : & /d/ \quad [\eth] \\
/s/ & : & /z/ \\
/x/ & : & /g/ \quad [\gamma].
\end{array}
$$

In each case, the alternation was phonetically between voiceless and voiced spirant. This set-up has been partly concealed in the daughter languages, by restructurings of the consonant system; for instance, in OE /θ/ is a spirant but the alternating /d/ always a stop, and /s/ is a spirant but the alternating /r/ neither stop nor spirant.

512

The neat Proto-Germanic situation is even more tempting than OE for internal reconstruction, and there is, indeed, no reason why we cannot apply internal reconstruction to a language known only through the comparative method as well as to a language known more directly—provided the evidence is such as to render it possible. In the present case, as in the specific case of OE, the evidence does not get us very far. We can rest reasonably assured that at some pre-Proto-Germanic stage the alternation had not yet developed, but if we try to get at the details via internal reconstruction we can make nothing but guesses.

If the Germanic languages stood alone, with no known related languages outside the Germanic group, this would be as far as we could carry the matter. But Germanic is a subgroup of the Indo-European family, which includes also a good many other well-attested languages. Under these circumstances, it is possible, by a special method which can be called *inverted reconstruction*, to carry our investigation further, and, in this instance, to discover the exact answer.

Inverted reconstruction is a logically different procedure from ordinary (external) reconstruction. In the latter, as already amply illustrated, we compare a set of two or more related languages and reconstruct their latest common ancestor. In inverted reconstruction, we also approach the particular proto-language from earlier stages, in turn determined by applying the comparative method to a larger group of related languages. In Figure 60.1, A and B, we show the difference. In A we see the historical Germanic languages stemming from the earlier common ancestor, Proto-Germanic; in B we see a larger picture in which Proto-Germanic, as well as Latin, Greek, Sanskrit, Proto-Slavic, and others we have not bothered to represent, trace back to *their* common ancestor, Proto-Indo-European. Now if we begin with the historical evidence, in either A or B, and aim towards the reconstruction of the common ancestor of *all* the directly attested languages, we are doing ordinary (external) reconstruction—within Germanic in the first instance, for Indo-European as a whole in the second. On the other hand, if in the situation depicted in B we aim towards a fuller understanding of Proto-Germanic, by approaching it from "behind" (reconstructed Proto-Indo-European) as well as from later (the historic Germanic languages), we are doing inverted reconstruction.

In Proto-Germanic, as reached via normal comparison, we must assume that there was a stress, which fell on the so-called "root" syllable of words just as it does in all the historic Germanic languages. A reexamination of cognate-sets (1) and (2) of §57.2 will show this: the daughter languages all show a stress on the first (and only) syllable of the word for 'fish,' and on the first syllable of the word for 'father,' and we consequently reconstruct Proto-Germanic */fískɔz/ and */fóder-/, with the stress on these same syllables. The principle is one we have

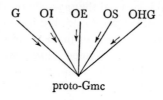

A

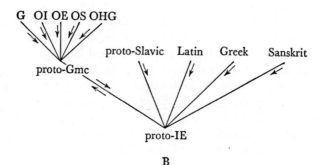

B

FIGURE 60.1

The arrows in A represent the direction of inference in ordinary reconstruction. The arrows in B represent the directions of inference, when inverted as well as ordinary reconstruction are involved, focussing on Proto-Germanic.

already expounded: if a (phonetic) feature appears in all the descendant languages, it is to be ascribed to the common ancestor unless there is convincing evidence against this conclusion.

However, this accentual situation was not that of Proto-Indo-European. In Greek and in Vedic Sanskrit, for example, we find an accent which fell now in one place in the word, now in another—as well on an inflectional ending as on the stem. Illustrating from Vedic Sanskrit, we find /várt-a-mi/ 'I turn' and /va-várt-a/ '(he) has turned' with the accent on the stem, but /va-vr̥t-imá/ 'we turned' and the participle theme /va-vr̥t-aná-/with the accent on an inflectional ending. It is impossible to account for the various placing of the accent in Greek and Vedic Sanskrit within the separate histories of those languages; it i necessary to assume that the accentual system of Proto-Indo-European showed much the same sort of variation, that it was inherited with only minor changes in Greek and in Vedic Sanskrit, and that the system of Proto-Germanic was a new development within the separate prehistory of Germanic, having occurred at a time earlier than the stage we reach via the comparative method within the Germanic branch.

This enables us to postulate a pre-Proto-Germanic stage in which the primary accent fell sometimes on the stem, sometimes on a suffix; when the primary accent was not on the stem, then there is reason to believe that a secondary accent (or something structurally equivalent thereto) appeared there. Let us call this Stage I, and call the stage of development reached by direct reconstruction Stage II. In Stage I, the ancestral forms of the consonant-alternating verb stems showed no such alternation: they ended, in all environments, with voiceless spirants /f θ s x/. But between Stage I and Stage II two developments took place, in the following order:

(1) /f θ s x/, by sound change, became voiced *non-initially in voiced surroundings when the next preceding vowel did not bear primary stress.* The voiced [z], produced from earlier /s/ by this sound change, was still a member of the same phoneme as the voiceless [s], since the two were in complementary distribution. But the voiced [v ð γ] fell together with spirantal allophones of /b d g/, and thus became further occurrences of those three phonemes.

(2) *The primary stress shifted to the stem syllable in all cases* (partly by sound change, probably in part by analogy). With this change, the older allophones [s] and [z] of the single earlier phoneme /s/ were thrown into contrast as distinct phonemes /s/ and /z/, since the basis of complementation was gone.

The consequence of these two changes was the situation we find in Stage II (Proto-Germanic as achieved via reconstruction).

The inflectional endings of the preterit plural and of the past participle were among those which, in Stage I, carried stress. This is not just speculation to make the theory fit the Germanic facts: it is based on inverted reconstruction, from the accentual situation in Vedic

Sanskrit. The Vedic forms cited earlier show the basis for the conclusion: the endings /-imá/ and /-aná-/ of the third and fourth forms cited are cognate with the preterit plural and past participle endings of Germanic. To show how the sequence of changes between Stage I and Stage II brought about the consonantal alternation in certain verbs, we give a table; all entries in the first three columns must be imagined to be preceded by an asterisk:

Stage I	after first change	after second change (Stage II)	historic
/sníjθɔnɔ/	/sníjθɔnɔ/	/sníjθɔnɔ/	OE /sní·θan/ 'to cut'
/snìθumí/	/snìdumí/	/snídumi/	OE /snídon/ 'we cut' (pret.)
	[snìðumí]	[sníðumi]	
/snìθɔnɔ́-/	/snìdɔnɔ́-/	/snídɔnɔ-/	OE /sníden/ (part.)
	[snìðɔnɔ́-]	[sníðɔnɔ-]	
/kíwsɔnɔ/	/kíwsɔnɔ/	/kíwsɔnɔ/	OE /kɔ́·san/ 'to choose'
/kùsumí/	/kùsumí/	/kúzumi/	OE /kúron/ 'we chose'
	[kùzumí]	[kúzumi]	
/tíjxɔnɔ/	/tíjxɔnɔ/	/tíjxɔnɔ/	OHG /tʂí·han/ 'to draw'/
/tìxumí/	/tìgumí/	/tígumi/	OHG /tʂígum/ 'we drew
	[tìɣumí]	[tíɣumi]	
/tìxɔnɔ́-/	/tìgɔnɔ́-/	/tígɔnɔ-/	OHG /(gi)tʂígan/ 'drawn.'
	[tìɣɔnɔ́-/	[tíɣɔnɔ-]	

(The OE preterit plural is historically the third-person subject form, extended analogically within pre-OE for use with all plural subjects; this accounts for OE /n/ in the ending instead of /m/.)

When we try to get at, say, the recent prehistory of OE by comparing the situation in OE with that in the other old Germanic languages, we are once again really using "inverted" reconstruction. That is, we use OE as well as OI, OS, OHG, and G to reconstruct Proto-Germanic; but at the same time we have to fill in the details of what happened between Proto-Germanic and each of its descendants, including OE. Thus, practically, regular reconstruction and inverted reconstruction go hand in hand. They are logically distinguishable, but are both techniques within the comparative method as a whole.

60.2. Historical Grouping via the Comparative Method. In beginning comparative work with a group of presumably related languages, one first inspects them to see whether there are any obvious degrees of difference in their interrelationships. Thus if one were starting out with English, German, and French, it would be clear at the outset that the first two are more closely related to each other than either is to the third. Accordingly, one would work first with the more closely related pair, reconstructing their common ancestor, and only then compare that reconstructed common ancestor with the third language. But in some cases there is no superficially obvious variation in the degree of relationship. When this is so, one assumes temporarily that the languages are all equally related. Then, as historical details get filled in, one is often (not always) able to see that this initial assumption was wrong.

The Germanic group is one for which the initial assumption of equal relationship is sensible. But, as comparison proceeds, it turns out that the relationship of G to the other languages is perhaps the most distant, and that that of OI to OE, OS, and OHG is perhaps somewhat more distant than those between OE, OS, and OHG. Which two of the last three should be grouped together as against the third is much more difficult to decide, and, as we shall see, it is possible that the question is not entirely meaningful.

One bit of evidence for the segregation of G is the fact that a widespread phenomenon usually called *umlaut* led to various effects in all the other languages, but does not show up in G. Umlaut is a type of sound change, with phonemic consequences, in which the vowel of one syllable is modified in the direction of the vowel (or a semivowel) in the next syllable. Thus G /háfjan/ 'to raise' is cognate to OI /héfja/, OE /hébban/, OS /hébbian/, and OHG /héffen/: the G form shows the unraised stem vowel (Proto-Germanic /ɔ́/), and the G, OI, and OS show the /j/ in the next syllable, through the influence of which, in all the languages but G, the stem vowel turns up as /é/. Similarly, one can compare G /twálif/ 'twelve' with OE /twélf/ (the influencing vowel in the second syllable having been lost late in pre-OE), or G /bádi/ 'bed' with OE /bédd/ and OHG /bétti/. When the vowel or semivowel of the next syllable is high and back, instead of high and front, one gets in OE a different result: G /síbun/ 'seven,' pre-OE */síbun/ becoming */sɨ́bun/ (with a high back unrounded vowel instead of /í/), and appearing in OE as /sɔ́fon/.

The phonemic results of umlauting as a trend in sound change vary from one of the non-Gothic Germanic languages to another, and therefore must have come about during the separate histories of those languages. But the trend itself, in sound change, probably went on for many centuries before it led to any phonemic consequences, and we may suspect that it started in the more westerly languages after the precursor of G had, in one way or another, already become fairly well separated from them.

Another innovation in all the languages but G is the loss, via syncretism and analogy, of the vocative case, kept separate from the nominative for some G nouns (§59.3). Still another is the change of Proto-Germanic /z/ to /r/, falling together with /r/ from Proto-Germanic /r/: G /húzd/ 'treasure' : OS/hórd/, OHG /hórt/; G /-iza/ '-er' (comparative ending for adjectives) : OE /-(e)ra/, OS /-ira/, OHG /-iro/; G masculine nominative singular ending /-s/ from Proto-Germanic /-ɔz/ : OI /-r/. The very earliest records of Scandinavian (Runic inscriptions, which antedate OI manuscripts by as much as a millenium) show a consonant of unknown phonetic nature distinct from both /r/ and /s/, but this does not necessarily imply that the consequent falling-together of this consonant and /r/ was independent of the comparable change in OE, OS, and OHG.

It is also possible to list some special developments in G which did not take place in the other languages: for example, Proto-Germanic /í/ and /é/ first fell together, and then were split into G /í/ and /é/, the latter before /r/ and /h/, the former otherwise, while parental /ú/ was split into G /ú/ and /ó/ on the same distributional basis (late pre-G changes account for the phonemic contrasts between /í/ and /é/, and /ú/ and /ó/, in G as attested in our documents). It is because of this that cognate sets (1), (7), (8), and others show /í í í í í/, set (11) rather /í é é é é/, set (39) /é é ó é é/ (with a special change in OE), and still others, of which we have had no examples, /é í í í í/. But this sort of evidence is not of much value. It does not require much time or separation (as such things go) for a language to develop features not shared by languages related to it. What counts is *common innovations* in two or more of a related group of languages.

Even a single common innovation does not carry much weight, especially if it is the sort of development which is known to take place in all sorts of languages with considerable frequency. The pre-OE splitting of Proto-Germanic /k/ and /g/ into two phonemes each, a front /ķ ĝ/ and a back /k g/, recurs in certain modern Low German dialects in the northeast of Germany. This need have no historical significance: the palatalization of a dorso-velar stop in the vicinity of a front vowel is one of the commonest trends in sound change. So many of the common innovations on which we have to rely for historical grouping are of this sort that it is rarely safe to put one's faith on a *single* common innovation: we look, rather, for several which set off the same subgroup of languages against the rest of those in the family.

One innovation shared by OE, OS, and OHG but not by either OI or G is a thorough-going doubling of medial consonants (other than /r/) after a stressed vowel before /j/. The cognate set cited above beginning with G /háfjan/ 'to raise,' illustrates this point: OI /héfja/ shows the effects of umlaut but no doubling, but OE /hébban/, OS /hébbian/, and OHG /héffen/ show the doubling. Another example is G /lágjan/ 'to lay': OE /léĝĝan/, OS /léggian/. Still another is G /skáθjan/ 'to injure': OE /skeθθan/.

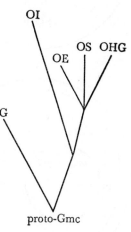

FIGURE 60.2

Another common innovation for this group of three is the development of the spirantal allophone of Proto-Germanic /d/ into a stop, surviving as [d] in OE and OS, but losing the voicing to appear in OHG as [t] (§58.3, C28, cognate sets 2, 15, 19). Still a third, much less weighty, is the complete loss of the masculine nominative singular ending /-ɔz/ (by sound change), which appears in G as /-s/, and in OI as /-r/.

From the comparative evidence for all five old Germanic languages, one would conclude that the varying degrees of relationship might be presented diagrammatically as shown in Figure 60.2. The vertical dimension represents time, increasing as one goes from bottom to top. G has been placed earlier than the other four languages because our records of it date from an earlier century. Read literally, the diagram would suggest that, after Proto-Germanic, first the speakers of what was

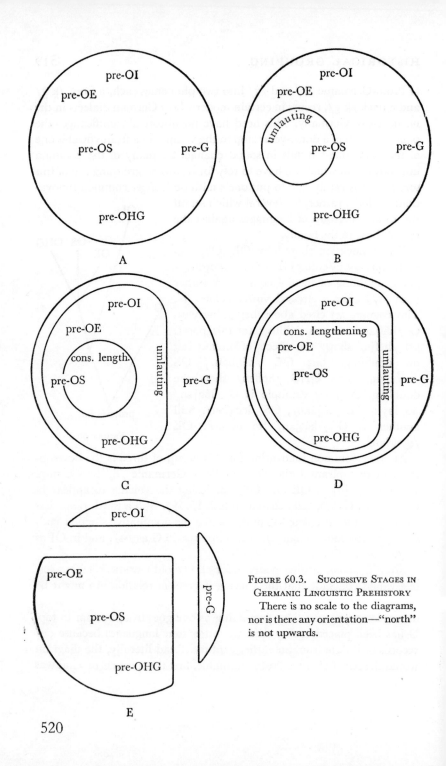

FIGURE 60.3. SUCCESSIVE STAGES IN GERMANIC LINGUISTIC PREHISTORY

There is no scale to the diagrams, nor is there any orientation—"north" is not upwards.

to become G split off from the rest (perhaps by migration), that somewhat later the speakers of what was to become OI moved away from the rest, and that, finally, the remaining group split three ways—the splits, in each case, being more or less sudden. Now such literal interpretation is not contrary to what sometimes happens in history. But it is dangerous to assume that this is always what has happened, because there are other ways in which divergence can come about.

One of these ways is shown in Figure 60.3, where the successive lettered parts show the situation at successive points in time. In A, we see the speakers of a non-uniform Proto-Germanic language spread over an area—the way the speakers of a language usually live—with those in certain regions marked, respectively, "pre-OE," "pre-OHG," and the like. In B, we see a type of phonetic habit (the tendency towards umlauting) begin at an arbitrarily selected point outside the territory of the pre-G speakers. In C, this habit has spread through much of the area, but not to the pre-G speakers; at the same time, at some point within the umlauting area the tendency towards lengthening posttonic consonants before /j/ has begun. In D, each of these trends has spread as far as it is destined to. In E we show the state of affairs in, say, the second century A.D., with OI and G apart from each other and from the other three groups, but the latter three still in contact.

In other words, the grouping of a set of related languages which we get by finding common innovations may well reflect something of the state of affairs when the distinct languages were still but divergent dialects of a single language. That languages X and Y share common innovations over against Z need not imply that X and Y shared a period of common development out of touch with Z: it can mean merely that X and Y were in closer contact with each other than with Z when all three belonged to a set of mutually intelligible dialects.

Sometimes, when we look for common innovations dividing the languages of a family into those that share the innovations and those that do not, we find them in abundance, but not in agreement with each other. This is what happens when we apply the techniques to Indo-European, taking Latin, Greek, Proto-Germanic, Proto-Celtic, Proto-Balto-Slavic, and certain other directly attested or reconstructed languages, as the separate daughter languages for the comparison. Some criteria group certain of these together; other criteria give a different grouping. Figure 60.4 shows this: the caption explains the criteria.

It is in a case of this sort that we are surest we have worked back, via the comparative method, to a period of mutually intelligible dialects of a single parent language. The general contours of the picture (Figure 60.4) are just the sort that turn up constantly in dialect-geographical work (§56), and the resemblance cannot be coincidental. Indeed, the comparative method has caused us to "overshoot" the

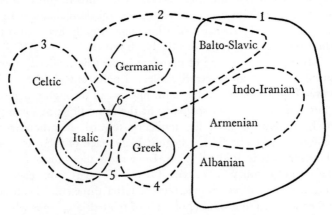

FIGURE 60.4. CROSS-CUTTING CLASSIFICATION OF IE LANGUAGES BY DIFFERENT CRITERIA

1. [s]- and [š]-type consonants from parental velar stops in certain forms.
2. Case-endings with /m/ instead of /bh/.
3. Verb forms in passive voice with /r/.
4. A prefix of type /e-/ in past tenses.
5. Feminine nouns with historically masculine endings.
6. Perfect tense used as a general past tense.

(Slightly redrawn from *Language*, by Leonard Bloomfield. By permission of Henry Holt and Company, Inc., Copyright 1933.)

period of the parent language, not necessarily to a genuine earlier state of affairs without dialect differentiation, but to a sort of hypothetical uniformity which may never have existed. The stage of mutually intelligible dialects is too far in the past to permit the application of the ordinary methods of dialect geography, so we are forced to accept our reconstruction as the best portrayal that can be obtained. The fact that we can at best see the parent language only as through a glass darkly in no way means that we should abandon the comparative method as "inaccurate." It is imperative for us to remember that our reconstruction wears a disguise of greater preciseness than can validly be ascribed to it, but to throw it out for this reason would be folly.

60.3. Cultural Deductions from Reconstruction. The reconstructed vocabulary of a parent language is like any vocabulary in any language: grammatical forms have phonemic shapes and also meanings. From the shapes, we are able to proceed, as illustrated in the foregoing discussion, toward a picture of the design of the language. From the meanings, in some favorable cases, and if we use great care, we are able to draw some tentative conclusions about the nonlinguistic culture of the speakers of the parent language.

Here, slightly paraphrased, is Leonard Bloomfield's summary of the deductions that have been drawn in this way about the speakers of Proto-Indo-European:

The noun and the verb *snow* appears so generally in the Indo-European languages that we can exclude India from the range of possible dwellings of the Proto-Indo-European community.[1] The names of plants, even where there is phonetic agreement, differ as to meaning; thus, Latin *fāgus*, OE /bo·k/ mean 'beech-tree,' but Greek *phēgós* means a kind of oak. Similar divergences of meaning appear in other plant-names, such as our words *tree*, *birch*, *withe* (German *Weide* 'willow'), *oak*, *corn*, and the types of Latin *salix* 'willow,' *quercus* 'oak,' *hordeum* 'barley' (cognate with German *Gerste*), Sanskrit /jávah/ 'barley.' The type of Latin *glans* 'acorn' occurs with the same meaning in Greek, Armenian, and Balto-Slavic.

Among animal-names, *cow*, Sanskrit /ga·wh/, Greek *bôus*, Latin *bōs*, Old Irish /bo·/, is uniformly attested and guaranteed by irregularities of form. Other designations of animals appear in only part of the territory; thus, *goat* is confined to Germanic and Italic; the type Latin *caper* : OI /háfr/ 'goat' occurs also in Celtic; the type Sanskrit /ajáh/, Lithuanian /oži·s/ is confined to these two languages; and the type of Greek *áiks* appears also in Armenian and perhaps in Iranian. Other animals for which we have one or more equations covering part of the Indo-European territory, are horse, dog, sheep (the word *wool* is certainly of Proto-Indo-European age), pig, wolf, bear, stag, otter, beaver,

[1] From pages 319f of *Language*, by Leonard Bloomfield. By permission of Henry Holt and Company, Inc., Copyright 1933.

goose, duck, thrush, crane, eagle, fly, bee (with *mead*, which originally meant 'honey'), snake, worm, fish. The types of our *milk* and of Latin *lac* 'milk' are fairly widespread, as are the word *yoke* and the types of our *wheel* and German *Rad* 'wheel,' and of *axle*. We may conclude that cattle were domesticated and the wagon in use, but the other animal-names do not guarantee domestication. Verbs for weaving, sewing, and other processes of work are widespread, but vague or variable in meaning. The numbers apparently included 'hundred' but not 'thousand.' Among terms of relationship, those for a woman's relatives by marriage ('husband's brother,' 'husband's sister,' and so on) show widespread agreement, but not those for a man's relatives by marriage; one concludes that the wife became part of the husband's family, which lived in a large patriarchal group. The various languages furnish several equations for names of tools and for the metals gold, silver, and bronze (or copper). Several of these, however, are loan-words: so certainly Greek *pélekus* 'axe,' Sanskrit /paraśúh/ is connected with Assyrian *pilakku*, and our *axe* and *silver* are ancient loan-words. Accordingly, scholars place the Proto-Indo-European community into the Late Stone Age.

The clear separation of loan-words from inherited vocabulary obviously has important implications for culture-history. It is also useful, when possible, to know something of the relative dates of importation of different loans, and in this the comparative method can help. English *cheese* and *wine* recur in several Germanic languages, and can be reconstructed for Proto-Germanic, but were clearly borrowed into early Germanic from Latin: both items must have been obtained by the Germanic tribes, as trade articles, from the Romans. English *abbot, altar, canon, cowl, noon, pope,* and some others (§48.3) are also from Latin; some of these words recur in some of the other Germanic languages, but not in shapes which encourage the reconstruction of Proto-Germanic prototypes, and it would seem that these were borrowed into English from the Latin of Christian missionaries in the 7th century. It is not surprising to find that the Menomini terms for card-playing are loans from French; it is perhaps more significant that some of them must have come indirectly, via Ojibwa, along with words from Ojibwa which the latter had not earlier obtained from French.

Any effort to draw cultural deductions from linguistic prehistory is fraught with danger. The Central Algonquian languages show apparently cognate words for 'gun' and for 'whisky,' and, if one knew nothing of the history of the tribes, one would proceed to reconstruct prototype forms in Proto-Central-Algonquian with these same two meanings. We do not know the date of Proto-Central-Algonquian, but at the very latest it antedated the arrival of Europeans by several centuries. The chief source of difficulty, obviously, is the fact that meanings can, and do, change in many whimsical and uncodifiable ways. But all this does not mean that we should abandon our efforts; it means merely that we must proceed with great caution and always regard our conclusions as tentative.

NOTES

New terms: *inverted reconstruction; common innovations.*

Bloomfield, 1933 chapters 18–27, gives many examples of cultural deductions from historical linguistic procedures, or of results obtained by the combined use of linguistic and ordinary historical or cultural methods. See also the journal *Wörter und Sachen*, and Sapir 1916, 1936.

61·

GLOTTOCHRONOLOGY

61.1. Kinds of Dating. Any study of the past, be it of human history, of organic evolution, or of geology, involves *dating*.

There are two kinds of dating, *metric* and *topological*. The former turns on the *measurement of elapsed time* between events, especially between some past event and the present. The latter turns exclusively on *before* and *after*. To say that the Declaration of Independence was signed in 1776 A.D. is to say, indirectly—as of the moment of this writing, in 1955 A.D.—that it was signed 179 years ago: this is metric dating. To say that the signing of the Declaration preceded the drawing-up of the Constitution is to speak in topological terms.

Metric dating is sometimes precise and sometimes vague, but vagueness does not destroy its metric status. It is perfectly metric to assert that the Declaration was signed in the 1770's, instead of specifying the year 1776, or even to say merely that it was signed in the second half of the eighteenth century. Such statements are as valid as it is to give the distance from New York to San Francisco as approximately 3000 miles, instead of specifying the airline distance along a great circle course as 2571 miles. Various factors contribute to the determination of how precise a metric date *can* be; within the limits thus established, other factors determine how precise the measurement *need* be for a specific purpose.

One special variety of metric dating is what we shall call the *likelihood* variety. Suppose that we are confronted with a middle-aged man who does not remember the year of his birth, and whose vital records have been destroyed. All human beings undergo certain physiological changes as they grow older, but the rate at which these changes occur

526

varies from one person to another. Hence we cannot determine the year of our subject's birth in an exact way by, say, counting the wrinkles on his forehead, as it is alleged one can fix the age of a tree by counting the annual growth rings. Nevertheless, medical statistics enable us to make a fairly good guess as to the subject's age, by observing his current physical condition and comparing it with that of individuals of known ages. At best, the results would appear as shown in Figure 61.1. Along the abscissa are marked successive years. The

bell-shaped curve means that the most likely date of birth is that marked by the highest point of the curve, and that any earlier or later date is correspondingly less likely.

In Figure 61.1 appear two limits, to either side of the maximum of the curve, marked "nine-tenths confidence level." The meaning of this is as follows: if one made the likelihood dating determination in a large number of cases, where comparable evidence could be used for each, the actual date of birth would fall, in nine-tenths of the cases, within the indicated limits. Consequently, when examining just a single case, we say that

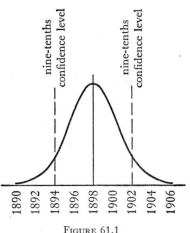

FIGURE 61.1

the date of the event in question occurred, with a nine-tenths likelihood, within the interval so marked. We speak here of "likelihood" rather than of "probability" because there is no *objective* indeterminacy about the event in question: the subject was actually born at a specific time, and the curve (and the confidence-level) is only a formal representation of our ignorance.

It is possible to view all metric dates as of the likelihood sort; the only difference is in the contour of the curve. In Figure 61.2 we show the sort of curve that would be drawn for the dating of the signing of the Declaration of Independence, or any other event where the available evidence makes pinpointing possible.

61.2. Dating in Historical Linguistics. A review of the methods of historical linguistics which have been discussed in the last few sections will show that most of them do not yield very satisfactory dating. Of course, where we are able to draw linguistic deductions from dated documents, we can often at least give a precise date before which, or after which, a certain linguistic change must have occurred. But many important documents bear no overt date. And when we rely on internal reconstruction, dialect geography, or the comparative method, usually the best we can achieve is topological dating.

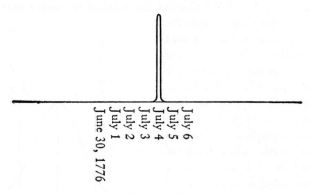

FIGURE 61.2

Thus we can obviously deduce, from internal reconstruction and the comparative method, that Proto-Indo-European was spoken earlier than was Proto-Germanic. We can tentatively guess that Pre-Gothic became effectively separated from the rest of early Germanic before the antecedents of the other historic languages drifted apart; in §60.2 we showed why this particular deduction is not very certain. We can deduce clearly that the split of Proto-Germanic /k/ and /g/ into pre-English /k k̲ g ĝ/ preceded the umlauting of Proto-Germanic /u o/ to /y ö/. The shape of the word *cheese*, in NE and in OE, shows that it was borrowed from Latin before the split of /k/ into /k/ and /k̲/; otherwise we should now say /kíjz/. The shape of the word *pope* shows that it was borrowed from Latin before the restructuring of the late OE (or early ME) vowel system described in §53.2: a later borrowing would yield NE /péjp/ or /pǽp/, or even, if recent enough, /pávpə/.

Topological dating is not to be belittled: knowing the temporal sequence of events is a considerable gain over no dating knowledge at all. Nevertheless, even the vaguest sort of metric dating would be better.

If we could assert, for example, that Proto-Germanic was with highest likelihood being spoken in 500 B.C., though conceivably as early as 1100 B.C. or as late as 100 A.D., this would be far more satisfactory than the loose (though absolutely certain) assertion that Proto-Germanic postdated Proto-Indo-European and predated, say, historic Gothic.

It is this kind of likelihood dating that the recently developed technique known as *glottochronology* or *lexicostatistics* may be able to supply. The method is still undergoing tests and modifications, so that we cannot yet be certain of its eventual value.

61.3. The Basis of Glottochronology. The assumptions which, if valid, form the basis for glottochronology are as follows:

(1) There are certain recurrent things and situations, or kinds of things and situations, for which every community of human beings, regardless of differences of culture or environment, has words. The words used by a given human group for these omnipresent things and situations constitute the *basic vocabulary* of the group's language. It should be noted that "basic vocabulary" is defined in semantic terms.

(2) As time goes by, some items in the basic vocabulary of a language will be replaced; the mechanisms of such replacement are numerous, and have been discussed in preceding sections (§§44–54). There is no guarantee that the rate of replacement will be unvarying; indeed, we know perfectly well that *over short periods of time* the rate varies. One need only remember the impact of Norman French on English. Between 1200 and 1300 A.D. the use of French in England was on the wane; former bilinguals were making increasing use of English, but would resort to a French word when momentarily they could not remember the English. Consequently, more inherited English words (of the basic vocabulary and otherwise) were replaced during this century than during the one immediately preceding. However, it is postulated that *over long periods of time*, measured perhaps only to the nearest millenium or half-millenium, such short-term variations in rate of replacement level out, so that one can treat the rate as constant.

Suppose that the rate of replacement of basic vocabulary items per thousand years is such that, at the end of a millenium, N percent of the earlier basic vocabulary will survive. In another thousand years, only N percent of this surviving N percent will still have resisted replacement, so that the unreplaced residuum in two millenia will be N^2 percent.

Suppose, next, that at a certain time a parent language becomes effectively split into two descendants. After a thousand years, each of the descendants will be expected to retain N percent of the basic vocabulary of the parent, but the particular items retained in each will be independent of those retained in the other. Consequently, the percentage of *shared* (i.e., cognate) basic vocabulary items in the two descendants at the end of a thousand years should be, once again, N^2.

Suppose, now, that we know the basic vocabulary of a language at stage A and at a later stage B, but do not know, through other sources, the elapsed time between A and B. We can determine the percentage of the basic vocabulary of stage A which is still retained at stage B, and from this can compute the elapsed interval of time. Or, again, suppose that we have information on two related languages but no direct documentary information on their common ancestor. We can determine the percentage of shared items in the basic vocabulary of the two, and from this deduce the likely date of the common ancestor.

61.4. Difficulties. The theoretical presentation just given seems perfectly straightforward, but in application one encounters many difficulties. Here are the chief ones:

(1) Do languages actually include well-defined basic vocabularies, in the sense described above? If so, what meanings does the basic vocabulary provide for? Is English *two* in the basic vocabulary? *Ten? See? Think? Book?* Only extended trial-and-error, comparing languages and cultures, can assemble the proper reference-list of meanings; this trial-and-error work continues, and the reliable list seems to get smaller and smaller as more languages and cultures are taken into account. The number of meanings for which a human language *must* have words seems amazingly small.

(2) Given a tentatively accepted reference-list of meanings, our evidence for a particular stage of some language may or may not tell us the word for a given meaning on the list. Where the information is lacking, we are forced to strike the item from the list. This reduces even further the effective sample-size for the investigation. Even when we can find the proper pair of words for two languages (or two stages of a single language), we often cannot be sure whether the two words are cognate or not, and under these conditions, also, the item has to be discarded. The mathematical methods which are to be applied to the data

are of a statistical nature: the smaller the sample, the more vague the results. If the sample is too small, the computations are useless. If we make it large by being careless in our selection of items and in our decisions as to whether pairs of words are cognate or not, the purely mathematical results become sharper but this increased sharpness may not mean much empirically. It is certain that the optimum compromise between these two extremes has not yet been worked out.

(3) If languages indeed include well-defined basic vocabularies, to what extent is it true that the rate of replacement in the basic vocabulary is approximately constant over long periods of time? The only way to find out is to take as many cases as possible where accurate metric dating can be achieved by other methods: English between Alfred's times and our own; classical Latin to contemporary French; classical Attic Greek to modern Greek; and so on. This also involves extensive trial-and-error, for if one reference-list of meanings shows too great a variation in rate of replacement (from one sample to another), a different list may reduce the variation.

The above sources of uncertainty are such that, no matter how much the technique is refined, the only dating that it can yield will be of the likelihood variety, with fairly flat dating curves rather than the spiked type of Figure 61.2. What is more, by its very nature the technique can be applied only to intermediate time-depths. For very short intervals of time, variations in the rate of replacement loom so large that dates based on the assumption that it is constant are worthless. For extremely long intervals, the dating curve becomes very flat: obviously it is not helpful to find that, though the most likely date of an event is 40,000 years ago, the nine-tenths confidence level defines a span running from 90,000 years ago to a date 10,000 years in our own future!

61.5. Tentative Results. The reference-list of meanings which has been most thoroughly tested so far, and most often used in applications, contains just 200 items (a simpler number to handle in computations than, say, 201 or 198). In many cases, as already stated, the usable number has been smaller. There is little point in presenting the full list here: some examples appear in the following small-scale illustration of its use. In the first column of the illustration, we give OE forms, and in the second column the NE semantic equivalents. The second column also serves to define the areas of meaning being used. In the third column the pairs in the first and second columns are marked as cognate (a plus-sign) or not (a minus-sign). The fourth, fifth, and sixth columns repeat in terms of Latin and Spanish:

eall	/ál/	*all*	+	*omnēs*	*todos*	—
and	/ónd/	*and*	+	*et*	*y*	+
dēor	/dó·r/	*animal*	—	*animal*	*animal*	+
æsc	/æ̰sk/	*ashes*	+	*cinis*	*cenizas*	+
æt	/æ̰t/	*at*	+	*in*	*a*	—
bæc	/bæk/	*back*	+	*dorsum*	*espalda(s)*	—

To underscore the basis for the procedure, let us note again that the pairing-off of forms is purely in terms of semantics, the scoring as plus or minus in terms of cognation. OE *dēor* survives in NE as *deer*, but the OE word meant 'animal' and is therefore properly paired off with NE *animal*. The OE word for 'deer' does not occur on the list at all, nor does the NE word *deer*, because this semantic item is not in the basic vocabulary. Minor changes in inflectional pattern are ignored. English and Spanish *ashes* and *cenizos* are generally used in the plural, while OE *æsc* and Latin *cinis* were common enough in the singular, but this change of habit does not lead us to score the pairs negative instead of positive.

Using the 200-item list as, by definition, our basic vocabulary, a number of independent determinations of the rate of replacement (and, conversely, the rate of retention) have been made where the actual elapsed interval of time could be determined by other means. Between Classical Latin of 50 B.C. and present-day Rumanian, the measured rate of retention per thousand years is 76%. At the other extreme, between the Plautine Latin of 200 B.C. and the Spanish of 1600 A.D., the measured rate of retention per thousand years is 85%. A computation based on these and a number of other measurements yields 81% as the best "constant" estimate of rate of retention to use in cases where dating is to be achieved by glottochronological methods. That is, in a millenium a language will retain, unreplaced, approximately 81% of the items in its basic vocabulary; in a millenium of separate history after divergence from a common parent, two languages will be most likely to show $81\% \times 81\% = 66\%$ cognate items within the basic vocabulary.

The indefiniteness of the latter measure is shown graphically in

Figure 61.3. The heavy line shows the most probable percentagewise retention for a pair of related languages (along the ordinate) after separation for a given length of time (along the abscissa); or, conversely, the most likely length of time since separation (along the abscissa) if the basic vocabularies of the two show a certain percentage of cognates

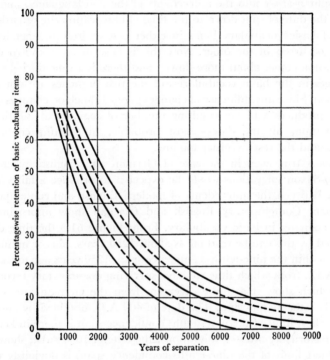

FIGURE 61.3.   NOMOGRAPH FOR GLOTTOCHRONOLOGICAL DETERMINATION OF TIME
DEPTH OF RELATIONSHIP
(Redrawn from *Workbook in Descriptive Linguistics* by H. A. Gleason, Jr. By permission of Henry Holt and Company, Copyright 1955.)

(along the ordinate). The dashed curves show the nine-tenths confidence level when the full 200-pair sample is available; the light solid curves show the nine-tenths confidence level when it is possible to use only 50 pairs out of the basic list. We see, thus, that the definiteness and reliability of dating of a common ancestor decrease both as the usable sample becomes smaller, and as the time-depth increases. The curves do not start from the zero date (date of no separation at all) because they are meaningless for time depths of less than, say, half a millenium. The measure graphed in Figure 61.3 has to be corrected, in application, on another basis. The assumption behind the computations on which the graph is made is that the common ancestor of two languages was split *suddenly* into the antecedents of the two languages, and that from the date of split down to the time of observation the retention or loss of basic vocabulary items in either was entirely independent of what occurred in the other. Now this is false in most known cases: separation comes about more slowly, and there is a time during which changes in the basic vocabularies of the two branches are not independent. Since any influence of changes in one branch on changes in the other produces a higher resulting number of cognates at the time of observation, all the dates—most probable, nine-tenths confidence limits, and the rest—register too low.

This is true even in the case of German and English, where the Anglo-Saxon migrations would be expected to produce a fairly clean break between the antecedents of modern English and contemporary German. Contemporary English and German show approximately 59% cognates in basic vocabulary. From Figure 61.3 the time depth implied by this can be read off as about 1250 years, plus or minus 300 years within the nine-tenths confidence span. 1250 years ago takes us to 700 A.D., from which time we have surviving documentary records of OE which show it as quite divergent from the German attested by slightly later manuscripts. The date of 400 A.D. obtained by going to the earliest limit of the nine-tenths confidence span is more in keeping with historically attested migrations; the date of 1000 A.D., shown by the latest limit of the nine-tenths confidence span, is obviously to be disregarded.

We can never know exactly how much allowance to make for this factor, except when there is other evidence for migrations, invasions, and the like. Nootka and Kwakiutl, two Indian languages spoken on Vancouver Island, show about 30% cognates in basic vocabulary. This points, by the chart, to a time-depth of some 2800 years; if a full sample of 200 items was used for the determination, then the nine-tenths confidence span is a band about 1000 years wide, with the 2800 year figure in the middle. If the speakers of the two languages have always been, as they now are, in some contact with each other, then this figure is doubtless too low. But if the early antecedents of one of the present-day groups migrated away from the antecedents of the other, and only after a considerable interval came back to establish the side-by-side settlement-pattern in which the tribes are now found, then the figure may be more accurate, or may even be too high. It is possible that archeology, or some comparison of Nootka-Kwakiutl cognates versus recent loans between the two languages, may in time tell us which of these is more likely. Glottochronological dating, after all, does not work in a vacuum: one supplements it with any other sort of evidence one can find.

The ultimate results that we seek through glottochronology are not yet available: all work done so far is experimental, as much to test and improve the method as to obtain a yield. But no development in historical linguistics in many decades has showed such great promise.

NOTES

New terms: *lexicostatistics* (= glottochronology); *metric* versus *topological* dating; *likelihood* dating; *nine-tenths* (or other) *confidence level; basic vocabulary.*

The techniques of glottochronology have been developed mainly by Swadesh 1952; see also Lees 1953.

Gleason *Workbook* (1955b), page 87, gives an interesting problem in glottochronological computation.

WRITING

62.

WRITING

62.1. At the outset of this book (§1.2) we underscored the distinction between language and writing. Though writing is not the linguist's primary concern, he is interested in it, as any educated member of our society of course is, and also for two special reasons. One is that our records of past speech, until the extremely recent invention of the phonograph, take the form exclusively of documents and inscriptions. The other is that writing is itself of tremendous importance in human life, and that the nature and history of writing can only be clearly understood in terms of the workings of language.

The systematic study of writing and writing systems, to which the present section is devoted, may be called *graphonomy*. Writing, like language, is a culturally-transmitted institution; therefore graphonomy and linguistics stand side-by-side as sister branches of the more inclusive field, cultural anthropology.

62.2. Kinds of Writing Systems. Any utterance in any language consists wholly of an arrangement of *morphemes*. Suppose we devise a large number of visually distinct hen-scratches, and quite arbitrarily assign one such hen-scratch to each morpheme in a language. Suppose, further, that we agree on some linear order on a flat surface—say, left to right and top to bottom, or top to bottom and left to right—which equally arbitrarily will be equated with the single unidirectional dimension, time (§3.1). We are then equipped to put down an array of hen-scratches to represent any possible utterance in the language.

For example, let us assign the graphic shape "1" to the morpheme *I*, "2" to *want*, "3" to *to*, "4" to *go*, "5" to *home*, "6" to *do*, and "7" to *you*. We can then write any English utterance which involves (neglecting intonation) only these few morphemes; for instance:

1 2 3 4 5
6 7 2 3
1 2 7

Of course, the example is in miniature: for real use we should have to invent thousands and thousands of additional graphic shapes. But the principle should be clear. A system worked out in this way is called a *morphemic writing system*. Several systems currently in use, and some known from antiquity, are essentially of this sort.

A morphemic writing system works, but is laborious to learn because the number of morphemes in any language is very large. There is a second variety of writing system which is much simpler. It is true that any utterance in a language consists wholly of an arrangement of morphemes; but it is also true that any utterance consists wholly of an arrangement of phonemes. In a *phonemic writing system*, graphic shapes are assigned, in an arbitrary fashion, not to the morphemes of the language, but to the phonemes or to some sort of recurrent combinations of phonemes (say syllables). Fewer graphic shapes are needed, and such a writing system is consequently learned much more quickly. As an example, we need only cite the phonemic notation for English developed in §§3–7.

62.3. Complications. Pure writing systems of either of the sorts we have described are rare. In most systems there are certain complications. We can deal with these under four headings:

(1) *Omissions.* In all traditional systems some morphemes (or some phonemes) are simply left out. English writing largely omits any indication of intonation, and no known system provides for all intonational contrasts. The customary traditional writing of Hebrew and Arabic usually omitted indication of vowels, though a supplementary system of "vowel points" was utilized in certain kinds of texts. We must not be surprised that such truncation leaves what is written intelligible, much of the time, to the literate native speaker; remember redundancy (§10.3). In the case of Hebrew and Arabic, an additional factor was that the contentives of Semitic often consist of a skeleton of three consonants, around and between which a speaker intercalates the vowels which represent inflectional and derivational material (modern Egyptian Arabic /katab/ 'he wrote,' /ka·tib/ 'a writing (person),' /kita·b/ 'book'). The omission of vowel indication in the writing was

thus, in effect, largely the omission of the stigmata of certain functors, sharply delimiting the range within which the reader had to guess from context.

(2) *Sequence Deviations.* Apart from omissions, if there are *n* successive elements, in an utterance, of the kind regularly represented in the writing system (morphemes, phonemes, or some kind of groupings of phonemes), then one would expect its written representation to include just *n* unit graphs. But there are deviations from this in two directions.

Thus, in Chinese writing (essentially morphemic), some morphemes are longer than a single syllable, and are represented graphically by as many successive marks as there are syllables. On the other hand, some morphemes are shorter than a single syllable, but in this case a graph is written for each morpheme. By way of exception, there is one complicated graph—recent, and optional, to be sure—which represents the whole three-morpheme sequence *túshūgwǎn* 'library.' This is perhaps more like a "monogram" in our culture—the intertwined initials put on silver or napkins—than like a regular element of the writing system, except that the distinction is a more difficult one to make in the Chinese context.

In English orthography (largely phonemic), the letter "x" most often represents the two-phoneme sequence /ks/ ("ox") or /gz/ ("exist"). Contrariwise, the two-letter sequences "th," "ch," and "sh" usually represent the single phonemes /θ/ or /ð/, /č/, and /š/.

(3) *Inadequate and Superfluous Representation.* In a "pure" system, either morphemic or phonemic, a single graph would represent always one and the same linguistic element (be it morpheme, phoneme, or sequence of morphemes or phonemes), and that linguistic element would never be represented by any other graph. For phonemic writing systems, English orthography affords the horrible example of how far one can get from this pure situation. The letter "s" represents /s/ ("sing"), /z/ ("rose"), and /š/ ("sugar"). /s/ is also represented by "c" ("rice"), by the digraph "ss" ("fuss"), by "sc" ("crescent"), and by "sch" ("schism"). The letter "a" represents a wild array of phonemes and phoneme clusters in "table", "tablet", "father", "all"; "o" is even worse, as shown by "hope", "pot", "log", "nothing", "worm", "women". The syllabic /ow/ is represented in half a dozen ways: "so", "sew", "sow" (ambiguous for /sów/ and /sáw/), "though", "depot", "doe", "beau".

In morphemic writing systems this sort of deviation does not ordinarily go so far. Instances in Chinese are isolated, though they can be found: *syíng* 'to work, be effective, be OK' and *háng* 'line of business or trade' are written with the same graph, while the morpheme *chyǔ* 'to get, obtain, withdraw' is written with one graph in most contexts, but in a different way in the context of obtaining a woman in marriage. However, part of the Japanese writing system is morphemic, and in this part multiplicity and inadequacy of representation is probably as extensive as it is in English writing.

(4) *Mixture of Basis.* The complexities of English spelling cannot be accounted for completely on the assumption that the system is phonemic with irregularities of the sort listed under (2) and (3). It is necessary to assume that the system is partly phonemic and partly morphemic. To show this, consider the three written words "so," "sew," and "sow." The differences of spelling correlate with nothing at all in the phonemic system of the language, since the three words are pronounced identically. But the three words are different morphemes. The child learning to spell English can keep these three spellings straight only by remembering which spelling correlates with which morpheme.

In most other traditional writing systems there is at least some trace of mixed basis, though usually one or the other basis predominates. In Japanese there is a special sort of mixed system in which—speaking roughly but not too inaccurately—contentives (§31.1) are represented morphemically, functors (and recent loanwords) phonemically in a syllabary.

62.4. The History of Writing. We are fortunate in that some of the earliest writing produced by the human race was put on durable materials—stone, bone, shell, baked clay—which have survived several thousand years of weathering and can still be examined. As a result, we can describe the evolution of the institution in fairly precise terms.

Something approaching writing has been developed at various times and places in human history. We may consider, as an example, the so-called "picture writing" of the Indians of the North American Plains. This was a system of communication which operated freely between speakers of a number of different languages, but communication was possible only about a limited number of practical matters. The symbols used in the system were more or less stylized pictures of the things represented. The semantic conventions of the pictures, insofar as they were not immediately obvious, were shared by all the tribes concerned. The members of a given tribe might talk matters over in their language before writing out a message in this system, and, at the receiving end, it might be roughly "translated" into the language of the recipients before being acted on; but there was no particularly close tie between the various graphic elements and words or other linguistic elements in any of the languages spoken by the different tribes. That is, the semantic conventions of the system were *direct* associations between pictorial features and the things or situations that were being communicated about. We can only assume that, despite the functioning of this system across the boundaries between speech communities, it arose by the mechanism described in §36.3.

In theory, such a system of graphic-visual communication might become increasingly complex, until in the end it achieved all the subtlety and flexibility of expression which we find in language, without ever coming to be tied in with the latter. In fact, this has never happened. There is an always an easier way to achieve such subtlety and flexibility, without losing the various advantages of permanent marks in contrast with rapidly-vanishing sound waves. The users of a picture writing system already have a system of communication characterized by endless subtlety and flexibility: their language. Instead of developing a second means of communication in complete independence of the first, what people have done is to make an apparently small change in lines of association between graphic symbols, things, and words.

The nature of this step is simple enough. We shall illustrate by imagining speakers of English who are illiterate except for a picture writing system in which a sketchy picture of a bee is the graphic symbol for a bee. The picture means a bee; the English morpheme {bee} also means a bee. In the picture writing stage, the picture and the morpheme are related only indirectly, in that they are both symbols for the same thing. The step to true writing is then a realignment of associations: the picture comes to be a representation, not directly of a bee, but of the morpheme {bee}. The connection between the picture and the bee has ceased to be immediate; instead, it is mediated by the morpheme.

The step from picture writing to true morphemic writing must have involved much stumbling and temporary retrogression. After all, a picture of a bee *looks* like a bee, and it seems highly artificial to insist that it does not directly mean what it looks like. But other things about which one may wish to communicate in writing are harder to draw pictures of—love, honor, common sense, piety, plurality, past time, contingency. And despite the difficulty in the readjustment, the step is known to have been taken independently at least three times in the history of the human race, and possibly also a fourth: once in ancient Egypt, once in ancient China, and once, much later, among the Maya of Yucatan. The possible fourth time was in ancient Mesopotamia, where we cannot be certain that Egyptian influence was not responsible. All known writing systems trace back to these origins, all but a few to early Egypt and Mesopotamia.

The statement just made implies that phonemic writing, of any sort, is a more recent development than morphemic writing and that it grew out of the latter.

Suppose that our hypothetical community of speakers of English have now developed a full-fledged morphemic writing system, in which the graph for the morpheme {bee} is still a rough picture of a bee. Someone, about to write something down, finds that he cannot remember the proper way to represent the morpheme {be}, or, perhaps, the first morpheme of a word like behold, beseech, bemuse. Instead of delaying his work, he uses the graph for {bee}, hoping that his readers will supply the regular phonemic representation of this morpheme, and gather his meaning through the pun. This practice, and others like it, becomes widespread, with the ultimate result that the graphs of the system no longer have a tie to morphemes, but only to syllables (or the like) as strings of phonemes: one then has a phonemic writing system of the syllabary type.

A certain amount of such transferred use of graphs took place in ancient China. The currently used graph for the morpheme meaning 'come' formerly stood only for a (then) homonymous morpheme meaning 'wheat.' But such transfer, in China, never led to a real break with the morphemic principle. Similarly, in Egypt certain graphs very early came to represent syllables rather than morphemes, and some even came to represent, if our interpretations are correct, individual consonants: but these phonemic graphs were always used together with morphemic ones, not replacing the latter.

The further development from a syllabary to an alphabetical writing system involves two steps. The first was taken by the Phoenicians—and, so far as we know, only by them. Graphic shapes which had earlier been, representations of whole syllables came to be used for single consonants, with vowels left out. Superfluous graphs were weeded out, until there were just enough graphs to match the consonant phonemes of the language. The second step was taken by the Greeks, when they borrowed the Phoenician writing system to use for their own language. Some of the Phoenician symbols represented consonants that were not like any in Greek, and the Greeks reassigned them to vowels, thus at last achieving a phonemic writing system in which there was something approaching one-to-one assignment of symbols to segmental phonemes. All *alphabetic* writing stems from this development among the Phoenicians and Greeks.

It is important to note, however, that, quite apart from the history of writing, the phonemic patterning of languages has played a crucial part in the development of human communicative systems outside language. The Mazateco Indians of Mexico speak a language with four phonemically distinct tones (§11.8); they also have a system of *whistle-talk*, in which one matches, in a whistle, the distinctive features of stress, pitch, and duration of utterances, necessarily leaving out vowels and consonants: the whistles are understandable through context and because of redundancy (§10.3). Similarly, the drum signals of West Africa are derived from the tonal and rhythmic phonemic features of some of the languages spoken by their users. Like all other human communicative systems, these were worked out by the mechanism of "non-linguistic idiom-formation" discussed in §36.3. As for true writing, language played the further role of a structural model to be followed in devising the details of the new system. Later, writing rather than language sometimes plays this latter role: telegraphy mocks writing, rather than language, in the matching of its units to letters in an alphabetical writing system.

When an alphabetical writing system is first invented or introduced for a language, it is almost always reasonably accurate and free from ambiguities. But, as time passes, it does not remain so. The language changes, as languages always do; but for some reason people are more conservative about writing systems than about any other human institution that can be named—even religion. Perhaps this conservatism is a natural result of the most outstanding feature of writing as opposed to language: the factor of some *permanence*, by which the receiver of a message can be separated from the transmitter not only in space but in time. In any case, the writing system gets out of step with the changing language, and in the end one has irregularities and complexities of the sort we find in current English.

62.5. The Communicative Properties of Writing. As pointed out earlier, no traditional writing system has ever provided for the graphic representation of everything that counts (morphemically or phonemically) in speech. Certain linguistic distinctions are always left out; this renders particularly apposite the traditional lay phrase "*reduce* a language to writing."

The factor of reduction can be shown by an analogy with telegraphy. In the latter, the message to be transmitted takes the form of a stretch of writing, but this is encoded into a series of voltage pulses for transmission. The conventions of the Morse Code provide for twenty-six letters and certain punctuation marks, but not for the distinction between capital and lower case letters. Thus one might receive the following telegram:

JUST APPOINTED MANAGER NEW YORK BRANCH OFFICE

—and think that the sender was referring to New York City, when actually he is referring to a new branch office in York, Pennsylvania. Ordinary English orthography keeps these two clear by writing "New York" versus "new York". And, of course, the content of the telegram could easily have been reworded so as to remove the ambiguity imposed by telegraphy. Indeed, people who communicate a great deal via telegraphy or teletypy develop a *telegraphic style* of writing—partly for the sake of conciseness to save cost, but also sacrificing conciseness in conventionally established ways when necessary in order to avoid ambiguity.

Just as the restrictions of telegraphy compress writing and lead to the development of a special telegraphic style of writing, in the same way the limitations of a writing system impose certain restrictions on what is to be transmitted in it, and lead to the development of a special *writing style* of the language. We do not write English as we speak it (§16.3). Read a transcription of a conference which has been taken down stenotypically or on a tape recorder and then written out: those who have had this experience need no convincing of the assertion just made. English Composition courses in College are (or should be) designed first and foremost to teach literate native speakers of English what they can and what they cannot do effectively in writing. The special conventions of the writing style of English have never been completely described, in terms of the economy of the language as a whole and the specific constraints of the English writing system. Yet the special conventions are there, and we notice it when someone fails to follow them. Here is a curiously ambiguous headline, which in speech would not be ambiguous at all:

15 KILLED, SEVEN OF THEM
DROPPING PARATROOPERS
STRUCK BY DISABLED PLANE

But if the above discussion tends to focus attention on what might be thought of as "shortcomings" in writing systems, writing also has tremendous advantages, for certain uses, as over against speech.

Foremost of these, of course, is the fact that the recipient of a written message does not have to be in the immediate vicinity of the sender at the time of transmission. Even a modern device like the radio eliminates only the first of these restrictions. A radio message is *broadcast*, so that anyone with proper equipment, within range, can receive it if he is listening at the right moment; but a written message is a sort of *temporal broadcast*, which can be received over and over again, at will, by anyone literate in the language, as long as the hen-scratches have not faded or the surface withered away. Archeologists today receive written messages carved in stone several thousand years ago in the dry regions of the Near and Middle East.

Furthermore, the sender of a written message can at some later time become the receiver: writing serves as a sort of *external memory*, supplementing what people can keep inside their heads. The technological importance of this is beyond calculation. Imagine what it would be like to be the member of an illiterate but technologically advanced community whose sole duty was to keep the five-place common logarithms of all numbers in one's head, ready to supply them as needed! It is certain that, without writing, even devices far simpler than logarithms would never have been invented.

The functioning of such "external memory" need not span much time to prove its usefulness. If one multiplies 2397 by 852, one uses pencil and paper, putting down the results of certain partial steps before reaching the final answer, and thus avoiding the need to keep all the intermediate results in one's head.

There are three other ways in which writing does things for us that language probably would not. One is in clear indication of *scope*. If I say *two times five minus three plus seven*, this may work out to 18, 11, −10, 14, or 0, depending on how the operations are grouped. In writing there are devices for keeping these clear:

$$2 \times (5 - 3 + 7)$$
$$2 \times (5 - 3) + 7$$

and so on. It is possible to achieve freedom from ambiguity in the spoken form by pauses of various lengths at various places, but it is difficult; and in more complex operations it soon becomes impossible.

Another is in *two-dimensionality*. Speech is essentially linear: distinctive arrangements in contrast with each other must largely turn on whether element A precedes or follows element B. But in writing there is a two-dimensional surface at hand, and although traditional writing systems prescribe some convention by which the two-dimensional array of graphs is to be read off in a certain linear sequence, it is always possible to break this convention for some purposes. Thus—again in mathematics—the arrangements

$$\begin{matrix} a & b \\ c & d \end{matrix} \quad \text{and} \quad \begin{matrix} a & c \\ b & d \end{matrix}$$

may be distinctively different.

Finally, there are ways in which writing systems go beyond the associated languages, developing conventions of direct semantic relevance in addition to those which are mediated through phonemes or morphemes. The distinction between capital and lower case letter, which is a relatively recent development of Western culture, does not directly reflect anything in speech. Other comparable contrasts are those between lightface and boldface, or Roman and Italic, or print and cursive. In the West there are a few traces, not really very important, of an esthetic aspect in writing, by which some type faces are preferred to others; in China this has gone much further, and calligraphy is classed among the fine arts. As one writes it is always possible to incorporate visual shapes which are not writing in the narrow sense at all—pictures, diagrams, graphs, and so on. In some cases, such non-writing items and "real" writing get so entangled that it is hard to tell what part is to be interpreted in one way and what part in the other.

The status of writing and of speech in the eyes of the law is interesting, though inconsistent. The document usually called a "contract" is, in law, not the contract, but a *record* thereof; the contract itself is the agreement reached by the contracting parties. On the other hand, a man's surname is legally a sequence of letters, not a linguistic form. A man named "Smith" /smíθ/ has a different name, legally, from one named "Smythe" /smíθ/, despite the identity of pronunciation; the latter has the "same" name legally as one named "Smythe" /smáj∂/.

We see, thus, that the linguist's emphatic generalization about writing—that it is merely a record of what people have said—is not strictly the case. It is nearer the truth than is the ordinary lay view (§1.2), but it is not the *whole* truth. As with most easy generalizations, the truth is more complicated.

NOTES

New terms: *graphonomy;* types of writing-system: *morphemic, phonemic* (including *syllabic* and *alphabetic*); *mixed basis* (partly morphemic, partly phonemic), *omissions* in writing, *sequence deviations,* and *inadequate and superfluous representation; writing style* of a language.

On the history of writing see Bloomfield 1933 chapter 17; Diringer 1948, Gelb 1952. Gleason (1955a, chapter 22) speaks in terms of what he calls "written languages," which may be fairly well equated with our "writing style" of a language—the term "written language" is not desirable. His examples are numerous and interesting. On recent "direct" relationships to meaning: Bolinger 1946.

LITERATURE

63·

LITERATURE

63.1. Literature is an art form, like painting, sculpture, music, drama, and the dance. Literature is distinguished from other art forms by the medium in which it works: language. Insofar as speech forms occur in other arts—sung words in music, speaking as well as action in drama—these other arts have literary aspects. The linguist is concerned with literature because it is his business to discover wherein literary discourse differs from everyday non-literary discourse. So far, relatively few generalizations have been worked out along this line of investigation. In this section we merely report what little seems to be reasonably well established. If our remarks are seemingly trivial, it is because we must be more concerned with truth than with profundity.

Let us, in imagination, join a circle of Nootka Indians who are resting around the campfire after their day's work. One old man tells a story, which runs as follows in English translation:

Kwatyat caught sight of two girls.[1] "Whose daughters are you?" said Kwatyat to the two girls. The girls did not tell him who their father was. Many times did Kwatyat ask them who their father was, but they would not tell. At last the girls got angry. "The one whose children we are," said they, "is Sunbeam." For a long time the girls said this.

And then Kwatyat began to perspire because of the fact that their father was Sunbeam. Kwatyat began to perspire and he died. Now Kwatyat was perspiring and he swelled up like an inflated bladder, and it was because of the girls. Now Kwatyat warmed up and died. He was dead for quite a little while, and then he burst, making a loud noise as he burst. It was while he was dead that he heard how he burst with a noise.

[1] From Edward Sapir and Morris Swadesh, *Nootka Texts*. Linguistic Society of America, Philadelphia (1939).

The individual words and phrases of this story are mostly intelligible, but the narrative as a whole makes little sense to us—we might as well have heard it in the original Nootka. Yet as we look around the fire we note that the speaker is being followed with close attention and interest. The Nootka audience is getting something from the performance that we, as outsiders, cannot get. Furthermore, inquiry reveals that this same story has been told many times in the past; it is new to no one in the audience save ourselves.

Our own reaction to the story, be it bewilderment, boredom, disgust, or curiosity, is for our present purposes quite irrelevant. The point is that the participants in Nootka culture appreciate and value the story. Nor is it at all helpful for us to say, after recognizing this fact, that it is indicative of low or crude literary taste on the part of the Nootkas. This would simply be to resort, in a more indirect way, to our own personal responses. What we are after is at least the beginnings of an *objective* understanding of literature.

In every society known to history or anthropology, with one insignificant exception, there are some discourses, short or long, which the members of the society agree on evaluating positively and which they insist shall be repeated from time to time in essentially unchanged form. *These discourses constitute the literature of that society.*

The one insignificant exception to this generalization and definition is our own complex Western social order. For us, also, some discourses are highly valued and others are not; but, peculiarly—and unlike anything known in other societies—the discourses which the literary specialist values most highly tend to be most despised by the layman. One result of this strange situation is that Western society is a very bad point of departure if we want to understand the typical nature of literature. We are forced to look elsewhere at first, and only later turn to a self-examination.

Yet even when we do look closely enough at smaller and more homogeneous societies, we find inconsistencies and disagreements: the literary status of a discourse turns out to be a matter of degree rather than kind. One story may be repeated very often, another rarely. One story may be valued by a whole tribe, another only by some small segment. One story may retain its literary status for generations, while another may hold it only for a year or so.

Another question that immediately arises is: how changed can the form of a discourse be from one recounting to another, and still leave it "essentially" unchanged? There seems to be much variation in this; in general the degree of objective identity (that could be determined, for example, by carefully recording two successive recountings and listing the differences) seems to be irrelevant, and what is relevant is rather a feeling on the part of the members of the society that at a given time the discourse being told is one that has been told before.

63.2. Common Features of Literary Discourse. When the literature of a society has been collected, the analyst faces the problem of determining wherein it differs from ordinary non-literary discourse in the same society. This is not the problem of *definition*—we already know that the discourses in question are literary for the society in which they occur. Rather, it is the problem of *describing* or *characterizing* that which has already been defined.

For the most part this study has to be carried out separately for each society. But two general characteristics seem to be quite common, if not universal: *excellence of speech* and *special style*.

Excellence of Speech. Apparently in every society it is generally recognized that some individuals are more effective users of the machinery afforded by the society's language than are others. The Menomini Indians, for example, can name certain people who are unusually good speakers of Menomini, and others who are unusually poor. Some do very little hemming and hawing; others speak in badly disconnected spurts (§16.3). The good speaker keeps his pronominal references and his concord, government, and cross-reference clear; the poor speaker gets lost in the emerging grammatical complexities of what he is trying to say. In other words, though the grammatical machinery is different, variations of effectiveness and fluency of control are much as they are with us.

Now it is very generally required, in an illiterate or a literate society, that literary discourse be characterized by excellence of speech. The story-teller must be a fluent and effective speaker; the writer in a literate society must write in such a way that reading can be fluent and effective. However, the converse of this generalization does not hold: not all excellent speech qualifies as literary.

It is easy to think one has found an exception when, in fact, one has not. For example, the Plains Cree have a favored manner of delivery for certain very familiar stories, in the form of a succession of short disconnected sentences which merely allude to the chief episodes. The hearers, knowing the details, are supposed to fill them in for themselves. This style seems like "poor speech" to us only because we do not have anything comparable. Actually, it calls for skill and judgment on the part of the narrator.

Special Style. The term "style" is not easy to define precisely. Roughly speaking, two utterances in the same language which convey approximately the same information, but which are different in their linguistic structure, can be said to differ in style: *He came too soon* and *He arrived prematurely*, or *Sir, I have the honor to inform you* and *Jeez, Boss, get a load of dis*. Stylistic variations within a single language are universal, and in many cases there are certain special styles which are felt to be peculiarly appropriate to certain circumstances. An Oneida chief, making a speech, begins with the style of pronunciation of everyday conversation, but gradually lapses into a special quavery sing-song. We all know the special style used by a minister at the pulpit, reciting the words of a hymn which is about to be sung, or intoning his share during responsive reading of a psalm. None of us would venture to use this style of speech in ordering groceries or in asking a girl for a date.

It is very common for literary discourse to differ from everyday speech in describable stylistic ways. In Fox, one recounts what happened to one in town yesterday using verb forms in the modes of the so-called independent order; but one tells a literary story using verb forms in the modes of the conjunct order. Conjunct order verbs in everyday speech mark dependent clauses; independent order verbs in literary narrative, on the other hand, mark direct quotations of things said by characters or else parenthetical explanations addressed to the hearer. Sometimes, in other societies, the stylistic differences are much less prominent than this; sometimes they are much more prominent. But where a clearly literary narrative does not differ at all stylistically from everyday speech, it seems that there is always something special about the content. Everyday discourse about everyday content seems never to qualify as literature.

Related to this is a customary use of a special manner of speech whenever the words of some recurrent character or type of character are quoted. The customary recounting of *Goldilocks and the Three Bears* incorporates such a device. We also use it, in serious writing as well as in vaudeville jokes, when we quote the prototypical Irishman, Scotsman, or Brooklynite. In Nootka mythological narratives the characters Deer and Mink regularly distort the phonemic structure of words in one fashion (turning all occurrences of /s c c'/ and /š č č'/ into laterals /ł ƛ ƛ'/), Raven in another, and Kwatyat in a third. A story-teller who forgets to make the proper changes may lose prestige.

Extensive use of figures of speech (§37.5), or of one or another type of figure of speech, can mark stylistic differences, and may serve to distinguish literary from non-literary discourse, as well as the literature of one community from that of another. The figures of speech common in the literature of the aboriginal New World are not the same as those most familiar to us: translations into English of "classic" Indian speeches are apt to lose the native stylistic values and replace them by those more familiar in our own literature. This shows up even in non-literary contexts. Such place-names as *Father-of-Waters* (for the Mississippi) and *Cheop's Temple* (for a butte in the Grand Canyon) are Old-World in style and were invented by Europeans; the Fox Indian word /mešisi·pi/, whence our *Mississippi*, means merely 'big river,' and the Havasupai Indian word for the mountains which include Cheop's Temple means merely 'Buckskin mountains.'

The stylistic examples given above are all on a low size-level—that of words, phrases, sentences, or even that of phonemes (Nootka phoneme-replacement in the speech of certain characters). Comparable phenomena at higher size-levels are not usually classed as style by literary specialists, but as "structure." The relatively precise machinery of analysis which linguists have developed does not yet enable us to make effective statements about stylistic or structural features of longer segments of discourse—conversations, narratives, "paragraphs," or whole stories. Literary scholars have a battery of terms, *plot, counterplot, introduction, climax, anticlimax, dénouement* with which they describe the larger-grained structure of certain types of literary discourse. A whole novel, we must assume, has some sort of a determinate IC-structure, its ICs in turn consisting of still smaller ones, and so on down until we reach individual morphemes. The terminological arsenal of the literary scholar applies, often very well, to the largest size-levels of this structure; that of the linguist applies equally well to the smallest size-levels; but there is at present a poorly explored terrain in between.

63.3. Types of Literature. The literature of a society may be anything but homogeneous. Usually there are two or more sharply different categories of literary discourse, occurring perhaps under different circumstances. Folklorists make use of various classificatory terms—"proverbs," "riddles," "folktales," "myths," "origin myths," and the like. But the use of such terms requires great care, for what we must always seek, in the first instance, is an indigenous classification—one overtly given by the participants of the society in question, or indicated by their differential behavior.

For example, the Plains Cree distinguish between an /a·tayo·hke·win/ or 'sacred story,' on the one hand, and an /a·cimo·win/—any other sort of narrative—on the other. The former deals with events in an earlier stage of the history of the world, before things had settled into the familiar fixed patterns which now surround us: the characters are part animal, part human, and part spirit, and are prototypes of the actual animals and people of today. Any /a·tayo·hke·win/ under aboriginal conditions was by definition literary. An /a·cimo·win/, on the other hand, might or might not be, for the term is quite inclusive. The indigenous Cree classification may well be more complicated than just described, but of this two-way differentiation we are sure.

Whatever other sort of indigenous classification may appear in a society, the segregation of the sacred tale from all other kinds is very widespread; certainly it is found in many social groups within our own Western society.

63.4. Prose and Poetry. Poetry is widespread, though not certainly known to exist in all societies. It is everywhere distinguished from prose in the same fundamental way, but the distinction is one of degree, not of kind.

Most poetry can be described as literature in the form of *verse*. Verse, in turn, can be defined as discourse in which the speaker binds himself in advance to follow certain more or less closely defined patterns of rhythm, regardless of the topic of the discourse. The rhythm is variously achieved in different languages: sometimes it is a spacing of stresses, lengths, or tones; sometimes it is a spaced recurrence of vowels or consonants or both (yielding *rhyme* and *assonance*). No matter how alien the pattern may be to our ears, the factor of controlled rhythm is present or the discourse cannot qualify as verse. The definition of verse obviously depends on phonological rather than grammatical properties of the discourse.

But not all poetry conforms neatly to the above description. Probably a better basic definition of poetic discourse is that in it as much as possible is made of the secondary associations of the shapes which represent morphemes (§35), as a means of reinforcing the obvious literal meaning of the words. The emergence in poetry of rhythm, rhyme, and assonance then comes about as one formal means to the end. The works of Walt Whitman clearly count as English poetry under this basic definition, though they conform to no simple verse pattern. Contrariwise, discourse can be produced in the strictest verse pattern without being poetry—because it fails to qualify as literature.

It is clear that the exact grammatical and phonemic shape of a poem is important. Poetry under conditions of illiteracy tends to retain its shape from one recounting to another much more precisely than does prose literature, for obvious reasons. Even so, poetry passed down by word-of-mouth is subject to a remarkable amount of modification in course of time, as the most casual study of the folksongs of our own country will show.

63.5. The Impact of Writing on Literature. Most of our discussion so far has applied especially to the literature of illiterate societies. The development of writing in relatively recent times (the last few thousand years, and only in certain parts of the world) has brought about certain transformations. We shall take these up under three headings: *the impact of writing style, the survival factor,* and *emphasis on authorship.*

The Impact of Writing Style. Orally transmitted literature is, of course, not cast in a writing style (§62.5). This often proves embarrassing to the collector of folk-tales, who faces the task of producing a written record of what has not previously been written.

But if a literary artist lives in a community where his products will be cast in written form to begin with, the situation is different. The raw-materials of his trade are not simply the whole language, but rather the writing style of the language. This is not an uncompensated loss, for, as shown in §62.5, although some elements of speech can be written only inaccurately, if at all, writing systems make up for this by developing devices which are independent of language and go beyond it. All of these devices are available to the writer in a literate community.

A few trivial examples must suffice. In the West there is an established special typographical convention for verse, by which certain rhythmic units are written in successive lines—and, because of this, are called "lines." Thus we have:

The day is done, and the darkness
Falls from the wings of Night,
As a feather is wafted downward
From an eagle in his flight.

The rhythmic organization of this poem is actually—save for the presence of rhyme—very similar to (though not identical with) that of *Evangeline:*

| The | dáy | is | dóne and the | dárkness ‖ |
| | Thís is the | fórest   pri- | méval ‖ |

| | fálls from the | wíngs   of | níght |
| the | múrmuring | pínes and the | hémlocks |

(Remember that English has stress-timed rhythm, so that the number of stresses in a passage is the main determinant of its duration; §5.4.) If Longfellow had followed the same orthographic convention here as he did for *Evangeline*, it would superficially seem like a major alteration, but we must conclude that the difference is not to any great extent linguistic.

A few writers have chosen to attain a special effect (we shall not venture to describe it) by printing their verses in solid paragraphs, like prose. Illustrating with the same poem, we should have:

The day is done, and the darkness falls from the wings of Night, as a feather is wafted downward from an eagle in his flight. I see the lights of the village gleam through the rain and the mist, . . .

There have been experiments with other typographical arrangements. George Herbert (early 17th century) wrote a poem called *The Altar* with long first and last lines, short and centered middle ones, so that the arrangement of print on the page forms a rough picture of an altar. Lewis Carroll's verse beginning *Fury said to a mouse* was originally printed so that the words formed a mouse's tail curling down the page.

One of the subjects studied by analysts and historians of literature is the stylistic peculiarities of different writers, the sources thereof, and the way in which one writer affects another along such lines. Individual styles are related to the general writing style of a language in that each of the former is some sort of specialization within the confines of the latter, just as the latter—save for the late-developed independent features of writing—is a specialization of the language as a whole.

The Survival Factor. In an illiterate society a story or other literary work will survive only as long as it continues to be learned by at least one person in each generation. If this process of transmission fails, either through changing taste or through accident, the story is gone.

With the introduction of writing the conditions for survival change. When a discourse is written down, it can be kept in essentially unchanged form much more easily; the exact degree of ease depends on the type of writing-materials, the ease with which copies are made (witness the tremendous impact of the invention of printing), and the extent to which it is the habit to make them.

There is no guarantee, however, that only discourse considered to have literary merit will be committed to writing. For example, the accidents of history have preserved for us a highly erratic collection of writings from the first few centuries of English-speaking Britain: *Beowulf*, parts of some other poems of various kinds, lives of the saints, laws, recipes for remedies, charms, historical chronicles, and so on. Specialists in Old English ignore no slightest scrap of this, but such specialists are not literary scholars in the narrow sense of the term; rather, they seek, through the sifting of all the available evidence, to determine as much as they can about the pattern of life in early England. Even for narrower literary purposes this background work is essential, for without it we cannot hope to find out which discourses or types of discourses, preserved or not, were actually literature for the Anglo-Saxons.

Literacy may preserve a discourse past the period in the history of a society during which it qualifies as literature. This, again, is unlikely or impossible in an illiterate society. Having thus survived, a discourse may be rediscovered by a later generation, and regain its literary status. This happened, in a way, to various of the works of classical Greek and Roman authors, which were nowhere read or appreciated during the earlier Middle Ages of Europe, but which are now once again treasured by a certain few elements of our society, if not by the man on the street.

Poetry, and literature which verges on the poetic, is sometimes valued primarily for reasons of style rather than content. But language constantly changes, and this means that the frame of reference for the rhythmic and associative features which constitute poetic style is also constantly changing. In an illiterate society the precise shape of a poem may gradually be modified, a word replaced here, a rhythm or rhyme brought up to date there, in such a way as to keep pace with the changing language. On this score the introduction of writing has some implications which might be called unfortunate. Once a poem is written down it is fixed: it has lost its ability to grow with the language. Sooner or later, the poem is left behind.

This has happened to Anglo-Saxon poetry in the last thousand years: it is meaningless to us unless we first study Old English as we would study French or Chinese, and no amount of labor can make it sound to us as it did to our ancestors. The poetry of Shakespeare, written only four-hundred-odd years ago, is still largely understandable, and was so extremely well contrived that it still moves many of us deeply. Yet nothing can prevent it from suffering, in the end, the same fate: its stylistic merits will in due time be lost forever to all but a handful of antiquarians.

Sufficiently strong motivation, such as that based in religious conviction, can fight a partially effective delaying action against this. The King James translation of the Bible is still with us, and preferred by many to the newer versions; the ritual discourses of the Church of England are even older. The ultimate outcome of this sort of delaying action appears in the use of a totally alien language for certain purposes: Latin in the Catholic Church, so-called Classical Arabic by Mohammedans. In extreme cases like these, the emotional attachment and positive valuation come first, and are by fiat, rather than because of the intrinsic properties of the discourses, associated with the latter.

Emphasis on Authorship. In an illiterate society the literary artist is the individual who recounts the traditional stories or recites the traditional poetry in a way which is pleasing and proper to his contemporaries. There is no distinction between creator and performer: the two are bound up in a single individual, whose discourse is largely that passed down to him from his predecessors, but who makes his own minor alterations, deletions, and additions, in keeping with the contemporary language of everyday affairs, current conditions of life, and his own personality. This does not mean, of course, that "folktales" are invented by the "folk" in any mystic sense. Every single element of a given folktale was invented by some specific artisan somewhere in the tale's past history.

We can find the same thing in the literature of literate communities. The Faust legend is much older than Marlowe; his was not the first treatment in written form, and his successors have included Goethe, librettists working for Gounod and for Boito, Thomas Mann, and many others. We could regard the legend itself as "the" literary unit, and think of all the writers and dramatists we have mentioned as passers-on of the legend, each adding his own modifications, just as in an illiterate society.

But there is a sharp difference. In the illiterate society no one is apt to be acquainted with more than two or three slightly differing manipulations of a single theme—one old man may put episode A before episode B, and another may reverse this order. In a literate society a single generation has access to many different treatments of a single theme, both those worked out by contemporaries and those inherited from earlier times. Thus we *have* Marlowe's play, and Goethe's, and Gounod's opera, and Boito's, and Thomas Mann's *Doktor Faustus*, and *The Devil and Daniel Webster*, to say nothing of rewrites of the same plot in one variety of contemporary pulp fiction. For the literary scholar this changes the emphasis. It is naturally worthy of note that a single legend threads through all these varied treatments; but of much greater interest are the differences: the creative artisanship of each writer, the ways in which he individually reflects—or repudiates—the temper of his own times and the pattern of his own language. Thus arises the *emphasis on authorship.*

This emphasis makes itself felt not alone in the work of the literary scholar or critic. It permeates the appreciation of literature by the layman, and, most important, invades the activity of the would-be literary artist and molds his work. The writer is forced by the nature of a literate literary tradition to drive towards individuality, towards the unique and different. This is no place to discuss the possible consequences, save to point out that such an orientation may well be directly antithetical to the original and fundamental nature of literature.

63.6. Language, Literature, and Life. A common notion holds that great writers, such as Shakespeare and Milton, are the "architects of the English language"; that is, that individuals of special literary ability are those primarily responsible for the shape a language takes in the mouths of subsequent generations of ordinary speakers.

This theory is consonant with the emphasis on authorship of which we have just spoken, and is held with amazing tenacity by some scholars. Yet there is not a shred of evidence in its support. The scholars in question dip badly calibrated depth-gages into the river of language: they overestimate the extent and durability of the "surface froth" and underestimate the deeper more slowly flowing layers. Suppose, for example, that we examine Shakespeare's usage of English in comparison with our own. We find the following classes of forms and usages:

(1) Numerous items shared by Shakespeare and ourselves, but inherited by Shakespeare from the everyday speakers who preceded him: the bulk of the grammatical pattern, most short idioms, and even slang phrases like *there's the rub*.

(2) A few idioms invented by Shakespeare and now used, though only by some people and under rather special circumstances, because he used them (*allusions* and *quotations*): *to be or not to be, the most unkindest cut of all*. These are "surface froth."

(3) Some passages which we cannot understand without help, because the words and phrases involved have since fallen into disuse:

> If I do prove her haggard,
> Though that her jesses were my dear heart-strings,
> I'd whistle her off, and let her down the wind,
> To prey at fortune.

The reference is to falconry, now largely a lost art.

Surprising as it may be, a comparable examination of, say, the King James Bible yields much the same results. The "architects" of our language are not literary artists, but the masses of people who use the language for everyday purposes. The greatness of a literary artist is not measured in terms of his stylistic novelty—if he does not operate within the body of shared conventions which constitute ordinary language, he can hope only for a short faddistic following—but by the extent to which he can develop freedom and variety of expression *within* the constraints imposed by the language. So far as language is concerned, the greatest of literary artists is infinitely more a recipient than a donor.

If we must thus conclude that the impact of literature on language is trivial, no comparable conclusion is justified about the impact of literature on the business of living. The existence of a stock of positively evaluated and oft-repeated discourses is a phenomenon made possible by language: it is patent that dogs and apes, having no language, also have no literature. One of the most important things about human language is that it serves as the medium for literature. The literary tradition of a community, in turn, is a vital mechanism in the training of the young in culturally approved attitudes and patterns of behavior; it serves to transmit the moral fiber of the community from one generation to the next. Speaking of Menomini sacred tales, Bloomfield wrote:

[These stories deal] with a far-off time when the world as we know it was in process of formation.[1] The spirit animals enter in human or semi-human form, and the powers of the sky still dwell on earth. These stories are considered as true; they are told to inform and instruct; they often explain the origin of things, especially of plants and animals, and of customs. Even the lovable ineptitudes of [the culture hero] indicate by contrast the correct human way of obtaining food and the like.

"Marginal men," their aboriginal heritage undermined by the intrusion of Western ways, lose their literature—if the stories are remembered, the evaluations are gone—and the cultural orientation which it provides. Perhaps this is not unrelated to the peculiar state of literature in Western society itself.

NOTES

New terms: *excellence of speech; special style; poetry* versus *prose; verse.*

The definition of *literature* is essentially that of Martin Joos (unpublished). Nootka: Sapir and Swadesh 1939. Sapir 1915. Menomini: Bloomfield 1928 (the quotation is from page xii), 1927. Cree: Bloomfield 1930 and 1934. Fox: Jones 1917. Oneida: fide Floyd Lounsbury. Old English literary study: Hulbert 1947. Old World versus New World genres: Boas 1927, chapter 7.

The peculiar status of Western literature is obvious in the work of almost any literary critic, not excluding those few, such as Richards (1929, 1934) and Wellek and Warren (1949), who try to bring certain linguistic techniques to bear on literary analysis. These specialists are *participants* in the Western literary tradition, not merely observers; as such, it is in no sense improper for them to make value judgments, or even to reject, for the specific purposes they seek, the cross-cultural orientation aimed at in the present section.

[1] From Leonard Bloomfield, *Menomini Texts*. Publications of the American Ethnological Society 12, New York (1928).

MAN'S PLACE IN NATURE

64·

MAN'S PLACE in NATURE

64.1. Our last task in this book is to explore, as best we can with the information currently available, the bearing of language on Man's place in the universe. From time immemorial, the animals and spirits of folklore have had human characteristics thrust upon them, including always the power of speech. But the cold facts are that Man is the only living species with this power, and that no other living species can reasonably be presumed to have had the power at some earlier time and to have lost it since. The appearance of language in the universe—at least on our planet—is thus exactly as recent as the appearance of Man himself. We should like to know how language evolved from what was not language, and how its emergence shaped the ensuing life and destiny of those organisms which developed it. The detailed answers to these questions are not available and probably never will be. But we have the obligation of pinning things down as closely as the evidence allows, and the right to go somewhat further along the line of educated guesses.

As a frame of reference we need a purview of Man's position in the zoological family tree. All living human beings are members of a single species, *Homo sapiens*. The more distant genetic affiliations of *Homo sapiens* are as follows:

Genus: *Homo*. In geologically Recent times (approximately the last 30,000 years), *H. sapiens* has been the only representative of this genus. In Pleistocene times (from approximately 700,000 to about 30,000 years ago) there was at least one other species, *H. neanderthalensis*, known from Europe, the Middle East, and Central Asia, which shared with *H. Sapiens* his unusually large brain.

Family: Hominidae. *Homo* is the only genus of this family surviving

569

into Recent times. Pleistocene fossils attest to two other genera: *Pithecanthropus*, known from Java and China, and *Australopithecus*, from South Africa. These did not share with *Homo* the especially large brain of the latter, but the earliest use of crude tools and of fire for warmth (not for cooking, and not the making of fire) date from the early Pleistocene and were not confined to *Homo*.

Superfamily: Hominoidea. In addition to the Hominidae, this super-family includes a now extinct family and the still represented family Pongidae. Present-day gibbons belong to one subfamily of the Pongidae; contemporary orang-utans, chimpanzees, and gorillas to another. The earliest Hominoidea may have lived in the late Oligocene or early Miocene; the latest common ancestors of *H. sapiens* and the great apes presumably lived ten to fifteen million years ago.

Suborder: Anthropoidea (including also monkeys): oldest known fossils are Oligocene.

Order: Primates (including also lemurs, tarsiers, etc.): earliest fossils are Eocene.

Cohort: Unguiculata (including Insectivora, bats, anteaters): earliest fossils late Cretaceous.

Infraclass: Eutheria (placental mammals).

Subclass: Theria (placental mammals and marsupials like the kangaroos).

Class: Mammalia (the above and the monotremes): earliest fossils Jurassic.

Subphylum: Vertebrates (fishes, amphibians, reptiles, birds): from Ordovician.

Phylum: Chordata: from Cambrian.

Kingdom: Animalia.

64.2. Animal Communication. Although *Homo sapiens* is the only living species with the power of speech, Man is by no means the only animal which carries on communication of some sort. Part of the problem of differentiating Man from the other animals is the problem of describing how human language differs from any kind of communicative behavior carried on by non-human or pre-human species. Until we have done this, we cannot know how much it means to assert that only Man has the power of speech. Therefore we shall consider briefly several examples of non-human animal communication.

First, bees (which belong to a different Phylum of the animal

Kingdom from Man). When a worker bee finds a source of nectar, she returns to the hive and performs a dance. It has been shown that certain features of the dance transmit to the other workers information about the location of the source of nectar: one feature specifies the direction of the source from the hive, and another feature specifies its distance. The worker bee performs the appropriate dance, or understands the dance of another worker (that is, flies properly to the new nectar source), on the basis of instinct: the semantic conventions of the system are built into her by her genes, and do not have to be learned or taught. A worker can report on a source of nectar at a location at which neither she nor her fellows have ever previously found nectar. Thus, within narrow limits, the system is flexible. But bees cannot communicate about anything except nectar—or, if they do, it is via other equally specialized small systems, not through further variations of the dance. The reader will detect certain similarities and certain differences between bee dancing and human language, but we postpone our discussion of these until the rest of our animal examples have been given.

Next, the courtship behavior of a type of fish known as the three-spined stickleback (*Gasterosteus aculeatus*, of the same Phylum and Subphylum as Man, but of a different and vastly older Class). Our account reports both observations made of the fish in its natural environment and the results of certain experiments in aquaria. During the breeding season, the male builds a nest on the floor of ocean, river, or aquarium, then swims upwards, spies a female whose abdomen is distended with eggs, and performs a zigzag dance around her, turning first towards her and then away. The reaction of the female is to follow the male, who then leads her to the nest. At this season, the male stickleback has a bright red belly and bright blue eyes. A crude wooden model will induce the courtship dance from a male; the precise details of shape and coloring of the female do not have to be matched, but it is essential that the distension of the abdomen be represented, or the male will not react. Similarly, a crude wooden model of the male will induce the female to follow: most details, even the blue eye, can be left out, but the red underside is crucial, and the zigzag dance must be roughly imitated. Arriving at the nest, the male turns to a vertical position, nose downwards, and points at the nest, into which the female swims. The female's response can be elicited by proper pointing with a wooden model, without any nest at all. The female then ejects her eggs when the male

rubs her abdomen with its nose: properly rhythmic rubbing with any
object leads to the same result. The female then goes away, and the
male ejects his sperm. In this train of behavior we see a highly specific
sequence of signals passed back and forth between the male and the
female, each signal serving as all or part of the stimulus for the next.
The behavior is undeniably communicative under any reasonable
definition of the latter term, but, if anything, it is even less flexible than
bee dancing. Like the latter, its conventions are acquired genetically,
not through learning.

Third, the pattern of caring for the young manifested by herring
gulls (*Larus argentatus*, a kind of bird, and thus of the same Phylum and
Subphylum as sticklebacks and men, but of a different Class, more
recent than Fishes but probably older than mammals). Soon after the
eggs of a pair of herring gulls have hatched, the brooding parent rises
and lets the chicks up. They begin to beg for food by aiming pecking
motions at the parent's bill. The parent responds by regurgitating a
bit of half-digested food, taking a piece of it between the bill tips, and
offering it to the chicks. The chicks continue their pecking until one
of them manages to get hold of the morsel, and to swallow it; then the
parent offers another morsel. The process ends when the chicks stop
the begging, presumably because they are no longer hungry. The
general outlines of this chain of interstimulation are beyond doubt
genetically determined. But in the successive pecks of an individual
chick we can perhaps discern an element of learning: earlier pecks are
more random, later ones, or pecks on later feeding occasions, are more
effective. It is not certain that such an increase in accuracy shows that
learning is taking place; it may be that the process is entirely one of
maturation—the unfolding of genetically determined behavior patterns. Even if there is some learning, there is clearly none of what we
would call *teaching*. The actions of the parents, in building the nest and
then in regurgitating and offering food, produce or constitute factors
in the environment of the chick; but we would speak of "teaching" only
if these actions of the parents were themselves learned, and clearly
they are not.

Fourth, the calls of gibbons (several species of the genus *Hylobates*,
Superfamily Hominoidea, and thus among our closest surviving non-
human kin). Gibbons stimulate each other in various ways, including
posturing and gesturing, but the most language-like of their communi-

cation is their system of calls. Field investigations with the gibbons of northern Thailand have shown that these gibbons have a stock of at least nine different calls, differing from each other in sound, in antecedents, and in consequences. One of these is emitted typically when the group is surprised by a possible enemy: it takes the form of a sort of high-pitched shout; those gibbons who hear it often repeat the call, and manifest what can only be regarded as "avoidance behavior." An entirely different sort of call occurs in connection with friendly approaches among young gibbons, and reinforces other play behavior. Still a third sort of call seems to serve to keep the members of a band from scattering too far as they move through the woods together in search of food. Communicatively, the most important property of this system is its lack of flexibility. Whatever the exact number of calls actually is, it is in any case finite and small. No matter what situation a gibbon may encounter, his vocal reaction is constrained to be one or another of this small finite number: a gibbon does not react to some partly novel situation by producing a new kind of call, built out of parts of two or more of the stock of calls already at hand. True, any one of the calls can apparently be varied in loudness or in the number of repetitions, but this resembles the variability of the "auditory aura" about human speech discussed in §6.5, not anything within language proper. The call-systems of different species of gibbons, and perhaps of different bands of the same species, show some differences. This differentiation may rest entirely on genetics, but we cannot yet be sure. It is possible that the differentiation reflects some element of *cultural transmission:* that is, learning of the system by the young, and teaching of the system by the adults.

The fact that we class the four examples given above, along with human language, as communicative behavior implies something of our general definition of communication: communicative behavior is those acts by which one organism triggers another. Thus, also, we would class as communicative the fact that the roaring of lions puts gazelles to flight, or that the mating-calls of birds may entice predators, or that a husband may wash his hands and go to the dining room when he observes his wife setting the table. On the other hand, if a burly bartender gets rid of an objectionable patron by picking him up bodily and throwing him out, the event is not communicative, since the bartender does not *trigger* the patron's change of location, but brings it about by a direct application of energy. And it is not communicative if a man prepares for bed when he sees the sun going down, because even though the connection is one of triggering rather than of direct action, the sun is not an organism.

64.3. The Key Properties of Language. It can avail us nothing merely to assert—no matter how justifiably—that the difference between human language and any non-human communicative system is "great." We must know *in what ways* the great difference comes about. Now human language has seven important properties which do not recur, as a whole set, in any known non-human communicative system, although individually some of them do. These seven we shall call *duality, productivity, arbitrariness, interchangeability, specialization, displacement,* and *cultural transmission.* Table 64.1 shows how each of these

TABLE 64.1

	bee dancing	stickleback courtship	herring gull care of offspring	gibbon calls	language
duality	no(?)	no	no	no	yes
productivity	yes	no	no	no	yes
arbitrariness	slight	—	—	slight	great
interchangeability	yes	no	no	yes	yes
specialization	yes	some	?	yes	yes
displacement	yes	no	no	no	yes
cultural transmission	no	no	no	no(?)	yes

seven turns up, or fails to turn up, in the communicative systems we have chosen as representative examples. Below we discuss each of the seven briefly.

Duality. Any utterance in a language consists of an arrangement of the phonemes of that language; at the same time, any utterance in a language consists of an arrangement of the morphemes of that language, each morpheme being variously represented by some small arrangement of phonemes. This is what we mean by "duality": a language has a phonological system and also a grammatical system.

The duality principle is convenient in any communicative system where a fairly large number of messages must be distinguished. If Paul Revere and his colleague had needed a total repertory of several hundred messages, instead of just two, it would have been inconvenient and expensive to have on hand, in the Church tower, several hundred lanterns. But it could have been agreed that each message would take the form of a row of five lights, each of which would be either red, or yellow, or blue. Only fifteen lanterns would then be needed (one of each color for each position), but the system would allow a total of $3^5 = 243$ different messages. The meanings, we assume, would be assigned to the whole messages, just as in the system described by Longfellow: thus "red light in first position" would not have any separate meaning of its own, but would merely serve to distinguish some messages from others, as the recurrent initial /b-/ of the English morphemes *beat, bat, but, bottle* distinguishes these from morphemes like *meat, rat, cut, mottle* without having any meaning of its own.

This system would then manifest duality: its "phonological" subsystem would involve the five positions and the three colors, while its "grammatical" subsystem would involve only the whole messages and the semantic conventions established for each. But here the terms "phonological" and "grammatical" make too direct a reference to human language; it will be better to introduce two new terms for general applicability: *cenematic* and *plerematic*. The cenematic structure of language is phonology; the plerematic structure of language is grammar. Phonemes are linguistic *cenemes;* morphemes are linguistic *pleremes*. Positions and colors are the cenemes of the revised Paul Revere system; the whole arrays of five lanterns are the pleremes.

A good many of Man's recent communicative systems show duality: for example, telegraphy with Morse code, where the cenemes are dots and dashes and silences of several durations, while the pleremes are combinations of cenemes to which meanings have been assigned (e.g., two dots means the letter "I"), or the Ogam script used by the speakers of Old Irish. Figure 64.2 shows the latter.

Table 64.1 shows that none of our four selected animal examples manifests duality. It is possible, however, that duality does appear in some other sub-human communicative systems.

Productivity. We have already mentioned the commonplace that a speaker of a language may say something that he has never said nor heard before, and be understood perfectly by his audience, without either speaker or audience being in the slightest aware of the novelty. We have also discussed the mechanism by which this comes about, which can be summed up by the term *analogy* (§50.1); in our treatment of linguistic ontogeny (§41.3) we pointed out that each child, at some point in time, produces his first analogically constructed novel utterance, and that only after this event can his speech habits be slowly molded in the direction of the adult speech around him.

Productivity implies that some messages in the system—old ones as well as the new one—are *plerematically complex:* that they consist

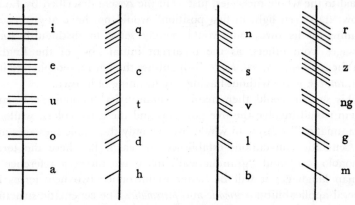

FIGURE 64.2. THE OGAM SCRIPT

The vertical base-lines represent the edges of stones on which the inscriptions were made. The horizontal and slanting strokes constitute the letters of the system. Each letter represented a phoneme of Old Irish, with some irregularities and holes of the usual sort; the Latin letters printed alongside the Ogam letters roughly indicate these values. Thus, each Ogam letter was a plereme. But the letters are composed of from one to five strokes, at one or another of three angles from the base-line, and extending either in both directions or only in one or the other: these facts are indicative of the cenematic structure of the system. "Direction," "angle," and "number" do not in themselves mean anything, but they serve to keep the whole letters (pleremes) apart.

of an arrangement of two or more pleremes, instead of each consisting of a single indivisible plereme. If one starts with a system with no plerematic complexity, then there is only one variety of analogy by which a new message can be coined: *blending* (§51.2). We shall see the importance of this fact later on.

Productivity must be distinguished from duality. In the modified Paul Revere system described earlier, the semantic conventions assign entirely discrete meanings to each whole message, so that each message is a single plereme, and there is no plerematic complexity. The system thus has duality, but no productivity. Conversely, bee dancing is productive, in that a worker can report on an entirely new source of nectar, but bee dancing has no duality. The smallest independently meaningful aspects of a given dance are not composed of arrangements of meaningless but differentiative features, of the sort that would constitute cenemes. The other animal systems which we have discussed show no productivity at all.

Arbitrariness. A plereme means what it does *iconically* if there is some element of geometrical similarity between the plereme and its meaning. Otherwise the semantic relationship is *arbitrary*. At the lowest size-level of most, or all, iconic systems one finds a layer of arbitrariness. Thus a road-map means the territory it represents iconically down to a certain level, but there is no precise correlation between the width of the line representing a road or a river and the actual width of road or river— these features are not represented to scale. Similarly, in English writing the letter-sequence "man" is iconic to the extent that the linear sequence of three letters represents a linear (though temporal) sequence of three English phonemes, while the semantic connection between "m" or "a" or "n" and the phoneme /m/, /æ/, or /n/ is quite arbitrary. It is only when one has reached this breaking point between iconic and arbitrary, going down the size scale, that one can proceed to determine whether a system involves duality or not. In the Ogam script (Figure 64.2), the level of arbitrariness is reached when one comes to the individual letters of the system, since there is no geometrical similarity between the shape of a letter and the shape of an Old Irish phoneme represented by it. Below this level one finds a cenematic structure, as indicated by the caption to the Figure, showing that the system has duality.

Bee dancing is almost wholly iconic. There is a continuum of possible directions to a source of nectar, and another continuum of possible distances. In the choice of one aspect of the dance to represent the former, and another to represent the latter, one finds arbitrariness, but from that point on the system is iconic. The direction is mapped continuously into one continuously variable aspect of the dance, and the distance is mapped continuously into another continuously variable aspect: discrepancies in actual performance are like any discrepancy in accuracy of measurement.

Human language, on the other hand, is almost entirely arbitrary in its semantic conventions. The exceptions are the vague traces of iconicity in onomatopoetic or partially onomatopoetic forms (§35.3), and we have seen that even in these there is a large arbitrary element.

The advantage of arbitrariness over iconicity, in human language versus bee communication, is the same as the advantage of a true writing system over against a picture writing system (§62.4), or the advantage for purposes of wide application of a digital computer over an analog computer. An analog computer, a picture writing system, or bee dancing, can be beautifully adapted for a narrow function, and at the same time worthless for anything else. Human beings can talk about anything; bees can only talk about nectar.

Interchangeability. By this we mean that any participating organism equipped for the transmission of messages in the system is also equipped to receive messages in the same system, and vice versa. For language, any speaker of a language is in principle also a hearer, and is theoretically capable of saying anything he is able to understand when someone else says it. Bee dancing and gibbon calls also involve interchangeability, but our other animal systems do not. In the courtship signalling of sticklebacks, for example, it is obvious that the male and the female cannot exchange roles. Nor can one imagine gazelles roaring and lions fleeing.

Specialization. Any communicative activity, by definition, involves triggering. But the fact that an action of one organism leads, via triggering, to some behavior of another organism does not prevent the triggering activity from leading also to direct physical consequences. In order to determine the extent to which a communicative system is specialized, we compare the trigger consequences and the direct physical consequences of the messages or acts in the system: if they are closely related, then the system is not specialized, but if they have no particular relationship, the system is specialized.

Thus if one sees one's wife setting the table at the right time of day, one knows that dinner is about to be served, and one may wash one's hands and go to the dining room. The table-setting activity has the direct physical consequence that the table is set, ready for dinner. The triggering consequences are that the other members of the family are alerted. The two are obviously interrelated to the highest degree, and the communicative aspect of table-setting is thereby not specialized, but only marginal. On the other hand, the direct consequences of making the verbal announcement *Dinner is almost ready* are some very minor flurries in the air about the speaker. The triggering consequences are the same as those of the observed table-setting. Here there is no functional interrelationship at all, and the system of communication within which the verbal announcement has its place is highly specialized.

Specialization is thus a matter of degree, and our entries in Table 64.1 indicate this. For example, the distension of the abdomen of the female stickleback constitutes an essential ingredient in the "signals" transmitted by her to the courting male; this distension is produced by direct energetic action by the accumulation of roe, and the ultimate outcome of the courtship sequence involves the expulsion of the roe and thus the disappearance of the distension. This element of the signalling system is thus not specialized. On the other hand, the redness of the male's belly seems to be involved largely or exclusively in a triggerwise fashion, and thus shows more specialization. Thus the most that we can assert about human language on this score is that it shows much more extensive specialization than known examples of animal communication.

Displacement. A message is *displaced* to the extent that the key features in its antecedents and consequences are removed from the time and place of transmission. A great deal of human speech is displaced in this sense. So far as has been observed, gibbon calls never are. The search for instances of displacement in still lower animals is apparently quite vain—except, once again, for bees, who are no longer in the presence of the source of nectar when they dance. Even the bee, though, does not delay her announcement indefinitely, as a human being may: she returns directly to the hive and makes it.

Cultural Transmission. In order for an organism to participate in any communicative system, the conventions of that system have to be built into the organism in some way. There are two biological mechanisms by which this is accomplished. One is the *genetic* mechanism: the genes of a given individual, inherited from its parent or parents, govern the pattern of growth and thus the behavioral patterns of the individual. The other is the *cultural* mechanism. The acquisition of a habit via the cultural mechanism involves learning, as when a rat learns to run a maze or a child learns a language, but learning alone is not enough to render a habit cultural. The element of *teaching* must also be present, and the teaching activities of those about the focal organism must themselves have been learned from even earlier teachers. Thus if there is indeed some element of learning in the successive pecks of herring gull young, there is nevertheless no cultural transmission, since the complementary conditioning behavior of the adult herring gulls is itself entirely instinctive.

The genetic mechanism is coterminous, so far as we know, with life itself. The cultural mechanism is far more limited. A certain genetic make-up is obviously prerequisite for the development of cultural transmission: animals other than man can be "enculturated" by human intervention only to slight degrees. Man stands alone, in the modern world, at least in the depth and complexity of his culture, though it is not so certain that he stands alone in an absolute sense: other surviving species of the Superfamily Hominoidea, or even species more distantly related to man, may be suspected of having culture of a thin sort. The observations on which proof or disproof of this hypothesis must be based are exceedingly difficult to make, and the answer is at present not known.

The importance of cultural transmission as a biological mechanism is that it vastly speeds up the rate and the finesse with which a species can adapt to its environment and to changes therein. A cultureless species can "learn," as a whole species, in the sense that in enough time natural selection breeds out unfavorable traits and spreads those which are favorable in the given environment. But even if an individual organism of a cultureless species should manage to work out, ontogenetically, some particularly good adaptation to its environment, there is no way in which this adaptation can be passed on to later generations. Only culture makes this kind of cumulative learning possible.

There can be no question but that the conventions of human language are transmitted culturally, rather than genetically, from one generation to the next. This is true of no known pre-human communicative system, unless in due time it is shown to hold to some extent for gibbon calls or for the communicative behavior of other non-human Hominoidea.

One apparently important ingredient for cultural transmission is *imitation:* a type of interstimulation in which the conditioning behavior of one individual stimulates *similar* behavior from another. Humans surpass all other species in the ability or tendency to imitate, but other Primates, particularly Anthropoidea, have some of this—as indicated by our customary use of the word *ape* as a verb.

64.4. Language and Human Origins. The various recurrences of one or another of the key properties of human language in non-human communicative systems are not all of equal significance in trying to work out Man's own early history. The most extensive and striking parallelism is that between language and bee dancing, which share productivity, interchangeability, some displacement, and some specialization. But there are no proto-bees in Man's lineage, so that the functional parallels are like the fact that some invertebrates, some reptiles, most birds, and two mammals (bats and men) have all, quite independently, acquired the power of flight.

If we confine our attention to Man's own lineage, plus, at most, developments among near collaterals, then we see that the seven fundamental properties of language as a communicative system could not have emerged in just any temporal sequence. Some of them either unquestionably or with high likelihood imply the prior existence of some of the others.

Some degree of specialization seems to be the earliest of all, since it appears in the communicative behavior of birds and of fishes.

Gibbon calls share with human language the properties of interchangeability and specialization, and perhaps to a limited extent that of cultural transmission. It is in this connection that the imitative tendencies of many primates are worthy of notice: they suggest that the seeds for the later development of cultural transmission, displacement, and interchangeability may have been planted in pre-Hominoid times. Imitation involves displacement just as soon as the young of a species are sometimes taught a habit out of the exact context in which the response will normally be evoked. The relationship of imitation and interchangeability is obvious, once it is given that the young of a species will be developing habits through learning rather than through genetically driven maturation.

Nowhere in Man's lineage, prior to language itself, do we find the property of productivity, nor that of arbitrariness which seems to go along with it, and these do not recur among surviving non-human Hominoidea. We conclude, therefore, that this property developed at some point in time subsequent to the era of the latest common ancestors of all the Hominoidea—some time during the last ten or fifteen million years. Furthermore, we regard this as the one crucial development setting Man off against his surviving cousins. As of this development, those who had it were *man*, and what they had was genuine *language*.

We cannot tell whether duality appeared before or after productivity, since its known recurrences in the non-human world are far away and not helpful. The most we can say is that, if productivity preceded duality, duality must have been added very soon: there is no other economical way of obtaining a sufficiently large number of different signals.

Conceivably, productivity and duality developed at the same time. We can imagine a band of pre-humans possessed of a stock of plerematically unstructured vocal signals somewhat like present-day gibbon calls. We can imagine the occasional production of a new call, built from parts of two old ones by the type of analogy called blending; we can imagine these innovations usually not being understood by the hearers, but occasionally—and increasingly often—being effective, so that the habit of building such new calls in time gained ground. Such a sequence of events would lead both to genuine productivity and to duality, the latter because of the partial physical resemblances of new calls to old ones. It would also, almost inevitably, lead to arbitrariness, at least as the system enlarged and became more readily productive. The fact that a given analogical innovation—the "first," for example, if there was a "first"—must have occurred quite suddenly at a certain time and place in no wise implies that the whole process was sudden. The slow trial-and-error process which began with an unproductive system of the gibbon-call type and ended with something recognizably like modern language may have gone on for twenty thousand years, or for a million, or for five million.

At the time of the earliest foreshadowings of productivity, there may have been striking differences in the genetically determined abilities of various groups of Hominoidea to acquire culturally transmitted communicative habits, and correspondingly striking differences in the "languages" and quasi-languages found among the groups. But the workings of natural selection, on both the genetic and the cultural level, eliminated the inefficient strains and the inefficient culturally transmitted habits in relatively short order, so that what we know now as human language is, and for many millenia has been, about equally efficient for all human communities. If the impact of different present-day languages on the other behavior of their speakers shows any meaningful variation at all, the differences are of the order that can be discerned, as it were, only through a cultural microscope; whatever the differences may be, there is no reason to believe that they are a residue of the presumably much vaster differences of the early times of which we are now speaking.

One of the strongest bits of evidence for the hypothesis just stated is Man's extreme biological isolation—for thirty thousand years or more the only surviving species of the only surviving genus of the family Hominidae, his nearest surviving relatives sharing ancestors only as of ten or fifteen million years in the past. Why should this be? Why should there not also still be a whole string of species bridging the gap between chimpanzee or gorilla and Man? Biogeographers assert that two closely related species cannot live side by side in a single ecological niche. It seems that if a set of related species or strains are in competition in a single ecological niche, the one which has made the most successful adaptation in time crowds out those most similar (and genetically closest) to it, though more distantly related other species or strains may survive because they are not so directly in competition with the first. It is a race in which the winner destroys—or interbreeds with—the runner-up. This is one of the mechanisms by which strains become separate species: they destroy the intermediate types and become isolated by so doing.

In the case of the adaptation or adaptations which changed prehumans into humans—first, and quite early, the genetic changes which were permissive for cultural transmission, and later those which were permissive for language—the differential advantage was enormous, for a wide variety of ecological niches: no half-way genetic adaptation among kindred strains had a chance.

The emergence of the relatively large brain shared by all the Hominidae may have correlated with the first of these two crucial developments (easier learning, and thus cultural transmission); this is supported also by the use, attested by archeological remains, of simple tools and of fire for warmth by several different early Pleistocene Hominidae. The emergence of the extremely large brain of all species of *Homo* may similarly have been correlated with the second (true language). Such inferences, however, are doubtful. In particular, we must eschew the easy assumption that a genetically determined increase in brain size or complexity necessarily *preceded* some crucial functional development. The reverse could be true: a new functional development, such as productive language, might be the key factor favoring a genetic selection for larger brains.

We have been led in the above to the tentative conclusion that cultural transmission was earlier than plerematically complex communication; but the inception of language must in turn have been the biggest shot in the arm ever administered to cultural transmission. The relevance of language for cultural transmission can be shown easily. Once the language of a community has begun to be acquired by any new member of the community, the portion already learned serves as a powerful carrier for the acquisition of the rest, as well as for the acquisition of other communicative systems and of aspects of culture which are not usually thought of as communicative. Learning via already understood symbols may obviate the considerable dangers involved in learning via direct participation. The boy who is destined to become a hunter for his tribe hears a great deal about hunting before he goes along in person. On his first hunt, he certainly learns in part by demonstration, but it has been communicatively determined that he *should* do so, and he is also *told* how things are to be done and why. A child is repeatedly *told*, at apt moments, "we do it this way," or "such-and-such just isn't done." Parts of the environment which an individual has not yet experienced directly are described to him, accurately or inaccurately as may be, in terms of parts which he has already experienced. Verbalization penetrates into every cultural nook and cranny of tribal life. Individuals are told not only how to seek their goals, but in numerous cases are told *what goals to seek*. Without productive, culturally-transmitted, language, the proliferation of human culture as a whole would never have taken place.

Conversely, given a Hominoid possessed of cultural transmission and of the earliest imaginable form of genuine language, it is hard to see how the proliferation of human culture as we know it could be avoided. A genuinely productive communicative system at once begins modifying both itself and other aspects of the behavior of its possessors along the lines discussed under Idiom Formation (§36.2,3); and this is precisely the process of drawing more and more types of activity into the domain of the cultural. Language is a technological device of the greatest importance and increases the chances of survival of those who have it. At the same time, it changes an undifferentiated Hominoid into a very special kind of creature. As a Hominoid, Man shares all the biological drives or motives found for organisms in general—hunger, sex, the elimination of waste, and so on, each with its characteristic periodicity. Above and beyond these, the vital role of communicative behavior in human life has brought about a drive which probably cannot be reduced to those shared with other animals: the drive to *be in communication* with others. This does not mean active reciprocal triggering; it implies only being in a state in which triggering is possible. Even the actual transmission of signals does not always lead to gross behavioral consequences. A telegrapher clicks his key a bit to let other operators know that the channel is open and that he is on the job. People indulge in chit-chat about nothing for much the same reason. A housewife leaves the radio on as she goes about her chores, not bothering to listen most of the time. The term *phatic communion* has been proposed for this sort of minimal communicative activity which has no obvious consequence save to inform all concerned that the channels are in good working order for the transmission of more "important" messages. It is almost certain that phatic communion plays a major role in those human activities usually classed as artistic—painting, sculpture, the dance, music, literature, and so on—which seem to have certain communicative-like features but which are hard to deal with completely in communicative terms. Typically human states of "mental" well-being or neurosis are likewise communicative: they relate to communication and to phatic communion as malnutrition and measles relate to food and bacteria.

Put in another way, *much human communication is itself about communication*, rather than about the corn crop, the arrival of raiders from a neighboring tribe, or the like. Many animals, indeed, seem to like to be in the company of their own kind, at least at certain crises; but they do not often indulge in communicative behavior merely for the sake of the activity. With most species, communication occurs only in four contexts: mating, the care of the young, cooperation in obtaining food or territory, and fighting within the species or against predators. There is a vast quantity of human communication which cannot possibly be related, even mediately, to any of these four factors. Man does not live by bread alone: his other necessity is communication.

NOTES

Man's zoological classification: Le Gros Clark 1955, Simpson 1945.
Animal communication: Tinbergen 1953, Frisch 1950, Carpenter 1940.

Coon, 1954, LaBarre 1954, and Hooton 1946 attempt to trace the whole of Man's history; only LaBarre gives more than lip-service to the role of language. Kroeber 1955 suggests a new and important type of investigation of animal behavior in comparison with human. Our definition of culture is consonant with only some of those surveyed by Kroeber and Kluckhohn 1952. Bloomfield 1935 and 1939 deals with the importance of language for technology and science; Hockett 1948b is more general. Ruesch and Bateson 1950 discuss the communicative basis of neurosis; somewhat different is the approach of the "General Semanticists," especially Korzybski 1948, Hayakawa 1941, 1949, Rapoport 1950. Whorf (essays collected in Carroll, ed., 1956) tries to investigate the differential impact of differing linguistic systems; a recent conference on this is reported in Hoijer, ed., 1954.

APPENDIX of
LANGUAGE-NAMES

The following is an alphabetical list of all names of languages, language families, and other groupings of languages mentioned anywhere in the text. Omitted are a few, such as "North American Indian languages," too obvious to require any comment. Names generally interpreted as referring to single languages are printed in lower-case letters (e.g., "English"), while those usually thought of as subsuming groups or families are printed in capitals (e.g., "GERMANIC"). In some instances a reference to the Bibliography (which follows this appendix) gives the source of the writer's information. Geographical location and dates are given in more "exotic" cases, but not for familiar languages like English, French, and German. Whenever two or more languages of a single family have been mentioned in the text, the detailed information is given under the name of the family, and the separate language names are followed merely by cross-reference to the family.

General references of value in this connection are Meillet and Cohen 1952, Matthews 1951, Voegelin and Voegelin 1944, Hoijer 1946, McQuown 1955, Greenberg 1949–1950, Bloomfield 1933, Gray 1939.

A

Adyge.—See CAUCASUS, LANGUAGES OF.

AFRO-ASIATIC (formerly called HAMITO-SEMITIC or SEMITIC-HAMITIC).

SEMITIC:

EASTERN SEMITIC (extinct): Babylonian and Assyrian. Cuneiform form inscriptions from about 2500 B.C.

WESTERN SEMITIC:

NORTHERN branch: Canaanite (1400 B.C.), Moabite (ninth century B.C.), Phoenician (ninth century B.C. and later, in Phoenicia and Carthage), and Aramaic (eighth century B.C. through about 650 A.D.), all now extinct; Hebrew (ninth century B.C. on; superseded by Aramaic about second century B.C., but continued in religious and learnèd use, and now being revived in Israel as a language learned by children).

SOUTHERN branch: South Arabic (800 B.C. through 6th century A.D., surviving along south coast of Arabia); Arabic (328 A.D. on;

587

now actually a group of closely related languages spread—by Islam —from Morocco and Algiers through North Africa, Arabia, and the Levant); Ethiopian (from fourth century A.D.; now several languages in and near Ethiopia).

EGYPTIAN (known from 4000 B.C.; a later form, Coptic, surviving into the Christian era but swamped in the seventh century A.D. by Arabic).

BERBER (Libyan inscriptions from 4th century B.C.); CUSHITE; and CHAD; all represented today by languages in Africa.

Albanian.—See INDO-HITTITE.

ALGONQUIAN.

CENTRAL-EASTERN branch:

EASTERN division: a number of languages, spoken aboriginally in an Atlantic Coastal strip from Nova Scotia through Virginia. Most of these are now extinct.

CENTRAL division: Cree (in many dialects in a large territory south-west, south, southeast, and east of Hudson's Bay); Ojibwa (in many dialects, in a belt just south of Cree, touching on most of the Great Lakes); Menomini (aboriginally in northern Wisconsin and Michigan, now on one reservation in Wisconsin); Fox (with Sauk and Kickapoo; aboriginally in southern Wisconsin, now on reservations in Iowa and Oklahoma); Potawatomi (aboriginally in southern Michigan, now in Wisconsin, Oklahoma, and Kansas); Shawnee (aboriginally migratory in Ohio, Indiana, and perhaps Illinois, now mainly in Oklahoma); several now extinct languages. In §38.3 the terms "Shawnee," "Sauk-and-Fox," "Kickapoo," and "Ojibwa" refer to the dialects of four present-day communities.

ARAPAHO-ATSINA-NAWATHINEHENA branch; in Plains: we mention only Arapaho.

Blackfoot branch and Cheyenne branch: each composed of one language, in the plains.

APACHEAN.—See ATHAPASKAN.

Arabic.—See AFRO-ASIATIC.

Arapaho.—See ALGONQUIAN

Armenian.—See INDO-HITTITE.

Assyrian.—See AFRO-ASIATIC.

ATHAPASKAN.

NORTHERN branch: a large number of languages, including Chipewyan, spoken by scattered migratory tribes in a vast continuous area of northwestern Canada and the interior of Alaska.

PACIFIC branch: a number of languages, some now extinct, in isolated spots near the Pacific Coast in Oregon and California.

SOUTHERN or APACHEAN branch: the languages of the various Apache tribes and of the Navaho, in the Southwest.

B

Badaga.—See DRAVIDIAN.

BALTO-SLAVIC.—See INDO-HITTITE.

BANTU LANGUAGES.—The BANTU group, in Central Africa in the Congo basin and southwards, includes a large number of dialects and languages. This constitutes one subdivision of about fifteen main branches of the NIGER-CONGO family, other representatives of which cover a broad belt stretching northwards and westwards into the Niger basin.

Basque.—In the western Pyrenees in France and Spain. Known from written records only as of the sixteenth century A.D. Probably related to some of the ancient languages of the Iberian Peninsula which were otherwise swamped by Latin, but there are no other proved, or even strongly supported, affiliations.

Bella Coola.—See SALISHAN.

Bengali.—See INDO-HITTITE.

Bihari.—See INDO-HITTITE.

Breton.—See INDO-HITTITE.

Bulgarian.—See INDO-HITTITE.

C

Catalan.—See INDO-HITTITE.

CAUCASUS, LANGUAGES OF.—The Caucasus region includes a large number of languages, few of which have any proved relationships outside the area; so far as is known, they fall into a number of distinct families. Adyge, in the north, belongs to one small family; Georgian, the most important language of the southern region, to another.

CELTIC.—See INDO-HITTITE.

Cherokee.—See IROQUOIAN.

Chinese. Hockett 1947, 1950, and unpublished materials; Chao 1947. Our references are usually to the variety of so-called "Mandarin" spoken in Peiping, but occasionally, when so marked, to Cantonese.—See SINO-THAI.

Chinese Pidgin English.—See INDO-HITTITE.

Chipewyan.—See ATHAPASKAN.

Chitimacha.—Formerly spoken on the Gulf Coast of Louisiana just west of the mouth of the Mississippi; now extinct or nearly so. Probably related to a few other languages of the same region, all also either extinct or nearly so, in a TUNICAN family.

Choctaw.—Belongs to the MUSKOGEAN group of the NATCHEZ-MUSKO-GEAN family; these languages were spread in aboriginal times in a belt touching the Gulf Coast in Louisiana, Mississippi, and Alabama. We sometimes use the word "Choctaw" in the text not specifically of this language, but merely as a means of implying general applicability of an assertion.

Cree.—See ALGONQUIAN.

D

Dalmatian.—See INDO-HITTITE.

Danish.—See INDO-HITTITE.

DRAVIDIAN.—A large family in the Indian subcontinent: includes Tamil, Malayalam, Canarese, and several other languages spoken by millions of people, plus a number spoken only by hundreds or thousands in isolated places. Badaga and Kota are of the latter type: both are spoken in the Nilgiri Hills.

Dutch.—See INDO-HITTITE.

Duwamish.—See SALISHAN.

E

EGYPTIAN.—See AFRO-ASIATIC.

English.— See INDO-HITTITE.

Eskimo. Swadesh 1946b.—Forms are cited in the text from the South Greenlandic dialect described by Swadesh. All the dialects of the arctic coastal strip, including those of the north shore of Alaska, seem to be mutually intelligible. Greater variety is found on the west and south shores of Alaska; there are probably two or three distinct languages in all. These constitute ESKIMOAN, which belongs in turn to the ESKIMO-ALEUT family; the other branch, ALEUT, includes the languages of the Aleutian Islands.

Esperanto.—In origin an invented language, now slightly Creolized. If its origin were not known, scholars would doubtless class it as a deviant type of ROMANCE (see INDO-HITTITE).

Etruscan.—An extinct language of Pre-Roman and Roman Italy, known to us only through inscriptions which have not been deciphered in full. Its affiliations are thus unknown, except that it is in all probability *not* INDO-EUROPEAN.

F

Fijian. Churchward 1941.—See MALAYO-POLYNESIAN.

Finnish.—See FINNO-UGRIAN.

FINNO-UGRIAN.—A family with about six main branches, most of which are confined to Asiatic Russia or to the northeastern part of European Russia. Two branches are represented in Europe proper. One of these includes Finnish, together with Esthonian, Lappish, and some less well-known varieties with few speakers (or now extinct). The other consists of Hungarian. Finnish and Hungarian have both been written since the thirteenth century A.D.

Flemish.—See INDO-HITTITE.

Fox. Bloomfield 1924b; Hockett unpublished materials.—See ALGONQUIAN.

French.—See INDO-HITTITE.

G

Georgian. Vogt 1936; Hockett unpublished materials.—See CAUCASUS, LANGUAGES OF.

German.—See INDO-HITTITE.

Germanic.—See INDO-HITTITE.

Gothic.—See INDO-HITTITE.

Greek.—See INDO-HITTITE.

H

Haitian Creole French.—See INDO-HITTITE.

HAMITO-SEMITIC. An older term for AFRO-ASIATIC.

Havasupai.—See YUMAN.

Hawaiian.—See MALAYO-POLYNESIAN.

Hebrew.—See AFRO-ASIATIC.

HELLENIC.—See INDO-HITTITE.

Hindi.—See INDO-HITTITE.

Hopi. Whorf in LSNA.—Western New Mexico. In UTO-AZTECAN (see under Zuni).

Hungarian.—See FINNO-UGRIAN.

I

ICELANDIC.—See INDO-HITTITE.

INDO-ARYAN.—See INDO-HITTITE.

INDO-EUROPEAN.—See INDO-HITTITE.

INDO-HITTITE.

ANATOLIAN branch: several languages in Anatolia, all now long since extinct, but known through inscriptions. Our knowledge is most detailed in the case of Hittite (cuneiform inscriptions begin around 1400 B.C.).

Armenian branch: one language (written records from the fifth century A.D.). This may properly belong as a subdivision of the next branch listed.

INDO-EUROPEAN branch:

INDO-IRANIAN:

INDO-ARYAN or INDIC: the oldest written records are in Sanskrit, known from documents which are not themselves much older than the Christian era, but which transmit a form of speech from as early as 1200 B.C. Modern languages of this group include Bengali, Bihari, Hindi (Hindustani), Marathi, and others.

IRANIAN: oldest records in Old Persian (sixth to fourth centuries B.C.) and Avestan (texts composed perhaps as early as 600 B.C., but manuscripts later); now modern Persian, Kurdish, Pashto (Afghanistan), Ossetic (in the Caucasian area) and some others.

TOCHARIAN: extinct; manuscript fragments of 6th century A.D., found in Chinese Turkestan.

HELLENIC: Ancient Greek, with many dialects, the earliest records from the middle of the second millenium B.C. (see *Language* 32.505, 1956). All modern Greek dialects but one are descended from the ancient dialect of Athens; the exception, Tsakonian, comes from the ancient dialect of Sparta and vicinity.

Albanian: written records only from the seventeenth century A.D.

ITALIC: Various extinct languages of ancient Italy, including Oscan and Umbrian. Latin is recorded from 300 B.C. on. The modern descendants of Latin are called the ROMANCE languages: Portuguese, Spanish, Catalan in the Iberian Peninsula (the first two also overseas as the result of the post-Medieval European expansion); French (of which Haitian Creole French is a recent aberrant variety); Italian; Ladin or Rhaeto-Romance in Switzerland; Dalmatian (extinct; in what is now Yugoslavia); Rumanian; Sicilian and Sardinian are sometimes interpreted as separate and sometimes counted as marginal forms of Italian.

BALTO-SLAVIC:

BALTIC: Lithuanian (written from the 16th century A.D. on); Lettish (the same); Old Prussian now extinct but known from records of the fifteenth and sixteenth centuries.

SLAVIC: Lusatian, Polabian (extinct), Polish, Czech, Slovak, Russian, Bulgarian, Serbian, Croatian, Slovene. Earliest records from the ninth century A.D.

GERMANIC:

EAST GERMANIC group: Gothic, known from sixth-century manuscripts reflecting a fourth-century original; survived in and tuguese.—See INDO-HITTITE.

awatomi. Hockett 1948 and unpublished materials.—See ALGONQUIAN.

Q

chua or Kechua.—Probably a family of related languages rather than a single language; our references are to the variety of Cuzco in Peru. The languages or dialects cover the high plateaus of Ecuador and Peru, and parts of Bolivia and northwestern Argentina.

leute.—Spoken aboriginally on the Pacific Coast of Washington, south of Cape Flattery. Now probably extinct. Related to Chemakum, in the CHIMAKUAN family; more distant affiliation with WAKASHAN has been suspected.

R

aeto-Romance or Ladin.—See INDO-HITTITE.

MANCE.—See INDO-HITTITE.

manian.—See INDO-HITTITE.

sian.—See INDO-HITTITE.

S

LISHAN.—A family of the aboriginal Northwest, spread over much of the state of Washington and southern British Columbia, with some groups in Idaho, Montana, and Oregon. Bella Coola was and is spoken on the coast of British Columbia just north of the northern end of Vancouver Island. Duwamish and Snoqualmie were on the Washington coast; Tillamook on the northernmost coast of Oregon.

skrit.—See INDO-HITTITE.

k-and-Fox.—See ALGONQUIAN.

on, Old.—See INDO-HITTITE.

ANDINAVIAN.—See INDO-HITTITE.

MITIC.—See AFRO-ASIATIC.

MITIC-HAMITIC.—An older term for AFRO-ASIATIC.

wnee.—See ALGONQUIAN.

rra Miwok. Freeland 1951.—See PENUTIAN.

O-THAI.—A family with two chief branches: Chinese and TAI. Chinese covers most of China, in many widely different dialects, and has been carried elsewhere—particularly to Indo-China and Indonesia—by immigration in the last half-millenium. The earliest written records of Chinese go back close to 2000 B.C. TAI includes Thai (the language of

near the Crimea until the sixteenth century, but now extinct. Other varieties known only through mention in classical literature, and all now extinct.

NORTH GERMANIC or SCANDINAVIAN group: a scattering of Runic inscriptions from as early as the second century A.D.; Old Icelandic from manuscripts from the twelfth century. The modern languages are Danish, Swedish, Norwegian, and Icelandic.

WEST GERMANIC group:

English is attested in manuscripts from the end of the seventh century A.D. The term Old English (OE) refers to the language of the period of Alfred, or more loosely to the period from the Germanic Invasions of England to the Norman Conquest; Middle English (ME) refers to the language of Chaucer's time, or more loosely to the period from the Norman Conquest to about 1600 A.D.; Modern English (NE) to our own speech, or, more loosely, the period from 1600 A.D. to the present. Melanesian and Chinese Pidgin English are extremely aberrant varieties of Modern English.

Frisian is spoken on the coast and the coastal islands along the North Sea in The Netherlands; Old Frisian texts date from the second half of the thirteenth century.

The remaining continental dialects of West Germanic are split roughly into Low German and High German. The former includes the dialects of The Netherlands, Belgium, and the northern part of Germany: standard forms in the first two countries are called Dutch and Flemish respectively (they are very close: Afrikaans, in South Africa, belongs in the same subgroup). High German dialects cover the rest of Germany, plus Austria and some two thirds of Switzerland. The standard German taught in schools in this country is a standard form based largely on High German. Yiddish is the High German dialects of Jews who migrated to Eastern Europe in the late Middle Ages. Pennsylvania German is a variety deriving from the High (South) German dialects of immigrants. The earliest Low German records are Old Saxon texts from the ninth century A.D.; the earliest High German records are Old High German texts from the same period.

CELTIC: Includes Irish (Old Irish manuscripts from the eighth century A.D. on), Scotch Gaelic, Manx; Welsh and Breton (also from the eighth century on); Cornish (known from the ninth century A.D., but extinct around 1800).

IRANIAN.—See INDO-HITTITE.

Irish.—See INDO-HITTITE.

IROQUOIAN. Lounsbury 1953 and unpublished materials.—Includes Oneida and several other languages spoken aboriginally in upstate New York and adjacent territory (now on reservations and reserves in New York, Wisconsin, and Canada), plus Cherokee, formerly in the Southeastern Woodlands, now there and in Oklahoma.

Isthmus Zapotec.—See MACRO-OTOMANGUIAN.

Italian.—See INDO-HITTITE.

ITALIC.—See INDO-EUROPEAN.

J

Japanese. Bloch 1946a, b, c, 1950.—The language of Japan, Okinawa, and the Ryukyu Islands. No known external affiliations. Written records from the eighth century A.D.

K

Kechua.—See Quechua.

KHMER.—A family to which Vietnamese may belong. Represented also in the Nicobar Islands, and by Cambodian and some other languages in separate spots on the Indo-China mainland; perhaps (not certainly) in the Indian subcontinent.

Kickapoo.—See ALGONQUIAN.

Korean. Martin 1951, 1954.—The language of Korea, with only minor dialect differentiation. No known external affiliations.

Kota.—See DRAVIDIAN.

Kwakiutl.—See WAKASHAN.

L

Ladin or Rhaeto-Romance.—See INDO-HITTITE.

Latin.—See INDO-HITTITE.

Lithuanian.—See INDO-HITTITE.

M

MACRO-OTOMANGUIAN.—A tentatively posited family. If valid, it includes, among others, the ZAPOTECAN and the MIXTECAN groups. ZAPOTECAN includes Isthmus Zapotec, spoken on the Isthmus of Tehuantepec, Mexico; MIXTECAN includes about thirteen languages, one of which is Mixteco, spoken west of the Isthmus.

Maidu.—See PENUTIAN.

MALAYO-POLYNESIAN.—A far-flung language family, Micronesia, much of Indonesia, all of the Philippines (a few points on the Indo-Chinese mainland, and Mac branch, POLYNESIAN, includes Maori (New Zeala Fijian falls outside of POLYNESIAN but is relatively

Maori.—See MALAYO-POLYNESIAN.

Marathi.—See INDO-HITTITE.

Maya.—The MAYAN family includes almost sixty differer today in Yucatan and adjacent parts of Mexico, Honduras, and Salvador. The Mayan inscriptions are l from Yucatan, and represent an older form of the M same area today. The inscriptions cannot yet be read i literacy was wiped out by the Spanish.

Mazateco. Oaxaca; OTOMANGUIAN.

Melanesian Pidgin English.—See Indo-Hittite.

Menomini. Bloomfield 1924a, 1928b, 1939a, and unpublish ALGONQUIAN.

Miwok, Sierra. Freeland 1951.—See PENUTIAN.

Mixteco.—See MACRO-OTOMANGUIAN.

N

Navaho.—See ATHAPASKAN.

Nootka. Sapir and Swadesh 1939.—See WAKASHAN.

Norwegian.—See INDO-HITTITE.

O

Ojibwa. Bloomfield unpublished materials.—See ALGON(

Oneida.—See IROQUOIAN.

Oscan.—See INDO-HITTITE.

Ossetic.—See INDO-HITTITE.

P

Pennsylvania German.—See INDO-HITTITE.

PENUTIAN.—A tentatively posited family of languages Oregon. Includes Miwok (central California east of the area; Sierra Miwok is one dialect); Costanoan; Yokut foothills of the southern San Joaquin Basin; Yawelm Maidu; Wintun; Takelma; Kalapuya; and Chinookan along both banks of the Columbia River; Wishram is

Persian.—See INDO-HITTITE.

Phoenician.—See AFRO-ASIATIC.

POLYNESIAN.—See MALAYO-POLYNESIAN.

Thailand or Siam), Laotian, and a number of languages spoken by small
groups in the hilly parts of Indo-China and southern China. Relation to
Tibetan and Burmese is speculative.

SLAVIC.—See INDO-HITTITE.

Snoqualmie.—See SALISHAN.

Spanish.—See INDO-HITTITE.

Swedish.—See INDO-HITTITE.

T

Tagalog. Luzon, Philippines.—See MALAYO-POLYNESIAN.

Thai.—See SINO-THAI.

Tillamook.—See SALISHAN.

Totonac. East Central Mexico; affiliation unknown.

Turkish.—Spoken in Turkey. Belongs to the TURCO-TARTAR family, which
includes also languages spoken in various parts of Central Asia as far east
as the Yenisei River. Siberian inscriptions from the 8th century A.D.;
Turkish proper in manuscripts from the 11th century A.D.

U

Umbrian.—See INDO-HITTITE.

Umotina. Lounsbury unpublished materials.—One of about sixteen languages
of the BOROTUQUE family, in the Matto Grosso of Brazil and nearby.

V

Vietnamese.—The chief language of Vietnam and Vietminh (formerly French
Indo-China). Affiliation unknown; possibly KHMER, possibly SINO-
THAI.

W

WAKASHAN.—A family including Nootka and Kwakiutl (no others for certain). Nootka is spoken on the western half of Vancouver Island; Kwakiutl
on the eastern part and on the shore of the mainland.

Welsh.—See INDO-HITTITE.

Wishram.—See PENUTIAN.

Y

Yawelmani.—See PENUTIAN.

Yiddish.—See INDO-HITTITE.

Yuma.—See YUMAN.

YUMAN.—A family aboriginally in western Arizona, southern California, and
the northern part of Lower California. Yuma was spoken near the site of
the present city of that name, and upstream along the Gila River. Havasupai was spoken by a tribe with main headquarters in Cataract Canyon,
an arm of the Grand Canyon west of the present National Park Headquarters. Both languages, and a number of others, still survive. YUMAN
may possibly be affiliated with some groups of languages in California, in a
larger HOKAN family.

Z

Zapotec, Isthmus.—See MACRO-OTOMANGUIAN.
Zoque. Wonderly, 1946.—See MACRO-OTOMANGUIAN.
Zuni.—The language of Zuni Pueblo in New Mexico. No fully established rela-
tionships, but probably belongs, together with Kiowa (southern Plains),
TANOAN (eastern Pueblos), and UTO-AZTECAN (many languages,
from Aztec or Nahuatl in the Valley of Mexico north into Wyoming and
Montana), to an AZTECO-TANOAN family.

BIBLIOGRAPHY

The following is an alphabetical ordering of all books and articles referred to in the text and in the Appendix of Language Names. It does not pretend to be anything like a complete bibliography of linguistics. Available bibliographical references on some specialties have been referred to at the ends of appropriate sections. The bibliography in Bloomfield 1933 (pp. 525–45) is remarkably full for the period up through about 1930. In 1949–50, the Comité International Permanent des Linguistes, under a subvention from UNESCO, published a *Bibliographie linguistique des années 1939–47* (Utrecht and Brussels), and supplementary volumes are being issued annually.

All abbreviations used in the following are themselves entered in proper alphabetical order, with explanation. A superscript numeral after a title indicates the edition.

Abbott, E. A., 1872. A Shakespearian Grammar. London.

AmSp = American Speech. Baltimore 1925–32, New York 1933–.

Baugh, Albert C., 1935. A history of the English language. New York.

Bloch, Bernard. Studies in colloquial Japanese:

    1946a. I. Inflection. JAOS 66.97–109.

    1946b. II. Syntax. Lg 22.200–48.

    1946c. III. Derivation of inflected words. JAOS 66.304–15.

    1950. IV. Phonemics. Lg 26.85–125.

Bloomfield, Leonard, 1924a. The Menomini language. Proceedings of the Twenty-First International Congress of Americanists 336–43. The Hague.

———, 1924b. Notes on the Fox language. IJAL 3.219–32.

———, 1927. Literate and illiterate speech. AmSp 2.432–41.

———, 1928. Menomini texts. Publications of the American Ethnological Society 12. New York.

———, 1930. Sacred stories of the Sweet Grass Cree. National Museum of Canada Bulletin 60 (Anthropological Series 11). Ottawa.

———, 1933. Language. New York.

———, 1934. Plains Cree texts. Publications of the American Ethnological Society 16. New York.

———, 1935. Linguistic aspects of science. Philosophy of Science 2.499–517.

———, 1939a. Menomini morphophonemics. Travaux du Cercle Linguistique de Prague 8.105–15.

———, 1939b. Linguistic aspects of science. International Encyclopedia of Unified Science 1:4. Chicago.

Boas, Franz, 1927. Primitive art. Oslo and Cambridge Mass.

Bolinger, Dwight L., 1946. Visual morphemes. Lg 22.333–40.

———, 1950. Rime, assonance, and morpheme analysis. Word 6.117–36.

Brown, Roger W. 1955. Review of Wissemann 1954. Lg 31.84–91.

Carnap, Rudolf, 1937. The logical syntax of language. London.

Carpenter, C. R., 1940. A field study in Siam of the behavior and social relations of the gibbon. Comparative Psychology Monographs 16:5.

Carroll, John B., 1953. The study of language. Cambridge, Mass.

———, ed., 1956. Language, thought, and reality: selected writings of Benjamin Lee Whorf. New York.

Chace, H. L., 1956. Anguish Languish. Englewood Cliffs, N. J.

Chao, Yuenren, 1947. Cantonese primer. Cambridge, Mass.

Chomsky, Noam, 1957. Syntactic structures. 's-Gravenhage.

Churchward, C. Maxwell, 1941. A new Fijian grammar. [Sydney?]

Coon, Carleton S., 1954. The story of man. New York.

Curme, G. O., 1931. Syntax. In G. O. Curme and H. Kurath, A grammar of the English language, v. 3. New York.

Diringer, D., 1948. The alphabet. New York.

Freeland, L. S., 1951. The language of the Sierra Miwok. Indiana University Publications in Anthropology and Linguistics 6.

Fries, Charles C., 1952. The structure of English, an introduction to the construction of English sentences. New York.

Frisch, K. von, 1950. Bees, their vision, chemical senses, and language. Ithaca.

Gelb, Ignace J., 1952. A study of writing. Chicago.

Gleason, Henry A. Jr., 1955a. An introduction to descriptive linguistics. New York.

———, 1955b. Workbook in descriptive linguistics. New York.

Gray, Louis H., 1939. Foundations of language. New York.

Greenberg, Joseph H. Studies in African linguistic classification:

  1949a. I. The Niger-Congo family. SJA 5.79–100.

  1949b. II. The classification of Fulani. SJA 5.190–8.

  1949c. III. The position of Bantu. SJA 5.309–17.

  1950a. IV. Hamito-Semitic. SJA 6.47–63.

  1950b. V. The Eastern Sudanic family. SJA 6.143–60.

  1950c. VI. The Click languages. SJA 6.223–37.

  1950d. VII. Smaller families; index of languages. SJA 6.388–98.

Guérard, Albert L., 1922. A short history of the international language movement. New York.

Hale, Wm. Gardner, and Carl D. Buck, 1903. A Latin grammar. Boston and London.

Hall, Robert A. Jr., 1943. Melanesian Pidgin English: grammar, texts, vocabulary. Baltimore.

————, 1944. Chinese Pidgin English grammar and texts. JAOS 64.95–113.

————, 1951a. Idiolect and linguistic super-ego. Studia Linguistica 5.21–7.

————, 1951b. American linguistics 1925–1950. Archivum Linguisticum 3.101–25.

————, 1953. Haitian Creole: grammar, texts, vocabulary. American Anthropological Association Memoir 74; also American Folklore Society Memoir 43.

Harris, Zellig S., 1951. Methods in structural linguistics. Chicago.

————, 1957. Co-occurrence and transformation in syntactic structure. Lg 33.283–340.

Haugen, Einar, 1950. The analysis of linguistic borrowing. Lg 26.210–31.

————, 1953. The Norwegian language in America; a study in bilingual behavior. 2v. Philadelphia.

Hayakawa, S. I., 1941. Language in action. New York.

————, 1949. Language in thought and action. (Revision of the preceding.) New York.

Hickerson, Harold, Glen D. Turner, and Nancy P. Hickerson, 1952. Testing procedures for estimating transfer of information among Iroquois dialects and languages. IJAL 18.1–8.

Hockett, Charles F., 1947. Peiping phonology. JAOS 67.253–67.

————, 1948a. Potawatomi. IJAL 14.1–10, 63–72, 139–49, 213–25.

————, 1948b. Biophysics, linguistics, and the unity of science. American Scientist 36.558–72.

————, 1950. Peiping morphophonemics. Lg 26.63–85.

————, 1954. Two models of grammatical description. Word 10.210–34.

————, 1955. A manual of phonology. Indiana University Publications in Anthropology and Linguistics 11.

Hoenigswald, Henry, 1943. Internal reconstruction. SiL 2.78–87.

————, 1946. Sound change and linguistic structure. Lg 22.138–43.

————, 1950a. Morpheme order diagrams. SiL 8.79–81.

————, 1950b. The principle step in comparative grammar. Lg 26.357–64.

————, 1952. The phonology of dialect borrowing. SiL 10.1–5.

Hoijer, Harry, 1946. Introduction. LSNA 9–29.

————, editor, 1954. Language in Culture. Chicago.

Hooton, E. A., 1942. Man's poor relations. Garden City N. Y.

————, 1946. Up from the ape.[2] New York.

Hulbert, James R., 1947. [Survey of Old English literature.] In James W. Bright, Old English Reader, revised by James R. Hulbert. New York.

IJAL = International Journal of American Linguistics. New York 1917–35, Baltimore 1944–.

Jakobson, Roman, 1941. Kindersprache, aphasie, und allgemeine lautgesetze. Uppsala.

————, 1957. Shifters, verbal categories, and the Russian verb. Harvard University.

JAOS = Journal of the American Oriental Society. Boston 1843–49; New York v. 2–5, New Haven v. 6–72, Baltimore v. 73–.

Jespersen, Otto, 1909–49. A modern English grammar on historical principles. Parts 1–7. Heidelberg.

————, 1925. Mankind, nation, and individual from a linguistic point of view. Oslo and Cambridge Mass.

————, 1933. Essentials of English grammar. New York.

Jones, William, 1917. Fox texts. Publications of the American Ethnological Society 1. Leiden and New York.

Joos, Martin A., 1948. Acoustic phonetics. Baltimore.

Korzybski, Alfred, 1948. Science and sanity.[3] Lancaster Penn.

Kroeber, Alfred L., 1919. On the principle of order in civilization as exemplified by changes in fashion. American Anthropologist 21.235–63.

————, 1955. On human nature. SJA 11.195–204.

———— and Clyde Kluckhohn, 1952. Culture: a critical review of concepts and definitions. Cambridge Mass.

———— and Jane Richardson, 1940. Three centuries of women's dress fashions; a quantitative analysis. University of California Anthropological Records 5:2.111–54.

Kruisinga, E., 1925. A handbook of present day English.[4] Utrecht. (Part 2 in a fifth edition, Groningen 1931–2.)

Kuhn, Sherman M., and Randolph Quirk, 1953. Some recent interpretations of Old English digraph spellings. Lg 29.143–56.

————, 1955. The Old English digraphs: a reply. Lg 31.390–401.

Kurath, Hans, 1949. A word geography of the eastern United States. Ann Arbor.

LaBarre, Weston, 1954. The human animal. Chicago.

Lees, Robert B., 1953. The basis of glottochronology. Lg 29.113–27.

————, 1957. Review of Chomsky 1957. Lg 33.375–407.

Le Gros Clark, W. E., 1955. The fossil evidence for human evolution. Chicago.

Leopold, Werner F., 1952. Bibliography of child language. Evanston.

Lg = Language, Journal of the Linguistic Society of America. Baltimore, 1925–.

Lounsbury, Floyd G., 1953. Oneida verb morphology. Yale University Publications in Anthropology 48.

LSNA = Harry Hoijer and others, Linguistic structures of native America. Viking Fund [now Wenner-Gren] Publications in Anthropology 6, 1946.

Martin, Samuel E., 1951. Korean phonemics. Lg 27.519–33.

————, 1954. Korean morphophonemics. Baltimore.

Martinet, André, 1955. Économie des changements phonétiques. Berne.

Matthews, W. K., 1951. The languages of the U.S.S.R. Cambridge, England.
McDavid, Raven I., 1948. Postvocalic /r/ in South Carolina: a social analysis. AmSp 23. 194–203.
McQuown, Norman A., 1955. The indigenous languages of Latin America. American Anthropologist 57.501–70.
Meech, Sanford B., and Harold Whitehall, 1935. Middle English dialect characteristics and dialect boundaries. University of Michigan Essays and Studies in English and Comparative Literature 12.
Meillet, Antoine, 1912. Introduction a l'étude comparative des langues indo-européennes.³ Paris. Seventh edition 1934. New edition, corrected and augmented by Emile Benveniste, 1953.
———, and Marcel Cohen, editors, 1952. Les langues du monde.² Paris.
Menke, Frank G., 1953. The encyclopedia of sports. New York.
Moore, Samuel, 1951. Historical outlines of English sounds and inflections. Revised by Albert H. Marckwardt. Ann Arbor.
Moulton, William G., 1954. The stops and spirants of early Germanic. Lg 30.1–42.
Nida, Eugene, 1949. Morphology, the descriptive analysis of words.² University of Michigan Publications in Linguistics 2.
Palmer, Harold E., 1924. A grammar of spoken English. Cambridge England.
Pedersen, Holger, 1931. Linguistic science in the nineteenth century. Translated by J. Spargo. Cambridge Mass.
Pierce, Joe E., 1952. Dialect distance testing in Algonquian. IJAL 18.208–18.
Pike, Kenneth L., 1945. The intonation of American English. University of Michigan Publications in Linguistics 1.
Pop, Sever, 1950. La dialectologie: Aperçu historique et methodes d'enquêtes linguistiques. 2v. Louvain.
Quine, Willard O., 1951. Mathematical logic.² Cambridge Mass.
Rapoport, Anatol, 1950. Science and the goals of man. New York.
Read, Allan Walker, 1949. English words with constituent elements having independent semantic value. Philologica: The Malone Anniversary Studies, edited by T. A. Kirby and H. B. Woolf. Baltimore.
Richards, Ivor A., 1929. Practical criticism. New York.
———, 1934. Principles of literary criticism.⁵ London and New York.
Ruesch, Jurgen, and Gregory Bateson, 1951. Communication; the social matrix of psychiatry. New York.
Sapir, Edward, 1915. Abnormal types of speech in Nootka. National Museum of Canada Memoir 62 (Anthropological Series 5). Reprinted SWES.
———, 1916. Time perspective in aboriginal American culture; a study in method. National Museum of Canada Memoir 90 (Anthropological Series 13). Reprinted SWES.
———, 1921. Language. New York.

————, 1936. Internal linguistic evidence suggestive of the northern origin of the Navaho. American Anthropologist 38.224–35. Reprinted SWES.

————, and Morris Swadesh, 1939. Nootka texts. Philadelphia.

Shannon, Claude, and Warren Weaver, 1949. The mathematical theory of communication. Urbana.

SiL = Studies in Linguistics. 1942– (New Haven; Washington; Norman, Okla.)

Simpson, George G., 1945. The principles of classification and a classification of the mammals. American Museum of Natural History Bulletin 85.

SJA = Southwestern Journal of Anthropology. Albuquerque 1945–.

Sledd, James, 1955. Review of Trager and Smith 1951 and of Fries 1952. Lg 31.312–45.

————, 1956. Superfixes and Intonation patterns. Litera 3.35–41.

Smith, Henry Lee Jr., 1955. The communication situation. Multilithed, Foreign Service Institute, Department of State, Washington.

Stockwell, Robert P., and C. Westbrook Barritt, 1951. Some Old English graphemic-phonemic correspondences. Studies in Linguistics Occasional Papers 4.

————, 1955. The Old English short digraphs: some considerations. Lg 31.372–89.

Sturtevant, Edgar H., 1947. An introduction to linguistic science. New Haven.

Swadesh, Morris, 1946a. Chitimacha. LSNA 312–36.

————, 1946b. South Greenlandic Eskimo. LSNA 30–54.

————, 1948. Sociologic notes on obsolescent languages. IJAL 14.226–35.

————, 1952. Lexico-statistic dating of prehistoric ethnic contacts, with special reference to North American Indians and Eskimos. Proceedings of the American Philosophical Society 96.452–63.

Sweet, Henry, 1885. The oldest English texts. London.

SWES = Selected writings of Edward Sapir. Edited by David G. Mandelbaum. Berkeley and Los Angeles, 1951.

Thorndike Century Senior Dictionary. Chicago 1941.

Tinbergen, N., 1953. Social behavior in animals. London and New York.

Trager, George L., and Henry Lee Smith Jr., 1951. An outline of English structure. Studies in Linguistics Occasional Papers 3.

Voegelin, Carl F., and Zellig S. Harris, 1951. Methods for determining intelligibility among dialects of natural languages. Proceedings of the American Philosophical Society 95.322–9.

Voegelin, Carl F., and E. W. Voegelin, 1944. Map of North American Indian languages. American Ethnological Society and Indiana University, New York.

Vogt, Hans, 1936. Esquisse d'une grammaire de géorgien moderne. Oslo.

Wallace, Wilson D., 1945. Inference of relative age of culture traits from magnitude of distribution. SJA 1.142–60.

Weinreich, Uriel, 1953. Languages in contact: findings and problems. Publications of the Linguistic Circle of New York 1.

Wellek, Rene, and Austin Warren, 1949. Theory of literature. New York.

Wells, Rulon S., 1947. Immediate constituents. Lg 23.81–117.

———, Automatic alternation. Lg 25.99–116.

Wissemann, Heinz, 1954. Untersuchungen zur Onomatopöie: 1 Teil, Die sprachpsychologischen versuche. Bibliothek der allgemeinen sprachwissenschaft, 2. Reihe. Heidelberg.

Wonderly, William L., 1946. Phonemic acculturation in Zoque. IJAL 12.92–5.

Wörter und Sachen. Heidelberg 1909–.

INDEX

References are to pages. Authors' names appearing in the Bibliography (p. 599) are not listed below.

607